Handbook of Healthcare Analytics

Wiley Series in Operations Research and Management Science

Operations Research and Management Science (ORMS) is a broad, interdisciplinary branch of applied mathematics concerned with improving the quality of decisions and processes and is a major component of the global modern movement towards the use of advanced analytics in industry and scientific research. The Wiley Series in Operations Research and Management Science features a broad collection of books that meet the varied needs of researchers, practitioners, policy makers, and students who use or need to improve their use of analytics. Reflecting the wide range of current research within the ORMS community, the Series encompasses application, methodology, and theory and provides coverage of both classical and cutting-edge ORMS concepts and developments. Written by recognized international experts in the field, this collection is appropriate for students as well as professionals from private and public sectors including industry, government, and nonprofit organizations who are interested in ORMS at a technical level. The Series is comprised of four sections: Analytics; Decision and Risk Analysis; Optimization Models; and Stochastic Models.

Handbook of Healthcare Analytics

Theoretical Minimum for Conducting 21st Century Research on Healthcare Operations

Edited by
Tinglong Dai and Sridhar Tayur

WILEY

This edition first published 2018

Registered Office
John Wiley & Sons, Inc., 111 River Street, Hoboken, NJ 07030, USA

Editorial Office
111 River Street, Hoboken, NJ 07030, USA

For details of our global editorial offices, customer services, and more information about Wiley products visit us at www.wiley.com.

Wiley also publishes its books in a variety of electronic formats and by print-on-demand. Some content that appears in standard print versions of this book may not be available in other formats.

Library of Congress Cataloging-in-Publication Data:

Names: Dai, Tinglong, editor. | Tayur, Sridhar, editor.
Title: Handbook of healthcare analytics : theoretical minimum for conducting 21st century research on healthcare operations / edited by Tinglong Dai, Sridhar Tayur.
Description: Hoboken, NJ : Wiley, 2018. | Series: Wiley series in operations research and management science | Includes bibliographical references and index. |
Identifiers: LCCN 2018007641 (print) | LCCN 2018007950 (ebook) | ISBN 9781119300953 (pdf) | ISBN 9781119300960 (epub) | ISBN 9781119300946 (hardback)
Subjects: LCSH: Medical care–Data processing. | Medical care–Information services. | BISAC: BUSINESS & ECONOMICS / Management Science.
Classification: LCC R858 (ebook) | LCC R858 .H3216 2018 (print) | DDC 610.285–dc23
LC record available at https://lccn.loc.gov/2018007641

Cover Design: Wiley
Cover Image: © marysuperstudio/Shutterstock

Set in 10/12pt WarnockPro by SPi Global, Chennai, India

Printed in the United States of America

V10004334_090618

Healthcare markets are in need of redesign. This timely Handbook showcases what analytics have to offer.

–Alvin E. Roth, *Nobel Laureate in Economics*
Craig and Susan McCaw Professor of Economics, Stanford University

This project is a very smart move. This is the book I have been looking for. There are too many "one-off" papers, but I get confused about the "big picture" in reading them. To build a stronger Operations Management community, we need to know context, research methods, issues, findings, and missing gaps.

–Christopher S. Tang
University Distinguished Professor, University of California, Los Angeles
Editor-in-Chief, Manufacturing & Service Operations Management

It is an impressive volume indeed and will hopefully get more bright minds to work on addressing the healthcare issues that so urgently need to be fixed.

–Nitin Nohria
Dean and George F. Baker Professor of Administration,
Harvard Business School

As a healthcare professional interested in analytics, especially as related to development of national health policy, I found that this work was able to expand my horizons.

–John P. Roberts, MD
Professor of Surgery, Division of Transplant Surgery
Endowed Chair in Abdominal Transplantation
University of California, San Francisco

TD: To Audrey, Carl, and Ricci.
ST: To his parents.

Contents

List of Contributors

Mustafa Akan	Carnegie Mellon University
Itai Ashlagi	Stanford University
Barış Ata	University of Chicago
Turgay Ayer	Georgia Institute of Technology
Qiushi Chen	Pennsylvania State University
Soo-Haeng Cho	Carnegie Mellon University
Tinglong Dai	Johns Hopkins University
Donald R. Fischer	Highmark Inc.
John J. Friedewald	Northwestern University
Srinagesh Gavirneni	Cornell University
Joel Goh	Harvard University; National University of Singapore
Diwas KC	Emory University
Vidyadhar G. Kulkarni	University of North Carolina at Chapel Hill
Nadia Lahrichi	Polytechnique Montréal
Jay Levine	Massachusetts Institute of Technology; ECG Management Consultants
Nan Liu	Boston College
Karthik V. Natarajan	University of Minnesota
Rema Padman	Carnegie Mellon University
A. Cem Randa	University of Chicago
Louis-Martin Rousseau	Polytechnique Montréal
Alan Scheller-Wolf	Carnegie Mellon University
Hummy Song	University of Pennsylvania
Jayashankar M. Swaminathan	University of North Carolina at Chapel Hill
Sridhar Tayur	Carnegie Mellon University
Van-Anh Truong	Columbia University
Willem-Jan Van Hoeve	Carnegie Mellon University
Senthil Veeraraghavan	University of Pennsylvania
Hui Zhao	Pennsylvania State University

Preface

Why another handbook on healthcare?

In developing the conceptual framework of this book, we interviewed an internationally acclaimed expert, who, like several others, articulated the need: "Operations Management researchers should be given a window into the reality of the *weirdness* of healthcare under a fee-for-service model (or other payment methods). Notably, hospitals more or less don't give two hoots about making people healthy; they are all about the margin and rejiggering services toward high-margin services. Also, many hospitals simply do not have anyone on the floor with serious training in analytics beyond lean manufacturing; the horsepower is on the finance side, and with the payers not the providers."

Provocative as the above quote was intended to be, in reality the situation is quite complex, and there is some truth to that frustration. Although physicians for the most part indeed intend to provide the best care for each patient, they are part of a larger entrenched organizational and cultural system where financial considerations (and other habitual procedures) and performance metrics sometimes do play an outsized role and have unintended consequences that may not be readily apparent. Our survey of existing handbooks on healthcare operations shows that although these references are in general quite elaborate about how quantitative-modeling efforts may lead to improvements, actual widespread and sustainable benefits have been difficult to accomplish; thus, there is a strong and real demand and need for a volume that places the hurdles that can impede change—including incentive, metrics, behavioral, and organizational issues—more *centrally* in discussing *healthcare operations.*

We believe that the Operations Research/Management Science (OR/MS) community can be of greater value to healthcare operations, but only if we understand what is really driving decision-making in this domain and appropriately incorporate the role of incentives and institutions—and, if appropriate, demand for structural disruptions with superior alternatives—in our framing, models, and recommendations for change. Of course, the study of incentive, behavioral, and organizational issues in healthcare has been the theme of the decades-old discipline of *health economics,* but it remains to be seen whether such theoretical studies (which are based on stylized models) can yet improve the design, organization, and day-to-day operations in healthcare without incorporating operational realities and levers.

In light of the above observations, it is not surprising that there is an ongoing, lively discussion on US healthcare, which has touched virtually every stakeholder in the system and influenced similar efforts throughout the world, and increasingly calls for fresh approaches that can actually be implemented. Three key issues have emerged from this discussion: cost, quality, and access, which are jointly referred to as the "iron triangle" of healthcare:

- The *cost* of providing healthcare is excessively high—17.7% of the GDP of the US, whereas none of the other OECD countries report more than 11.9%. The healthcare expenditure is projected to grow at an annual rate of 5.8% during the next decade, 1% faster than the expected annual growth rate of the economy.
- The *quality* of care, however, is not as high as in other countries. A 2013 National Institutes of Health (NIH) study found that the US performs worse than almost all the other 17 high-income countries in critical quality measures such as the prevalence of infant mortality, heart and lung disease, and sexually transmitted infections.
- The *access* to health insurance coverage, particularly for the low-income population, has been vastly expanded under the Patient Protection and Affordable Care Act. However, unless the mismatch of supply and demand is addressed, expanded coverage will not immediately translate into expanded care. Consider the ongoing organ shortage crisis: about 18 people die each day in the US while waiting for transplants, and a new candidate is added to the waiting list every ten minutes. In the meantime, the waiting list of transplant candidates outgrows the registry of potential organ donors: between 1989 and 2009, the number of people wait-listed for an organ increased by almost five times, but the number of registered organ donors grew by less than 1.5 times.

Clearly, there is an urgent need to study these "*big issues*" (cost, quality, and access) in the US healthcare industry. OR/MS researchers can contribute to this need, given that so much has been done to analyze and solve supply-demand mismatch problems of virtually any scale. Yet the literature of healthcare operations management has *focused too narrowly* on applications of Operations Research techniques to specific healthcare scenarios, such as nurse scheduling, appointment scheduling, facility design, and patient flow management. Little attention from the Operations Management community has been paid to incentive issues in healthcare operations. On the other hand, the health economics literature has significantly enhanced our understanding of the incentive issues in healthcare, but there is a paucity of operations-level modeling. For example, health economists tend to treat patients' waiting time before access to healthcare services as the healthcare provider's unilateral, self-concocted decision variable rather than an output variable that depends on the physician and patients' joint strategic decision-making.

Dedicated to the next generation of healthcare operations scholars, this volume has a dual purpose: first, it provides a refreshing healthcare context for OR/MS researchers, and second, it offers an actionable introduction to quantitative tools ranging from operations research, economics, and econometrics, to data sciences. The primary audience of the handbook is doctoral students and faculty in business and engineering schools, and the secondary audience is healthcare practitioners. We wish to instill a way of thinking that genuinely incorporates incentive considerations in operational changes and create a habit of weighing incentives in understanding and analyzing healthcare operations management problems; in the future, we expect the need for healthcare operations researchers – as in other subjects such as supply chain management and sustainable operations – to justify themselves if their models lack any consideration for incentive issues.

Framework Development

We take this opportunity to create a classification – a taxonomy – based on frameworks and suggestions already in the literature as well as our ongoing survey of contemporary healthcare research. We thus create a structure, and a vocabulary, for communicating *what we do and how it fits and why it matters* within our community and beyond, and lift the fog from this seemingly disorganized and uncoordinated, large inventory of research papers. Due to the complex nature of healthcare services, the field of healthcare operations is exceedingly broad, diversified, and fluid. To build a systematic, inclusive, and forward-looking theoretic framework, we have conducted a survey of prevailing taxonomy of healthcare literature, including

- the *Health Research Classification System* (HRCS) developed by UK Clinical Research Collaboration (UKCRC) Partners
- *Journal of Economic Literature* (JEL) Classification Codes, particularly its Part C ("Mathematical and Quantitative Methods") and Part I ("Health, Education, and Welfare")
- the enumeration of research topics by major health economics journals such as *Journal of Health Economics* and *Health Economics*

We use Part C of the *Journal of Economic Literature* (JEL) Classification Codes as the starting point as we identify key tools essential for research on healthcare operations. In addition, we classify major research themes into three broad categories: macro-level thrusts, meso-level thrusts, and micro-level thrusts. For details on our classification system, readers are referred to an invited OM Forum article (Dai and Tayur 2018) for *Manufacturing & Service Operations Management* (*M&SOM*).

Tools

Operations Research Methods (OR)
- OR1: Markov Decision Process
- OR2: Deterministic Mathematical Programming
- OR3: Stochastic Programming
- OR4: Robust Optimization
- OR5: Queuing (and Rational Queuing) Theory
- OR6: Decision Analysis
- OR7: Simulation

Econometric Methods (EM)
Game Theory and Information Economics (GTIE)
Data Science (DS)

Thrusts[1]

Macro-level Thrusts (MaTs)
- MaT1: Supply of and Demand for Health Services [2]
- MaT2: Access to Health Services
- MaT3: Organizational Structure
- MaT4: Health Network Flows (Costing, Contracting, and Coordination)
- MaT5: Financing of Health Services
  - Health service reimbursement
  - Health Insurance
  - Clinician compensation
- MaT6: Design of Health Market

Meso-level Thrusts (MeTs)
- MeT1: Resource Allocation
  - Organ Transplantation
  - Global Health
  - Quality-Speed Tradeoff
  - Humanitarian Logistics
- MeT2: Design of Delivery
  - Infection Prevention and Control
  - Detection and Screening (Population Health)
  - Diagnosis Under Uncertainty
  - Gatekeepers

---

1 The three-tiered organizational structure—classifying research into macro-, meso-, and micro-level thrusts—was motivated by an OM Forum article by Linda Green (2012, The vital role of operations analysis in improving healthcare delivery. *Manufacturing Service Oper. Management* **14**(4) 488–494).

2 Demand and supply involve resources such as hospitals, drugs, beds, emergency rooms, physicians, nurses, and imaging equipment.

  - Treatments and Therapeutic Interventions
  - Chronical Diseases Management
- MeT3: Precision Medicine
  - Individualized Therapy
- MeT4: Organization Design
  - Clinician Workload and Workflow
  - Patient Safety
  - Patient Flow
- MeT5: Innovation
  - New Drug Development
  - Health Innovations
- MeT6: Conflicts of Interest
- MeT7: Healthcare Supply Chain

Micro-level Thrusts (MiTs)

- MiT1: Ambulatory Care
- MiT2: Emergency Care
- MiT3: Surgical Care
- MiT4: Inpatient Care
- MiT5: Residential Care
- MiT6: End-of-Life Care
- MiT7: Telemedicine
- MiT8: Concierge Medicine

Based on the above framework, the handbook is designed to cover a subset of the tools and thrusts. The thrusts covered in Part I are representative of the healthcare research landscape, whereas the tools covered in Part II are among the most powerful and versatile ones with the potential to solve important problems in the healthcare domain.

A "thrust" chapter aims to provide (a) essential facts, statistics, and tradeoffs this thrust entails, (b) important, interesting, and nonobvious aspects the thrust presents, (c) essential quantitative tools (if any) useful for research into this thrust, (d) two or three examples, (e) the most useful reference books, lecture notes, and online resources for deeper learning about the thrust, (f) the most influential papers relevant to this thrust, (g) behavioral, incentive, and policy issues relevant to this thrust, and (h) the most promising venues for future research into this thrust.

A "tool" chapter aims to provide (a) a conceptual-level introduction to the tool, with simple and specific motivating examples from healthcare, (b) a brief summary of applications of the tool in various healthcare thrusts, (c) venues of future healthcare applications empowered by the tool, (d) the most effective reference books, lecture notes, and online resources for deeper learning about the tool, and (e) the most influential healthcare papers and applications using the tool.

Overview of the Handbook

Part I of this handbook, titled "Thrusts," includes Chapters 1 through Chapter 13. This part can be broadly divided into three groups.

Chapters 1 through 3 constitute the **macro-level thrusts**, in that they directly tackle society-level issues facing healthcare operations management researchers. In Chapter 1 ("Organizational Structure"), Jay Levine (MIT/ECG Management Consultants) provides a perspective on how institutions crucial for delivering care are organized and structured. Donald Fischer, MD (previously Chief Medical Officer at Highmark), in Chapter 2 ("Access to Healthcare"), raises key questions facing US healthcare reform, which "has become a national obsession," and outlines "opportunities for actions." Chapter 3 ("Market Design"), written by Itai Ashlagi (Stanford University), provides an introduction to market design, a topic that has received considerable attention from economists and OR/MS scholars over the past several years, thanks to successful initiatives such as the National Residency Matching Program and Kidney Exchange.

Chapters 4 through 9 cover the **meso-level thrusts**, which bridge macro- and micro-level issues in healthcare operations management. In Chapter 4 ("Competing Interests"), Joel Goh (Harvard University/National University of Singapore) provides a comprehensive and forward-looking review of the growing literature on the conflict between healthcare providers' professional calling and various political, economic, and social forces—a topic that is "paradoxically both patently obvious and overwhelmingly complex." Hummy Song and Senthil Veeraraghavan (both of the University of Pennsylvania), in Chapter 5 ("Quality of Care"), based on an extensive survey of published and ongoing research on the quality of care, build a framework that can guide further research in this space. In Chapter 6 ("Personalized Medicine"), Turgay Ayer (Georgia Institute of Technology) and Qiushi Chen (Massachusetts General Hospital) discuss the mathematical, computational, and statistical models in personalized medicine. Karthik Natarajan (University of Minnesota) and Jay Swaminathan (University of North Carolina), in Chapter 7 ("Global Health"), provide a comprehensive discussion of resource (including funding, inventory, and capacity) allocation problems in global health. In Chapter 8 ("Healthcare Supply Chain"), Soo-Haeng Cho (Carnegie Mellon University) and Hui Zhao (Pennsylvania State University) present supply chain management issues in the healthcare industry, featuring examples from generic injectable drugs and influenza vaccine. Barış Ata and Cem Randa (both of the University of Chicago) and John Friedewald (Northwestern University), in Chapter 9 ("Organ Transplantation"), synthesize the progress in the applications of operations research methods to organ transplantation, and lay out avenues for further research.

Chapters 10 through 13 discuss operations issues—**micro-level thrusts**—in the delivery of care in specific areas, including "Ambulatory Care" (Chapter 10, by Nan Liu of Boston College); "Inpatient Care" (Chapter 11, by Van-Anh Truong of Columbia University); "Residential Care" (Chapter 12, by Nadia Lahrichi and Louis-Martin Rousseau, both of École Polytechnique de Montréal, and Willem-Jan Van Hoeve of Carnegie Mellon University); and "Concierge Medicine" (Chapter 13, by Nagesh Gavirneni of Cornell University and Vidyadhar Kulkarni of University of North Carolina). Of these four areas, the first two are relatively well studied, with a large volume of extant literature. That said, Nan Liu and Van-Anh Truong connect these areas to meso- and macro-level thrusts and present fruitful research agendas for future researchers. The other two areas are relatively new domains for healthcare researchers, and we expect growing interest in these topics as healthcare increasingly moves to a continuum covering the entire spectrum of the population.

Part II of this handbook, titled "Tools," presents both traditional and contemporary methods for conducting healthcare research. These tools include *Markov Decision Process* (Chapter 14, by Alan Scheller-Wolf of Carnegie Mellon University); *Game Theory and Information Economics* (Chapter 15, by Tinglong Dai of Johns Hopkins University), *Queuing Games* (Chapter 16, by Mustafa Akan of Carnegie Mellon University), *Econometric Methods* (Chapter 17, by Diwas KC of Emory University), and *Data Sciences* (Chapter 18, by Rema Padman of Carnegie Mellon University).

It is impossible to cover all the topics within healthcare operations in one introductory volume: notably absent from our collection are (a) macro-level thrusts such as health insurance design, physician compensation, and health service reimbursement (or simply "financing healthcare"); (b) meso-level thrusts such as design of delivery and organizational design; and (because many good articles have recently covered them) micro-level thrusts such as emergency care and surgical care.

We recognize that, for a beginner, this field can be dauntingly broad in terms of application areas being studied and the range of tools being applied. We hope that this handbook provides an accessible and structured gateway to this important area of research. We have borrowed "Theoretical Minimum" in our subtitle from books in physics in the expectation that some scientific sparkle will rub off on our field as we generate useful knowledge in a disciplined manner.

Tinglong Dai and Sridhar Tayur

Reference

Dai, T., S. Tayur. (2018). Healthcare Operations in the Twenty-First Century. Working Paper.

Glossary of Terms

Academic medical center A medical center consisting of medical schools, faculty practice plans, and teaching hospitals. (Chapter 1)

Access to care The attainment of timely and appropriate health care by patients. (Chapter 5)

Activities of daily living (ADL) Activities such as bathing, clothing, transfer, toilet use, feeding and walking, which reflect the patient's ability to heal. (Chapter 12)

Adverse events Injuries caused by medical management and resulting in a measurable disability. (Chapter 5)

Adverse selection An agency issue that arises before two parties enter into a contractual arrangement, when one party has better information about himself than the other party does. (Chapter 15)

Ambulatory care Health services that are provided on an outpatient basis and without the need to admit patients to an inpatient facility. Ambulatory care is provided in a variety of settings, including, but not limited to, the offices of healthcare providers, hospital outpatient departments, outpatient surgical centers, diagnosis clinics, labs, dialysis clinics, and (freestanding) emergency departments. (Chapter 10)

Ambulatory surgery center Non-hospital facilities that exclusively provide surgical services that do not require patients to be admitted for hospital stays. (Chapter 4)

Asymmetric information A situation in which one party has an informational advantage over the other party. (Chapter 15)

Boutique medicine A type of business model in which physicians cater only to their fee-paying customers, which means that those unwilling to pay the additional concierge fee must choose another physician. (Chapter 13)

Case-based reasoning An Artificial Intelligence (AI) method that formalizes the process of solving a new problem based on the experience from past cases. (Chapter 6)

Classification algorithm A method of labeling unknown data to target variables through training a classification model using labeled data. Examples of classification algorithms include logistic regression and naïve Bayes algorithms. Classifications algorithms are also called *supervised learning algorithms*. (Chapter 18)

Clinical pathways Indications of the most widely applicable order of treatment interventions for specific health conditions or particular patient groups. (Chapter 18)

Clinical practice guidelines (CPGs) Lists of recommendations for various treatments based on evidence from randomized clinical trials (RCTs) or the consensus opinions of clinical experts. (Chapter 18)

Competing interests in healthcare Secondary, nonclinical, objectives that can potentially influence how healthcare is delivered, evaluated, and reported. (Chapter 4).

Concierge medicine A system of fee-based priority access. In a typical concierge medicine practice, physicians see both fee-paying patients and those who appear on a conventional fee-for-service basis. (Chapter 13)

Conflicts of interest in healthcare Circumstances in which secondary interests (pecuniary or otherwise) may exert undue influence over a physician's decisions or judgment. (Chapter 4)

Deceased-donor organ transplant A form of organ transplant carried out by procuring donor's organs after brain death or cardiac arrest. (Chapter 9)

Deferred acceptance (DA) algorithm An algorithm which outputs a stable matching, meaning that no doctor and hospital who are not matched with other doctors and hospitals prefer to match with others over their current matches. (Chapter 3)

Disease dynamics model A model reflecting change of a patient's health condition over time. (Chapter 6)

Donor service area (DSA) An area consisting of potentially multiple transplant centers and one organ procurement organization (OPO). United Network of Organ Sharing (UNOS) has established 11 geographic regions that further subdivided into 58 local donor service areas (DSAs). (Chapter 9)

Dynamic prediction models Prediction models that account for the continually changing states of the patient's health and exploit the longitudinal nature of patient data are critical to capture the nuances of care delivery and health outcomes, particularly mortality and hospitalizations. In contrast to static models, dynamic models provide the opportunity to update an individual prediction when a patient's condition progresses over time and covariates, such as laboratory measurement, are observed longitudinally. (Chapter 18)

Effectiveness in resource allocation How well the need for services are met, that is, whether service recipients receive what they originally requested. (Chapter 7)

Efficiency in resource allocation The ratio of inputs to outputs (or outcomes). (Chapter 7)

Equity in resource allocation The measure of fairness of the services offered. (Chapter 7)

Evidence-based medicine A critical prerequisite for achieving coordinated, patient-centered, and effective healthcare, which entails conscientiously and systematically using best available evidence to reach medical decisions. (Chapter 18)

Game theory An analytical basis for modeling and predicting human interactions (e.g., between a patient and a physician). (Chapter 15)

General acute care hospital A hospital that provides care across many specialties, such as adult care, pediatric care, surgical care, obstetrical care, etc. (Chapter 1)

Healthcare supply chain A supply chain in the healthcare industry, which may be a pharmaceutical supply chain, a medical device supply chain, or a supplies supply chain. (Chapter 8)

Homecare service A service to support activities of daily living (ADL) and instrumental activities of daily living (IADL). (Chapter 12)

Home health care A type of care covering a wide range of activities, which differ in the level of required expertise, frequency, and duration. It includes wound care for pressure sores or a surgical wound, patient and caregiver education, intravenous or nutrition therapy, injections, and monitoring serious illness and unstable health status. (Chapter 12)

Hospice care A bundle of comprehensive services for terminally ill patients with a medically determined life expectancy of six months or less. The provided care emphasizes the management of pain and symptoms. (Chapter 12)

Individualized medicine see *personalized medicine.* (Chapter 6)

Information design A branch of information economics that focuses on the design of information structure that maximizes the utility of an information designer. Typically, the information designer has information but no ability to change the mechanism specific to agents' actions. (Chapter 15)

Information economics An analytical framework that characterizes how information, or lack thereof, drives decision making. (Chapter 15)

In-home care see *homecare service.* (Chapter 12)

Inpatients A type of patients who are formally admitted (hospitalized) for at least one night, taking up a room, a bed, and board. Inpatient areas in a hospital include intensive care units, general nursing wards, delivery wards, and neonatal care units. (Chapter 11)

Instrumental activities of daily living (IADL) Everyday tasks such as light housework, meal preparation, taking medication, buying groceries or clothing, using the phone, and managing money, which allow the patient to live independently in their community. (Chapter 12)

Investor-owned hospital A hospital owned by a group of investors. Approximately 20% of US hospitals are investor owned. Most investor-owned hospitals are operated by large hospital corporations that operate facilities in multiple states. (Chapter 1).

Iron triangle of healthcare cost of providing healthcare, quality of care, and access to care. (Preface)

Length of stay (LOS) The total amount of time a patient spends in an inpatient (e.g. hospital) or outpatient (e.g. ED) setting. (Chapter 5)

Living organ donation A form of organ donation occurring between a recipient and a consenting (living) donor. (Chapter 9)

Lucas critique The view, attributed to the Economist Robert Lucas, that individuals will change their behavior after the rules governing the functioning of the system have changed. (Chapter 15)

Macro-level healthcare thrusts System-level healthcare scenarios relevant to the supply of and the demand for healthcare services and how supply and demand are matched through marketplaces. (Chapter 15)

Marketplace A public good that enables economic transactions between the market participants according to a given set of rules. (Chapter 3)

Meso-level healthcare thrusts Healthcare scenarios that bridge micro-level and macro-level applications. (Chapter 15)

Micro-level healthcare thrusts Specific healthcare operational functions, including, for example, ambulatory care, inpatient care, surgical care, and emergency care (Chapter 15)

Moral hazard An agency issue that arises when one party, after entering into a contractual arrangement, takes actions not perfectly observable to the other party. (Chapter 15)

Not-for-profit hospitals Hospitals qualifying for tax-exempt status under Section 501(c)(3) of the Internal Revenue Code. Approximately 58% of US hospitals fall into this category. (Chapter 1)

Outpatient surgery center see *ambulatory surgery center*. (Chapter 4)

Organ procurement organizations (OPOs) The organizations that procure donated organs after donor's brain death. (Chapter 9)

Organ procurement and transplantation network (OPTN) The network of transplant centers and OPOs established by US Congress under the NOTA in 1984. OPTN facilitates the interaction among all professionals involved in organ donation and transplantation. (Chapter 9)

Outcome measures of quality of care The measures of the effects of care on the health status of patients and populations resulting from healthcare services. These measures can be either intermediate- or long-term, and may include improvements in the patient's knowledge concerning care and the degree of the patient's satisfaction with care. (Chapter 5)

Palliative care Acute care delivered in a holistic approach to the person with a severe, progressive, or terminal illness. The goal of palliative care is to relieve physical pain and other symptoms but also to take into account psychological, social, and spiritual suffering. Palliative care extends the principles of hospice care to a broader population that could benefit from receiving this type of care earlier in the illness or disease process. (Chapter 12)

Patient experience Patients' observations and participation in health care. Typically, patient-experience measures consist of ratings or mean scores from patient satisfaction surveys, such as the Consumer Assessment of Healthcare Providers and Systems (CAHPS) family of surveys overseen by AHRQ. (Chapter 5)

Personalized medicine Tailoring clinical interventions (including screening, diagnosis, and treatment) to the characteristics (including demographic, clinical, and genetic) of individual patients. (Chapter 6)

Physician-induced demand An agency issue specific to the healthcare industry, which arises when a physician directly influences patients' usage of medical resources. (Chapter 16)

Precision medicine Treatments targeted to the needs of individual patients on the basis of "omics" (e.g. genomics, proteomics) data. (Chapter 6)

Primary care The day-to-day healthcare including care for acute symptoms, (multiple) chronic illness, health maintenance, and mental/social health issues, among others. Primary care is usually delivered in the office of primary care providers (PCPs), e.g. primary care physicians, pediatricians, or nurse practitioners. (Chapter 11)

Private physician medicine see *boutique medicine*. (Chapter 13)

Process measures of quality of care The measures of the healthcare-related activities that are performed, that is, what is actually done in delivering and receiving care. These measures are generally calculated as the ratio of the number of patients who receive a particular service (numerator) in comparison to the total number of patients for whom a particular service is indicated (denominator). (Chapter 5)

Program coverage The number of people served by a global health program. (Chapter 7)

Public hospitals Hospitals funded by the public, including: (a) the Veterans Administration (VA) operates dozens of hospitals, (b) public universities with medical schools sometimes own and operate university hospitals, (c) cities or counties operate public hospitals that often provide care to underserved populations, (d) local public community hospitals supported by regions of the country with tax districts, and (e) states operate public psychiatric hospitals. About 22% of US hospitals are public hospitals. (Chapter 1)

Quality management The discipline of measuring results, reengineering processes, and continuously improving, all of which aim to higher quality and lower costs. (Chapter 2)
Queueing discipline The specification of the order in which to serve the customers waiting in line. (Chapter 16)
Queueing games A type of queueing theoretic models in which customers are assumed to strategic and forward-looking. (Chapter 16)
Queueing theory The mathematical analysis of customers waiting for service. (Chapter 16)
Rational queueing see *queueing games.* (Chapter 16)
Residential care see *home health care.* (Chapter 12)
Scientific Registry of Transplant Recipients (SRTR) An organization devoted to studying the transplant candidates' decisions for specific organ offers and developing prediction models to take into account the donor and recipient characteristics. UNOS uses this model to evaluate the proposals for changes to allocation policy. To be more specific, kidney pancreas simulation allocation model (KPSAM) and liver simulation allocation model (LSAM), which are also developed by SRTR, are used to test policy proposals in order to predict the number of transplantations, number of deaths while waiting, and several other performance measures under the proposed changes. (Chapter 9)
Self-referrals Referrals to entities financially connected to the referring provider (or the provider's family members). (Chapter 4)
Specialty hospitals A type of hospitals with a specific and narrow clinic focus. Two most common types of such hospitals are orthopedic hospitals and cardiac hospitals. (Chapter 4)
Stopping time problems in healthcare A type of decision concerning when to initiate a one-shot treatment or intervention. (Chapter 14)
Strategic queueing see *queueing games.* (Chapter 16)
Structure The capacity attributes of the setting in which care is delivered. It encapsulates a healthcare organization's or a clinician's capacity to provide high quality healthcare. (Chapter 5)
Structural estimation A empirical methodology (1) driven by the notion that observed empirical data results from a data-generating process dictated by an underlying theoretic model and (2) aimed to uncover the parameters of that model. (Chapter 17)
Structural method A type of econometric model that specifies (1) data-generating process defined by an underlying economic theory and (2) statistic relationships between observed and unobserved variables. (Chapter 17)
Structural issues in healthcare Issues that affect how healthcare services are developed and delivered, including, for example, organizational design, material resources, and human resources. (Chapter 5)

Supervised learning algorithms An algorithm that learns from datasets that contain "correct answers" to the output variables of interest. See also *classification algorithms*. (Chapter 6)

Supplier-induced demand see *physician-induced demand*. (Chapter 16)

Surgery center see *ambulatory surgery center*. (Chapter 4)

Specialty Hospital A facility that provides highly specialized care to targeted patients such as orthopedic patients, children, women, psychiatric patients, etc. (Chapter 1)

Tax-exempt hospitals see *not-for-profit hospitals*. (Chapter 1)

Teaching hospital Member of the Association of American Medical Colleges' Council of Teaching Hospitals. There are approximately 400 teaching hospitals in the US, comprising about 7% of US hospitals. (Chapter 1)

Temporary care Post-surgery or hospitalization support. The services address very specific needs: change dressings, help manage medications, or ensure that the recommendations of the care team are being followed. (Chapter 12)

Triple Aim of healthcare simultaneously improving population health, improving the patient experience of care, and reducing per capita cost. (Chapter 1)

Turnaround time Waits that occur after the patient has begun his or her treatment process (i.e. time until test results are returned once the test has been initiated). (Chapter 5)

Uniformization A mathematical technique that transform a continuous-time model to an equivalent discrete-time model. (Chapter 14)

United Network of Organ Sharing (UNOS) A private nonprofit organization that administers the OPTN under contract with Health Resources and Services Administration of the US Department of Health and Human Services. (Chapter 9)

Unsupervised learning algorithms Algorithms that identifies latent groups in the data. Unlike classification, unsupervised learning does not have true labels, and users need to predefine the number of latent groups. (Chapter 18)

Upcoding Systematic erroneous reporting that result in financial benefit. (Chapter 4)

Acknowledgements

This Handbook could not have happened without the enthusiasm, contributions and support from the healthcare operations management community, to which we are greatly indebted to. In particular, the October 2016 Johns Hopkins Symposium on Healthcare Operations in Baltimore, Maryland and a July 2017 authors' meeting in Chapel Hill, North Carolina helped shape the development of the book.

We appreciate Susanne Steitz-Filler, Kathleen Pagliaro, and the production team of Wiley for their timely and quality engagement.

We thank our institutions, Johns Hopkins and Carnegie Mellon, for their support.

Tinglong Dai and Sridhar Tayur

1

Organizational Structure

Jay Levine

Massachusetts Institute of Technology; ECG Management Consultants (retired)

> *We now have an unparalleled opportunity to make healthcare better for the people we serve and to make it better for the people who choose this noble profession. Each of you who are involved in healthcare have a demanding and stressful job. But when you go home tired, and spent, and stressed out, ask yourself, 'What would I rather be doing?' What could be more worthwhile than caring for the thing others consider to be the most precious—their lives? (Charles Sorensen, MD, former president, Intermountain Healthcare)*

Selected attributes of the organization, management, and financing of healthcare services differentiate this industry from all others in the United States. These unique attributes create challenges for those conducting research and analysis focused on enhancing health outcomes, improving operational efficiencies, expanding patient access, and optimizing the financial performance of healthcare delivery systems. A firm grasp of these attributes, coupled with an understanding of the organizational design of healthcare services, will provide a foundation for the conduct of research and analysis focused on improving performance, outcomes, and patient satisfaction.

Handbook of Healthcare Analytics: Theoretical Minimum for Conducting 21st Century Research on Healthcare Operations, First Edition. Edited by Tinglong Dai and Sridhar Tayur.

1.1 Introduction to the Healthcare Industry

The healthcare industry is among the most regulated industries in the United States.[1,2] Federal and state statutes and regulations, along with licensure and industry accreditation requirements for hospital services, physician services, and services provided by other healthcare professionals (nurses, therapists, pharmacists, technicians, etc.), create a complex web of requirements that define the context within which patient care is delivered. Such regulations dictate where, how, when, and by whom healthcare services are provided. For the most part, these industry regulations and licensure/accreditation requirements have evolved over the past 100 years and are focused on ensuring the safety and efficacy of services provided to patients.

The healthcare industry encompasses numerous entities that interact (sometimes efficiently and sometimes inefficiently) to enhance or preserve the health status of patients. These entities include

- Physicians
- Hospitals
- Post-acute facilities and services
- Payers
- Other types of providers such as ambulatory surgical centers

Each of these entities plays a critical role in healthcare delivery. However, hospitals are likely the most complex among these entities and are central to the delivery of the most sophisticated care provided to patients.

Before we consider the operational complexity of hospitals, it is useful to review the various types of hospitals that operate in the United States. Hospitals can be classified in many ways, and multiple classifications can be attributed to a single institution. Outlined below are key types of hospitals.

- General Acute Care Hospitals. Most hospitals in the US are general acute care hospitals that provide care across many specialties such as adult care, pediatric care, surgical care, obstetrical care, etc.
- Specialty Hospitals. Selected facilities provide highly specialized care to targeted patients such as orthopedic patients, children, women, psychiatric patients, etc.
- Public Hospitals. The Veterans Administration (VA) operates dozens of hospitals. Public universities with medical schools sometimes own and operate university hospitals. Some cities and counties operate public

1 Field, R.I. (2007). *Healthcare Regulation in America: Complexity, Confrontation, and Compromise.* Oxford University Press.

2 Cochran, J. (May 2014). "Who Regulates and Oversees Healthcare Facilities in California?" California Healthcare Foundation. May 2014. http://www.chcf.org/publications/2014/05/regulate-oversight-tool

hospitals that often provide care to underserved populations. Some regions of the country have formed tax districts to support the budgets of local public community hospitals. And some states operate public psychiatric hospitals. Approximately 22% of US hospitals are public hospitals.[3]
- Not-for-Profit/Tax-Exempt Hospitals. Many community hospitals operate as not-for-profit/tax-exempt institutions. Approximately 58% of US hospitals fall into this category.
- Investor-Owned Hospitals. Approximately 20% of US hospitals are investor owned. Most investor-owned hospitals are operated by large hospital corporations that operate facilities in multiple states.
- Teaching Hospitals. There are approximately 400 teaching hospitals in the US, comprising about 7% of US hospitals.

Individual hospitals can be categorized by multiple typologies. For example, most specialty hospitals and public hospitals are also teaching hospitals. Some general acute care hospitals are investor-owned facilities. And teaching hospitals can be categorized into every typology cited above.

The mission of a hospital is in part a function of its type. Obviously, VA hospitals exist to meet the healthcare needs of US veterans. But most VA hospitals also maintain affiliations with medical schools and as such conduct educational programs for medical students, residents, fellows, and others. Similarly, teaching hospitals exist to provide patient care and to educate medical students and train residents, fellows, and other healthcare professionals. Public hospitals often exist to care for underserved populations, but many also operate teaching programs—all of which is reflected in their missions. And one public hospital (National Institutes of Health Clinical Center) exists exclusively for the conduct of clinical research. The missions of investor-owned hospitals can become somewhat muddied by virtue of the possible conflicts that may emerge between the investors' objectives and the missions to provide patient care to an underserved population and operate teaching programs as the principle teaching hospital of a medical school. The complexities attributable to such intersecting missions have implications for every aspect of an institution's operations, strategy formulation, financial performance, and public perception.

Beyond the comprehensive regulation of healthcare services and the multifaceted components of health delivery systems, the structure, economics, and financing of healthcare delivery differentiates healthcare from other industries in several important ways, as briefly outlined below.

1. Resource management and consumption. Physicians serve as the gatekeepers of patient access to most healthcare services. Patients cannot be admitted to a hospital, obtain ancillary services such as radiology and laboratory services, or obtain prescription medications without an order from

3 http://www.aha.org/research/rc/stat-studies/fast-facts.shtml

a physician. As such, physicians control access to the most sophisticated and expensive healthcare resources. Yet, interestingly, although the healthcare industry is highly regulated, the manner by which physicians order healthcare services for their patients (i.e., consume expensive resources) is generally not highly regulated. In fact, the practice styles of physicians and associated costs can vary dramatically, not only from physician to physician, but also from one region of the country to another.[4] Furthermore, physician practice styles drive hospital financial performance, yet hospitals can exercise only modest influence over how physicians consume expensive hospital resources. Most physicians are not employees of hospitals and consequently hospitals exert little managerial control over physician practice styles and resource consumption. Moreover, hospitals are dependent upon physicians who admit patients to the hospital. Without an adequate supply of physicians who admit patients to a hospital and who perform surgeries and other clinical procedures at that hospital, the patient census and associated patient care revenue will be inadequate to support the hospital. In summary, the organizational relationship between doctors and hospitals is complex, symbiotic, and potentially challenging to manage.

2. Payment for healthcare services. Only 11%[5] of healthcare expenses (~$330 billion in 2014) are paid for directly by patients out of pocket. In fact, patients are generally insulated from the direct financial implications of decisions they and their physicians make regarding their care and associated resource consumption. Some have argued that this dynamic is contributing to escalating healthcare costs[6]. Accordingly, some employers who pay much of the cost of health insurance premiums for their employees, as well as insurance companies and government payers who bear the financial burden for resource consumption decisions made by physicians and patients, have begun to seek strategies to shift some of the financial burden for such decisions to patients. For instance, employers shifting an increasing portion of premium costs to employees and insurance companies increasing policy deductibles and patient co-payments represent strategies for shifting this dynamic. Additionally, insurance companies have become increasingly selective regarding the physicians and hospitals that are included in their networks of approved providers in an effort to exclude those that are deemed too costly. In summary, physicians drive many of the patient care decisions that affect cost, while hospitals, insurance companies, government payers, and employers who finance insurance premiums incur

4 Gawande, A. "The Cost Conundrum." *The New Yorker*. June 1, 2009. http://www.newyorker.com/magazine/2009/06/01/the-cost-conundrum

5 Centers for Medicare and Medicaid Services. https://www.cms.gov/research-statistics-data-and-systems/statistics-trends-and-reports/nationalhealthexpenddata/nhe-fact-sheet.html

6 Cleverly, William O; Cleverly, James O; Song, Paula H. *Essentials of Healthcare Finance*. Jones and Bartlett Learning, LLC, Sudbury, MA, 2011. Page 140.

the expenses, and patients are generally insulated from much of the cost attributable to their care.

3. Initiatives to control costs. Policy experts, third-party payers, large employers, congress, and others have been seeking strategies to reduce the rate of increasing healthcare costs for decades. In 1971, President Richard Nixon imposed caps on healthcare wages and other healthcare expenditures. In 1978 and 1979, President Jimmy Carter proposed legislation to limit hospital cost increases. In 1982, the Tax Equity and Fiscal Responsibility Act created the framework for the Prospective Payment System to replace cost reimbursement for Medicare payments to hospitals[7]. During the late 1980s and throughout the 1990s, large employers collaborated with third-party payers in a failed effort to shift health insurance to a capitated model of payment to hospitals and physicians. And in 2010, President Barack Obama signed into law the Patient Protection and Affordable Care Act (ACA). In addition to its many provisions related to the availability of health insurance, the act established the Center for Medicare and Medicaid Innovation within the Centers for Medicare and Medicaid Services of the Department of Health and Human Services. Among the initiatives of the Innovation Center was development of bundled payments for care improvement. This innovative payment model has been applicable to three targeted categories of Medicare cases: joint replacements, some cardiac cases, and selected neurosciences cases. Under bundled payments, Medicare makes one payment to a participating health delivery system for a covered procedure, and that payment encompasses reimbursement for pre-procedure testing, hospitalization, physician/surgeon services, implant and device costs, and usually post-discharge care. It is then incumbent upon the delivery system to allocate the bundled payment accordingly, including payment to the involved physicians. Bundled payments are designed to align the financial interests of the physicians and the hospital, incentivize quality outcomes, and cap Medicare expenditures for applicable cases.[8]
4. Complexity of hospital operations and finance. The missions of hospitals contribute the complexity of their organizational design, operations, and financial structures; moreover, there is variability among these missions. Large teaching hospitals and academic medical centers, for instance, embrace a tripartite mission of patient care, teaching, and research. Community hospitals exist principally to meet selected patient care needs of their local communities. A research hospital, the National Institutes of Health Warren Grant Magnuson Clinical Center in Bethesda, Maryland, exists solely to conduct research to advance medical science and clinical

7 http://www.commonwealthfund.org/publications/from-the-president/2009/bending-the-health-care-cost-curve

8 Conversation with Jim Donohue, ECG Management Consultants, Inc., Boston MA. January 18, 2017.

care. And almost 20% of hospitals in the United States are investor owned,[9] which suggests that they operate, at least in part, to benefit shareholders. Thus, the organizational design, management structures, financing, and operations of these institutions vary considerably. Furthermore, some challenges and complexities are common among all hospitals and some challenges and complexities are unique to each category of hospital. The remainder of this chapter will describe the organizational design of healthcare delivery systems with a focus on the organizational design of hospitals and their interface with physicians. In light of the complex role, scale, and importance of teaching hospitals and academic medical centers (AMCs), much of the chapter will focus on those institutions.

Two basic financial data points will establish the context for this review. National health expenditures reached $3 trillion in 2014, or $9,523 per capita. The two largest categories of expenses included hospital expenses (32.1%) and physician and related clinical services (19.9%).[10] Hospitals and physicians are not only key components of the cost equation, but they also tend to drive the other elements of the healthcare cost equation, such as prescription drug costs (9.8% of national health expenditures) and nursing and other post-acute care facility costs (5.1%). Furthermore, much of the most sophisticated and therefore expensive healthcare services are provided at AMCs/teaching hospitals that generally provide care to the sickest patients.

1.2 Academic Medical Centers

There are approximately 400 teaching hospitals in the United States,[11] yet they constitute only 7% of all US hospitals. However, these ~400 teaching hospitals account for:

- 75% of burn care units
- 40% of neonatal intensive care units (ICUs)
- 61% of pediatric ICUs
- 61% of Level I trauma units
- 50% of surgical transplant services
- 44% of Alzheimer centers
- 22% of cardiac surgery services

9 American Hospital Association. http://www.aha.org/research/rc/stat-studies/fast-facts.shtml

10 National Center for Health Statistics. Centers for Disease Control and Prevention. http://www.cdc.gov/nchs/fastats/health-expenditures.htm

11 Defined as members of the Association of American Medical Colleges' Council of Teaching Hospitals.

- 41% of all hospital charity care
- 25% of Medicaid hospitalizations[12]

Teaching hospitals are one organizational component of AMCs; the other two are medical schools and faculty practice plans. These three organizational components share a tripartite mission of teaching, research, and patient care. However, each organizational component of the AMC plays a unique role and therefore places different levels of emphasis on the elements of the tripartite mission. Moreover, within the AMC, teaching, research, and patient care can all take place simultaneously in the same setting, involving the same patients, clinicians, researchers, students, and others. Clearly, these overlapping and simultaneous functions contribute to a highly complex organizational, managerial, and financial construct.

Although there can be some limited variability from one AMC to another, generally speaking, the role of each component of an AMC can be described as follows.

1. Medical schools exist to provide undergraduate (post-baccalaureate) medical education to medical students. Almost all medical school curricula require four years and include approximately two years of basic science/preclinical study and two years of clerkship/patient-related experience in a clinical setting.[13] The clinical setting may include the teaching hospital, community hospitals, clinics, and physician offices. Medical schools also serve as the site for most of the basic science and clinical research conducted at AMCs. In summary, the focus of medical schools is to direct and advance the academic enterprise: teaching and research. However, as we will address later, the clinical enterprise (i.e., the remaining two components of the AMC) finances much of the budget of medical schools, creating an important synergy for sustaining the AMC.
2. Teaching hospitals serve as the clinical site for much of the teaching and clinical research that occurs at AMCs. Medical students conduct clerkship rotations at teaching hospitals (undergraduate medical education) and resident physicians and fellows[14] continue their clinical training at teaching

---

12 Association of American Medical Colleges' Council of Teaching Hospitals https://www.aamc.org/download/47496/data/howdothservecommunities.pdf

13 In recent years selected medical schools have blended the preclinical and clinical components of the curriculum, and a few schools have implemented a three-year curriculum.

14 Resident physicians are medical school graduates who are continuing their training in a specialized field, such as internal medicine, pediatrics, general surgery, etc. A medical school graduate must complete a residency training program in order to practice medicine. Fellows are physicians who are continuing their training beyond residency in a sub-specialty field such as hand surgery, hematology-oncology, pediatric cardiology, etc.

hospitals (graduate medical education). In fact, teaching hospitals are the principle site for resident and fellow training, and Medicare reimburses teaching hospitals for some (but not all) of the costs associated with such training programs. However, the principle focus of teaching hospitals is to provide inpatient and outpatient care. In summary, teaching hospitals manage and finance the overlapping, integrated, and sometimes competing functions related to graduate medical education and patient care.

3. Faculty practice plans are the organized medical practices of the full-time faculty of medical schools. The faculty physician members of practice plans treat patients as a component of their responsibilities to teach medical students and supervise the clinical activities of residents and fellows. Some of the patient care and teaching activities take place in the hospital, and some of those functions take place in clinics, doctor offices, and other outpatient settings. Faculty practice plans provide the infrastructure necessary to support the faculty's clinical functions, including billing and collecting the professional fees generated through the patient care functions conducted by faculty physicians. Practice plans also compensate the faculty physicians for the patient care they provide.[15] In summary, faculty practice plans manage and finance the clinical activities of faculty physicians as they provide patient care services in association with their teaching activities.

Although the functional roles of the three components of AMCs are generally consistent from one AMC to another, there is variability in the organizational design of AMCs. Much of this variability is a function of history. However, recent market dynamics, changes in hospital and physician reimbursement by Medicare, Medicaid, and commercial insurers, and other elements of health reform have begun to cause shifts in the organizational design of AMCs.

Figure 1.1[16] depicts the five organizational constructs of AMCs. Each construct represents a unique set of organizational interrelationships and implies variability in the roles of the CEOs. Model 1 indicates that each component of the AMC is organized independently of the others. In other words, the teaching hospital and the faculty practice plan are both organizationally

---

15 The employment status of faculty physicians varies at AMCs. Some are employed solely by one organizational component of the AMC. At other AMCs, the faculty may be employed by multiple AMC entities. Accordingly, the flow of funds necessary to compensate faculty physicians for their teaching, research, and clinical activities is often quite complex and generally reflects elements of compensation directly attributable to their clinical and academic responsibilities. It is typical that faculty physician compensation consists of a modest base salary augmented by compensation that reflects clinical and academic productivity/performance. It is important to note that compensation for clinical activities is substantially more lucrative than for academic activities. It is well recognized by faculty that an hour spent in the operating room is much more lucrative than an hour spent conducting research in a laboratory.

16 Levine, J. "Considering Alternative Organizational Structures for Academic Medical Centers." *Academic Clinical Practice*. Association of American Medical Colleges. Washington, DC. Summer 2002. 14:2.

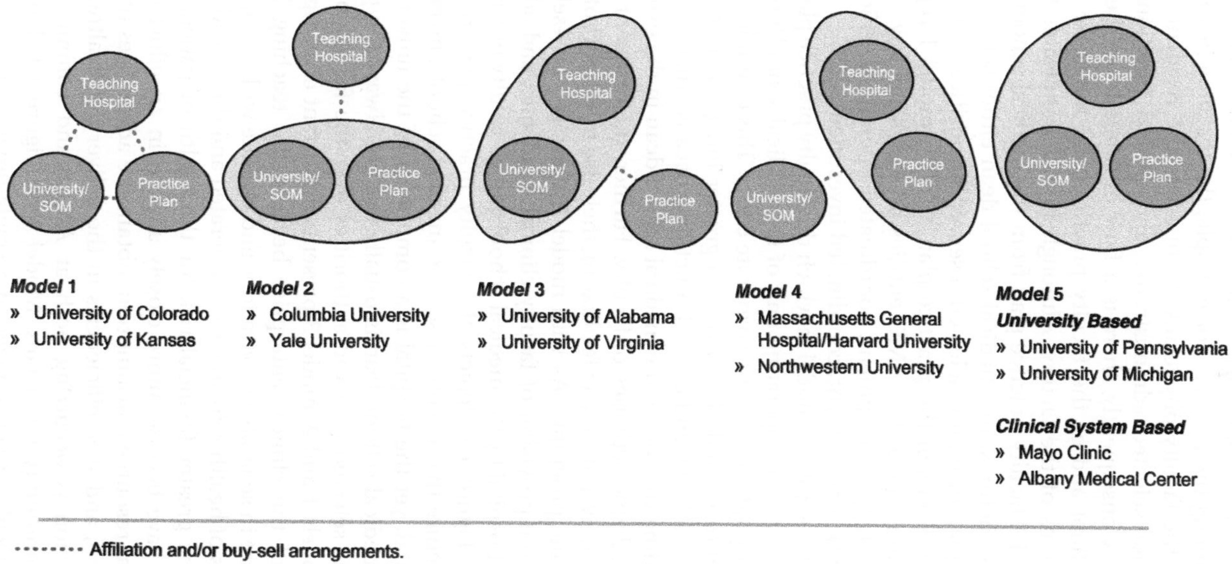

Figure 1.1 AMC Organizational Structures.

and corporately separate from the medical school and its parent university. A series of affiliation and buy-sell agreements defines the working and financial relationships among the entities. For example, the teaching hospital requires the services of the faculty physicians to supervise the residents and fellows and to carry out selected administrative and clinical functions on behalf of the hospital. Consequently, there is a flow of funds from the hospital to the medical school and/or the faculty practice plan for those clinical and academic activities of the faculty. Although model 1 indicates the separate relationship of the faculty practice plan from the medical school, in many of these types of structures, the medical school dean either serves as the CEO of the practice plan or retains selected reserved authorities over key strategic and financial decisions of the practice plan. Clearly, model 1 represents the weakest affiliation among the AMC entities and presents key challenges to coordinated strategy development, coordinated operations, efficient patient flow, effective risk management, coordinated investment, etc.

Selected AMCs employ a model in which the faculty practice plan is an organizational component or operating unit of the medical school/university, and the teaching hospital is a separate corporate entity. This example is depicted as model 2 on Figure 1.1 and often fosters a greater integration or coordination of the faculty's academic and clinical functions, because there is generally no question regarding the role of the medical school dean in the oversight of the clinical and academic activities of faculty. Further, the assets of the practice plan are clearly university assets facilitating their use in support of the medical school's academic programs. As with model 1, there is a buy-sell agreement that describes the provision of faculty clinical, academic, and administrative services to the hospital by the medical school and its faculty practice plan.

Model 3 on Figure 1.1 depicts the faculty practice plan outside of the corporate structure that encompasses the medical school/university and the teaching hospital, yet the hospital is a component of the university. As with model 1, the medical school dean is usually but not always the practice plan CEO or retains selected reserved authorities over the faculty practice plan. And, as do models 1 and 2, model 3 presents important challenges regarding coordination of the clinical enterprise because the teaching hospital and practice plan are in separate corporations and operate with less integration.

As the forces of health reform have accelerated and the providers of clinical services assume greater financial risk for the health of patients, physicians and hospitals have become more closely aligned in an effort to effectively manage clinical resource consumption, obtain the advantages of scale, attain market strength, and seek efficiencies in the delivery of healthcare services. This phenomenon is occurring both at AMCs and community hospitals and among community physicians. Model 4 on Figure 1.1 depicts teaching hospitals and faculty practice plans in a single organizational construct that is separate from the medical school/university. Due to the practice plan's integration with the teaching hospital, the medical school dean may not retain a role in the clinical practice of the faculty physicians. The dean's role is focused principally on the academic enterprise, and the hospital CEO exercises leadership over the clinical enterprise, that is, the hospital and the faculty practice plan. In recent years, selected AMCs have transitioned from model 1 (e.g., Northwestern University/Northwestern Medical Faculty Foundation /Northwestern Memorial Hospital) and model 2 (e.g,. University of Massachusetts/UMASS Memorial Medical Center) to model 4. It is not unreasonable to expect the trend toward greater integration/consolidation of the clinical enterprise to continue at both AMCs and community hospitals.

The most highly integrated AMCs are those represented by model 5 on Figure 1.1. This organizational construct combines all three components of the AMC under a single leader overseeing the academic and clinical enterprises. Model 5 is certainly positioned to avail the AMC of the synergies and efficiencies that can accrue from a close working relationship among the hospital, medical school, and faculty practice plan. Interestingly, most of the AMCs that fit this typology are centered at universities and embrace a highly academic focus with substantial investment in research and other academic initiatives often found at universities. However, a small subset of these highly integrated AMCs are based at clinical systems rather than based at universities (e.g., Mayo Clinic/Mayo Medical School, Albany Medical Center/Albany Medical College, and Geisinger Health System/Geisinger Commonwealth School of Medicine). As we reflect on the tripartite mission of AMCs, it is clear that the mission emphasis may vary in a university-based, integrated AMC (such as University of Pennsylvania) and a clinical system-based AMC (such as Mayo Clinic).

There is substantial synergy and complexity/competition in the interrelationship among the three organizational components of AMCs and between the academic enterprise (research and teaching) and the clinical enterprise (patient care). Much of this complexity can be attributed to

- Financial interdependencies
- Strategic interdependencies
- Operational interdependencies
- Competition for resources

Even a cursory review of the budgets that support medical schools demonstrates the stark dependence of the academic enterprise upon the clinical programs of the teaching hospital and the faculty practice plan. Figure 1.2 shows that in all 136 medical schools accredited by the Liaison Committee for Medical Education, 61% of the schools' revenue is derived from the faculty practice plan (42%) and the teaching hospital (19%). The 42% derived from the practice plan is overwhelmingly devoted to compensation of the medical school faculty physicians. A modest amount of practice plan revenue is used

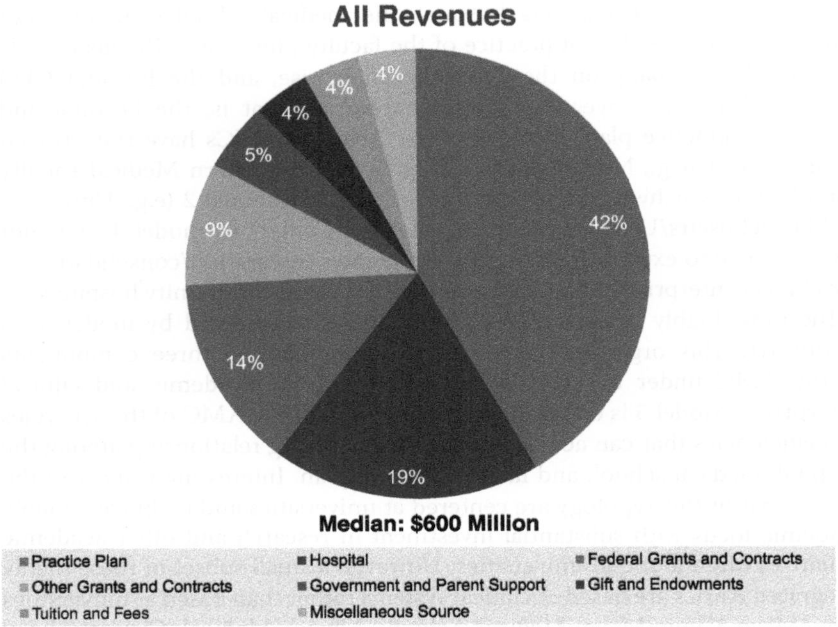

Figure 1.2 Fully-Accredited Medical School Revenue by Source 136 Medical Schools, FY 2016. *Source*: Association of American Medical Colleges Analysis of LCME Part I-A Annual Financial Questionnaire Data, https://www.aamc.org/data/finance/480314/figures1-2.html.

by deans and department chairs to finance new programs, to support the unfunded portion of research, and/or to support selected initiatives that are not self-sufficient. Similarly, the funds derived from the teaching hospital compensate medical school faculty who are providing clinical, administrative, and teaching services for the hospital.

High-performing AMCs generally recognize this financial interdependence and manage their enterprises accordingly. On the other hand, some AMCs are immersed in conflict over the flow of funds from the clinical enterprise to support teaching and research. This conflict can be a major source of tension and distraction for boards, executives, physicians, and others. Specifically, several of the AMCs depicted by models 1 and 2 on Figure 1.1 are embroiled in ongoing controversy regarding the magnitude of support for the academic enterprise provided by the practice plan and/or teaching hospital. In cases where the teaching hospital is investor owned and shareholder return on investment complicates the hospital's traditional tripartite mission, it is not difficult to envision protracted conflict between the medical school/university and its affiliated teaching hospital, related to financial support of the shared academic enterprise.

Case I: The AMC is in a relatively depressed urban center. The medical school is a component of a public university, and the AMC is depicted as model 1 on Figure 1.1; however, the medical school dean is president of the practice plan corporation. Due to its role in providing care to an underserved population, the hospital suffers from a poor payer mix and a challenging financial position. In an effort to "turn around" the hospital, it was converted from not-for-profit/tax-exempt to investor-owned and divested to a large national proprietary hospital corporation.

The hospital's investor-owned status complicates its traditional mission to provide care to the underserved inner city population and foster the academic enterprise. In response to deteriorating financial performance, the hospital reduced its financial support of the medical school (see Figure 1.2), and the medical school responded by indicating that it must seek an alternative teaching hospital partner that is better able to foster a shared academic mission. (The medical school and hospital share a campus and have been AMC partners for a century.) The hospital fears the loss of faculty physicians who admit and care for its patients and began an effort to lure physicians from the medical school to become hospital-employed physicians. The city has no other teaching hospitals of the scale necessary to support the academic programs of the medical school and serve as the practice site for the faculty physicians.

This controversy has been simmering for years, and in an effort to salvage the hospital-medical school partnership/AMC, the national hospital corporation has replaced the hospital CEO. The issues remain unresolved.

The synergy between the academic and clinical enterprises is critically important to AMCs. Teaching hospitals are dependent upon faculty physicians to admit and care for patients who generate hospital revenue. Without a busy faculty practice plan/medical staff, the hospital patient census and associated revenues will suffer. The most lucrative hospital patients are those who require complex surgeries or other complex medical interventions performed by sub-specialty physicians. Such physicians are generally attracted to AMCs with fellowship training programs in their specialty fields and with research conducted in their areas of expertise. Consequently, teaching hospitals are generally willing to finance the costs of fellowship programs in selected (lucrative) clinical areas as well as research in fields that complement the targeted clinical specialties. Clearly, there is value in coordinating the academic enterprise and clinical enterprise across the organizational components of the AMC.[17] Such balance is more likely to occur at those AMCs reflected in model 5 on Figure 1.1.

Although health reform has caused some AMCs to more closely align the components of the clinical enterprise (teaching hospital and faculty practice

---

17 "Synchronizing the Academic Health Center Clinical Enterprise and Education Mission in Changing Environments." The Blue Ridge Academic Health Group. Report 20. Winter 2016.

plan), AMC faculty physicians remain organized into specialty-based clinical departments: internal medicine, pediatrics, surgery, radiology, etc.[18] The department chair, usually jointly appointed by the medical school dean and hospital president, serves as the department CEO. The clinical department structure contributes to several operational, strategic, financial, and other challenges confronting AMCs due to the following:

- Although AMC policy guides the operation of each clinical department, departments operate with a relatively high degree of autonomy.
- Department chairs are usually evaluated based upon the academic, clinical, and financial performance of their departments. This can foster competition among departments for scarce resources such as space, institutional investment, philanthropy, patient referrals, etc.
- The financial performance of individual departments is, to a great extent, a function of how third-party payers reimburse physicians for patient care services. For example, some clinical services (e.g., anesthesia, surgery, radiology) are reimbursed at higher rates than other services (e.g., pediatrics, general internal medicine, psychiatry).

The clinical organization of faculty physicians creates a series of silos that can impede operational efficiencies, coordinated investment, and integrated strategies.

A closer look at the funds flow within an AMC clinical department will further highlight the interdependencies among the components of an AMC, the competing attributes of the tripartite mission, and the effects of the traditional silo structure of clinical departments. Figure 1.3 shows a typical funds flow for a clinical department. The revenue streams include professional fees attributable to patient care provided by department faculty physicians, hospital payments for graduate medical education (GME), administration of clinical services (e.g., intensive care units) and occasionally patient care that is not reimbursable by professional fees, and grants and contracts for research and special patient care programs. An academic enrichment fund (sometimes called a dean's tax) is charged against professional fees and is the only source of discretionary or flexible funds for the dean. The department pays its operating expenses, including the unreimbursed portion of indirect research expenses.[19]

Remaining funds are distributed in part to physicians as incentives for clinical and academic performance. Remaining funds also provide flexible funds

18 The clinical department structure is replicated across the three organizational components of the AMC such that there is, for example, a department of internal medicine in the medical school, in the teaching hospital, and in the faculty practice plan. The department chair directs and coordinates the internal medicine faculty physicians across all three organizational entities.

19 Even the best research grants, such as those from the National Institutes of Health, pay only a portion of indirect costs. The balance must be covered by the institution receiving the grant. At medical schools, the unreimbursed cost is financed by the clinical practice of the faculty physicians.

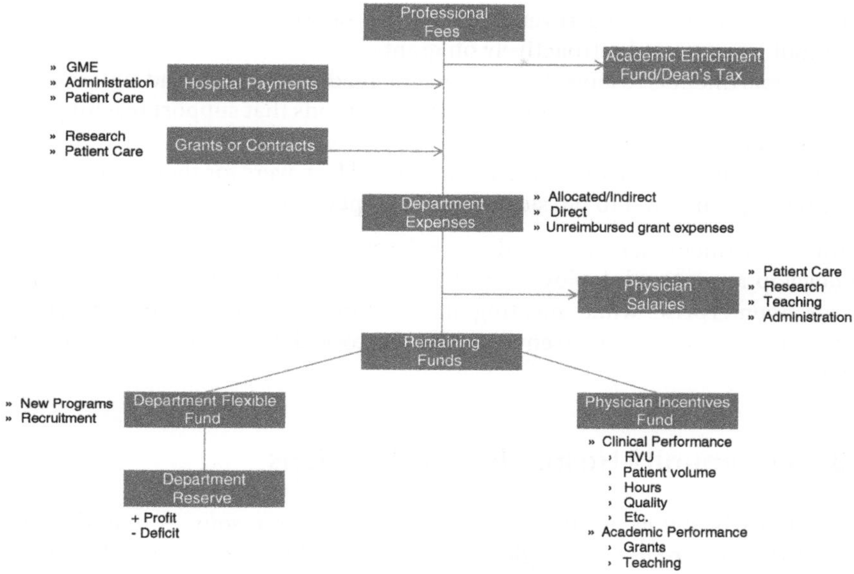

Figure 1.3 AMC Clinical Department Funds Flow.

for the department to finance new academic and clinical programs and to finance new faculty recruitments. Any remaining funds accrue to department reserves and to offset any previous operating deficits. Although there are some exceptions, many clinical departments operate on a razor-thin margin. Further, the vagaries of the professional fee reimbursement system favors some specialties (e.g., anesthesia) at the expense of others (e.g., pediatrics). Often, the dean must use the academic enrichment fund to offset losses in under-reimbursed or underperforming departments.

Case II: The department of pediatrics is suffering financial shortfalls that may be attributable to one or more of the following factors:

- The department has a large research enterprise that brings prestige to the AMC and university. However, grants support only a portion of indirect costs associated with the research enterprise.
- In order to generate successful grant applications, the department deploys several faculty physicians to develop research protocols and associated grant applications.
- The time that faculty devote to such activities takes them away from patient care functions that generate professional fee revenue. Some faculty physicians devote multiple years to developing research protocols and grant applications, and not all grant applications are funded. Consequently, their

work is not generating revenue, and their salary and other related costs cannot be recouped retroactively on grants.
- The department is responsible for teaching medical students and supervising residents and fellows. As at other AMCs, the funds that support teaching are constrained.
- Pediatricians are generally under-reimbursed by payers for their patient care activities, compared to physicians in other specialties.

The department has generated several years of deficit and is challenged to develop an optimal deployment of faculty that can continue to foster the research enterprise while meeting its teaching obligation and generating sufficient professional fee revenue to offset historic deficits and foster financial viability.

1.3 Community Hospitals and Physicians

Community hospitals are the "hub" of the healthcare resources that support the delivery of care to every region of the country. Most community hospitals are not-for-profit/tax-exempt, although there are many examples of public and investor-owned community hospitals. Not-for-profit/tax-exempt community hospitals generally include the following attributes:

- Governing board composed of community leaders who are responsible for the oversight, operations, and strategic direction of the facility.
- Medical staff composed of voluntary physicians, that is, doctors who are not employed by the hospital or an affiliated entity.

An important synergy, as well as a dynamic tension, exists between voluntary physicians and community hospitals. Voluntary physicians are not hospital employees and in most cases have no direct business or financial arrangement with the community hospitals. Instead, they volunteer their time to serve on a community hospital medical staff. In return for the privilege of admitting patients and practicing medicine at the hospital, voluntary physicians are obligated to participate on selected clinical committees of the hospital, such as infection control, quality assurance, and process improvement. They also agree to take call in the hospital's emergency department, which means that they agree to treat emergency department patients who require their specialty expertise. Obligations to treat these patients extend to all such patients, irrespective of their ability to pay for physician services. In return for the volunteered time[20] and expertise, the hospital bestows upon the physicians admitting, surgical, and other clinical privileges that entitle the physicians to

20 A recent trend has been that some physicians demand compensation by the hospital for taking emergency department call. Additionally, some community hospitals with modest patient

admit and treat patients at the hospital. The hospital imposes limitations on its physicians and provides clinical privileges specific to each physician's training and expertise.

The synergy in this voluntary medical staff structure is that the hospital is dependent upon the voluntary physicians to admit and care for patients, which generates revenue to support the hospital. Further, the physicians are dependent upon the hospital for the provision of sophisticated services (e.g., laboratory, radiology) necessary for the care and treatment of their patients. Physicians are also dependent upon the hospital to provide the clinical setting (e.g., operating rooms, intensive care units) and associated staff required by their patients.

In small and remote communities with a single hospital, the voluntary medical staff arrangement is not particularly complex to manage. However, in larger communities with competing hospitals, it is not unusual for voluntary physicians to maintain privileges at multiple/competing hospitals and admit their patients to the institutions that can provide the most attractive benefits. Such benefits may include easy scheduling of patients for surgery and convenient operating room start times. (Surgery patients are among the most lucrative for a hospital, so it is not uncommon for community hospitals to compete for the busiest surgeons in the community.) The shift of lucrative surgeries from one hospital to another can have a substantial effect on hospital financial performance.

In the voluntary medical staff model, the physicians do not have a financial or employment relationship with the hospital. This has important implications for resource consumption and operating costs for the hospital. To understand such implications, note that among the themes conveyed to medical students and residents during undergraduate and graduate medical education are

- Think for yourself.
- Trust your training and insights.
- You are the responsible party.

These themes can occasionally contribute to challenges for hospital management related to operational efficiencies, resource consumption, and staff morale. The manner in which the physician delivers care in the hospital and interacts with hospital staff has direct implications on hospital costs and operating efficiency. For example, three different physicians may require three different manufacturers of expensive surgical supplies, thereby causing the hospital to increase its inventory. Each physician may require alternative versions of the same medication, driving up pharmacy costs. And certain

---

volumes must supplement the professional fee revenue generated by hospital-based physicians (anesthesiologists, emergency medicine, pathologists, and radiologists) in order to recruit an adequate number of such physicians to meet the clinical needs of the hospital.

physicians may routinely keep their patients in the hospital beyond the number of days for which Medicare or other payers reimburse the hospital and thereby generate unreimbursed hospital costs.

Voluntary physicians may be reluctant to modify their traditional practice styles or schedules. As a result, scheduling physician access to operating rooms can be highly contentious. For instance, it seems that all surgeons prefer an early start time in the operating room on Monday morning. Conversely, none want the 2:00 Friday afternoon start time—for numerous reasons, including the likely requirement that they see their postsurgical patients during the weekend. Effective/efficient scheduling of surgeries can have dramatic implications for hospital operations and cost performance. The voluntary nature of the medical staff arrangement makes it challenging for hospital management to achieve operational efficiencies and cost savings. In fact, this community hospital dilemma is sometimes characterized as follows: Physicians influence hospital efficiency, operations, and hospital operating costs, but who manages the physicians?

Selected AMCs and Health Maintenance Organizations[21] have adopted a closed medical staff model that involves employment and management of the physicians by an organization affiliated with the hospital.[22] In the case of AMCs, the employing entity may be the medical school/university or faculty practice plan. In the case of health maintenance organizations (HMOs), the employing entity may be an affiliated multispecialty medical group.[23] This physician employment arrangement can provide institutions with the managerial mechanisms to align the interests of the hospital with those of the physicians. In a closed medical staff model, managerial influence can more effectively be brought to bear on issues related to resource consumption, operational efficiency, patient satisfaction, patient outcomes, and other considerations.

Although every hospital devotes substantial managerial expertise to optimizing performance of the physician component of the delivery system, the challenge is most daunting for community hospitals with a voluntary medical staff, especially for hospitals in markets where multiple hospitals compete for physician services and patient admissions. The challenge for such hospitals is to attract physicians and their patients by offering convenience, customer service (keep in mind that the customer is often the patient as well as the physician), and high-quality patient care. As insurers, employers, and others who finance patient care become increasingly concerned with cost, competition now also extends to cost performance.

---

21 Such as Henry Ford Medical Group and Kaiser Permanente Medical Group.

22 Many state corporate practice of medicine statutes preclude hospitals from directly employing physicians.

23 Such as the Kaiser Permanente Medical Group.

In most, if not all hospitals, convenience, customer service, quality of care, and cost performance are directly related to the composition, training, size, and management of the employed hospital staff. In excess of 50% of hospital operating cost is attributable to labor expense,[24] and the largest subset of labor cost is related to hospital nurses. Hospital nurses generally deliver the patient care as specified by the physicians. Of course this physician-nurse dynamic is complicated by the fact that in many cases at community hospitals and at some AMCs, the physicians operate outside of the managerial construct of the hospital, yet their clinical decisions and style of practice have a direct impact on nurse staffing and performance and the staffing and performance of other hospital departments. Furthermore, physicians and nurses interact on a daily basis in operating rooms, intensive care units, nursing units, emergency departments, etc. Those professional interactions are highly complex because they impact patient care, clinical outcomes, operating efficiencies, patient satisfaction, physician satisfaction, employee satisfaction, and other considerations—all of which influence the quality of patient care and financial performance of the hospital.

One of the key indicators that hospital executives monitor on a daily, weekly, monthly, and annual basis is nursing cost and nursing full-time equivalents per occupied bed. Even a slight shift in these ratios can have material impact upon quality of care, patient outcomes, patient safety, patient satisfaction, and hospital financial performance. Complicating this management challenge is the fact that the nursing population in the US is aging, which drives up hourly wages due to the seniority of nurses in the employment pool. Furthermore, a nurse shortage has loomed for decades. In 1980, 54% of nurses were under the age of 40. In 2008, only 29.5% of nurses were under the age of 40.[25]

1.4 Conclusion

The recent confluence of three related initiatives have brought the healthcare industry into its current era of reform. In 2000, the Institute of Medicine (IOM, but now the National Academy of Medicine) published a landmark report entitled "To Err Is Human."[26] This report drew attention to the opportunities to enhance quality of care, patient safety, and patient outcomes. The report provided a roadmap toward safer health delivery systems and began a national conversation focused on improving the quality of patient care. Eight years after the IOM report, the Institute for Health Improvement (IHI) first described

---

24 http://www.aha.org/content/11/11costtrendspricediffreport.pdf

25 http://www.nursingworld.org/MainMenuCategories/ThePracticeofProfessionalNursing/workforce/Fast-Facts-2014-Nursing-Workforce.pdf

26 *To Err Is Human: Building a Safer Health System.* Institute of Medicine of the National Academy of Sciences. Washington DC. 2000

the Triple Aim of simultaneously improving population health, improving the patient experience of care, and reducing per capita cost.[27] The Triple Aim entered the lexicon and represented an early expression of the objectives of health reform. In 2010, Congress passed and President Obama signed into law the Patient Protection and Affordable Care Act. In addition to the well-known provisions related to expanded access to health insurance, the new law made substantial changes to how Medicare pays for hospital and physician services. The overarching purpose of these reimbursement changes is twofold: (1) to begin the shift away from paying physicians based upon the volume of services provided to patients; and (2) to begin to consider quality indicators as a component of the reimbursement mechanism. Similarly, hospital reimbursement was revised to place hospitals at modest risk for the continuing health status of Medicare patients who were discharged from the hospital. As has typically been the case for the past 50 years, revisions in Medicare reimbursement to physicians and hospitals greatly influence the reimbursement mechanisms employed by commercial health insurance companies. Likewise, a shift in reimbursement across the healthcare industry has resulted from the Affordable Care Act.

The confluence of these three events has created new and increased pressures for hospitals and physicians. As has occurred in other industries[28] disrupted by major regulatory changes, the healthcare industry is currently experiencing significant reorganization that can be characterized by

- New entrants to the market
- Focus on consumers
- Pressure to reduce cost/improve productivity
- Consolidation
- Shakeout

The complexity of healthcare delivery in association with recent regulatory changes and industry disruption has created substantial opportunity for health services researchers to bring their expertise to bear on the challenges confronting the organization, management, delivery, and financing of healthcare. The application of sophisticated analytical approaches will undoubtedly be important to health delivery systems as they are transformed in response to the IOM report, IHI's Triple Aim, and health reform that has been accelerated by the Affordable Care Act.

---

27 http://www.ihi.org/engage/initiatives/tripleaim/Pages/default.aspx
28 Airlines, telecommunications, banking, etc.

2

Access to Healthcare

Donald R. Fischer

Highmark Inc.

2.1 Introduction

Health has become a national obsession. The mainstream media presents a nearly continuous focus on health-related topics, covering anything from extremely fit individuals who focus on nutrition and exercise for chronic disease prevention to those who are already chronically ill and clamor for appropriate healthcare and insurance coverage. Yet, the current healthcare "system" often fails to deliver value to its customers. Whether we're ultra-fit and determined to live forever or we're living a lifestyle that invites chronic disease, we all eventually need healthcare in some fashion. Ideally, we will all be insured against catastrophic financial losses from the costs of such healthcare. However, despite the universal need for healthcare, we buy it directly or indirectly with little objective guidance on quality, and Americans spend more than any other country per capita on the service. The national conversation about the percentage of uninsured individuals has been politically charged and is front and center once again in the coming years as a new administration controls Washington.

Although the United States generally enjoys the availability of the newest, most advanced, and innovative medical procedures and health technology, there is no question that variation in quality of care across regions and populations is large, and that the value derived from new discoveries is not being fully captured. The major issues dominating the lay press have been poor quality of care, excessive costs, and a large uninsured population. Employer-based insurance has been the model for health coverage in the United States for decades, but as the employers' costs of providing health benefits to their employees have skyrocketed, employers have become a major driver in demanding value from the dollars they spend in this sector.

Quality management in the manufacturing world has been a focus of research since the work of J. Edwards Deming in post–World War II Japan—work that

Handbook of Healthcare Analytics: Theoretical Minimum for Conducting 21st Century Research on Healthcare Operations, First Edition. Edited by Tinglong Dai and Sridhar Tayur.

fostered the discipline of measuring results, reengineering processes, and continuously improving, all of which led to higher quality and lower costs.[1] And for most products, the lay public has access to transparent information that demonstrates comparative value among products that they seek to buy. Health care, on the other hand, has been slow to embrace a similar culture. A patient choosing a physician for an elective procedure has virtually no information on which to base a decision about which provider adheres to standardized care processes or has better outcomes. In fact, poor outcomes, as evidenced by malpractice suits, are purposefully hidden from the public as a matter of law. In addition, price transparency is virtually nonexistent.

The current state of the problem is multifactorial:

1. **Insurance products are complicated and confusing.**
   For example, consider the options of the Medicare-eligible retired individual who is over the age of 65. It is quite likely that this person had a group policy through his employment until the point of retirement, and that very few choices of plan were offered by that employer. The individual was provided basic comparison information at the time of enrollment in order to assist selection of the plan that best fit his needs and budget. But most of the work to screen options had been done by the company's human resource department.
   The difference with Medicare is striking; the handbooks explaining both the public and private options are difficult to comprehend, and there is no HR department equivalent to serve as a navigator. Though the general public sees Medicare as a "single payer" with a standard product, on closer examination it is far more complex. An individual can choose an "off-the-shelf" traditional Medicare policy directly from the government for both hospital services (Part A) and for physician services (Part B), but must pay an income-based contribution for the Part B aspect of the plan, which will be deducted from any social security payment made to that individual. In addition, the enrollee may select a Part D plan (drug coverage) from a variety of private health insurers. However, careful inspection of the coverage provided by standard Medicare reveals many gaps that could put an enrollee at substantial financial risk if no other action is taken. For example, coverage for specialty pharmaceutical drugs is based on 20% coinsurance on the part of the individual, translating to a cost of $2,000 for a drug costing $10,000. As a result, most Medicare-eligible individuals decide to cover those gaps with a policy bought from a private insurer, either through a Medigap product superimposed on traditional Medicare or through a Medicare Advantage product from a private plan that rolls Part A, Part B, and Part D together into a comprehensive wrap-around policy that limits financial exposure.

1 Deming, W.E. (1954). On the teaching of statistical principles and techniques to people in industry. *Bulletin of the International Statistical Institute* Tome XXXIV Part 2.

To complicate matters further, each type of private plan varies in benefit structures, provider networks, deductibles, copays, and associated premiums. Even the most sophisticated professionals struggle to navigate the nuances of these products and make decisions that are in their best interest. The world of individual products for the under-65 population is similarly confusing.

2. **Insurance coverage allows the individual member to be distanced from actual costs.**

   Depending on the policy, a member may have little incentive to pay any attention to the real cost of services. Patients receive meager guidance from their physicians about the cost of care or the value of various options; this lack of dialogue about choices means that decisions tend to be dictated by provider recommendations. This is especially true when insurance benefits are rich in their design, providing nearly all of the cost reimbursement necessary to pay for the service.

   As an example, consider the recommendation for a patient to have an outpatient MRI performed for an acute ankle sprain. The list prices of MRI tests vary considerably, and the actual member contribution toward the service depends on her health plan's discounted reimbursement rate with the various vendors and on her benefits (deductibles and copays). In the case of a plan with first dollar coverage, a member would have no incentive to choose the lowest cost provider or to even question whether the test was necessary. On the other hand, an individual with a $2500 deductible would have a real interest in assuring that the test was actually essential. He might be inclined to ask, "Can I just ice my ankle and keep weight off it for a few days?" If necessity is indeed confirmed, then the patient should be motivated to choose the provider that charges the lowest fee (say $250 versus $1000), if that information is readily available. But finding that actionable information is often difficult.

3. **The uninsured population adds costs to the healthcare system that are borne by those who have insurance.**

   The uninsured population was estimated to be as high as 50 million individuals prior to the rollout of the individual product marketplace in late 2013. Over the next three years, over 20 million individuals secured health plan coverage as a result of the Affordable Care Act, still leaving upwards of 30 million uninsured.[2] Why does this matter? First, lack of insurance leads to poor health status. Second, uninsured individuals still seek and receive care, often by appearing in a hospital emergency department when they are quite ill and must be treated based on a longstanding federal law. Their care leads to substantial unreimbursed costs at the hospital level, resulting

2 Key facts about the uninsured population. http://www.kff.org/uninsured/fact-sheet/key-facts-about-the-uninsured-population/

in institutional requests for disproportionate increases in reimbursement at the time of renegotiation of contracts with insurers. Insurers end up paying larger increases than would be warranted from their own book of business, in order to assure that struggling hospitals stay solvent. And as this happens, care costs and premiums for employer-based plans escalate out of proportion to actual incurred costs. There is strong evidence that the reduction in the uninsured population that occurred as a result of the ACA has improved hospitals' bottom lines, and has blunted the overall rate of rise of per capita healthcare costs.[3,4]

Alternatively, if the uninsured rate rises again, disproportionate increases in premiums will again be seen by those with employer-based coverage, leading more employers to drop coverage, and triggering the much-discussed "death spiral" for health coverage on the private market.

4. **Financial incentives for hospitals, physicians, and other providers are not aligned with patient value.**

   Most hospitals, physicians, and other provider types are compensated based on the volume of services that they deliver, following the dominant "fee-for-service" reimbursement model. In a business plan to increase revenue, the major lever is to generate more encounters with patients and to generate more procedures and tests for each patient seen. In many instances, additional physician payment is tied to prescribing specific high-cost pharmaceuticals and biologic treatments, creating a perverse incentive to overprescribe.

   For instance, in an oncology service line, a percentage of the cost of a chemotherapy drug is paid to the practice as additional compensation. If a medical oncologist is seeing a patient with lung cancer who requires chemotherapy, the physician will generally receive three sources of revenue for that patient encounter: a professional fee for seeing the patient, an administration fee for infusing the chemotherapy drug, and as much as 6% of the price of the drug given to the patient. While the first two are generally based on a fixed fee schedule from Medicare or the private plan, the drug surcharge is directly related to the cost of the drug. In this model, giving the most expensive drug yields the greatest physician revenue. Similarly, there is an incentive to continue a patient on chemotherapy beyond when there is a truly therapeutic advantage. Patients are generally unaware of this conflict of interest.

   Increasingly, there is a call for financial incentives to be tied to better quality or documented improvement in outcomes; however, these metrics are

3 Blumenthal D., Abrams M., Nuzum R. (2015). The Affordable Care Act at 5 years. *New England Journal of Medicine* 372:2451–2458.

4 Searing A. (2016). Beyond the reduction in uncompensated care: Medicaid expansion is having a positive impact on safety net hospitals and clinics. Georgetown University Health Policy Institute June 2016:1–6.

hard to obtain, and provider pushback to document performance metrics is substantial.

5. **Medical care is disjointed.**
   Poor communication among providers caring for the same patient hampers optimal care delivery. This is particularly problematic for the patient with multiple medical and surgical conditions who is seen in disparate venues. A fully interoperable electronic health record (EHR) can provide full information at the point of care, yet penetration of interoperable systems within the provider community is not high. Let's consider a common scenario: an older patient with dementia and a variety of chronic diseases appears in an emergency room of a hospital system where the patient has not been seen before. In the absence of a reliable medical historian or any paper or electronic record, the medical team often resorts to an extensive battery of tests to rediscover what other providers may already know. This not only results in wasteful costs, but can also directly lead to harm if unnecessary testing is associated with a complication—for example, sedating an agitated patient for an unnecessary CT scan, which then leads to a respiratory arrest.
   Full information at the point of care is the gold standard. Twenty years ago, that might have been achieved only by gathering all of a patient's paper charts and manually perusing them to determine the core problem lists, test results, medications, and plan. But if the patient was being seen in multiple locations, full information was never possible. In the era of EHRs, the most sophisticated health systems and population centers are able to facilitate such information for the provider so that key issues are not overlooked. And decision support is embedded in the best EHR systems to facilitate the best course of action based on medical evidence. The travesty is that available technology has not spread quickly, and cooperation among competing health systems has often prevented interoperability among various health systems' EHRs, even within the same community.
6. **Measuring success is primitive.**
   There is little reliance on measuring outcomes for populations of patients within and between provider practices. Pay for value programs have been promulgated by health plans to drive improved quality, initially providing bonus payments for adhering to standardized processes and, more recently, rewarding on the basis of better outcomes. For example, pediatricians would all agree with the evidence that immunizing all children against measles, mumps, rubella (MMR) on a schedule that is approved by the American Academy of Pediatrics is a desirable activity. Not only is it desirable, but the rate of immunizing should also approach 100% of the population who are of the appropriate age. Using a population-based approach, a large employer might then expect that over 95% of the dependent children of the appropriate age who receive health insurance coverage from them should have received the MMR vaccine, assuming that there may be some children with

contraindications or some parents who refuse vaccines that would prevent the immunization rate from being 100%. However, there is a rather broad variation in immunization rates for this and all other vaccines. Assuring high immunization rates requires a systematic approach, and providers must be accountable for making certain that their patient population is adherent. One tactic may be recalling children who are overdue for their MMR, rather than simply relying on parents to remember to do so. Yet, many providers see such population measurements as intrusive, requiring laborious record keeping that adds unnecessarily to their workload.

Many other processes can also be measured and tied to reimbursement. Much more problematic are rewards based on outcomes. Physicians tend to dislike being measured and dislike the implications that such metrics can be used to differentiate physicians based on quality. They prefer to rely on their reputations as experts and expect the public to accept their word that they perform well compared to their peers.

7. **Spread of best practices is glacial.**

   Historically, new information and best practices spread slowly in the medical world; research has suggested that new knowledge doesn't become incorporated into standard medical practice for 17 years.[5] Even if this timeline is exaggerated, there is no doubt that knowledge and change in behavior spread slowly in healthcare. The causes include the following:

   - Physicians are usually at their most knowledgeable about current medicine when they finish residency because they have recently been immersed in highly academic environments surrounded by brilliant faculty and supported in their need to learn while they deliver care.
   - Residents are trained by clinical mentors at academic medical centers who may be propagating long-standing biases about approaches to care.
   - Education after residency training tends to be haphazard and is driven by an individual physician's interests.
   - Reading the latest journal articles on new science is time-consuming and becomes a last priority in a busy practitioner's day.
   - The quantity of new information in medicine is growing exponentially.
   - The best and brightest physicians are still human; they cannot remember everything.

   New methods of spreading the latest evidence and facilitating best practices beyond didactic education are needed, perhaps accommodated by electronic tools at the point of care.

---

5 Bauer M., Damschroder L., Hagedomk H., Smith J, Kilbourne A.M.: An introduction to implementation science for the non-specialist. *BMC Psychol* 3(1):32. 2015.

2.2 Goals

Considering that everyone uses the healthcare system and most expect to receive optimal care, it should be a goal to ensure that the money that we spend on healthcare truly brings better outcomes. The travesty of the current system is that the United States spends more on healthcare per capita and as a percentage of GDP than any other country, yet we rank as low as 39th among all countries in the World Health Organization (WHO) metrics of health quality. Don Berwick, founder of the Institute for Healthcare Improvement (IHI) and a former acting administrator of CMS, has proposed that the industry pursue the Triple Aim,[6] which embraces the following improvement goals:

1. Improve the patient experience of care (quality and satisfaction)
2. Improve the health of populations
3. Reduce per capita cost of care

The goals are clear, concise, and ambitious. The tactics to achieve the goals are myriad and will be enhanced if traditional health providers and payers can partner with bright minds in other disciplines to seek new solutions and tools to achieve transformation. For too long, healthcare policy and care delivery have been isolated fields, dependent on the life sciences to drive innovation. Although that method has yielded great benefits in developing new cures, new clinical procedures, and new diagnostics, it has not generated disruptive innovation in systems improvement, reengineering of processes, and delivery of value. A great opportunity lies in engaging scientists in the spheres of computer science, engineering, and business to think creatively about an industry crying for fresh solutions. This handbook is focused on posing questions that beg for answers from nontraditional sectors that might be able to design disruptive innovations to bring value to our healthcare spending.

Potential tactics include the following:

1. Develop tools to reliably and simply measure the health of populations, enabling easy comparisons among populations managed by competing providers or managed in different ways. Health plan claims costs have been extremely useful in beginning to look at unwarranted variation in practice as defined by process metrics, but they are generally not useful in measuring outcomes of care. It will be necessary to capture appropriate outcomes from interoperable electronic health records in a manner that requires little

6 Berwick D., Nolan T., Whittington J. The Triple Aim: Care, Health and Cost. *Health Affairs* 27:759–769. 20

work for the providers beyond capturing data, both from their own work and from the patients themselves.

2. Provide transparent actionable information about performance of providers and payers, as well as reliable cost and price data, to enable the public to comparison shop. These data should include both overall cost of services and accurate predictions of an individual's personal financial responsibility based on his insurance product design.
3. Design a reimbursement model that eliminates moral hazards. The fee for service model that predominates today provides an incentive to overtreat, creating overuse and misuse errors that cause harm and add unwarranted cost. The typical capitation model that dominated in the 1990s provided an incentive to undertreat, as revenue that flowed on a per-patient basis was associated with the highest profit margin if patient encounters and treatments were minimized. Ultimately the public good is best served if financial rewards for providers are aligned with better outcomes, lack of harm, satisfied patients, and reasonable costs (the Triple Aim).
4. Reengineer the care team to capitalize on the appropriate skill sets for the tasks required. The current reimbursement model often requires that a service be delivered by a physician in order for payment to be made. Yet many care delivery tasks can be handled by a trained professional with a different skill set whose hourly rate is less costly. For instance, while a pediatrician is knowledgeable and well trained to handle routine well child care, nurse practitioners and child development experts can handle many of the well child visits. Using a pediatrician's time for routine tasks like anticipatory guidance is not the best use of time for a physician who spent at least three years in pediatric residency managing highly complex patient needs. Yet, if payment for managing a patient happens only if the physician performs the encounter, we propagate a system where clinicians are not "practicing to the top of their license." Systems improvement is needed to develop an integrated care team that achieves the most effective proportion of physicians and other health professionals, thus assuring that the right person is delivering the right service to the right patient at the right time.
5. Use technology to meet patients where they live and work. The concept of requiring in-person visits for care delivery is archaic. Although direct patient contact is critical to develop a trusting relationship and will almost always be necessary for initial evaluation and management of a new patient, much of the follow up and management of a patient with a clearly defined treatment plan can be handled remotely, aided by technology. Developing the right tools and assuring a reimbursement model that accommodates such methodology is essential to changing the paradigm. It is quite likely that embracing digital monitoring and accommodating frequent remote communications with the care team will improve adherence to prescribed

regimens, allow early interventions for declining health status, and improve patient satisfaction.

Process flow mapping is a standard technique to assign value to each step in a process. Non-value-added steps are those that are ripe for elimination. In a process flow mapping of in-person ambulatory visits, the following are all non-value-added steps: traveling to an appointment, parking the car, registering for the appointment, waiting to be placed in an examining room, waiting for the physician once a patient is in a room, checking out, retrieving the car, traveling to the pharmacy, waiting for a prescription to be filled, and traveling home. The value-added steps, on the other hand, are short in duration and limited to personal communication with the physician and pharmacist. How much time and money can be saved on the part of both patient and provider if the non-value-added steps are minimized?

6. Medicine is increasingly complex, with the burden of new information and knowledge accelerating every year. A physician in the past may have been able to rely on innate intelligence, an excellent memory, and a commitment to staying current with the medical literature in order to provide reliable care. That is no longer possible, and decision support to assist in management of complex patients is necessary to guarantee that current standards of care are met. We need to accelerate the adoption of new evidence, rather than waiting 17 years for knowledge to spread into practice. And we need to ensure that the complex patient who is seeing multiple physicians is certain that all of their information is available at the time of every encounter. The role of informatics and analytics in assessing individual practice patterns and populations of patients will be critical in assuring continuous learning and enhancing care.

2.3 Opportunity for Action

The key to transformation in healthcare delivery will depend on abandoning traditional assumptions that have been intrinsic to the development of our current "non-system" of care. Traditional medical training has relied on recruitment of bright minds who have a proven ability to work autonomously. Physicians have been confident in their abilities to absorb information and use it independently to handle the problem at hand for each patient. But being smart and having a good memory do not comprise a reliable system for either population health or individual patient management.

Instead, we must use actionable clinical and cost data, analytical tools, and computer modeling to design a true system of care that meets the needs of populations of patients. The success of medicine depends on recognizing that it is truly a collaborative effort driven by population data and by our understanding of science that is constantly changing. The multidisciplinary team needed for this transformation must include clinical professionals at varying skill levels as well as process engineers, data analytics experts, behavioral scientists, information systems engineers, and many others. Huge opportunities await scientists outside of the life sciences, to engage with the care delivery community and resolve the current problems of poor quality, lack of affordability, patient dissatisfaction, and poor access to care to assure that we truly obtain value for the healthcare dollar.

3

Market Design

Itai Ashlagi

Stanford University

3.1 Introduction

A marketplace enables economic transactions between the market participants according to a given set of rules. When a social planner has all the information, traditional operations and optimization can be applied directly to achieve optimal outcomes. But it is often the case that participants hold private information not directly accessible to the planner; engineering the rules (or the strategy sets) carefully is often crucial to allow the market to operate smoothly and reach desired outcomes. Another important piece of market design is paying attention to institutional details, which impose constraints on the planner and hence market outcomes, as in traditional operations.

Researchers have not only developed elegant theories in the area of market design, but also contributed to improving the operations of real marketplaces in collaboration with practitioners. This chapter provides a brief overview of two healthcare marketplaces, the National Residency Matching Program and Kidney Exchange, while emphasizing some of their design issues and ongoing challenges. These marketplaces might seem to be nonstandard due to the lack of monetary transfers or prices, but we shall see that they share some similar economic principles with classic markets.

3.2 Matching Doctors to Residency Programs

3.2.1 Early Days

Every year, thousands of doctors who graduate from medical school start a residency, specialty training, in the United States. In 2017 alone, more than 27,000 doctors began their first year of residency. Between the years 1900 and 1945,

Handbook of Healthcare Analytics: Theoretical Minimum for Conducting 21st Century Research on Healthcare Operations, First Edition. Edited by Tinglong Dai and Sridhar Tayur.

hospitals competed to hire doctors and the market in decentralized manner, and the market suffered from unraveling: offers to doctors were made earlier each year, until that doctors were often being hired more than a year before the completion of their training, which in turn led to inefficiency due to mismatching (Roth, 2008, 2002).[1]

In 1945, American medical schools agreed that all offers would be made on a specified day. Although this consensus solved the unraveling problem, it led to other frictions. Hospitals quickly noticed that when their first offer was rejected, other candidates had already accepted offers from other hospitals. This congestion further led hospitals to make exploding offers to which doctors had to reply immediately.[2] Finally, in the early '50s the American medical associations decided to use a centralized clearinghouse to match doctors to residency programs. The idea was that, within this new framework, after doctors interviewed with residency programs, both doctors and hospitals would submit ranking lists representing their match preferences, and an algorithm would determine matches based on these and on programs' capacities. The organization that runs the match is called the National Residency Matching Program (NRMP).

3.2.2 A Centralized Market and New Challenges

Before we describe the algorithm adopted by the NRMP, one natural question would be what objectives should such matching algorithm achieve? A common answer is to maximize some weighted function based on the rankings (an extreme version would be to maximize the number of doctors who are matched to their top choice). Such algorithms, however, may provide doctors misreporting their ranking of programs; that is a doctor who is interested in a highly demanded residency may be concerned that if she doesn't get that assignment, her second choice will be taken by another doctor who listed it as her first choice. Thus a doctor who does not get her first choice may well get a bad choice.

The NRMP adopted instead an algorithm that is similar to the *deferred acceptance* (DA) algorithm which outputs a *stable* matching. A matching of doctors to programs is stable if no doctor and hospital who are not matched to each other, prefer each other over their match (Roth, 1984; Gale and Shapley, 1962). The theory of stable matching was initiated by Gale and Shapely in their seminal paper "College admissions and the stability of marriage" where they also introduced the DA algorithm.

The DA algorithm takes the input rankings and simulates a natural process where agents on one side propose and agents on the other side evaluate offers.

1 There is much literature on unraveling in labor markets (see, e.g., Roth and Xing, (1994); Ünver (2001); Niederle and Roth, (2003)).

2 For congestion in labor markets, see, e.g., Avery et al., (2001); Roth and Xing (1997).

The *doctor-proposing DA algorithm* works as follows (the hospital-proposing version works similarly): at each stage of the algorithm, unmatched doctors propose to their favorite program, which they have not previously proposed to. Programs tentatively keep their favorite offers so far and reject all other offers. The algorithm stops if all doctors are matched, or, every unmatched doctor has applied to all the programs on her list. In addition to finding a stable matching, the doctor-proposing DA algorithm is strategyproof for doctors; in other words, it is always safe for doctors to report their true preferences. The original algorithm used by the NRMP was in fact similar to the hospital-proposing DA algorithm (Roth, 1984). It is interesting to note that the set of stable matchings has a lattice structure, and the DA algorithm generates the stable matching that is most (least) preferred by each agent on the proposing (courted) side.

But over the years, more women attended medical school, and the number of married doctors (couples) on the residency job market has grown. The NRMP began to face a real challenge because the DA algorithm allowed doctors to submit preferences only individually, and couples often had to find residencies outside the match (to avoid working in different cities).

Stability is arguably one of the keys to the success of the NRMP (Roth, 2002; Kagel and Roth, 2000). But in the case of couples who introduce complementary preferences, stability may not even exist (Klaus and Klijn, 2005; Roth, 1984). Despite this challenge, Roth and Peranson (1999) engineered a new algorithm, which has been in use by the NRMP since 1998. The key idea was to allow couples to apply together, by ranking pairs of hospitals. Roth and Peranson (1999) also switched from the hospital-proposing DA to a version based on the doctor-proposing DA.

The theory of stable matching hasn't provided guidelines for how to design the market with complementarities (a common issue in mechanism design), yet insights from the existing theory together with careful engineering have made this marketplace successful once again. Dozens of labor markets now use the stable matching mechanisms in different entry-level labor markets.[3]

3.2.3 Puzzles and Theory

Stability is arguably an important part of the success of the NRMP and other two-sided markets that adopt matching mechanisms (Roth, 2008). However, until recently various puzzles still remained.

One challenge is that when couples are part of the market, a stable matching may not exist. Roth and Peranson (1999) report that in every year they examined, there was a stable matching with respect to the reported preferences. Kojima et al. (2013) and Ashlagi et al. (2014) studied a large market model with

---

3 The deferred acceptance algorithm is also used in various cities around the world to assign a students to schools (Abdulkadiroğlu and Sönmez, 2003; Abdulkadiroğlu et al., 2005a,b).

random preferences and showed that as long as the number of couples grows more slowly than the number of single doctors, a stable matching will be found with high probability.[4]

Another longstanding challenge has to do with the multiplicity of stable matchings in a two-sided matching market (without couples). Multiplicity of stable matching raises several issues. First, which stable matching should be implemented? The one that is best for the doctors, the one that is best for the hospitals, or something in between? Another related issue concerns incentives. Roth (1982) and Dubins and Freedman (1981) find that no stable matching mechanism is strategy-proof for all agents (so there are some instances in which an agent will benefit from misreporting her preferences). Demange et al. (1987) further find that opportunities to misreport preferences successfully will arise only if an agent has multiple stable partners.

Even though artificial markets with a large set of stable matchings can be easily constructed, empirical evidence from the NRMP suggests that this set is small (Roth and Peranson, 1999), with very few agents having more than one stable partner.[5]

When preferences are highly correlated, we would expect the core (the set of stable matchings) to be small (for example there is a unique stable matching if all doctors have the same preferences over programs). So the question is whether a large core can arise with uncorrelated preferences. Pittel (1992) and Knuth et al. (1990) study a two-sided matching market with n men and n women and find that almost every man has multiple stable partners as the market grows large, when preferences for each man and each woman over all the agents on the other side are drawn independently, at random from a uniform distribution.

Following simulations by (Roth and Peranson, 1999), Immorlica and Mahdian, (2005) find that if one side ranks (uniformly at random) only a constant fraction of agents on the other side, or alternatively when the ratio between supply and demand (competition) is large, then as the market grows large, almost all agents have a single stable partner.

More recently, Ashlagi et al. (2017) find that even with the slightest competition, the core is small: in a market with n men and $n + k$ women (for any $k \geq 1$) and preferences drawn independently and uniformly at random over all agents from the other side, almost all agents have a single stable partner as n grows large. This result provides a generic reason for why two-sided markets typically have a small core. Therefore, which side proposes in a the DA algorithm is not a real concern, and it is safe to recommend all participants to report their true preferences.

---

4 Recent studies established the existence of stability in more general large markets (Che et al., 2015; Azevedo and Hatfield, 2012).

5 A small core was found also in online dating markets with respect to estimated preferences (Hitsch et al., 2010).

3.3 Kidney Exchange

3.3.1 Background

Kidney transplantation is the preferred treatment for end-stage renal disease, increasing life expectancy by ten years on average (Wolfe et al., 1999). Transplantation also saves several hundred thousands of dollars over remaining on dialysis.[6] Currently, the vast majority of Medicare spending on kidney failure is directed to dialysis costs.

Unfortunately, there is a large shortage of organs, and there are currently more than 97,000 patients on the waiting list for cadaver kidneys in the US. Another source of transplants is live donation. In fact, transplantation from a live-donor kidney is also preferable to a cadaver kidney. However, not everyone who is healthy enough to donate a kidney can donate to her intended recipient because a successful transplant requires the donor and recipient to be blood-type and immunologically compatible. Incompatibility between a donor and her intended recipient creates the demand for *kidney exchange*: an incompatible patient-donor pair can donate a kidney to a compatible recipient and receive a kidney from a compatible donor.

Note that it is illegal to buy or sell organs for transplantation in almost all countries (see Roth (2007) and Leider and Roth (2010)).[7] Kidney exchange thus represents an attempt to organize a barter economy.

The first kidney exchange took place in Korea in 1991.[8] Until 2003, few exchanges have taken place in the US, but in 2016 the number of transplants from kidney exchanges had reached more than 640 (the number is higher because some transplants are recorded as anonymous donations rather than as kidney exchanges), and are more than 11% of all living donor transplants in the US.

Forms of exchanges: cycles and chains. One form in which exchanges are organized is a *cycle*, which involves only incompatible patient–donor pairs, with each patient receiving a kidney from a compatible donor of another pair. Another form is a chain, which is initiated by an altruistic donor (with no intended recipient) and donates to a pair, whose donor donates to the next pair, and so forth.[9] Exchanges are organized such that no patient–donor

6 In 2014, Medicare paid $87,638 per year per dialysis patient, but only $32,586 per year per transplant patient. Given a median waiting time of 3.5 years for a deceased donor kidney, the difference adds up to a cost savings of about $192,682 (United States Renal Data System, 2016).
7 In the US, the National Organ Transplant Act (NOTA 1984) makes it illegal to obtain organs for valuable consideration. For discussion in favor of compensation for donors see, e.g., Becker and Elias (2007).
8 See Rapaport (1986) who first raised the idea of kidney exchange and Ross et al. (1997) and Ross and Woodle (2000) for discussions regarding ethical considerations.
9 Chains typically end with a patient on the waiting list who has no intended donor.

pair donates a kidney prior to receiving a kidney. This means that cycles are conducted simultaneously, since the cost of a broken link would be high to a pair that first donated a kidney and later failed to receive one. Due to logistical barriers, cycles are typically short including or three pairs. But chains can be organized nonsimultaneously without breaking this requirement, and therefore can be longer (Saidman et al., 2006). The majority of kidney exchange transplants in the US are now conducted through chains.

Compatibility between a donor and recipient. For a transplant to take place, a patient must be both blood-type (ABO) and tissue-type compatible with a donor. Thus, an O donor is valuable because O is ABO compatible with any other patient. Tissue-type compatibility means that the patient has no antibodies to the donor's antigens. The common measure for patient sensitivity is the Panel Reactive Antibody (PRA), which captures the likelihood that, based on her antibodies, the patient is tissue-type incompatible with a random donor in the population.

We survey some important steps in the progress of kidney exchange in the US, while emphasizing the economic and operational perspectives. Due to the shortage of space, we elaborate on only about handful of (more recent) issues.

3.3.2 Creating a Thick Marketplace for Kidney Exchange

The first proposal for organizing kidney exchange on a large scale involved integrating cycles of patient–donor pairs while considering patients' preferences (Roth et al., 2004). However, in the early days, only pairwise exchanges were conducted.[10] Subsequent work suggested that allowing only slightly larger, three- and four-way exchanges, would increase efficiency (Saidman et al., 2006; Roth et al., 2007). Common to these studies is taking a centralized approach (clearinghouse) to kidney exchange and in particular using *optimization*.[11]

Efficiency in Large Markets

Roth et al. (2007) characterize efficient allocations using cycles in a large market and find no need for cycles longer than four. Their large market assumption assumes that compatibility between patient and donors depends only on blood types.[12]

The characterization follows from the blood-type structure. To get some intuition consider, for example, the set of A-O and O-A patient–donor pairs. A

10 Roth et al. (2005) proposed a mechanism for conducting pairwise exchanges.

11 See also Segev et al. (2005).

12 This prediction is true even when patients' PRAs are included, by building on the Erdős-Renyi random graph theory (Ashlagi and Roth, 2014) because in a sufficiently large market, the PRA will not be a barrier, and the blood-type structure will determined the efficient allocation (In fact, there is no need for cycles longer than 3.)

kidney exchange pool is likely to have fewer A-O pairs than O-A pairs because many A-O pairs are compatible and select to go through a direct live-donor transplant.[13] If there were only A-O pairs and O-A pairs, in a sufficiently large market, it would be efficient (and possible) to match every A-O pair with a different O-A pair in a two-way cycle.[14] In particular, some pairs are *overdemanded* and some are *underdemanded*; the former will all match whereas some fraction of the latter will remain unmatched in an efficient outcome.

It is not hard to extend the characterization to show that under large market assumptions also chains need not be long.[15] However, the experience of kidney exchange platforms suggested that chains in fact play a crucial role.

Optimization

Kidney exchange platforms often use optimization to find matches through cycles and chains. The optimization problem of maximizing the number of matches is NP-complete (Abraham et al., 2007) and various algorithms have been developed to help programs with this task, following Roth et al. (2007) and Abraham et al. (2007).[16]

The Need for Chains

After the first nonsimultaneous chain (Rees et al., 2009), which involved more than ten transplants, chains became common. Today the average chain length is between four and five. The two longest chains so far contained 30 and 35 transplants in 2012 and 2014, respectively. The pairs in a chain, especially longer ones, are not all identified at once. The last donor in a chain segment either ends the chain by donating to a patient on the waiting list or becomes a *bridge donor* and initiates a chain segment in a future period.

One reason that chains have become ubiquitous is the large fraction of (very) highly sensitized patients in kidney exchange networks (Ashlagi et al., 2012). Another reason, which we elaborate in our discussion on incentives (Section 3.3.4), is that hospitals often match internally easy-to-mach pairs and enroll the pairs they cannot match. As a result, the compatibility graphs induced from the patient–donor pairs in real kidney exchange pools are sparse.[17] Data-driven simulations by Ashlagi et al. (2011a,b) and Dickerson

13 An A-O pair is incompatible if the A patient is tissue-type incompatible with the O donor.
14 A-O pairs can potentially match with each other, but this is a waste, as each such pair could potentially help a different O patient.
15 Altruistic donors can initiate chains that can be at most of length three, including at most two underdemanded pairs and one patient on the cadaver waiting list.
16 Abraham et al. (2007) develop an algorithm that can identify an optimal solution in a large pool using cycles up to length three. Researchers have expanded this line of work to include chains as well as various objectives (e.g., Biro et al. (2009), Glorie et al. (2012), Anderson et al. (2015), Constantino et al. (2013), Klimentova et al. (2014), Dickerson et al. (2012c)).
17 See Ashlagi et al. (2012, 2013) for a theoretical models based on Erdős Renyi graphs (in static and dynamic settings), in which the the key ingredient is the sensitivity of the patient (and blood

et al. (2012a) reveal that nonsimultaneous chains increase efficiency in a dynamic environment.[18]

3.3.3 Dynamic Matching

Early theoretical papers took a static approach and focused on the importance of the *matching technology*. But kidney exchange pools are dynamic, with pairs arriving and being matched over time; thus, it is natural to ask how the platform should match in this dynamic environment.

The *policy* employed by the clearinghouse, which determines which exchanges to implement and when, also affects the efficiency of the marketplace. One natural policy is a *greedy* policy, where the clearinghouse forms exchanges as soon as an opportunity arises. Another possibility is to adopt a *batching* policy, which identifies a (weighted) optimal allocation within the pool every number of periods. More sophisticated policies may take into account both the compatibility graph and the future.

Kidney exchange platforms in the US have gradually moved to small batches and thus frequently identify exchanges. The Alliance for Paired Donation (APD) and the National Kidney Registry (NKR) identify exchanges on a daily basis, and the UNOS program identifies matches twice a week. These are national programs, in which multiple hospitals participate in. A major concern is that this behavior is driven by platform competition. However, Methodist at San Antonio (MSA), which is a single center program and faces no competition, also matches on a daily basis. In contrast, national exchange programs in several countries such as Canada, United Kingdom, Netherlands, and Australia, search for exchanges every three or four months (Ferrari et al., 2014; Malik and Cole, 2014; Johnson et al., 2008). We briefly discuss recent research on this front.

In a simulation study, Ashlagi et al. (2018) looked at the effect of batching policies on efficiency (measured by the fraction of matched pairs and waiting times), using empirical data from the APD and MSA programs, which have different pool compositions, partially because participating hospitals in national pools often match easy-to-match pairs internally. Pairs in the simulation arrive according to a Poisson process and depart according to an exponential random variable, unless they are matched earlier. (Ashlagi et al. also model various frictions such as delays due to blood shipping and match cancellations.) They find that there is essentially almost no harm in matching frequently. Figure 3.1 plots the fraction of matched pairs and the average waiting time under different

types are ignored); the models explain the relationships between the fraction of highly sensitized patients and the need for long chains.

18 Ashlagi et al. (2011a,b) have been also part of an ongoing debate regarding the importance of chains (see also Gentry and Segev (2011) and Gentry et al. (2009)).

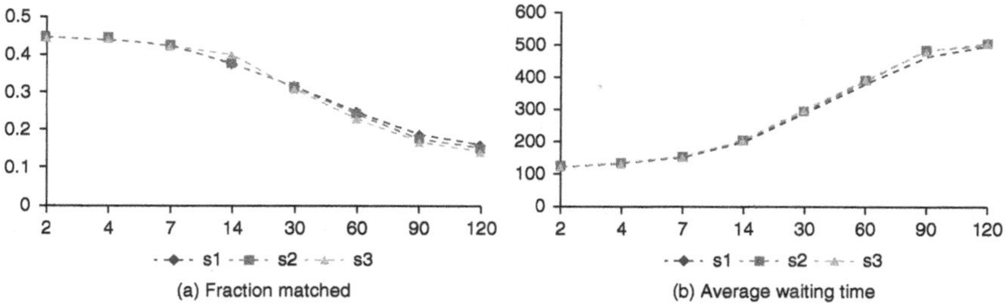

Figure 3.1 Statistics using APD data (taken from Ashlagi et al.). The x-axis represents the time interval between two match-runs. Each plot, S1-S3, stands for different prioritizations/weights assigned to pairs based on the patients' PRA.

matching frequencies and different sets of weights. Assigning high priority to highly sensitized patients increases their match rate but at the expense of other pairs.

Intuitively, matching frequently does not harm the fraction of transplanted patients because both underdemanded pairs and highly-sensitized patients accumulate in the pool. For instance, when an A-O patient-donor arrives, if the A patient is not too sensitized, there is likely an immediate match with an O-A pair. But if the A-O cannot match with an O-A pair, a match with any pair arriving in the near future is also unlikely; thus delaying other pairs from matching is also unlikely to help this pair. In other words, when the departure rate is low, many hard-to-match pairs accumulate in the pool, and waiting with a newly arriving, easy-to-match pair is unnecessary, because it is likely to match a hard-to-match pair. When the departure rate is high, matching infrequently will result in many departures of easy-to-match pairs.

Artificially thickening the market does not increase the fraction of matched pairs, but Ashlagi et al. (2018) also find that increasing the arrival rate increases the fraction of matched pairs up to a certain point (which is the fraction matched in a large market). Figure 3.2 plots the fraction of matched pairs under different arrival rates. Note that there is a diminishing return to scale. Note also, however, that the waiting time will keep decreasing as the arrival rate increases, even when the fraction of matched pairs does not increase anymore.

Consequently, increasing participation rate is much more important than artificially thickening the market. Rough intuition is that, at a low arrival rate, some O donors may match A patients, whereas at a large arrival rate, such A patients can be matched by other A donors.

Theoretical frontiers

Ünver (2010) first studied the problem of dynamic matching under large market assumptions. He found that a greedy algorithm that uses two-way and

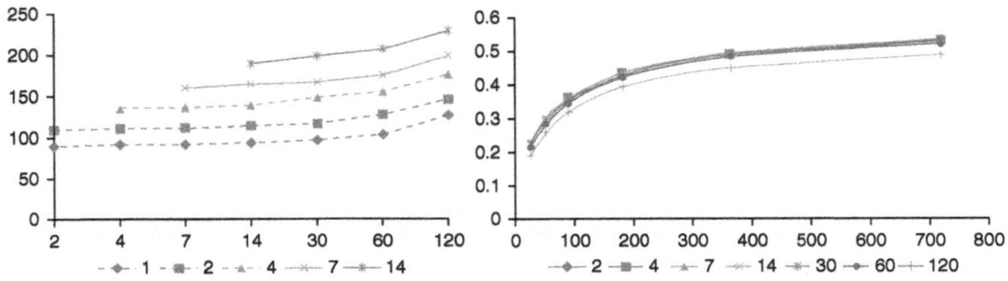

Figure 3.2 Varying arrival rates using APD data (taken from Ashlagi et al.). (Left) The x-axis represents the time interval between two match-runs, and each plots represents a different arrival rate. (Right) The x-axis represents the number of arrivals per year and y-axis the fraction of matched pairs.

three-way cycles is almost optimal and minor gains would be achieved by holding up some pairs.

Motivated by the sparsity of kidney exchange pools, various authors have studied dynamic matching in random graph-based models while abstracting away from blood types (Ashlagi et al., 2013; Anderson et al., 2017; Akbarpour et al., 2014).

Anderson et al. (2017) looked at homogenous agents and considered three settings distinguished by the types of feasible exchanges: two-way cycles, two- and three-way cycles, and a single chain. They found that a greedy algorithm is approximately optimal. Furthermore, allowing three-way cycles results in significantly lower waiting times than only two-way cycles, and a single unrestricted chain reduces the waiting times even more. This result sheds light on the importance of chains in sparse pools. Akbarpour et al. (2014) looked at a similar model with departures and found that if departure times are known to the planner, matching patients just before they depart reduces the loss rate significantly in comparison to a greedy algorithm, but without this information, greedy matching is approximately optimal.

Ashlagi et al. (2013) allow for two types of agents, hard- and easy-to-match, and ask how the market thickness, as determined by arrival rates, affects efficiency under a class of myopic policies. They found a tight connection between the market thickness and the desired matching technology. When easy-to-match agents arrive more frequently to the market, two-way cycles are approximately optimal; otherwise, using chains is important.

More sophisticated policies, which consider the future, have been developed in the computer science literature. Dickerson et al. (2012b) learn the potential of different nodes in the compatibility graph to determine whether to match them or not (see also Dickerson and Sandholm (2014)).

In practice, myopic algorithms (which optimize periodically) are ubiquitous, and there is no evidence that such sophisticated algorithms lead to significant benefits. Moreover, when the market is sufficiently thick, simple matching rules are essentially optimal (Ünver, 2010). Otherwise, as figure 3.2 suggests, increasing arrival rates is arguably more important than designing the perfect algorithm.

3.3.4 The Marketplace for Kidney Exchange in the United States

In the last decade several national platforms emerged in the US, which seek to organize kidney exchange at a large scale. Participation, however, is not mandatory, and hospitals may decide to engage only partially in these platforms by enrolling some of their pairs and internally matching others. It is therefore natural to ask: How common is this behavior? Is efficiency harmed, and if so by how much? How can the platform align incentives to increase efficiency? Can full efficiency even be achieved?

The current national platforms vary according to size, operations, and algorithms. The major national platforms, the Alliance for Paired Donation (APD), United Network for Organ Sharing kidney exchange program (UNOS), and the National Kidney Registry (NKR) all involve the participation of many hospitals. Other platforms involve fewer hospitals and even single hospitals, such as Methodist at San Antonio (MSA). Typically, large scale programs use optimization algorithms to identify exchanges and may vary in how they prioritize patients or how frequently they search for exchanges.

Why Should Hospitals' Incentives Matter?

By and large, patients rely on hospitals (surgeons), and hospitals benefit from conducting more transplants (Sönmez and Ünver, 2013; Ashlagi and Roth, 2014). Let us see how hospitals may benefit from participating only partially in kidney exchange platforms. Consider a hospital A with two pairs, $a1$ and $a2$, which it can match internally through a two-way cycle. Suppose A enrolls both pairs to the platform, and the platform can either match $a1$ with $a2$ or match $a1$ with some other pair $b1$ that does not belong to A. If $b1$ has the highest priority, than $a1$ will remain unmatched. Thus hospital A is better off matching internally $a1$ and $a2$. Suppose there is another pair $b2$ that can only match with $a2$. If A would match $a1$ and $a2$ internally, only two transplants will happen instead of four.

Roth and Sonmez and Unver find that there is there is no efficient strategyproof mechanism ((Sönmez and Ünver, 2013; Roth, 2008)). Ashlagi and Roth (2014) studied extensively the free riding problem and found that under large market assumptions the cost from requiring allocations to be individually rational is low (see also Toulis and Parkes (2015)). They further suggest to adopt a "frequent flyer program" that will encourage hospitals to enroll their easy-to-match pairs. Therefore, optimizing without considering hospitals' incentives may potentially result in a large loss due to hospitals' behavior. But how big of an issue is this in practice?

Market Failure in Kidney Exchange

In a recent paper, Agarawal et al. (2017) accumulated data from various sources to study the kidney exchange marketplace in the US, quantified the efficiency loss, and offer solutions for how to fix it. They proposed a stylized model based on producer theory that predicts the sources of inefficiency and pursues these objectives empirically.

The first dataset they used is from the NKR, the largest platform in the US and includes all submissions (medical data of all incompatible pairs and altruistic donors) and transplants conducted between the years 2012–2014. Another dataset, obtained from UNOS, is the list of all live-donor transplants ever conducted in the US, and whether they are due to an exchange or not.

Agarawal et al. (2017) find that the US kidney exchange market is *highly fragmented*, with more than 60 percent of transplants conducted through internal matches (that are not facilitated by the NKR). Furthermore, larger hospitals are more likely to participate at the NKR, though hospitals vary in their level of participation. Importantly, they find that the NKR is *selected to have harder-to-match pairs*: the smaller the fraction of pairs a hospital enrolls, the more sensitized the patients within these enrolled pairs. They further provide smoking-gun evidence for large efficiencies: **while** *2.5 percent of the transplanted O kidneys go to non-O recipients at the NKR, more than 11 percent of such transplants occur within internal matches.*[19] Recall that in a large market it is efficient to transplant O kidneys in O recipients.

Agarawal et al. (2017) propose to model the kidney exchange as a platform that receives submissions and produces transplants. They take a steady-state approach (where submissions and transplants are per time period, say per year), but do not adhere to the previous large market assumptions. The platform is associated with a *production function* f, which receives vectors of submissions and generate transplants. The platform rewards hospitals with transplants, either immediately or in the future. Agarawal et al. (2017) considered the problem of maximizing welfare subject to two constraints. First, hospitals submit pairs optimally to maximize their own utility, and second, the platform is constrained from promising more transplants than it can generate.

One insight from the model is that to maximize welfare, optimal rewards should equal marginal products minus some adjustment term (the adjustment terms is zero when the platform operates at a constant returns to scale regime). In particular, hospitals should be rewarded based on their marginal contribution to the platform. This provides a simple explanation why current algorithms, which essentially attempt to maximize the number of transplants don't provide hospitals with the right incentives.

---

19 Large gaps remain even when restricting the non-O recipient to be low sensitized.

The finding by Agarawal et al. (2017) suggests that platform incentives can be solved by simply using point systems. Hospitals will maintain a point balance of transplants, and the platform will break ties in favor of hospitals that have a larger amount. For platforms that operate at constant returns to scale regime, the exact rewards can be computed by estimating the derivatives of the production function. The idea is that hospitals will earn points based on their marginal contribution to the platform, whereas the platform will favor favor hospitals with higher balances during the matching process (for example through tie-breaking). For implementation details and challenges, see Agarawal et al. (2017).

Agarawal et al. (2017) further quantify the inefficiency in the data. Estimating the production function reveals that the NKR is operating at the constant returns to scale regime, but many hospitals that match internally operate at an inefficient scale. They find that misaligned incentives account for around 200–400 transplants per year.

Finally, Agarawal et al. (2017) find that platform incentives do not account for all inefficiency. The remaining inefficiency is due to agency problems. This prediction, also generated by their model, is also supported by significant efforts in recent years to organize financial agreements between insurance companies and hospitals (Rees et al., 2012; Held et al., 2016; Irwin et al., 2012; DHHS, 2016). One challenge was to engage private insurance companies in a standard acquisition charge to reimburse for expenses prior to transplants.

As Agarawal et al. (2017) point out, kidney exchange, which is a seemingly unusual market, faces classic market failures, which can be addressed using market and nonmarket tools. It will be interesting to see how this market evolves in the next few years, now that some of these agency problems have been alleviated and platforms such the NKR have adopted point systems.

3.3.5 Final Comments on Kidney Exchange

Kidney exchange is now responsible for more than 11 percent of live-donor transplants in the United States. Despite this success, many challenges still remain in order to allow platforms to operate more smoothly, as well as to grow this marketplace. Although optimization plays a role in kidney exchange, increasing participation is a first-order consideration in order to increase the number of of transplants. In the US creating one national pool is more challenging than in other countries, arguably due to institutional structure. However, small countries that seek to work together in order to increase matching opportunities may face similar concerns. For a thorough survey of kidney exchange practices in European countries, see Biro et al. (2017).

There are ongoing efforts towards new innovations, such as the Global Kidney Exchange that aims to overcome medical and financial incompatibilities by matching pairs in developed countries that lack transplantation facilities with pairs in developed countries (Rees et al., 2016). But similar to other innovations in the field of transplantation, ethical considerations are an integral part of the process toward implementation. Indeed, Global Kidney Exchange sparked a loud debate in the transplantation community (Delmonico and Ascher, 2017; Roth et al., 2017; Rees et al., 2017). It remains to be seen how this potential new market will develop.

Marketplaces such as platforms for kidney exchanges are usually part of a larger market. Little is still known about the design of marketplaces that face outside competition.

References

Abdulkadiroğlu, A., Pathak, P. and Roth, A. (2005a). The New York City High School Match. *American Economic Review*, 95(2), pp. 364-367.

Abdulkadiroğlu, A. and Sönmez, T. (2003). School Choice: A Mechanism Design Approach. *American Economic Review*, 93(3), pp. 729-747.

Abdulkadiroğlu, A., Pathak, P., Roth, A. and Sönmez T. (2005b). The Boston Public School Match. *American Economic Review*, pp. 368–371.

Abraham, D.J., A. Blum, and T. Sandholm. (2007). Clearing Algorithms for Barter Exchange Markets: Enabling Nationwide Kidney Exchanges. In *Proceedings of the 8th ACM conference on Electronic commerce*, pp. 295–304, 2007.

Agarawal, N., I. Ashlagi, E. Azavedo, C. Featherstone, and O. Karaduman. (2017). "Market Failure in Kidney Exchange." Working paper.

Akbarpour, M., S. Li, and S. Oveis Gharan. (2014). "Dynamic matching market design." Working paper.

Anderson, R., I. Ashlagi, Y. Kanoria, and D. Gamarnik. (2017). Efficient dynamic barter exchange. *Operations Research* 56(6):1446–1459.

Anderson. R., I. Ashlagi, D. Gamarnik, and A.E. Roth. (2015). Finding long chains in kidney exchange using the traveling salesman problem. *Proceedings of the National Academy of Sciences*, 112(3):663–668.

Ashlagi, I., and A.E. Roth. (2014). Free riding and participation in large scale, multi-hospital kidney exchange. *Theoretical Economics*, 9(3):817–863.

Ashlagi, I., D.S. Gilchrist, A.E. Roth, and M.A. Rees. (2011a). Nonsimultaneous Chains and Dominos in Kidney Paired Donation—Revisited. *American Journal of Transplantation*, 11:984–994.

Ashlagi, I., D. S. Gilchrist, A. E. Roth, and M. A. Rees. NEAD Chains in Transplantation. *American Journal of Transplantation*, 11:2780–2781, 2011b.

Ashlagi, I., Adam Bingaman, Maximilien Burq, Vahideh Manshadi, David Gamarnik, Cathi Mur- phey, A.E. Roth, Marc L. Melcher, and Michael A. Rees. The effect of match-run frequencies on the number of transplants and waiting times in kidney exchange. (2018). *American Journal of Transplantation.* 18(5): 1177–1186.

Ashlagi, I., David Gamarnik, Michael A Rees, and Alvin E Roth. The need for (long) chains in kidney exchange. Technical report, National Bureau of Economic Research, 2012.

Ashlagi, I., P. Jaillet, and V.H. Manshadi. (2013). Kidney exchange in dynamic sparse heterogenous pools. In *In ACM Conference on Electronic Commerce*. Citeseer, 2013.

Ashlagi, I., M. Braverman, and A. Hassidim. (2014). Stability in large matching markets with complementarities. *Operations Research*, 62(4):713–732.

Ashlagi, I., Y. Kanoria, and J.D. Leshno. (2017). Unbalanced random matching markets: The stark effect of competition. *Journal of Political Economy*, 125(1):69–98.

Avery, C., C. Jolls, R.A. Posner, and A.E. Roth. (2001). The market for federal judicial law clerks. *The University of Chicago Law Review*, 68(3):793–902.

Azevedo, E.M. and J.W. Hatfield. (2012). Complementarity and multidimensional heterogeneity in matching markets. *Unpublished mimeo*.

Becker, G.S. and J.J. Elias. (2007). Introducing incentives in the market for live and cadaveric organ donations. *The Journal of Economic Perspectives*, 21(3):3–24.

Biro, P., L. Burnapp, H. Bernadette, A. Hemke, R. Johnson, J. van de Klundert, and D. Manlove. (2017). First Handbook of the COST Action CA15210: European Network for Collaboration on Kidney Exchange Programmes (ENCKEP).

Biro, P., D.F. Manlove, and R. Rizzi. (2009). Maximum weight cycle packing in directed graphs, with application to kidney exchange programs. *Discrete Mathematics, Algorithms and Applications*, 1(04):499–517.

Che, Y-K, J. Kim, and F. Kojima. (2015). Stable matching in large economies. *Department of Economics, Columbia University*. Working paper.

Constantino, M., Xenia Klimentova, A.V., and A. Rais. (2013). New insights on integer-programming models for the kidney exchange problem. *European Journal of Operational Research*, 231(1):57–68.

Delmonico, F.L. and N.L. Ascher. (2017). Opposition to irresponsible global kidney exchange. *American Journal of Transplantation*, 17(10):2745–2746.

Demange, G., D. Gale, and M. Sotomayor. (1987). A further note on the stable matching problem. *Discrete Applied Mathematics*, 16(3):217–222.

DHHS. Medicare Provider Reimbursement Manual, Part 2. (2016). www.cms.gov/Regulations-and-Guidance/Guidance/Transmittals/Downloads/R7PR241.pdf.

Dickerson, J.P., A.D. Procaccia, and T. Sandholm. (2012a). Optimizing Kidney Exchange with Transplant Chains: Theory and Reality. *Proceedings of the 11th International Conference on Autonomous Agents and Multiagent Systems.*

Dickerson, J.P., A.D. Procaccia, and T. Sandholm. (2012b). Dynamic matching via weighted myopia with application to kidney exchange. In *AAAI Workshop: Modern Artificial Intelligence for Health Analytics.*

Dickerson, J.P., A.D. Procaccia, and T. Sandholm. (2012c). Optimizing kidney exchange with transplant chains: Theory and reality. In *Proceedings of the 11th*

International Conference on Autonomous Agents and Multiagent Systems—Volume 2, pp. 711–718. International Foundation for Autonomous Agents and Multiagent Systems.

Dickerson, J.P. and T. Sandholm. (2014). Balancing efficiency and fairness in dynamic kidney exchange. In *AAAI Workshop: Modern Artificial Intelligence for Health Analytics*.

Dubins, L.E. and D.A. Freedman. (1981). Machiavelli and the Gale-Shapley algorithm. *The American Mathematical Monthly*, 88(7):485–494.

Ferrari, P., Willem Weimar, Rachel J Johnson, Wai H Lim, and Kathryn J Tinckam. (2014). Kidney paired donation: principles, protocols and programs. *Nephrology Dialysis Transplantation*, 30 (8):1276–1285.

Gale, D. and L.L. Shapley. (1962). College Admissions and the Stability of Marriage. *American Mathematical Monthly*, 69:9–15.

Gentry, S.E., R. A. Montgomery, B. J. Swihart, and D. L. Segev. (2009). The Roles of Dominos and Nonsimultaneous Chains in Kidney Paired Donation. *American Journal of Transplantation*, 9: 1330–1336.

Gentry, S.E. and D.L. Segev. (2011). The honeymoon phase and studies of nonsimultaneous chains in kidney paired donation. *American Journal of Transplantation*, 11:2778–2779.

Glorie, K., A. Wagelmans, and J. van de Klundert. (2012). Iterative branch-and-price for hierarchical multi-criteria kidney exchange. Technical report.

Held, P.J., F McCormick, A Ojo, and John P Roberts. (2016). A cost-benefit analysis of government compensation of kidney donors. *American Journal of Transplantation*, 16(3):877–885.

Hitsch, G.J., A. Hortaçsu, and D. Ariely. (2010). Matching and sorting in online dating. *American Economic Review*, 100(1):130–163.

Immorlica, N. and M. Mahdian. (2005). Marriage, honesty, and stability. In *Proceedings of the sixteenth annual ACM-SIAM symposium on Discrete algorithms*, pp. 53–62. Society for Industrial and Applied Mathematics.

Irwin, F.D., AF Bonagura, SW Crawford, and M Foote. (2012). Kidney paired donation: a payer perspective. *American Journal of Transplantation*, 12(6):1388–1391.

Johnson, R.J., J.E. Allen, S.V. Fuggle, J.A. Bradley, C. Rudge et al. (2008). Early experience of paired living kidney donation in the United Kingdom. *Transplantation*, 86(12): 1672–1677.

Kagel, J.H. and A.E. Roth. (2000). The dynamics of reorganization in matching markets: A laboratory experiment motivated by a natural experiment. *The Quarterly Journal of Economics*, 115(1): 201–235.

Klaus, B. and F. Klijn. (2005). Stable matchings and preferences of couples. *Journal of Economic Theory*, 121(1):75–106.

Klimentova, X., F. Alvelos, and A. Viana. (2014). A new branch-and-price approach for the kidney exchange problem. In *International Conference on Computational Science and Its Applications*, pp. 237–252. Springer.

Knuth, D.E., R. Motwani, and B. Pittel. (1990). Stable husbands. *Random Structures & Algorithms*, 1(1):1–14.

Kojima, F., P.A. Pathak, and A.E. Roth. (2013). Matching with couples: Stability and incentives in large markets. *The Quarterly Journal of Economics*, 128(4):1585–1632.

Leider, S. and A.E. Roth. Kidneys for sale: Who disapproves, and why? (2010). *American Journal of transplantation*, 10(5):1221–1227.

Malik, S. and Edward Cole. (2014). Foundations and principles of the Canadian living donor paired exchange program. *Canadian Journal of Kidney Health and Disease*, 1(1):6, 2014.

Niederle, M. and A.E. Roth. (2003). Unraveling reduces mobility in a labor market: Gastroenterology with and without a centralized match. *Journal of Political Economy*, 111(6):1342–1352.

Pittel, B. (1992). On likely solutions of a stable matching problem. In *Proceedings of the third annual ACM-SIAM symposium on Discrete algorithms*, pp. 10–15. Society for Industrial and Applied Mathematics.

Rapaport, F.T. (1986). The case for a living emotionally related international kidney donor exchange registry. *In Transplantation proceedings, volume* 18(3), pp. 5–9.

Rees, M., T. Dunn, S. Rees, J. Rogers, L. Reece, A. Roth, C. Kuhr, O. Ekwenna, D. Fumo, K. Krawiec, et al. (2016). Global kidney exchange. In *American Journal of Transplantation*, volume 16, pp. 352–352. Wiley Online Library.

Rees, M.A., J.E. Kopke, R.P. Pelletier, D.L. Segev, M.E. Rutter, A.J. Fabrega, J. Rogers, O.G. Pankewycz, J. Hiller, A.E. Roth, T. Sandholm, M.U. Ünver, and R.A. Montgomery. (2009). A non-simultaneous extended altruistic donor chain. *New England Journal of Medicine*, 360: 1096–1101.

Rees M.A., S. Paloyo, A.E. Roth, K.D. Krawiec, O. Ekwenna, C.L. Marsh, A.J. Wenig, and T.B. Dunn. (2017). Global kidney exchange: Financially incompatible pairs are not transplantable compatible pairs. *American Journal of Transplantation.*

Rees, M.A., M.A. Schnitzler, E.Y. Zavala, J.A. Cutler, A.E. Roth, F.D. Irwin, S.W. Crawford, and A.B. Leichtman. (2012). Call to develop a standard acquisition charge model for kidney paired donation. *American Journal of transplantation*, 12(6):1392–1397.

Ross, L.F. and E.S. Woodle. (2000). Ethical issues in increasing living kidney donations by expanding kidney paired exchange programs. *Transplantation*, 69(8):1539–1543.

Ross, L.F., D.T. Rubin, M. Siegler, M.A. Josephson, J.R. Thistlethwaite Jr., and E.S. Woodle. (1997). Ethics of a paired-kidney-exchange program.

New England Journal of Medicine 336:1752–1755. DOI: 10.1056/NEJM199706123362412.

Roth, A.E. (2008). What have we learned from market design? *Economic Journal*, 118:285–310.

Roth, A.E. and E. Peranson. (1999). The redesign of the matching market for American physicians: Some engineering aspects of economic design. *American Economic Review*, 89:748–780.

Roth, A.E., T. Sönmez, and M. U. Ünver. (2004) Kidney exchange. *Quarterly Journal of Economics*, 119: 457–488.

Roth, A.E., T. Sönmez, and M. U. Ünver. (2005). Pairwise kidney exchange. *Journal of Economic Theory*, 125:151–188.

Roth, A.E, T. Sönmez, and M. U. Ünver. (2007). Efficient kidney exchange: coincidence of wants in markets with compatibility-based preferences. *American Economic Review*, 97:828–851.

Roth, A.E. (2002). The Economist as Engineer: Game Theory, Experimentation, and Computation as Tools for Design Economics. *Econometrica*, 70:1341–1378.

Roth, A.E. (1982). The economics of matching: Stability and incentives. *Mathematics of Operations Research*, 7(4):617–628.

Roth, A.E. (1984) The evolution of the labor market for medical interns and residents: a case study in game theory. *Journal of political Economy*, 92(6):991–1016.

Roth, A.E. (2007). Repugnance as a constraint on markets. *The Journal of Economic Perspectives*, 21 (3):37–58.

Roth, A.E. and Xiaolin Xing. (1994). Jumping the gun: Imperfections and institutions related to the timing of market transactions. *The American Economic Review*, pp. 992–1044.

Roth, A.E. and X. Xing. (1997). Turnaround time and bottlenecks in market clearing: Decentralized matching in the market for clinical psychologists. *Journal of Political Economy*, 105(2):284–329.

Roth, A.E., K.D. Krawiec, S. Paloyo, O. Ekwenna, C.L. Marsh, A.J. Wenig, T.B. Dunn, and M.A. Rees. (2017). People should not be banned from transplantation only because of their country of origin. *American Journal of Transplantation*, 17(10):2747–2748.

Saidman, S.L., A.E. Roth, T. Sönmez, M.U. Ünver, and F.L. Delmonico (2006). Increasing the Opportunity of Live Kidney Donation by Matching for Two and Three Way Exchanges. *Transplantation*, 81:773–782.

Segev, D.L., S.E. Gentry, D.S. Warren, B. Reeb, and R.A. Montgomery (2005). Kidney paired donation and optimizing the use of live donor organs. *JAMA*, 293(15):1883–1890.

Sönmez, T. and M.U. Ünver. (2013). Market design for kidney exchange. *The Handbook of Market Design*, pp. 93–137.

Toulis, P. and D.C. Parkes. (2015). Design and analysis of multi-hospital kidney exchange mechanisms using random graphs. *Games and Economic Behavior*, 91:360–382.

United States Renal Data System. *2016 USRDS annual data report: Epidemiology of kidney disease in the United States*, volume 3. (2016). Bethesda, MD: National Institutes of Health, National Institute of Diabetes and Digestive and Kidney Diseases.

Ünever, M.U. (2010). Dynamic Kidney Exchange. *Review of Economic Studies*, 77(1):372–414.

Utku, M.U. (2001). Ünver. Backward unraveling over time: The evolution of strategic behavior in the entry level British medical labor markets. *Journal of Economic Dynamics and Control*, 25(6):1039–1080.

Wolfe, R.A., V.B. Ashby, E.L. Milford, A.O. Ojo, R.E. Ettenger, L.Y.C. Agodoa, P.J. Held, and F.K. Port. (1999). Comparison of mortality in all patients on dialysis, patients on dialysis awaiting transplantation, and recipients of a first cadaveric transplant. *New England Journal of Medicine*, 341(23):1725–1730.

4

Competing Interests

Joel Goh

Harvard University; National University of Singapore

4.1 Introduction

Whatever houses I may visit, I will come for the benefit of the sick.
— The Hippocratic Oath, translation from the original Greek by Ludwig Edelstein (1943).

I will apply, for the benefit of the sick, all measures which are required.
— Modern adaption of the Hippocratic Oath, by Louis Lasagna, former Academic Dean of the School of Medicine, Tufts University (Tyson, 2001)

The Oath of Hippocrates, estimated to be written in 400 BCE, is one of the earliest known declarations of medical ethics. Historical scholars believe that it was originally used as part of an initiation ceremony into a medical apprenticeship (Miles, 2005). Much of the historical oath is now anachronistic, and modern versions of the oath or other statements of medical ethics substantially depart from it. Nevertheless, a central tenet that has been preserved from the original oath through the ages, as exemplified in the two quotes above, is a concept that one might refer to as *beneficience*, which, plainly stated, means that a physician should act with the primary objective of delivering care that benefits the patient.

The purpose of this chapter is to introduce and discuss an important issue that can impede both physicians and healthcare delivery organizations in their efforts to fulfill this primary objective. Specifically, this chapter focuses on *competing interests* in healthcare, which we will define as secondary nonclinical objectives that can potentially influence how healthcare is delivered, evaluated, and reported. These interests include, of course, the secondary objective of financial gain, which is most commonly discussed in the public arena, studied

Handbook of Healthcare Analytics: Theoretical Minimum for Conducting 21st Century Research on Healthcare Operations, First Edition. Edited by Tinglong Dai and Sridhar Tayur.

in academic journals, targeted for regulatory action, and is consequently also the focus of the present chapter. Nonetheless, it is worth recognizing that other nonpecuniary objectives exist and also represent potential competing interests, such as careerism or even overzealousness for scientific knowledge (Levinsky, 2002). These are much harder to objectively quantify, which likely explains why they have not yet been the subject of sustained academic attention, although they have been noted in the popular press.

Public and academic discourse on this subject traditionally belongs to the field of medical ethics. Although the present chapter does not depart substantially from this tradition, it will focus more explicitly on the impact of competing interests on healthcare management and operations. Our choice of the term *competing interests* is wholly intentional, and designed to be distinct from what the medical community refers to as "conflicts of interest." The latter is typically applied to individual physicians and refers to circumstances in which secondary interests (pecuniary or otherwise) may exert undue influence over a physician's decisions or judgment (Thompson, 1993). Our present use of (admittedly) nonconventional terminology is to signal a focus that is more inclusive, encompassing both the traditional conflicts of interest for physicians as individual decision-makers, but also for organizations that contribute to the delivery of healthcare in their daily operations.

The problem of competing interests in healthcare delivery is, paradoxically, both patently obvious and overwhelmingly complex. With regard to the former, there is little question that competing interests are detrimental and can pose immediate danger to patient health and safety, for example, if a physician chooses to conduct a risky medical procedure out of financial considerations instead of the concerns for patient's well-being. In the long run, competing interests can be more broadly damaging, by eroding patients' confidence and trust in healthcare providers and institutions. On the other hand, even though the detriments of competing interests are clear, a simple solution to this problem has been elusive. A major hurdle is the fact that competing interests are often difficult to conclusively determine and, consequently, harder still to manage. One reason is that even though evidence-based medicine has been practiced since the early 20th century and accelerated since the 1970s (Claridge and Fabian, 2005), modern medicine still relies heavily upon the subjective expert judgment on the part of the physician. As Lisa Rosenbaum, a cardiologist at Brigham and Women's Hospital in Boston and national correspondent for the New England Journal of Medicine, notes, "[there is] tremendous uncertainty upon which most of medicine is practiced—an uncertainty that eludes hard and fast rules governing" (Rosenbaum, 2013).

Competing interests in healthcare have been studied extensively, in part because of their importance and the managerial challenges that they bring. This chapter reviews some of the representative research on this subject and has two main objectives. First, this chapter aims to provide readers with a broad overview of the research on competing interests at various points along the healthcare supply chain. We endeavor to fulfill this objective in section 4.2 by conducting an extensive review of key research studies and providing an organizing framework for these studies. Second, this chapter highlights avenues for future research on competing interests and healthcare operations as well as some of the tools that can potentially be directed to this effort. We tackle this objective in section 4.3 through an in-depth discussion of two concrete examples that have been studied in recent literature. Finally, section 4.4 concludes with a brief summary and some observations about specific gaps in the literature that could be fruitful subjects of future research inquiry.

4.2 The Literature on Competing Interests

This section reviews of the literature on competing interests in healthcare. Most of the work on this subject is empirical. At a very high level of abstraction, these works share a common theme: they find evidence of medical decisions influenced by various forms of competing financial interests.

The review is organized by going downstream in the healthcare supply chain. We begin at the most upstream level of the chain in section 4.2.1, reviewing studies that investigate how competing interests may affect the development and evaluation of pharmaceutical products. Going further downstream, in section 4.2.2, we review studies that investigate the impact of how physician ownership interests in the supply of healthcare delivery affect their decisions. Finally, in section 4.2.3, we review the evidence for the impact of competing interests on the accuracy of reported medical outcomes. Throughout this review, unless otherwise noted, all references to statistical significance will implicitly refer to significance at the 5 percent level.

4.2.1 Evaluation of Pharmaceutical Products

Of all the arenas where competing interests in healthcare have been studied, the one subject to the most intense debate and scrutiny is that of competing interests in the development and evaluation of pharmaceutical products (drugs and medical devices). This is not entirely surprising, given the large size of the pharmaceutical industry in the United States. What is perhaps less apparent is that competing interests in this space have intensified in recent years as the dividing line between academic and commercial research gets increasingly blurred, as industry collaborations are ubiquitous, and as industry funding for biomedical research has been steadily growing (Ehrhardt et al., 2015).

As a consequence of these trends, since around the 1990s, there have been concerns that the growing influence of the industry might bias the scientific objectivity of researchers in reporting and evaluating clinical evidence. A number of studies have found associations between ties to industry (e.g., through funding, collaborations, gifts) and how clinical evidence is reported and evaluated. Most studies find that statistical bias exists; that is, on average, linkages to the industry tend to result in scientific conclusions that are more favorable toward the industry. These studies cut across different drug classes, study designs, and time periods.

We review some of the major studies below, beginning with studies that focus narrowly on individual drug classes, broadening to studies that span multiple drugs and clinical interventions, and ending with studies that focus on medical reviews. Interested readers are referred to the systematic review by Bekelman et al. (2003) for further reading on the topic.

4.2.1.1 Individual Drug Classes

In the mid 1990s, the medical community was sharply divided over the safety of calcium-channel blockers, a class of drugs used to treat hypertension. Stelfox et al. (1998) surveyed the medical literature from March 1995 to September 1996, and developed a list of 70 articles (including primary studies, reviews, letters to the editor) on each side of the debate. They surveyed the authors of these articles to identify financial relationships (including speaking engagements, support for research/teaching, employment/consultation) with manufacturers of these and other drugs. They found that authors who had such financial relationships with these manufacturers (of calcium-channel blockers or other drugs), in general, more likely to be supportive of use of the drug.

Another study that focused on a different class of drugs had similar findings. Friedberg et al. (1999) surveyed the medical literature from 1988–1998 for published economic analyses of six different oncology drugs, to investigate if study conclusions were associated with whether the study was funded by a pharmaceutical company or nonprofit entities. The authors identified 44 studies: 20 that were funded by pharmaceutical companies and 24 by nonprofits. The authors found that unfavorable qualitative conclusions were reached in 5 percent of company-sponsored studies (1 out of 20), a significantly smaller fraction than the thirty-eight percent of nonprofit-funded studies (9 out of 24) that reached such unfavorable conclusions. They also investigated their sample of studies for "overstatement" of results; that is, having more favorable qualitative conclusions than was warranted by the quantitative results. They found that company-sponsored studies tended to overstate their results more frequently (30%, 6 out of 20) than non-profit-sponsored studies (13%, 3 out of 24), but this result was not statistically significant.

4.2.1.2 Multiple Interventions

Similar associations were found by other studies, which did not focus on individual drug classes but which cast a wide net on various clinical interventions. One study, by Ridker and Torres (2006), focused on the medical speciality of cardiology and reviewed randomized cardiovascular trials on the efficacy of an array of therapeutic interventions (including drugs, devices, behavioral interventions) published in three major medical journals (Journal of the American Medical Association, The Lancet, and the New England Journal of Medicine) from January 2000 to July 2005. Their sample comprised 303 trials that listed funding sources: 104 trials funded solely from not-for-profit organizations, 137 trials funded solely by for-profit organizations, and 62 trials that were jointly funded. They found that in their sample, trials that were solely for-profit funded tended to reach positive conclusions (that favored new treatments over existing standards of care) significantly more frequently (67.2%) than trials that were solely not-for-profit funded (49%); trials that were jointly funded reached favorable conclusions in 56.5 percent of their sample.

Consistent findings were also obtained by other studies that did not focus on specific drugs or diseases. Yaphe et al. (2001) performed a broad search for randomized clinical trials that were published in five major medical journals in from October 1992 through October 1994. They found that of the 209 industry-funded studies, a favorable outcome was reached by 87 percent; in contrast, only 65 percent of the 96 non-industry-funded studies reached favorable conclusions.

Kjaergard and Als-Nielsen (2002) reviewed all randomized clinical trials published in the British Medical Journal from 1997 to June 2001, finding 159 such trials across 12 medical specialties. They calculated a favorability score for each trial's findings, and categorized trials according to whether authors had no competing interests (94 trials), competing interests as a consequence of funding from for-profit organizations (27 trials), competing interests because of combined funding from both for-profit and not-for-profit organizations (19 trials), or other forms of competing interests (19 trials), including personal or political interests. They found that trials that had declared competing interests stemming from for-profit funding had significantly higher favorability scores than the other three categories; that is, they tended to report more favorable results than trials with either no competing interests or other forms of competing interests.

Such associations were not confined to studies published in standard issues of medical journals. Cho and Bero (1996) reviewed 152 drug studies published both in peer-reviewed medical journals and in medical symposia. (A symposium is a "collection of papers published as a separate issue or as a special section in a regular issue of a medical journal" (Bero et al., 1992)). Of these studies, 40 were sponsored by drug companies, and 112 were not. The authors found that of the company-sponsored studies, 98 percent (39 of 40) had conclusions that favored the drug of interest. This was a significantly higher proportion than the 79 percent (89 of 112) of non-sponsored studies.

4.2.1.3 Review Articles

The studies referenced above investigated bias among empirical studies on primary data. Other studies, reviewed below, have also found evidence of such bias among secondary data, namely, review articles. Jørgensen et al. (2006) did a matched pairwise comparison of industry-sponsored drug reviews with Cochrane reviews, which are reviews that have to adhere to strict guidelines and are often viewed as objective. Each pair of matched reviews studied the same two drugs targeting the same disease and had to be published within two years of each other. They found that industry-sponsored reviews tended to be less transparent, contain less methodological reservations about the data, and reach more favorable conclusions.

Studies of bias have also been conducted on evaluations of evidence on subjects pertaining to public health. Barnes and Bero (1998) identified 106 review articles published over a 15-year period from 1980 to 1996 about the health effects of passive smoking, that is, exposure to secondhand smoke. They found that 37 percent (39 of 106) of the articles concluded that such exposure posed no health risks, but of those 39 articles, there was a disproportionate fraction (74%, representing 29 of the 39 studies) were authored by investigators who had either received funding from or participated in activities that were sponsored by the tobacco industry. In regression analyses that controlled for other observable characteristics of the study (e.g, quality, year of publication), whether or not study authors had tobacco-industry affiliations was the only variable significantly associated with a conclusion that passive smoking had no negative health effects.

4.2.2 Physician Ownership

Moving further along the healthcare supply chain, this subsection focuses on competing interests faced by physicians if they have ownership interests in medical facilities that supply healthcare services or in companies that supply medical products.

The presence of competing financial interests for physicians opens several avenues of concerns from the standpoint of the overall health system. First, because of the promise of financial gain, physicians may induce patients to over-utilize medical services or products unnecessarily or, more egregiously, at the cost of unwarranted risks to their health. This potential for abuse is further exacerbated by the asymmetry of information and trust implicit in a typical patient–provider relationship: patients place their trust in the superiority of a provider's expertise and are often willing to comply with provider recommendations. Second, physician ownership constitutes a form of market power that can inhibit competition for similar goods and services, contributing to higher prices and overall inefficiency in the marketplace (Kahn, 2006).

On the other hand, proponents of various forms of physician ownership argue that because physicians have a more intimate knowledge of medical services or products, they can deliver higher quality care and at lower costs and therefore have higher levels of patient satisfaction. Proponents also argue that there has not been clear evidence that such ownership stifles competition (Greenwald et al., 2006; Babu et al., 2011).

In the United States, specific pieces of legislation were passed in the 1990s that established prohibitions on physicians from performing self-referrals (i.e., referrals to "entities in which the provider or the provider's family members have a financial interest" (U.S. Government Accountability Office, 2012)) for services billed to federal health care programs (e.g., Medicare or Medicaid). Two particularly relevant laws are the Stark law (42 USC section 1395 nn) and the anti-kickback statute (42 USC section 1320a-7b(b)), that prohibit such referrals. Our objective here is simply to make readers aware of the existing legal context under which this competing interest is regulated; details of these laws and their enforcement are beyond the scope of this review and interested readers are referred to Manchikanti and McMahon (2007) and references therein for further study. For our purposes, it suffices to note that there are exceptions to these laws that allow self-referral in some circumstances, allowing the associations between the competing interests posed by these exceptions and the delivery of healthcare to be studied by researchers.

What follows is a review of the studies that have investigated associations between differences in physician practice patterns and differences or changes in physician ownership. Throughout, we will use the term ***physician ownership*** to refer broadly to settings where physicians have any financial or direct investment interest in providers of medical services or suppliers of medical products.

This portion of the review is structured in a manner that follows roughly the same chronology as the public and academic interest in this subject. We review studies that examine physician ownership in medical facilities that supply ancillary services (§4.2.2.1), outpatient surgical services (§4.2.2.2), and specialty hospitals that provide services in dedicated specialties (§4.2.2.3). We conclude in section 4.2.2.4 with the contemporary issue of competing interests from physician ownership of medical device distributors.

4.2.2.1 Physician Ownership of Ancillary Services

The studies reviewed below are those that investigated how differences in physician ownership of facilities that supply limited medical services (e.g., physical therapy, radiation therapy, diagnostic imaging) were associated with differences in the physicians' patterns of referrals or service usage.

Studies in the early 1990s found positive correlations between physician ownership and higher utilization of various types of ancillary medical services. Mitchell and Scott (1992) surveyed freestanding facilities in Florida that provided physical therapy services and comprehensive rehabilitation services in 1989. These were facilities that provided such services outside of a regular physician's practice. A facility was classified as a "joint venture" if physicians who referred patients for services at that facility had any ownership or investment stake in the facility. They found that, compared to non-joint-venture facilities, joint ventures were on average, more profitable (2–3 times higher operating margins), generated more revenue (30–40% higher net revenue per patient), had a larger number of patient visits (approximately 50% higher), and used less skilled labor per visit (38–42% less time spent by licensed medical workers per patient visit). The authors also argued that these differences did not stem from any disparity in underlying health status between the patients using each type of facility but could have been driven partially by differences in social class. In a follow-up study with additional data, Mitchell and Sass (1995) provided evidence to argue that this observed increased utilization of medical services is more likely a consequence of demand creation by physicians instead of a mechanism to ensure quality.

Using a dataset comprising all health reimbursement claims administered by the United Mine Workers of America Health and Retirement Funds in the calendar years 1988–1999, Hillman et al. (1992) studied ten clinical presentations that commonly led to referrals for diagnostic imaging. They found that self-referring physicians had a significantly higher usage of diagnostic imaging compared to physicians who referred to external radiologists across all the ten different presentations. The extent of this increase ranged between 1.7 to 7.7 times, depending on the presentation.

Findings of similar positive associations continue to persist in modern studies. Baker (2010) used Medicare reimbursement claims data from 1998–2005 to study the behavior of orthopedists and neurologists before and after the event of "acquisition"—billing directly for MRI scans—and thereby gaining an financial interest in those scans. He found that physicians tended to order significantly more scans after acquisition than before and that this effect appeared to persist over time.

Several recent governmental reports on physician ownership of radiology equipment have shown associations between ownership changes and increased utilization of radiologic services. The U.S. Government Accountability Office used Medicare claims data to study patterns of MRI and CT between 2008, comparing "switchers"—providers who only began self-referring 2009—to non-switchers. The report noted that switchers had marked increases in their overall referral rates for such services, having approximately 67 percent higher referrals in 2010 compared to 2008. In contrast, providers who did not change their referral practices all had mild decreases in referral rates (U.S. Government

Accountability Office, 2012, Table 4). Similar findings were reported for therapeutic radiology services. In another study, the same office studied referrals for intensity-modulated radiation therapy for treatment of prostate cancer between 2007 and 2009. They found that switchers had 47 percent higher rates of referral in 2009 compared to 2007, whereas non-switchers had roughly stable referral rates (U.S. Government Accountability Office, 2013).

4.2.2.2 Physician Ownership of Ambulatory Surgery Centers

Ambulatory surgery centers (ASCs), also known as outpatient surgery centers or surgicenters, are nonhospital facilities that exclusively provide surgical services that do not require patients to be admitted for hospital stays (e.g., cateract surgery, endoscopy). In the United States, the numbers of ASCs have been steadily growing. As of 2013, there were more than 5,000 ASCs in operation (MedPAC, 2015), more than ten times the roughly 400 ASCs in 1983 (Winter, 2003). Surveys have indicated that many ASCs tend to feature a relatively high level of physician ownership; in 2004, 83 percent of ASCs had some level of physician ownership, and their average percentage of ownership was 43 percent (Choudhry et al., 2005).

Unsurprisingly, ASCs have been the subject of several studies of the potential effects of competing interests from physician ownership. An early case study by Lynk and Longley (2002) studied changes in patterns of referral by physicians on the medical faculty of an acute-care hospital in Hammond, Lousiana, before and after a new ASC opened in 1996. The ASC had ownership interests from several physicians on the faculty. The study authors reported that after the ASC opened, physician owners of the ASC had substantially higher levels of referrals to the ASC compared to non-physician owners.

Competing interests from physician-owned ASCs may not only induce physician owners to preferentially refer patients to these centers, but also induce them to cherry-pick and refer patients who are healthier (i.e. have lower acuity) and who are therefore more profitable to ASCs. This concern has been recognized and raised repeatedly by the community in various forums (Casalino et al., 2003; Carey et al., 2011). Some studies have found evidence that suggests, although not definitively, that this may be happening. Gabel et al. (2008) studied referral patterns of approximately 1 million patient discharges in Pennsylvania in 2003. One of their key findings pertained to a sample of physicians who had high levels of referrals to physician-owned ASCs (this group was a proxy for physician owners). They found that when faced with a well-insured patient, these physicians referred such a patient to a physician-owned ASC in 90–98 percent of such cases. In contrast, when faced with a poorly-insured patient (i.e. on Medicaid), they referred such a patient to a physician-owned surgicenter in only 55 percent of such cases, and directed the remaining 45 percent to hospital outpatient departments. Similarly, in cross-sectional analyses of surgical claims data from 1998 from Medicare beneficiaries, Winter (2003) found that, compared to hospital outpatient departments, ASCs tended to treat patients who were less medically complex.

Other studies used longitudinal analyses to study changes in referral and usage patterns before and after physician ownership status changed. Hollingsworth et al. (2010) focused on five common outpatient procedures performed at ASCs and collected data on all such procedures conducted in Florida from 2003–2005. In addition to finding that physician-owners had significantly higher rates of performing all five procedures, they found through longitudinal analyses, that switching from non-owner to owner status was associated with an increased use of four of the five procedures.

4.2.2.3 Physician Ownership of Speciality Hospitals

Another important class of medical facilities that tends to feature high levels of physician ownership is specialty hospitals. These are hospitals which have "a specific clinical focus such as an anatomic region or patient population" (Babu et al., 2011), and the two most common types of such hospitals are orthopedic hospitals and cardiac hospitals. Overall, estimates indicate that there were less than 50 physician-owned specialty hospitals in operation in 2002, but approximately 235 in operation in 2013 (Baum, 2013). These hospitals tend to have fewer beds (Babu et al., 2011) and limited emergency services (Kahn, 2006; Office of Inspector General, 2008). The concerns about competing interests from physician ownership in such hospitals are analogous to those for ASCs reviewed above.

Mitchell (2008) used claims from a large workers' compensation database in Oklahoma covering the calendar years 2000 to 2004 (inclusive) in order to study how referral patterns of physicans were affected by ownership in a specialty hospital. Two physician-owned specialty hospitals (an orthopedic hospital and a spine hospital) began operations in one metropolitan area of Oklahoma during the study period, instigating an exogenous shock that formed the basis of a differences-in-differences analysis. Mitchell (2008) found that physician owners increased their usage of a number of surgical and diagnostic services to a greater extent than physician non-owners, who typically kept their levels of usage approximately constant across several procedures (e.g., complex spinal fusion surgery, epidurals, fluoroscopy), with moderate levels of increase across others (e.g., MRI scans).

A study by Greenwald et al. (2006) assessed the differences between physician-owned specialty hospitals and community hospitals, finding that physicians who had financial interests in specialty hospitals were more likely to refer patients to their own specialty hospitals in general, but also were more likely to refer patients with lower acuity (and who were therefore more profitable) to their hospitals as well. However, the authors caution against interpreting their findings as indicating that physicians are unduly influenced by their financial incentives, pointing to a number of other factors, including typically small ownership shares that physicians hold in these hospitals, physician convenience, and patient preferences as possible reasons for their findings.

Other studies on this subject used individual hospitals, instead of individual physicians, as the unit of analysis. Two papers (Stensland and Winter, 2006; Nallamothu et al., 2007) studied the emergence of physician-owned cardiac hospitals across the 306 hospital referral regions in the United States between the mid 1990s to early 2000s, investigating how the entry of these hospitals affected the rate at which invasive cardiac surgeries (comprising coronary artery bypass grafts and percutaneous coronary interventions) were performed on Medicare beneficiaries. The rate of such procedures in a region was measured as the volume of procedures normalized by the total number of beneficiaries in that region. Stensland and Winter (2006) found that regions where new cardiac hospitals were opened had significantly higher growth rates of coronary artery bypass graft procedures compared to other regions. Nallamothu et al. (2007) used a slightly different time window and segmented comparison groups and found that the growth rate of cardiac procedures (in aggregate, and individually) was significantly higher in regions with new cardiac hospitals compared to regions with general hospitals that had new cardiac programs and compared to regions with no new cardiac programs. In other words, the latter study found that the increase in usage of such procedures at physician-owned cardiac hospitals appeared to exceed what we would expect as a consequence of increased capacity for these procedures.

4.2.2.4 Physician-Owned Distributors

A contemporary form of physician ownership and one that has sparked intense debate in the medical, academic, and political arenas is that of physician-owned distributors (PODs). These are business entities that supply medical products to healthcare facilities and that are partially or wholly owned by physicians. PODs that supply devices for spinal surgeries, in particular, have come under the most attention.

At the time of writing this chapter, academic studies on this topic are scant, likely because of the recency of the growth of PODs. Nonetheless, because PODs represent a modern and important evolution of competing interests in healthcare and could be a fruitful avenue of future academic inquiry, we will briefly highlight what is known about PODs and some relevant statistics.

A report published by the U.S. Department of Health and Human Services Office of Inspector General (Office of Inspector General, 2013) describes the present state of affairs of PODs. The report details the results of an in-depth study of a sample of 971 Medicare reimbursement claims for spinal fusion surgery in FY2011 from 596 hospitals. According to the report, almost 20 percent of such surgeries used devices that were supplied by PODs, and approximately one in three hospitals in the sample reported ever purchasing spinal devices from PODs. In these hospitals, rates of spinal surgery increased by about 15 percent after they began to purchase from PODs, which was higher than the 5 percent growth rate in spinal surgeries from hospitals who were not supplied by PODs across matched time periods.

Another published governmental report (United States Senate Finance Committee Majority Staff, 2016) showed that as of 2016, PODs were estimated to be operating in 43 states. The report also contained the results of a preliminary study comparing the utilization of spinal surgeons who had ownership interests in PODs with non-owners, which found that surgeon owners tended to see more patients and perform more surgeries than non-owners.

4.2.3 Medical Reporting

In this final portion of the review, we focus on the issue of reporting of medical outcomes, a process that is further yet downstream in the healthcare supply chain, typically commencing *after* healthcare delivery for a given patient is complete. In this context, competing financial interests may create incentives for providers to inaccurately report medical outcomes to insurance payers in order to increase reimbursements. Because such reporting inaccuracies come usually in the form of incorrect billing codes, the term *upcoding* has been used to refer to systematic erroneous reporting that results in financial benefit. We note, however, that upcoding may refer to either willful or unintentional errors. The literature, reviewed below, is mostly unconcerned with the intention behind upcoding but focuses instead on finding evidence that upcoding exists.

The potential for upcoding arises, in part, because the financial incentives for doing so can be substantial. On a national scale, the U.S. Department of Health and Human Services estimated that across FY12 through FY15, between 8.5 and 12.7 percent of all Medicare dollars spent on claims were inaccurate; in particular, in FY15, this percentage was 12.09 percent, representing a total of 43.3 billion dollars in expenditure of Medicare (U.S. Department of Health and Human Services, 2016, Table 1A). On the scale of individual diseases, incentives for erroneous reporting can be large, too. For example, Psaty et al. (1999) used follow-up data from the Cardiovascular Health Study on 485 Medicare patients who were diagnosed with heart failure and tried to validate each patient's diagnosis by reviewing of a combination of evidence for each patient (medical records, interviews with the patient, proxies, and/or physicians, and any available death certificates). They were able to positively validate a diagnosis of heart failure in only 62.5 percent of the cases. In the remaining 182 patients, the authors write that they were "not able to find even modest levels of supporting evidence for the diagnosis of heart failure" (Psaty et al., 1999, p 109). By scaling their estimates nationally, they suggest that miscoding for heart failure could potentially cost Medicare $993 million a year.

Ambiguity is another factor that allows upcoding to occur. In addition to the ambiguity around medical diagnoses, which present opportunities for competing interests to surface in general, upcoding is further enabled by ambiguity in billing codes, specifically, because they generally do not map cleanly onto medical diagnoses. For example, the primary mechanism through which inpatient services are reimbursed in the United States and several other countries is by classifying patients into diagnosis-related groups (DRGs). However, as one study notes, "[c]linically ... many medical DRGs are not mutually exclusive. Often patients may reasonably be assigned to two or more DRGs" (Iezzoni and Moskowitz, 1986). Specifically, a given clinical diagnosis can potentially be mapped into different DRGs with different reimbursement levels depending on its severity, creating incentives (and the opportunity) for providers to exaggerate a patient severity, to gain higher reimbursement.

This portion of our review is organized into two portions. We begin with studies that have studied DRG upcoding in inpatient settings in section 4.2.3.1, which represents the classical setting under which upcoding has been studied, and move in section 4.2.3.2 to more contemporary studies that investigate non-DRG variants of upcoding.

4.2.3.1 DRG Upcoding

Studies on DRG upcoding broadly share a common analytical strategy. They identify pairs (or more generally, sets) of DRGs that represent the same clinical diagnosis, but of different severities and reimbursements, and compute an "upcoding ratio"—the proportion of discharges in these DRG sets that contain the code yielding the highest reimbursement over a given time window. They then try to find patterns in how these upcoding ratios differ across provider types or times.

Silverman and Skinner (2004) used a sample of Medicare claims data over 19 years from 1989 to 1998 to study the billing patterns of for-profit, not-for-profit, and government hospitals. They focused on pneumonia, which had four possible distinct DRGs. The authors computed the average upcoding ratio for each of the three classes of hospital ownership, and found that the class of for-profit hospitals featured much higher ratios than not-for-profit or government hospitals for every year in their study window. In particular, not-for-profit and government hospitals had ratios that fluctuated between 20 and 30 percent in the study window, whereas for profit hospitals had ratios ranging from 28 to 52 percent. In this study, the authors also provided evidence that their results were not a consequence of patient selection or more efficient billing on the part of for-profit hospitals.

Expanding the scope of DRG upcoding from one clinical condition to multiple different conditions, Dafny (2005) performed a study of approximately 7 million Medicare patients from FY85-FY91 and 95 DRG pairs. Each DRG pair represented the same principal clinical diagnosis, but the top and bottom codes of the pair differed in severity and reimbursement. Her analysis exploited a policy shock, namely, a change in reimbursement rates in FY88 that had the average effect of increasing the "spread"—the disparity in reimbursement between the top and bottom codes in each pair—which in turn increased hospitals' financial incentives to upcode. Her results suggested that coding practices were influenced by financial incentives. In particular, DRG pairs that had larger changes in spread (as a consequence of the policy change) tended to also have higher fractions of diagnoses that were assigned to the higher reimbursement code of the pair.

Studies have also uncovered differences in upcoding patterns even *within* the class of not-for-profit hospitals. Heese et al. (2016) hypothesized that hospitals that had higher levels of beneficience—those that served higher proportion of indigent patients and supported more medical residents—would face lower regulatory scrutiny and would consequently be more prone to upcoding. To investigate their hypothesis, they considered a sample of Californian not-for-profit hospitals from 1996 to 2007 and focused on three distinct groups of DRGs that were particularly prone to upcoding, general respiratory conditions, disorders of the circulatory system, and metabolic disorders (including diabetes). They calculated the upcoding ratio for each hospital, in each year, for each DRG and found strong support for their hypothesis: Even after controlling for possible confounding factors, hospitals that served more indigents and had higher resident-to-bed ratios tended to have higher upcoding ratios.

4.2.3.2 Non-DRG Upcoding

Beyond the inpatient setting, other studies have investigated upcoding in the outpatient setting. Brunt (2011) used Medicare Part B claims, which are used for reimbursement of outpatient visits, from 2001–2003, focusing on a group of four procedure codes for general assessments of health that were ordered in terms of intensity of service, and therefore, reimbursement. He used a mixed logit model to estimate the probability that physicians would choose one of the four codes and studied how the extent of the marginal benefit/cost of using a higher/lower reimbursement code influenced this selection probability. The results suggested that coding choice was influenced by reimbursement levels. After controlling for various confounders, a given code tended to be selected with higher probability when (a) the marginal cost of reducing the code's intensity to a lower-reimbursement code was higher, and (b) the marginal benefit of increasing the code's intensity to a higher-reimbursement code was lower.

Another recent form of upcoding that has been studied pertains to financial incentives around hospital-acquired infections (HAI). In an effort to reduce the incidence of HAIs in hospitals, Medicare developed a list of HAIs that were deemed to be important and preventable, and revised their reimbursement policy in 2008 to reduce reimbursements to hospitals if a patient incurred one of these HAIs during their stay. If, on the other hand, the infection was present-on-admission (POA), that is, the patient was infected when he/she arrived at the hospital, then the hospital would be fully reimbursed. This created financial incentives for a new form of upcoding for patients who actually had HAIs, to either incorrectly report them as having infections that were POA, or for these HAIs to be omitted altogether. We will refer to these incentives collectively as HAI upcoding because both forms of errors would financially benefit the hospital. The two studies reviewed below investigated HAI upcoding by using detailed reviews of medical records to validate the true HAI/POA status of patients and reached mixed findings. In section 4.3.2, we present an in-depth discussion of another study, which takes a different approach to HAI upcoding.

A study by Meddings et al. (2010) provided evidence in support of the existence of HAI upcoding. The authors reviewed 80 patient records that listed a urinary tract infection as a secondary diagnosis. They engaged a physician to do a full review of each medical record, including both physician and nursing notes, to distinguish whether the urinary tract infection was a HAI or POA. This was considered the *correct* code for the patient. The authors compared this to the actual code that had been assigned to the patient by medical coders and found substantial discrepancies, in the direction that financially benefited the hospital. In particular, the proportion of POA in the actual codes (75%) was substantially higher than the proportion of correct POA codes (50%).

On the other hand, a report by Snow et al. (2012) using similar methods found that HAI upcoding was not widespread. They reviewed a set of patients' medical records and linked them to Medicare claims data. They segmented their study into the two different types of inaccuracy noted above: HAI underreporting, where a HAI was truly present, but was absent in the claims report; and POA overreporting, where a HAI condition was reported as POA. Snow et al. (2012) found that the average prevalence of both types of inaccuracy was low. For the former, in each of three different conditions (approximately 250 cases in each condition), they found between 0 and 6 percent of HAI underreporting. For the latter, they grouped five different conditions (290 cases in all) and found that the POA overreporting rate was 8 percent.

4.3 Examples

In this section, we review in detail two examples of problems on the topic of competing interests in healthcare, which are simplified and adapted versions of problems that have been the subject of recent papers by Dai et al. (2017) and Bastani et al. (2018), respectively. These examples were chosen to highlight (a) nascent research problems in the interface of competing interests and healthcare operations, and (b) the methodological tools that can be fruitfully applied to tackle these problems.

The first example, adapted from Dai et al. (2017) by employing constructs by Dranove (1988), is model-based and focuses on developing predictions about how physicians will act when they are faced with competing interests. Our goal in discussing this study is to highlight basic decision-analytic modeling principles that can be deployed to analyze problems in this domain. The second example is a simplified version of the study by Bastani et al. (2018) that focuses on finding empirical evidence for HAI upcoding. Our goal in discussing this is to highlight one possible empirical strategy for conducting such a study.

A common modeling feature that runs through these two examples and that makes competing interests a salient feature in influencing medical decisions is that a patient's true health status is not perfectly observable. This ambiguity creates the opportunity for a provider to recommend a course of action (in the first example) that is not fully aligned with what is in the patient's best interests or make a report (in the second example) that is not aligned with the best interests of the overall healthcare system.

4.3.1 Example 1: Physician Decisions with Competing Interests

In this example, we assume a stylized model of physician decision-making. Specifically, suppose that a physician (she) observes a test result of a patient (he), and has to decide whether or not to recommend a certain medical intervention to the patient. For simplicity, we will assume that the patient will always agree with what the physician recommends. Extensions to this model could potentially model the patient's decision to accept or reject the recommendation in so-called "games of persuasion" (Dranove, 1988; Milgrom, 1981). Because the test is an inexact measure of the true health status of the patient, the physician may face two sources of erroneous decision-making: (a) the physician might have conducted the intervention when it was not warranted or appropriate (this is akin to a Type I error in statistics); or (b) the intervention was necessary, but the physician did not perform the intervention (this is akin to a Type II error in statistics). The competing interest faced by the physician is the possibility of financial gain from performing the procedure.

Formally, let $X \in \{0, 1\}$ be a random variable that indicates whether the intervention is appropriate for the patient. This is unobserved and can be interpreted as the latent "type" of the patient. Let $p := \mathbb{P}(X = 1)$, which represents the unconditional probability that the patient needs the intervention, and assume for simplicity that $0 < p < 1$.

Let Z be a $[0, 1]$-valued random variable that represents the patient's severity level (e.g., from symptoms or test results), which is observed by the physician. We will interpret larger values of Z as being more severe, or, in other words, X and Z are positively correlated. We let $f_Z(\cdot|X = j)$ denote the conditional density of Z on $X = j$, for $j \in \{0, 1\}$. To avoid technical minutiae, we assume that $f_Z(z|X = j)$ is strictly positive and continuous for all $z \in (0, 1)$ and $j \in \{0, 1\}$. For ease of exposition, we will also let $Z_j, j = 1, 2$ represent a random variable with a density equal to $f_Z(\cdot|X = j)$. Throughout, we implicitly assume that there is a well-defined probability space $(\Omega, \mathcal{F}, \mathbb{P})$ upon which all these random variables are constructed.

A concept that we will use in our exposition is that of a likelihood ratio ordering between random variables, which we define below in our context.

Definition 4.1 Given two [0,1]-valued random variables, U and V, with respective densities $f_U, f_V : [0, 1] \to \Re_{++}$, we say that V is larger than U in the likelihood ratio order, and write $U \leq_{lr} V$ if $\frac{f_V(t)}{f_U(t)}$ is increasing in t on $[0, 1]$.

It is a routine exercise to show that $U \leq_{lr} V$ in turn implies that V is stochastically larger than U, which we will write as $U \leq_{st} V$ (see, e.g., Shaked and Shanthikumar, 2007).

To model competing interests in this context, we leverage a class of models that have been developed in the health economics literature, which assumes that the physician's utility is jointly increasing in her patient's utility as well as her own financial return (e.g., Farley, 1986; De Jaegher and Jegers, 2000). Here, we will use a simple special case of this general model that nonetheless allows us to capture the essential features of competing interests.

We assume that the physician's net utility from not performing the intervention is zero (this is without loss of generality). If the intervention is performed, we assume that the physician gains an incremental financial benefit of r. For the patient, we assume that he gains an incremental utility of $b > 0$ if the intervention was appropriate (i.e., $X = 1$) and suffers an incremental disutility of $-h$ if the intervention was not appropriate (i.e., $X = 0$), where $h > 0$.

We let the exogenous parameter $\phi \in [0, 1]$ represent the level of (financial) competing interest, and that the physician's net utility is a convex combination of her financial reward and the patient's utility, weighted by ϕ, such that a higher value of ϕ represents a stronger competing interest. Therefore, the physician's expected utility, conditional upon Z is

$$U := \begin{cases} \phi r + (1 - \phi)[b\mathbb{E}(\mathbf{1}_{\{X=1\}}|Z) - h\mathbb{E}(\mathbf{1}_{\{X=0\}}|Z)] & \text{if the intervention is taken} \\ 0 & \text{otherwise} \end{cases} \tag{4.1}$$

We assume that the physician is rational and chooses an intervention policy that maximizes her expected utility upon observing Z. Her policy may be equivalently represented as a set $\Theta \subseteq [0, 1]$ so that she will intervene iff $Z \in \Theta$ and do nothing otherwise. In other words, after simplifying, we may write

$$\Theta := \{z \in [0,1] : \phi r - (1-\phi)h + (1-\phi)(b+h)\mathbb{P}(X=1|Z=z) \geq 0\}. \tag{4.2}$$

From Eq. (4.2), we can immediately observe that for high enough levels of competing interest, the physician will always conduct the intervention.

Proposition 4.1 Define $\phi^{**} := \frac{h}{r+h}$. For $\phi \geq \phi^{**}$, the physician will always choose to conduct the intervention, irrespective of the value of Z.

On the other hand, for moderate values of ϕ below ϕ^{**}, whether or not the physician recommends the intervention will, in general, depend upon her observation of Z, and the structure of her decision policy further depends on the functional dependence of $\mathbb{P}(X=1|Z=z)$ on z. Since Z represents the patient's severity, and it is natural to assume that higher levels of severity should make it more likely that the treatment is appropriate, it should not be surprising that a simple structural result follows from assuming that $\mathbb{P}(X=1|Z=z)$ is increasing in z. In particular, Θ will have a threshold structure. The following lemma presents an equivalent characterization of this assumption in terms of model primitives.

Lemma 4.1 $\mathbb{P}(X=1|Z=z)$ is increasing in z if and only if $Z_0 \leq_{lr} Z_1$.

Proof: Let $\eta(z) := \mathbb{P}(X=1|Z=z)$ and $L(z) := \frac{f_Z(z|X=1)}{f_Z(z|X=0)}$. Our objective is to show that $\eta(z)$ is increasing iff $L(z)$ is increasing. By Bayes's rule, we have

$$\eta(z) = \frac{f_Z(z|X=1)p}{f_Z(z|X=0)(1-p)+f_Z(z|X=1)p} = \frac{L(z)\frac{p}{1-p}}{1+L(z)\frac{p}{1-p}},$$

from which the result follows because the mapping $y \mapsto \frac{y}{1+y}$ is a strictly increasing mapping. □

Henceforth, we will assume that the assumption that $Z_0 \leq_{lr} Z_1$ holds, and for ease of exposition, we will in fact assume a stronger condition, that the likelihood ratio between Z_1 and Z_0 is *strictly* increasing.

Proposition 4.2 Suppose that $\phi < \phi^{**}$ and let $L(z)$ represent the likelihood ratio function between Z_1 and Z_0, that is, $L(z) = \frac{f_Z(z|X=1)}{f_Z(z|X=0)}$. Assuming that the likelihood ratio between Z_1 and Z_0 is strictly increasing, Θ admits the characterization, $\Theta = [\underline{z}, 1]$, where $\underline{z} = \underline{z}(\phi)$ is the unique value of z that solves

$$L(z) = \frac{1-p}{p}\left[\frac{h - \frac{\phi}{1-\phi}r}{b + \frac{\phi}{1-\phi}r}\right].$$

In other words, under these assumptions, the physician will choose to recommend the intervention if Z exceeds the threshold $\underline{z}$. Straightforward comparative statics will show that this threshold is decreasing in the conflict of interest parameter, as the next proposition shows.

Proposition 4.3 $\underline{z}(\phi)$ is decreasing in ϕ

In other words, as a physician's competing interest increases, she will tend to recommend intervention for lower severities.

For a given level ϕ, the interval $[\underline{z}(\phi), \underline{z}(0)]$ intuitively represents the range of patient severity in which the effect of the physician's competing interest has the most important ramifications. Specifically, when the patient's severity level is in this interval, the physician recommends the intervention (to maximize her utility), but this is suboptimal for the welfare of the patient, who would have gotten a higher expected utility if the intervention had not been performed.

One extension of this basic model that has been pursued by Dai et al. (2017) and briefly reviewed here, is to introduce the option of taking another measurement to gain more information about the patient's condition, which we will refer to as an "advanced test." This may provide additional revenue to the physician but at an added risk to the patient. To model this extension, the physician's decision becomes a two-stage process, where she can now choose from three options in the first stage (do nothing, perform the intervention, or do the advanced test). The second stage materializes only if the advanced test is chosen, in which she receives the result of the test and then faces two decisions (do nothing or intervene). This two-stage extension is analyzed by the approach of backward induction. This approach is standard; therefore, we will refrain from performing an in-depth analysis, referring readers to Dai et al. (2017) for an example of how such an analysis can be done.

Instead, we will present an approach to modeling this advanced test that is similar in spirit, but differs slightly in specifics from the presentation in Dai et al. (2017). Specifically, let Y represent a $[0, 1]$-valued random variable that represents the result of the new test. We will describe an assumption on the distribution of Y that captures the salient features of the problem and allows tractable analysis. As before, for notational simplicity, we let $Y_j, j = 1, 2$ represent a random variable that has the same distribution as $Y|X = j$. Our key assumption is stated below.

Assumption 4.1 $Y_0 \leq_{lr} Z_0$ and $Z_1 \leq_{lr} Y_1$.

First, this assumption results in a simple threshold decision rule for the physician, which allows analysis to be tractable. This is because the assumption above implies that $Y_0 \leq_{lr} Y_1$ (from the earlier assumption that $Z_0 \leq_{lr} Z_1$ and the transitive property of the likelihood ratio ordering). Because this holds, for the physician's second stage decision, we will arrive at a threshold-type result that is similar in structure and spirit to Proposition 4.2.

Second, this assumption captures the idea that the second test is more accurate than the first. To motivate this, we will show that this assumption implies that the Type I and II errors for the second test (i.e., from Y) are both lower than that of the first test (i.e., from Z), for any common decision threshold. To see this, we note that for any $u \in (0, 1)$,

$$\begin{aligned}
&\text{Type I error from first test using threshold } u \\
&\quad = \mathbb{P}(Z > u | X = 0) \\
&\quad = \mathbb{P}(Z_0 > u) && [\text{Definition of } Z_0] \\
&\quad \geq \mathbb{P}(Y_0 > u) && [Y_0 \leq_{lr} Z_0 \Rightarrow Y_0 \leq_{st} Z_0] \\
&\quad = \mathbb{P}(Y > u | X = 0) && [\text{Definition of } Y_0] \\
&\quad = \text{Type I error from second test using threshold } u
\end{aligned}$$

and similarly for the Type II error.

4.3.2 Example 2: Evidence of HAI Upcoding

In this example, we review the approach taken by Bastani et al. (2018) for the detection of HAI upcoding for a given class of infections (e.g., urinary tract infections). Focusing solely on patients who were diagnosed as having the infection upon discharge, we find two distinct possibilities for any given patient. One, the patient may have arrived at the hospital with the infection already present (we say that this patient is a true POA), or the infection was hospital-acquired (we say that this patient is a true HAI). The potential for the hospital to upcode stems from the fact that the hospital receives only a noisy signal of the patient's true infection status.

For a true POA patient, there is some probability ϵ_1 that the hospital erroneously codes the patient as having a HAI, and a further probability ϵ_2 that the hospital misses the condition altogether and does not code it. For a true HAI patient, there is some other probability δ_1 that the hospital erroneously codes the patient as being POA, and a further probability δ_2 that it misses the condition and does not code it. These error probabilities are summarized in Table 4.1 For a true HAI patient, both errors are considered *upcoding* because they would result in a more favorable reimbursement for the hospital.

One simple way of detecting upcoding in this context is to find an exogenous variation in hospitals that separates them into treatment (T) and control (C) groups, and to investigate whether δ_1 or δ_2 (or their sum) significantly differ between these groups. The variation that Bastani et al. (2018) exploit in their methodology is the variation of the strength of state-level regulation and enforcement of HAI reporting across different states, as classified in a report by the U.S. Department of Health and Human Services Office of

Table 4.1 Frequency of different codes assigned to a true POA patient and a true HAI patient. r_{POA}: frequency of reported POAs, r_{HAI}: frequency of reported HAIs. Assumption: $\delta_1 + \delta_2 < 1$ and $\epsilon_1 + \epsilon_2 < 1$

Actual	Coded as POA	Coded as HAI	No Code
True POA	$1 - \epsilon_1 - \epsilon_2$	ϵ_1	ϵ_2
True HAC	δ_1	$1 - \delta_1 - \delta_2$	δ_2
Observed	$r_{POA} := 1 - \epsilon_1 - \epsilon_2 + \delta_1$	$r_{HAI} := 1 - \delta_1 - \delta_2 + \epsilon_1$	$\delta_2 + \epsilon_2$

Inspector General. Their treatment group T comprised states that had "weak" regulations, and their control group comprised the states that had "strong" regulations.

In this setting, Bastani et al. (2018) investigated the following hypothesis: Relative to hospitals in states with stronger regulations, hospitals in states with weaker regulations tended to upcode true HAIs more frequently, or tended to upcode true HAIs into POAs more frequently in particular. Formally, letting $\Delta\delta_i, \Delta\epsilon_i, i = 1, 2$ respectively represent the difference in δ_i and ϵ_i between the treatment and control group, they investigated the composite hypothesis listed below.

Hypothesis. $\Delta\delta_1 + \Delta\delta_2 > 0$ or $\Delta\delta_1 > 0$.

One source of complexity that their methodology had to overcome was that ϵ_i and δ_i could not be easily estimated from data. Put another way, the data only revealed what the reported frequencies of POA and HAI were, but not their true frequencies. Their approach handled this problem in two main steps:

First, they argued that $\Delta\epsilon_i \geq 0, i = 1, 2$. In other words, the claim is that hospitals who face stronger state regulations (the control group) tended to have lower errors in misreporting true POAs. The intutive argument supporting this claim is as follows. For such (true POA) patients, all hospitals have a financial incentive to be code accurately, and the level of reporting accuracy is largely a function of the hospital's ability to assess and detect these conditions in a timely fashion. This often requires a well-developed infrastructure, which the presence of a strong regulatory environment tends to encourage. Beyond this intuitive argument, the authors cited separate evidence showing that hospitals in the control group had higher quality and were generally more responsive in delivering care.

Second, they showed that if the assumption that $\Delta\epsilon_i \geq 0, i = 1, 2$ holds, then, analyzing the reported POA and HAI rates would be sufficient to determine their hypothesis. This is reproduced in the following proposition.

Proposition 4.4 ***(Bastani et al. (2018))*** Let $\Delta r_i, i \in \{POA, HAI\}$ represent the respective differences in observed reporting rate of POAs and HAIs between the treatment and control groups. If $\Delta \epsilon_i \geq 0, i = 1, 2$, then

$$\Delta r_{POA} > 0 \qquad \text{and} \qquad \Delta r_{HAI} < 0$$

implies

$$\Delta \delta_1 + \Delta \delta_2 > 0 \qquad \text{or} \qquad \Delta \delta_1 > 0.$$

The authors used their approach on inpatient claims data from Medicare, focusing on two important classes of HAIs, cathether-associated urinary tract infections and central line-associated bloodstream infections. Their empirical results supported their main hypothesis: Hospitals in the treatment group (those who faced lower state-level regulations) did have higher levels of reported POAs and lower levels of reported HAIs, even after controlling for major confounders, such as patient-level demographic factors and comorbidities, and local sociodemographic factors. Under further assumptions, they estimated that roughly 18.5 percent of true HAI claims were inaccurately reported as POAs.

4.4 Summary and Future Work

To summarize, in this chapter we have provided (a) a broad overview of the research on competing interests in healthcare and (b) a deep dive into two specific examples of recent work on this subject that intersect with healthcare operations. Through this review, several gaps stand out as possible opportunities for future research on this subject.

First, there is still a need for empirical research as new forms of competing interests emerge from the combination of policy changes, new business models, or new models of healthcare delivery or financing. For example, as noted in section 4.2.2.4, there is comparatively little academic inquiry into the extent to which clinical decisions are affected by competing interests posed by the nascent growth of physician-owned distributors. As another example, many existing studies on this subject are based on the fee-for-service model of reimbursement. As newer, and supposedly improved, models of healthcare financing become more prevalent (e.g., accountable care organizations or more general capitation models), research should empirically assess whether or not these reimbursement models actually deliver upon their promises, in particular to mitigate the impact of competing interests that drive inefficiencies in healthcare delivery.

Second, there is also a need for empirical research that goes after stronger causal interpretations of findings instead of only demonstrating correlations.

This is likely to be a challenging task, given the challenges in appropriate counterfactuals in existing work. Nonetheless, this remains an area that appears to be underserved and thus far pursued only by a minority of studies.

Third, the literature that uses the lens and methods of operations management to study problems of competing interests in healthcare operations is very thin at various levels of the healthcare supply chain. Given the widespread prevalence of such competing interests at multiple levels, the enormity of financial stakes that can be involved, and the potential detriment to patient health and safety, the dearth of work on this subject using operations management methodologies is somewhat surprising. On the other hand, this gap suggests that much insight could be derived from such methods, which are presently waiting for new research to uncover. Specific issues that seem particularly promising are assessing the effectiveness of various forms of regulation (e.g., mandated disclosure, prohibitions) in mitigating the impact of competing interests and, relatedly, whether there are optimal ways of managing these competing interests given certain conditions or settings.

In conclusion, competing interests in healthcare is a topic that remains ripe for future academic study. A deeper understanding of both the impact of such competing interests in new and future healthcare delivery models as well as insights into how the competing interests can be better managed will be important to our holistic understanding of effective healthcare operations management.

References

Babu, M.A., J.M. Rosenow, and B.V. Nahed. (2011). Physician-owned hospitals, neurosurgeons, and disclosure: lessons from law and the literature. *Neurosurgery* 68(6) 1724–1732.

Baker, L.C. (2010). Acquisition of MRI equipment by doctors drives up imaging use and spending. *Health Affairs* 29(12) 2252–2259.

Barnes, D.E. and L.A. Bero. (1998). Why review articles on the health effects of passive smoking reach different conclusions. *JAMA* 279(19) 1566–1570.

Bastani, H., J. Goh, and M. Bayati. (2018). Evidence of upcoding in pay-for-performance programs. Management Science, forthcoming/

Baum, N. (2013). Physician ownership in hospitals and outpatient facilities. *Center for Healthcare Research & Transformation* 1–8.

Bekelman, J.E., Y. Li, and C.P. Gross. (2003). Scope and impact of financial conflicts of interest in biomedical research: a systematic review. *JAMA* 289(4) 454–465.

Bero, L.A., A. Galbraith, and D. Rennie. (1992). The publication of sponsored symposiums in medical journals. *New England Journal of Medicine* 327(16) 1135–1140. doi: 10.1056/NEJM199210153271606. http://dx.doi.org/10.1056/NEJM199210153271606.

Brunt, Christopher S. (2011). CPT fee differentials and visit upcoding under Medicare Part B. *Health Economics* 20(7) 831–841.

Carey, K., J.F. Burgess, and G.J. Young. (2011). Hospital competition and financial performance: The effects of ambulatory surgery centers. *Health Economics* 20(5) 571–581. doi: 10.1002/hec.1617. http://dx.doi.org/10.1002/hec.1617.

Casalino, L.P., K.J. Devers, and L.R. Brewster. (2003). Focused factories? Physician-owned specialty facilities. *Health Affairs* 22(6) 56–67. doi:10.1377/hlthaff.22.6.56. http://content.healthaffairs.org/content/22/6/56.abstract.

Cho, M.K. and L.A. Bero. (1996). The quality of drug studies published in symposium proceedings. *Annals of Internal Medicine* 124(5) 485–489. doi: 10.7326/0003-4819-124-5-199603010-00004. http://dx.doi.org/10.7326/0003-4819-124-5-199603010-00004.

Choudhry, S., N.K. Choudhry, and T.A. Brennan. (2005). Specialty versus community hospitals: what role for the law? *Health Affairs, suppl* 24 W5–361–372.

Claridge, J.A. and T.C. Fabian. (2005). History and development of evidence-based medicine. *World Journal of Surgery* 29(5) 547–553.

Dafny, L.S. (2005). How do hospitals respond to price changes? *The American Economic Review* 95(5) 1525–1547.

Dai, T., X. Wang, and C-W Hwang. (2017). Clinical ambiguity and conflicts of interest in interventional cardiology decision-making. *Working Paper*.

De Jaegher, K. and M. Jegers. (2000). A model of physician behaviour with demand inducement. *Journal of Health Economics* 19(2) 231–258.

Dranove, D. (1988). Demand inducement and the physician/patient relationship. *Economic Inquiry* 26(2) 281–298.

Edelstein, L. (1943). *The Hippocratic Oath: Text, translation and interpretation*. Baltimore: The Johns Hopkins Press.

Ehrhardt, S., L.J. Appel, and C.L. Meinert. (2015). Trends in National Institutes of Health Funding for Clinical Trials registered in clinicaltrials.gov. *JAMA* 314(23) 2566–2567. doi: 10.1001/jama.2015.12206. http://dx.doi.org/10.1001/jama.2015.12206.

Farley, P.J. (1986). Theories of the price and quantity of physician services: A synthesis and critique. *Journal of Health Economics* 5(4) 315–333.

Friedberg, M., B. Saffran, T.J. Stinson, W. Nelson, C.L. Bennett. (1999). Evaluation of conflict of interest in economic analyses of new drugs used in oncology. *JAMA* 282(15) 1453–1457.

Gabel, J.R. C. Fahlman, R. Kang, G. Wozniak, P. Kletke, J.W. Hay. (2008). Where do I send thee? Does physician-ownership affect referral patterns to ambulatory surgery centers? *Health Affairs* 27(3) w165–w174. doi:10.1377/hlthaff.27.3.w165. http://content.healthaffairs.org/content/27/3/w165.abstract.

Greenwald, L., J. Cromwell, W. Adamache, S. Bernard, E. Drozd, E. Root, K. Devers. (2006). Specialty versus community hospitals: Referrals, quality, and community benefits. *Health Affairs* 25(1) 106–118. doi:10.1377/hlthaff.25.1.106. http://content.healthaffairs.org/content/25/1/106.abstract.

Heese, J., R. Krishnan, and F. Moers. (2016). Selective regulator decoupling and organizations strategic responses. *Academy of Management Journal* 59(6) 2178–2204.

Hillman, B.J., G.T. Olson, P.E. Griffith, J.H. Sunshine, C.A. Joseph, S.D. Kennedy, W. R. Nelson, L.B. Bernhardt. (1992). Physicians' utilization and charges for outpatient diagnostic imaging in a Medicare population. *JAMA* 268(15) 2050–2054.

Hollingsworth, J.M. Z. Ye, S.A. Strope, S.L. Krein, A.T. Hollenbeck, B.K. Hollenbeck. (2010). Physician-ownership of ambulatory surgery centers linked to higher volume of surgeries. *Health Affairs* 29(4) 683–689. doi:10.1377/hlthaff.2008.0567. http://content.healthaffairs.org/content/29/4/683.abstract.

Iezzoni, L.I. and M.A. Moskowitz. (1986). Clinical overlap among medical diagnosis-related groups. *JAMA* 255(7) 927–929.

Jørgensen, A.W., J. Hilden, and P.C. Gøtzsche. (2006). Cochrane reviews compared with industry supported meta-analyses and other meta-analyses of the same drugs: Systematic review. *BMJ* 333(7572) 782.

Kahn, N. (2006). Intolerable risk, irreparable harm: The legacy of physician-owned specialty hospitals. *Health Affairs* 25(1) 130–133. doi:10.1377/hlthaff.25.1.130. http://content.healthaffairs.org/content/25/1/130.abstract.

Kjaergard, L.L. and B. Als-Nielsen. (2002). Association between competing interests and authors' conclusions: epidemiological study of randomised clinical trials published in the BMJ. *BMJ* 325(7358) 249. doi:10.1136/bmj.325.7358.249. http://www.bmj.com/content/325/7358/249.

Levinsky, N.G. (2002). Nonfinancial conflicts of interest in research. *New England Journal of Medicine* 347(10) 759–761. doi:10.1056/NEJMsb020853. http://dx.doi.org/10.1056/NEJMsb020853.

Lynk, W.J. and C.S. Longley. (2002). The effect of physician-owned surgicenters on hospital outpatient surgery. *Health Affairs* 21(4) 215–221. doi:10.1377/hlthaff.21.4.215. http://content.healthaffairs.org/content/21/4/215.abstract.

Manchikanti, L. and E. Brisbay McMahon. (2007). Physician refer thyself: is Stark II, phase III the final voyage? *Pain Physician* 10 725–741.

Meddings, J., S. Saint, and L.F. McMahon Jr., (2010). Hospital-acquired catheter-associated urinary tract infection: Documentation and coding issues may reduce financial impact of Medicare's new payment policy. *Infection Control and Hospital Epidemiology* 31(6) 627–633.

MedPAC. (2015). Ambulatory surgical center services. *Report to the Congress: Medicare Payment policy* 115–135.

Miles, Steven H. (2005). *The Hippocratic oath and the ethics of medicine.* Oxford University Press. Milgrom, Paul R. (1981). Good news and bad news:

Representation theorems and applications. *The Bell Journal of Economics* 380–391.

Mitchell, J.M. (2008). Do financial incentives linked to ownership of specialty hospitals affect physicians practice patterns? *Medical Care* 46(7) 732–737.

Mitchell, J.M. and T.R. Sass. (1995). Physician ownership of ancillary services: Indirect demand inducement or quality assurance? *Journal of Health Economics* 14(3) 263–289. doi: 10.1016/0167-6296(95)00003-Z. http://www.sciencedirect.com/science/article/pii/016762969500003Z.

Mitchell, Jean M. and E. Scott. (1992). Physician ownership of physical therapy services: Effects on charges, utilization, profits, and service characteristics. *JAMA* 268(15) 2055–2059. doi: 10.1001/jama.1992.03490150107033. http://dx.doi.org/10.1001/jama.1992.03490150107033.

Nallamothu, B.K., M.M. Rogers, M.E. Chernew, H.M. Krumholz, K.A. Eagle, J.D. Birkmeyer. (2007). Opening of specialty cardiac hospitals and use of coronary revascularization in Medicare beneficiaries. *JAMA* 297(9) 962–968. doi:10.1001/jama.297.9.962. http://dx.doi.org/10.1001/jama.297.9.962.

Office of Inspector General. 2008. Physician-owned specialty hospitals' ability to manage medical emergencies. Tech. Rep. OEI-02-06-00310, U.S. Department of Health and Human Services.

Office of Inspector General. 2013. Spinal devices supplied by physician-owned distributors: Overview of prevalence and use. Tech. Rep. OEI-01-11-00660, U.S. Department of Health and Human Services.

Psaty, B.M., R. Boineau, L.H. Kuller, R.V. Luepker. 1999. The potential costs of upcoding for heart failure in the United States. *The American Journal of Cardiology* 84(1) 108–109.

Ridker, P.M. and J. Torres. (2006). Reported outcomes in major cardiovascular clinical trials funded by for-profit and not-for-profit organizations: 2000–2005. *JAMA* 295(19) 2270–2274.

Rosenbaum, L. (2013). When is a medical treatment unnecessary? *The New Yorker* www.newyorker.com/tech/elements/when-is-a-medical-treatment-unnecessary. Accessed December 22, 2016.

Shaked, M. and G. Shanthikumar. (2007). *Stochastic Orders*. Springer Science & Business Media.

Silverman, E. and J. Skinner. (2004). Medicare upcoding and hospital ownership. *Journal of Health Economics* 23(2) 369–389.

Snow, C.A. et al. (2012). Accuracy of coding in the hospital-acquired conditions present on admission program final report. Tech. Rep. CMS contract no. HHSM-500-2005-00029I, RTI International.

Stelfox, H.T., G. Chua, K. O'Rourke, A.S. Detsky. (1998). Conflict of interest in the debate over calcium-channel antagonists. *New England Journal of Medicine* 338(2) 101–106.

Stensland, J. and A. Winter. (2006). Do physician-owned cardiac hospitals increase utilization? *Health Affairs* 25(1) 119–129. doi:10.1377/hlthaff.25.1.119. http://content.healthaffairs.org/content/25/1/119.abstract.

Thompson, D F. (1993). Understanding financial conflicts of interest. *New England Journal of Medicine* 329 573–573.

Tyson, P. 2001. The Hippocratic Oath today. http://www.pbs.org/wgbh/nova/body/hippocratic-oath-today.html. Accessed Jan 10, 2017.

United States Senate Finance Committee Majority Staff. (2016). Physician owned distributorships: An update on key issues and areas of congressional concern. Tech. rep., United States Senate Finance Committee.

U.S. Department of Health and Human Services. (2016). FY 2016 agency financial report. Tech. rep., U.S. Department of Health and Human Services.

U.S. Government Accountability Office. (2012). Higher use of advanced imaging services by providers who self-refer costing Medicare millions. Tech. Rep. GAO-12-966, U.S. Government Accountability Office.

U.S. Government Accountability Office. (2013). Higher use of costly prostate cancer treatment by providers who self-refer warrants scrutiny. Tech. Rep. GAO-13-525, U.S. Government Accountability Office.

Winter, A. (2003). Comparing the mix of patients in various outpatient surgery settings. *Health Affairs* 22(6) 68–75. doi:10.1377/hlthaff.22.6.68. http://content.healthaffairs.org/content/22/6/68.abstract.

Yaphe, J., R. Edman, B. Knishkowy, J. Herman. (2001). The association between funding by commercial interests and study outcome in randomized controlled drug trials. *Family Practice* 18(6) 565–568. doi:10.1093/fampra/18.6.565. http://fampra.oxfordjournals.org/content/18/6/565.abstract.

5

Quality of Care

Hummy Song and Senthil Veeraraghavan

University of Pennsylvania

5.1 Frameworks for Measuring Healthcare Quality

Quality of service is an instrumental component of the service provision process. Through a large corpus of theoretical and empirical research in service operations, we now have an increasingly better understanding of how to calibrate and measure quality in various service settings. Nevertheless, despite the vast literature on service quality, there exists little consensus in the operations research/management science (OR/MS) community around what constitutes a good measure of healthcare quality and which aspects of quality should be emphasized. Furthermore, there is an operations management literature recognizing the complex interactions between various service attributes, such as service quality and service speed (Anand et al., 2011), which is relevant to our understanding of service quality in the healthcare setting as well.

While the research on healthcare quality might be relatively nascent in the field of OR/MS, there exist well-established frameworks around quality measurement in the field of health services research. Our overview in this work presents a helpful starting point for OR/MS scholars to position, enhance, and contribute further to the study of healthcare quality.

5.1.1 The Donabedian Model

The most widely-used framework for quality measurement in health services research originates from the seminal framework proposed by Avedis Donabedian (1966). In later work, Donabedian (1988) sets forth a framework of methods for evaluating healthcare quality, which we address as the Donabedian Model, depicted in Figure 5.1. The Donabedian Model formalizes an interacting triptych of healthcare quality attributes and measures: *Structure, Process*, and *Outcome.*

Handbook of Healthcare Analytics: Theoretical Minimum for Conducting 21st Century Research on Healthcare Operations, First Edition. Edited by Tinglong Dai and Sridhar Tayur.

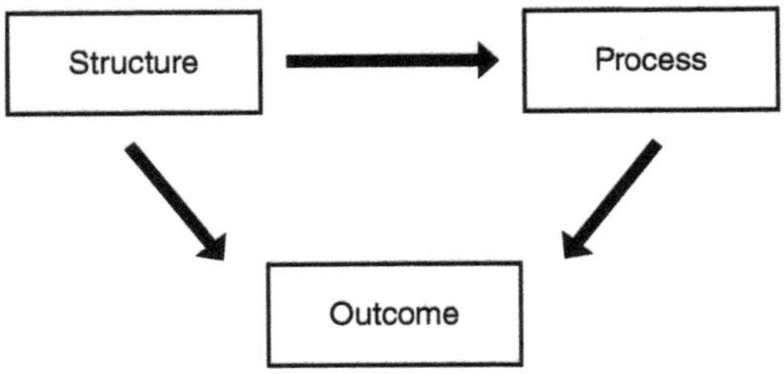

Figure 5.1 The Donabedian Model. *Note*: Arrows indicate the direction of influence.

Structural attributes influence outcomes either directly or through their impact on processes. (Processes also directly impact outcome.) Structure denotes the capacity attributes of the setting in which care is delivered. Thus, it encapsulates a healthcare organization's or a clinician's capacity to provide high quality healthcare. Structure would typically include facets such as material resources, human resources, and organizational structure.

Process measures capture the healthcare-related activities that are performed, that is, what is actually done in delivering and receiving care. They are generally calculated as the ratio of the number of patients who receive a particular service (numerator) in comparison to the total number of patients for whom a particular service is indicated (denominator).

Outcome measures encompass the effects of care on the health status of patients and populations resulting from healthcare services. They can be either intermediate- or long-term measures. Broadly defined, they may even include improvements in the patient's knowledge concerning care and the degree of the patient's satisfaction with care. We summarize these definitions and provide examples of structure, process, and outcome measures in Table 5.1.

Table 5.1 Domains of the Donabedian Model and accompanying examples.

Domain	Definition	Selected Examples
Structure	Attributes of the setting in which care is delivered, including material resources, human resources, and organizational structure	Nurse-to-patient ratios, levels of clinician expertise or skill, use of an electronic medical record system, reimbursement method
Process	What is actually done in giving and receiving care; what healthcare-related activities are performed	Percent of diabetic patients being checked for hemoglobin A1C levels, percent of patients receiving surgery for whom a surgical safety checklist was followed
Outcome	Effects of care on the health status of patients and populations resulting from healthcare services	Blood pressure control rate, 30-day mortality, functional status, changes in patient's health-related behaviors

5.1.2 The AHRQ Framework

More recently, the Agency for Healthcare Research and Quality (AHRQ) supplemented the Donabedian framework by adding two more domains of quality: *access* and *patient experience* (Institute of Medicine, 1990). Figure 5.2 illustrates the AHRQ framework. Access denotes the attainment of timely and appropriate healthcare by patients. Similar to process measures, access measures are generally calculated as a proportion of patients who had access to a service among all patients who should have had access to that service. Patient experience captures patients' observations and participation in healthcare. Typically, patient experience measures consist of ratings or mean scores from patient satisfaction surveys, such as the Consumer Assessment of Healthcare Providers and Systems (CAHPS) family of surveys, overseen by AHRQ.

Using these frameworks, health services researchers have identified large variations in the quality of care (McGlynn et al., 2003), suggesting that there is significant room for improvement. For instance, extant research has identified concerns around patient safety and medical errors associated with poor quality care (e.g., Brennan et al., 1991). There also exists a large literature around the overuse, underuse, and misuse of care (Chassin, 1991; Chassin and Galvin, 1998). Due to the pervasiveness of these concerns, organizations such as the *National Quality Forum* have worked on structures and guidelines with the goal of improving quality and quality measurement (National Quality Forum, 2017).

We adapt the extant frameworks in health services research to classify measures of quality relevant to healthcare operations. To this end, the remainder of our work is organized as follows. In section 5.2, we apply the AHRQ framework in reviewing the existing literature in OR/MS related to healthcare and formalize our current understanding of quality measurement in healthcare

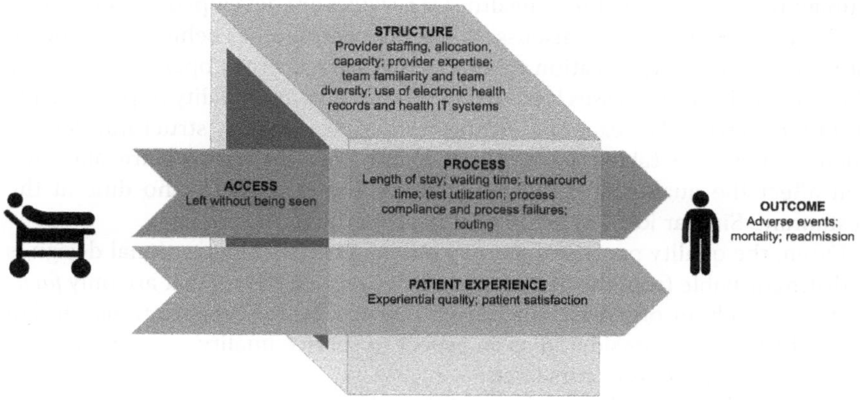

Figure 5.2 A Framework based on AHRQ measures of quality. *Note*: Adapted from Society for Maternal-Fetal Medicine Quality and Safety and Health Policy Committees et al. (2016).

operations. In section 5.3, we identify critical interactions of interest among various measures of healthcare quality and propose exciting open areas for future research by OR/MS scholars. We conclude in section 5.4.

5.2 Understanding Healthcare Quality: Classification of the Existing OR/MS Literature

To understand the extent to which healthcare-related OR/MS research has explored various aspects of healthcare quality, we apply the frameworks in health services research to classify the existing literature. Specifically, we consider each of the five domains of quality as captured in the AHRQ framework described in section 5.1.2, and focus on works that consider these domains of quality. Whereas most papers focus on one particular aspect of healthcare quality (e.g., waiting time), some consider interactions among multiple domains. Our classification allows us to formalize complex interactions among the different domains, which in turn helps us to identify areas of interest for future research. For the sake of brevity, in the remainder of this section, we focus our discussion on specific research papers to exemplify the types of OR/MS research within that framework. We also classify the body of recent OR/MS literature that directly or peripherally considers one of the five domains of quality, and present a more extensive list of research in tables within each section.

5.2.1 Structure

Structural issues—such as organizational design, material resources, and human resources—affect how healthcare services are developed and delivered. As Vera and Kuntz (2007) discuss, this is the central tenet behind the concept of process-based organization design. Structuring a firm's operations around the core business processes leads to cost reductions and quality improvements in other metrics. For example, in the restaurant industry, structural designs such as how the tables are organized and how the waiters are allocated can affect the quality of the experience for the customers who dine at the restaurant. Similar ideas apply to healthcare settings.

Often, the quality perceived *directly due to* a better organizational design is indistinguishable from the experience due to service efforts that are only *facilitated by* such an organizational design. Hence, better organizational design is itself frequently considered as an aspect of service quality, even though the actual service process occurs later.

In what follows, we discuss some of the salient structural attributes of quality that research in healthcare operations has considered to date. For a list of selected works, see Table 5.2.

Table 5.2 Research papers related to Structure.

Measure	Published and Working Papers in OR/MS
Provider Staffing, Allocation, and Capacity	Armony et al. (2016), Armony et al. (2017), Bavafa et al. (2014), de Véricourt and Jennings (2011), Kuntz and Scholtes (2013), Kuntz and Sülz (2013), Li et al. (2016), Miedaner et al. (2016), Wang and Gupta (2014), Ward et al. (2015), Zhan and Ward (2015)
Team Structure	Aksin et al. (2016), Huckman et al. (2009), Huckman and Staats (2011), Staats (2012), Valentine and Edmondson (2015)
Expertise	KC and Staats (2012), KC and Terwiesch (2011), KC et al. (2013), Kuntz and Sülz (2013), Staats and Gino (2012)
Use of EHR and Health IT Systems	Devaraj and Kohli (2003), Devaraj et al. (2013), Kohli and Devaraj (2004), Kohli and Kettinger (2004), Piontek et al. (2010), Ward et al. (2013), Ward et al. (2014), Ward et al. (2014), Ward et al. (2015)

Provider Staffing, Allocation, and Capacity Nurse staffing is probably the most often analyzed structural measure of quality in the OR/MS literature. One example is Armony et al. (2016), which examines the staffing and sizing of critical care units in answering the question of when and how a step-down unit (SDU) can be useful in managing patient flow in a hospital. This staffing decision can be considered a structural component of quality, as the decision of how many providers to staff and how to allocate them precedes the actual service provision. Other aspects of organizational design, such as nursing-led, cross-level collaborations (Senot et al., 2016a), and the level of workaround difficulty (Tucker, 2016) are aspects of structure that have been examined vis-à-vis healthcare quality.

Whereas provider staffing and allocation have been typically discussed with respect to nursing, service capacity has been predominantly discussed in the context of individual physicians (e.g., the size of a physician's patient panel, the service rate of a given physician). As one would expect, structural choices, such as panel sizes, interact with the other measures of quality (e.g., patient experience). For instance, Bavafa et al. (2014) study the relationship between the size of a physician's patient panel, his or her decision regarding a patient's revisit frequency, and the expected health status of patients. A careful study of structural measures of quality reveals other intricate tradeoffs. In this case, there exists a tension around the optimal size of a physician's patient panel, as small panel sizes are likely to lead to reductions in process efficiency (Terwiesch et al., 2011), whereas large panel sizes will likely lead to appointment delays, which in turn may reduce access. In fact, such appointment delays are well understood through queueing models and can be seen in studies of many other service contexts (Tan and Staats, 2016). Some recent papers have also started explicitly accounting for discretion in physician service capacity and how this may affect aspects of healthcare quality relating to process and outcomes (Armony et al., 2017).

Expertise The expertise of physicians and nurses is often identified with better structural quality. Despite the significant effects found in health services research on the development of expertise and the influence of expertise on outcomes, few papers in healthcare operations address issues related to the role of expertise. A notable exception is KC and Staats (2012). The authors study cardiothoracic surgeons conducting a class of minimally invasive cardiac procedures known as off-pump coronary artery bypass. Examining 6,516 such surgeries performed by 71 surgeons in the state of Massachusetts, the authors find that when physicians develop focal skills, rather than related skills, their expertise leads to significant improvements in health outcomes. At this juncture, it is natural to ask, in our continuing efforts to understand structure, if physician expertise itself can be considered as a proxy for (structural) quality, and if so, how to measure that expertise.

Team Structure Given that multiple providers or multiple types of providers are often involved in the care delivery process, how the care delivery team is structured is also an important element that impacts quality. Most of the literature that examines provider effects has tended to focus solely on one provider, but some research in OR/MS has considered the effects of *who* comprises a team and *how* their varying prior experiences may impact the team's overall performance, specifically with regard to their team familiarity and partner diversity.

The earliest works on the topic of team familiarity in teams with unstable membership and organization are by Huckman and coauthors (Huckman et al., 2009; Huckman and Staats, 2011), who explore team performance in the context of the software services industry. Team familiarity—defined as individuals' previous experience working with other members of their current team—is positively associated with team performance, unlike conventional measures of individual team members' experience levels, which do not consistently exhibit this relationship. Valentine and Edmondson (2015) build on this stream of work to define and examine the effects of team scaffolds, which are organizational structures that bound a set of roles and give team members collective responsibility for a whole task. More recently, others have also started to explore how partner diversity in fluid teams may affect team performance in ambulance transport settings (Aksin et al., 2016).

Electronic Health Records One of the structural improvements at the center of focus in the past decade is the implementation of electronic health record (EHR) systems and other health information technology (IT) systems (e.g., patient portals). Despite the expected benefits, the implementation of EHRs has seen mixed results and poses several yet-to-be resolved operational challenges. For example, in a survey of physicians, only about a quarter of responding physicians reported that they perceive EHRs to have a positive effect on their care delivery (Emani et al., 2014). There are also reports of unintended consequences, such as the processing of refills of unintended medications (Allen and Sequist, 2012). For a more detailed discussion of the benefits and challenges associated with EHR implementation as discussed in the health services research literature, we refer readers to section 4.2.1 of Song and Tucker (2016).

In the OR/MS literature, a series of papers by Michael Ward, Craig Froehle, and coauthors has examined the benefits and the pitfalls of the EHR implementation process and its aftermath (Ward et al., 2013, 2014, 2015). For instance, they note that the frequency of laboratory testing, overall radiologic imaging, radiographs, computed tomography scans, and electrocardiograms all increased due to EHR implementation. Although some amount of additional testing could lead to better clinical quality through improved diagnostic accuracy, it may also lead to increases in waiting times and delays, which would in turn negatively affect process quality. For further exploration of tradeoffs between diagnostic accuracy and service time interactions, we refer the reader to Alizamir et al. (2013), Anand et al. (2011), Deo et al. (2015), and Zheng et al. (2018).

In part, the implementation of EHR systems is driven by the need to reduce errors. However, Ward et al. (2015) report an *increase* in data errors after EHR implementation in the study's emergency department (ED). Such changes may arise from implementation complexities, but a careful study of pre- and post-implementation error rates across multiple settings would also help researchers better calibrate the costs and benefits of EHR implementation. Despite the increasing trends in EHR adoption and the increasing awareness of complexities in its implementation, several issues still remain to be addressed within the purview of OR/MS healthcare research.

5.2.2 Process

Though structural attributes are typically invariant across patients, process attributes can vary widely across heterogeneous patients undergoing treatment and across heterogeneous physicians providing treatment, even when they are all within the same structural network. Identifying and documenting the sources of such variability and improving quality through process engineering has been at the heart of research in healthcare operations.

In what follows, we discuss some of the salient process attributes of quality considered in the healthcare operations literature to date. For a list of selected works, see Table 5.3. We note that our measures expand understanding of process measures as originally conceptualized by health services researchers (proportion of a patient population that received a specific healthcare-related activity).

Length of Stay Length of stay (LOS) is the total amount of time a patient spends in an inpatient (e.g., hospital) or outpatient (e.g., ED) setting. Though

Table 5.3 Research papers related to Process.

Measure	Published and Working Papers in OR/MS
Length of Stay (incl. processing time)	Bartel et al. (2016), Batt and Terwiesch (2017), Bavafa et al. (2016), Berry Jaeker and Tucker (2016), Berry Jaeker and Tucker (2017), Best et al. (2015), Chan et al. (2016b), Chan et al. (2016a), Deo and Jain (2016), Freeman et al. (2016a), Freeman et al. (2017), KC and Terwiesch (2009), KC and Terwiesch (2011), KC and Terwiesch (2012), Kim et al. (2015), Kim et al. (2016), Kuntz and Sülz (2013), Kuntz et al. (2015), Lee et al. (2010), McCarthy et al. (2012), Pick et al. (2014), Piontek et al. (2010), Saghafian et al. (2012), Saghafian et al. (2014), Song et al. (2015), Song et al. (2017), Traub et al. (2015), Traub et al. (2016), Wang et al. (2016), Ward et al. (2014), Ward et al. (2015), Wiler et al. (2011), Zhang et al. (2016)
Waiting Time	Ang et al. (2016), Batt and Terwiesch (2015), Batt and Terwiesch (2017), Berry Jaeker and Tucker (2016), Bolandifar et al. (2016), Chan et al. (2016a), Laker et al. (2014), Liu et al. (2018), Lucas et al. (2014), Osadchiy and KC (2016), Paç and Veeraraghavan (2016), Park et al. (2016), Pines et al. (2011), Saghafian et al. (2012), Savva et al. (2017), Song et al. (2015), Song et al. (2017), Terwiesch et al. (2011), Ward et al. (2015), White et al. (2011), Wiler et al. (2011), Xu and Chan (2016), Yuan et al. (2016), Zhan and Ward (2014), Zhan and Ward (2015), Zhang et al. (2016)
Turnaround Time	Aksin et al. (2016), Clark et al. (2013), Deo and Sohoni (2015), Deo et al. (2015), Halsted and Froehle (2008), Ibanez et al. (2017), Torabi et al. (2016)
Test Utilization	Batt and Terwiesch (2017), Berry Jaeker and Tucker (2016), Dai et al. (2017), Deo and Jain (2016), Song et al. (2015), Song et al. (2017), Ward et al. (2014)
Process Compliance and Process Failures	Staats et al. (2017), Tucker (2004), Tucker (2014), Tucker (2016),
Routing	Dobson et al. (2013), Freeman and Scholtes (2016), Kuntz et al. (2016), Saghafian et al. (2012), Saghafian et al. (2014), Tan and Staats (2016), Traub et al. (2016), Zhan and Ward (2014)

earlier healthcare operations papers initially considered LOS an outcome measure itself, it is now more often (and in our view, perhaps more accurately) identified as a process measure of quality that influences outcome measures.

Dozens of papers in healthcare operations have reported on LOS as a process measure of quality (see Table 5.3). Many have also considered certain portions of LOS (e.g., excluding waiting time or boarding time) to more precisely define treatment times or processing times. One of the first papers in OR/MS to empirically examine LOS as a process measure of quality is KC and Terwiesch (2009) that studies the effect of workload and overwork on changes in service time and mortality. The authors find that a 10 precent increase in workload can lead to reduced LOS (as much as 20%) due to worker speedup. Attaining such shorter LOS may be preferred as an efficiency goal; however, there may be downsides. The authors find that sustained periods of increased workload (i.e., overwork) are associated with an increased likelihood of patient mortality (KC and Terwiesch, 2009).

As research in healthcare operations has evolved, a more nuanced understanding of LOS has emerged. We now know that *how* and *for whom* LOS is reduced has a significantly different impact on outcomes such as mortality. As an illustrative example, we discuss Chan et al. (2016b) that examines how SDU care affects LOS and mortality. The authors find that for patients discharged from the intensive care unit (ICU) and low-severity patients being admitted from the ED, SDUs may be a cost-effective way to reduce remaining hospital LOS without affecting mortality. However, for high-severity patients who should be admitted to the ICU but are off-placed into the SDU (typically due to limited ICU capacity), SDU care can lead to increases in both remaining hospital LOS and mortality risk.

In addition to thinking of LOS as a process measure that affects other outcomes, we can also think of it as intricately influenced by the design of the healthcare delivery process. For example, how relative performance feedback (RPF) is provided to physicians may affect physician workflow, which in turn may affect patients' LOS and physician processing times.[1] Song et al. (2017) compare these measures, among others, at two EDs, one of which adopted public RPF while the other continued to provide private RPF. The authors identify that the public disclosure of RPF, and the best practice sharing that this enabled, led to significant improvements in physician productivity as measured by reductions in physician processing times. Furthermore, they find a significant reduction in the variation in processing times across physicians.

Waiting Time Longer waiting times for healthcare services are detrimental from both an efficiency perspective and a social value perspective. Within the healthcare context, researchers have studied various types of waiting times. Some approaches combine the waiting time to access a healthcare facility and the waiting time prior to treatment initiation (e.g., *door-to-needle times* in Torabi et al. (2016) and *door-to-balloon times* in Bradley et al. (2006)). Other studies focus on waiting times from one stage of treatment to another (e.g., *boarding times* in Pines et al. (2011)).

Building on the rich history of analysis of waiting times in queueing theory and service operations, several OR/MS papers address waiting times in healthcare settings (see Table 5.3). Some of this literature has discussed waiting times in the context of reducing patient waiting times through the provision of

1 Physician processing time can be thought of as the portion of a patient's LOS that is most directly attributable to the physician.

information. For example, Xu and Chan (2016) examine how admission control and diversion policies utilizing predictive information can help to improve efficiency by achieving shorter waiting times while serving the same number of patients. Other works examine how waiting times are affected as a consequence of adjusting operations.

The implementation of well-established theory in the queueing literature can reveal surprising complexities germane to healthcare operations. In an ED setting, Song et al. (2015) find that having a dedicated queueing system (with some fairness constraint) can reduce the average LOS by 17 percent and the average wait time by 9 percent compared to having a pooled queueing system (with the same fairness constraint). Such improved performance stems from the dedicated queueing system providing physicians with more ownership and responsibility over patients and resources, which enables them to strategically adjust their work routines to manage patient flow.

Another stream of work considers waiting times for patients in relation to unused physician capacity as two types of inefficiencies that arise from dynamic supply-demand mismatches. Osadchiy and KC (2016) show that some of these costly mismatches could be addressed by a combination of scheduled appointments and accepting unscheduled patients. Specifically, the authors discuss how appointment wait times can be optimized based on the differences among patients in their levels of willingness to wait.

In addition, waiting times are sometimes exacerbated by overtreatment in credence services (Debo et al., 2008; Paç and Veeraraghavan, 2016). Some of these delays could be reduced or impacted by simple process changes. Berry Jaeker and Tucker (2016) show how the removal of a justification step for ordering an ultrasound in the ED affects rates of ordering this test and also overall ED waiting times. They find that the removal of the justification step more than doubles the probability that a patient with abdominal pain will receive an ultrasound (from 8% to 19%). Furthermore, the removal of this justification step leads to a 26 percent increase in expected waiting times. Recent work by Dai et al. (2017) also shows that excessive diagnostic tests can increase waiting times at hospitals without a significant corresponding improvement in outcomes.

Turnaround Time Turnaround time is a process measure of quality that is related to, but distinct from overall waiting time. Turnaround time refers to waits that occur after the patient has begun his or her treatment process (i.e., time until test results are returned once the test has been initiated). For instance, consider the distinct effects of waiting time in service versus waiting time in queue in Anand et al. (2011).

Although processing times are typically assumed to be short in theoretical research, turnaround times can be long and can adversely impact patient health, especially in global health settings (see Deo and Sohoni, 2015; Deo et al., 2015). In an early infant diagnosis network for pediatric HIV in Mozambique, turnaround time constitutes the gap between the time the blood is drawn from a potential HIV patient to the time when the test results are communicated to patients (see Figure 5.1 in Deo and Sohoni (2015, p. 192)). In these settings, because patients are less likely to collect test results in a timely manner when there are processing, batching, clinical, and transportation delays, longer turnaround times are associated with a higher risk of adverse outcomes.

Turnaround time optimization can also lead to freeing up valuable physician capacity. For instance, Halsted and Froehle (2008) examine the design and launch of a paperless workflow management system and find improvements in case turnaround times (i.e., the time between when a case is made available and when the radiology staff sign off on the final interpretation). This reduction in turnaround times allowed the staff to handle an increased caseload volume and led to some improvements in patient perceptions of the timeliness of service.

Test Utilization Waiting times and idle capacity are both ramifications of short-run mismatches in supply and demand. As such, the utilization of diagnostic tests, which are often ordered to facilitate more informed and more accurate medical decisions (Alizamir et al., 2013), can be either efficient and informative or unnecessary and expensive. Often the usage of low-yield diagnostic tests are driven by economic and operational needs (referred to as supplier-induced demand) rather than a patient's medical needs. For an excellent study of the underlying economics of physicians' test-ordering behaviors in outpatient services, see Dai et al. (2017). As evident in Berry Jaeker and Tucker (2016), these tests can lead to increased waiting times.

A deliberate, across-stage, load-dependent, operational ordering policy can reduce waiting times and make service delivery more efficient. Batt and Terwiesch (2017) examined more than 140,000 ED visits to identify diagnostic testing behaviors that can improve the system. By incorporating early task initiation (i.e., having the upstream stage proactively initiate tasks that are normally handled downstream) into system procedures, the authors found that the ED is able to cut treatment times by 20 minutes (regardless of the length of the queue).

Process Compliance and Process Failures Another aspect of process that has been considered in the OR/MS literature relates to process compliance and process failures. Staats et al. (2017) build on the larger stream of work on standard processes in operations to explore how individual electronic monitoring may help or hinder compliance with previously established standardized processes. In the context of hand hygiene in healthcare delivery settings, they find that compliance rates initially increased before gradually declining—in some cases declining below pre-intervention levels in cases where the electronic monitoring was discontinued. This highlights the need for caution in utilizing and sustaining similar interventions.

Using years of organizational primary and secondary data, interviews, surveys, and experiments, Anita Tucker has used qualitative and quantitative methodologies to investigate the causes and effects of operational process failures in hospitals (Tucker, 2004, 2014, 2016). Tucker (2014) finds that nurses can spend more than 10 percent of their time working around operational failures, which is often due to low levels of interconnectedness across departments. These workarounds result in a significant loss in productivity (Tucker, 2004). Therefore, whether there exist process failures and, if so, how providers either continue to engage in workarounds or are able to learn from these failures are important process measures of quality. In an excellent study utilizing a series of laboratory experiments, Tucker (2016) finds important differences in nurses' responses to operational failures, depending on whether it was easy or difficult to work around them. Namely, when operational failures are difficult to work around and nurses have a high level of access to process owners, they are most likely to contribute ideas for rectifying process failures.

Routing Even given similar levels of provider staffing, allocation, and capacity, how incoming patients are routed through the process can lead to varying outcomes in service quality. A significant portion of the literature on call center service operations has focused on routing design and its effects on service quality. For instance, Zhan and Ward (2014) examine the effects of routing on waiting time and call resolution. Also, Tan and Staats (2016) investigate routing to different servers in the context of the restaurant industry. In a similar spirit, several papers dealing with the ED setting have examined the effects of routing as well. For instance, Traub et al. (2016) compare two routing systems: automatic rotational patient assignment and physician self-assignment. They find that the former led to increased quality as measured through "left without being seen" (LWBS) rates (see definition in section 5.2.5) and LOS (defined in section 5.2.2). An operational question that remains open in the health services research literature is whether certain routing structures lead to improved quality regardless of the specific context of application.

In the United States, the healthcare market has seen a growing agglomeration of large hospital networks. Scholars such as Christiansen et al. (2009) have suggested operationally separating large hospitals into two types of organizations: "value-adding process clinics" for routine patients and "solution shop hospitals" for more complex patients. An excellent OR/MS paper by Kuntz et al. (2016) tests this theory by studying the routing of patients of differing health complexities to different hospitals. They found a beneficial effect of a hospital's focus on a particular disease group, suggesting that value-adding process clinics are best organized as focused factories. On the other hand, the data suggests that a disease focus does not necessarily improve quality for the most complex patients. One suggestion is that solution shop hospitals may continue to maintain a broad portfolio of patient services. Perhaps a disease-based admission regime might lead to stronger societal benefits than a treatment-based admission regime would. Such a policy calls for admitting patients who have a complex healthcare need rather than adopting an admission policy that is more focused on the utilization of resources in the treatment facility.

5.2.3 Outcome

Measuring outcomes is perhaps the most fundamental assessment of the quality of healthcare services. Outcomes measured after care delivery can span a vast array of health states: mortality, physiological measures (e.g., blood pressure), laboratory test results (e.g., cholesterol levels), or even patient self-reported symptoms. We should note that due to patient heterogeneity and treatment contexts, it is difficult to directly infer the quality of the service provided from the observed health state. In this section, we discuss three outcome measures that have been widely studied in OR/MS research. We present a list of related works in Table 5.4.

Mortality Mortality is surely one of the most undesirable outcomes in healthcare settings. The Centers for Medicare & Medicaid Services (CMS) now releases data on hospitals' 30-day mortality rates as a measure of quality and uses this information to determine reimbursement levels. The National Quality Foundation also recommends using the 30-day mortality rate as a measure of hospital quality. The 30-day mortality rate is essentially a *postdischarge* outcome measure, that may (or may not) be strongly related to inpatient process measures. To measure how accurately process measures affect 30-day mortality rates as an outcome measure, Bartel et al. (2016) examined data on all inpatient hospitalizations from 2000 to 2011 for Medicare fee-for-service beneficiaries, and argue in favor of using 30-day mortality as an outcome measure of quality.

It is well known that the occupancy levels in EDs and in acute care hospitals show significant variation because the demand for urgent care services is often unpredictable. Typically, hospitals buffer excess capacity in anticipation of high periods of demand. However, at peak demand, these buffers are depleted, and there is thus a need for scarce resources. As a result, providers may need to cut corners to make sure they can attend to more patients (i.e., manage a higher workload). Hence, if utilization exceeds a certain critical tipping point, there could be adverse health outcomes. A recent paper by Kuntz et al. (2015) delves into the relationship between hospital occupancy and mortality outcomes, and finds a substantial increase in mortality after a "tipping-point" of high occupancy. Two solutions are offered: (i) to semi-flexibly expand capacity, where beds are fully resourced but staffing is flexibly deployed in response to surges in demand/occupancy and (ii) to pool capacities across hospitals.

Adverse Events Another type of outcome measure considered by some works in healthcare operations regards adverse events, which are defined as injuries caused by medical management and resulting in a measurable disability (Brennan et al., 1991). One example of an adverse event is a hospital-acquired infection (HAI), for which Medicare now penalizes hospitals in calculating their levels of reimbursement.

This is a topic of interest for several studies, as the monitoring of medical care and the quality of care is beset with issues of agency. Despite the nonpayment (i.e., reimbursement penalty) for HAIs, there has been little impact on the true incidence of them. Bastani et al. (2016) argue that this may be driven by *upcoding*. Given the penalty for HAIs, hospitals have a strong incentive to underreport them, either by reporting a HAI as a present-on-admission infection or by failing to report a HAI. By exploiting the heterogeneity in state-level regulations, the authors are able to identify the extent of upcoding, and they report that providers in weakly regulated states upcode more frequently than their strongly regulated counterparts. Given the prevalence of performance-based contracts in reimbursements, it is natural to examine reimbursement rates as a measure of quality at the provider level. See Kohli and Devaraj (2004) and Kohli and Kettinger (2004) for further analyses on the interactions between structural measures (e.g., IT and decision support systems) and providers' rates of reimbursement.

Readmission Readmission rates constitute another important outcome measure of quality. As is the case in HAIs, hospitals with high levels of readmissions are penalized by CMS. Several papers in healthcare operations assess readmission rates, not only because these rates are a measure of quality, but also because they have implications for capacity utilization.

KC and Terwiesch (2012) examine these relationships in their work on patient flows and capacity utilization in a cardiac ICU. They find that high occupancy in the ICU can sometimes lead to early discharges, which in turn leads to an increased likelihood of readmission to the ICU at a later point. Such "bounce-backs" have important implications on capacity utilization in the ICU. Specifically, an aggressive discharge policy applied to patients with lower clinical severity frees up capacity in the ICU, which is then used by bounce-backs of high clinical severity patients, which thereby constrains the ICU's capacity.

Some other work more explicitly examines the relationship between readmissions and costs. Using 793 hospital visits for heart failure, Bayati et al. (2014) constructed a model for patient-specific readmission risk to predict the likelihood of a patient's readmission within 30 days of discharge. They argue that by using these predictions to guide decisions about post-discharge interventions, the hospital would be able to significantly reduce 30-day readmissions, which would lead to increased capacity utilization and better cost savings. Zhang et al. (2016) conduct a detailed theoretical and empirical analysis of CMS's Hospital Readmissions Reduction Program and argue that 4 to 13 percent of the 3,000 hospitals in the US remain unincentivized by the current policy and prefer to pay a penalty than to reduce costly readmissions. To reduce the unintended consequence of the extant competitive policy, the authors suggest establishing a localized benchmarking process to mitigate competitive effects.

5.2.4 Patient Experience

Better health outcomes drive patient satisfaction and well being. Nevertheless, patients with comparable outcomes can differ significantly in their

Table 5.4 Research papers related to Outcome.

Measure	Published and Working Papers
Mortality	Armony et al. (2016), Bartel et al. (2016), Chan et al. (2016b), Chan et al. (2016), Hu et al. (2016), Huckman and Pisano (2006), KC and Terwiesch (2009), KC and Staats (2012), KC and Terwiesch (2011), KC et al. (2013), Kim et al. (2016), Kuntz et al. (2015), Kuntz et al. (2016), Piontek et al. (2010), Savva et al. (2016), Shwartz et al. (2016), Song et al. (2015), Song et al. (2017), Wang et al. (2016), Wiler et al. (2011), Zenios et al. (2011)
Adverse Events	Bastani et al. (2016), Bastani et al. (2016), Goh et al. (2015), Saghafian et al. (2014), Shwartz et al. (2015), Zarling et al. (1999)
Readmission	Armony et al. (2016), Bastani et al. (2016), Bayati et al. (2014), Chan et al. (2012), Chan et al. (2016b), KC (2014), KC and Terwiesch (2012), Kim et al. (2015), Kim et al. (2016), Piontek et al. (2010), Senot et al. (2016), Shwartz et al. (2016), Song et al. (2015), Song et al. (2017), Traub et al. (2016), Wang et al. (2016), Zhang et al. (2016)
Clinical Severity	Berry Jaeker and Tucker (2017), Lee and Zenios (2012)

realized experiences and resulting levels of satisfaction. The inclusion of the *patient experience* domain in the AHRQ framework indicates the increasingly important role of patient perspectives in understanding healthcare quality.

To date, only a small fraction of the health services research literature has focused on measuring patient experience (see Table 5.5 for a list of selected works). In fact, the attention on assessing patient experience is relatively recent, as it emerged with the spread of the patient-centered medical home (PCMH) model. PCMHs place an emphasis on care coordination across the care-delivery spectrum to ensure that patients receive the necessary care, when and where they need it, and in a manner they understand. Recent healthcare legislation, such as the Patient Protection and Affordable Care Act of 2010, has many provisions for the promotion of PCMH models.

Given the fact that measuring patient experience is relatively new, even in the health services research literature, it is not surprising that only a few papers in the OR/MS literature have explored this aspect of quality. The papers most closely aligned with patient experience are by Claire Senot and coauthors, who explore the role of experiential quality in patient satisfaction (Senot et al., 2016a).

Existing work suggests there may be a few ways to improve patient experiences through operational change. For example, smoothing workflow management systems can lead to improved process efficiency, which might increase patient satisfaction (Halsted and Froehle, 2008).

Table 5.5 Research papers related to Patient Experience.

Measure	Published and Working Papers
Experiential Quality	Chandrasekaran et al. (2012), Senot et al. (2016), Senot et al. (2016a), Senot et al. (2016b)
Patient Satisfaction	Das Gupta et al. (2016), Halsted and Froehle (2008), Miedaner et al. (2016), Pick et al. (2014), Shwartz et al. (2016), Song et al. (2017), Traub et al. (2016), Wang and Gupta (2011), Ward et al. (2014), Wiler et al. (2011)

5.2.5 Access

The AHRQ framework also adds *access* to the Donabedian Model as an important domain of healthcare quality. Access to healthcare can be thought of as comprising two interacting components: *timely access* and *appropriate access*. Timely access can be obtained by improving patients' access to good healthcare services through operational efficiency. Appropriate access can be attained by considering better mechanism designs, structural improvements, and financial and social improvements. In Table 5.6, we provide a list of selected works that relate to access.

Left Without Being Seen Rates One measure of access quality that is often tracked is the left without being seen (LWBS) rate. This measure is related to the concept of *abandonments* in the theoretical queueing literature, and can be thought of as the fraction of joining customers who abandon a queue without completing their service. For a representative study in this stream of healthcare research, see Wiler et al. (2011) and references therein.

In the healthcare context, the corresponding measure of quality captures the rate of patients who leave the system after having joined the queue but before being seen by a provider. Unsurprisingly, high levels of LWBS are associated with decreased levels of patient satisfaction. We note that because LWBS can occur due to a slow, suboptimally-designed process, it may also be considered a process measure of quality, as is the case in Batt and Terwiesch (2017).

Improving Access to Timely and Appropriate Care Few papers in the OR/MS literature focus on the study of improving quality by improving access. For an exception, see the discussion by Werner et al. (2014) in the context of primary care. The authors observe that patients who do not access primary care are often poor and postulate that improving access to primary care may reduce ED visits. To this end, they conduct a longitudinal study of 627,276 patients and 6,398 primary care providers within the Veterans Health Administration in 2009, and find that the availability of primary care physicians during weekdays is a key driver in the reduction of ED visits.

Policymakers have long been interested in approaches that can enhance patient access to healthcare. One such approach that has garnered much

Table 5.6 Research papers related to Access.

Measure	Published and Working Papers
Left Without Being Seen	Batt and Terwiesch (2015), Bolandifar et al. (2016), Lucas et al. (2014), Traub et al. (2015), Traub et al. (2016)
Access to Timely and Appropriate Care	Bavafa et al. (2016), Bavafa et al. (2018), Green et al. (2007), Gupta and Denton (2008), KC and Terwiesch (2017), Werner et al. (2014)

attention is using electronic visits (e-visits), especially for primary care—the idea being that this could enable cost reductions and larger panel sizes without reducing the quality of care. Recently, papers by Bavafa and coauthors have shed more light on the operational effects of e-visits on access quality, with initial findings indicating that the benefits of e-visits may have been overestimated. For instance, Bavafa et al. (2018) find that e-visits do not free up capacity and may instead trigger additional phone calls and office visits without large benefits to patient health. This finding is driven by the observation that e-visits are predominantly sought out by healthier patients rather than sicker patients. As a result, overall access may not improve, and the additional capacity may be disproportionately used by healthier patients who may already have better access.

5.3 Open Areas for Future Research

Research in healthcare operations has expanded rapidly, due to the burgeoning interest of OR/MS scholars in the intricacies of healthcare delivery. The large compendium of published papers and working papers that focus on aspects of healthcare quality—many of which are referenced in this chapter—is indicative of this rapid growth.

Our classification of the expanding literature offers a perspective, especially regarding key areas of interest in which OR/MS research is still nascent or perhaps even nonexistent. In this section, we identify these research areas and comment briefly on interesting directions for future research. We believe that structure, patient experience, and access are relatively unexplored domains, all of which significantly impact—and interact with—various process and outcome measures of healthcare quality.

5.3.1 Understanding Structures and Their Interactions with Processes and Outcomes

As evident in section 5.2.1, several aspects of structural quality have been considered in the healthcare operations literature. Yet, in light of the innovations in healthcare delivery and its changing landscape, there remain many open areas for future research.

One important structural aspect concerns the ownership of healthcare organizations (e.g., physician-owned hospitals). Some works in health services research have begun examining the effects of these organizations; for example, Blumenthal et al. (2015) study whether and how physician ownership of hospitals affects access to healthcare services (which also relates to our discussions on improving access to care). In addition to hospital ownership, care delivery models are evolving. Most recently, accountable care organizations (ACOs) have garnered much attention. These are groups of doctors, hospitals, and healthcare providers who come together with the agreement to be accountable for the quality, cost, and overall care of their patients. What are the effects on other domains of quality that may accompany the adoption of these newer models, given the changes they bring to structural aspects of quality?

Relatedly, how various leadership and management practices affect performance is another important question that remains. Some works in health services research have begun to explore this. For example, Tsai et al. (2015) find that hospitals with higher-rated hospital boards and more effective management practices also provide higher-quality care. Adler-Milstein et al. (2014) find that leadership can aid in utilizing electronic health records appropriately, which can improve hospital performance. As OR/MS scholars, we are well situated to extend this area of inquiry by examining how managerial leadership and operational interventions may impact various aspects of clinical quality.

Finally, there is also a need for more research on the interactions between organizational structures, organizational learning, and performance in healthcare settings. Some recent work using experimental approaches has started to shed significant light on how organizational structures may influence problem-solving processes and learning approaches (Tucker, 2016). We encourage more work in this stream, especially concerning the interaction between organizational structures and operational processes.

5.3.2 Understanding Patient Experiences and Their Interactions with Structure

As mentioned in section 5.2.4, the focus on patient experience is relatively new, even in the health services research literature. Thus, there is much room for further study in healthcare operations around how operational choices may impact patient experience. For example, one such operational choice around structure may include the adoption of EHRs and other health IT systems. Some work by Ward et al. (2014) examines changes in patient experience during EHR implementation in the ED. More work on the interaction between structural aspects of quality and patient experience is warranted.

Some of these structural aspects of interest naturally arise from the emergence of new models of healthcare delivery (e.g., PCMHs, ACOs, etc.) and the accompanying set of new regulations. Concurrently, a new set of patient experience measures continues to evolve as well. Singer et al. (2013) develop and validate a survey instrument to measure the integration of patient care as experienced by patients. A research paper by Hibbard and Greene (2013) explores the relationship between patient activation (i.e., being able to engage in their healthcare) and outcomes (including health outcomes and patient experiences). In studying their relationships with outcomes, Pick et al. (2014) use measures assessing provider empathy, communication with providers, and familiarity with providers.

A challenge that remains in utilizing measures of patient experience that are assessed through postdischarge surveys is the generally low rates of response and limited degree of variation. Therefore, we encourage researchers to consider developing, validating, and using measures that capture patient experiences as they are being manifested or at least closer to that point in time. Researchers might also consider other sources of data that serve as a strong proxy for patient experience, especially as more varied types of data are being collected on a real-time basis.

5.3.3 Understanding Processes and Their Interactions with Outcomes

An area worth highlighting, even though it is not necessarily understudied, is that of the interaction between process measures and outcome measures—specifically, what we have come to think of as *speed–quality tradeoffs* in the queueing and service operations literatures (Anand et al., 2011; Oliva and Sterman, 2001).

In many papers in healthcare operations, researchers have considered the effects of speed (e.g., LOS, treatment times) on outcome measures and *vice versa*, with the underlying assumption that there may exist a tradeoff between speed and quality. For example, Batt and Terwiesch (2017) show that early task initiation may significantly reduce treatment times, but potentially at the expense of overtesting. Yet, this relationship need not always be a tradeoff; it may at times be one of complementarity. For example, in their study of queueing systems in the ED, Song et al. (2015) examine whether the time savings accompanying dedicated queueing systems are also associated with reductions in outcome quality. Regarding mortality and revisits, they do not find evidence of lower quality. Thus, it is important for future research to further explore how processes and outcomes may interact and under what conditions a speed-quality tradeoff may manifest versus not.

5.3.4 Understanding Access to Care

Access to care is perhaps the most salient measure of quality that has remained understudied in the OR/MS literature. Using capacity as an example, we consider how our understanding of how to improve access has become more nuanced, with more research.

In general, investing in capacity has been suggested as a solution for resolving issues of low healthcare access and coverage. Thanks to recent papers, we are in the process of enhancing our understanding of the effects of additional capacity on access to care. For instance, Bavafa et al. (2018) examine expanding availability through e-visits. The authors find that despite the additional capacity and lower friction created by the introduction of e-visits, the overall access to healthcare services may not improve because the additional capacity may be disproportionately used by healthier patients, many of whom already have better access. Such findings confirm and bring to attention the problems of fairness and equity in relation to the provision of healthcare services—a concern that has long been a focus of attention for health services researchers and policymakers.

Much of the ongoing healthcare debate rests at the intersection of socioeconomic, demographic, and geographic variations in access to care, and the interactions of disparate access with other metrics of healthcare quality. As policies and regulations evolve, they create many new constraints within which we must answer questions regarding access. We believe OR/MS scholars are well situated to contribute to this literature through both theoretical and empirical research.

5.4 Conclusions

As we conclude, we note that a significant proportion of the research in healthcare operations has been focused on aspects of healthcare quality in the US. As we discussed in section 5.3, we still need to make progress in understanding healthcare operations in the US. Nevertheless, there is much room (and need) for OR/MS research in global settings beyond the US as well. This would allow us to enhance our understanding of global issues in healthcare operations, especially vis-à-vis developing economies. Understanding global healthcare quality is beneficial in two ways: (i) it provides a venue for immediate operational improvement, and (ii) it provides a benchmark for understanding quality of care in the US healthcare system. Given the differences in political, economic, and social conditions in the provision of healthcare services in various countries, the scope for further OR/MS research is expansive. We believe that our framework continues to apply in global contexts, presenting an approach to classify and explore global healthcare quality-related issues.

In fact, a steady and growing interest in healthcare operations in many settings beyond the US has already started to fill this research gap. In the last five years (2013-2017), Operations scholars have begun to significantly advance our understanding of healthcare operations across several countries in the world: Canada (Park et al., 2016), Germany (Kuntz and Scholtes, 2013; Kuntz and Sülz, 2013; Kuntz et al., 2015, 2016; Pick et al., 2014), India (Deo and Jain, 2016), Mozambique (Deo and Sohoni, 2015; Deo et al., 2015), and the United Kingdom (Aksin et al., 2016; Freeman et al., 2016a; Freeman et al., 2017; Freeman and Scholtes, 2016). We believe there are future research avenues in global heath care operations that are rewarding not only from the perspective of knowledge enhancement, but also from their potential for social impact.

Finally, we hope that our classification of the research in healthcare operations and the identification of new research avenues are beneficial to many OR/MS scholars in exploring new ideas and in positioning their work. As OR/MS researchers ourselves, we too look forward to contributing to the growing understanding of healthcare quality.

Acknowledgments

We thank colleagues and researchers who shared their perspectives with us through email and discussions during our exploration of research papers in healthcare quality. All errors remain our own.

References

Adler-Milstein, J., K. Woody Scott, and A. K. Jha (2014). Leveraging electronic health records to improve hospital performance: The role of management. *American Journal of Managed Care 20* (11 Spec No. 17), SP511–SP519.

Aksin, Z., S. Deo, J.O. Jonasson, and K. Ramdas (2016). Learning from Many: Partner Diversity and Team Familiarity in Fluid Teams. Working paper.

Alizamir, S., F. de Véricourt, and P. Sun (2013). Diagnostic Accuracy under Congestion. *Management Science* 59 (1), 157–171.

Allen, A. S. and T. D. Sequist (2012). Pharmacy dispensing of electronically discontinued medications. *Annals of Internal Medicine* 157 (10), 700–705.

Anand, K. S., M.F. Paç, and S. Veeraraghavan (2011). Quality–Speed Conundrum: Trade-offs in Customer-Intensive Services. *Management Science* 57 (1), 40–56.

Ang, E. et al. (2016). Accurate Emergency Department Wait Time Prediction. *Manufacturing & Service Operations Management* 18 (1), 141–156.

Armony, M., C.W. Chan, and B. Zhu (2016). Critical Care Capacity Management: Understanding the role of a Step Down Unit. Working paper.

Armony, M., G. Roels, and H. Song (2017). Pooling Queues in Discretionary Services. Working paper.
Bailit, J.L., J.D. Gregory, S. Srinivas, T. Westover, W.A. Grobman, and G.R. Saade. (2016). Current approaches to measuring quality of care in obstetrics. *American Journal of Obstetrics and Gynecology* 215 (3), B8–B16.
Bartel, A. P., C. W. Chan, and S.-H. Kim (2016). Should Hospitals Keep Their Patients Longer? The Role of Inpatient and Outpatient Care in Reducing Readmissions. Working paper.
Bastani, H., M. Bayati, M. Braverman, R. Gummadi, and R. Johari. (2016). Analysis of Medicare Pay-for-Performance Contracts. Working paper.
Bastani, H., J. Goh, and M. Bayati (2016). Evidence of Upcoding in Pay-for-Performance Programs. Working paper.
Batt, R.J. and C. Terwiesch (2015). Waiting Patiently: An Empirical Study of Queue Abandonment in an Emergency Department. *Management Science* 61 (1), 39–59.
Batt, R.J. and C. Terwiesch (2017). Early Task Initiation and Other Load-Adaptive Mechanisms in the Emergency Department. *Management Science* 63 (11), 3531–3551.
Bavafa, H., A. Canamucio, S. Marcus, C. Terwiesch, and R. Werner. (2016). The Impact of Primary Care Workload on Emergency Room Visits: An Econometric Analysis. Working paper.
Bavafa, H., L. Hitt, and C. Terwiesch (2018). The Impact of E-Visits on Visit Frequencies and Patient Health: Evidence from Primary Care. *Management Science* (ePub ahead of print)
Bavafa, H., L. Ormeci, and S. Savin (2016). Optimal Mix of Elective Surgical Procedures Under Stochastic Patient Length of Stay. Working paper.
Bavafa, H., S. Savin, and C. Terwiesch (2014). Managing Office Revisit Intervals and Patient Panel Sizes in Primary Care. Working paper.
Bayati, M., M. Braverman, M. Gillam, K.M. Mack, G. Ruiz, M.S. Smith, and E. Horvitz. (2014). Data-Driven Decisions for Reducing Readmissions for Heart Failure: General Methodology and Case Study. *PLoS ONE* 9 (10), e109264.
Berry Jaeker, J. and A.L. Tucker (2016). The Value of Process Friction: An Empirical Investigation of Justification to Reduce Low-Yield Medical Services. Working paper.
Berry Jaeker, J.A. and A.L. Tucker (2017). Past the Point of Speeding Up: The Negative Effects of Workload Saturation on Efficiency and Patient Severity. *Management Science* 63 (4), 1042–1062.
Best, T.J., B. Sandkcç, D.D. Eisenstein, and D.O. Meltzer. (2015). Managing Hospital Inpatient Bed Capacity Through Partitioning Care into Focused Wings. *Manufacturing & Service Operations Management* 17 (2), 157–176.
Blumenthal, D.M., E.J. Orav, A.B. Jena, D.M. Dudzinski, S.T. Le, and A.K. Jha. (2015). Access, quality and costs of care at physician owned hospitals in the United States: Observational study. *BMJ* 351, h4466.

Bolandifar, E., N. DeHoratius, T. Olsen, and J.L. Wiler. (2016). Modeling the Behavior of Patients Who Leave the ED Without Being Seen. Working paper.

Bradley, E.H. et al. (2006). Achieving rapid door-to-balloon times: how top hospitals improve complex clinical systems. *Circulation* 113 (8), 1079–1085.

Brennan, T. A., L. L. Leape, N. M. Laird, L. Hebert, A. R. Localio, A. G. Lawthers, J. P. New- house, P. C. Weiler, and H. H. Hiatt (1991). Incidence of adverse events and negligence in hospitalized patients. Results of the Harvard Medical Practice Study I. *New England Journal of Medicine* 324 (6), 370–376.

Chan, C.W., J. Dong, and L. V. Green (2016a). Queues with Time-Varying Arrivals and Inspections with Applications to Hospital Discharge Policies. *Operations Research* 65 (2), 469–495.

Chan, C.W., V. F. Farias, N. Bambos, and G. J. Escobar. (2012). Optimizing Intensive Care Unit Discharge Decisions with Patient Readmissions. *Operations Research* 60 (6), 1323–1341.

Chan, C.W., V.F. Farias, and G.J. Escobar. (2016). The Impact of Delays on Service Times in the Intensive Care Unit. *Management Science* 63(7):2049–2072.

Chan, C.W., L.V. Green, L. Lu, S. Lekwijit, G. Escobar. (2016b) Assessing the Impact of Service Level when Customer Needs are Uncertain: An Empirical Investigation of Hospital Step-Down Units, *Management Science, forthcoming.*

Chandrasekaran, A., C. Senot, and K.K. Boyer (2012). Process Management Impact on Clinical and Experiential Quality: Managing Tensions Between Safe and Patient-Centered Healthcare. *Manufacturing & Service Operations Management* 14 (4), 548–566.

Chassin, M.R. (1991). Quality of care: Time to act. *JAMA* 266 (24), 3472–3473.

Chassin, M.R. and R.W. Galvin (1998). The urgent need to improve health care quality. Institute of Medicine national roundtable on health care quality. *JAMA* 280 (11), 1000–1005.

Christiansen, C., J.H. Grossman, and J. Hwang (2009). *The Innovator's Prescription: A Disruptive Solution for Health Care.* McGraw Hill Education.

Clark, J.R., R.S. Huckman, and B.R. Staats (2013). Learning from Customers: Individual and Organizational Effects in Outsourced Radiological Services. *Organization Science* 24 (5), 1539–1557.

Dai, T., M. Akan, and S. Tayur (2017). Imaging Room and Beyond: The Underlying Economics Behind Physicians' Test-Ordering Behavior in Outpatient Services. *Manufacturing & Service Operations Management* 19 (1), 99–113.

Das Gupta, A., U.S. Karmarkar, and G. Roels (2016). The Design of Experiential Services with Acclimation and Memory Decay: Optimal Sequence and Duration. *Management Science* 62 (5), 1278–1296.

de Véricourt, F. and O.B. Jennings (2011). Nurse Staffing in Medical Units: A Queueing Perspective. *Operations Research* 59 (6), 1320–1331.

Debo, L.G., L.B. Toktay, and L.N. Van Wassenhove (2008). Queuing for expert services. *Management Science* 54 (8), 1497–1512.

Deo, S., J. Gallien, and J.O. Jonasson (2015). Improving HIV early infant diagnosis supply chains in sub-Saharan Africa: Models and application to Mozambique. Working paper.
Deo, S. and A. Jain (2016). Slow first, fast later: Empirical evidence of speed-up in service episodes of finite duration. Working paper.
Deo, S. and M. Sohoni (2015). Optimal Decentralization of Early Infant Diagnosis of HIV in Resource-Limited Settings. *Manufacturing & Service Operations Management* 17 (2), 191–207.
Devaraj, S. and R. Kohli (2003). Performance Impacts of Information Technology: Is Actual Usage the Missing Link? *Management Science* 49 (3), 273–289.
Devaraj, S., T.T. Ow, and R. Kohli (2013). Examining the impact of information technology and patient flow on healthcare performance: A Theory of Swift and Even Flow (TSEF) perspective. *Journal of Operations Management* 31 (4), 181–192.
Dobson, G., T. Tezcan, and V. Tilson (2013). Optimal Workflow Decisions for Investigators in Systems with Interruptions. *Management Science* 59 (5), 1125–1141.
Donabedian, A. (1966). Evaluating the quality of medical care. *Milbank Memorial Fund Quarterly* 44 (3), 166–206.
Donabedian, A. (1988). The Quality of Care: How can it be assessed? *JAMA* 260 (12), 1743–1748.
Emani, S., D.Y. Ting, M. Healey, S.R. Lipsitz, A.S. Karson, J.S. Einbinder, L. Leinen, V. Suric, and D.W. Bates. (2014). Physician beliefs about the impact of meaningful use of the EHR: a cross-sectional study. *Applied Clinical Informatics* 5 (3), 789–801.
Freeman, M., N. Savva, and S. Scholtes (2016a). Economies of Scale and Scope in Hospitals. Working paper.
Freeman, M., N. Savva, and S. Scholtes (2016b 2017). Gatekeepers at Work: An Empirical Analysis of a Maternity Unit. *Management Science* 63(10):3147–3167.
Freeman, M. and S. Scholtes (2016). Gatekeeping Under Uncertainty: An Empirical Study of Referral Errors in the Emergency Department. Working paper.
Goh, J., M.V. Bjarnadóttir, M. Bayati, and S.A. Zenios. (2015). Active Postmarketing Drug Surveillance for Multiple Adverse Events. *Operations Research* 63 (6), 1528–1546.
Green, L.V., S. Savin, and M. Murray (2007). Providing Timely Access to Care: What is the Right Patient Panel Size? *The Joint Commission Journal on Quality and Patient Safety* 33 (4), 211–218.
Gupta, D. and B. Denton. (2008). Appointment Scheduling in Health Care: Challenges and Opportunities. *IIE Transactions* 40, 800–819.
Halsted, M.J. and C.M. Froehle (2008). Design, Implementation, and Assessment of a Radiology Workflow Management System. *American Journal of Roentgenology* 191 (2), 321–327.

Hibbard, J.H. and J. Greene (2013). What the evidence shows about patient activation: Better health outcomes and care experiences; fewer data on costs. *Health Affairs* 32 (2), 207–214.

Hu, W., C.W. Chan, J.R. Zubizarreta, and G.J. Escobar. (2016). An Examination of Early Transfers to the ICU Based on a Physiologic Risk Score. Working paper.

Huckman, R.S. and G.P. Pisano (2006). The Firm Specificity of Individual Performance: Evidence from Cardiac Surgery. *Management Science* 52 (4), 473–488.

Huckman, R.S. and B.R. Staats (2011). Fluid Tasks and Fluid Teams: The Impact of Diversity in Experience and Team Familiarity on Team Performance. *Manufacturing & Service Operations Management* 13 (3), 310–328.

Huckman, R.S., B.R. Staats, and D.M. Upton (2009). Team Familiarity, Role Experience, and Performance: Evidence from Indian Software Services. *Management Science* 55 (1), 85–100.

Ibanez, M.R., R.S. Huckman, J.R. Clark, and B.R. Staats. (2017). Discretionary Task Ordering: Queue Management in Radiological Services. *Management Science* (ePub ahead of print).

Institute of Medicine (1990). *Medicare: A strategy for quality assurance.* Washington, DC: National Academies Press.

KC, D.S., B.R. Staats, and F. Gino (2013). Learning from My Success and from Others' Failure: Evidence from Minimally Invasive Cardiac Surgery. *Management Science* 59 (11), 2435–2449.

KC, D.S. (2014). Does Multitasking Improve Performance? Evidence from the Emergency Department. *Manufacturing & Service Operations Management* 16 (2), 168–183.

KC, D.S. and B.R. Staats (2012). Accumulating a Portfolio of Experience: The Effect of Focal and Related Experience on Surgeon Performance. *Manufacturing & Service Operations Management* 14 (4), 618–633.

KC, D.S. and C. Terwiesch (2009). Impact of Workload on Service Time and Patient Safety: An Econometric Analysis of Hospital Operations. *Management Science* 55 (9), 1486–1498.

KC, D. S. and C. Terwiesch (2011). The Effects of Focus on Performance: Evidence from California Hospitals. *Management Science* 57 (11), 1897–1912.

KC, D.S. and C. Terwiesch (2012). An Econometric Analysis of Patient Flows in the Cardiac Intensive Care Unit. *Manufacturing & Service Operations Management* 14 (1), 50–65.

KC, D.S. and C. Terwiesch (2016). Benefits of Surgical Smoothing and Spare Capacity: An Econometric Analysis of Patient Flow. Working paper.

Kim, S-H., C.W. Chan, M. Olivares, and G. Escobar. (2015). ICU Admission Control: An Empirical Study of Capacity Allocation and Its Implication for Patient Outcomes. *Management Science* 61 (1), 19–38.

Kim, S-H., C.W. Chan, M. Olivares, and G.J. Escobar. (2016). Association Among ICU Congestion, ICU Admission Decision, and Patient Outcomes. *Critical Care Medicine* 44 (10), 1814–1821.

Kohli, R. and S. Devaraj (2004). Contribution of institutional DSS to organizational performance: Evidence from a longitudinal study. *Decision Support Systems* 37 (1), 103–118.

Kohli, R. and W.J. Kettinger (2004). Informating the Clan: Controlling Physicians' Costs and Outcomes. *MIS Quarterly* 28 (3), 363–394.

Kuntz, L., R. Mennicken, and S. Scholtes (2015). Stress on the Ward: Evidence of Safety Tipping Points in Hospitals. *Management Science* 61 (4), 754–771.

Kuntz, L. and S. Scholtes (2013). Physicians in leadership: The association between medical director involvement and staff-to-patient ratios. *Health Care Management Science* 16 (2), 129–138.

Kuntz, L., S. Scholtes, and S. Sülz (2016). Separate & Concentrate: Accounting for Patient Complexity in General Hospitals. Working paper.

Kuntz, L. and S. Suülz (2013). Treatment speed and high load in the Emergency Department: Does staff quality matter? *Health Care Management Science* 16 (4), 366–376.

Laker, L.F., C.M. Froehle, C.J. Lindsell, and M.J. Ward. (2014). The Flex Track: Flexible Partitioning Between Low- and High-Acuity Areas of an Emergency Department. *Annals of Emergency Medicine* 64 (6), 591–603.

Lee, D.K.K., G.M. Chertow, and S.A. Zenios (2010). Reexploring Differences among For-Profit and Nonprofit Dialysis Providers. *Health Services Research* 45 (3), 633–646.

Lee, D.K.K. and S. A. Zenios (2012). An Evidence-Based Incentive System for Medicare's End-Stage Renal Disease Program. *Management Science* 58 (6), 1092–1105.

Li, F., D. Gupta, and S.P. Potthoff. (2016). Improving Operating Room Schedules. *Health Care Management Science* 19 (3), 261–278.

Liu, N., S.R. Finkelstein, M.E. Kruk, and D. Rosenthal. (2018). When Waiting to See a Doctor is Less Irritating: Understanding Patient Preferences and Choice Behavior in Appointment Scheduling. *Management Science* 65 (4), 1975–1996.

Lucas, J., R.J. Batt, and O.A. Soremekun (2014). Setting wait times to achieve targeted left-without-being-seen rates. *The American Journal of Emergency Medicine* 32 (4), 342–345.

McCarthy, M.L., R. Ding, J. M. Pines, C. Terwiesch, M. Sattarian, J.A. Hilton, J. Lee, and S.L. Zeger. (2012). Provider Variation in Fast Track Treatment Time. *Medical Care* 50 (1), 43–49.

McGlynn, E.A., S.M. Asch, J. Adams, J. Keesey, J. Hicks, A. DeCristofaro, and E.A. Kerr. (2003). The quality of health care delivered to adults in the United States. *New England Journal of Medicine* 348 (26), 2635–2645.

Miedaner, F.. (2016). The role of nursing team continuity in the treatment of very-low-birth-weight infants: Findings from a pilot study. *Journal of Nursing Management* 24 (4), 458–464.

National Quality Forum (2017). Measures, Reports, and Tools.

Oliva, R. and J.D. Sterman (2001). Cutting corners and working overtime: Quality erosion in the service industry. *Management Science* 47 (7), 894–914.

Osadchiy, N. and D. KC (2016). Are Patients Patient? The Role of Time to Appointment in Patient Flow. *Production and Operations Management* 26 (3), 469–490.

Paç, M.F. and S. Veeraraghavan (2016). False Diagnosis and Overtreatment in Services. Working paper.

Park, E., Y. Ding, M. Nagarajan, and E. Grafstein. (2016). Patient Prioritization in Emergency Department Triage Systems: An Empirical Study of Canadian Triage and Acuity Scale (CTAS). Working paper.

Pick, V., K. Halstenberg, A. Demel, V. Kirchberger, R. Riedel, R. Schlößer, C. Wollny, C. Woopen, L. Kuntz, and B. Roth (2014). Staff and parents are discriminators for outcomes in neonatal intensive care units. *Acta Paediatrica* 103 (11), e475–e483.

Pines, J.M., R.J. Batt, J.A. Hilton, and C. Terwiesch (2011). The Financial Consequences of Lost Demand and Reducing Boarding in Hospital Emergency Departments. *Annals of Emergency Medicine* 58 (4), 331–340.

Piontek, F., R. Kohli, P. Conlon, J.J. Ellis, J. Jablonski, and N. Kini (2010). Effects of an adverse-drug-event alert system on cost and quality outcomes in community hospitals. *American Journal of Health-System Pharmacy* 67 (8), 613–620.

Saghafian, S., W.J. Hopp, M.P. Van Oyen, J.S. Desmond, and S.L. Kronick (2012). Patient Streaming as a Mechanism for Improving Responsiveness in Emergency Departments. *Operations Research* 60 (5), 1080–1097.

Saghafian, S., W.J. Hopp, M.P. Van Oyen, J.S. Desmond, and S.L. Kronick (2014). Complexity-Augmented Triage: A Tool for Improving Patient Safety and Operational Efficiency. *Manufacturing & Service Operations Management* 16 (3), 329–345.

Savva, N., T. Tezcan, and O. Yildiz (2016). Yardstick Competition for Service Systems. Working paper.

Senot, C., A. Chandrasekaran, and P.T. Ward (2016a). Collaboration between service professionals during the delivery of health care: Evidence from a multiple-case study in U.S. hospitals. *Journal of Operations Management* 42-43, 62–79.

Senot, C., A. Chandrasekaran, and P.T. Ward (2016b). Role of Bottom-Up Decision Processes in Improving the Quality of Health Care Delivery: A Contingency Perspective. *Production and Operations Management* 25 (3), 458–476.

Senot, C., A. Chandrasekaran, P.T. Ward, A.L. Tucker, and S.D. Moffatt-Bruce (2016). The Impact of Combining Conformance and Experiential Quality on

Hospitals' Readmissions and Cost Performance. *Management Science* 62 (3), 829–848.

Shwartz, M., A.B. Cohen, J.D. Restuccia, Z.J. Ren, A. Labonte, C. Theokary, R. Kang, and J. Horwitt (2016). How well can we identify the high-performing hospital? Working paper.

Shwartz, M., J.D. Restuccia, and A.K. Rosen (2015). Composite Measures of Health Care Provider Performance: A Description of Approaches. *The Milbank Quarterly* 93 (4), 788–825.

Singer, S.J., M.W. Friedberg, M.V. Kiang, T. Dunn, and D.M. Kuhn. (2013). Development and preliminary validation of the patient perceptions of integrated care survey. *Medical Care Research and Review* 70 (2), 143–164.

Song, H. and A. Tucker (2016). Performance Improvement in Health Care Organizations. *Foundations and Trends in Technology, Information and Operations Management* 9 (3-4), 153–309.

Song, H., A.L. Tucker, and K.L. Murrell (2015). The Diseconomies of Queue Pooling: An Empirical Investigation of Emergency Department Length of Stay. *Management Science* 61 (12), 3032–3053.

Song, H., A.L. Tucker, K.L. Murrell, and D.R. Vinson (2017). Closing the Productivity Gap: Improving Worker Productivity through Public Relative Performance Feedback and Validation of Best Practices. *Management Science*. (ePub ahead of print).

Staats, B.R. (2012). Unpacking team familiarity: The effects of geographic location and hierarchical role. *Production and Operations Management* 21 (3), 619–635.

Staats, B.R., H. Dai, D. Hofmann, and K.L. Milkman. (2017). Motivating Process Compliance Through Individual Electronic Monitoring: An Empirical Examination of Hand Hygiene in Healthcare. *Management Science* 63 (5), 1563–1585.

Staats, B.R. and F. Gino (2012). Specialization and Variety in Repetitive Tasks: Evidence from a Japanese Bank. *Management Science* 58 (6), 1141–1159.

Tan, T. and B.R. Staats (2016). Behavioral Drivers of Routing Decisions: Evidence from Restaurant Table Assignment. Working paper.

Terwiesch, C., D. KC, and J.M. Kahn (2011). Working with capacity limitations: operations management in critical care. *Critical Care* 15 (4), 308.

Torabi, E., C.M. Froehle, C.J. Lindsell, C.J. Moomaw, D. Kanter, D. Kleindorfer, and O. Adeoye. (2016). Monte Carlo Simulation Modeling of a Regional Stroke Team's Use of Telemedicine. *Academic Emergency Medicine* 23 (1), 55–62.

Traub, S.J., C.F. Stewart, R. Didehban, A.C. Bartley, S. Saghafian, V.D. Smith, S.M. Sil- vers, R. LeCheminant, and C.A. Lipinski. (2016). Emergency Department Rotational Patient Assignment. *Annals of Emergency Medicine* 67 (2), 206–215.

Traub, S.J., J.P. Wood, J. Kelley, D.M. Nestler, Y.-H. Chang, S. Saghafian, and C.A. Lipinski. (2015). Emergency Department Rapid Medical Assessment: Overall Effect and Mechanistic Considerations. *The Journal of Emergency Medicine* 48 (5), 620–627.

Tsai, T.C., A.K. Jha, A.A. Gawande, R.S. Huckman, N. Bloom, and R. Sadun. (2015). Hospital board and management practices are strongly related to hospital performance on clinical quality metrics. *Health Affairs* 34 (8), 1304–1311.

Tucker, A.L. (2004). The impact of operational failures on hospital nurses and their patients. *Journal of Operations Management* 22 (2), 151–169.

Tucker, A.L. (2014). Designed for Workarounds: A Qualitative Study of the Causes of Operational Failures in Hospitals. *The Permanente Journal* 18 (3), 33–41.

Tucker, A.L. (2016). The Impact of Workaround Difficulty on Frontline Employees' Response to Operational Failures: A Laboratory Experiment on Medication Administration. *Management Science* 62 (4), 1124–1144.

Valentine, M.A. and A.C. Edmondson (2015). Team scaffolds: How mesolevel structures enable role-based coordination in temporary groups. *Organization Science* 26 (2), 405–422.

Vera, A. and L. Kuntz (2007). Process-based organization design and hospital efficiency. *Health Care Management Review* 32 (1), 55–65.

Wang, G., W.J. Hopp, J. Li, F.L. Fazzalari, and S.F. Bolling. (2016). Using Patient-Centric Quality Information to Unlock Hidden Health Care Capabilities. Working paper.

Wang, L., I. Gurvich, K.J. O'Leary, and J.A.V. Mieghem. (2016). Collaboration, Interruptions and Setup Times: Model and Empirical Study of Hospitalist Workload. Working paper.

Wang, W.Y. and D. Gupta. (2011). Adaptive Appointment Systems with Patient Preferences. *Manufacturing and Service Operations Management* 13 (3), 373–389.

Wang, W.Y. and D. Gupta. (2014). Nurse Absenteeism and Staffing Strategies for Hospital Inpatient Units. *Manufacturing and Service Operations Management* 16 (3), 439–454.

Ward, M. J., Y.B. Ferrand, L.F. Laker, C.M. Froehle, T.J. Vogus, R.S. Dittus, S. Kripalani, and J.M. Pines. (2015). The Nature and Necessity of Operational Flexibility in the Emergency Department. *Annals of Emergency Medicine* 65 (2), 156–161.

Ward, M.J., C.M. Froehle, K.W. Hart, S.P. Collins, and C.J. Lindsell. (2014). Transient and Sustained Changes in Operational Performance, Patient Evaluation, and Medication Administration During Electronic Health Record Implementation in the Emergency Department. *Annals of Emergency Medicine* 63 (3), 320–328.

Ward, M.J., C.M. Froehle, K.W. Hart, and C.J. Lindsell. (2013). Operational data integrity during electronic health record implementation in the ED. *American Journal of Emergency Medicine* 31 (7), 1029–1033.

Ward, M.J., K.A. Marsolo, and C.M. Froehle (2014). Applications of business analytics in healthcare. *Business Horizons* 57 (5), 571–582.

Ward, M.J., W.H. Self, and C.M. Froehle (2015). Effects of Common Data Errors in Electronic Health Records on Emergency Department Operational Performance Metrics: A Monte Carlo Simulation. *Academic Emergency Medicine* 22 (9), 1085–1092.

Werner, R.M., A. Canamucio, S.C. Marcus, and C. Terwiesch. (2014). Primary Care Access and Emergency Room Use Among Older Veterans. *Journal of General Internal Medicine* 29 (S2), 689–694.

White, D.L., C.M. Froehle, and K.J. Klassen (2011). The Effect of Integrated Scheduling and Capacity Policies on Clinical Efficiency. *Production and Operations Management* 20 (3), 442–455.

Wiler, J.L., R.T. Griffey, and T. Olsen (2011). Review of Modeling Approaches for Emergency Department Patient Flow and Crowding Research. *Academic Emergency Medicine* 18 (12), 1371–1379.

Xu, K. and C.W. Chan (2016). Using Future Information to Reduce Waiting Times in the Emergency Department via Diversion. *Manufacturing & Service Operations Management* 18 (3), 314–331.

Yuan, X., T. Dai, L.G. Chen, and S. Gavirneni. (2016). Co-opetition in Services with Waiting-Area Entertainment. Working paper.

Zarling, E.J., F.A. Piontek, and R. Kohli (1999). The utility of hospital administrative data for generating a screening program to predict adverse outcomes. *American Journal of Medical Quality* 14 (6), 242–7.

Zenios, S., G. Atias, C. McCulloch, and C. Petrou. (2011). Outcome differences across transplant centers: comparison of two methods for public reporting. *Clinical Journal of the American Society of Nephrology* 6 (12), 2838–45.

Zhan, D. and A.R. Ward (2014). Threshold Routing to Trade Off Waiting and Call Resolution in Call Centers. *Manufacturing & Service Operations Management* 16 (2), 220–237.

Zhan, D. and A.R. Ward (2015). Incentive Based Service System Design: Staffing and Compensation to Trade Off Speed and Quality. Working paper.

Zhang, D.J., I. Gurvich, J.A. Van Mieghem, E. Park, R.S. Young, and M.V. Williams. (2016). Hospital Readmissions Reduction Program: An Economic and Operational Analysis. *Management Science* 62 (11), 3351–3371.

Zhang, Z., B.P. Berg, B.T. Denton, and X. Xie. (2016). Appointment Scheduling and the Effects of Customer Congestion on Service. Working paper.

Zheng, R., T. Dai, and K. Sycara (2018). Jumping the Line, Charitably: Analysis and Remedy of Donor-Priority Rule. Working paper.

6

Personalized Medicine

Turgay Ayer[1] *and Qiushi Chen*[2]

[1] *Georgia Institute of Technology*
[2] *Pennsylvania State University*

6.1 Introduction

Personalized medicine (PM) refers to tailoring clinical interventions (including screening, diagnosis, and treatment) to the characteristics (including demographic, clinical, and genetic) of individual patients. Although the term *personalized medicine* is often used interchangeably with *precision medicine*, their meanings are not exactly the same (Jameson and Longo 2015). Although these terms are not universally defined, precision medicine is typically used to refer to treatments targeted to the needs of individual patients on the basis of "omics" (e.g., genomics, proteomics) data, whereas personalized medicine (aka *individualized medicine*) is a broader term that refers to a departure from one-size-fits-all, population-based strategies to interventions centered on individuals. Regardless of the nuances in their definitions, the objective in both personalized and precision medicine is to maximize clinical outcomes for individual patients while avoiding or minimizing unnecessary side effects and costs for those less likely to benefit from a particular intervention. By enabling each patient to receive improved risk assessments, diagnoses, and ultimately treatment, PM offers opportunities for higher-quality care delivered at lower costs. As an example, this may include avoiding an unnecessary diagnostic exam as such a cardiac CT scan (as well as its potential radiation effect and high cost) for a patient who would not benefit from it or offering radioimmunotherapy to a chemotherapy-resistant cancer patient. Some example uses of PM are illustrated below:

- *Guide the selection of optimal therapy.* For example, in clinical practice, oncology patients show significant heterogeneity, and interventions can be tailored to their demographic, clinical, and genetic factors.

Handbook of Healthcare Analytics: Theoretical Minimum for Conducting 21st Century Research on Healthcare Operations, First Edition. Edited by Tinglong Dai and Sridhar Tayur.

- *Avoid adverse events.* For example, genotype-guided dosing of blood thinners, such as warfarin, can lead to significant reductions in adverse events, such as readmissions.
- *Prepositioning disease, shift emphasis to earlier intervention/prevention.* For example, breast cancer prevalence is higher in breast cancer (BRCA) gene mutation carriers, and effectively identifying and managing such patients may lead to effective prevention of future cancers.
- *Reduce the overall healthcare cost.* For example, by limiting the use of expensive drugs to targeted populations who would benefit most from such drugs, overall healthcare costs could be reduced.

The area of personalized medicine has blossomed in parallel with incredible advancements in genomics research, but the concept of PM is not new. Clinicians have a long history of using the term personalized medicine to refer to patient-centered clinical practice. In the early 1900s, the laboratory-based medicine—which focused on diseases rather than individuals and promoted one-size-fits-all universal clinical guidelines—was challenged by the "patient-a-person" initiative. While acknowledging the value of laboratory-based findings, this new initiative emphasized differences among individual patients and hence the need for tailored interventions (Tutton, 2012). Starting from Garrod's work in 1902 (Garrod, 1902), which is often cited as a major influence on the emergence of the pharmacogenetics area, much of the literature has documented variations in individuals' responses to drugs. More recently, starting from 1990s, large investments from the government and the pharmaceutical industry into genomics have substantially shaped the area of pharmacogenomics and the contemporary definition of precision medicine. By considering genetic variations in drug development and targeting biomarkers that some some individuals shared with others, pharmacogenomics offered great promise in stratifying groups of individuals and treating them accordingly. Although pharmacogenomics greatly influenced the area of personalized medicine, limiting the definition of personalized medicine to pharmacogenomics is considered a form of reductionism, where nongenetic determinants of disease and drug response are marginalized (Tutton, 2012).

In this study, we introduce important concepts in personalized medicine and discuss the role that mathematical/computational/statistical models can play in the advancement of this field. By drawing examples from published literature, we illustrate the use of models in various problems related to personalized medicine. Further, we discuss challenges and promising research directions for the modeling community. We categorize personalized medicine-focused studies in the literature by the modeling approaches they use, based on the following hierarchy:

- *Disease modeling approach.* Modeling studies in this category usually formulate the disease course explicitly as a dynamic process. Development of such disease models requires a thorough understanding of the epidemiological and clinical contexts, and large datasets for model parameterization. Depending on the specific research question and the type of decisions that need to be made, different modeling paradigms can be used. In particular, two high-level approaches are commonly used in the disease modeling literature:

- *Sequential decision disease models with health information updates.* Many chronic disease prevention and management problems involve sequential decisions over a long time horizon. Information collected over time, based on the outputs of the previous decisions, allows further tailoring of future decisions for individual patients. These problems typically lead to large-sized models and require access to longitudinal data for parameterization.
- *One-time decision disease models with risk stratification.* One-time decision disease models aim to stratify patients into subgroups based on subtype testing and guide intervention decisions accordingly. Studies in this category usually focus on *static* personal factors at the cellular, molecular, or genetic level. This class of problems is mostly relevant in the growing area of *precision medicine.* Although one-time decisions about subtype testing are simpler than sequential decisions, an underlying disease model is still needed to fully capture the long-term impact over the disease course, and systematically determine the best use of interventions with respect to clinical benefit and cost-effectiveness.

- *Artificial Intelligence (AI)-based approaches.* The major distinction of this approach from the disease modeling approach is that AI-based methods typically do not explicitly model disease progression. Instead, such models usually learn some hidden relationships directly from the data without an underlying predefined model, which may ultimately lead to improved personalized decisions.

In the remainder of this chapter, we describe each of these approaches in detail and illustrate their uses via several examples from the published literature.

6.2 Sequential Decision Disease Models with Health Information Updates

For many chronic diseases, detection and later management involve a sequence of interventions over a long time period. Examples include annual/biennial breast screening in women over age 40, or multiline treatment in indolent cancers such as leukemia.

Due to patient-level heterogeneity and inherent uncertainty in the clinical process, the same sequence of interventions is not necessarily optimal for all patients. In clinical practice, interventions can be personalized, based on a patient's past history of health status, test results, and responses to any previous interventions. To model such a dynamic decision-making process, several key issues need to be addressed.

- Health state. Many health-related attributes of a patient can be used to define the health state in a model, such as demographic factors, disease stages, risk scores, and critical clinical measures, among others. States can be categorical or numerical, or discrete or continuous, depending on the nature of the disease. Even though a patient has many attributes, keeping track of only those attributes that may influence the decisions in the context of the problem studied is a good modeling practice.
- Disease dynamics. A disease model captures changes in a patient's health condition over time. Static factors could be captured easily in the model and used to stratify models into different risk groups or subpopulations. On the other hand, capturing dynamically changing factors/conditions typically imposes modeling, computational, or estimation challenges. Various state space models, such as Markov chains, linear Gaussian systems, or differential equations, can be utilized to characterize the stochastically evolving disease natural history, as well as responses to a given intervention. Parameterizing such dynamic models usually requires access to large, longitudinal datasets.
- Observations. In many practical cases, knowing the exact health state of a patient (e.g., existence or staging of a tumor) is not possible. Instead, providers can draw observations from the patient and make inferences about the patient's health state based on these observations. Such inferences can then be updated as new information emerges, and decisions can be tailored to individual patients based on the updated information collected. Observations are typically collected from medical tests (e.g., a blood draw, X-ray, MRI), and these tests are usually imperfect with some inherent uncertainty. More specifically, medical tests typically do not have perfect *sensitivity*, that is, a true positive rate, leading to false-negative outcomes, and perfect *specificity*, that is, a true negative rate, leading to false-positive outcomes.
- Information update. Because medical tests typically provide imperfect signals, the decision-makers usually do not have perfect knowledge about the true underlying disease state. When a new observation is made, this observation can be used to update the current information about the underlying disease state. Such an *iterative* information update procedure can indeed take into account the patient's entire history of state, actions, and observations.

Several stochastic optimal control and estimation models naturally fit in the above described modeling framework, such as dynamic programming-based approaches (e.g., Markov decision process (MDP), partially observable MDP (POMDP)), and stochastic filtering (e.g., Kalman filter). In the following two case studies, we demonstrate the use of POMDP and Kalman filter models, respectively, in personalized screening for breast cancer (Ayer, 2012) and glaucoma (Helm, 2015). Then we will briefly review other relevant studies that use a similar modeling approach.

6.2.1 Case Study: POMDP Model for Personalized Breast Cancer Screening

Breast cancer is the most common type of cancer among US women. Although mammography is a proven screening modality for early detection, it has relatively high false-positive rates, leading to further unnecessary and often invasive diagnostic procedures, such as a biopsy. In such cases, aggressive screening leads to an increased number of false-positives, unnecessary further invasive tests, and a reduction in quality of life. The current population-based mammography screening guidelines consider only age and are controversial. For example, whereas the American Cancer Society (ACS) recommends annual screening over age 40, the US Preventive Services Task Force (USPSTF), an influential organization in health coverage decisions, recommends every two year screening between ages 50–74. Furthermore, both guidelines recommend discussing screening decisions with physicians and personalizing intervals to women outside these intervals. On the other hand, although age is an important risk factor for breast cancer, there exists also many other known risk factors, such as a family history, prior biopsies, fertility, and ages at menarche and menopause. While current breast cancer screening guidelines are "one-size-fits-all" type, even though a personalized approach for breast cancer screening is identified as "crucial to improve the early detection of breast cancer" in the 2005 Institute of Medicine report (Petitti et al., 2005).

Ayer et al. (2012) present a POMDP model as the first analytical framework for developing personalized mammography screening policies. In this model, personalized screening decisions are driven by an individual's risk estimate, which can capture the above-mentioned known risk factors, and which is updated dynamically, based on the underlying disease progression, prior screening history, and prior test outcomes. In the following, we illustrate the key modeling components and discuss practical implications of such personalized policies.

Health states. Core state $s_t \in S = \{0, \cdots, 5\}$ represents the underlying health state at time period t, including no cancer (0), non-invasive cancer (1), invasive cancer (2), non-invasive cancer under treatment (3), invasive cancer under treatment (4), and death state (5). States $S^{PO} = \{0, 1, 2\}$ are not fully observable. Instead, the decision-maker can have a belief $b_t \in \mathcal{B}$ about the underlying states, representing a probability distribution over states S^{PO}.

Actions, observations, and system dynamics. At every time point t, the decision-maker decides to either screen the woman or defer the screening action. That is, the decision-maker chooses either *Wait* or *Mammography* action a at each time period (i.e., $a \in \{W, M\}$). Depending on the outcomes of these actions, an observation o is made. In particular, upon a *Mammography* action, either a positive ($M+$) or a negative mammogram ($M-$) output is observed. On the other hand, upon a *Wait* action, the woman can make either a self-detection ($SD+$) or no self-detection ($SD-$). That is, if $a = W$, $o \in \Theta_W = \{SD+, SD-\}$; and if $a = M$, $o \in \Theta_M = \{M+, M-\}$. Given that mammography and breast self-exams are not perfect, the observation o cannot capture the exact true health state. Instead, it provides an imperfect but useful signal. Hence, the observation o follows the observation probability $K_t^a(o|s)$, $s \in \mathcal{S}^{PO}$, representing the probability of making an observation o, given the underlying state s, and action taken a at time t. These observation probabilities are determined by the sensitivity and specificity of the tests—in this case, mammography and breast self-exams.

Based on the action a and observation o, the transition from health state s to s' takes place in period t with the probability $P_t^{(a,o)}(s'|s)$. For $(a, o) \in \{(W, SD+), (W, SD-), (M, M-)\}$, no intervention is initiated, and the state transition follows the natural history of the disease. If $(a, o) = (M, M+)$, that is, a positive mammography outcome is observed, then the patient undergoes a perfect diagnostic exam such as a biopsy to confirm the diagnosis. If the biopsy reveals that $s \in \{1, 2\}$ (i.e., true-positive mammogram), the patient starts treatment and enters state $\{3, 4\}$ respectively; on the other hand, if $s = 0$ (i.e., false-positive mammogram), the state transition again follows the natural history, with $P_t^{(M,M+)}(s'|0) = P_t^{(M,M-)}(s'|0)$.

Information updates. A decision-maker updates his belief b after making action a and observing o. Let $\tau[b, a, o]$ be the updated belief at time $t + 1$, representing the probability of being in state $s' \in \mathcal{S}^{PO}$, given prior belief b, action taken was a, and the observation made was o. Unless a positive mammogram is observed, belief is updated as follows:

$$\tau[b, a, o](s') = \frac{\sum_{s \in \mathcal{S}^{PO}} b(s) K_t^a(o|s) P_t^{(a,o)}(s'|s)}{\sum_{s \in \mathcal{S}^{PO}} b(s) K_t^a(o|s)} \quad \text{if } (a, o) \in \{(W, SD+), (W, SD-), (M, M-)\}. \tag{6.1}$$

Otherwise, if a positive mammogram is observed, that is, $(a, o) = (M, M+)$, and it turns out that the patient is indeed cancer-free, her risk estimate is reset and her updated risk estimate in the next period simply follows the probability of developing cancer in this period:

$$\tau[b, a, o](s') = P_t^{(a,o)}(s'|0) \quad \text{if } (a, o) = (M, M+). \tag{6.2}$$

Optimal screening decision. The objective is to maximize the total expected health outcomes, measured by quality-adjusted life years (QALYs). Intermediate QALY reward $r_t(s, a, o)$ is collected at every time point, based on the state, action, and observation. On the other hand, when a patient is diagnosed with cancer and starts treatment, she is assigned a lump-sum QALY $R_t(s), s \in \{1, 2\}$. Then, the value function $V_t^a(b)$ for a given action a and belief b, which represents the reward-to-go from period t onward under action a, is defined recursively as follows:

$$V_t^W(b) = \sum_{s\in S^{PO}} b(s) \sum_{o\in\Theta_W} K_t^W(o|s)\,(r_t(s, W, o) + V_{t+1}^*(\tau[b, W, o])), \tag{6.3}$$

$$\begin{aligned} V_t^M(b) = &\sum_{s\in S^{PO}} b(s)K_t^M(M-|s)\,(r_t(s, M, M-) + V_{t+1}^*(\tau[b, M, M-])) \\ &+ b(0)K_t^M(M+|s)\,(r_t(s, M, M+) + V_{t+1}^*(\tau[b, M, M+])) \\ &+ \sum_{s\in\{1,2\}} b(s)K_t^M(M+|s)R_t(s), \end{aligned} \tag{6.4}$$

Then, the optimal value function $V_t^*(b)$ is given by:

$$V_t^*(b) = \max\{V_t^W(b), V_t^M(b)\},$$

and the optimal action $a_t^*(b)$ is selected as $\arg\max_a V_t^a(b)$.

This POMDP model is parameterized using multiple sources, including a validated microsimulation model for state transitions, cancer registry data for breast cancer treatment survivals, and published medical literature for test accuracies. The initial belief state is calculated using the Gail model, a validated risk estimation model for breast cancer (Gail and Green, 2000).

The optimal solution to the POMDP model shows that there exist age-specific threshold risks for non-invasive and invasive cancers, above which mammogram is the preferred action. The optimal policy can inform the optimal screening decision for any given age and for the current risk estimate. As new information is collected and a patient's estimated risk is updated, her screening interval is adapted, based on this up-to-date risk estimate. Compared with population-based policies, the optimal personalized screening policy is shown to improve the total QALYs, while significantly decreasing the number of mammograms and false-positives.

The results also show that the screening history matters: patients of the same age may have different optimal screening intervals, depending on their screening histories. For example, if a 60-year-old patient has 20 negative mammograms in the past and another 60-year-old patient is receiving her first mammography exam, it is plausible to recommend shorter future screening intervals for this latter patient. The authors remark that while capturing prior screening history can significantly improve performance of breast cancer screening policies, such information is not considered by existing guidelines.

In a follow-up study, Ayer et al. (2015) extend their model to address the heterogeneity in women's adherence behaviors in further personalizing breast cancer screening decisions. In this extension study, recommendations of wait or annual/biennial/triennial mammograms depend on estimates from both underlying cancer states and adherence levels. Their results show that the patients with high adherence could be adversely affected by the screening policy that is optimized for an average adherence level and that adherence levels should be explicitly considered in breast cancer screening recommendations.

6.2.2 Case Study: Kalman Filter for Glaucoma Monitoring

Glaucoma is an eye disease that typically progresses asymptomatically and can eventually lead to vision loss if left untreated. By closely monitoring the disease progression via quantitative tests, patients can receive timely interventions to slow down the deterioration.

However, these is no consensus on the ideal testing frequency. Obviously, a too-long monitoring interval is not desirable, as it may lead to a missed opportunity for timely treatment. On the other hand, a too-short interval is not ideal, either; given the noisy measurement from the test and slow progression of the disease, too-frequent monitoring may result in increased patient discomfort at an overall higher cost of testing.

In an attempt to address this tradeoff in glaucoma monitoring, Helm et al. (2015) developed a Kalman filter-based algorithm to predict the state and determine the optimal time to next test. In particular, they first built a Kalman filter that updates the estimate of state distribution from previous observations and projects the future state distribution. Then, based on the projected state trajectory, they identified the optimal time to next test as the minimum time to reach a prespecified progression level at a given confidence level. This way the testing interval is optimized to balance the increased discomfort and cost from too-frequent monitoring and the potential delay in a timely intervention from a too-infrequent monitoring. In the following, we provide a more detailed overview of the modeling approach and summarize the key findings from this study.

In the glaucoma monitoring problem, the disease status, $\alpha_t \in \mathbb{R}^n$, is measured by a visual field test and intraocular pressure (IOP) test, and is characterized by three critical clinical numerical measures: mean deviation (MD), pattern standard deviation (PSD), and IOP. The disease state is then defined as a vector:

$$\alpha_t = [MD, MD', MD'', PSD, PSD', PSD'', IOP, IOP', IOP'']^\top, \quad (6.5)$$

where X' and X'' (e.g., MD', MD''), respectively, represent the first- and second-order derivative of X. Such a state definition allows capturing nonlinear dynamics in the form of a linear system, which simplifies the subsequent analysis. More specifically, disease dynamics can be formulated as a discrete-time linear Gaussian process as follows:

$$\alpha_t = \mathbf{T}\alpha_{t-1} + \eta, \quad t = 1, \cdots, N, \quad (6.6)$$

where $\mathbf{T}$ represents the state transition matrix, and η represents a Gaussian random vector with mean $\mathrm{E}[\eta] = 0$ and covariance matrix $\mathrm{Var}[\eta] = \mathbf{Q}_{n\times n}$. Let

$z_t \in \mathbb{R}^m$ be the observations, specifically the observed values of MD, PSD and IOP, at time t, which is determined by the following measurement equation:

$$z_t = \mathbf{Z}\alpha_t + \epsilon, \quad t = 1, \cdots, N, \tag{6.7}$$

where ϵ represents the measurement noise with mean $\mathrm{E}[\epsilon] = 0$ and covariance matrix $\mathrm{Var}[\epsilon] = \mathbf{H}_{m\times m}$, and matrix $\mathbb{Z}_{m\times n}$ maps the state space to the observation space. Next, we describe the two important steps of a Kalman filter approach: prediction and update.

Prediction. Let $\hat{\alpha}_{t|t}$ and $\hat{\Sigma}_{t|t}$ represent the estimates of mean and variance for the current state at time t, respectively, and let $\hat{\alpha}_{t+l|t}$ and $\hat{\Sigma}_{t+l|t}$ represent the prediction at time l-step ahead at time $t + l$ given the information up to time t. The Kalman filter predicts the state (i.e., mean and covariance) in the period $t + l$ as

$$\hat{\alpha}_{t+l|t} = \mathbf{T}^l \hat{\alpha}_{t|t}, \quad \hat{\Sigma}_{t+l|t} = \mathbf{T}^l \hat{\Sigma}_{t|t} (\mathbf{T}^l)^\top + \sum_{j=0}^{l-1} \mathbf{T}^j \mathbf{Q} (\mathbf{T}^j)^\top. \tag{6.8}$$

Intuitively, Equation (6.8) implies that mean values of states follow the linear state transition l times as if in a deterministic way; meanwhile, the uncertainty of the predicted states is propagated over l periods. The l-step update can also be interpreted as the state update without new observations from time $t + 1$ to $t + l$.

Update. When a new observation z_{t+1} is made, earlier prediction $\hat{\alpha}_{t+1|t}$ and $\hat{\Sigma}_{t+1|t}$ can be adjusted with such new information. The updated state estimates $\hat{\alpha}_{t+1|t+1}$ and $\hat{\Sigma}_{t+1|t+1}$ are calculated as follows:

$$\hat{\alpha}_{t+1|t+1} = \hat{\alpha}_{t+1|t} + \mathbf{K}_{t+1} \cdot (z_{t+1} - \mathbf{Z}\hat{\alpha}_{t+1|t}) \tag{6.9}$$

$$\hat{\Sigma}_{t+1|t+1} = \hat{\Sigma}_{t+1|t} - \mathbf{K}_{t+1} \mathbf{Z} \hat{\Sigma}_{t+1|t}, \tag{6.10}$$

where the matrix $\mathbf{K}_{t+1}$ is called the *optimal Kalman gain*, which minimizes the mean squared error of the new estimates and is determined by

$$\mathbf{K}_{t+1} = \hat{\Sigma}_{t+1|t} \mathbf{Z}^\top (\mathbf{Z}\hat{\Sigma}_{t+1|t} \mathbf{Z}' + \mathbf{H})^{-1}. \tag{6.11}$$

The link between the state estimates to the treatment decision is established by the progression function, which maps physiological indicators x (including disease states and additional clinical factors of a patient) to the probability of progression and the treatment decision is initiated when the estimated value of the progression probability reaches a certain critical value. The progression function $f(x)$ is defined as a logistic function as follows:

$$f(x) = \frac{1}{1 + e^{-w(x)}}, \tag{6.12}$$

where $w(x)$ is a linear function with variables including current readings of MD, MD$'$, MD$''$, PSD baseline value, current PSD value, and patient's age. Based on such a function, a confidence region of a predicted state can be translated into a set of predicted progression probabilities. Then, the largest value, representing the "worst case" progression by prediction, can be used as the threshold value to indicate treatment. The l-step prediction, following a Gaussian distribution with mean $\hat{\alpha}_{t+l|t}$ and covariance $\hat{\Sigma}_{t+l|t}$, has a $100\rho\%$-confidence region given by

$$\mathcal{D}_\rho(\hat{\alpha}_{t+l|t}, \hat{\Sigma}_{t+l|t}) = \left\{x : (x - \hat{\alpha}_{t+l|t})^\top \hat{\Sigma}_{t+l|t}^{-1}(x - \hat{\alpha}_{t+l|t}) \leq \chi^2(1-\rho, n)\right\}, \tag{6.13}$$

and the point of maximum progression (POMP) can be defined by the function

$$h_\rho(\hat{\alpha}_{t|t}, \hat{\Sigma}_{t|t}, l) = \max_{x \in \mathcal{D}_\rho(\hat{\alpha}_{t+l|t}, \hat{\Sigma}_{t+l|t})} f(x). \tag{6.14}$$

Because the objective is to identify the earliest time point that the disease progression risk reaches a critical threshold level τ, the optimal time to next test $F_{\rho,\tau}(\hat{\alpha}_{t|t}, \hat{\Sigma}_{t|t})$ can then be computed by:

$$F_{\rho,\tau}(\hat{\alpha}_{t|t}, \hat{\Sigma}_{t|t}) = \min_{l \in \mathbb{Z}^+} l, \quad \text{s.t. } h_\rho(\hat{\alpha}_{t|t}, \hat{\Sigma}_{t|t}, l) \geq \tau. \tag{6.15}$$

The model has two parameters that can be set by clinical decision-makers: the threshold τ and confidence level ρ. A lower value of τ indicates a lower tolerance for missing progressions, and a higher ρ reflects a more risk-averse attitude on the state estimates, both leading to more frequent tests with shorter intervals.

At time $t' = t + F_{\rho,\tau}$, new observations are made, which are then used to update the state estimates $\hat{\alpha}_{t'|t}$ and $\hat{\Sigma}_{t'|t'}$. This way, the test outcome history for a patient can be incorporated to predict his personal risk of disease progression and to eventually identify a personalized monitoring strategy.

Longitudinal data from two randomized trials are utilized to calibrate the model. Comparing with common practice (using a fixed interval of 1, 1.5, and 2 years), the authors find that the model-based monitoring provides a higher accuracy of detecting progression, and lower delay of diagnosing progression, and thus dominates the fixed-interval schedules.

6.2.3 Other Relevant Studies

In addition to the above examples, several other studies in the literature examine personalized decisions of screening and/or treatment in many disease areas, using various modeling tools and algorithms. Earlier studies use MDP models to identify the optimal timing of initiating HIV treatment based on a patient's CD4 categories (Shechter et al., 2008), optimal timing of statin initiation for patients with type 2 diabetes based on each individual's lipid ratio (Kurt et al., 2011), initiation of blood pressure and cholesterol medications based on a patient's systolic blood pressure, total cholesterol, and high-density lipoprotein level (Mason et al., 2014), and the optimal timing of liver transplant given a patient's model for end-stage liver disease (MELD) scores (Alagoz et al., 2004, 2007; Sandikci et al., 2008).

Kotas and Ghate (2016) present a stochastic dynamic programming (DP) framework to determine the optimal response-guided dose of biologic drugs for treating rheumatoid arthritis. A patient's disease activity score (DAS, the lower the better) is affected by the biologic dose and follows a dose-response function with stochastic noise. The model balances a better disease control and the increased costs from a higher dose. Numerical results based on clinical trial data show that optimal dosing policy increases with worsening disease conditions. They extend the formulation with general dose-response and cost functions and show that monotone dosing policy is optimal under a certain structure of the dose-response and cost function. Sinha et al. (2016) later extend the model of Kotas and Ghate (2016) using a robust stochastic DP approach, which considers an interval uncertainty set of the probability distribution of the stochastic noise term for the state transition and minimizes the worst-case total expected cost.

Ibrahim et al. (2016) developed a two-stage analytical framework to personalize the warfarin dose in anticoagulation therapy. The framework discerns an individual patient's sensitivity parameter—an unobservable and individual-specific factor affecting the patient's response to warfarin dose—to a certain confidence level, using a POMDP model in the first initiation stage, and then determines the optimal dose to minimize the cumulative risks of bleeding and strokes, using an MDP model in the second maintenance stage. They derive a closed-form expression for belief updates in the POMDP model and find that the constant dose throughout the maintenance stage is optimal to the MDP model. They validate the model using real clinical data and draw useful implications about the length of initiation stage and the importance of properly assessing sensitivity.

Personalized decisions for cancer screening and diagnosis have been studied in the literature for various types of cancers. Erenay et al. (2014) develop a POMDP model to optimize the personalized colonoscopy screening policy to prevent colorectal cancer (CRC). The colonoscopy decision is tailored to the individual's risk by static (gender) and dynamic factors (history of CRC and polyp, age). They find that optimal colonoscopy screening policies are generally more aggressive and result in higher QALYs with lower mortality, compared with the current recommended policies. Akhavan-Tabatabaei et al. (2016) developed an MDP model to optimize the screening policy for cervical cancer prevention in Colombia. The optimal screening policy determines whether to screen and if so, which test (pap test or colposcopy) to use, based on individual's risk category, age, and previous screening history. Chhatwal et al. (2010) formulated an MDP to study the optimal biopsy decisions for breast cancer detection based on individualized risk estimates. The patient's breast cancer risk was evaluated using mammographic features and demographic factors via a validated Bayesian network risk model. They found the risk threshold for biopsy increases with age. Zhang et al. (2012) solved a POMDP model to determine the optimal biopsy decisions for prostate cancer. The biopsy referral decision is driven by the individual's cancer risk, which is updated based on previous prostate-specific antigen (PSA) screening tests. In addition to determining an age-dependent risk threshold, their empirical study presents the optimal stopping time for PSA screening. Lavieri et al. (2012) considered an optimal timing problem for prostate cancer treatment, in other words, when a patient's PSA reaches the lowest value (PSA nadir) for initiating radiation therapy. They used a Kalman filter to update an individual's PSA dynamics based on his previous PSA readings and to predict the PSA nadir. Through numerical analysis, they showed that their proposed strategies can effectively reduce the difference between the radiation treatment time and the estimated PSA nadir, compared with the currently used protocol in British Columbia.

6.3 One-Time Decision Disease Models with Risk Stratification

In addition to sequential dynamic decisions as reviewed in Section 6.2, many decisions in personalized medicine are one-time decisions (e.g., selecting the optimal one out of multiple treatment alternatives for a patient). The optimal choice usually depends on many individual factors, including demographic, clinical, and genetic factors. Recent advancements in science and technology enables identifying molecular factors, such as biomarkers (e.g., genetic variant, cellular characteristics), to more accurately predict a patient's clinical outcomes in response to a given therapy. For example, patients with a mutated KRAS gene are known to be less likely to respond to the cetuximab and panitumumab treatment for colon cancer (Lievre et al., 2006). Better assessing or predicting such gene mutations allows the decision-makers to better tailor intervention strategies to individual patients.

Although personalizing treatment to individual patients based on biomarker-level information rather than providing a one-size-fits-all treatment option, is ideal, such decisions are typically nontrivial. Biomarkers can be assessed via different tests with different levels of accuracy, availability/access, and cost. Whether a *testing-first-then-treatment* approach is preferred to the *one-size-fits-all* approach may depend on test accuracy, health outcome (e.g., survival rate) differences between treatment options, as well as cost. Several questions rise in this context—for example, which test (or test combination) should be used? What is the best algorithm for the testing-and-treatment protocol? How should the development of new testing or targeted therapy be prioritized, given the current level of uncertainty?

A modeling-based analysis is useful in integrating the multiple aspects of the decision problem and synthesizing the existing evidence to improve the quality of decisions. In the clinical literature, decision models for *precision medicine* usually follow a similar framework with several important model elements:

- *Disease course.* A state transition model is typically used to capture the disease course a patient is experiencing, and compare the outcomes of the decisions made. The model may include a sequence of a priori defined interventions based on predefined protocols (e.g., multiple lines of treatment, and supportive care); however, unlike as in the previous section, one-time decisions (e.g., treatment A vs. B) are made this time based on biomarker-level information.
- *Test accuracy.* The existence of certain biomarkers, or any other stratification factor, is assessed by medical tests. Some tests are considered as the gold standard with 100 percent accuracy (e.g., gene expression profile [GEP] test), while others have imperfect accuracies. Imperfect accuracy allows for the chance to make a mistake in stratification and misclassify a patient's subtype.
- *Intervention assignment based on test outcomes.* Interventions (e.g., treatment) are assigned to patients based on the observed subtype from the test. On the other hand, the actual clinical outcomes (e.g., survival) of a patient is determined by the treatment and patient's true subtype, which may or may not be accurately revealed by the test. Therefore, a testing-first-then-treatment strategy may or may not lead to a clinical improvement, compared with a one-size-fits-all strategy, depending on the prevalence of subtypes, test accuracy, and differences in treatment options.

In the following, we illustrate the modeling framework and analysis for such decision problems through an example of subtype-based treatment for diffuse large B-cell lymphoma (DLBCL) based on Chen et al. (2017).

6.3.1 Case Study: Subtype-Based Treatment for DLBCL

Diffuse large B-cell lymphoma is the most common aggressive type of lymphoma (Shipp et al., 2002). First-line treatment with rituximab, cyclophosphamide, doxorubicin, vincristine, and prednisone (RCHOP) therapy has been the standard of care for DLBCL patients. However, patients with DLBCL experience widely divergent outcomes. DLBCL is composed of two major biological subtypes: germinal center B-cell-like (GCB) and activated B-cell-like (ABC) subtypes, and the ABC subtype has been shown to be associated with markedly worse outcomes compared with GCB DLBCL (three-year overall survival [OS]: 85% for GCB and 69% for ABC) (Fu et al., 2008). The subtype can be assessed by gene expression profiling (GEP) or an immunohistochemistry (IHC) test.

Preliminary evidence suggests that novel agents like lenalidomide can improve ABC DLBCL survival when added to RCHOP (Nowakowski et al., 2014), which motivates the implementation of precision medicine treatment strategies stratified by GCB/ vs ABC subtype. To compare alternative strategies, Chen et al. (2017) present a mathematical model where considered first-line treatment strategies include:

(1) Administering RCHOP for all patients (as the current standard of care),
(2) Administering novel treatment for all patients,
(3) Performing subtype testing first and subsequently administering RCHOP to patients with GCB subtype and the novel treatment to those with ABC/non-GCB subtype.

A patient's disease course is captured by a simple Markov model with three health states: progression-free, relapsed, and deceased (Figure 6.1a). The transition from the progression-free state to relapsed or dead state is determined by progression-free survival and overall survival of the first-line treatment; the transition from relapsed to death is determined by the overall survival of salvage chemotherapy followed by autologous stem cell transplant (ASCT) as the current standard of care.

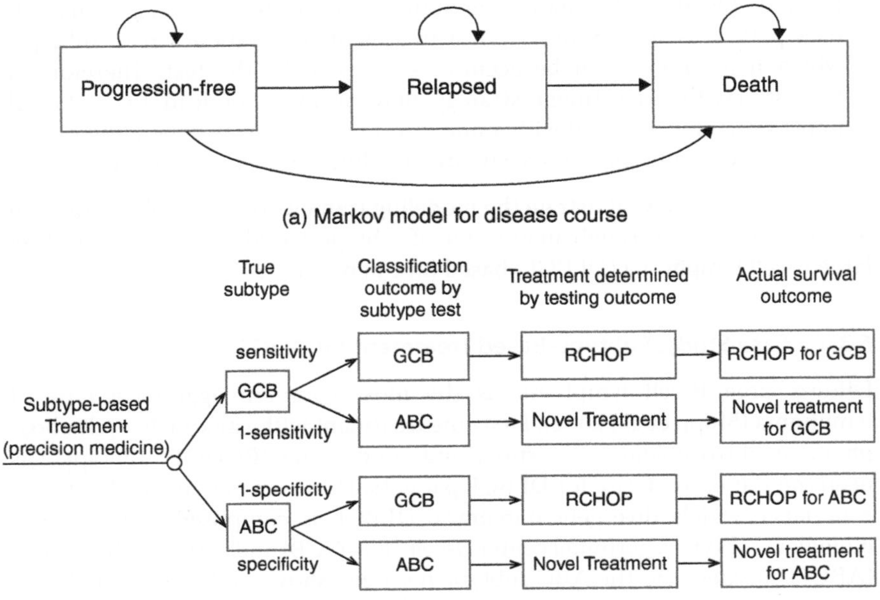

Figure 6.1 Decision model of first-line treatment for DLBCL. (Note. Non-GCB and ABC are used interchangeably)

For the subtype-based treatment strategy (Strategy 3), the first-line treatment is assigned based on the classification results of the subtype test (see Figure 6.1b). GEP is considered the gold standard with perfect accuracy, whereas IHC tests are less accurate (sensitivity and specificity varying across different IHC algorithms) but more accessible in clinical practice. Thus, the generic model allows the possibility of a suboptimal treatment assignment.

Using this Markov model, the DLBCL patient cohort is simulated to evaluate the average health and cost outcomes under different treatment strategies. The true subtype of a patient is generated according to the subtype prevalence. As patients follow different clinical pathways as defined by state transitions, health outcomes (e.g., QALYs) and cost outcomes (e.g., costs due to treatment, administration, adverse event management) are accumulated over time. With such a model, a series of analyses can be conducted to answer different research questions, including but not limited to the following:

Is the subtype-based treatment cost-effective based on the current evidence? Chen et al. (2017) parameterized their model using the survival data from published clinical studies and meta-analysis and estimate costs based on Centers for Medicare and Medicaid Services (CMS) data. They found that the subtype-based treatment strategy is cost effective with either the GEP or IHC test and that the universal novel treatment has dominated (i.e., lower health outcomes at a higher cost). This is mainly because of the imbalanced survival benefit of the novel treatment: novel has limited survival improvement for patients with the GCB subtype who make up nearly half of the overall DLBCL cohort; for such a patient subgroup, the additional cost of the novel treatment is not justified by the limited survival benefit.

For potential new treatment and subtype tests, in what parameter ranges does the subtype-based treatment strategy remain optimal? As new data arise and further advancements are made in science, technology, and drug development, one may want to know within what range of parameters a certain strategy remains favorable. For example, in the context of DLBCL, other novel treatment and testing assays are expected to emerge in the near future. In order to answer such a question, Chen et al. (2017) varied the values of various parameters and identified the cost frontier for the novel treatment, which shows the maximum cost of the novel treatment where the subtype-based treatment strategy remains cost-effective.

What is the value of personalized care, considering various factors such as a patient's insurance coverage, uncertainty in test accuracy, and technology diffusion trajectory? How should research and investments be prioritized? Such questions are also applicable in the context of DLBCL, but they are not limited to DLBCL. In order to study such problems, Basu et al. (2016) propose a generic framework to assess the expected value of individualized care (EVIC). Their framework can incorporate several aspects of behavior at the patient, physician, and payer levels. They demonstrate the EVIC analysis using an example from personalized breast cancer treatment stratified by a genomic assay (OncotypeDx), show the EVIC calculations, and discuss the implications of their findings on the coverage decisions by insurers and investment decisions by manufacturers of medical tests. The EVIC framework is generalizable to other diseases and can help to analyze the benefits of and guide the use of personalized medicine from various perspectives.

6.3.2 Other Applications

Customizing treatment based on molecular factors (e.g., genotype or phenotype) of individual patients has been studied in the contexts of many other types of cancers. For metastatic non-small-cell lung cancer (NSCLC), crizotinib is found to significantly improve the survival in both untreated (Solomon et al., 2014) and previously treated patients with ALK rearrangement (Shaw et al., 2013), and ceritinib is later found to overcome the resistance of crizotinib for ALK+ patients (El-Osta et al., 2015). However, the significant survival benefits for ALK+ patients do not necessarily translate to a cost-effective *test-treat* approach for general NSCLC patients. In particular, economic evaluation studies found that ALK testing with crizotinib treatment for ALK+ patients is not cost-effective, given the low biomarker frequency and high drug cost (Djalalov et al., 2014; Atherly et al., 2012), and first-line treatment for metastatic NSCLC, guided by multiplexed genetic testing for multiple biomarkers (i.e., EGFR mutation and ALK rearrangement), also leads to a high incremental cost-effectiveness ratio (Romanus et al., 2015).

For breast cancer, HER2 testing with adjuvant trastuzumab treatment for HER+ patients is shown to be cost-effective for patients with early-stage breast cancer (Lidgren et al., 2008). Elkin et al. (2004) evaluated such a strategy for metastatic breast cancer and identified the most cost-effective use of different types of tests. Multiple genes can be tested simultaneously to guide the treatment decision. Lyman et al. (2007) showed that treatment guided by a 21-gene recurrence score assay is cost-effective for early-stage breast cancer.

In addition to guiding therapeutic options, subtype testing also shows its value in disease prevention and early intervention. For example, it is well known that women with BRCA mutations are at significantly higher risks of developing breast or ovarian cancer (King et al., 2003). Thus, the BRCA mutation test enables the differentiation of screening and treatment strategies based on a patient's BRCA status. Previous studies have found that the BRCA test can be cost-effective in prevention of breast and ovarian cancers among certain populations with high BRCA mutation prevalence (Manchanda et al., 2015; Rubinstein et al., 2009), and in preventing the occurrence of secondary cancer among breast cancer survivors (Kwon et al., 2010).

Precision medicine based on genotype testing can also help to prevent adverse events and improve treatment safety. An early systematic review has found that use of pharmacogenomics could reduce adverse drug reactions (Phillips et al., 2001). For example, in the context of HIV treatment, genotypic antiretroviral resistance testing may guide the choice of initial and subsequent treatment to reduce drug resistance (Weinstein et al., 2001); HLA-B*5701 genetic screening can help to identify patients with a high risk of hypersensitivity to abacavir, and HLA-B*5701 genetic testing can guide first-line antiretroviral therapy (Schackman et al., 2008).

Another interesting example of precision medicine is genotype-guided dosing of the blood thinner warfarin. Due to marked interpatient variability of responses to the drug, it is difficult to establish the optimal dose of warfarin. Two gene variations have been identified as major predictors of responses (Higashi et al., 2002). Although earlier data did not provide sufficient evidence to support the routine use of genotype-guided warfarin dosing (Kangelaris et al., 2009; Sanderson et al., 2005), a later prospective comparative effectiveness study warfarin sensitivity genotyping found that genotype-guided dosing significantly reduces the hospitalization rate (Epstein et al., 2010). On the other hand, the cost-effectiveness of such a strategy remains indefinitive (Patrick et al., 2009; Eckman et al., 2009), which calls for a wise use of genotype-guided dosing in properly selected patients.

More examples of genetic testing and their health economic evaluations can be found in systematic reviews (Jarrett et al., 2006; Giacomini et al., 2003; Carlson et al., 2005; Rogowski, 2006). Although the above examples cover only a small subset of existing testing techniques (48,000+ tests for 16,000+ genes (The genetic testing registry)), we believe these examples illustrate some fundamental research questions in this area and the general modeling paradigms for biomarker testing and stratified intervention strategies. Before closing this section, we remark that, in addition to health outcomes, the value of diagnostic information and non-health outcomes are also important factors to consider in such decisions. A well-designed modeling analysis can help fully assess the predictive value and the best use of the biomarker testing beyond the analysis of cost-effectiveness, which could in turn further motivate the innovation of therapeutic agents targeting the identified biomarkers.

6.4 Artificial Intelligence-Based Approaches

In the era of data explosion, numerous levels of data in medicine—from the genetic level to patient medical records—have become available. This abundance of data could help better inform clinical decision-making, as it enables the use of artificial intelligence (AI)-based approaches to translate the information embedded in the data into knowledge and ultimately guide personalized clinical decisions. Indeed, AI-based approaches have been extensively studied and applied in various areas within healthcare, including image reading and processing, bioinformatics, and pharmacogenomics. Numerous models have been validated and used for risk prediction, disease diagnosis, classification, medical imaging process, treatment selection, and drug development.

The major distinction of artificial intelligence-based approaches from the approaches presented in the previous sections is that AI-based approaches typically (1) do not build upon a predefined model structure, but instead discover some information knowledge in the data and (2) do not explicitly model the progression of the disease. Instead of identifying the optimal solution based on a mathematical model that captures disease progression over time, AI-based approaches learn the underlying connection between a patient's health information and decisions directly from existing data. Once an AI model is trained, this trained model can then be used to tailor decisions for an individual patient.

Given that it is not possible to provide a comprehensive review of all the existing AI-based approaches and algorithms in personalized medicine, we limit our attention to two main types of learning in this section: *learning from existing health data* and *learning from trial-and-error*. In addition to describing key ideas in these approaches, we further draw several examples from the literature to illustrate how these methods are applied in specific clinical contexts.

6.4.1 Learning from Existing Health Data

With the growing adoption of electronic health records (EHR), large clinical datasets collected and stored in the electronic environment have become available. The availability of such extensive electronic medical records (EMR) motivates development of efficient learning algorithms to extract clinically useful knowledge possibly hidden in such datasets and improve clinical practice. EMR data and the potentially hidden relations in them can be learned in two different ways: via *supervised learning* and via *unsupervised learning*.

Supervised learning algorithms learn from datasets that contain "correct answers" to the output variables of interest (Friedman et al., 2001). These correct answers in some sense play the role of a teacher to correct any potential mistakes, hence the name "supervised learning." For example, using a large dataset that contains mammograghic and demographic information as well as cancer outcomes (0/1 indicating nonexistence/existence of cancer) from more than 65,000 women, Ayer et al. (2010) predicted the likelihood of having breast cancer. In particular, they built an artificial neural network using mammographic and demographic risk factors, train this model using cancer outcomes, and validate it using a 10-fold cross validation. Compared with radiologists, they found that their proposed methods increase the overall detection rate by about 10 percent while reducing false-positive rates by about 50 percent.

Another commonly used AI method in personalized medicine is case-based reasoning (CBR), which formalizes the process of solving a new problem based on experience from past cases. Due to its similarity to the reasoning process in real clinical practice, CBR has been a well-recognized and established method in clinical decision-making (Begum et al., 2011). For example, Miotto and Weng (2015) used CBR to identify patients eligible for clinical trials, where EHR data from past cases include medication, diagnosis, laboratory results, and clinical notes. Their results show that the CBR approach shows good classification accuracy and demonstrates the feasibility of using EHR data to determine patient's eligibility for clinical trials. In another problem context, Ahmed et al. (2013) applied the CBR to a pulse rate and oxygen saturation monitoring problem, where the CBR system collects an individual's data from sensors, predicts the health outcomes, and generates an alarm when an intervention is necessary.

Unlike supervised learning, *unsupervised learning* aims to mine some hidden structures and patterns in the data in the absence of a teacher, that is, true "output variables." As an example, Lasko et al. (2013) developed a feature-learning approach and apply it to a longitudinal uric-acid EMR data. Their approach identified distinct phenotypical features that suggest the existence of multiple disease subpopulations and accurately distinguished two known diseases. Miotto et al. (2016) developed a deep neural network to identify features that may predict various diseases. They applied their approach to a large-scale EHR dataset with 700,000+ patients and 40,000+ factors, and showed that the proposed approach can effectively predict multiple diseases (e.g., severe diabetes, schizophrenia, and various cancers), and is superior to several other feature learning methods (e.g., principle component analysis, k-means clustering).

6.4.2 Learning from Trial and Error

In addition to learning directly from data, another set of problems within AI deal with learning from interactions with the world. Such problems are typically studied by a machine learning approach known as *reinforcement learning* (Sutton et al., 1998). In reinforcement learning, the agent interacts with the (unknown) dynamic environment and learn to behave optimally through a smart "trial-and-error" approach.

In reinforcement learning (RL), the crucial trade-off is between *exploitation* of the best option based on up-to-date knowledge versus *exploration* of other options to acquire more information about the uncertain (and possibly dynamic) environment. In the clinical context, many sequential intervention problems face a similar trade-off: treat current patients with best known possible interventions under current knowledge versus explore new strategies to identify potentially better treatment options for future interventions. Unlike the sequential decision-making problems with an explicit disease dynamics model we reviewed earlier in Section 6.2, in RL-based studies, the underlying dynamics of the disease are usually unknown and are learned over time.

RL has been applied to many personalized treatment problems. For example, Wang and Powell (2016) present a knowledge gradient-based policy to guide the treatment through rapid learning, and apply it to a case study in knee replacement. Their results show that the optimal learning approach-guided assignment of physician and caregiver significantly improves success rates. Daskalaki et al. (2016) developed a model-free Actor-Critic (AC) algorithm for personalized insulin infusion and glucose regulation. They evaluate the AC algorithm using an FDA-accepted simulator for type 1 diabetes, and the results show that the AC algorithm adapts to individual patients' characteristics and maintains the glucose level at a targeted range.

RL-based methods have also been used in identifying optimal dynamic treatment regimens (DTR) and individualized treatment rules (ITR), mainly in the statistics community (see Schulte et al. [2014] for a detailed introduction of Q-learning and A-learning methods and their applications for learning optimal DTR). Several other studies use reinforcement learning for clinical trial design as an alternate to the standard randomized controlled trials for treatment evaluations (Murphy, 2003; 2005). For example, Zhao et al. (2011) developed a clinical reinforcement trial design of two lines of treatment for patients with lung cancer. Through simulation experiments, they showed that Q-learning-based RL successfully identifies the optimal DTR (optimal first- and second-line treatment, and timing of initiating second-line treatment) tailored to patient subpopulations. Deng et al. (2011) considered a clinical trial design problem as a minimax bandit model and developed an active learning policy to optimize the patient recruitment process (i.e., patient selection and treatment assignment) for learning ITR. Minsker et al. (2016) proposed an active learning framework to efficiently learn optimal ITRs by recruiting the "most informative" patient in the clinical trial. Simulation results showed that their proposed approach can learn the optimal ITR from data with significantly reduced size.

6.5 Conclusions and Emerging Future Research Directions

Unlike one-size-fits-all type approaches, personalized medicine-based approaches have the potential to improve overall health outcomes at a lower cost. The current state-of-the-art quantitative models in personalized medicine either explicitly consider disease progression or directly learn from data, and aim to adapt the intervention strategies to individual patients.

Recent advancements in computing, data storage, and wide implementation of EHRs have allowed for the collection of larger sets of individual-level digital data. Wide EHR adoption became possible only recently, after the Affordable Care Act. Given that collection of data itself does not lead to improved decisions, the next critical stage is the "meaningful use" of these rich datasets. The use of quantitative models allows for systematic analysis of this data and may lead to improved decisions. As designing RCTs typically requires enrolling thousands of patients over time with excessive costs, such quantitative PM models may be invaluable in supplementing RCTs or in offering an alternate evidence-based solution when the design of RCTs is unethical, time-prohibitive, or cost-prohibitive.

Given the aging population, increasing prevalence of chronic disease, and increased occurrences of multiple comorbid conditions, long-term followup on a regular basis becomes even more important. As wearable devices that enable continuous monitoring of various conditions become widely available, we anticipate the emergence of cloud-based algorithms that would allow near-real time personalized monitoring and control of patients.

Another potential promising direction is in developing evidence-based clinical practice guidelines for molecular testing for various diseases. As new biomarkers are discovered, testing strategies need to be identified for detecting these biomarkers, and for tailoring interventions based on such test results. Such clinical practice guidelines may address several open questions—Which patients should be tested for various gene mutations? When should a patient specimen be tested for mutations? Is the use of other molecular markers cost-effective for the entire population or only for specific subpopulations?

Another promising direction is the design of *one-person trials*. Traditional clinical trials involve thousands of people, which are not only time-consuming and costly, but which also typically yield results that apply to a large portion of patients. For example, in the context of cardiovascular diseases, most drugs are effective only in a small fraction (<10%) of the patient population, and the remaining majority of the patients (>90%) are unnecessarily exposed to side effects without any clinical benefit (Mukherjee et al., 2002). The availability of big data in healthcare has led to a heated discussion about a paradigm shift in trial designs. In particular, instead of N-patient trials, designing 1-person trials (or N-of-1 trials) is appealing. In such trials, person-level longitudinal data will be collected, and various alternative interventions will be tested to identify what works and what does not work for an individual patient, rather than populations (Schork, 2015). Indeed, physicians have long done these, but often in an ad hoc way. Wider availability of digital data and advanced quantitative models may lead to promising avenues in formalizing such a process and help in the design of one-person trials.

References

Ahmed, M.U., H. Banaee, and A. Loutfi. (2013) Health monitoring for elderly: An application using case-based reasoning and cluster analysis. *ISRN Artificial Intelligence*, 2013.

Akhavan-Tabatabaei, R., D.M. Sánchez, and T.G Yeung. (2016) A Markov decision process model for cervical cancer screening policies in Colombia. *Medical Decision Making*, p. 0272989X16670622.

Alagoz, O., L.M. Maillart, A.J. Schaefer, and M.S. Roberts. (2004) The optimal timing of living-donor liver transplantation. *Management Science*, 50 (10), 1420–1430.

Alagoz, O., L.M. Maillart, A.J. Schaefer, and M.S. Roberts. (2007) Determining the acceptance of cadaveric livers using an implicit model of the waiting list. *Operations Research*, 55 (1), 24–36.

Atherly, A. and D. Camidge. (2012) The cost-effectiveness of screening lung cancer patients for targeted drug sensitivity markers. *British journal of cancer*, 106 (6), 1100–1106.

Ayer, T., O. Alagoz, and N. Stout. (2012) OR Forum: A POMDP approach to personalize mammography screening decisions. *Operations Research*, 60 (5), 1019–1034.

Ayer, T., O. Alagoz, J. Chhatwal., J.W. Shavlik, C.E. Kahn, and E.S. Burnside. (2010) Breast cancer risk estimation with artificial neural networks revisited. *Cancer*, 116 (14), 3310–3321.

Ayer, T., O. Alagoz, N.K. Stout, and E.S Burnside. (2015) Heterogeneity in women's adherence and its role in optimal breast cancer screening policies. *Management Science*, 62 (5), 1339–1362.

Basu, A., J.J. Carlson, and D.L. Veenstra. (2016) A framework for prioritizing research investments in precision medicine. *Medical Decision Making*, 36 (5), 567–580.

Begum, S., M.U. Ahmed, P. Funk, N. Xiong, and M. Folke. (2011) Case-based reasoning systems in the health sciences: a survey of recent trends and developments. *IEEE Transactions on Systems, Man, and Cybernetics, Part C (Applications and Reviews)*, 41 (4), 421–434.

Carlson, J.J., N.B. Henrikson, D.L. Veenstra, and S.D. Ramsey. (2005) Economic analyses of human genetics services: a systematic review. *Genetics in Medicine*, 7 (8), 519–523.

Chen, Q., A. D., Staton, T., Ayer, D. A., Goldstein, J. L., Koff and C. R., Flowers. (2017) Exploring the potential cost-effectiveness of precision medicine treatment strategies for diffuse large B-cell lymphoma Leukemia & Lymphoma, 1–10.

Chhatwal, J., O. Alagoz, and E. Burnside. (2010) Optimal breast biopsy decision-making based on mammographic features and demographic factors. *Operations Research*, 58 (6), 1577–1591.

Daskalaki, E., P. Diem, and S.G. Mougiakakou. (2016) Model-free machine learning in biomedicine: Feasibility study in type 1 diabetes. *PloS one*, 11 (7), e0158 722.

Deng, K., J. Pineau, and S. Murphy. (2011) Active learning for developing personalized treatment, in *Proceedings of the Twenty-Seventh Conference on Uncertainty in Artificial Intelligence*, AUAI Press, pp. 161–168.

Djalalov, S., J. Beca, J.S. Hoch, M. Krahn, M.S. Tsao, J.C. Cutz, and N.B. Leighl. (2014) Cost effectiveness of eml4-alk fusion testing and first-line crizotinib treatment for patients with advanced alk-positive non–small-cell lung cancer. *Journal of Clinical Oncology*, 32 (10), 1012–1019.

Eckman, M.H., J. Rosand, S.M. Greenberg, and B.F. Gage. (2009) Cost-effectiveness of using pharmacogenetic information in warfarin dosing for patients with nonvalvular atrial fibrillation. *Annals of internal medicine*, 150 (2), 73–83.

Elkin, E.B., M.C. Weinstein, E.P. Winer, K.M. Kuntz, S.J. Schnitt, and J.C. Weeks. (2004) Her-2 testing and trastuzumab therapy for metastatic breast cancer: a cost-effectiveness analysis. *Journal of Clinical Oncology*, 22 (5), 854–863.

El-Osta, H. and R. Shackelford. (2015) Personalized treatment options for alk-positive metastatic non-small-cell lung cancer: potential role for ceritinib. *Pharmacogenomics and personalized medicine*, 8, 145.

Epstein, R.S., T.P. Moyer, R.E. Aubert, D.J. O'Kane, F. Xia, R.R. Verbrugge, B.F. Gage, and J.R. Teagarden, (2010) Warfarin genotyping reduces hospitalization rates: results from the mm-wes (medco-mayo warfarin effectiveness study). *Journal of the American College of Cardiology*, 55 (25), 2804–2812.

Erenay, F.S., O. Alagoz, and A. Said. (2014) Optimizing colonoscopy screening for colorectal cancer prevention and surveillance. *Manufacturing & Service Operations Management*, 16 (3), 381–400.

Friedman, J., T. Hastie, and R Tibshirani. (2001) *The elements of statistical learning*, vol. 1, Springer series in statistics Springer, Berlin.

Fu, K., D.D. Weisenburger, W.W. Choi, K.D. Perry, L.M. Smith, X. Shi, C.P. Hans, T.C. Greiner, P.J. Bierman, R.G. Bociek, *et al.* (2008) Addition of rituximab to standard chemotherapy improves the survival of both the germinal center b-cell–like and non–germinal center b-cell–like subtypes of diffuse large b-cell lymphoma. *Journal of Clinical Oncology*, 26 (28), 4587–4594.

Gail, M.H. and M.H Greene. (2000) Gail model and breast cancer. *The Lancet*, 355 (9208), 1017.

Garrod, A. (1902) The incidence of alkaptonuria: a study in chemical individuality. *The Lancet*, 160 (4137), 1616–1620.

Giacomini, M., F. Miller, and B.J. O'Brien,. (2003) Economic considerations for health insurance coverage of emerging genetic tests. *Public Health Genomics*, 6 (2), 61–73.

Grosse, S.D., S. Wordsworth, and K. Payne. (2008) Economic methods for valuing the outcomes of genetic testing: beyond cost-effectiveness analysis. *Genetics in Medicine*, 10 (9), 648–654.

Helm, J.E., M.S. Lavieri, M.P. Van Oyen, J.D. Stein, and D.C. Musch. (2015) Dynamic forecasting and control algorithms of glaucoma progression for clinician decision support. *Operations Research*, 63 (5), 979–999.

Higashi, M.K., D.L. Veenstra, L.M. Kondo, A.K. Wittkowsky, S.L. Srinouanprachanh, F.M. Farin, and A.E. Rettie. (2002) Association between cyp2c9 genetic variants and anticoagulation-related outcomes during warfarin therapy. *JAMA*, 287 (13), 1690–1698.

Ibrahim, R., B. Kucukyazici, V. Verter, M. Gendreau, and M. Blostein. (2016) Designing personalized treatment: An application to anticoagulation therapy. *Production and Operations Management*, 25 (5), 902–918.

Inwards, D.J., I.N. Micallef *et al.* (2014) Lenalidomide combined with r-chop overcomes negative prognostic impact of non–germinal center b-cell phenotype in newly diagnosed diffuse large b-cell lymphoma: A phase II study. *Journal of Clinical Oncology*, 33 (3), 251–257.

Jameson, J.L. and D.L. Longo. (2015) Precision medicine—personalized, problematic, and promising. *Obstetrical & Gynecological Survey*, 70 (10), 612–614.

Jarrett, J. and M. Mugford. (2006) Genetic health technology and economic evaluation. *Applied health economics and health policy*, 5 (1), 27–35.

Kangelaris, K.N., S. Bent, R.L. Nussbaum, D.A. Garcia, and J.A. Tice. (2009) Genetic testing before anticoagulation? A systematic review of pharmacogenetic dosing of warfarin. *Journal of general internal medicine*, 24 (5), 656–664.

King, M.C., J.H. Marks, J.B. Mandell *et al.* (2003) Breast and ovarian cancer risks due to inherited mutations in BRCA1 and BRCA2. *Science*, 302 (5645), 643–646.

Kotas, J. and A. Ghate. (2016) Response-guided dosing for rheumatoid arthritis. *IIE Transactions on Healthcare Systems Engineering*, 6 (1), 1–21.

Kwon, J.S., A.M. Gutierrez-Barrera, D. Young, C.C. Sun, M.S. Daniels, K.H. Lu, and B. Arun. (2010) Expanding the criteria for BRCA mutation testing in breast cancer survivors. *Journal of Clinical Oncology*, 28 (27), 4214–4220.

Lasko, T.A., J.C. Denny, and M.A. Levy. (2013) Computational phenotype discovery using unsupervised feature learning over noisy, sparse, and irregular clinical data. *PloS one*, 8 (6), e66 341.

Lavieri, M.S., M.L. Puterman, S. Tyldesley, and W.J. Morris. (2012) When to treat prostate cancer patients based on their psa dynamics. *IIE Transactions on Healthcare Systems Engineering*, 2 (1), 62–77.

Lidgren, M., B. Jönsson, C. Rehnberg, N. Willking, and J. Bergh. (2008) Cost-effectiveness of her2 testing and 1-year adjuvant trastuzumab therapy for early breast cancer. *Annals of oncology*, 19 (3), 487–495.

Lievre, A., J.B. Bachet, D. Le Corre, V. Boige, B. Landi, J.F. Emile, J.F. Côté, G. Tomasic, C. Penna, M. Ducreux *et al.* (2006) Kras mutation status is predictive of response to cetuximab therapy in colorectal cancer. *Cancer research*, 66 (8), 3992–3995.

Lyman, G.H., L.E. Cosler, N.M. Kuderer, and, J. Hornberger. (2007) Impact of a 21-gene rt-pcr assay on treatment decisions in early-stage breast cancer. *Cancer*, 109 (6), 1011–1018.

Manchanda, R., R. Legood, M. Burnell, A. McGuire, M. Raikou, K. Loggenberg, J. Wardle, S. Sanderson, S. Gessler, L. Side *et al.* (2015) Cost-effectiveness of population screening for BRCA mutations in Ashkenazi Jewish women compared with family history–based testing. *Journal of the National Cancer Institute*, 107 (1), dju380.

Mason, J.E., B.T. Denton, N.D. Shah, and S.A. Smith. (2014) Optimizing the simultaneous management of blood pressure and cholesterol for type 2 diabetes patients. *European Journal of Operational Research*, 233 (3), 727–738.

Minsker, S., Y.Q. Zhao, and G. Cheng. (2016) Active clinical trials for personalized medicine. *Journal of the American Statistical Association*, 111 (514), 875–887.

Miotto, R. and C. Weng. (2015) Case-based reasoning using electronic health records efficiently identifies eligible patients for clinical trials. *Journal of the American Medical Informatics Association*, 22 (e1), e141–e150.

Miotto, R., L. Li, B.A. Kidd, and J.T. Dudley. (2016) Deep patient: An unsupervised representation to predict the future of patients from the electronic health records. *Scientific reports*, 6. doi: 10.1038/srep26094.

Mukherjee, D. and E.J. Topol. (2002) Pharmacogenomics in cardiovascular diseases. *Progress in cardiovascular diseases*, 44 (6), 479–498.

Murphy, S.A. (2003) Optimal dynamic treatment regimes. *Journal of the Royal Statistical Society: Series B (Statistical Methodology)*, 65 (2), 331–355.

Murphy, S.A. (2005) An experimental design for the development of adaptive treatment strategies. *Statistics in medicine*, 24 (10), 1455–1481.

Nowakowski, G.S., B. LaPlant, W.R. Macon, C.B. Reeder, J.M. Foran, G.D. Nelson, C.A. Thompson, C.E. Rivera, D.J. Inwards, I.N. Micallef, *et al.* (2014). Lenalidomide combined with r-chop overcomes negative prognostic impact of non–germinal center b-cell phenotype in newly diagnosed diffuse large b-cell lymphoma: A phase II study. *Journal of Clinical Oncology*, 33 (3), 251–257.

Patrick, A.R., J. Avorn, and N.K. Choudhry. (2009) Cost-effectiveness of genotype-guided warfarin dosing for patients with atrial fibrillation. *Circulation: Cardiovascular Quality and Outcomes*, 2 (5), 429–436.

Petitti, D.B., E.E. Penhoet, J.E. Joy, *et al.* (2005) *Saving women's lives: strategies for improving breast cancer detection and diagnosis*, National Academies Press.

Phillips, K.A., D.L. Veenstra, E. Oren, J.K. Lee, and W. Sadee. (2001) Potential role of pharmacogenomics in reducing adverse drug reactions: a systematic review. *JAMA*, 286 (18), 2270–2279.

Rogowski, W. (2006) Genetic screening by DNA technology: a systematic review of health economic evidence. *International journal of technology assessment in health care*, 22 (03), 327–337.

Romanus, D., S. Cardarella, D. Cutler, M.B. Landrum, N.I. Lindeman, and G.S. Gazelle. (2015) Cost-effectiveness of multiplexed predictive biomarker screening in non-small-cell lung cancer. *Journal of Thoracic Oncology*, 10 (4), 586–594.

Rubinstein, W.S., H. Jiang, L. Dellefave, and A.W. Rademaker. (2009) Cost-effectiveness of population-based brca1/2 testing and ovarian cancer prevention for Ashkenazi Jews: a call for dialogue. *Genetics in Medicine*, 11 (9), 629–639.

Sanderson, S., J. Emery, and J. Higgins. (2005) Cyp2c9 gene variants, drug dose, and bleeding risk in warfarin-treated patients: A hugenet™ systematic review and meta-analysis. *Genetics in Medicine*, 7 (2), 97–104.

Sandikçi, B., L. Maillart, A. Schaefer, O. Alagoz, and M. Roberts. (2008) Estimating the patient's price of privacy in liver transplantation. *Operations Research*, 56 (6), 1393–1410.

Schackman, B.R., C.A. Scott, R.P. Walensky, E. Losina, K.A. Freedberg, and P.E. Sax. (2008) The cost-effectiveness of hla-b* 5701 genetic screening to guide initial antiretroviral therapy for HIV. *AIDS (London, England)*, 22 (15), 2025.

Schork, N.J. (2015) Personalized medicine: time for one-person trials. *Nature*, 520 (7549), 609–611.

Shaw, A.T., D.W. Kim, K. Nakagawa, T. Seto, L. Crinó, M.J. Ahn, T. De Pas, B. Besse, B.J. Solomon, F. Blackhall, *et al.* (2013) Crizotinib versus chemotherapy in advanced alk-positive lung cancer. *New England Journal of Medicine*, 368 (25), 2385–2394.

Shechter, S.M., M.D. Bailey, A.J. Schaefer, and M.S. Roberts. (2008) The optimal time to initiate HIV therapy under ordered health states. *Operations Research*, 56 (1), 20–33.

Shipp, M.A., K.N. Ross, P. Tamayo, A.P. Weng, J.L. Kutok, R.C. Aguiar, M. Gaasenbeek, M. Angelo, M. Reich, G.S. Pinkus, *et al.* (2002) Diffuse large b-cell lymphoma outcome prediction by gene-expression profiling and supervised machine learning. *Nature medicine*, 8 (1), 68–74.

Sinha, S., J. Kotas, and A. Ghate. (2016) Robust response-guided dosing. *Operations Research Letters*, 44 (3), 394–399.

Solomon, B.J., T. Mok, D.W. Kim, Y.L. Wu, K. Nakagawa, T. Mekhail, E. Felip, F. Cappuzzo, J. Paolini, T. Usari, *et al.* (2014) First-line crizotinib versus chemotherapy in alk-positive lung cancer. *New England Journal of Medicine*, 371 (23), 2167–2177.

Staton, A.D., Q. Chen, T. Ayer, D. Goldstein, J.L. Koff, and C.R. Flowers. (2015) Cost-effectiveness of subtype-based treatment strategies for diffuse large b-cell lymphoma patients (DLBCL). *Blood*, 126 (23), 4476–4476.

Sutton, R.S. and A.G. Barto. (1998) *Reinforcement learning: An introduction*, vol. 1, Cambridge: MIT press Cambridge.

The genetic testing registry, https://www.ncbi.nlm.nih.gov/GTR/. Accessed: 2017-02.

Tutton, R. (2012) Personalizing medicine: futures present and past. *Social Science & Medicine*, 75 (10), 1721–1728.

Wang, Y. and W. Powell. (2016) An optimal learning method for developing personalized treatment regimes. *arXiv preprint arXiv:1607.01462.*

Weinstein, M.C., S.J. Goldie, E. Losina, C.J. Cohen, J.D. Baxter, H. Zhang, A.D. Kimmel, and K.A. Freedberg. (2001) Use of genotypic resistance testing to guide HIV therapy: clinical impact and cost-effectiveness. *Annals of internal medicine*, 134 (6), 440–450.

Zhang, J., B. Denton, H. Balasubramanian, N. Shah, and B. Inman. (2012) Optimization of prostate biopsy referral decisions. *Manufacturing & Service Operations Management*, 14 (4), 529–547.

Zhao, Y., D. Zeng, M.A. Socinski, and M.R. Kosorok. (2011) Reinforcement learning strategies for clinical trials in nonsmall cell lung cancer. *Biometrics*, 67 (4), 1422–1433.

7

Global Health

Karthik V. Natarajan[1] *and Jayashankar M. Swaminathan*[2]

[1] *University of Minnesota*
[2] *University of North Carolina at Chapel Hill*

7.1 Introduction

Over the last twenty-five years, there has been an increased push and commitment from developed nations towards addressing some of the pressing health issues prevalent in developing countries. During this period, the total funding contribution from developed nations, bilateral agencies, and NGOs toward improving health conditions in developing countries witnessed a roughly 500 percent increase (from $6.8 billion in 1990 to $35.8 billion in 2014; Dieleman et al. 2014). The increase in funding, combined with concerted efforts and targeted interventions at the national, regional, and local levels have led to significant improvements in health conditions across the globe and saved millions of lives. However, the improvements have been uneven across countries, and in some cases, the disparities in care across regions, gender, and economic conditions have increased over this period. The uneven improvements and the increased disparities in some cases have led to a renewed focus on the three key pillars of resource allocation—efficiency, effectiveness, and equity (see Swaminathan, 2003; Savas 1978). Efficiency is defined as the ratio of inputs to outputs or outcomes. Effectiveness refers to how well the need for services are met; in other words, do service recipients receive what they requested? Finally, equity is tied to the fairness or equality of the services offered.

In many global health programs, resource allocation decisions are driven primarily by the notion of allocation efficiency, which is a systematic way to compare the costs relative to the health gains that are expected to be achieved through various interventions (Jamison et al., 2006). However, analyses focusing on allocation efficiency often suffer from one key limitation: they do not take into account the potential interactions between the interventions, which could lead to underestimating or overestimating the benefits of the

Handbook of Healthcare Analytics: Theoretical Minimum for Conducting 21st Century Research on Healthcare Operations, First Edition. Edited by Tinglong Dai and Sridhar Tayur.

interventions. More recent resource allocation models, including some of the ones discussed in this chapter, overcome this limitation by allowing for the possibility of interaction effects. Despite advances in improving allocation efficiency, a frequent criticism of these models is that they do not focus on the effectiveness and equity in allocation, often leading to widening gaps in access to prevention and treatment across different population groups (Johri and Norheim, 2012). More recently, there has been an increased push to explicitly incorporate equity constraints in resource allocation models. These models could serve as a valuable tool to policy-makers in exploring the efficiency-equity trade-off inherent in resource allocation decisions.

Depending on the level of decision-making (e.g., national, regional, etc.) and the underlying disease condition, many different types of resource allocation decisions arise in global health programs. Most of the existing literature in operations management, operations research, and public health focuses on allocation decisions for three main types of resources, namely, funding, inventory, and infrastructural capacity. In this survey, we will focus on these three types of resources, but we wish to point out that other types of resources (e.g., human resources) also play an important role in the operation and management of global health programs. Before providing details regarding the resource allocation models developed in the literature, we present a broad overview of some key dimensions along which these models differ from one another.

Prevention versus treatment programs: The nature and type of resource allocation decisions change significantly depending on whether a particular health program focuses on disease prevention or treatment. In the case of prevention programs, the goal is to minimize the number of new infections or cases; hence, the focus is on picking the right interventions (from a given set) to allocate resources. In the case of treatment programs, the goal is to provide treatment to as many people as possible to lower the disease burden and/or improve the quality of life of patients. In such programs, the resources available to provide treatment often have to be allocated among various groups of patients, and in some cases, resources need to be split among various entities that are involved in providing treatment.

Time horizon: Resource allocation decisions also change based on whether we look at single-period or multi-period models. In general, single-period models capture the impact of an intervention or resource allocation decision as an aggregated, one-time effect, as opposed to multi-period models, which explicitly model the time-evolution of the effect of the allocation decisions. Even within multi-period models, there are differences in terms of when the allocation decisions are made. In some cases, the allocation decision is made at the beginning of the planning horizon, whereas in others, the decision is made in every period, based on the most recent information available.

Deterministic versus stochastic models: Resource allocation models also differ in terms of taking into account the potential uncertainty in demand as well as the availability of resources. Several existing works assume deterministic demand and predictable resource availability, but a growing number of papers consider demand uncertainty and/or uncertainty in resource availability.

In what follows, we provide details of representative works that deal with resource allocation issues that arise in global health settings. For clarity and ease of exposition, we group the models based on the type of resource in question. In section 2, we discuss the issue of funding allocation in global health and some relevant papers. Sections 3 and 4 focus on inventory and capacity allocation in global health, respectively. In section 5, we discuss some future research directions and conclude the chapter.

7.2 Funding Allocation in Global Health Settings

The nature of funding allocation decisions and the underlying models that drive these decisions vary significantly between disease prevention and treatment programs. We first discuss some funding allocation models that focus on lowering disease incidence and the number of new infections.

7.2.1 Funding Allocation for Disease Prevention

Several researchers have focused on allocating limited funding toward interventions aimed at reducing the number of new infections and/or improving the quality of life for existing patients within a target population over a finite period of time. The interventions could be wide-ranging, serving a variety of purposes. For example, some interventions are aimed at reducing the "contact rate" between infected and susceptible individuals. Other interventions are aimed at changing the rate of disease progression for infected individuals. Interventions could also be carried out in order to move individuals from a high-risk group to a low-risk group for infection.

Zaric and Brandeau, (2001) study the problem of allocating limited funding among n interventions that could potentially reduce the negative impact from an epidemic. The target population consists of sub-populations (e.g., high-risk and low-risk groups), and each sub-population contains a mix of infected and uninfected individuals. A sub-population and disease state pair (for example, high-risk uninfected or high-risk infected) is referred to as a "compartment" and there could be contact both within and across compartments, leading to disease transmission. Through appropriate interventions, it is possible to influence the number of people in the different compartments at any given point in time. An attractive feature of Zaric and Brandeau, (2001) is that they allow for interaction effects across interventions — many earlier works in resource allocation (Weinstein and Zeckhauser, 1973; Chen and Bush, 1976;

Stinnett and Paltiel, 1996) assume that the benefits of interventions are independent and that all combination of interventions are feasible. Under such assumptions, it is optimal to pick interventions in the decreasing order of cost-effectiveness until the entire budget is consumed. However in reality, interventions frequently have interaction effects; it may not be possible, therefore, to isolate the benefits from each intervention.

In Zaric and Brandeau (2001), a key decision is the amount to be invested in each of the n interventions. The interventions go into effect instantaneously at time 0, but their effect on the compartment sizes (i.e., the number of people in the different compartments) lasts until time T. The relationship between the investment in the interventions and the parameters that impact the compartment sizes is referred to as the ***production function***. The time evolution of the compartment sizes and the effect of interventions on them are captured using a system of differential equations.

In global health contexts, it is well-known that disease conditions impact the quality of life. Accordingly, the authors assume that people in the different compartments have different quality adjustments for life years lived in a particular compartment. Zaric and Brandeau consider two objectives that could be relevant in epidemic settings: (1) maximize the total quality-adjusted life years experienced by the population until time T, and (2) minimize the number of new infections until time T. In general, deriving closed-form expressions for the compartment sizes as a function of the investments in interventions is challenging, making it difficult to analytically solve the above-described resource allocation problem. Hence, the authors develop first- and second-order approximations of the compartment sizes. Using those approximations, they derive optimal investment levels for some special cases of the resource allocation problem. For the general resource allocation problem, the authors propose four heuristics, including simulation and knapsack-based approaches. Based on a computational study, they evaluate the effectiveness of the compartment size approximations and perform a comparative analysis of the four heuristics.

In a related paper, Brandeau et al., (2003) considered the problem of allocating limited funding for epidemic control among multiple independent populations. The model studied in the 2003 paper is somewhat simpler than the one considered in Zaric and Brandeau, (2001). For example, Brandeau et al., (2003) consider only one type of intervention whereas Zaric and Brandeau, (2001) consider $n > 1$ potential interventions. Moreover, in Zaric and Brandeau (2001), contact can occur both within and across sub-populations, and the interventions can also have interaction effects. In Brandeau et al., (2003), the different population groups are independent (i.e., they do not come into contact with each other), and intervention in one population has no impact on the epidemic spread rate in another population. The simplified epidemic model is more tractable than the one considered in

Zaric and Brandeau, (2001); thus, the authors are able to develop analytical results regarding the structure of the optimal allocation policy.

Similar to Zaric and Brandeau (2001), Brandeau et al. (2003) considered two objective functions: (1) Maximize the total QALYs experienced (summed over all populations) over the T periods, and (2) minimize the number of new infections across all populations over the T periods. The key decision in Brandeau et al., (2003) is the amount invested in reducing the contact rate within each population; contact rates determine the rate of transmission between infected people and susceptible people who come in contact with them. The authors provide several theoretical results regarding the structure of the two objective functions with respect to the resource allocation levels. In addition, the authors characterize the structure of the optimal allocation policy for different types of cost functions; for example, investments to reduce the contact rate could exhibit increasing, decreasing, and constant returns to scale. For health programs that have increasing returns to scale, the resource allocation problem has an all-or-nothing greedy type of solution, whereas in the case of decreasing returns to scale, the allocation problem has an interior solution that could involve sharing the limited funding among all populations.

The two papers mentioned above focus on resource allocation at a single level. However, in reality, funding allocation for epidemic prevention frequently involves multiple levels, including allocation at the central, regional, and local levels. Lasry et al. (2007) studied multi-level funding allocation for epidemic control, specifically HIV prevention. They analyze a setting where a central authority has limited funding B available that needs to be split between two regions. There are two subpopulations within each region, namely, low-risk and high-risk groups, and both groups consist of a mix of adults and children. Taking the funding allocated to each region as given, the regional authorities decide how the available funding should be allocated between the two subpopulations. The funding allocated to each subpopulation can be used for two types of interventions: (1) Reducing the contact rate within the subpopulation (to reduce the transmission rate between infected and susceptible individuals), and (2) reducing the mother-to-children transmission rate in the case of newborns.

In Lasry et al. (2007), the objective is to identify the right mix of investments in the two interventions across subpopulations, to minimize the number of new infections until time T. The authors consider four possible versions of the two-stage allocation model. In the first version, the allocations at the central and regional levels are both done in an optimal fashion. The regional allocation decisions are taken into account by the central decision maker using backwards induction. In the second version, the central allocation is done optimally, but at the regional level, funding allocation is equity-based—in other words, the amount allocated to each subpopulation is proportional to the number of infected individuals within the subpopulation. In the third version, the central allocation is equity-based, whereas at the regional level, funding allocation is done optimally. In the fourth version, funding allocation at the central and regional levels are both equity-based. Based on a numerical study, the authors perform a comparative analysis of the four funding allocation schemes. They find that the performance gaps between allocation schemes 1 and 3 as well as 2 and 4 are both small (< 1%), while the gap between allocation schemes 2 and 3 is high (7%). This finding highlights the importance of making the right funding allocation decisions at the regional level and suggests that lower-level allocation is of much greater consequence than resource allocation decisions at higher levels as it relates to epidemic control.

Several complex epidemiological models have been used to study funding allocation problems in epidemic contexts, but there are few papers specifically devoted to developing allocation approaches suitable for implementation in practice. Richter et al. (2008), for instance, focus on allocating a given amount of HIV prevention funds among various priority groups (e.g., high-risk heterosexuals or female injection drug users) across different regions. The allocation decision is made based on two key inputs: (1) The number of new infections that could potentially be averted for any given priority group in a particular region, and (2) the relative importance of each priority group, as ranked by the community planning groups (CPG) within each region. These two factors are multiplied together to create what is known as a *potential impact index*. In addition to the potential impact index, information regarding the cost of offering a particular intervention to each priority group in the different regions is also required to make the allocation decision.

An attractive feature of the allocation model developed in Richter et al. (2008) is that along with the impact-based allocation focusing on efficiency, the model can also incorporate equity constraints. For example, it would be easy to set minimum and maximum limits on the funding allocated to the different priority groups across regions. Naturally, the addition of equity constraints could impact the number of potential new infections averted; therefore, the model sheds light onto the efficiency-equity trade-off as it relates to HIV prevention. The resource allocation model presented in Richter et al. (2008) has been implemented in the form of an Excel-based tool that could be used by state and local authorities to make HIV prevention resource allocation decisions.

Another paper that focuses on the efficiency-equity trade-off in HIV prevention funding allocation is Kaplan and Merson (2002). Given a fixed HIV prevention budget, the authors address the question of how much funding should be given to each risk group across different states within the country. States exhibit differences in terms of the annual number of new infections and the number of individuals in the different risk groups. The central focus is to understand the implications of the equity–based allocation scheme used in practice. Under the equity-based approach, the funding allocated to a particular risk group in a state is proportional to the number of new infections within that risk group in that state. The authors evaluate the performance of the equity–based allocation scheme against an allocation scheme that aims to maximize allocation efficiency.

Kaplan and Merson (2002) use a linear program to identify the optimal allocation levels. Their model is unique, in that they allow for a certain portion of the total funding to be earmarked for proportional allocation. This reserved funding will be distributed among the different risk groups across states in a equity–based fashion. The remaining funding is allocated with the goal of maximizing allocation efficiency. The authors vary the percentage of funds that are earmarked from 0 to 100 percent, which correspond to the cases of pure efficiency–based allocation and pure equity–based allocation, respectively. They find that a system with 60 percent earmarked funding achieves five sixths of the reduction in new infections obtained by pure efficiency-based allocation. This implies that moving away from pure equity-based allocation allows for significant improvements in health outcomes while still maintaining an acceptable level of equity and fairness in allocation.

Overall, funding allocation models for prevention programs generally operate under the assumptions of deterministic funding availability and predictable demand. However, the interactions among the different interventions and subpopulations often make it difficult to develop analytical solutions to the funding allocation problem. Thus, several authors have resorted to heuristics, and they numerically evaluate the performance of the proposed allocation approaches.

Next, we look at funding allocation models that are applicable to programs focusing on disease treatment. There is a wide variety and significant diversity among funding allocation models for disease treatment, in terms of the underlying disease condition, entities/interventions that are targets for funding allocation, and whether treatment involves caring for patients by offering an array of services or simply getting a product into the hands of targeted patients. In what follows, we provide some representative examples of funding allocation issues that arise in treatment programs under healthcare services and product settings, respectively.

7.2.2 Funding Allocation for Treatment of Disease Conditions

7.2.2.1 Service Settings

Griffin et al. (2008) analyzed a funding allocation problem that arises in the context of primary healthcare services. The paper focuses on the location and service offerings of community health centers (CHCs). Examples of primary care services offered by CHCs include general health (diabetes, blood pressure, asthma, arthritis, flu, hepatitis C, etc.), OBGyn, dental services, and mental health and substance abuse (M/SA) counseling. There are fixed costs associated with operating a CHC, and each service offering entails both fixed and variable costs. Given limited funding availability, the decision-maker needs to determine the optimal location of the CHCs as well as the type and amount of services to be offered at each center. The objective is to maximize the total weighted number of persons served, with the weight assigned to a disease being proportional to its impact on the overall health of individuals.

An attractive feature of the paper is the use of publicly available data sources to estimate the demand for the different health services at each CHC by incorporating disease prevalence rates and the probability of potential patients visiting a particular health center. Griffin et al. also used publicly available data to estimate the fixed and variable costs of service offerings at the different health centers. Additionally, the model incorporates geographical constraints; that is, only people within a certain distance are likely to access a health center, even if the desired services are offered. Based on data available from the state of Georgia, the authors analyzed the impact of optimal facility location and service level decisions. They compared the network configuration derived from their mixed integer linear programming model to the existing CHC network using different performance measures, including total percent demand served for a given budget, number of uninsured served, and number of new people served. Performance improvements range between 15–20 percent for all measures when compared to the existing CHC network. The authors also compared the optimal solution to different heuristics, including making facility location decisions based on the number of uninsured people in a given area or using the medically underserved areas (MUA) index.

Deo et al. (2015) studied a funding allocation and planning problem for HIV screening, testing and care at the Veterans Health Administration (VA). They focus on identifying the appropriate screening rate for patients and determining the right staff level at the screening, testing and clinical care areas. Patients who access the VA are of two types: ones who have no opportunistic infections and who are asymptotic and ones who have opportunistic infections and who display symptoms. They assumed that patients who display symptoms are always tested. Hence, the screening rate decision is relevant only in the case of patients who are asymptotic.

There are costs associated with testing a patient and providing care, which could change with the patient's health state. In addition, there are labor costs that include the salaries paid to physicians, nurses, and lab technicians. The VA has a limited budget, and its objective is to maximize the total QALYs gained across the entire patient population over a finite planning horizon.

The above-described funding allocation and planning problem is hard to solve, and determining the optimal solution is computationally intensive. Thus, the authors develop four heuristics that could be implemented in practice and evaluate the performance of the heuristics relative to an upper bound. Based on an extensive computational study, they find that all four heuristics perform well, with an average performance gap of 1.5 percent.

Mehrotra and Natarajan (2016) analyzed funding allocation and incentive design issues that arise in budget-constrained humanitarian healthcare programs that offer a particular service (e.g., immunization, maternal health services, etc.) to a target population. In their work, the focus is on allocating the available funding between the supply and demand sides. Funding allocated to the supply side is targeted at increasing the availability of healthcare services whereas demand-side funding is utilized to mobilize demand for the services that are offered. In developing countries, humanitarian and non-profit organizations frequently enter into contracts with private providers to deliver healthcare services, and the focus of their work is on such contracted settings. More specifically, they consider linear performance-based contracts with the healthcare provider where the provider receives a fixed amount, which is adjusted to account for the quality of care provided, for every patient treated. On the demand side, they consider per-capita incentives (e.g., vouchers or conditional cash transfers) for patients to encourage them to seek care.

Mehrotra and Natarajan developed a two-stage model that captures the interaction between the humanitarian healthcare organization, the healthcare provider, and patients. In their model, the provider decides the service rate and service quality in response to the incentive offered by the humanitarian organization. Patients decide whether or not to seek care depending on the per capita offered by the humanitarian organization and the opportunity cost of seeking care, including waiting times. The organization has limited funding available and the goal is to identify the right incentives to offer to the provider and patients, to maximize the number of people treated (weighted by the quality of care). Mehrotra and Natarajan (2016) found that relative to some incentive schemes commonly used in practice, humanitarian organizations can improve program performance by as much as 200 percent by using the right combination of incentives for patients and the provider. They also find that fundraising efforts will yield little to no benefits unless the right incentives are in place for patients to seek care and for providers to offer the best possible care.

One feature that is different in Mehrotra and Natarajan (2016) relative to the other two papers discussed in this section is the focus on performance improvement through incentive design. Traditionally, resource allocation models have focused on identifying the optimal allocation level among a fixed set of entities/interventions, and the central idea behind these models is that an increased allocation to any given entity/intervention will naturally lead to improvements in system performance, ceteris paribus. This assumption is likely to be valid in centralized systems where the decision-maker can directly control how investments in interventions/entities translate into health outcomes. However, in decentralized systems, there is an added layer of complexity. In addition to making allocation decisions, the decision-maker needs to design the right contract to incentivize the agents so that the allocated funds are put to the best use to achieve the desired health outcomes. In the following section, we look at funding allocation in product settings and discuss incentive-design issues that arise in decentralized global health settings.

7.2.2.2 Product Settings

Taylor and Xiao (2014) consider the problem of allocating donor funding in the form of subsidies to improve the availability of malaria drugs. The product is sold through private profit-maximizing retailers. The authors consider an infinite horizon setting, and the market condition in period t is given by M_t. They assume that $M_1, M_2, \ldots$ are independent and identically distributed. In every period, after observing the realized value of the market condition m, the retailer sets price p, resulting in demand $D(m, p)$. In addition to setting the price, the retailer decides how much to order. Although the price is set after observing the market condition m, the ordering decision is made before m is known.

The donor's objective is to maximize sales/consumption of the malaria drug subject to a budget constraint. The donor achieves this objective by designing sales and purchase subsidies for the retailer subject to the constraint that the sum of the expected per-period purchase subsidy payment and the expected per-period sales subsidy payment cannot exceed the budget available. One of the key results is that the donor should offer only purchase subsidy and no sales subsidy should be provided. This result holds true for several extensions of the base model, for example, multiple heterogeneous retailers, inventory perishability, and cases where the retailer sets the price before the market condition is realized.

Natarajan and Swaminathan (2016) analyzed the operations of a humanitarian organization offering a health product (e.g., malaria bed nets, reproductive health supplies) to people within a particular community. The organization was budget-constrained, and the authors analyzed how the limited funding should be allocated between procuring inventory and engaging in activities to mobilize demand. Identifying the right balance between inventory procurement and demand mobilization was important in ensuring that the health product reaches as many people as possible, given the limited funding availability.

Using a single-period model with effort-dependent (unpredictable) demand, they studied the above-described funding allocation problem. Relative to the supply-side focused allocation that is frequently observed in practice, the authors found that by optimally allocating resources between demand mobilization and inventory procurement, program coverage (defined as the number of people served) can be increased significantly, by as much as 100 percent in some cases.

Oftentimes, in developing countries, humanitarian organizations are not directly involved in demand mobilization. Rather, demand mobilization is carried out by agents, for example, community health workers or public health employees. For such decentralized settings, Natarajan and Swaminathan (2016) focused on identifying the optimal form of contract to motivate agents to engage in demand mobilization. They find that a bonus contract (or a contract that closely resembles the bonus contract) is the optimal contract in decentralized settings. In addition, they numerically evaluate how some contracts commonly used in practice perform relative to the bonus contract.

Before concluding this section, we wish to highlight the work by Alistar et al. (2014). The papers discussed so far focus on resource allocation in either prevention or treatment settings. However, Alistar et al. (2014) is unique, in that the authors considered funding allocation between prevention and treatment interventions for HIV epidemic control. The funding allocated toward prevention reduced the sufficient contact rate for infection transmission between infected and susceptible individuals. The funds allocated for treatment reduce the infectivity of treated infected individuals. The overall objective was to minimize the "basic reproduction number," a measure that indicates whether the disease will spread to the entire population or eventually fizzle out over time.

In Alistar et al. (2014), the authors presented structural results regarding the optimal funding allocation for prevention and treatment for several settings, including single population, multiple non-interacting populations, and two interacting populations. In addition to presenting the analytical results, they conducted sensitivity analysis to investigate the impact of different input parameters, including the cost and effectiveness of interventions. An attractive feature of their work is the use of real data from two countries to estimate the parameters of the epidemiological model used in the sensitivity analysis.

In the next section, we look at inventory allocation models for global health settings. As we did in this section, we look at inventory allocation issues that arise in disease prevention and treatment programs.

7.3 Inventory Allocation in Global Health Settings

7.3.1 Inventory Allocation for Disease Prevention

Samii et al. (2012) analyze inventory allocation and reservation policies for influenza vaccines. The vaccine is used to immunize two classes of customers: high priority and low priority. The demand from each priority class is unpredictable, and the total available inventory is limited, with no replenishment opportunities within the time frame under consideration. In this context, inventory allocation and reservation assume significance because in some cases, it might be beneficial to reserve a certain amount of inventory to serve the high-priority patients who might show up in the future.

Samii et al. (2012) considered a continuous time, finite horizon model to study the inventory allocation and reservation problem. Demand from the two priority classes modeled using a Poisson distribution. The authors focused on comparing the performance of three allocation mechanisms that could be potentially used in practice. Under the partitioned allocation (PA) mechanism, r units of inventory are reserved exclusively for high priority patients and $x - r$ units are reserved for the low-priority class (assuming total vaccine availability is x units). Under standard nesting (SN), high-priority patients first consume the r units exclusively reserved for that class. Once the r units are exhausted, then both the priority classes compete on a first-come, first-served basis for any remaining unreserved vaccine inventory. Finally, under theft nesting (TN), patients from both priority classes first compete for the unreserved vaccine inventory. Once the unreserved inventory is exhausted, only high-priority patients are served from the reserved inventory.

The authors developed exact expressions for the fill rate and service rate under the three allocation schemes. Then using these expressions, they investigate how the fill rate and service rate for the two classes differ under the different allocation schemes for various starting inventory levels and demand rates. They found that there is no dominant allocation mechanism that consistently outperforms — different allocation mechanisms emerge as the best, depending on the demand rate and starting inventory level.

Smalley et al. (2015) considered vaccine allocation strategies to minimize the incidence of cholera. The target population consisted of those living in regions classified based on their risk profile, that is, regions at a high-risk, medium-risk, and low-risk of acquiring the disease in the absence of vaccinations. Each region is further subdivided based on age (1–4 years, 5–14 years and >15 years). The disease incidence rate varied for each age group and risk-profile combination. Administering the vaccination has the potential to lower the disease incidence rate, but the model allows for the possibility that vaccinations may not be perfect; in other words, they may have less than 100 percent efficacy.

The authors develop a mixed integer programming model to determine the optimal vaccine allocation strategy to minimize the cases of cholera over a finite time period. Using data from Bangladesh as a case study, they analyze the effectiveness of the optimal allocation strategy by comparing it to strategies that allocate based only on age or region. Further, they analyze how changes in vaccine efficacy and increase in vaccine supply impact the number of number of new cases of cholera over a finite time period.

Smalley et al. (2015) focused on inventory allocation strategies during epidemics in an intracountry context. However, some epidemics have the potential to spread on a global scale. In such cases, it is critical to take steps to prevent the spread of the disease beyond the country(ies) of origin to reduce the possibility of a pandemic. Global reallocation of stockpiles of drugs and vaccines is an important element of this effort and forms the focus of the next paper.

Sun et al. (2009) analyzed inventory reallocation strategies for minimizing the number of new infections over a finite time period in the case of influenza pandemics. The pandemic is assumed to start in country 0 and has the potential to spread to other countries $1,2,\ldots,m$. Only country 0 has infected individuals at time $t = 0$ but over time, the disease could spread both within and across countries. The inventory reallocation question arises because country 0 has no stockpile of antiviral drugs but other countries $1, 2,\ldots, m$ have limited stockpiles. The drug has the potential to reduce susceptibility to infection in the case of uninfected individuals and reduce the infectiousness of infected individuals. By donating their limited stockpiles to country 0, each country can increase the possibility of the disease being confined within country "0." However, by donating, they run the risk of not having enough stock on hand to treat their own population in case the disease spreads beyond country 0.

Sun et al. (2009) assumed that the population size remains the same over time within each country. They used a two-period model with an uncertain number of new infections in each country, where the number of new infections is modeled using a binomial distribution with allocation-dependent success probability. The objective was to minimize the number of new infections within a country, which is equivalent to maximizing the number of susceptible/uninfected individuals, given the fixed population assumption. Each country needs to decide how much of the stockpile to retain to serve its own population and how much to donate to other countries, including country 0.

The paper provides several analytical results regarding the optimal allocation. For example, they show that when the between-country transmission rate is small enough, no country will donate to a country other than country 0. Moreover, if the within-country transmission rate is less than a certain threshold, then it is optimal for the country to give all of its stockpile to country 0. Otherwise, it is best for the country to retain all of its stockpile. Through an extensive numerical study, the authors conclude that selfish, decentralized allocation (described above) leads to the same allocation as in the centralized setting (where a central planner allocates all the stockpiles) in roughly 50 percent of the cases. However, in other cases, the allocations do not match, resulting in a significant negative impact on the number of new infections.

Next, we look at inventory allocation models in global health programs that focus on disease treatment. Though the specific model details are different, there are some common themes among the papers, which we outline in the next section.

7.3.2 Inventory Allocation for Treatment of Disease Conditions

A common feature across all the resource allocation models that we have discussed so far is the assumption that the amount of resources available to be allocated is known with certainty. In addition, the aforementioned papers assume that the resources are available to the decision-maker in entirety before any allocation decision is made. However as Swaminathan et al. 2009 point out, in many settings, there is significant uncertainty about how many units of resources are available, and these resources may not become available as they are needed. Moreover, the resources may become available in small chunks over time, not all at once up front. Such uncertainty and delays in resource availability make operations planning difficult, leading to significant inefficiencies and reducing the potential value derived from the available resources (Swaminathan et al., 2009). The uncertainty and delays in resource availability also create particular challenges for resource allocation in settings where the resource in question has to be allocated between different groups of patients/recipients. In such settings, the effect of treatment often varies across the different groups of patients. If future resource availability is uncertain, then decision-makers have to think about whether it would be better to use all resources available on-hand to meet current demand or whether there is value in reserving a portion of the available resources to meet future demand from certain groups of patients. The following two papers tackle the problem of allocating inventory among different patient groups in settings where the future inventory availability is unpredictable.

Deo et al. (2017) analyze an inventory allocation problem that arises in HIV programs. More specifically, the program receives a random amount of ARV drugs in every period, and the program administration needs to identify the best way to allocate this limited amount of ARV drugs between two groups of patients: previously treated and previously untreated. Given that future supply is unpredictable, they might also reserve a certain amount of drugs for future periods, even if that means not treating some patients today. Allocating the drugs to previously treated patients can prevent treatment interruption and the associated complications. However, this could imply delaying the initiation of treatment for previously untreated patients, which could result in health deterioration and lower quality of life. This trade-off is a key factor that influences the inventory allocation decision.

If treatment is interrupted, patients develop drug resistance, captured by the parameter γ. $\gamma=0$ refers to the case where patients do not develop drug resistance, and $\gamma=1$ implies that treatment interruptions always lead to drug resistance. Deo et al. (2017) used a multi-period stochastic dynamic program to analyze the inventory allocation problem. The objective is to maximize the quality of life across a fixed patient population over a time horizon of N periods. Identifying the optimal policy is difficult for problems with more than two periods because the optimal policy depends critically on the drug-resistance coefficient. The authors therefore look at some special cases of the inventory allocation problem, including problems with two periods and the general N-period allocation problem with $\gamma=0$ and $\gamma=1$. For an N-period problem with $0 < \gamma < 1$, the authors propose a heuristic (called the two-period heuristic) based on the structure of the optimal policy for the special cases. In addition to considering the two-period heuristic, the authors consider a safety-stock heuristic motivated by practice. The safety-stock heuristic sets aside enough so that all patients who are currently in the "treated" group will continue to receive treatment in the next period. The authors perform a computational study to evaluate the performance of the heuristics and find that the two-period heuristic performs particularly well (less than 4% performance gap) for all realistic combinations of parameter values.

Natarajan and Swaminathan (2017) considered inventory allocation and rationing issues that arise in multi-treatment humanitarian health settings with resource constraints. In 'multi-treatment' settings, each patient/customer requires more than one unit or dosage of the product for complete cure. The number of doses required for complete cure and the treatment response depend on the patient's health state. Examples include tuberculosis and the treatment protocol for malnutrition. In their work, the total funding available to procure inventory is limited, and the funding is received in installments throughout the planning period, with uncertainty in terms of both the installment amounts and installment timing. The funding dynamics in Natarajan and Swaminathan (2017) are similar to Natarajan and Swaminathan (2014) but the key difference is that in Natarajan and Swaminathan (2014), patients/customers are homogeneous in their health state; hence, the issue of resource allocation between patients in the different health states does not arise. However, when patients are heterogeneous in terms of their health states and the available inventory is limited, humanitarian organizations need to determine the best strategy to allocate the limited inventory between patients in the different health states who are currently seeking treatment. Moreover, in light of the future funding uncertainty, organizations also need to think about whether it would be valuable to reserve a certain portion of the funding available on hand to treat the more severe patients who might seek care in the future periods.

Natarajan and Swaminathan (2017) use a multi-period stochastic dynamic program with funding constraints to analyze the multi-treatment inventory allocation problem. In their model, a random number of new patients enter the system in every period, and they can be in either a less-severe health state or a more-severe state. Depending on both treatment and non-treatment, health state transitions take place, and there is a disability score associated with being in each health state. The objective is to allocate the available inventory between patients in the two health states in every period, to minimize the disease-adjusted life periods lost over a finite time horizon.

The authors present analytical results regarding the impact of funding timing and funding uncertainty on the disease-adjusted life periods lost. However, determining the optimal inventory allocation strategy is difficult for problems with more than two periods, so the authors develop two heuristics that humanitarian organizations can use to make inventory allocation decisions.

Both heuristics perform significantly better (up to 36.2% improvement) than the first-come, first-served heuristic commonly used in practice. In addition to developing new heuristics, they present several interesting findings based on a numerical study regarding the impact of funding uncertainty and delays in donor funding.

Yang et al. (2013) developed an optimization model to determine which children (from a cohort) should receive treatment for malnutrition, given limited funding availability to procure inventory. In their model, the funding can be used to procure either ready-to-use therapeutic food or supplemental food, both of which are given to children suffering from malnutrition. In Yang et al. (2013), there is no uncertainty with respect to demand or funding availability. They capture the health state of a child using height-for-age (HAZ) and weight-for-height (WHZ) scores, and they model the evolution of the HAZ and WHZ scores under both treatment and nontreatment.

Using a multi-period dynamic programming model, they analyze the problem of allocating a limited amount of ready-to-use therapeutic or supplemental food among a fixed cohort of children over a finite time period T. Identifying the optimal allocation strategy is computationally intensive and difficult for reasonable-sized problems. Hence, the authors focus attention on a restricted class of policies where the decision to provide ready-to-use therapeutic food (or supplemental food or no treatment) depends on whether a child's health score, obtained as a function of the HAZ and WHZ numbers, is above or below a certain threshold. Through a numerical study, they find that the proposed allocation policy can lead to a 9 percent reduction in the disease-adjusted life years lost relative to benchmark policies currently used in practice.

Based on the three papers discussed in this section, we can identify a common framework that applies to inventory allocation models in disease treatment settings. In such models, the key decision is how to allocate a limited amount of inventory among patients who are in different stages of a particular health condition. Depending on both treatment and nontreatment, health state transitions take place. The objective is to make inventory allocation decisions to improve health outcomes. Although this common framework does apply to all three papers discussed in this section, the specific modeling details and application contexts are different, leading to differences in their proposed solution approaches and heuristics.

The aforementioned papers discussed in this section focus on inventory allocation strategies that maximize allocation efficiency. However, they do not take into account the other two pillars of resource allocation, namely effectiveness and equity. Swaminathan et al. (2004) are among the few who focus on all three pillars as they relate to inventory allocation. The authors describe the drug-allocation policies that were developed for the Medpin program in California. The Medpin program received over $171 million worth of drugs from 21 different companies as part of a settlement; the program's resulting objective was to distribute the drugs to different clinics, hospitals, and non-profit health centers in a fair and equitable fashion.

Swaminathan et al. (2004) present a nonlinear optimization model to make the allocation decision. The optimization model has two objectives: the first one focuses on maximizing allocation efficiency (by minimizing the quantity of drugs that remain unallocated), and the second objective is to minimize the difference between allocations made and the weighted orders from clinics, thereby focusing on effectiveness and equity. The model also takes into account several important constraints that are relevant in practice. For example, every company will make available only a pre-agreed quantity of a certain drug in every period and there could also be an upper limit on the total dollar amount of drugs that can be requested from a company in any given period. In addition, there could be minimum order quantity restrictions for the clinics and hospitals. Despite the numerous practical constraints, the drug allocation mechanism reported in Swaminathan et al. (2004) proved to be successful in allocating almost 99 percent of the drugs provided to the program.

In the next section, we look at the third type of resource allocation decision that arises in global health settings, namely infrastructural capacity.

7.4 Capacity Allocation in Global Health Settings

Few papers study capacity allocation issues in global health contexts, and these papers tend to focus on resources that are available to clinics to treat or address certain health conditions.

Deo et al. (2013) analyzed the problem of how available clinic capacity should be allocated to maximize health outcomes in a chronic care setting, more specifically childhood asthma. The clinic has fixed capacity C, and the capacity has to be allocated among a fixed population of I patients. The capacity allocation is done through the decision to either treat or not treat a particular patient in a given period. When making the decision to schedule a patient, the healthcare provider does not know the health state with certainty. Instead, the healthcare provider has a belief system that captures the probability of the patient being in health states $0, 1, 2, \dots, K-1$. Different transition matrices govern the health transitions in the presence and absence of treatment.

In Deo et al. (2013), the objective was to maximize the quality of life (QoL) across the entire population over a finite time period. Each health state has an associated quality score and naturally, the better the health state, higher the quality score. The capacity allocation problem described above is PSPACE-complete, making it analytically intractable. Thus, the authors derived the optimal capacity allocation policy for a problem with two health states. For problems with multiple health states, the authors showed structural properties of the optimal policy for settings where the transition matrices satisfy certain properties.

For more general cases, the authors considered myopic heuristics. They identified conditions under which the myopic policy is optimal. For settings where the myopic policy is not optimal, the authors characterized the goodness of the myopic heuristic using a numerical study. The computational study was carried out using a model calibrated with data from the Mobile C.A.R.E Foundation (MCF). They found that the average optimality gap is less than 0.40 percent. Moreover, their analysis indicated that the myopic heuristic can improve health outcomes by up to 15 percent over policies currently employed in practice.

McCoy and Lee (2014) analyzed a transportation capacity allocation problem that frequently arises in humanitarian healthcare programs in developing countries. Oftentimes, healthcare clinics are located in urban centers, and people living in rural areas face numerous difficulties in accessing these clinics. One strategy to reduce the disparity in care is for the clinic to conduct outreach visits to rural areas, but clinics typically have limited transportation capacity at their disposal to perform outreach. McCoy and Lee (2014) analyzed how a clinic should allocate the limited transportation capacity between different outreach sites within its catchment area. The relative benefit of visiting each outreach site could be different based on a variety of factors, and each visit to an outreach site consumes a certain amount of transportation capacity. The decision variables correspond to how many outreach visits to allocate to each site, given a fixed transportation capacity. The paper considers maximizing α-fairness as the objective. When $\alpha = 0$, the focus is on maximizing allocation efficiency. $\alpha = 1$ implies proportionally fair allocation (proportional to the value derived from visiting an outreach site), and $\alpha = \infty$ means egalitarian (i.e., equal) allocation. Hence, by increasing α from 0 to ∞, the paper offers insights into the efficiency versus fairness trade-off involved in health delivery fleet management.

McCoy and Lee (2014) demonstrate that at α=0, only the outreach site with the highest benefit–cost ratio is allocated all the visits and other sites get zero visits. As α increases, the allocation becomes more uniform until $\alpha = \infty$, at which point the allocation is totally egalitarian (equal allocation). The paper also considers extensions to the base model, including the case where there is an alternate (slower) mode of transportation available and when the value of visiting additional sites exhibits a diminishing rate of return.

The authors extended the single-clinic capacity allocation problem to a two-stage allocation problem. In the two-stage problem, a central planner has access to M units of transportation capacity. This capacity is to be allocated among N different clinics, which in turn decide how to use the capacity allocated to them to conduct visits to outreach sites within their catchment area. In the centralized case, the central planner directly decides how many visits to allocate to each outreach site across the N clinics. In the decentralized case, the central planner decides the capacity allocation to each clinic. The clinics then independently decide how to allocate that capacity for outreach visits within their catchment area. Using field data from Riders for Health, a not-for-profit organization, the authors analyzed how the status quo allocation differs from the allocation proposed by the decentralized two-stage model in terms of total number of outreach visits, equity in allocation, and percentage of sites visited. They found that the two-stage model is slightly lower in efficiency (i.e., number of site visits) but leads to significant improvements in fairness and coverage.

7.5 Conclusions and Future Directions

Identifying the best strategies to allocate the available resources is critically important to advance global health outcomes, especially at a time when aid funding to developing countries is beginning to flatline. In this chapter, we have described some representative examples of models that have been developed to make resource allocation decisions in disease prevention and treatment settings. These models have contributed immensely to the theory and practice of global health resource allocation. However, several avenues and directions are open for future research. First, allocation models focusing on disease prevention assume that the effects of interventions are known with certainty. However, the effects of new interventions and treatments may not be fully known in the initial stages, and additional information regarding their efficacy may become available over time. A potential avenue for future research is to develop dynamic resource allocation models with learning effects where the efficacy of certain interventions is revealed over time. Such models could be especially useful in settings where newly–developed interventions are to be considered alongside existing interventions for resource allocation decisions. The decision-maker in these settings faces an exploration-versus-exploitation trade-off because learning the efficacy of the newly developed interventions involves investing resources in the new interventions as opposed to investing in an intervention with a known efficacy.

Second, current resource allocation models do not consider the possibility that resource availability may evolve over time. This is especially true with respect to funding availability because funding for a particular disease often changes dynamically, based on changes in donor priorities and preferences. For example, sudden disasters like earthquakes and hurricanes or disease outbreaks (e.g., ebola) could divert resources from long-term development programs. In the aftermath of such events, the funding outlook of global health organizations remains fluid, and information regarding future funding availability evolves over time as the response to the disaster or disease outbreak gets underway. Future research could focus on developing models to make resource allocation decisions in settings where the uncertainty around future funding availability dynamically evolves over time.

Finally, there is a growing need for resource allocation models that can incorporate multiple objectives (i.e., efficiency, effectiveness, and equity) and support evidence–based decision-making by policy makers. Some existing papers, including the ones discussed in this chapter, explicitly consider equity constraints, but more work is needed. For example, discrepancies in access to treatments (tied to equity of allocation) between the different patient groups could impact future demand from certain groups; consequently, it would be valuable to develop models that take into account the effect of allocation equity on future demand. In a similar vein, by focusing solely on improving allocation efficiency, decision-makers may fail to take into account the preferences and needs of the target population (tied to the effectiveness of the allocation), which in turn may impact future demand. Understanding and accounting for the impact of allocation effectiveness on future demand is another potential area for future research.

References

Alistar, S.S., E.F. Long, M.L. Brandeau, E. J. Beck. (2014). HIV epidemic control—a model for optimal allocation of prevention and treatment resources. *Health Care Management Science* 17(2) 162–181.

Brandeau, M.L., G.S. Zaric, A. Richter. (2003). Resource allocation for control of infectious diseases in multiple independent populations: beyond cost-effectiveness analysis. *Journal of Health Economics* 22(4) 575–598.

Chen, M.M., J.W. Bush. (1976). Maximizing health system output with political and administrative constraints using mathematical programming. *Inquiry* 13(3) 215–227.

Deo, S., C.J. Corbett, S. Mehta. (2017). *Dynamic allocation of scarce resources under supply uncertainty*. Working paper, Indian School of Business.

Deo, S., S. Iravani, T. Jiang, K. Smilowitz, S. Samuelson. (2013). Improving health outcomes through better capacity allocation in a community-based chronic care model. *Operations Research* 61(6) 1277–1294.

Deo, S., K. Rajaram, S. Rath, U.S. Karmarkar, M.B. Goetz. (2015). Planning for HIV screening, testing, and care at the Veterans Health Administration. *Operations Research* 63(2) 287–304.

Dieleman, J.L., C.M. Graves, T. Templin, E. Johnson, R. Baral, K. Leach-Kemon, A.M. Haakenstad, C.J.L. Murray. (2014). Global health development assistance remained steady in 2013 but did not align with recipients disease burden. *Health Affairs* 33(5): 878–886.

Griffin, P.M., C.R. Scherrer, J.L. Swann. (2008). Optimization of community health center locations and service offerings with statistical need estimation. *IIE Transactions* 40(9) 880–892.

Jamison, D.T., Breman J.G., A.R. Measham. (2006). *Priorities in health.* Washington (DC): The International Bank for Reconstruction and Development/The World Bank.

Johri, M., O.F. Norheim. (2012). Can cost-effectiveness analysis integrate concerns for equity? Systematic review. *International Journal of Technology Assessment in Health Care* 28(2) 125–132.

Kaplan, E.H., M.H. Merson. (2002). Allocating HIV-prevention resources: balancing efficiency and equity. *American Journal of Public Health* 92(12) 1905–1907.

Lasry, A., G.S. Zaric, M.W. Carter. (2007). Multi-level resource allocation for {HIV} prevention: A model for developing countries. *European Journal of Operational Research* 180(2) 786–799.

McCoy, J.H., H.L. Lee. (2014). Using fairness models to improve equity in health delivery fleet management. *Production and Operations Management* 23(6) 965–977.

Mehrotra, M., K.V. Natarajan. (2016). *Optimal provider and patient incentives in funding-constrained humanitarian healthcare service settings.* Working paper.

Natarajan, K.V., J.M. Swaminathan. (2016). *Coordinating demand and supply in funding-constrained developing country health supply chains.* Working paper.

Natarajan, K.V., J.M. Swaminathan. 2017. Multi-treatment inventory allocation in humanitarian health settings under funding constraints. *Production and Operations Management*, 26(6), pp. 1015–1034.

Natarajan, K.V., J.M. Swaminathan. (2014). Inventory management in humanitarian operations: Impact of amount, schedule, and uncertainty in funding. *Manufacturing & Service Operations Management* 16(4) 595–603.

Richter, A., K.A. Hicks, S.R. Earnshaw, A.A. Honeycutt. (2008). Allocating HIV prevention resources: a tool for state and local decision making. *Health Policy* 87(3) 342–349.

Samii, A., R. Pibernik, P. Yadav, A. Vereecke. (2012). Reservation and allocation policies for influenza vaccines. *European Journal of Operational Research* 222(3) 495–507.

Savas, E. S. (1978). On equity in providing public services. *Management Science* 24(8) 800–808.

Smalley, H.K., P. Keskinocak, J. Swann, A. Hinman. (2015). Optimized oral cholera vaccine distribution strategies to minimize disease incidence: a mixed integer programming model and analysis of a Bangladesh scenario. *Vaccine* 33(46) 6218 – 6223.

Stinnett, A.A., A.D. Paltiel. (1996). Mathematical programming for the efficient allocation of health care resources. *Journal of Health Economics* 15(5) 641–653.

Sun, P., L. Yang, F. de Vricourt. (2009). Selfish drug allocation for containing an international influenza pandemic at the onset. *Operations Research* 57(6) 1320–1332.

Swaminathan, J. M., M. Ashe, K. Duke, L. Maslin, L. Wilde. (2004). Distributing scarce drugs for the Medpin program. *Interfaces* 34(5) 353–358.

Swaminathan, J.M. (2003). Decision support for allocating scarce drugs. *Interfaces* 33(2) 1–11.

Swaminathan, J.M., A.D. So, W. Gilland, C.M. Vickery. (2009). A supply chain analysis of ready-to-use therapeutic foods for the Horn of Africa: the nutrition articulation project. Available at http://www.unicef.org/supply/files/supply_chain_analysis_of_ready_to_use_therapeutic_foods_for_the\ignorespaceshorn_of_africa.pdf.

Taylor, T.A., W. Xiao. (2014). Subsidizing the distribution channel: Donor funding to improve the availability of malaria drugs. *Management Science* 60(10) 2461–2477.

Weinstein, M., R. Zeckhauser. (1973). Critical ratios and efficient allocation. *Journal of Public Economics* 2(2) 147–157.

Yang, Y., J. Van den Broeck, L.M. Wein. (2013). Ready-to-use food-allocation policy to reduce the effects of childhood undernutrition in developing countries. *Proceedings of the National Academy of Sciences* 110(12) 4545–4550.

Zaric, G.S., M.L. Brandeau. (2001). Resource allocation for epidemic control over short time horizons. *Mathematical Biosciences* 171(1) 33–58.

8

Healthcare Supply Chain

Soo-Haeng Cho[1] *and Hui Zhao*[2]

[1] *Carnegie Mellon University*
[2] *Pennsylvania State University*

8.1 Introduction

One of the biggest concerns in the healthcare system in the United States is its ever-increasing spending and its impact on the economy and social welfare. Though there are many reasons for this increase, supply chain costs are unarguably one of the major driving forces. Supply chains now account for nearly 25 percent of pharmaceutical costs and more than 40 percent of medical device costs (Ebel et al., 2013). For healthcare service providers, the supply chain is the second largest and fastest growing expense after labor cost (Pennic, 2013).

Such high supply chain costs are driven by the unique characteristics of healthcare supply chains. First, healthcare supply chains are usually long and complex, involving many parties and unique intermediaries, such as a Group Purchasing Organization (GPO), as well as very different products, such as brand and generic products. For example, major players in the pharmaceutical supply chain include manufacturers, distributors/wholesalers, pharmacies who buy from wholesalers and dispense to patients, pharmacy benefit managers (PBMs) who manage claims and set up networks of pharmacies, create drug formularies, and negotiate discounts and rebates with drug manufacturers, and health plans, covering prescription drugs for patients. According to research done by the USC Schaeffer Center for Health Policy & Economics 2017, the gross profit margins of the manufacturers, wholesalers, pharmacies, PBMs, and health plans are 71, 4, 20, 6, and 22 percent, respectively, and the corresponding net profit margins are 26.3, 0.5, 4, 2.3, and 3 percent, respectively. Different supply chain players also face different risks, for instance, drug development and sales risks for manufacturers, inventory risks for wholesalers and pharmacies, and medical risks for health plans. Second, with the dilemma facing most healthcare supply chains that buyers of products/services are

Handbook of Healthcare Analytics: Theoretical Minimum for Conducting 21st Century Research on Healthcare Operations, First Edition. Edited by Tinglong Dai and Sridhar Tayur.

not the consumers, nor are they payers or price-setters, potential conflicts of interest among many supply chain players often arise, adding to the complexity of the supply chains. Third, healthcare supply chains are heavily regulated, incurring additional costs for quality and procedure compliance. As products become more complex to meet patients' needs (such as biological products), such costs can be significant. Fourth, although revenue maximization and cost containment are important objectives, many of these parties must also consider other factors, such as social welfare. Finally, given that the last link in healthcare supply chains is patients, any mistakes could potentially threaten human health/lives; hence, failure can be intolerable. The increasing drug recall cost is one example of this.

To drive supply chain savings to the next level, the Health Industry Distributors Association (HIDA) together with McKinsey & Company identified top four recommendations (Health Industry Distributors Association 2015), which are: (1) Fix the contracting process; (2) implement and champion data standards; (3) address end-to-end supply chain cost; and (4) expand the scope of products in distribution. This chapter presents an extensive review of past research efforts in healthcare supply chains and provides two particular examples. Although both examples focus on fixing contracts (mentioned in (1) above) and illustrate how supply chain efficiency can be improved through a better design of supply contracts that align incentives of different members in supply chains, they address the end-to-end supply chain costs (mentioned in (3) above) by considering many different players along the supply chain. Specifically, the first example studies the redesign of drug purchasing contracts for generic injectables to mitigate drug shortages, and the second example studies the redesign of supply contracts for influenza vaccines to address a mismatch between supply and demand. Corresponding to the characteristics of the healthcare supply chain as mentioned, in the first example, the authors treat social welfare together with many other parties' profitability or costs and how they take all parties' objectives into consideration when proposing a shortage-mitigating purchasing contract. Similarly, in the second example, we see how supply contracts between flu vaccine manufacturers and health care providers can be improved through coordinating contracts that align the incentives of the two parties. In the following, we provide some background of these two examples.

The current drug shortages faced by the US healthcare system primarily concern generic sterile injectable drugs, which account for 80 percent of the 127 shortage cases studied by the Food and Drug Administration (FDA) in 2010 and 2011 (FDA 2011). Several characteristics of generic sterile injectable drugs make them vulnerable to shortages. First, these drugs often have low profit margins, as most of them are long off-patent. Second, sterile injectable drugs require complex manufacturing processes that are vulnerable to quality problems violating the Current Good Manufacturing Practices (cGMPs), causing quality-related disruptions or even facility shutdowns for a substantial amount of time (FDA 2011). The combination of the above two characteristics makes these drugs unappealing to manufacturers, leading to a high market concentration and a high industry-wide capacity utilization.

Further, the high capacity utilization often implies less time for maintenance (exacerbating the drug supply chain's vulnerability to quality-related disruptions) and great challenges to responding effectively to disruptions, because disruptions that could otherwise be absorbed through a diversion of capacity can lead to cascading and persistent shortages (Assistant Secretary for Planning and Evaluation [ASPE] 2011, FDA 2011, Government Accountability Office [GAO] 2011). As a result, disruptions due to quality problems are linked to 54 percent of shortages (ASPE 2011), followed by lack of capacity or other delays (21%) (Piana 2012). At the same time, disruption durations are highly significant and uncertain, with an average duration of over nine months (GAO, 2011).

Generic injectables are prone to quality disruptions, yet holding these drugs to counter the problem is costly, due to the usual requirement of sterile, light- and temperature-regulated storage environments. Meanwhile, strikingly, a failure to meet customer orders incurs very low cost, even though most drug purchase contracts include failure-to-supply clauses (FTS). For example, many contracts compensate a buyer only if the buyer can find the same drug from an alternative source, and the contracts reimburse only the price difference. However, the high market concentration makes alternative sources unlikely during times of shortage. As a result, drug manufacturers, on average, compensate only 10 percent of buyers' losses due to FTS (ASPE 2011). Obviously, such weak FTS clauses do not help secure drug supply.

Various perspectives have been taken to report the drug shortage problem. Jia and Zhao (2017) studied this problem from a supply chain perspective, proposing to mitigate the US drug shortage through redesign of purchasing contracts. We will discuss challenges in addressing this problem, and provide a shortened version of their framework and analysis in section 8.3.1.

Our second example is related to influenza (flu) vaccine supply chains. More than 200,000 people in the US are hospitalized each year for illnesses associated with seasonal influenza virus infections (Centers for Disease Control and Prevention [CDC] 2016). Influenza vaccine is the first line of defense, but it is notoriously difficult to match its supply with demand. The challenges associated with the influenza vaccine *supply* are due to a limited time window for production and uncertainty in yield and lead time. Because influenza viruses change from year to year, influenza vaccines must be updated annually to include the viruses that will be likely to circulate in the upcoming season. This composition decision is made usually in February and March to collect sufficient information about virus activities. As a result, manufacturers must operate under a tight timeline for producing, testing, releasing, and distributing the vaccine. Yet, production yield and lead time are variable and unknown owing to their biological characteristics, especially when a vaccine strain is changed. The *demand* for the influenza vaccine is also uncertain largely due to unpredictable nature of influenza virus activities, and it is time-sensitive because the flu season is concentrated between December and February. Any leftovers after each season must be discarded.

To expand the time window for production, flu vaccine manufacturers usually start producing vaccines before the vaccine composition is finalized. However, this early production involves the risk that the virus chosen by manufacturers may differ from the virus included in the final composition; in this case, manufacturers must scrap entire production batches and redo the production. Accordingly, a supply contract needs to be designed that provides proper incentives for manufacturers to improve the mismatch between supply and demand.

Currently, most vaccine manufacturers distribute their products through two channels, each representing roughly 50 of vaccine sales/distribution (Health Industry Distributors Association 2011). In the first channel, manufacturers sell vaccines directly to retailers (pharmacies, hospitals, public agencies, etc.), whereas in the second channel, they sell vaccines through distributors who in turn deliver vaccines to their customers (primarily small physician offices). For simplicity, we focus on the first channel, but qualitative insights also apply to the second channel. These supply contracts between manufacturers and retailers are typically signed in January for vaccines to be delivered for the next flu season, starting in October. Dai et al. (2016) examined the ability of various contracts to coordinate members of this supply chain and proposed two coordinating contracts, such as a delivery-time-dependent quantity flexibility contract and a buyback-and-late-rebate contract. We present a simplified version of their model and an additional analysis in section 8.3.2.

The rest of this chapter is organized as follows. Section 8.2 reviews the broad literature on healthcare supply chains. Sections 8.3.1 and 8.3.2 present the models of supply chains for generic injectable drugs and for influenza vaccines, respectively, and characterize the performance of various supply contracts. In Section 8.4, we discuss promising future work and directions.

8.2 Literature Review

Operations researchers have frequently studied hospital operations, yet they have paid relatively little attention to healthcare supply chains. Healthcare supply chains include pharmaceutical supply chains, and medical devices and supplies supply chains. We will focus on pharmaceutical supply chains because, as will be seen, limited research exists on medical device supply chains, and most supply chains for medical supplies are similar to supply chains of other consumer products and hence do not warrant their own branch.

Burns et al. (2002) is a frequently cited general reference that analyzes the key elements and developments in US healthcare value chains. Schwarz (2010) describes the flow of products, dollars, and information in the supply chains for medical and surgical supplies, pharmaceuticals, and orthotic devices. A few authors have extensively studied pharmaceutical distribution supply chains. Specifically, Schwarz and Zhao (2011) provide, from a supply chain perspective, an overview of the pharmaceutical industry, the major players, and the challenges it faces. Based on the analysis of industry data and interviews with industry executives, the authors also examine the impact of the switch to Fee-for-Service (FFS) contracts (the prominent contracts governing brand-drug distribution) on pharmaceutical distributors and manufacturers. They concluded with a discussion of many current issues that are worth the attention of operations researchers. In terms of supply and distribution contracts, Zhao et al. (2012) analyzed the design and management of the brand drug supply chain under two contract models (FFS and Investment Buying) between a manufacturer and a distributor, and evaluate the value of information sharing enabled through FFS contracts. Martino et al. (2013) also looked at a direct shipment model for brand drugs. More recently, Jia and Zhao (2017) investigated the generic drug supply chain through the redesign of purchasing contracts to address a drug shortage problem. In addition to these papers on contracts, two papers have looked at the role of intermediaries in healthcare supply chains. Hu and Schwarz (2012) investigated the controversial role of GPOs widely used in the pharmaceutical and medical device industry. Kouvelis et al. (2015) looked at the impact of competition among PBMs on formulary design and drug pricing. In terms of inventory management, there is a stream of work on blood product management, for example, Pierskalla (2004), Zhou et al. (2011), and related references therein. Fleischhacker et al. (2014) studied the inventory allocation for drugs used in clinical trials. Ahuja and Birge (2016) also looked at clinical trials, but not from a supply chain perspective. Rather, the work proposes a better method to conduct clinical trials, that is, a response-adaptive way with simultaneous learning.

In addition to the above, there is a stream of research on the influenza vaccine supply chain. Most work on flu vaccines pertains to the issues related to the forecast and control of influenza through policy interventions in vaccinations (see, e.g., Philipson (2003) and Yamin and Gavious (2013)). Only recently, operations researchers have addressed various issues in the upstream of this supply chain or across different members of the supply chain. Chick et al. (2008) showed that if a central government purchases the entire volume of vaccines for consumers and a single manufacturer supplies all vaccines at a fixed price, a cost-sharing contract guarantees a sufficient supply of vaccines. In the United States, however, consumers make their own vaccination decisions and multiple manufacturers supply flu vaccines. Cho (2010) derived an optimal dynamic policy of the vaccine composition decision, taking into account subsequent production decisions of manufacturers. Özaltin et al. (2011) extend Cho (2010) by proposing a stochastic mixed-integer program that determines an optimal composition of a vaccine having three strains. Arifoğlu et al. (2012) studied the impact of yield uncertainty and self-interested consumers on inefficiency of the supply chain, and they analyzed the effectiveness of government interventions through partial centralization. Adida et al. (2013) studied how a central policy maker can induce a socially optimal vaccine coverage through the use of incentives for both consumers and vaccine manufacturers. Noting an important role of healthcare providers in this supply chain which has been ignored in all previous work, Dai et al. (2016) evaluated and improved the supply contracts used in practice between vaccine manufacturers and healthcare providers. They identified four sources of uncertainties in this supply chain: composition uncertainty, yield uncertainty, delivery uncertainty, and demand uncertainty. They developed and analyzed a tractable model that takes into account these sources of uncertainties.

In addition to the above analytical work, empirical studies look at pharmaceutical supply chains. Gray et al. (2015) examined how the location of pharmaceutical plants affects quality performance. Seeing the rise of specialty drugs (mostly biological products), Xu et al. (2016) investigated determinants of a distribution strategy for specialty drugs, using panel data on transactions between pharmaceutical manufacturers and distributors. Ball et al. (2016) looked at links between inspector experiences and product recalls in the medical device industry.

8.3 Model and Analysis

We now present two examples of the healthcare supply chain research, both of which redesign supply chain contracts to address current problems. All proofs of analytical results are presented in the appendix.

8.3.1 Generic Injectable Drug Supply Chain

In this section, we review the framework and analysis of the generic injectable drug supply chain in Jia and Zhao (2017). This research aims at redesigning purchasing contracts to mitigate the drug shortages facing the US pharmaceutical industry. As discussed earlier, while low profit margins are the *underlying* causes of drug shortages (GAO 2014), the weak FTS clauses, overlooked by the industry and literature, are also a direct cause, because they disincentivize drug manufacturers from maintaining sufficient inventory to satisfy customer demand. In the current drug purchase contracts, a contract price is often overemphasized, whereas the FTS clause seems nominal. Jia and Zhao (2017) propose the redesign of purchasing contracts to include *both price and FTS* as key contract parameters, to mitigate shortages. Such inclusion is nontrivial and requires a detailed analysis of the supply chain pertinent to drug shortages due to the price-capacity-inventory *triangular effect*. Intuitively, increasing prices can incentivize drug manufacturers to increase capacity. Given that demand is relatively insensitive to price (most of these drugs are medically necessary), the increased capacity would also reduce capacity utilization, improve quality maintenance, and potentially mitigate disruptions, hence, shortages. In the meantime, increasing prices can also incentivize manufacturers to hold more inventory. However, capacity and inventory are strategic *substitutes* (see, e.g., Angelus and Porteus 2002); increasing capacity may reduce inventory because with sufficient capacity, a manufacturer can easily ramp up production if needed and does not need to keep high inventory levels. Hence, the effectiveness of the proposed contract on shortage mitigation is not straightforward.

Modeling the drug shortage problem involves the key issues of having multiple supply chain parties who have distinct objectives and unique relationships. Specifically, while a drug manufacturer aims at maximizing its profit, the government, as the major payer (many of the drugs in shortage are covered by government programs such as Medicare), hopes to maintain its spending while reducing shortages. Healthcare providers are similarly keen to mitigate shortages to reduce suboptimal patient outcomes but are also concerned about cost. At the same time, a GPO, which represents its healthcare provider members and negotiates the drug purchase contract with the manufacturer, aims to improve its profit. Comprising these different parties, the drug supply chain possesses the unique characteristics furthering what we have mentioned at the beginning of the chapter for a typical healthcare problem: the buyer (provider) is not the payer (government) or the consumer (patient); the price setter (GPO in many cases) is not the payer or the buyer or even the consumer; and both the buyer and the payer have social welfare concerns beyond cost considerations. Accordingly, two important measures are taken to approach the shortage problem: (1) Instead of choosing an optimal contract for one party, Pareto-improving contracts are proposed, considering all the supply chain parties' objectives and their unique characteristics; and (2) in addition to monetary profits and costs, social welfare must be considered in some parties' objective functions.

To evaluate the effectiveness of the Pareto-improving contracts, Jia and Zhao (2017) investigated the drug supply chain through multiple research methodologies. First, they developed an analytical model of the drug supply chain, which captures all different parties' objectives and decisions, and incorporates key features of the problem, such as capacity-dependent disruption probability, uncertain recovery time, and mixed lost sales and backorders. Based on the model, the impact of the contract parameters on the objectives is characterized and analytical properties of the Pareto-improving contracts are explored. Next, the authors used scenario analysis and test the effectiveness of the proposal in three major scenarios developed based on key features of the problem and realistic industry data. For completeness, a full factorial analysis which covers a wide range of other scenarios also conducted. Finally, the authors reported their interactions with government agencies and industry practitioners, who provided additional insights on this proposal from various perspectives.

8.3.1.1 Model

In this section, we briefly review the model framework of the drug supply chain pertaining to shortages. Readers are referred to Jia and Zhao (2017) for more details. The supply chain consists of a major drug *manufacturer* (seller); a *GPO*, who represents a group of healthcare providers (buyers); and the *government*, who reimburses the drug through the Medicare program. The GPO and the manufacturer negotiate the purchasing contract, which includes a unit price p and a failure-to-supply (FTS) compensation s to buyers for *each* unit of demand the manufacturer cannot satisfy. The contract duration is typically 24–36 months (see, e.g., Navarro 2009), denoted by T. Notably, the random demand during the contract duration, denoted by D, does not depend on the contract parameters, p and s, due to the low price elasticity of demand (i.e., many of the drugs in shortage are medically necessary; FDA, 2011) and the fact that Medicare (instead of patients) pays for the drug. Given the purchase contract, let the drug shortage level be the average level of lost sales, $L(p, s)$, which will be derived when characterizing the manufacturer's decisions.

Next, we formulate the objective of each supply chain party as a function of the contract parameters (p, s), before we can obtain the Pareto-improving contracts. Although the objectives are affected by many factors, we focus on the most essential factors to capture the major trade-offs of the problem.

GPO

A GPO, which does not hold inventory, gains revenue mainly from two sources: a contract administration fee (CAF) from manufacturers as a percentage (α) commission on sales, and a membership fee from each participating healthcare provider. Note that CAF is the primary source of a GPO's revenue (Burns, 2002), and the flat membership fee can be viewed as a sunk cost (hence does not need to be modeled). With α as exogenous (since it is decided based on the sales of all drugs, not just the drugs on shortage), given a contract (p, s), the GPO's expected profit is

$$\Gamma_O(p, s) = \alpha p[1 - L(p, s)]D, \tag{8.1}$$

where $[1 - L(p, s)]$ is the percentage of sales (1 minus lost sales) and αp is the GPO's commission per unit of sales.

Drug Manufacturer

Given a contract (p, s), the drug manufacturer makes two major decisions: the production capacity for the T periods of contract duration and the production/inventory decisions in each of the T periods. Note that the capacity decision here is not the strategic capacity investment but rather the capacity allocation for the contract duration T because the strategic investment decision is usually made considering many other high-level strategic factors. For generic drug production, manufacturers often produce multiple drugs with similar manufacturing characteristics on the same production lines and adjust capacity allocation among the drugs based on needs and contracts (Ventola, 2011; GAO, 2014). Therefore, in this model, the manufacturer's capacity is set at the beginning of the contract period, and remains unchanged over all T periods.

Let κ_0 be the manufacturer's initial capacity for the drug at the beginning of the contract period. The manufacturer adjusts the capacity from κ_0 to κ with a cost of $G(\kappa - \kappa_0)$, which is a function of $\kappa - \kappa_0$. Thus, given a contract (p, s), the manufacturer aims to set a capacity κ to maximize its total expected profit:

$$\Gamma_M(p, s) = \max_{\kappa \geq 0} U(p, s, \kappa) - G(\kappa - \kappa_0), \tag{8.2}$$

where $U(p, s, \kappa)$ is the expected profit generated by the optimal inventory policy (detailed later) for a given contract (p, s) and capacity κ, which is derived in section 8.3.1.2.

Government

It is important to understand that in addition to the reimbursement costs of many drugs in shortage, the government also bears three types of shortage-related monetary or social welfare losses: (1) the reimbursement costs for alternative drugs or therapies (if any), which are usually more expensive than the original drugs; (2) social welfare losses due to suboptimal treatment outcomes and potentially higher future reimbursement costs due to these suboptimal outcomes; and (3) other social welfare losses such as the negative impact of gray markets (Cherici et al., 2011). Therefore, to fully capture the government's spending on drug shortages, we must consider both the monetary expenditure on reimbursement and the social welfare losses. Let $r(p)$ represent the unit reimbursement cost for a drug with wholesale price p. Under Medicare, the government currently reimburses drugs at 6 percent above their market wholesale prices. Let β_G be the government's aggregate unit loss due to drug shortages. The value of β_G varies for different drugs and is generally much higher than the drug price; medically necessary drugs have even higher β_G. Without loss of generality, we assume $\beta_G \geq r(p)$. It is estimated that β_G can range from 10 to 60 times the drug price (see Jia and Zhao (2017) for an example of estimating β_G for a drug in shortage). Using this notation, the total government spending under a contract (p, s) can be expressed as

$$\Gamma_G(p, s) = r(p)[1 - L(p, s)](D) + \beta_G L(p, s)(D), \tag{8.3}$$

where the first term is the total reimbursement cost for the expected sales of the drug under investigation, and the second term is the cost (loss) due to shortages.

Healthcare Providers

Similar to the government's loss β_G, when shortages occur, each unsatisfied unit incurs an average loss of β_P to the providers, which reflects the resultant negative effects (e.g., suboptimal treatment outcomes). The value of β_P varies for different drugs and is generally higher than the manufacturer's FTS compensation, s, that is, $\beta_P \geq s$. Thus, when purchasing through the GPO, the providers' expected cost is then

$$\Gamma_P(p,s) = [p - r(p)][1 - L(p,s)](D) + (\beta_P - s)L(p,s)(D), \qquad (8.4)$$

where the first term is the expected purchase cost less the reimbursement, and the second term is the loss due to shortages.

To evaluate the objectives of different parties, which all depend on the manufacturer's optimal production/inventory policy, $U(p,s,\kappa)$, and the shortage measure, $L(p,s)$, we next analyze the manufacturer's optimal policy.

8.3.1.2 Analysis

Given a contract (p,s) and a capacity decision κ, the drug manufacturer makes inventory decisions for each of the T periods of the contract duration. These decisions must consider production disruptions. To do so, define the production *reliability*, $\theta(\kappa)$, as the probability that *no* disruption occurs in a period. $\theta(\kappa)$ depends on the long-run average capacity utilization $(D)/(\kappa T)$ and is assumed to be increasing in κ, that is, the reliability is higher with higher capacity or lower utilization. Using shortage data from Yorukuglu (2014), Jia and Zhao (2017) infer the detailed structure of $\theta(\kappa)$ (see section 6.2 of the paper). In practice, production disruptions lead to a mixture of backorders and lost sales; backorders occur when production is normal, and lost sales occur when production is disrupted.

We now describe the sequence of events. The manufacturer starts period t $(= 1, 2, \ldots, T)$ with an initial inventory level x and a production status: normal or disrupted. If the production is normal, the manufacturer chooses a target postproduction inventory level y. The production incurs unit cost c and has a one-period lead time that reflects the complex manufacturing process. The manufacturer then observes the demand in period t, D_t, and uses the existing inventory x (instead of y due to the lead time) to meet the demand. Each unit of unsatisfied demand is backordered at a cost b. At the end of period t, the manufacturer observes whether or not the production batch in period t is disrupted. With probability $\theta(\kappa)$, the production succeeds, in which case the manufacturer carries the leftover units or backorders forward. The initial inventory in period $t+1$ is $y - D_t$ and the production status is again normal. With probability $1 - \theta(\kappa)$, the production is disrupted, in which case the entire batch with $y - x$ units fails (e.g., Tomlin 2006). The manufacturer announces the disruption according to the FDA's requirement (FDA 2016). All backorders at the end of period t, totaling $(D_t - x)^+$, become lost sales and incur an FTS compensation of s per unit. The manufacturer then starts period $t+1$ with an initial inventory of $(x-D_t)^+$, a production status as disrupted, and the number of periods since disruption $i=1$.

If the manufacturer starts period t with an inventory x, a production status as disrupted, and the disruption has lasted i periods, the manufacturer uses x to satisfy demand D_t (no new production available); unmet demand $(D_t-x)^+$ is lost. The manufacturer pays the FTS compensation, $s(D_t-x)^+$, and the holding cost, $h(x-D_t)^+$, for leftover units. Let R denote the entire random disruption duration. Given that the disruption has lasted i periods, it continues in period $t+1$ with probability $\lambda_i = P(R \geq i+1 | R \geq i)$ and ends in period $t+1$ with probability $1-\lambda_i$.

Under a contract (p,s) and a capacity κ, let $\mathcal{U}_t(x)$ be the manufacturer's optimal expected profit-to-go from the beginning of period t to the end of the planning horizon, given that the production is *normal* and the initial inventory is x in period t. Similarly, let $V_t(i,x)$ be the manufacturer's optimal expected profit-to-go from the beginning of period t onward, given that the production has been *disrupted* for i periods, and the initial inventory is x in period t. For simplicity, we have dropped the arguments p, s, and κ in the notation of $\mathcal{U}_t(x)$ and $V_t(i,x)$. The manufacturer aims to maximize its expected profit over the contract duration. For $1 \leq t \leq T$,

$$\begin{aligned}\mathcal{U}_t(x) = \max_{x \leq y \leq x+\kappa} \; & (1-\alpha)pD_t - c(y-x) - h(x-D_t)^+ \\ & - b(D_t-x)^+ + \theta(\kappa)\mathcal{U}_{t+1}(y-D_t) \\ & + [1-\theta(\kappa)]\{-[(1-\alpha)p+s](D_t-x)^+ + V_{t+1}(1,(x-D_t)^+)\}; \\ V_t(i,x) = {} & (1-\alpha)p\min\{x, D_t\} - s(D_t-x)^+ - h(x-D_t)^+ \\ & + \lambda_i V_{t+1}(i+1,(x-D_t)^+) + (1-\lambda_i)\mathcal{U}_{t+1}((x-D_t)^+). \end{aligned} \tag{8.5}$$

In period $T+1$, the boundary condition is set to be $\mathcal{U}_{T+1}(x) = cx^+ - [(1-\alpha)p+s]x^-$ and $V_{T+1}(i,x) = cx$, where $x^- = \max\{-x, 0\}$. In other words, at the end of the contract duration, if the production is normal, then the manufacturer recovers the production cost from leftover units, returns the revenue collected from all backorders, and pays the corresponding FTS compensation. If the production is disrupted in period $T+1$, then the manufacturer recovers only the production cost (no backorder exists in this case). This boundary condition maintains tractability.

As shown in Theorem 1 of Jia and Zhao (2017), even with the additional drug production features, given a contract (p,s) and a capacity κ, there exists a base-stock level k_t for the manufacturer in each period t, which is independent of x. Assuming that the manufacturer starts with zero initial inventory and normal production, his expected profit generated by the optimal inventory policy $\mathcal{U}(p,s,\kappa)$ in Eq. (8.2) is simply $\mathcal{U}_1(0)$ in Eq. (8.5). Given a contract (p,s), let $\kappa^*(p,s)$, or simply κ^*, denote the optimal capacity solution to Eq. (8.2).

Now we can calculate the shortage measure. Let $J_t(x)$ denote the cumulative lost sales from period t to the end of the contract duration, given that the production is normal and the initial inventory level is x in period t. Similarly, let $K_t(i, x)$ denote the cumulative lost sales from period t onward, given that the production has been disrupted for i periods, and the initial inventory is x in period t. Thus, for $1 \leq t \leq T$,

$$\begin{aligned} J_t(x) &= \theta(\kappa^*) J_{t+1}(y_t^*(x|\kappa^*) - D_t) + [1 - \theta(\kappa^*)] \\ &\quad [(D_t - x)^+ + K_{t+1}(1, (x - D_t)^+)]; \\ K_t(i, x) &= (D_t - x)^+ + \lambda_i K_{t+1}(i + 1, (x - D_t)^+) \\ &\quad + (1 - \lambda_i) J_{t+1}((x - D_t)^+). \end{aligned} \tag{8.6}$$

The boundary condition in period $T+1$ is: $J_{T+1}(x) = x^-$ and $K_{T+1}(i, x) = 0$. Again assuming that the production is normal and the initial inventory is zero at the beginning of the contract duration, we define the shortage measure as the *cumulative lost sales ratio* over the contract duration: $L(p, s) = J_1(0)/(D)$, where $D = \sum_{t=1}^{T} D_t$.

Next, we characterize the impacts of the contract parameters on different parties' objective functions and supply chain measures.

Proposition 8.1 ***(Proposition 1 in Jia and Zhao 2017)*** $\Gamma_O(p, s)$ increases in p and s; $\Gamma_M(p, s)$ increases in p and decreases in s; $\Gamma_G(p, s)$ decreases in s but is non-monotone in p; $\Gamma_P(p, s)$ and $L(p, s)$ decrease in p and s; and $y_t^*(x|\kappa)$ increases in p and s for any given capacity κ.

With these properties, we are ready to explore the Pareto-improving contracts. For a given p, let $s_\iota(p)$ be such that $\Gamma_\iota(p, s_\iota(p)) = \Gamma_\iota(p_0, s_0)$, where the subscript $\iota = O, P, M$, or G, represents GPO, provider, manufacturer, and government, respectively. Similarly, let $s_L(p)$ be such that $L(p, s_L(p)) = L(p_0, s_0)$. In other words, for a given p, $s_\iota(p)$ is the FTS penalty that leads to the same objective function value for player ι as under the original contract before re-design, (p_0, s_0), and $s_L(p)$ is the s value that leads to the same shortage value as under (p_0, s_0). Because Proposition 8.1 has shown that for any given p, strengthening s when redesigning the contract reduces the manufacturer's profit but improves all other measures (note that decreasing $\Gamma_G(p, s)$, $\Gamma_P(p, s)$, and $L(p, s)$ means improvement), the Pareto-improving s value must be above $s_O(p)$, $s_P(p)$, $s_L(p)$, $s_G(p)$ and below $s_M(p)$. In addition, realistically, because the price p and FTS compensation s should be adjusted only within reasonable ranges, we allow upper bounds for them, denoted by $\overline{p}$ and $\overline{s}$.

Proposition 8.2 ***(Theorem 3 in Jia and Zhao 2017)*** The set of Pareto-improving contracts is:

$$\Psi = \{(p, s) : p \in [p_0, \overline{p}], s \in [\max\{s_0, s_G(p)\}, \min\{\overline{s}, s_M(p)\}]\}.$$

Proposition 8.2 indicates that among the lower bounds $s_O(p)$, $s_P(p)$, $s_L(p)$, and $s_G(p)$, $s_G(p)$ are the tightest, so other bounds become redundant. Proposition 8.2 provides an expression of the Pareto-improving contracts. Unfortunately, further properties of how the bounding curves cross (e.g., number of crossings), are analytically intractable. The difficulty lies in the fact that both of the lower- and upper-bound curves for s involve the shortage measure $L(p, s)$, which has no analytical expression and has to be evaluated numerically by Eq. (8.6).

With the above theoretical expressions established, three major scenarios are developed, each covering a set of drugs with similar manufacturing characteristics. Numerical analysis linking these scenarios with the model parameters is conducted based on realistic industry data from various sources (public agencies as well as industry). This analysis focuses on calculating the proposed Pareto-improving contracts and their impact on shortage reduction and the different parties' objectives. Further, a full factorial analysis covering an even wider range of model parameters is also conducted to complement the scenario analysis. These numerical analyses show that Pareto-improving contracts exist in all scenarios tested with very effective shortage reduction. Readers are referred to the paper for details about the data and results.

This study generates several key findings. First, increasing drug prices only (referred to as IP), which has been advocated as a natural solution to the drug shortage problem in response to the current low profit margins, is unfortunately not very effective in mitigating drug shortages. Increasing drug prices must be paired with strengthened FTS clauses (referred to as IPS) to achieve consistent and significant shortage reduction. The effectiveness of this pairing is due to the triangular effect described earlier: an effective shortage mitigation requires a significant price increase to overcome the substitutional effect between capacity and inventory, but the IP approach does not render a large enough Pareto-improving space for price increase. The IPS approach, on the other hand, adds a significant dimension to resolve this problem and is shown to be much more effective over a wide range of scenarios. For all scenarios tested, a 30 percent price increase under IPS leads to a minimum, average, and maximum shortage reduction of 25, 53, and 70 percent, respectively. The readers are referred to Jia and Zhao (2017) for further discussion of the authors' interactions with industry and government agencies, the additional insights brought by these discussions, and the potential issues with implementations.

8.3.2 Influenza Vaccine Supply Chain

We next turn our attention to the influenza vaccine supply chain. In section 8.3.2.1, we briefly describe a simplified version of the model presented in Dai et al. (2016). In section 8.3.2.2, we analyze the model to characterize the performance of various contracts.

8.3.2.1 Model

Before a seasonal influenza vaccine is administered to consumers, several steps occur. Healthcare providers, pharmacies, government agencies, and distributors place orders mostly in January for vaccines to be used in the upcoming flu season, which begins in October or November. Soon after receiving orders, manufacturers begin their productions. This usually occurs before the FDA announces the final composition of vaccine typically in February or March based on the recommendation of the Vaccine and Related Biologic Products Advisory Committee. As soon as manufacturers complete production of each batch of vaccine, they test, release, and distribute vaccines to those who placed orders. Finally, consumers begin their vaccinations starting in October.

To model the above process, Dai et al. (2016) consider a supply chain with one influenza vaccine manufacturer and one retailer. The demand ξ for the vaccine is uncertain with a density f and a distribution F. There are two selling periods. All demands arrive at the beginning of the first period. If there is unmet demand during the first period due to limited supply, then a proportion $1-\gamma$ ($\in (0,1)$) of the unmet demand will return for vaccination at the beginning of the second period. Based on this demand projection, the retailer determines an order quantity Q. We assume that a retail price of vaccine is fixed at p.

After receiving the retailer's order, the manufacturer produces vaccines over two production periods. In the first "early" production period, the manufacturer produces vaccines without knowing the final composition. As a result, vaccines produced in this period may not have the same virus strains as in the final composition, in which case all produced vaccines will have to be discarded. To model this risk, we let β ($\in (0,1)$) denote the probability that the manufacturer's chosen strain in early production matches the final composition. We assume that vaccines produced in the "early' production period can always be delivered on time before the first selling period. The second "regular" production period begins after the announcement of the final vaccine composition. Although this regular production does not bear the mismatch risk in strains, there is a chance that the vaccines produced in this period will be delivered late. Let $\alpha \in (0,1)$ denote the probability that they will be delivered on time for the first selling period. With probability $(1-\alpha)$, the delivery will be late and the vaccines can be used to satisfy the demand only in the second selling period. Let c denote a per-unit cost for the manufacturer. The manufacturer decides on the first-period production quantity Q_e. If Q_e is successful with probability β, then the manufacturer produces only $Q-Q_e$ in the second period; otherwise, the manufacturer produces the entire order quantity Q in the second period.

Let Z denote sales quantity. We can express the expected sales as follows:

$$
\begin{aligned}
E[Z(Q,Q_e)] = {} & \alpha\left[\int_0^Q \xi dF(\xi) + \int_Q^\infty QdF(\xi)\right] \\
& + (1-\alpha)\beta\left\{\int_0^{Q_e} \xi dF(\xi) + \int_{Q_e}^{\frac{Q-\gamma Q_e}{1-\gamma}} [\gamma Q_e + (1-\gamma)\xi]dF(\xi)\right. \\
& \left. + \int_{\frac{Q-\gamma Q_e}{1-\gamma}}^\infty QdF(\xi)\right\} + (1-\alpha)(1-\beta) \\
& \times \left[\int_0^{\frac{Q}{1-\gamma}} (1-\gamma)\xi dF(\xi) + \int_{\frac{Q}{1-\gamma}}^\infty QdF(\xi)\right], \qquad (8.7)
\end{aligned}
$$

where the first term represents the expected sales quantity for the case when those vaccines produced in the regular production period are delivered on-time (so that the entire Q is delivered on-time), the second term represents the expected sales quantity for the case when the regular production is late and the early production is successful, and the third term represents the expected sales quantity when the regular production is late and the early production is not successful.

As a benchmark, consider a centralized supply chain and its expected profit $\pi_S(Q, Q_e)$. A decision-maker solves the following problem to determine the order quantity Q and the early production quantity Q_e that maximize $\pi_S(Q, Q_e)$:

$$\max_{Q>0,0\le Q_e\le Q} \pi_S(Q,Q_e) = pE[Z(Q,Q_e)] - [cQ + (1-\beta)cQ_e]. \qquad (8.8)$$

The solution of this problem is referred to as the first-best solution, denoted by (Q^{FB}, Q_e^{FB}). A contract is said to *coordinate* a decentralized supply chain if it induces the first-best solution (Q^{FB}, Q_e^{FB}) from the firms comprising the supply chain. We define the efficiency of the supply chain as a ratio of the supply chain's expected profit under a certain contract to that in the first-best solution. Under a coordinating contract, the supply chain efficiency is 100 percent. We focus on the realistic case where $Q_e^{FB} > 0$.

8.3.2.2 Analysis

A number of coordinating contracts have been proposed in the supply chain management literature (see, e.g., Cachon, 2003). We begin our analysis by evaluating two such contracts, namely revenue sharing and quantity flexibility contracts, in our setting. After demonstrating their limited ability to coordinate the influenza vaccine supply chain, we propose a new form of a supply contract that can coordinate this supply chain.

First, we analyze a revenue-sharing contract. Under this contract, the retailer pays the manufacturer a wholesale price w for each unit of order and a percentage ψ ($\in (0,1)$) of the retailer's revenue. Under this contract, the manufacturer's profit and the retailer's profit can be expressed respectively as follows:

$$\pi_M^{RS}(Q, Q_e) = \psi p E[Z(Q, Q_e)] + (w - c)Q - (c - \beta c)Q_e, \text{ and}$$
$$\pi_R^{RS}(Q, Q_e) = (1 - \psi) p E[Z(Q, Q_e)] - wQ.$$

It is well known that such a revenue-sharing contract can coordinate a traditional supply chain under uncertain demand. However, as shown in the next proposition, this contract cannot coordinate the influenza vaccine supply chain.

Proposition 8.3 If $(1 - \alpha)\beta\gamma(p - w) < (1 - \beta)c$, then a revenue-sharing contract always induces the manufacturer to choose $Q_e = 0$, and the efficiency of the influenza vaccine supply chain under this contract is lower than that under a wholesale price contract.

Proposition 8.3 shows, unlike the result in the traditional setting under uncertain demand, that the revenue-sharing contract fails to coordinate the supply chain and that it performs even worse than a wholesale price contract. The reason is as follows. Early production is intended to mitigate uncertainty in delivery. However, early production is risky to the manufacturer because it is undertaken before a final composition of vaccine is determined. A contract therefore needs to provide the right incentive for the manufacturer's early production. The result that $Q_e = 0$ in Proposition 8.3 suggests that the revenue-sharing scheme does not resolve the manufacturer's incentive problem. This, in conjunction with the observation that the retailer orders less under a revenue-sharing contract than under a wholesale price contract, implies that revenue sharing provides even less incentive to overcome double marginalization than a wholesale price contract.

To understand the condition given in Proposition 8.3, note that $\gamma(p - w)$ in its left-hand side represents the retailer's maximum proportion (γ) of lost net revenue ($p - w$) when late delivery occurs, and that $(1 - \alpha)\beta$ represents the probability that early production lessens the supply problem caused by late delivery of regular production. Thus, the left-hand side is the maximum expected benefit of early production to the retailer. The right-hand side of this condition is the expected additional cost of early production. Taken together, this condition implies that, even if the retailer shares all potential benefits of early production with the manufacturer, the manufacturer still lacks the incentive to undertake early production. When the condition is violated, we can still show that the manufacturer's chosen early production quantity is substantially lower than the first-best quantity.

Next, we analyze a quantity flexibility contract under which the manufacturer provides the retailer with full credit for leftover inventory up to a predetermined threshold. While there exist different specifications of the threshold, we focus on a quantity flexibility contract in which the threshold is a proportion of the order quantity (e.g., Tsay, 1999). Let $\kappa \in (0,1)$ denote a proportion of the retailer's ordering quantity Q that is allowed to return at the end of the flu season. The returning quantity, denoted by $R(Q, Q_e)$, is then $R(Q, Q_e) = \min\{\kappa Q, Q - Z(Q, Q_e)\}$, where $Q - Z(Q, Q_e)$ is the leftover inventory. Because the manufacturer provides full credit for returns, its transfer payment to the retailer $T(Q, Q_e)$ is equal to $wR(Q, Q_e)$. We can show that the returning quantity $R(Q, Q_e)$ takes three different forms as follows:

(Case i) Vaccines produced in the regular production period are delivered in time to the first selling period, with probability α:

$$R(Q, Q_e) = \begin{cases} \kappa Q & \text{if } 0 \leq \xi < (1-\kappa)Q \\ Q - \xi & \text{if } (1-\kappa)Q \leq \xi < Q \\ 0 & \text{if } \xi \geq Q. \end{cases}$$

(Case ii) Vaccines produced in the regular production period are delivered late to the second selling period with probability $(1-\alpha)$, and vaccines produced in the early production period match the final composition, with probability β:

- When $0 \leq \kappa < 1 - Q_e/Q$,

$$R(Q, Q_e) = \begin{cases} \kappa Q & \text{if } 0 \leq \xi < \frac{(1-\kappa)Q - \gamma Q_e}{1-\gamma} \\ Q - \gamma Q_e - (1-\gamma)\xi & \text{if } \frac{(1-\kappa)Q-\gamma Q_e}{1-\gamma} \leq \xi < \frac{Q-\gamma Q_e}{1-\gamma} \\ 0 & \text{if } \xi \geq \frac{Q-\gamma Q_e}{1-\gamma}. \end{cases}$$

- When $1 - Q_e/Q \leq \kappa \leq 1$,

$$R(Q, Q_e) = \begin{cases} \kappa Q & \text{if } 0 \leq \xi < (1-\kappa)Q \\ Q - \xi & \text{if } (1-\kappa)Q \leq \xi < Q_e \\ Q - \gamma Q_e - (1-\gamma)\xi & \text{if } Q_e \leq \xi < \frac{Q-\gamma Q_e}{1-\gamma} \\ 0 & \text{if } \xi \geq \frac{Q-\gamma Q_e}{1-\gamma}. \end{cases}$$

(Case iii) Vaccines produced in the regular production period are delivered late to the second selling period with probability $(1-\alpha)$, and vaccines produced in the early production period do not match the final composition, with probability $(1-\beta)$:

$$R(Q, Q_e) = \begin{cases} \kappa Q & \text{if } 0 \leq \xi < \frac{(1-\kappa)Q}{1-\gamma} \\ Q - (1-\gamma)\xi & \text{if } \frac{(1-\kappa)Q}{1-\gamma} \leq \xi < \frac{Q}{1-\gamma} \\ 0 & \text{if } \xi \geq \frac{Q}{1-\gamma}. \end{cases}$$

Proposition 8.4 When $Q_e^{FB} > 0$, a quantity flexibility contract cannot coordinate the influenza vaccine supply chain.

Although a quantity flexibility contract can coordinate a traditional supply chain under a set of conditions (see, for example, Cachon 2003), Proposition 8.4 shows that it cannot coordinate the influenza vaccine supply chain. Similar to a revenue sharing contract, a quantity flexibility contract fails to coordinate the influenza vaccine supply chain because it does not provide adequate incentive for the manufacturer to undertake early production. However, a numerical analysis shows that this contract performs better than a revenue sharing contract, especially when the profit margin is high. In this case, an optimal quantity flexibility contract provides a generous return allowance and hence motivates the retailer to place a large order. This in turn incentivizes the manufacturer to choose a high early production quantity.

In addition to revenue sharing and quantity flexibility contracts, Dai et al. (2016) have also examined other well-known contracts, including wholesale price and late rebate contracts that are used by some influenza vaccine manufacturers. Unfortunately, these contracts cannot coordinate the influenza vaccine supply chain, either. A common problem in these contracts is that they cannot induce the manufacturer to choose the first-best early production quantity. This causes the retailer to order less than the first-best order quantity. In practice, we have also seen some influenza vaccine manufacturers use a variation of a quantity flexibility contract, under which the maximum returning quantity depends on the timing of delivery. Although this contract, named the delivery-time-dependent quantity flexibility contract, does not always guarantee the coordination of the supply chain, it performs better than a conventional quantity flexibility contract (Dai et al. 2016).

Knowing that various conventional contracts are not effective in the influenza vaccine supply chain, we may wonder if there exists a specific form of a contract that can guarantee the coordination of this supply chain. Dai et al. (2016) show that a buyback-and-late-rebate (BLR) contract can always coordinate this supply chain with properly chosen contract parameters. This contract incorporates a late rebate term into a traditional buyback contract. Under a BLR contract, the manufacturer provides the retailer with a rebate $\rho \cdot w$ (where $\rho \in (0, 1)$) for each unit of late-delivered vaccine in addition to providing the retailer with a buyback credit b (where $b \in (0, w)$) for each unsold unit. This contract is based on two quantities that are observable to both the manufacturer and the retailer: the leftover inventory and the late-delivered quantity. Then the expected transfer payment from the manufacturer to the retailer can be written as

$$b\{Q - E[Z(Q, Q_e)]\} + \rho w[(1-\alpha)\beta(Q - Q_e) + (1-\alpha)(1-\beta)Q]. \quad (8.9)$$

In (8.9), the first term is the manufacture's expected buyback credit to the retailer, and the second term is the manufacturer's expected rebate, in which late-delivered quantity is 0 with probability α, $Q - Q_e$ with probability $(1-\alpha)\beta$, and Q with probability $(1-\alpha)(1-\beta)$; see three cases mentioned above for a quantity flexibility contract. The next proposition details the optimal contract parameters under which a BLR contract can coordinates the supply chain.

Proposition 8.5 ***(Proposition 8.3 of Dai et al. 2016)*** A BLR contract with the following contract parameters coordinates the influenza vaccine supply chain:

$$b = \frac{(\beta w - c)p}{\beta p - c} \quad \text{and} \quad \rho = \frac{(p-w)(1-\beta)c}{w(1-\alpha)(\beta p - c)}.$$

Dai et al. (2016) evaluated the performance of the sample contracts used in the industry, based on realistic parameter values in the US influenza vaccine market. They showed that the use of a coordinating contract improves the profitability of the supply chain by 12.14 percent and 15.55 percent on average over the late rebate and wholesale price contracts currently used in this industry, respectively. They further show that a coordinating contract together with a subsidy for the retailer can maximize social welfare that includes consumer welfare as well as supply chain profit.

This study generated several key findings. First, without proper contract design, a vicious incentive cycle may arise: A vaccine manufacturer lacks the incentive to improve on-time delivery, and anticipating that late delivery will cause lost sales, a healthcare provider reduces order quantity, which further discourages the manufacturer from improving its delivery performance. Second, well-known contracts that are capable of coordinating conventional supply chains have limited ability to align incentives of members of the influenza vaccine supply chain, due to the tension between overcoming double marginalization and incentivizing early production. Finally, a BLR contract can not only coordinate the supply chain, but it also provides flexibility in profit division. Such a coordinating contract can improve the overall profit of the supply chain as well as improve social welfare. These findings were featured in several industry magazines and news outlets, including *Pharmacy Times* and *Infection Control Today*, to inform practitioners.

8.4 Discussion and Future Research

We now turn our attention to ample future research opportunities in healthcare and pharmaceutical supply chains. The healthcare and pharmaceutical industry is vital to the US economy, and its supply chain efficiency directly affects the quality and cost of patient care. In this highly regulated industry, many of the questions faced also have significant implications for the government's healthcare policy. Most of the extant literature belongs to industry reports and white papers, but there is a great need for supply chain research because this unique industry is: (1) complex in its supply chain structure, with players who have objectives in different domains (profit, social welfare, and spending); (2) fairly closed and least familiar with supply chains (partly because of its nature to focus on innovation and discovery); yet (3) greatly challenged in its supply chain cost and efficiency while the healthcare industry faces dramatic pressure for cutting cost. These characteristics provide supply chain researchers with unprecedented opportunities, as the industry has passed the era when high margins can hide inefficiencies. Research in this area may encompass the whole supply chain, from R&D strategies, to drug manufacturing decisions, distribution, and inventory management, to various challenges faced by pharmacies, insurance, medical service providers, regulatory bodies, and patients. Research can also embrace both brand and generic drugs, and the nature of research can vary from tactical to strategic to public policy. In the following, we discuss a few research areas with potential impacts:

- *Incentives and Contracts:* As demonstrated by the examples in this chapter, healthcare supply chains involve many parties, with different objectives in different domains (profit, cost, social welfare). How to align these parties' incentives through contracts or other mechanisms remains an important approach to improving efficiency. This is also an interesting research area because the analysis of incentives usually exposes a different perspective on the problems from what the industry has normally seen. For example, as Jia and Zhao (2017) indicate, although using a higher fail-to-supply penalty compensated by a higher price to ensure better supply in a purchasing contract is quite common to other industries, it seems an intriguing idea to the pharmaceutical industry because the GPOs, who negotiate contracts with manufacturers on behalf of healthcare providers, are largely evaluated by prices but not explicitly penalized by supply shortage. Dai et al. (2016) also highlighted the important misalignment of incentives among different members of the influenza vaccine supply chain, which have caused mismatches between supply and demand for years. Further work is needed to study incentive issues in various healthcare supply chains, especially those involving intermediaries such as GPOs and PBMs.
- *Regulations and public policy:* As mentioned, the healthcare/pharmaceutical industry is heavily regulated. Regulations permeate the whole chain from drug discovery and approval, manufacturing, distribution and delivery, to reimbursement. Understanding the impact of regulations on different players in healthcare supply chains is an important area of study. For example, Gupta and Mehrotra (2015) studied the impact of bundle payments for healthcare delivery. Ahuja et al. (2015) looked at drug safety and developed

a data-driven approach to evaluate a drug's association with specific adverse reactions useful for the drug approval regulation. Recently, Xu, et al. (2017) analyzed the challenges faced by the FDA when managing the accelerated approval pathway and proposed various ways for the government agency to manage compliance to post-market study requirements, which is key to the success of the accelerated approval pathway. Other recent notable policy changes in the pharmaceutical industry include the track and trace legislature that is or will be implemented in several states as part of their healthcare policy reforms. Impacts of these changes on supply chains are compelling questions open for study.

- *Innovation and other current challenges:* Healthcare supply chains face many of their own specific challenges that are worth further research. For example, one of the prominent trends in the industry is the rise of specialty drugs. Although the number of specialty drugs approved has exceeded that of the traditional drugs in 2012, limited knowledge and insights exist regarding how to manage their supply chains. Xu et al. (2016) studied the determinants of the distribution strategy of specialty drugs, using large panel data on transactions between manufacturer and distributor. With most of the specialty drugs being bio-based, challenges in manufacturing bio-drugs, due to many uncertainties in the production phases, are also questions open to study. In addition, drug shortages remain a big challenge in the industry. Jia and Zhao (2017) proposed redesigning the purchasing contract to address this problem, but other approaches to this problem remain an interesting research direction. Further, inventory management and supply chain coordination along various drug supply chains have attracted little attention and yet are promising areas for study. Finally, downstream reimbursement policy and insurance plans are also of great importance and experiencing many innovations worth investigating.
- *Vaccine supply chains:* The influenza vaccine supply chain remains an interesting area, as it is a recurring challenge, and the dynamics of the vaccine supply chain may change as technology advances and consumers' attitudes toward vaccination changes. This problem is complex, due to myriads of uncertainties in yield, demand, flu virus activities, and vaccine composition. The model presented in section 8.3.2.1 focuses on a contract made *ex-ante*, usually in January, before uncertainty in demand and supply is resolved. In reality, retailers often place subsequent orders during a flu season after observing realized demands. Cho and Tang (2013) considered two-ordering opportunities of a retailer under a wholesale price contract. It will be intriguing to study more sophisticated contracts such as those contracts studied in this chapter combined with the second ordering opportunity during a flu season. Another avenue of research is to analyze the design of a contract in competitive environments. Federgruen and Yang (2008) studied a retailer's problem of selecting multiple manufacturers

under a fixed wholesale price, and Cho and Tang (2014) considered a supply chain with one manufacturer and multiple competing retailers and examine capacity allocation schemes under a wholesale price contract. Contracting problems between multiple manufacturers and multiple retailers under uncertain demand and supply will provide important avenues of research. Finally, it will be interesting to study an individual's problem of selecting when to get vaccinated considering the possibility of a supply shortage.

Finally, with the advance of technology in collecting and analyzing data, research in this area calls for data-driven approaches in all of the above areas. Fortunately, ample data is available in the pharmaceutical/healthcare industry, both from the public domain and private entities. However, as in all other industries, how to make use of this data remains a challenge. It is also worth mentioning that private data is more challenging to obtain in a highly competitive industry where public image plays a dramatic role. Researchers are encouraged to seek long-term relationships with the industry to obtain private data for research.

Appendix

Proof of Proposition 8.3. In preparation, we first show that $\psi < 1 - w/p$. From the expression of $\pi_R^{RS}(Q, Q_e)$, we can compute

$$\frac{\partial \pi_R^{RS}(Q, Q_e)}{\partial Q} = (1-\psi)p \cdot \frac{\partial E[Z(Q, Q_e)]}{\partial Q} - w.$$

Noting that

$$\frac{\partial E[Z(Q, Q_e)]}{\partial Q} = \alpha \bar{F}(Q) + (1-\alpha) \times \left[(1-\beta)\bar{F}\left(\frac{Q}{1-\gamma}\right) + \beta \bar{F}\left(\frac{Q-\gamma Q_e}{1-\gamma}\right)\right] < 1,$$

we have

$$\frac{\partial \pi_R^{RS}(Q, Q_e)}{\partial Q} < (1-\psi)p - w.$$

The right-hand side of this inequality must be positive because otherwise $\partial \pi_R^{RS}(Q, Q_e)/\partial Q < 0$ for any $Q > 0$. Thus, we have

$$\psi < 1 - \frac{w}{p}. \tag{8.10}$$

Using (8.10), we next prove that it is optimal for the manufacturer to choose $Q_e = 0$. From the expression of $\partial\pi_M^{RS}(Q, Q_e)/\partial Q_e$, we can compute

$$\begin{aligned}\frac{\partial\pi_M^{RS}(Q, Q_e)}{\partial Q_e} &= \psi p \partial E[Z(Q, Q_e)]/\partial Q_e - (1-\beta)c \\ &= \psi p(1-\alpha)\beta\gamma \left[F\left(\frac{Q-\gamma Q_e}{1-\gamma}\right) - F(Q_e)\right] - (1-\beta)c \\ &\leq \psi p(1-\alpha)\beta\gamma - (1-\beta)c.\end{aligned}$$

From (8.10), we can further simplify this inequality to

$$\frac{\partial\pi_M^{RS}(Q, Q_e)}{\partial Q_e} < (1-\alpha)\beta\gamma(p-w) - (1-\beta)c < 0,$$

where the last inequality is due to the condition given in the proposition.

Finally, we prove that a revenue sharing contract is dominated by a wholesale price contract. For this, it suffices to show that the retailer's order quantity Q decreases in ψ. This follows from the result that $\partial\pi_R^{RS}(Q, Q_e)/\partial Q = (1-\psi) p\partial E[Z(Q, Q_e)]/\partial Q - w$ decreases in ψ. □

Proof of Proposition 8.4. We prove that the marginal benefit of early production under a quantity flexibility contract is always lower than that of the first-best solution.

First, from Eq. (8.8), the marginal benefit of early production in the centralized supply chain is

$$p\frac{\partial E[Z(Q, Q_e)]}{\partial Q_e} = p(1-\alpha)\beta\gamma \cdot [F((Q-\gamma Q_e)/(1-\gamma)) - F(Q_e)].$$

Second, under a quantity flexibility contract, the manufacturer's expected profit is $\pi_M^{QF}(Q, Q_e) = (w-c)Q - (1-\beta)cQ_e - E[T(Q, Q_e)]$, where $E[T(Q, Q_e)]$ is the expected transfer payment from the manufacturer to the retailer. So, the marginal benefit of early production to the manufacturer is $-\partial E[T(Q, Q_e)]/\partial Q_e$ under this contract. We compute $-\partial E[T(Q, Q_e)]/\partial Q_e$ for the case when $0 \leq \kappa < 1 - Q_e/Q$ and for the case when $1 - Q_e/Q \leq \kappa < 1$. When $0 \leq \kappa < 1 - Q_e/Q$, we can compute

$$\begin{aligned}E[R(Q, Q_e)] &= \alpha\left[\int_0^{(1-\kappa)Q} \kappa Q dF(\xi) + \int_{(1-\kappa)Q}^{Q} (Q-\xi)dF(\xi)\right] \\ &+ (1-\alpha)\beta\left[\int_0^{\frac{(1-\kappa)Q-\gamma Q_e}{1-\gamma}} \kappa Q dF(\xi) + \int_{\frac{(1-\kappa)Q-\gamma Q_e}{1-\gamma}}^{\frac{Q-\gamma Q_e}{1-\gamma}} [Q-\gamma Q_e-(1-\gamma)\xi]dF(\xi)\right. \\ &+ (1-\alpha)(1-\beta)\left[\int_0^{\frac{(1-\kappa)Q}{1-\gamma}} \kappa Q dF(\xi) + \int_{\frac{(1-\kappa)Q}{1-\gamma}}^{\frac{Q}{1-\gamma}} [Q-(1-\gamma)\xi]dF(\xi)\right].\end{aligned}$$

From this, we have

$$-\frac{\partial E[T(Q,Q_e)]}{\partial Q_e} = w(1-\alpha)\beta\gamma\left[F\left(\frac{Q-\gamma Q_e}{1-\gamma}\right) - F\left(\frac{(1-\kappa)Q-\gamma Q_e}{1-\gamma}\right)\right]$$
$$< w\frac{\partial E[Z(Q,Q_e)]}{\partial Q_e}$$
$$< p\frac{\partial E[Z(Q,Q_e)]}{\partial Q_e},$$

where the first inequality is due to $Q_e < (1-\kappa)Q = \frac{(1-\kappa)Q-\gamma(1-\kappa)Q}{1-\gamma} < \frac{(1-\kappa)Q-\gamma Q_e}{1-\gamma}$ under the condition for κ. Next, when $1 - Q_e/Q \leq \kappa < 1$, we can similarly show that

$$-\partial E[T(Q,Q_e)]/\partial Q_e = w(1-\alpha)\beta\gamma \cdot [F((Q-\gamma Q_e)/(1-\gamma)) - F(Q_e)]$$
$$\times < p\partial E[Z(Q,Q_e)]/\partial Q_e.$$

Therefore, when $Q_e^{FB} > 0$, a QF contract cannot coordinate the supply chain. □

Acknowledgment

The authors of this chapter appreciate the contributions of Tinglong Dai, Justin Jia, and Fuqiang Zhang to their original work. They also benefitted from helpful discussions with several industry practitioners.

References

Adida, E., D. Dey, H. Mamani. (2013). Operational Issues and Network Effects in Vaccine Markets. *European Journal of Operational Research* 231(2) 414–427.

Ahuja, V., J. Birge, C. Syverson, E. Huang, M. Sohn. (2015). *Quality Management Using Data Analytics: An Application to Pharmaceutical Regulation*. Working paper. Southern Methodist University. Dallas, TX.

Ahuja, V., J. Birge. (2016). Response-Adaptive Designs for Clinical Trials: Simultaneous Learning from Multiple Patients. *European Journal of Operational Research* 248(2016) 619–633.

Angelus, A., E. Porteus. (2002). Simultaneous Capacity and Production Management of Short-Life-Cycle, Produce-to-Stock Goods under Stochastic Demand. *Management Science* 48(3) 399–413.

Arifoğlu, K., S. Deo, S. Iravani. (2012). Consumption Externality and Yield Uncertainty in the Influenza Vaccine Supply Chain: Interventions in Demand and Supply Sides. *Management Science* 58(6) 1072–1091.

ASPE. (2011). Economic Analysis of the Causes of Drug Shortages. *Tech. rep., Office of the Assistant Secretary for Planning and Evaluation*, U.S. Department of Health and Human Services.

Ball, G., E. Siemsen and R. Shah. (2017). Do plant inspections predict future quality? The role of investigator experience. *Manufacturing & Service Operations Management*, 19(4), pp.534–550.

Burns, L.R. (2002). *The Health Care Value Chain: Producers, Purchasers, and Providers*. John Wiley & Sons.

Cachon, G. (2003). Supply Chain Coordination with Contracts. In A.G. De Kok, S C. Graves, eds. *Handbooks in Operations Research and Management Science, Vol. 11. Supply Chain Management: Design, Coordination, and Operation*. Elsevier Science, Amsterdam, The Netherlands.

CDC. (2016). Influenza (Flu). https://www.cdc.gov/flu/. Accessed on November 4, 2016. Centers for Disease Control and Prevention.

Cherici, C., J. Frazier, M. Feldman, B. Gordon, C.A. Petrykiw, W.L. Russell, J. Souza. (2011a). *Navigating Drug Shortages in American Healthcare: A Premier healthcare alliance analysis*. Tech. rep.

Cherici, C., P. McGinnis, W. Russell. (2011b). *Buyer Beware: Drug Shortages and the Gray Market*. Tech. rep., Premier healthcare alliance.

Chick, S.E., H. Mamani, D. Simchi-Levi. (2008). Supply Chain Coordination and Influenza Vaccination. *Operations Research* 56(6) 1493–1506.

Cho, S.-H. (2010). The Optimal Composition of Influenza Vaccines Subject to Random Production Yields. *Manufacturing Service Operations Management* 12(2) 256–277.

Cho, S.-H., C.S. Tang. (2013). Advance Selling in a Supply Chain under Uncertain Supply and Demand. *Manufacturing Service Operations Management* 15(2) 305–319.

Cho, S.-H., C.S. Tang. (2014). Capacity Allocation under Retail Competition: Uniform and Competitive Allocations. *Operations Research* 62(1) 72–80.

Crama, P., B. Reyck, Z. Degraeve. (2008). Milestone Payments or Royalties? Contract Design for R&D Licensing. *Operations Research* 56(6) 1539–1552.

Dai, T., S.-H. Cho, F. Zhang. (2016). Contracting for On-Time Delivery in the U.S. Influenza Vaccine Supply Chain. *Manufacturing Service Operations Management* 18(3) 332–346.

Ebel, T., E. Larsen, K. Shah. (2013) *Strengthening Health Care's Supply Chain: A Five-Step Plan*. McKinsey & Company.

FDA. (2011). A Review of FDA's Approach to Medical Product Shortages. *Tech. rep., U.S. Food and Drug Administration*, U.S. Department of Health & Human Services.

FDA. (2013). Strategic Plan for Preventing and Mitigating Drug Shortages. *Tech. rep., U.S. Food and Drug Administration*, U.S. Department of Health & Human Services.

FDA. (2014). CMC Postapproval Manufacturing Changes to Be Documented in Annual Reports. *Tech. rep., U.S. Food and Drug Administration*, U.S. Department of Health & Human Services.

Federgruen, A., N. Yang. (2008). Selecting a portfolio of suppliers under demand and supply risks. *Operations Research* 56(4) 916–936.

Fleischhacker, A., A. Ninh, Y. Zhao. (2014). Inventory Positioning in Clinical Trial Supply Chains. *Production and Operations Management* 24 991–1011.

GAO. (2011). Drug Shortages: FDA's Ability to Respond Should Be Strengthened. *Tech. rep.*, U.S. Government Accountability Office.

GAO. (2014). Drug Shortages: Public Health Threat Continues, Despite Efforts to Help Ensure Product Availability. *Tech. rep.*, U.S. Government Accountability Office.

Gray J., E. Siemsen, G. Vasudeva. (2015). Collocation Still Matters: Conformance Quality and the Interdepedence of R&D and Manufacturing in the Pharmaceutical Industry. *Management Science* 61(11) 2760–2781.

Gupta, D., M. Mehrotra. (2015). Bundled Payments for Healthcare Services: Proposer Selection and Information Sharing. *Operations Research* 63(4) 772–288.

Health Industry Distributors Association. (2011). 2010–2011 Influenza Vaccine Production & Distribution.

Health Industry Distributors Association. (2015). Healthcare Supply Chain 2015: Insights from the Industry.

Hu, Q., L.B. Schwarz, N.A. Uhan. (2012). The Impact of Group Purchasing Organizations on Healthcare-Product Supply Chains. *Manufacturing & Service Operations Management* 14(1) 7–23.

Jia, Z., H. Zhao. (2017). Mitigating the U.S. Drug Shortages through Pareto-Improving Contracts. *Production and Operations Management* 26(8) 1463–1480.

Kouvelis, P., Y. Xiao, N. Yang. (2015). PBM Competition in Pharmaceutical Supply Chain: Formulary Design and Drug Pricing. *Manufacturing & Service Operations Management* 17(4) 511–526.

Martino, K., Y. Zhao, A. Fein. (2013). Resell versus Direct Models in Brand Drug Distribution. *International Journal of Pharmaceutical and Healthcare Marketing* 7 324–340

Navarro, R.P. (2009). *Managed care pharmacy practice*. 2nd ed. Jones and Bartlett Publishers.

Özaltin, O., O. Prokopyev, A. Schaefer, M. Roberts. (2011). Optimizing the Societal Benefits of the Annual Influenza Vaccine: A Stochastic Programming Approach. *Operations Research* 59(5) 1131–1143.

Pennic, J. (2013). 5 Ways Supply Chain Can Reduce Rising Healthcare Costs. Available at http://hitconsultant.net/2013/05/13/5-ways-supply-chain-can-reduce-rising-healthcare-costs/. Accessed on September 28, 2016.

Philipson, T. (2003). Economic Epidemiology and Infectious Diseases. A.J. Culyer, J.P. Newhouse, eds. *Handbook of Health Economics*, Vol. 1B. Elsevier Science, Amsterdam, 1761–1799.

Piana, R. (2012). Drug Shortages Hit Oncology Hard: Experts Weigh in on Challenges and Solutions. *The ASCO Post.*

Pierskalla, W. (2004). Blood Banking Supply Chain Management. *In Operations Research and Health Care, A Handbook of Methods and Applications*, M. Brandeau, F. Sainfort and W.P. Pierskella, editors. Kluwer Academic Publishers, New York, 104–145.

Schwarz, L. B. (2010). Healthcare-Product Supply Chains: Medical-surgical supplies, pharmaceuticals, and orthopedic devices. Y. Yi, ed. *Handbook of Healthcare-Delivery Systems*, CRC Press, Boca Raton, FL.

Schwarz, L., H. Zhao. (2011). The Unexpected Impact of Information-Sharing on US Pharmaceutical Supply-Chains. *Interfaces* 41 354–364.

Sood, N. (2017). Follow the Money: The Flow of Funds in the Pharmaceutical Distribution System. Presentation, USC Schaeffer Center for Health Policy & Economics.

Tsay, A. (1999). Quantity-Flexibility Contract and Supplier-Customer Incentives. *Management Science* 45(10) 1339–1358.

Tomlin, B. (2006). On the Value of Mitigation and Contingency Strategies for Managing Supply Chain Disruption Risks. *Management Science* 52(5) 639–657.

Ventola, C.L. (2011). The Drug Shortage Crisis in the United States: Causes, Impact, and Management Strategies. *Pharmacy and Therapeutics* 36(11) 740.

Xu, L., V. Mani, H. Zhao. (2016). *Not a Box of Nuts and Bolts: The Distribution Channel Decision of the Rising Specialty Drugs.* Working paper. Penn State University. University Park, PA.

Xu, L., H. Zhao, N. Petruzzi. (2017). *Post-Market Study Compliance for Drugs Under Accelerated Approval.* Working paper. Penn State University. University Park, PA.

Yamin, D., A. Gavious. (2013). Incentives' Effect in Influenza Vaccination Policy. *Management Science* 59(12) 2667–2686.

Yurukoglu, A. (2012). *Medicare Reimbursements and Shortages of Sterile Injectable Pharmaceuticals.* Working paper. Stanford University. Stanford, CA.

Zhao, H., C. Xiong, S. Gavirneni, A. Fein. (2012). Fee-For-Service Contracts in Pharmaceutical Distribution Supply Chains: Design, Analysis, and Management. *Manufacturing & Service Operations Management* 14(4) 685–699.

Zhou, D., L. Leung, W. Pierskalla. (2011). Inventory Management of Platelets in Hospitals: Optimal Inventory Policy for Perishable Products with Regular and Optional Expedited Replenishments. *Manufacturing & Service Operations Management* 13(4) 420–438.

9

Organ Transplantation*

Barış Ata[1], John J. Friedewald[2], and A. Cem Randa[1]

[1] University of Chicago
[2] Northwestern University

9.1 Introduction

The first successful solid organ transplantation was done in 1954 between identical twins (Merrill et al., 1956). With the discovery and rapid development of immunosuppressive drugs (Halloran, 2004), organ transplantation became widely available. These outstanding achievements changed the course of treatment of many end stage diseases and brought hope to countless patients suffering from them.

Solid organ transplantation can be carried out using organs from either living or deceased donors. The former is preferred because the graft failure risk of the organ is lower in that case (Trotter et al., 2002). At the same time, a living donor needs to continue having a productive life after the organ donation. Kidney transplants are the primary example of living-donor transplants because the nephrological functions of the human body can be handled by one kidney (Johnson et al., 1999). Living-donor partial liver transplants are another example (though they are much less common) because the liver itself is regenerative (Hashikura et al., 2002).

Living organ donation occurs between a recipient and a consenting (living) donor. The donor and the recipient are typically supposed to be biologically or emotionally related in this situation, and any type of monetary transactions are

*This work was supported in part by Health Resources and Services Administration contract 234-2005-37011C. The content is the responsibility of the authors alone and does not necessarily reflect the views or policies of the Department of Health and Human Services, nor does mention of trade names, commercial products, or organizations imply endorsement by the US Government.
†Baris.Ata@chicagobooth.edu
‡John.Friedewald@nm.org
§randa@chicagobooth.edu

Handbook of Healthcare Analytics: Theoretical Minimum for Conducting 21st Century Research on Healthcare Operations, First Edition. Edited by Tinglong Dai and Sridhar Tayur.

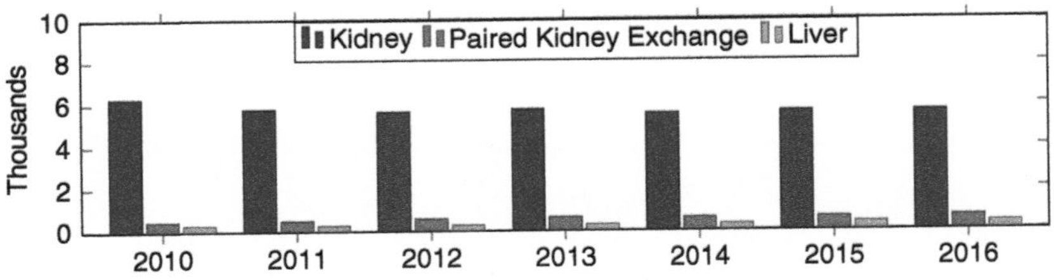

Figure 9.1 Total number of living organ donations over years. Based on OPTN data as of January 1, 2017.

strictly prohibited by the National Organ Transplantation Act (NOTA, 1984). A primary concern in living organ donation is to avoid the black market. For a comprehensive discussion of other ethical challenges in living-donor transplantation, see Gordon (2012).

Several researchers have explored decision problems involving living-donor transplants. David and Yechiali (1985) and Alagoz et al. (2004) studied the decision problem of a recipient–living-donor pair for a kidney and liver transplant, respectively. They characterized the optimal timing of the surgical operation under the objective of maximizing the quality adjusted life years (QALY) of the recipient from the transplant. Living-donor kidney transplants are more challenging than living-donor liver transplants, due to the increased complexity of histocompatibility. Although a person might be willing to donate her kidney to a specific patient, this might not be biologically feasible. When multiple such incompatible pairs are interested in a living-donor kidney transplant, an opportunity arises if the potential recipients are willing to exchange their donors. Such an exchange can facilitate a match between the new recipient–donor pairs. This is often referred to as the kidney exchange; see, for example, Zenios (2002), Roth et al. (2004, 2005), Segev et al. (2005), Ashlagi et al. (2011), and Glorie et al. (2014) for mechanism design and optimization approaches to facilitating kidney exchange. Although it is an active and important research area, see Figure 9.1, living-donor transplantation is beyond the scope of this chapter.

This chapter focuses on resource allocation problems arising in the deceased-donor kidney and liver transplant systems. A deceased-donor organ transplant is carried out by procuring a donor's organs after brain death or cardiac arrest.[1] It requires consent of the donors or their family. Although the deceased-donor transplants are performed for a range of organs, such as heart, lung, pancreas, and intestines, kidney and liver transplants constitute the great majority of the total number of deceased-donor organ transplants (see Figure 9.2). As such, we will focus attention on kidney and liver transplants.

1 To increase organ supply, donation after cardiac death is also permissible (Foley et al., 2005; Bernat et al., 2006).

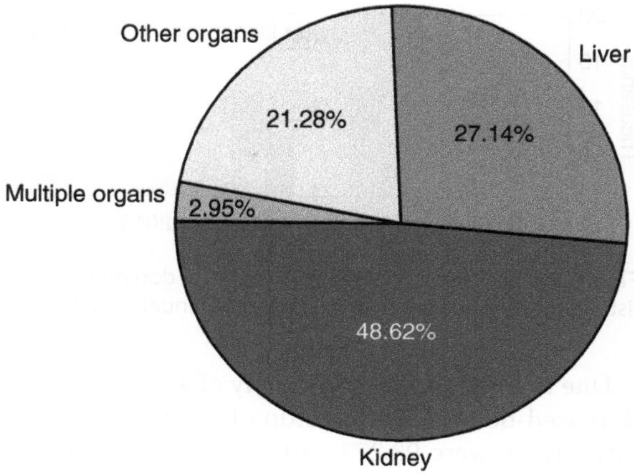

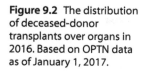

Figure 9.2 The distribution of deceased-donor transplants over organs in 2016. Based on OPTN data as of January 1, 2017.

9.2 The Deceased-Donor Organ Allocation System: Stakeholders and Their Objectives

The most prevalent aspect of the deceased-donor organ transplant system for our purposes is the severe organ shortage. Figures 9.3 and 9.4 show that the number of new patients in need of transplants far exceeds the number of organs available for transplant. Organ allocation is an instrument to match the limited supply of organs with the demand for them. However, the severe supply shortage turns the organ allocation problem essentially into a rationing problem. Several studies consider initiatives to boost the organ supply so that more patients can receive transplants. For example, Zheng et al. (2018) studied the effects of incentivizing living organ donation by prioritizing the donors in the case that they need an organ transplant in the future. Arikan et al. (2017) studied the impact of broader geographical sharing of low-quality organs on the deceased-donor organ procurement rates. Although such efforts can help to increase the organ supply, the severe shortage of organs available for transplant remains a key challenge.

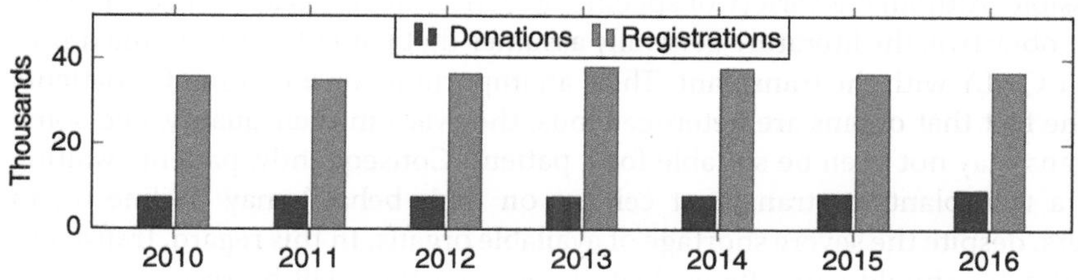

Figure 9.3 Number of deceased-donor kidney donations and new registrations to the waiting list over the years. Based OPTN data as of January 1, 2017.

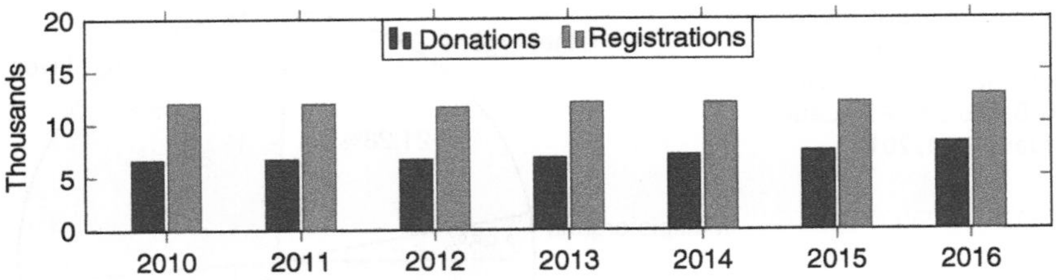

Figure 9.4 Number of deceased-donor liver donations and new registrations to the waiting list over the years. Based OPTN data as of January 1, 2017.

Due to the imbalance in supply of and demand for organs, the United States deceased-donor kidney waiting list has been growing at an alarming rate. In 2016, there were 98,272 patients registered on the waiting list, whereas only 13,431 candidates received transplants. A similar situation persists in the liver transplant waiting list, with 14,361 new patients registering and only 7,469 candidates receiving transplants in the same year.

The deceased-donor transplantation system comprises various stakeholders with different objectives. The key stakeholders are patients/transplant candidates, hospitals/transplant centers, the central planner (The Organ Procurement and Transplant Network [OPTN], a federal contract held by the United Network of Organ Sharing [UNOS]), organ procurement organizations (OPOs), and society.

The transplant candidates and their wellbeing are the main focus of the deceased-donor organ transplant system. For end-stage liver disease (ESLD) patients, transplantation is the only viable treatment. Without a transplant, the mortality rate of ESLD patients is quite high. In contrast, the end-stage renal disease (ESRD) patients are perhaps more fortunate because they may live up to ten years on dialysis. However, this treatment requires the patients to visit a dialysis center up to three times a week, which imposes a significant burden, potentially limiting the patients' opportunity for full-time employment. In addition, from the medical perspective, the desired therapy for ESRD patients is transplantation.

Presumably, a patient's primary objective is to live as long and well as possible. Although a variety of specific objective functions are consistent with that objective, the literature generally assumes that patients strive to maximize their QALY with the transplant. Thus, an important consideration for patients is the fact that organs are heterogeneous; they vary in their quality, and some organs may not even be suitable for a patient. Consequently, patients waiting for a transplant (or transplant centers on their behalf) may decline organ offers, despite the severe shortage of available organs. In this regard, transplant candidates should carefully evaluate how often they will be receiving organ offers of various quality and consider that factor when making an accept/reject decision when about an organ offer. Several researchers have studied dynamic programming formulations of patients' accept/reject decisions about possible organ offers; see, for example, Ahn and Hornberger (1996), Alagoz et al. (2007a,b) and Sandikci et al. (2008, 2013).

As mentioned above, organ donors are heterogeneous in terms of age or history of medical comorbidities such as diabetes or hypertension. As a result, the deceased-donor organs vary in their graft failure risk and useful life after transplantation. The graft failure risk of a kidney can be quantified in terms of some donor characteristics. Israni et al. (2014) introduced a the kidney donor profile index (KDPI), which is derived from the kidney donor risk index (KDRI). KDRI takes into account factors such as donor age, height, weight, ethnicity, and history of hypertension, and diabetes (Rao et al., 2009). KDPI is the percentile score of a kidney in terms of decreasing graft failure risk.

The graft failure risk of a deceased-donor liver can be predicted using several donor characteristics such as length of intensive care unit stay and antecedents of hypertension (Cuende et al., 2005); existence and degree of steatosis (Salizzoni et al., 2003); race, height, and involvement in a cerebrovascular accident (Feng et al., 2006); and age, blood type, and gender (Roberts et al., 2004). Transplant surgeons and candidates base their beliefs about graft survival of an organ mostly on this information. Candidates seek to transplant an organ that will survive for sufficiently long; consequently, they may decline organ offers if they are not satisfied with the organ quality.

Organ quality is not the sole predictor of a transplant candidate's decision. Transplant candidates themselves are heterogeneous, in terms of their own health status in particular. To be more specific, in the deceased-donor liver allocation system, transplant candidates are classified with respect to their likelihood of mortality. This classification also plays a key role in their prioritization by the liver allocation policy. If a candidate has a life expectancy of less than seven days without a liver transplant, she is classified as Status 1A. Candidates who are not eligible for Status 1A are assigned a score that reflects the probability of death within a three-month period. This scoring system is called the model for end-stage liver disease (MELD) scoring system which was first suggested by Malinchoc et al., (2000). A MELD score takes into account the serum concentrations of bilirubin and creatinine, the international normalized ratio for prothrombin (INR) time, and the cause of the underlying liver disease as predictors of survival. The maximum MELD score is 40, which means the probability of death within three months is 97 percent. If a patient has a MELD score of less than 6, she does not need a liver transplant. A patient's MELD score evolves over time as she waits for a transplant. Although the evolution is not necessarily for the worse, it is more likely that the health status of an ESLD patient will deteriorate over time. As a result, it is natural for the liver transplant candidate to lean more toward accepting an organ offer when the health condition gets more critical.

The mortality rate while waiting for a transplant does not vary as much across ESRD patients. However, the survival after a transplant depends on both the donor's characteristics and the recipient's health status (Clayton et al., 2014). The latter is quantified by the estimated post-transplant survival (EPTS) score, developed by the Scientific Registry of Transplant Recipients (SRTR) contractor upon request of the OPTN Kidney Transplantation Committee. The EPTS score of a patient takes into account her age, dialysis duration, prior solid organ transplantation, and diabetes status (Israni et al., 2014). Candidates with lower EPTS scores have a lower mortality risk after transplantation compared to those with higher EPTS scores. In addition, the EPTS score of a candidate gets worse with waiting because it increases with dialysis duration and age. This score can have a significant effect on the transplant candidate's tendency to accept organ offers. Even though the candidate may plan to wait for a high-quality kidney at first, her aspirations may change as she waits longer, because staying on dialysis for a long time may significantly lower the post-transplant graft survival, as captured by the EPTS score.

Healthcare professionals monitor and guide the candidates throughout the entire transplantation process. In the case of deceased-donor kidney transplants, candidates continuously visit dialysis centers until they receive a transplant. Dialysis centers keep track of their patients' schedule of visits and monitor their health status closely. They decide the best type of dialysis to offer according to health status of the patient; see, for example, Zenios and Fuloria (2000) and Lee et al. (2008). Because most patients wait a long time to receive a transplant, dialysis centers and their interactions with the candidates constitute an important part of the overall process. The involvement of healthcare professionals with liver patients can be even more dramatic. Many liver transplant candidates are hospitalized while they wait for a transplant. In both the liver and kidney transplant systems, healthcare institutions devote significant resources toward the well-being of their patients before any transplant surgery.

Transplant centers are involved in various administrative tasks, the surgery, and the pre- and post-transplant care of the patient. They register transplant candidates to the waiting list and are responsible for assessing each candidate's physical condition. The physicians and surgeons at a transplant center play a particularly important role. Because the candidates do not necessarily have the medical wisdom to assess their own situations, physicians and surgeons evaluate the organ offers and guide candidates through accepting or rejecting them. If the candidate accepts an organ offer, the transplant center facilitates the transplant surgery.

The performance of transplant centers is measured by risk-adjusted post-transplant outcomes. In fact, transplant centers are highly regulated under the Medicare Conditions of Participation (CoPs)[2], and centers that do not meet the

2 Department of Health and Human Services (ruling no: CMS-3835-F, March 30, 2007).

performance standards are flagged for performance review. Although CoPs are intended to protect the wellbeing of the transplant candidates, CoPs may also force transplant centers to be more risk-averse (Arikan et al., 2016; Delasay and Tayur, 2017).

To be specific, transplant centers are monitored for short-term patient and graft survival. This may have unintended consequences both when the transplant centers list the patients and when patients/surgeons make accept/reject decisions about organ offers. Patients with ESLD/ESRD go through an evaluation to decide their candidacy for organ transplantation. Moreover, once a patient is listed as a transplant candidate, he may need to undergo periodic testing to determine eligibility. The evaluation process prior to listing a patient tries to identify those patients who may benefit the most from transplantation, as well as those patients who may be placed at risk. Listing practices vary significantly across different transplant centers; whereas some transplant centers welcome risky patients, others do not.

The acceptance criteria for organ offers used by different transplant centers vary significantly as well. They may depend on a number of factors; including the risk tolerances of the transplant centers and the clinicians. Acceptance criteria can also be affected by the performance monitoring of transplant centers. The performance reports of all transplant programs are publicly available and have been used by insurance providers, prospective transplant candidates, the policy makers, and the public to evaluate transplant centers' performance. This provides a serious disincentive for the transplant centers to use high-risk organs. On the one hand, poor short-term outcomes are harmful both to the patients and the transplant centers. They can even jeopardize the viability of a transplant center. On the other hand, the deceased donor transplant system in the United States suffers from a high rate of discarded organs. Many attribute this, in part, to the institutional risk aversion, in addition to the various inefficiencies of the allocation system, which are discussed below.

OPOs procure donated organs after a donor's brain death. They assess the organ's characteristics and report it for a transplant candidate's evaluation. The procurement is done according to the Final Rule[3] issued by the Department of Health and Human Services (DHHS). The organ is procured unless one of the following occurs:

(i) The donor does not meet the criteria for eligible donors,
(ii) The organ has been ruled out by basic donor information or by laboratory data prior to the donor entering the operating room for excision of organs,
(iii) The family does not agree to donate the organ,
(iv) The search for a recipient for that organ has ended unsuccessfully prior to the donor's entrance into the operating room.

3 Department of Health and Human Services (ruling no: CMS-1543-R, Dec 21, 2006).

If none of these four conditions is true, the DHHS Final Rule states that "intent" is present, and the procurement may proceed.

Unfortunately, not every medically acceptable organ is procured and offered for transplantation, which is surprising, given the severe organ shortage. Organ procurement itself involves a surgical operation and takes significant time on the part of healthcare personnel and facilities. The heterogeneity of the deceased-donor organs may cause some of them not to be procured. Organ procurement rates vary significantly across different locations. For example, the lowest-quality kidney procured in New York is consistently of lower quality than the highest-quality kidney not procured in Utah, as observed by Arikan et al. (2017). Arikan et al. (2017) explore the reasons for these geographical differences in organ procurement rates and how changes to geographical sharing may increase organ procurement rates.

The Organ Procurement and Transplantation Network (OPTN) is the network of transplant centers and OPOs established by the US Congress under the NOTA in 1984. OPTN facilitates the interaction among all professionals involved in organ donation and transplantation. The United Network of Organ Sharing (UNOS) is a private nonprofit organization that administers the OPTN under contract with the Health Resources and Services Administration of the US Department of Health and Human Services.

A primary function of UNOS is to allocate (scarce) deceased-donor organs to transplant candidates. Given the imbalance between supply of and demand for organs, any allocation system that UNOS uses is bound to favor some candidates over others. Given the counteracting objectives of all the stakeholders involved in the transplantation system, it is virtually impossible to base deceased-donor organ allocation rules on a single metric. The 1984 NOTA mandates that the deceased-donor organ allocation system take into account both efficiency (i.e., patient and graft survival) and equity (i.e., fair allocation) (NOTA, 1984). There is also consensus in the transplant community that the overall objective of the allocation process should be to balance efficiency and equity (Kusserow, 1991; Zenios et al., 2000; Bertsimas et al., 2012; Akan et al., 2012). The equity can be achieved by providing all candidates with equal opportunity to receive a transplant. In other words, an equitable allocation policy should give patients with different demographics equal access to organs. Efficiency corresponds to maximizing the total QALYs from transplant for all candidates. One way to improve efficiency is to increase the overall post-transplant survival. This is one of UNOS's primary concerns, and it directly affects UNOS's choice of organ allocation policy. However, because the post-transplant survival depends on both the recipient's health status/characteristics and the donor's characteristics, it is not immediately obvious which policy will achieve this goal.

Another way to improve efficiency is to lower organ wastage, which occurs, in part due to the perishable nature of the procured deceased-donor organs.

The time lag between when an organ is procured and when it is transplanted, that is, cold ischemia time (CIT), is an important factor affecting the graft survival of an organ (Rao et al., 2009). As CIT increases, the graft failure risk increases. Donated organs that are not transplanted to a recipient within a reasonable time have to be discarded. Because of the severe organ shortage, minimizing organ wastage is important, yet remains challenging. One reason for this difficulty is that transplant candidates, for their own sake, reserve the right to reject organ offers. If an organ gets rejected by sufficiently many patients, the CIT for the organ may exceed the maximum allowable duration that it can be stored, and the organ has to be discarded. Therefore, addressing organ wastage requires UNOS to predict the transplant candidates' responses to organ offers, which itself is a challenging task.

As UNOS strives to balance efficiency and equity, it must also consider important biological constraints. In particular, a donated organ may not be a match for every transplant candidate on the waiting list. A transplanted organ can be perceived as a foreign intrusion, and the human body's immune system may put forth an effort to destroy the transplanted organ to protect itself. In order to avoid this mismatch, a prospective donor-recipient pair should satisfy certain match criteria (Weir and Lerma, 2014, Busuttil and Klintmalm, 2014).

One basic matching criterion is ABO blood type: A, B, O, or AB. Candidates can receive organs from donors of identical blood type. Blood type AB candidates are compatible to receive organs from donors of all other blood types, whereas blood type O donors are compatible to donate organs to candidates of all other blood types. If the donor-recipient pair is neither blood type identical nor compatible, it is ABO mismatched. ABO mismatched kidney transplantation is not allowed by UNOS. ABO mismatched liver transplantation is technically possible but not advised (Gugenheim et al., 1990). Accordingly, only candidates of severe health conditions receive liver offers with ABO mismatch.

Blood type matching is not the only criterion for histocompatibility. The human body contains human leukocyte antigens (HLAs), which define the familiarity of certain proteins to our organism. In the case of an organ transplant, the HLA antigens of the donor organ that do not match the recipient may be recognized as an intrusion by the recipient's body upon transplantation. Corresponding anti-HLA antibodies are formed in the recipient's immune system, which can cause acute and chronic rejection. To avoid this scenario, the candidate is treated with immunosuppressive drugs that prevent anti-HLA production mechanism. This treatment increases the candidate's access to organs, yet it may decrease the graft survival. Moreover, if the candidate has preformed HLA antibodies against the organ prior to the transplant, the donor-recipient pair is identified as a positive cross match, and the transplantation is ruled out.

Upon every organ donation, UNOS determines the eligible pool of candidates according to the above criteria. The eligible candidates can be located anywhere

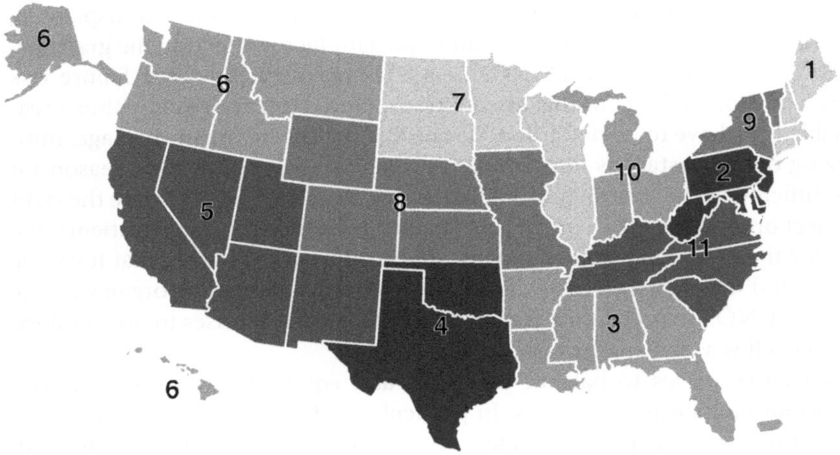

Figure 9.5 UNOS Regions, retrieved from http://optn.transplant.hrsa.gov

in the United States. To facilitate the allocation of organs, UNOS has established 11 geographic regions that are further subdivided into 58 local donor service areas (DSAs); see Figure 9.5 for an illustration of UNOS regions. A DSA consists of potentially multiple transplant centers and one OPO. A donated organ is first offered to the candidates waiting listed in the DSA of the OPO that is procuring the organ. If no transplant candidate within the DSA accepts the offer, then the organ is offered to the regional list. Similarly, if no one within the region accepts the offer, then it is offered to the national list.

At each step of the process, candidates are assigned points that depend on both the donor's and candidate's characteristics. UNOS follows two inherently different point systems for deceased-donor kidney versus liver allocation. Both point systems exhibit a variety of features promoting efficiency and equity.

Candidates who are listed for more than one organ transplant (e.g., kidney-pancreas) receive top priority from UNOS. These patients are in high urgency in terms of their medical situation. In addition, as shown in Figure 9.2, the number of patients who need multiple organ transplants is far fewer then the number of patients listed for a single organ transplant. Hence, their prioritization does not significantly impact the allocation system while it provides efficiency by contributing to their survival. The liver allocation rule follows a similar principle by first offering organs to Status 1A candidates who otherwise would die in a week.

To further improve medical utility, ESRD patients with better EPTS scores are matched with kidneys of better KDPI scores. To be specific, candidates in the top 20th EPTS percentile are given priority to receive kidneys in the top 20th KDPI percentile (so called longevity matching). Pediatric candidates, because their EPTS scores are better due to their youth, are preferentially offered kidneys in the top 34th KDPI percentile. These practices attempt to minimize the graft failure risk by exploiting the good health status of candidates before they wait on dialysis for too long.

Pediatric candidates receive further prioritization. These candidates are awarded with extra points, which presumably accelerates the process of receiving a transplant. This improves UNOS's objective of efficiency, because pediatric candidates have higher life expectancy. On the other hand, Bunzel and Laederach-Hofmann (2000) argue that the post-transplant noncompliance rate, that is, not adhering to immunosuppressive drug regimens, is high among pediatric recipients. This evidence raises the question of whether prioritizing the pediatric candidates necessarily results in higher efficiency.

One way in which the deceased-donor transplantation system builds equity in the kidney allocation policy is to award priority points to the patients commensurate with their waiting times. In most service systems, serving people (who have otherwise identical characteristics) on a first come, first-served basis is considered fair. In a similar vein, the deceased-donor kidney candidates begin to accrue waiting time points as soon as they are added to the wait list, and subsequently receive one point for each year they spend on the waiting list. All else being equal, the waiting time points ensure that whoever was listed earlier will also have access to organs earlier. The liver allocation system uses waiting time only as a tie breaker among patients who have identical MELD scores. Rather than accruing waiting time since the initial time they were listed, ESLD patients accrue waiting time for their historical MELD scores. In particular, the time they spend in each MELD category is recorded separately. Thus, a candidate's waiting time is the total waiting time spent at MELD scores higher than the current MELD score.

Sensitized patients (i.e., patients who have anti-HLA antibodies as a result of blood transfusion, pregnancy, or prior transplants) are at a disadvantage in terms of their likelihood of finding an eligible kidney and may wait twice as long as patients who are not sensitized. As previously mentioned, if a patient has anti-HLA antibodies that will counteract with at least one of the donor's HLAs, the pair is identified as a positive cross match. In this case, the transplantation is ruled out. Sensitized patients are more likely to have positive cross-match results. All transplant candidates are tested for anti-HLA antibodies and are assigned a calculated panel reactive antibody (CPRA) score, which is an estimate for how unlikely it is that a patient will find a matching kidney. For example, a patient with a CPRA score of 99 has only a 1 percent chance of finding an organ without a positive crossmatch. Patients who have CPRA scores greater than 20 are called sensitized and awarded extra points. Because they have a disadvantage in terms of finding a histocompatible organ, the extra points they receive stem from the desire to create an equitable allocation policy.

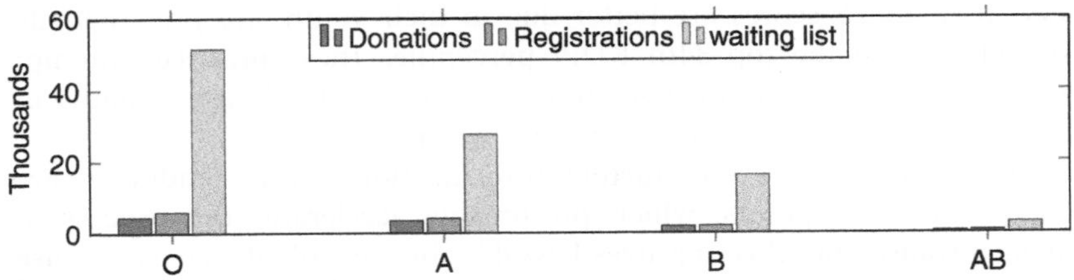

Figure 9.6 Number of deceased-donor kidney donations and new registrations in 2016, and the size of the current waiting list over blood types. Based on OPTN data as of May 26, 2017.

As discussed earlier, blood type compatibility is necessary for organ transplantation. On the other hand, the US population is not uniform in terms of ABO blood type distribution. This creates a discrepancy between organ supply and demand blood types for candidates of two blood types (see Figure 9.6). Blood type O donors are compatible with all other blood types. However, blood type O candidates can receive kidneys only from blood type O donors. This raises the risk that blood type O patients will have less access to organs if the organs are distributed on compatibility basis. On the other hand, blood type B is the most rare ABO blood type in the US population, which directly decreases the donations of blood type B. In order to ensure that blood type O and B candidates can receive transplants, donated kidneys with blood type O and B are first offered to blood type–identical candidates on the local, regional, and national lists. As a result, blood type O or B organs should be rejected by all the blood type–identical candidates on the local, regional, and national lists in order to be offered to any blood type compatible candidates. Exceptions occur only for transplant candidates with zero-HLA mismatch, when deceased-donor kidneys of blood type O and B are offered to candidates who do not have an identical blood type.

From an academic perspective, the interaction between UNOS and the transplant candidates can be viewed as strategic. Transplant candidates are forward looking and naturally seek to maximize their self interests. As such, they may decline organ offers without penalty. In an allocation system where waiting time matters, this can crucially influence the way candidates respond to organ offers. In particular, the transplant candidates close to the top of the waiting list tend to be more selective and reject more offers (Sandikci et al., 2008, 2013). This creates a dilemma for UNOS because the candidates who receive a higher risk organ offer first will likely decline it. In addition, Leshno (2015) shows that candidates who are expecting long waiting times tend to accept offers with mismatch, thus decreasing efficiency. Taking into account such incentives for the transplant candidates, UNOS has been making parallel offers using the online software DonorNet since 2007. DonorNet intends to expedite the organ placement by a system of electronic organ offers for organs refused by all centers in a given OPO. Through this system, offers are transmitted to transplant candidates outside of the donating OPO, with only three open offers allowed at a time and up to a one-hour allowance to decline an offer (Massie et al., 2009).

Using historical data, UNOS studies patients' past decisions to predict the responses to possible organ offers. The Scientific Registry of Transplant Recipients (SRTR) has studied transplant candidates' decisions about specific organ offers and has developed a prediction model that takes into account the donor and recipient characteristics; UNOS uses this model to evaluate the proposals for changes to allocation policy. In particular, the kidney pancreas simulation allocation model (KPSAM) and the liver simulation allocation model (LSAM), which were also developed by SRTR, are used to test policy proposals in order to predict the number of transplantations, number of deaths while waiting, and several other performance measures under the proposed changes. As a result, UNOS takes into account patient choice as it strives to improve allocation outcomes.

9.3 Research Opportunities in the Area

The complexity of the deceased-donor organ transplant system makes it challenging to come up with innovative solutions that improve the system and are broadly accepted by all stakeholders, especially given the inherent trade-off between efficiency and equity. Nonetheless, many researchers have been working on various aspects of the deceased-donor organ transplant system and have made important contributions over the last few decades. In what follows, we will discuss those as they relate to the resource allocation paradigm and operations research. We will also discuss some remaining challenges key to improving the deceased-donor kidney allocation system further.

9.3.1 Past Research on the Transplant Candidate's Problem

In evaluating any proposed change to the allocation policy and the resulting outcomes, it is important to take into account patient choice. Consider a transplant candidate who seeks to optimize her total QALYs. She may decline some organ offers, even though organs are scarce. Interestingly, it may be in her best interest to do so. Note that upon receiving an offer, the transplant candidate evaluates the expected life years that will result from accepting this offer. Then, she weighs this against the alternative and the likelihood of receiving a better organ in the future. As noted above, this reasoning can be formalized as an optimal stopping problem.

The organ quality is observable to the candidates when they are evaluating an offer. For kidneys, the graft failure risk is quantified by the KDPI score. Therefore, the candidate and the transplant surgeon can evaluate an organ in terms of the trade-off mentioned above. In the case of livers, the donor's age as well as comorbidities can be used to estimate the graft survival, which the physician can assess and communicate to the transplant candidate.

The organ characteristics are not the only deciding factors when a candidate is evaluating an organ offer. If the transplant candidate rejects an organ, she should consider when she is going to receive another organ offer. The motivation for doing so may differ for ESLD and ESRD patients. Because the mortality rate is high for liver transplant candidates, they reject an organ offer only if they are convinced that they will stay alive until another organ offer arrives. For kidney transplant candidates, the mortality rate is less of a concern. However, spending more time on dialysis decreases their EPTS score, hence the utility from a transplant. In both the deceased-donor kidney transplant system and the deceased-donor liver transplant system, a patient waiting for a transplant rejects an organ offer only if the expected benefit of doing so outweighs the expected cost.

To build intuition, let us consider the simpler case of deciding the optimal timing of a liver transplant from a living donor. Considering a living-donor–recipient pair provides significant insights on how recipient's behavior is affected purely by their health status. Because a living donor is involved, the candidates do not need to worry about the uncertainty in the timing of an organ offer from the waiting list. Additionally, the candidate does not need to account for uncertainty in organ quality. Alagoz et al. (2004) studied such a problem as a Markov Decision Process (MDP) in which an ESLD patient decides when to receive the transplant. They showed that the decision of the candidate follows a threshold policy over the MELD score and age of the living donor. David and Yechiali (1985) studied a similar problem for an ESRD patient. They characterized the optimal stopping decision of the patient as a function of the HLA match level with the living donor and the deteriorating health status of the patient.

If the candidate does not have a living donor, she needs to wait for an organ offer from the waiting list. For deceased-donor liver candidates, the likelihood of receiving an organ offer can accurately be inferred from the each candidate's MELD score. Alagoz et al. (2007a,b) modeled the deceased-donor liver offers to a specific candidate as a discrete time Markov Chain depending to the candidate's MELD score. Sandikci et al., (2008) built on the earlier models using perfect information from the waiting list as well as the MELD score. In reality, candidates do not get to observe their exact position on the waiting list. However, the fact that a candidate receives organ offers gives her some information about her position on the waiting list. Therefore, Sandikci et al. (2013) modeled the decisions of the candidate as a partially observed Markov decision problem. The candidate seeks to maximize QALY while the MELD score also evolves as a random walk. Under certain assumptions, the authors showed that the optimal policy is of threshold type, with respect to the monotone likelihood order on the space of probability measures.

Ahn and Hornberger (1996) and Hornberger and Ahn (1997) developed an empirical model for the decision process of a deceased-donor kidney candidate. They modeled the candidate's health as a discrete time Markov chain where the patient can have a status of on dialysis, ineligible for transplant, received a transplant, transplant failed, or deceased. They assumed that candidates apply a threshold policy to accept the deceased-donor kidney offers according to a one-year graft survival rate. The authors estimated this threshold using logistic regression.

9.3.2 Challenges in Modeling Patient Choice

A transplant candidate's decision cannot be studied in isolation from the decisions of the other candidates. For example, if the candidate has sufficient information about the waiting list, then she should consider the behavior of candidates who are ahead of her. In particular, the candidate should note that an organ offer will be available to her only if all candidates who have higher points reject the current organ offer. In other words, patients' choices should be studied in equilibrium. The specific equilibrium concept that is appropriate depends on both the informational assumptions and the tractability concerns. Sharpening these questions, and further studying the patients' accept/reject decisions in equilibrium is a fruitful future research direction.

However, considering the concept of equilibrium in the deceased-donor organ allocation system, we can reasonably believe that the candidates have little knowledge about the other candidates on the waiting list. This knowledge gap imposes a great deal of uncertainty when a candidate wants to forecast how the other candidates on the waiting list will behave. In a recent study, Bandi et al. (2016) modeled the US deceased-donor kidney system as a multiclass, multiserver queue where candidates have no information about other candidates and organ availability. The authors suggest a robust optimization solution methodology based on integer programming, and estimate waiting time given certain candidate characteristics.

Similar to most prior research, we postulate that a candidate's discrete choice of accepting or rejecting an organ offer is based on the difference between QALY after transplantation and the cost of waiting until receiving the specific type of organ. However, it may be too strong a position to take that the transplant candidate's behavior can be predicted as perfectly as the aforementioned analytical work suggests. In general, the candidate may take into account idiosyncratic factors that are unobservable to the researcher. Incorporating such idiosyncratic factors gives rise to the probabilistic discrete choice models that have been studied extensively in the literature; see, for example, Ben-Akiva and Lerman (1985) and Anderson et al. (1992).

Under such idiosyncratic factors or shocks to utility, the dynamic nature of the problem can be modeled as follows. A candidate has two choices upon every organ offer she receives: accepting the current offer or rejecting it to wait for a better-quality organ. The utility from accepting an organ offer is determined directly by the characteristics of the current organ under consideration, whereas the utility of rejecting the organ offer needs to take into account the utility to be gained from a possible offer accepted in the future and the cost of waiting as well as the possibility of death. This setting can be studied using the framework of dynamic discrete choice models. A closely related paper in the literature is Rust (1987), that used an optimal stopping problem to study a maintenance manager's decisions to either replace the engine of a bus and incur the cost of overhaul or not replace the engine and incurring the cost of unexpected failure. More recently, in the operations research literature, Aksin et al. (2013, 2017) proposed an optimal stopping model for empirically studying callers' abandonment behavior in a call center. Ata et al. (2017c) and Ata and Peng (2018) laid out the theoretical foundations of studying such optimal stopping models for call centers in an equilibrium framework, using queueing theory.

Ata et al. (2017b) used a dynamic discrete choice model to empirically study patients' accept/reject decisions for deceased-donor kidney offers in an equilibrium framework. The authors also conducted counterfactual studies to assess potential policy changes, taking into account possible changes in patient behavior.

9.3.3 Past Research on the Deceased-donor Organ Allocation Policy

One aspect of the allocation problem UNOS faces is geographic disparity. UNOS allocates deceased-donor organs according to geographic location. As noted above, UNOS divides the country into 11 regions, which are further divided into 58 DSAs. To be specific, the deceased-donor kidney allocation system works as follows: A deceased-donor kidney is first offered to the waiting lists in the DSA of the OPO. If the kidney is rejected by all candidates in the DSA, it is offered to the candidates in the region. Finally, if there are still no candidates willing to accept the offer, the kidney is offered to the national list. (The liver allocation system also uses a hierarchical geographical allocation rule.) Geographical hierarchy is at the heart of UNOS's allocation policy. More than 70 percent of the procured deceased-donor kidneys are shared locally (Davis, 2013). Although local sharing of organs may increase medical utility in some cases due to cold ischemia time, the volume of organ donations and recipient registrations vary significantly across DSAs owing to variety of demographic factors. This disparity dramatically impacts the waiting time of patients until they receive a transplant. For instance, the fraction of candidates who receive a transplant within five years can be as high as 67.3 percent in some DSAs, but this fraction can go as low as 25.5 percent for other DSAs, as shown in Figure 9.7. This illustrates a severe equity issue, and addressing such issues may create significant societal benefits (Ruth et al., 1985). The

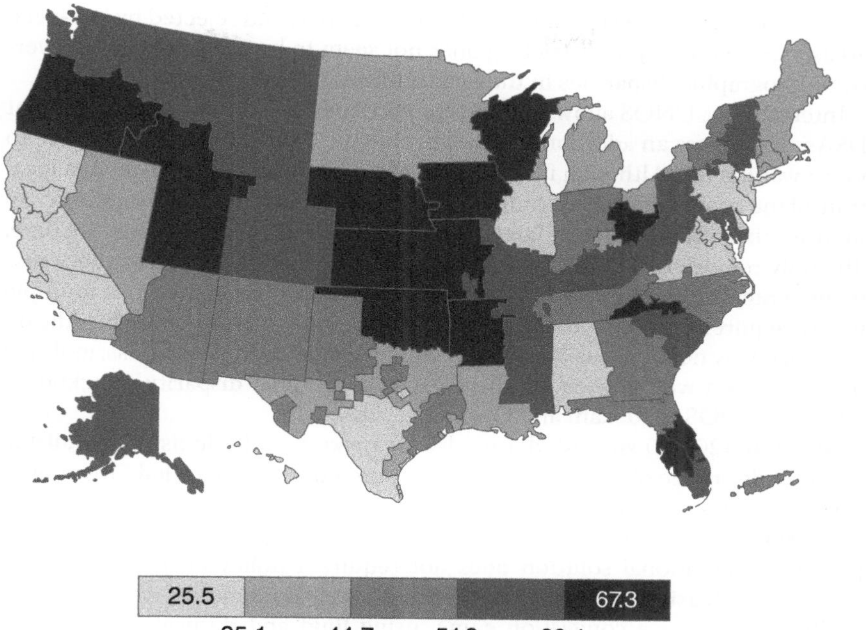

Figure 9.7 Percent of adult wait-listed patients, 2007, who received a deceased-donor kidney transplant within five years, by DSA (Hart et al., 2017).

inequality is in direct conflict with the 1998 final ruling of the Health and Human Services, which states[4]:

"In principle, and to the extent technically and practically achievable, any citizen or resident of the United States in need of a transplant should be considered as a potential recipient of each retrieved organ on a basis equal to that of a patient who lives in the area where organs or tissues are retrieved."

"Organs and tissues ought to be distributed on the basis of objective priority criteria, and not on the basis of accidents of geography."

Several researchers have used mathematical programming tools to improve upon the partitioning of the regions and DSAs; see, for example, Stahl et al. (2005), Kong et al. (2010), Gentry et al. (2013), and Davis et al. (2015). Although redistricting shows promising results in terms of both equity and efficiency, such approaches have met strong resistance from regions that already have a better supply/demand ratio. Washburn et al. (2011) summarized this fact by writing, "In general, any system that redistributes organs from areas of low need

4 Department of Health and Human Services (1998). OPTN, Final Rule (42 CFR Part 121). Federal Register 63, 12296–16338

to high-need will be accepted by the high-need areas and rejected by low-need areas." Consequently, redistricting does not seem to be a feasible way to overcome geographic disparities in the near future.

Interestingly, UNOS allows patients to join multiple waiting lists in different DSAs. This raises an additional choice problem for candidates about where to join a waiting list. Although it is convenient for candidates to register at a local transplant center, they may multiple-list in transplant centers elsewhere, to increase their chances of receiving a transplant and to lower their waiting time. The only requirement is that candidates should be able to travel to the transplant center within a reasonable amount of time. However, because multiple listing requires the ability to travel and navigate the subtleties of the healthcare system, it may not be a feasible option for many patients. Nevertheless, multiple listing offers a way to alleviate the current geographic disparity as acknowledged by UNOS (Ardekani and Orlowski, 2010).

Ata et al. (2017d) suggested a model for making multiple listings available to a broader range of people. The authors studied a service called OrganJet (a startup company providing private jet services for multiple-listing patients[5]) that brings people to the organs rather than bringing organs to people. The proposed operational solution does not require a policy change and hence is politically feasible. The authors modeled the DSA choice of candidates for multiple listing as a congestion game, using fluid and diffusion approximations, and identified the main routes that the jet service should offer. They thereby designed a implementable system that reduces geographic disparity via multiple listings.

Within the geographical hierarchy, UNOS further assigns patients priority points, determining which transplant candidate will be offered the next available organ. Due to the stochastic nature of the organ and candidate arrivals, the allocation problem is nontrivial even if the candidates do not potentially decline organ offers. Because many candidate and donor attributes need to be taken into account, the organ allocation problem has been viewed as a multidimensional stochastic dynamic optimization problem. Moreover, because waiting time is such an important contributor to organ allocation, queueing theory is extensively used in this area; see, for example, Zenios (1999), Gupta (2013), and Drekic et al. (2015).

Given the scarcity of resources, it is extremely important to allocate organs optimally. Early work by Righter (1989) and David and Yechiali (1995) consider nonstationary stochastic arrivals of organs and patients where the candidates are not allowed to turn down offers. Righter (1989) proved that a threshold policy over the value of a transplant, which is determined by the candidate characteristics, is socially optimal. David and Yechiali (1995) suggested that mismatched organs should be offered to candidates with the most rare attributes.

5 http://www.organjet.com

Zenios et al. (2000) built on the earlier work and suggested a dynamic allocation model for deceased-donor kidneys, using a fluid approximation; see Alagoz et al. (2009) for a detailed discussion of seminal work in this area.

Although these papers provide key insights, they do not incorporate patient choice; that is, the fact that organ offers may be declined. However, incorporating patients' accept/reject decisions into the organ allocation problem gives rise to a model that is challenging to study. This is because after an organ is rejected by a transplant candidate, it will be reallocated. Unfortunately, accounting for such phenomena is not always analytically tractable, given the complexity of the system. However, simulating such an allocation system is feasible. Zenios et al. (1999), Howard (2001), Su et al. (2004), Thompson et al. (2004), and Shechter et al. (2005) were among to first to incorporate candidate choice into allocation policies by simulation.

Under certain assumptions, the candidate choice can also be incorporated in analytical models. Akan et al. (2012) developed an optimal liver allocation policy, given probabilistic choices of candidates, which are static. They modeled the waiting list as an overloaded multi-class queue, and account for MELD score evolution of liver candidates. They propose allocating the organ to the patient class, which will have the highest marginal benefit upon every organ arrival.

Su and Zenios (2004) investigated the effect of patient choice on the deceased-donor kidney transplant system. The authors incorporated patient heterogeneity and show that, contrary to currently implemented deceased-donor kidney allocation, last-come, first-served policy will be more efficient.

Su and Zenios (2005) studied a model where candidates and kidneys are partitioned into exclusive groups according to their EPTS and KDPI scores, respectively. They matched the deceased-donor organs and recipients, based on longevity, disregarding the time that recipients spent on the waiting list. Under such a policy, efficiency is maximized. Moreover, a patient has no incentive to reject an organ offer, because waiting longer does not necessarily increase the quality of an organ offer in the future.

Su and Zenios (2006) recognized the fact that candidates may have private information about their life expectancy and life quality after transplantation. Consequently, a discrepancy emerges between the organ quality that a candidate is willing to receive and the quality of organs that the allocation policy offers to him. As a remedy, candidates are allowed to specify a quality range for the organs that they are willing to accept when they join the waiting list. Therefore, the waiting list is partitioned into multiple queues, and candidates choose which queue to join. The authors proved that such a system improves both efficiency and equity.

Bertsimas et al. 2013 developed a data-driven optimization model for a fundamentally different prioritization system. They constructed an additive point system of the characteristics that UNOS takes into account and determine the optimal weight of each characteristic. The authors test their proposed policy by a simulation study that suggests an 8 percent improvement in QALY.

9.3.4 Challenges in Modeling the Deceased-donor Organ Allocation Policy

UNOS evaluates proposals to change the allocation policy quantitatively, to assess the potential impact. Simulation studies are commonly used in the academic literature to illustrate the effectiveness of a new solution approach; see, for example, Su et al. (2004), Stahl et al. (2005), Akan et al. (2012), Gentry et al. (2013), Davis et al. (2015), and Bertsimas et al. (2013). Similarly, UNOS uses the liver simulation allocation model (LSAM) and the kidney pancreas simulation allocation model (KPSAM) to study the impact of possible changes to the liver and kidney allocation policies, respectively. In particular, KPSAM has been used extensively to assess the impact of potential changes in the deceased-donor kidney allocation system during the decade prior to the implementation of the new policy, that became effective in December 2014.

One key challenge of using simulation studies to compare alternative policy proposals for organ transplant systems is the endogenous nature of the transplant candidates' behavior. That is, as the policy changes, the candidates' behavior may change, too. Such changes in behavior have not been accounted for in previous simulation models. Rather, these models use historical data and assume that patient' behavior remains the same. However, the historical data may fail to capture the change in patient behavior, given the incentives provided by the new policy as articulated by Israni et al. (2014): "The KPSAM cannot account for changes in organ acceptance behavior. Therefore, if the new policy results in dramatic changes in organ acceptance behavior, the estimates of number of transplants from the simulations will differ from reality." This issue can lead to erroneous conclusions regarding the potential impact or unintended consequences of a proposed policy change—especially in the case of a major change. Clearly, incorporating patients' accept/reject decisions (and their endogenous nature) is an important challenge. Although this research avenue is largely unexplored, recent work by Ata et al. (2017a,b) explored the effects of such endogenous patient behavior. A related issue arising in the study of callers' abandonment behavior in call centers was explored by Ata et al. (2017c) and Ata and Peng 2017.

9.3.5 Research Problems from the Perspective of Other Stakeholders

Transplant centers are also involved in their patients' accept/reject decisions about organ offers. Transplant centers guide patients through the process of receiving a transplant. Making an accept/reject decision upon receiving an organ offer involves assessing the quality (and match) of the current organ and forecasting the availability of other organ offers in the future. The decision also involves consideration of how the patient's health may evolve. Given the complexity of the deceased-donor transplant system, these choices can be daunting for many patients. Transplant candidates, therefore, rely heavily on their physicians' guidance. In fact, Howard (2002) notes that the true decision-makers are surgeon-candidate pairs.

In this context, it is important to point out that a surgeon—and transplant centers in general—interact with multiple candidates on their waiting list. It is not entirely clear, then, whether a surgeon advises each patient on accept/reject decisions in isolation or whether considers all her other patients collectively (Roberts, 2016). Specifically, a surgeon may think that a current organ offer might be a better fit for another candidate on the same waiting list. If the surgeon is considering the welfare of the entire waiting list, she may discourage the current candidate from accepting the organ offer. Schummer (2016) suggests that this practice can significantly increase efficiency if the candidates are risk averse.

This discussion reasonably captures what may happen in a setting where there is only one transplant center in the DSA. The situation and the decision problem gets far more complex if there are multiple transplant centers in the same DSA. Such decisions involve the risk of losing the organ to the other transplant centers in the same local area. This constitutes an interesting decision problem for transplant centers, which is explored in Randa (2018).

In addition, transplant centers vary in the criteria they use to evaluate organ offers for their patients. For example, because the level of HLA mismatch does affect the graft survival of the transplanted organ, due to immunosuppressive drug use, transplant centers determine the maximum mismatch level that they are willing to accept for their patients. Transplant centers that have long waiting lists may be more lenient when they are offered with HLA mismatched organs and pass them along to their candidates. On the other hand, transplant centers with shorter waiting lists may be more strict about accepting HLA mismatched organs, to ensure high graft survival for their patients. The study of transplant center behavior offers a rich set of future research questions.

Organ procurement itself is a costly procedure and requires various resources (Jendrisak et al., 2002; Moazami et al., 2007). Therefore, the hospitals are reimbursed by the OPOs for procurement. Arora and Subramanian (2017) studied the reimbursement scheme and suggest improvements that take into account the OPO's financial objectives as well as the societal benefits of organ procurement. To the best of our knowledge, the financial aspects of transplant operations are not explored much in the literature, aside from few exceptions; see, for example, Abecassis (2006), Axelrod et al. (2010a,b), and Lee and Zenios (2012). Further research on the financial aspects of and incentives in transplant operations can further improve the system and outcomes.

As discussed above, the OPO procures a deceased-donor organ only if there is intent for transplantation. When the organ quality is low, it may not be procured. Arikan et al. (2017) observed that there is quite a bit of variation in the quality threshold for procuring organs across different locations, which seems to be driven by the variation in waiting times and the transplant center competition. The authors showed that broader sharing of low-quality organs can increase the intent for them and hence improve their procurement rates, more broadly, the supply can help improve the system significantly. Further research to increase the supply of organs can address the crux of the issue, that is the supply shortage (Tayur and Welsh, 2016).

9.4 Concluding Remarks

Stakeholders in the deceased-donor transplant system include transplant candidates, UNOS, transplant centers, and the OPOs. The problems facing the transplant candidates and UNOS have been studied by several researchers. As noted above, most papers in the extant literature focus on a single decision-maker, modeling other stakeholders passively; however, any major policy change affects the transplant candidates' subsequent behavior. Therefore, research that takes into account the change in patient behavior to assess the impact of possible policy modifications can be a great assistance to policymakers.

The problems that transplant centers and OPOs are facing have received scant research attention from the operations research community. The transplant centers' performances are monitored for short-term patient and graft survival. This system arguably leads to institutional risk aversion. In particular, these performance reviews can influence who the transplant centers sign onto their waiting lists and which organs they accept. Ultimately, these regulations may cause an increase in organ wastage and discourage innovation. Thus, this area deserves further research attention. Similarly, OPOs make the organ procurement decisions, and further research on potential ways of increasing the deceased-donor procurement rates can help increase the organ supply. Needless to say, any increase in the organ supply will improve the wellbeing of transplant candidates.

Finally, the availability of data makes it possible to utilize empirical/data-driven research methods, such as machine learning, reduced form empirical methods, and structural estimation. Empirical research on organ transplantation will help bridge the theory and practice.

References

Abecassis, M.M. (2006). Financial Outcomes in Transplantation—A Provider's Perspective. *American Journal of Transplantation* 6(6) 1257–1263.

Ahn, J., J.C. Hornberger. (1996). Involving patients in the cadaveric kidney transplant allocation process: A decision-theoretic perspective. *Management Science* 42(5) 629–641.

Akan, M., O. Alagoz, B. Ata, F.S. Erenay, A. Said. (2012). A broader view of designing the liver allocation system. *Operations Research* 60(4) 757–770.

Aksin, Z., B. Ata, S. M. Emadi, C. Su. (2017). Impact of Delay Announcements in Call Centers: An Empirical Approach. *Operations Research* 65(1) 242–265.

Aksin, Z., B. Ata, S.M. Emadi, C. Su. (2013). Structural Estimation of Callers' Delay Sensitivity in Call Centers. *Management Science* 59(12) 2727–2746.

Alagoz, O., L.M. Maillart, A.J. Schaefer, M.S. Roberts. (2004). The optimal timing of living-donor liver transplantation. *Management Science* 50(10) 1420–1430.

Alagoz, O., L.M. Maillart, A.J. Schaefer, M.S. Roberts. (2007a). Choosing among living-donor and cadaveric livers. *Management Science* 53(11) 1702–1715.

Alagoz, O., L.M. Maillart, A.J. Schaefer, M.S. Roberts. (2007b). Determining the acceptance of cadaveric livers using an implicit model of the waiting list. *Operations Research* 55(1) 24–36.

Alagoz, O., A.J. Schaefer, M.S. Roberts. (2009). *Optimizing Organ Allocation and Acceptance*, Springer US, 1–24.

Anderson, S.P., A. de Palma, J.F. Thisse. (1992). *Discrete Choice Theory of Product Differentiation*. MIT Press, Cambridge, MA.

Ardekani, M.S., J.M. Orlowski. (2010). Multiple listing in kidney transplantation. *American Journal of Kidney Diseases* 55(4) 717–725.

Arikan, M., B. Ata, J.J. Friedewald, R. Parker. (2017). Enhancing Kidney Supply Through Geographic Sharing in the United States. Working paper, University of Kansas School of Business.

Arikan, M., B. Ata, R. Parker. (2016). On the unintended consequences of risk adjusted evaluation of transplant centers. Working paper, University of Kansas School of Business.

Arora, P., R. Subramanian. (2017). Improving societal outcomes in the organ donation value chain. Working paper, Scheller College of Business, Georgia Institute of Technology.

Ashlagi, I., D.S. Gilchrist, A.E. Roth, M.A. Rees. (2011). Nonsimultaneous chains and dominos in kidney-paired donation–revisited. *American Journal of Transplantation* 11 984–994.

Ata, B., Y. Ding, S.A. Zenios. (2017a). The KDPI-Dependent Ranking Policies: Shaping the Alloca- tion of Deceased-Donor Kidneys in the New Era. Working paper, University of Chicago Booth School of Business.

Ata, B., J.J. Friedewald, A.C. Randa. (2017b). An empirical analysis of the effect of kidney allocation policies on patient behavior. Working paper, University of Chicago Booth School of Business.

Ata, B., P.W. Glynn, X. Peng. (2017c). An equilibrium analysis of a discrete-time Markovian queue with endogenous abandonments. *Queueing Systems* 86 141–212.

Ata, B., A. Skaro, S. Tayur. (2017d). OrganJet: Overcoming geographical disparities in access to deceased donor kidneys in the United States. *Management Science* 63(9) 2776–2794.

Ata, B., X. Peng. (2018). An equilibrium analysis of a multiclass queue with endogenous abandonments in heavy traffic. *Operations Research* 66(1) 163–183.

Axelrod, D.A., D. Millman, M.M. Abecassis. (2010a). US Health Care Reform and Transplantation. Part I: Overview and Impact on Access and Reimbursement in the Private Sector. *American Journal of Transplantation* 10 2197–2202.

Axelrod, D.A., D. Millman, M.M. Abecassis. (2010b). US Health Care Reform and Transplantation. Part II: Impact on the Public Sector and Novel Health Care Delivery Systems. *American Journal of Transplantation* 10 2203–2207.

Bandi, C., N. Trichakis, P. Vayanos. (2016). Robust wait time estimation in resource allocation systems with an application to kidney allocation. Working paper, Kellogg School of Management, Northwestern University.

Ben-Akiva, M., S. Lerman. (1985). *Discrete Choice Analysis: Theory and Application to Travel Demand*. MIT Press, Cambridge, MA.

Bernat, J.L., A.M. D'Alessandro, F.K. Port, T.P. Bleck, S.O. Heard, J. Medina, S.H. Rosenbaum, M.A. Devita, R.S. Gaston, R.M. Merion, M.L. Barr, W.H. Marks, H. Nathan, K. O'connor, D.L. Rudow, A.B. Leichtman, P. Schwab, N.L. Ascher, R.A. Metzger, V. Mc Bride, W. Graham, D. Wagner, J. Warren, F.L. Delmonico. (2006). Report of a national conference on donation after cardiac death. *American Journal of Transplantation* 6(2) 281–291.

Bertsimas, D., V.F. Farias, N. Trichakis. (2012). On the efficiency-fairness trade-off. *Management Science* 58(12) 2234–2250.

Bertsimas, D., V.F. Farias, N. Trichakis. (2013). Fairness, efficiency, and flexibility in organ allocation for kidney transplantation. *Operations Research* 61(1) 73–87.

Bunzel, B., K. Laederach-Hofmann. (2000). Solid Organ Transplantation: Are there any predictors for post transplant noncompliance? A Literature Overview. *Transplantation* 70(5) 711–716.

Busuttil, R.W., G.B. Klintmalm. (2014). *Transplantation of the Liver E-Book*. Elsevier Health Sciences.

Clayton, P. A., S. P. McDonald, J. J. Snyder, N. Salkowski, S. J. Chadban. (2014). External validation of the estimated posttransplant survival score for allocation of deceased donor kidneys in the United States. *American Journal of Transplantation* 14(8) 1922–1926.

Cuende, N., B. Miranda, J.F. Canon, G. Garrido, R. Matesanz. (2005). Donor characteristics associated with liver graft survival. *Transplantation* 79(10) 1445–1452.

David, I., U. Yechiali. (1985). A time-dependent stopping problem with application to live organ transplants. *Operations Research* 33(3) 491–504.

David, I., U. Yechiali. (1995). One-attribute sequential assignment match processes in discrete time. *Operations Research* 43(5) 879–884.

Davis, A.E. (2013). Addressing geographic inequities in kidney transplantation. PhD thesis, Northwestern University, Evanston, IL.

Davis, A.E., S. Mehrotra, J.J. Friedewald, M.S. Daskin, A.I. Skaro, M.M. Abecassis, D.P. Ladner. (2015). Improving geographic equity in kidney transplantation using alternative kidney sharing and optimization modeling. *Medical Decision Making* 35 797–807.

Delasay, M., S. Tayur. (2017). Cop: Inducing organ discards and patient deaths on transplant wait lists? Working paper, Tepper School of Business, Carnegie Mellon University.

Drekic, S., D.A. Stanford, D.G. Woolford, V.C. McAlister. (2015). A model for deceased-donor transplant queue waiting times. *Queueing Systems* 79(1) 87–115.

Feng, S., N.P. Goodrich, J.L. Bragg-Gresham, D.M. Dykstra, J.D. Punch, M.A. Debroy, S.M. Greenstein, R.M. Merion. (2006). Characteristics associated with liver graft failure: The concept of a donor risk index. *American Journal of Transplantation* 6 783–790.

Foley, D.P., L.A. Fernandez, G. Leverson, LT. Chin, N. Krieger, J.T. Cooper, B.D. Shames, Y.T. Becker, J.S. Odorico, S.J. Knechtle, H.W. Sollinger, M. Kalayoglu, A.M. D'Alessandro. (2005). Donation after cardiac death: the University of Wisconsin experience with liver transplantation. *Annals of Surgery* 242(5) 724–731.

Gentry, S.E., A.B. Massie, S.W. Cheek, K.L. Lentine, E.H. Chow, C.E. Wickliffe, N. Dzebashvili, P.R. Salvalaggio, M.A. Schnitzler, D.A. Axelrod, D.L. Segev. (2013). Addressing geographic disparities in liver transplantation through redistricting. *American Journal of Transplantation* 13(8) 2052–2058.

Glorie, K.M., J. J. van de Klundert, A.P.M. Wagelmans. (2014). Kidney exchange with long chains: An efficient pricing algorithm for clearing barter exchanges with branch-and-price. *Manufacturing & Service Operations Management* 16(4) 498–512.

Gordon, E.J. (2012). Informed consent for living donation: A review of key empirical studies, ethical challenges, and future research. *American Journal of Transplantation* 12(9) 2273–2280.

Gugenheim, J., D. Samuel, M. Reynes, H. Bismuth. (1990). Liver transplantation across ABO blood group barriers. *The Lancet* 336(8714) 519–523.

Gupta, Diwakar. (2013). *Queueing Models for Healthcare Operations*. Springer New York, New York, NY, 19–44.

Halloran, P.F. (2004). Immunosuppressive drugs for kidney transplantation. *The New England Journal of Medicine* 351 2715–2729.

Hart, A., J. M. Smith, M. A. Skeans, S. K. Gustafson, D. E. Stewart, W. S. Cherikh, J. L. Wainright, A. Kucheryavaya, M. Woodbury, J. J. Snyder, B. L. Kasiske, A. K. Israni. (2017). OPTN/SRTR 2015 Annual Data Report: Kidney. *American Journal of Transplantation* 17 21–116.

Hashikura, Y.S., S. Kawasaki, S. Miyagawa, M. Terada, T. Ikegami, Y. Nakazawa, K. Urata, H. Chisuwa, S. Ogino, M. Makuuchi. (2002). Recent advance in living donor liver transplantation. *World Journal of Surgery* 26(2) 243–246.

Hornberger, J.C., J. Ahn. (1997). Deciding eligibility for transplantation when a donor kidney becomes available. *Medical Decision Making* 17 160–170.

Howard, D.H. 2001. Dynamic analysis of liver allocation policies. *Medical Decision Making* 21 257–266.

Howard, D.H. (2002). Why do transplant surgeons turn down organs? A model of the accept/reject decision. *Journal of Health Economics* 21 957–969.

Israni, A.K., N. Salkowski, S. Gustafson, J.J. Snyder, J.J. Friedewald, R.N. Formica, X. Wang, E. Shteyn, W. Cherikh, D. Stewart, C.J. Samana, A. Chung, A. Hart, B.L. Kasiske. (2014). New National Allocation Policy for Deceased Donor Kidneys in the United States and Possible Effect on Patient Outcomes. *Journal of American Society of Nephrology* 25 1842–1848.

Jendrisak, M.D., K. Hruska, J. Wagner, D. Chandler, D. Kappel. (2002). Cadaveric-donor organ recovery at a hospital-independent facility. *Transplantation* 74(7) 978–982.

Johnson, E.M., J.K. Anderson, C. Jacobs, G. Suh, A. Humar, B.D. Suhr, S.R. Kerr, A.J. Matas. (1999). Long-term follow-up of living kidney donors: Quality of life after donation. *Transplantation* 67(5) 717–721.

Kong, N, A.J. Schaefer, B. Hunsaker, M.S. Roberts. (2010). Maximizing the Efficiency of the U.S. Liver Allocation System Through Region Design. *Management Science* 56(12) 2111–2122.

Kusserow, R.P. (1991). The distribution of organs for transplantation: Expectations and practices. Tech. rep., Department of Health and Human Services Office of Inspector General.

Lee, C.P., G.M. Chertow, S.A. Zenios. (2008). Optimal initiation and management of dialysis therapy. *Operations Research* 56(6) 1428–1449.

Lee, D.K.K., S.A. Zenios. (2012). An evidence-based incentive system for Medicare's end-stage renal disease program. *Management Science* 58(6) 1092–1105.

Leshno, J.D. (2015). Dynamic matching in overloaded waiting lists. Working paper, Columbia Business School.

Malinchoc, M., P.S. Kamath, F.D. Gordon, C.J. Peine, J. Rank, P.C. ter Borg. (2000). A model to predict poor survival in patients undergoing transjugular intrahepatic portosystemic shunts. *Hepatology* 31 864–871.

Massie, A.B., S.L. Zeger, R.A. Montgomery, D.L. Segev. (2009). The effects of DonorNet 2007 on kidney distribution equity and efficiency. *American Journal of Transplantation* 9(7) 1550–1557.

Merrill, J.P., J.E. Murray, J.H. Harrison, W.R. Guild. (1956). Successful homotransplantation of the human kidney between identical twins. *JAMA* 160(4) 277–282.

Moazami, N., O.H. Javadi, D.F. Kappel, J. Wagner, M.D. Jendrisak. (2007). The feasibility of organ procurement at a hospital-independent facility: a working model of efficiency. *The Journal of Thoracic and Cardiovascular Surgery* 133(5) 1389–1390.

NOTA. (1984). National Organ Transplantation Act. Tech. rep.

Randa, A.C. (2018). Essays on organ transplant operations. PhD thesis, University of Chicago Booth School of Business.

Rao, P.S., D.E. Schaubel, M.K. Guidinger, K.A. Andreoni, R.A. Wolfe, R.M. Merion, F.K. Port, R.S. Sung. (2009). A comprehensive risk quantification score for deceased donor kidneys: The kidney donor risk index. *Transplantation* 88(2) 231–236.

Righter, R. (1989). A resource allocation problem in a random environment. *Operations Research* 37(2) 329–338.

Roberts, J. (2016). Applying algorithms to organ transplantation. First Johns Hopkins Symposium on Healthcare Operations, October 1, 2016, Baltimore, MD.

Roberts, M.S., D.C. Angus, C.L. Bryce, Z. Valenta, L. Weissfeld. (2004). Survival after liver transplantation in the United States: A disease-specific analysis of the UNOS database. *Liver Transplantation* 10(7) 886–897.

Roth, A.E., T. Sonmez, M.U. Unver. (2004). Kidney exchange. *The Quarterly Journal of Economics* 119 457–488.

Roth, A.E., T. Sonmez, M.U. Unver. (2005). Pairwise kidney exchange. *Journal of Economic Theory* 125 151–188.

Rust, J. (1987). Optimal Replacement of GMC Bus Engines: An Empirical Model of Harold Zurcher. *Econometrica* 55(5) 999–1033.

Ruth, R.J., L. Wyszewianski, G. Herline. (1985). Kidney transplantation: A simulation model for examining demand and supply. *Management Science* 31(5) 515–526.

Salizzoni, M., A. Franchello, F. Zamboni, A. Ricchiuti, D. Cocchis, F. Fop, A. Brunati, E. Cerutti. (2003). Marginal grafts: Finding the correct treatment for fatty livers. *Transplant International* 16 486–493.

Sandikci, B., L.M. Maillart, A.J. Schaefer, O. Alagoz, M.S. Roberts. (2008). Estimating the patient's price of privacy in liver transplantation. *Operations Research* 56(6) 1393–1410.

Sandikci, B., L.M. Maillart, A.J. Schaefer, M.S. Roberts. (2013). Alleviating the patient's price of privacy through a partially observed model of the liver transplant waiting list. *Management Science* 59(8) 1836–1854.

Schummer, J. (2016). Influencing waiting lists. Working paper, Kellogg School of Management, Northwestern University.

Segev, D.L., S.E. Gentry, D.S. Warren, B. Reeb, R.A. Montgomery. (2005). Kidney paired donation and optimizing the use of live donor organs. *JAMA* 293(15) 1883–1890.

Shechter, S.M., C.L. Bryce, O. Alagoz, J.E. Kreke, J.E. Stahl, A.J. Schaefer, D.C. Angus, M.S. Roberts. (2005). A clinically based discrete-event simulation of end-stage liver disease and the organ allocation process. *Medical Decision Making* 25(2) 199–209.

Stahl, J.E., N. Kong, S.M. Shechter, A.J. Schaefer, M.S. Roberts. (2005). A methodological framework for optimally reorganizing liver transplant regions. *Medical Decision Making* 25(1) 35–46.

Su, X., S.A. Zenios. (2004). Patient choice in kidney allocation: The role of the queueing discipline. *Manufacturing & Service Operations Management* 6(4) 280–301.

Su, X., S.A. Zenios. (2005). Patient choice in kidney allocation: A sequential stochastic assignment model. *Operations Research* 53(3) 443–455.

Su, X., S.A. Zenios. (2006). Recipient choice can address the efficiency-equity trade-off in kidney transplantation: A mechanism design model. *Management Science* 52(11) 1647–1660.

Su, X., S.A. Zenios, G.M. Chertow. (2004). Incorporating recipient choice in kidney transplantation. *Journal American Society of Nephrology* 15(6) 1656–1663.

Tayur, S., C. Welsh. (2016). Nudge: Increasing nok consent rate. AMAT, September 29, 2016.

Thompson, D., L. Waisanen, R. Wolfe, R.M. Merion. (2004). Simulating the Allocation of Organs for Transplantation. *Health Care Management Science* 7 331–338.

Trotter, J.F., N. Stolpman, M. Wachs, T. Bak, M. Kugelmas, I. Kam, G.T. Everson. (2002). Living donor liver transplant recipients achieve relatively higher immunosuppressant blood levels than cadaveric recipients. *Liver Transplantation* 8(3) 212–218.

Washburn, K., E. Pomfret, J. Roberts. (2011). Liver allocation and distribution: possible next steps. *Liver Transplantation* 17 1005–1012.

Weir, M.R., E.V. Lerma. (2014). *Kidney Transplantation*. Springer New York.

Zenios, S.A. (1999). Modeling the transplant waiting list: A queueing model with reneging. *Queueing Systems* 31 239–251.

Zenios, S.A. (2002). Optimal Control of a Paired-Kidney Exchange Program. *Management Science* 48(3) 328–342.

Zenios, S.A., G.M. Chertow, L.M. Wein. (2000). Dynamic allocation of kidneys to candidates on the transplant waiting list. *Operations Research* 48(4) 549–569.

Zenios, S.A., P.C. Fuloria. (2000). Managing the delivery of dialysis therapy: A multiclass fluid model analysis. *Management Science* 46(10) 1317–1336.

Zenios, S.A., L.M. Wein, G.M. Chertow. (1999). Evidence-based organ allocation. *American Journal of Medicine* 107 52–61.

Zheng, R., T. Dai, K. Sycara. (2018). *Jumping the Line, Charitably: Analysis and Remedy of Donor-Priority Rule*. Johns Hopkins University Working Paper.

10

Ambulatory Care

Nan Liu

Boston College

10.1 Introduction

Ambulatory care is defined as "medical services performed on an outpatient basis, without admission to a hospital or other facility" (The Medicare Payment Advisory Commission, 2016). Ambulatory care is provided in a variety of settings, including, but not limited to, the offices of healthcare providers, hospital outpatient departments, outpatient surgical centers, diagnostic clinics, labs, dialysis clinics, and (freestanding) emergency departments. One unique feature of ambulatory care is that each episode of care consists of a single or multiple visits to a healthcare facility, and each of these visits last no more than one day.

Ambulatory care represents a large portion of the patient care delivered in the US. According to a 2013 National Ambulatory Medical Care Survey, there were 922.6 million ambulatory visits to nonfederal office-based patient care physicians, excluding anesthesiologists, radiologists, and pathologists (US CDC, 2016). This is equivalent to about three visits per person per year. In 2011, there were 125.7 million visits to hospital outpatient departments (excluding emergency rooms); this is equivalent to 0.4 visits per person per year (US National Center for Health Statistics, 2016b). While no data seem to be available yet on the total expenditures of ambulatory care in the past few years in the US, a 2011 study estimates that ambulatory care (office-based, hospital outpatient department, and hospital emergency room) costs approximately 309 billion dollars in 2008 (Machlin and Chowdhury, 2011), which is more than 10 percent of the total US health expenditures in the same period (US National Center for Health Statistics, 2016a).

In light of rising financial and regulatory pressures, providers and insurers are strongly incentivized to deliver care in an ambulatory environment, which is considered less costly, more efficient, and safer to patients (Mannino, 2012). At the same time, advances in medical care and technology allow many

Handbook of Healthcare Analytics: Theoretical Minimum for Conducting 21st Century Research on Healthcare Operations, First Edition. Edited by Tinglong Dai and Sridhar Tayur.

medical procedures that were traditionally done in an inpatient setting to be done in an outpatient setting, so that patients can be discharged on the same day of the procedure without admission to the hospital (Berg and Denton, 2012). From the patients' perspective, ambulatory care (versus hospital care) is also more preferable because the former is cheaper, more convenient, and often associated with lower risk of medical complications (Pugely et al., 2013; Mobin et al., 2013). Indeed, the shift from inpatient care to outpatient care, underway for several decades, has accelerated in recent years (Evans, 2015). It is more important than ever for healthcare organizations to be effective in managing their ambulatory care operations and business.

This chapter discusses operations management for ambulatory care. We focus on a key issue—which is also faced by other (service) industries—how to match supply and demand in a complex and dynamic environment where different stakeholders have competing objectives. Although different types of ambulatory care have different features, they all share a few common ones that are critical for operations management. We use *primary care* as a canonic example to illustrate how ambulatory care operations are managed in practice, the associated challenges, and the objectives of various stakeholders. Then we review operations management research in ambulatory care, and discuss some new trends in this care setting, as well as future research opportunities.

Other types of ambulatory care share similar management issues, except for, perhaps, emergency care.[1] Because of space limitations, we choose not to cover emergency care in this chapter. We refer readers to recent papers and literature reviews (e.g., Deo and Gurvich, 2011; KC, 2013; Cho et al., 2014; Saghafian et al., 2015; Batt and Terwiesch, 2015; and Xu and Chan, 2016) for discussion on operations management for emergency care.

10.2 How Operations are Managed in Primary Care Practice

Primary care is day-to-day healthcare. It involves the widest scope of healthcare, including care for acute symptoms, (multiple) chronic illness, health maintenance, and mental and social health issues (Starfield, 1994). Primary care is usually delivered in the office of primary care providers (PCPs), for example, primary care physicians, pediatricians, or nurse practitioners. Patients schedule medical appointments with their PCPs in advance. Walk-in patients, that is, those who have not booked their appointments but show up at a practice when they need care, are often accepted. Some (specialty) clinics, however, may only see scheduled patients.

1 Unlike other types of ambulatory care, emergency rooms run 24/7, most patients are nonscheduled, and emergency care is closely related to inpatient care.

Each PCP usually has a group of patients whose primary care needs she is held accountable for. This group of patients form the patient "panel" of this particular PCP. The size of this group is called the *panel size*, which is an important indicator for the workload of the PCP. All else being equal, the larger the panel size, the longer it takes for a patient to get an appointment with a PCP. Thus, when a PCP has a sufficiently large panel, she may choose not to accept any new patients to join her panel in order to ensure that existing patients on her panel receive care in a timely fashion. (Other types of ambulatory care providers, for example, dentists, also follow a similar practice.)

With a panel of patients in mind, each PCP manages her daily work by setting up daily *appointment templates* (also called appointment books or master schedules). These appointment templates are specific to individual PCPs and can vary by days; they specify the total office hour length (also called clinic session length), the number/types of patients expected to be seen in a day, and their expected service start and finish times. Appointment templates reflect the expected workload set by the PCP and/or her practice organization. For instance, PCPs in private practices (versus salaried physicians) may have stronger financial incentives to work longer and see more patients in a day. A resident usually sees far fewer patients than an attending physician because the resident is in medical training and often needs to spend a longer time with patients. PCPs working in an aging community (versus a younger community) need to reserve more slots with longer durations for patients with multiple comorbidities.

A critical question related to the use of appointment templates is how to design one—or more specifically—how many patients, and what type of patients should be contained in each appointment slot. A variety of factors affect the optimal design of daily appointment templates, such as patient no-show probabilities, provider consultation time variability, PCPs' willingness to work overtime, patients' tolerance for waiting, and the admission policy for walk-in patients. These factors may also influence the total number of patients included in a daily template (i.e., the expected daily workload). Appointment template design is an active research area in (healthcare) operations management, and we discuss it in Section 10.4.2 below.

Appointment templates are usually maintained in medical scheduling systems (e.g., SIEMENS Sorian Clinical Workflow System), which may be integrated with electronic medical record systems. In the current ambulatory care environment, patients have two ways to book appointments.

- First, patients call the practice. Then the scheduler, after examining the available slots in the appointment templates and discussing with the patient, schedules an appointment for the patient. Following an established scheduling protocol set by the practice, the scheduler may schedule differently depending on the patient. For instance, the scheduler may put a patient who is identified as a high risk no-show into an overbooked slot or suggest that the patient not book the appointment until one day before he really needs the appointment (to reduce the chance of no-shows). For a new patient, the scheduler may ask for the insurance information first, and then schedule this patient into a slot reserved only for new patients or with a provider who is looking for new patients. In specialty clinics, the scheduler may try to match patients' symptoms with providers' expertise areas.

- The second way for patients to get an appointment is via an online scheduling website (more on this in Section 10.5.1). Indeed, this scheduling method has become increasingly popular among patients and providers, given the rise of health information technologies. Such platforms offer patients an Amazon.com-like experience for seeking care. On these websites, patients can see a variety of provider options (including their reviews) and their available appointment days and times. One click on the computer or smartphone can secure an appointment slot for the patient.

Ambulatory care facilities plan their operations using appointment scheduling systems and may use one or both ways (telephone and online) to schedule their patients. These appointment systems are the primary entry point for patients to access ambulatory care. On the day of appointment, patients go through various stages of services, depending on the work flow of their PCPs and the purpose of their visits. We refer readers to Froehle and Magazine (2013) for an excellent, detailed discussion on potential work flows in a (complex) ambulatory care clinic.

10.3 What Makes Operations Management Difficult in Ambulatory Care

Even though the use of appointment scheduling significantly reduces the variation of patient demand and unpredictability of the system, a range of challenges makes ambulatory care a difficult practice environment to manage and operate. We discuss two main issues: competing objectives of multiple stakeholders and complex environmental factors that add uncertainties and are not easy to control.

10.3.1 Competing Objectives

Ambulatory care encompasses a number of important stakeholders, such as patients, providers, provider organizations, payers, and governments. At a high level, all stakeholders prefer timely and high-quality care at a low cost, but these objectives are competing (Carroll, 2012). At the operational level, different stakeholders have their own interests and objectives to achieve. It is possible that the objectives of multiple stakeholders are competing. Even the same stakeholder may have objectives that compete with each other, meaning that an operational change that improves one objective she cares about can compromise the other.

For example, patients desire timely access to care, shorter wait times in a clinic, and being seen by their own provider (or a high-quality provider they prefer). These objectives can be competing among themselves. For instance, seeing a particular provider may entail a longer delay in accessing the appointment. This conflict also exists on the provider side: providers want to ensure *continuity of care*[2] (by not allowing patients to see someone who is not their own PCP), but providers also want to reduce delays for patients (which may be achieved by relaxing the requirement above). It is possible that providers' objectives compete with patients' objectives: scheduling more patients in a day increases utilization of a provider's time, but potentially leads to longer waits for patients.

Froehle and Magazine (2013) discuss common operational objectives of patients, providers, and health organizations in ambulatory care. They also highlight that devising and achieving balanced combinations of competing performance metrics is vital and challenging in operations management for ambulatory care.

10.3.2 Environmental Factors

A number of environmental factors add uncertainties, sometimes unpredictable, to the daily operations of ambulatory care, and thus present significant management hurdles. These factors are critical to consider in order to achieve desired management goals. As the previous literature has thoroughly reviewed these factors (see, e.g., Gupta and Wang (2012) and Ahmadi-Javid et al. 2017), we shall provide only a brief outline.

- *Patient No-show and Cancellation*: Patient no-show occurs when patients break their scheduled appointments without notifying the clinic in advance. Patients may also cancel their appointments in advance; however, a last-minute cancellation is effectively a no-show. Factors that contribute to no-shows and cancellation can be categorized into patient-related reasons (e.g., forgetting), scheduling problems (e.g., long delays), environmental and financial factors (e.g., transportation); see, e.g., Turkcan et al. (2013). Interventions (e.g., reminders) may reduce no-shows and cancellations but cannot eliminate them (Macharia et al., 1992).
- *Patient Preferences and Choice*: Patients may prefer certain dates and times and to be seen by a particular provider; see, for example, Rubin et al. (2006), Liu et al. (2018). If their preferences cannot be accommodated, they may seek alternatives (e.g., walk-in urgent care centers) or skip care altogether.

---

2 Continuity of care refers to an ongoing personal relationship between the patient and the care provider that is characterized by personal trust and responsibility (Saultz, 2003).

- *Patient Unpunctuality*: Patients may arrive earlier or later than their scheduled appointment times (Cayirli and Veral, 2003). Patient unpunctuality may lead to the so-called "wait-preempt" dilemma, in which an available physician decides whether to see a patient who has arrived early or to wait for the patient scheduled next (Samorani and Ganguly, 2016).
- *Provider Service Time Variability*: Providers may spend a random amount of consultation or procedure time with each patient. The length and distribution of service times may depend on provider and patient characteristics. A range of distributions has been considered to model service times, for example, exponential, phase-type, Gamma, log-normal, discrete, and general distributions (Cayirli and Veral, 2003; Cayirli et al., 2006).
- *Interruption*: Interruptions may occur for reasons such as ancillary tasks (e.g., writing medical notes), emergency patient arrival, and breakdown of equipment. Physician lateness or physician-initiated cancellation may also cause interruptions to daily work flows. Interruption may be just a short break from the current task or may preempt the current work and require attention to new tasks. After interruption, the service may resume or restart (as a new task). Interruptions are often inevitable, and they present important challenges to management.

10.4 Operations Management Models

As discussed above, a PCP manages her practice by first setting up the panel of patients she serves. She then figures out her "ideal" daily workload and designs the daily appointment template, with which she manages the daily patient flow to her practice. Following this logic, we introduce three streams of operations management modeling work, which provide solutions and insights for the operational decisions above that need to be sequentially made by a PCP. For each stream, we also discuss potential future research directions.

10.4.1 System-Wide Planning

At the system-wide level, a PCP has two main decisions to make when managing the practice: (1) the panel size, and (2) the daily workload (which can be thought of as the number of patients to be scheduled in a single day). These strategic decisions require careful considerations because they have a significant impact on daily operations, and more importantly, these decisions, once made, cannot be changed often.

Several key tradeoffs affect these decisions. Specifically, a larger panel size leads to longer delay in care, but a smaller panel size presents a waste of healthcare resources. Scheduling more patients in a day can be done via overbooking (i.e., scheduling two or more patients into one appointment slot).

This may help reduce overall delays to care for all patients and is a way to hedge against the risk that some patients do not show up (e.g., due to long delays to care); however, sometimes the patients may all show up, leading to undesirable patient wait times and staff overtime. There is a "sweet spot" for all these decisions—extremes are not desirable.

Queueing models are excellent tools that allow OM researchers to analyze these tradeoffs. Green and Savin (2008) were the first to investigate the choice of panel size using queueing models. Liu and Ziya (2014) and Zacharias and Armony (2017) studied joint decisions of panel sizing and overbooking for outpatient care. We briefly review the modeling framework in these studies and their key results below. For ease of presentation, we follow the notation of Liu and Ziya (2014).

Suppose that the provider has an established panel of N patients. Appointment requests from any patient in this panel arise according to a Poisson process with rate λ_0, independent from those of others. Thus, the overall demand to the provider also follows a Poisson process with rate $\lambda = N\lambda_0 > 0$. When patients request appointments, it is assumed that they will be (offered and) scheduled in the *earliest* appointment slot available.[3]

The appointment backlog of the provider is referred to as the "queue." This queue is in fact a *virtual* waitlist of scheduled patients yet to be seen by the provider. Note that these are not patients waiting in clinic, but those who hold appointments and have not yet visited the PCP. Thus, the waiting, if any, that occurs in this queue can be viewed as the appointment delay (i.e., the time from a patient's request for an appointment to the actual time of the appointment).

To see how this model approximates reality, imagine for now that the provider has exactly μ appointment slots in a day; that is, each appointment slot is deterministic, with length $1/\mu$ day.[4] During the day, patients request appointments and will be added to the queue in an first-come, first-served order (FCFS). As time passes, the provider serves the patients on the schedule and makes the queue shorter. When the provider is off duty, no patients call to join the queue, and no patients are served or leave the queue either; the queue remains unchanged. From a modeling perspective, we can disregard the non-office hours of the provider and "coalesce" the office hours together to consider a continuous queueing process.

At patient appointment times, patients arrive on time if they show up, but they may not show up. As discussed earlier, high no-show probabilities are often positively correlated with long appointment delays. To capture this empirical relationship, we assume that if a patient sees j patients ahead of her upon her appointment request, this patient will be scheduled as the $(j + 1)$th

---

3 An underlying assumption is that patients have strong preferences for speedy access to care and thus would take the first appointment slot that is available.

4 There may be some variability in the service time, but it suffices to assume that the provider can serve each patient within one appointment slot.

patient in the system and show up with probability $p_j \in [0, 1]$; furthermore, $p_j \geq p_{j+1}$ for $j \in \{0, 1, 2, \dots\}$. To track system performance, we suppose that for every scheduled patient who shows up, the system accrues one nominal unit of reward. If a scheduled patient does not show up or there are no scheduled patients in the queue, the provider sits idle.

Define $\Pi_j(\lambda, \mu)$ to be the steady-state probability that there are j appointments in the queue, including the ongoing service (which may be a "no-show service"). Let $T(\lambda, \mu)$ denote the long-run average reward that the system will collect. As the arrival process is Poisson, $\Pi_j(\lambda, \mu)$ is also the probability that there are j scheduled appointments at the arrival time of a new appointment in a steady state. With probability p_j this appointment will be filled in by the patient who makes the appointment. Thus, we have

$$T(\lambda, \mu) = \lambda \sum_{j=0}^{\infty} \Pi_j(\lambda, \mu) p_j \tag{10.1}$$

Although this model seems simple, it is fairly flexible and allows researchers to consider various types of decisions. In Eq. (10.1), λ can be viewed equivalently as the panel size, and μ is the service capacity of the system, which can be viewed as the number of patients to be scheduled in a day. If μ is fixed, the manager can optimize the system throughput by choosing λ. The manager may also add a service-level constraint to enforce a requirement on patient appointment delays, for example, to ensure that the average delay is no larger than a threshold.

This model also allows us to analyze the optimal number of appointments to be scheduled per day (or equivalently, the overbooking level). Clearly, the more patients are scheduled per day, the higher the daily cost the clinic incurs. One can use $\omega(\mu)$ to represent this daily cost, which is a function of the service rate μ the clinic sets. Let $M \geq 0$ be the regular daily capacity of the clinic and assume that $\omega(\mu) = 0$ if $\mu \leq M$. That is, there is a sunk cost of serving up to M patients a day. Thus, $\max\{0, \mu - M\}$ can be thought of as the overbooking level. We let $\omega(\cdot)$ be convexly increasing on (M, ∞) to capture the overbooking cost. This cost can be seen as the direct financial cost (e.g., overtime cost for the staff) and/or the indirect cost of patient dissatisfaction as a result of long waits on the day of the appointment and less time devoted to the care of each patient. Taking the overbooking cost into account, the expected daily net reward for the service provider can be written as

$$R(\lambda, \mu) = T(\lambda, \mu) - \omega(\mu), \tag{10.2}$$

where $T(\lambda, \mu)$ is given by Eq. (10.1) and $\omega(\mu)$ is the overbooking cost. The objective of the service provider is to maximize $R(\lambda, \mu)$ by choosing λ (panel size) and/or μ (overbooking level). Again, a service-level constraint may be added to consideration.

The models above are stylized in nature and are meant mainly to derive managerial insights. But they are still helpful to generate a first-order approximation of real appointment systems. Green and Savin (2008) focus on the panel size decisions for a clinic that uses "open access" scheduling. Open access is a scheduling paradigm that tries to give all patients same-day or next-day appointments, to the extent possible (Murray and Tantau, 2000). The objective of open access is to improve patient attendance and clinic capacity utilization by reducing patient no-show rates via cutting appointment delays short. Clearly, an overly large panel will lead to long delays and make open access fail. Green and Savin (2008) consider both an M/M/1/K queue and an M/D/1/K queue (and realistic simulation models as well) to investigate the appropriate panel size that would enable a practice to adopt open access. Specifically, they identify patient demand rates under which a large proportion, say 85 percent, of the patients can access care on the same day of their appointment requests. One notable feature of their model is that patients, if they do not show up at their appointment, have a certain probability to reschedule another appointment (i.e., to join the back of the queue).

Liu and Ziya (2014) used M/M/1 queueing models to model the appointments scheduled for a provider, and they considered two different problems. In the first problem, the service capacity is fixed and the decision variable is the panel size; in the second problem, both the panel size and the service capacity (i.e., overbooking level) are decision variables. They characterized the optimal decisions that maximize the net reward collected by the clinic, and analyzed how optimal decisions depend on patients' no-show behavior in regards to their appointment delays. They found that in addition to the magnitudes of patient showup probabilities, patients' sensitivity to incremental delays is an important determinant of how demand and capacity decisions should be adjusted in response to anticipated changes in patients' no-show behavior.

Zacharias and Armony (2017) addressed the joint problem of determining the panel size of a medical practice and the number of offered appointment slots per day, so that patients do not face long backlogs and the clinic is not overcrowded. They explicitly modeled the two time scales involved in accessing medical care: appointment delay (order of days, weeks) and clinic delay (order of minutes, hours). They derived closed-form expressions for the performance measures of interests based on diffusion approximations and provided theoretical and numerical support for the optimality of an open access policy in outpatient scheduling when accounting for both types of delay.

The research stream above has mainly modeled patient no-show behavior in a queueing framework. One important avenue for future research is to consider other types of patient behaviors. In addition to no-shows, patients may cancel in advance or reschedule their appointments. These patient behaviors can leave "holes" in the appointment queue. In this case, a first-come, first-served queue may not be an accurate representation, and some sort of approximation is required to derive analytical insights. The other significant patient behavior to model is balking; that is, patient chooses upon arrival not to book the appointment (because he observes a long queue ahead). It is possible that the patient retries joining the queue later or even abandons the panel after some unsuccessful retrials (and seeks an alternative provider). It would be interesting to study the optimal decision-making in such an elaborate patient behavioral framework.

The other promising research direction is to study system-wide decisions other than panel size and overbooking level. One such decision is the scheduling window, that is, how far into the future an appointment can be scheduled. A smaller scheduling window enforces shorter appointment delays (and thus lower no-show rates), but increase the blocking probability (i.e., patients are refused due to a full appointment backlog). Liu (2016) provides some initial thoughts on how to set an optimal scheduling window when patient no-show probability increases with appointment delay. More research is called for to examine the connection between the appointment window size and the operational efficiency of ambulatory care facilities in broader settings.

Another interesting research direction is to consider group practice. A traditional group practice involves multiple physicians who work together to co-manage a panel of patients. With a severe shortage of (primary) care workforce (Petterson et al., 2012), nonphysician providers (e.g., nurse practitioners) become important alternatives to provide less costly but high-quality care (Mundinger et al., 2000). These nonphysician providers often team up with physicians to form a care team. Previous work has investigated the productivity and capacity allocation issues in a group practice (Green et al., 2013; Balasubramanian et al., 2013). However, intriguing team dynamics arise in care teams (Song et al., 2015, 2017), and it would be compelling to study the impact of these team dynamics on the operational function of a group practice and study how to form an effective care team.

10.4.2 Appointment Template Design

Daily appointment templates are typically set up in the following way. They divide a clinic session into small, discrete time slots, say 15 or 20 minutes. Most routine primary care visits take one slot. Some patient visits may involve a longer consultation time with PCPs, and thus use multiple slots, for example, new patient visits, annual physical checkups, patients with chronic diseases, or in-office procedures. Daily appointment templates specify the use of each time slot. Some slots are used only for routine visits, and multiple consecutive slots may be reserved for complex visits. It is possible that more than one patient can be scheduled into a single slot (this is called overbooking); overbooking is often used by a practice to deal with the problem of patient no-shows (i.e., patients break their scheduled appointments without notifying the practice in advance).

Some appointment slots may be reserved in anticipation of potential walk-in (and urgent) patients; these slots cannot be booked in advance.

Appointment times tell patients when to arrive at the clinic (not the time they will see the PCP). After patients arrive, they first check in with the front desk staff, who verifies their basic information and registers the patients. Then patients will be seen by the PCP when the PCP becomes available. During a patient's visit, she may see multiple health professionals (such as nurses, nutritionists, social workers, etc.), depending on the purpose of her visit. Lab tests may also be ordered; patients may have to wait for the lab test results and see the PCP again, if necessary. Upon discharge, patients may be asked to schedule a follow-up appointment if a single visit does not complete this episode of care.

A well-designed appointment template ensures a smooth clinic patient flow. In theory, if scheduled patients always show up and always arrive on time, and if the provider's service time is deterministic, this is an easy task. However, in practice, patient no-shows, unpunctuality, and service time variability are common. These uncertainties in the system lead to several competing objectives when designing the appointment template. To ensure high capacity utilization and reduce potential overtime work, one prefers to schedule patients early in the day, but this unfortunately increases patient wait time. The central goal of appointment template design is to achieve a fine balance among these competing objectives.

Design of appointment templates has been studied extensively in the (health) OM literature; see in-depth reviews by Cayirli and Veral (2003), Gupta and Denton (2008), and Ahmadi-Javid et al. (2016). A common theme of this literature is to develop mathematical programming models to optimize the tradeoff between patient in-clinic waiting and provider utilization. Two types of decision variables have been considered. The first type of decision scenario is concerned with the exact appointment time for each patient (decision variables are *continuous*). If patients are heterogeneous (e.g., their no-show probabilities or service time distributions are different), then sequencing is also of interest. Some recent representative work includes Denton and Gupta (2003), Hassin and Mendel (2008), Begen and Queyranne (2011), Begen et al. (2012), Kong et al. (2013), Ge et al. (2013), Mak et al. (2014a), and Mak et al. (2014b). The second type of decision scenario divides a day into a certain number of appointment slots and determines the number of patients assigned to each slot (decision variables are *integers*); see, for example, Kaandorp and Koole (2007), Robinson and Chen (2010), LaGanga and Lawrence (2012), and Zacharias and Pinedo (2014).

Although both types of decision variables can find applications in practice, the first type (i.e., continuous appointment intervals) is used more often in the (ambulatory) surgical scheduling setting, and the second decision scenario (i.e., deciding the number of patients assigned to each slot) is more common in outpatient (primary) care clinics (Gupta and Wang, (2012)). In this chapter, we focus on the second type of decision variable.

We start by describing a basic modeling framework. We consider a clinic session with T appointment slots, where the provider needs to schedule N patients in these slots.[5] Suppose that the service time of each patient is exactly one appointment slot, and that each patient will not show up for her appointment with probability p. Let $\mathbf{x} := \{x_t, t = 1, 2, \dots, T\}$ be the number of patients scheduled for slot t (this is our decision variable). Note that we do not allow booking patients beyond time slot T. Let $z_t = (z_{t-1} - 1)^+ + x_t$ be the maximum possible number of patients in the system during slot t, with $z_0 = 0$. Denote by $\pi_t(k)$ the probability that k patients present in the system at the beginning of time slot t before any service. Let $b(k|z, \theta) = \binom{z}{k} \theta^k (1-\theta)^{z-k}$ be the probability mass function for the binomial distribution. Then, we have the following recursive definition for $\pi_t(k)$:

$$\pi_t(k) = b(k|x_t, 1-p)\pi_{t-1}(0) + \sum_{j=1}^{k-j+1} b(k-j+1|x_t, 1-p)\pi_{t-1}(j),$$

where the calculation of $\pi_t(k)$ is conditional on whether there are zero or more than zero patients during time slot $t-1$. It follows that the expected overtime is

$$O(\mathbf{x}) = \sum_{k=1}^{z_T} (k-1) \cdot \pi_T(k), \tag{10.3}$$

and the expected total length of the provider's day is

$$D(\mathbf{x}) = T + \sum_{k=1}^{z_T} (k-1) \cdot \pi_T(k).$$

The expected amount of time that the provider is working is $N \cdot (1-p)$. Subtracting this expected workload from the expected total length gives the provider's expected idle time:

$$I(\mathbf{x}) = D(\mathbf{x}) - N \cdot (1-p). \tag{10.4}$$

The expected total patient wait time is

$$W(\mathbf{x}) = \sum_{t=1}^{T-1} \sum_{k=1}^{N} (k-1)\pi_t(k) + \sum_{k=1}^{N_S} \left[\sum_{j=1}^{k} (j-1) \right] \pi_T(k). \tag{10.5}$$

Assuming that the unit time cost rates for provider idling, overtime, and patient waiting are C_I, C_O and C_W, respectively. Without loss of generality, we

5 N itself can also be a decision variable, but most literature assumes that it is a given number reflecting the provider's expected workload.

normalize $C_W = 1$. Then, the optimization problem faced by the provider can be formally expressed as follows:

$$\min_{\mathbf{x}} W(\mathbf{x}) + C_I I(\mathbf{x}) + C_O O(\mathbf{x}) \tag{10.6}$$

$$\sum_{t=1}^{T} x_t = N,$$

$$\mathbf{x} \in \mathbb{Z}_+^T,$$

$W(x)$, $I(x)$, $O(x)$ are defined in Eqs. (10.5), (10.4), and (10.3), respectively.

The Model Eq. (10.6) above is perhaps the simplest model for appointment template design. It assumes homogeneous patient no-show probability, deterministic and equal patient service times, patient punctuality, and no walk-in patients. Even with these simplifications, the model is still difficult, given its combinatorial nature. The existing literature has considered a range of variants of the basic model above. Most research efforts have been focused on proving the structural properties of the objective function and/or the optimal schedule; these properties can be used to devise efficient solution algorithms.

Robinson and Chen (2010) consider a model similar to Eq. (10.6), but assume that patients can be purposefully scheduled beyond the Tth time slot. They show that the optimal policy contains no "holes." That is, if patients are scheduled into a slot t, then any slot before slot t should contain at least one patient. This "no-hole" property drastically reduces the search space for the optimal schedule, making enumeration a viable approach for realistically-sized problem instances. They also identify conditions under which it is optimal to assign each patient to an individual time slot.

Kaandorp and Koole (2007) extend Model Eq. (10.6) by considering exponentially distributed service times. They are the first to show that the objective function is *multimodular*. This elegant property ensures that a local search procedure converges to the optimal schedule.

Zacharias and Pinedo (2014) consider heterogeneous patients. Specifically, they allow that the cost of waiting to depends on the patient and consider two classes of patients, depending on their no-show rates. They (partially) characterize the optimal schedule and introduce a new sequencing rule that schedules patients according to a single index that is a function of their characteristics. Recently, the same group of researchers studied a multiserver system in which the number of patients to be scheduled is also a decision variable (Zacharias and Pinedo, 2017). They prove the *discrete convexity* of the resultant optimization model. This property restricts the search space for the optimal schedule and guarantees that a local search algorithm terminates with a globally optimal schedule.

In recent work, Wang et al. (2016) develop perhaps the first optimization model to determine the optimal appointment schedule in the presence of potential walk-ins. They show that the natural formulation of the problem, which is difficult to deal with directly, can be reformulated as a two-stage stochastic integer program with a simple and tractable structure. Their model can accommodate exponentially distributed service times, and patient-dependent and time-dependent no-show probabilities.

Even though there has been significant research progress in the study of appointment template design in recent years, a range of "open" and practical problems remains yet to be studied. One important issue is patient unpunctuality; that is, patients may arrive earlier or later than their scheduled appointment times. Patient unpunctuality complicates the analysis significantly because if a patient is not punctual, the provider may choose to serve a patient who holds an appointment scheduled later than the other patient if the former patient arrives earlier. In other words, service order may not be the same as the arrival order (i.e., the order of appointment times). Previous research has studied how to evaluate a service system with a finite number of customer arrivals with stochastic and heterogeneous customer interarrival times and service times; see, for example, Wang et al. (2014). This research assumes an FCFS service order, and may be useful in the analysis of an appointment system with unpunctual patients. However, it is not clear whether FCFS (according to arrival times) is the exact service order used in practice when patients are not punctual. A recent study analyzes the wait-preempt dilemma[6] optimally for the two-patient case (Samorani and Ganguly, (2016)), and finds that in contrast to preemption which is adopted by practice, sometimes it is optimal to wait. In general, however, how to model how a provider prioritizes her service when patients are not punctual and how to optimize the appointment template under patient unpunctuality remain open research questions.

Besides considering patient unpunctuality, future research may consider the design of appointment templates in a complex clinic environment, which may become even more complex with the advance of ambulatory care (Froehle and Magazine, (2013)). One common assumption made by most previous work is that the physician is the bottleneck of the system; thus, it suffices to consider a single server in the system. This assumption is valid in many cases (Berg and Denton, (2012)). However, patient care paths in reality can be more complicated than those modeled in a single server queueing system. Multiple stages (e.g., registration, nursing station, exam room, and recovery room in the case of an in-clinic procedure) and multiple service providers (e.g., registration staff, nurse, physician, and social worker) may be involved. Patients may also share care paths; for example, multiple patients may join a group visit to receive service from the same provider (team) at the same time. Thus, it would be interesting to investigate how to schedule patients who need to move through a service network (rather than a single server system).

6 As discussed earlier, this dilemma is referred to as whether an available provider should see an early patient right away (preempt) or wait for the patient scheduled next.

Futhermore, interruptions are likely to occur in a complex environment, and add another layer of difficulty. Luo et al. (2012) study the optimal appointment policies in a single-server system where the service of scheduled patients can be interrupted by emergency requests that have a higher priority. Future research may be directed to consider other types of interruptions, for example, nonpreemptive interruptions by customer arrivals, or server vacation.

10.4.3 Managing Patient Flow

The last section concerns the *static* design of daily appointment templates, and this section discusses how to manage patient flow after that — more specifically, how to *dynamically* schedule patients into service sessions upon their requests. There are typically two ways how patients are scheduled for service: advance scheduling and allocation scheduling. Advance scheduling refers to scheduling patients into an exact future day and time to receive service upon their requests of an appointment. This is commonly used in many ambulatory care services. Allocation scheduling uses a wait list to keep patients who request for service. Patients are then selected from the wait list and scheduled for service on the basis of urgency and availability of clinical resources. Allocation scheduling is commonly used in managing surgical schedules in single-payer health systems, such as UK and Canada. We refer readers to Gerchak et al. (1996) and Huh et al. (2013) for discussion on allocation scheduling. In this chapter, we focus on advance scheduling.

We start by describing a basic modeling framework, following the notion of Liu et al. (2010). We consider how to schedule patients into different days in the future for service upon their requests for appointments, based on the current appointment schedule. Let A^t denote the number of appointment requests that arrive on day t. Assume that $\{A^t, t = 1, 2, \dots\}$ is a sequence of independent and identically distributed (i.i.d.) random variables. Suppose that the clinic uses a scheduling window of T days so that no patient can be scheduled more than T days ahead.

For any given day t, we define type (i, j) patients as those who called on day $t - i$, were given appointments for day $t + j$, and have not canceled their appointments by the beginning of day t. All patients of type (i, j) have an appointment delay of $i + j$ days; thus, we must have $i + j \leq T$. Let X_{ij}^t denote the number of type (i, j) patients at the beginning of day t and let $\mathbf{X}^t = \{X_{ij}^t : 1 \leq i + j \leq T, i = 1, 2, \dots, T\}$. So $\mathbf{X}^t$ contains the information on the number of patients of each type in the appointment schedule at the beginning of day t. We refer to $\mathbf{X}^t$ as the *schedule* on day t, based on which the provider schedules the incoming appointment requests.

There are three possible outcomes for each appointment made. The patient may show up for her appointment, she may cancel her appointment on or before the day of the appointment, or she may not cancel but simply not show up for her appointment. We assume that each patient's behavior is independent of that of others and the arrival process. To model these patient behaviors, we let α_{ij} be the probability that a patient who is currently of type (i,j) will show up for her appointment and β_{ij} be the probability that a patient who is currently of type (i,j) will not cancel her appointment before her appointment day.

Assume that events occur in the following order on each day. First, new patients call in and are given appointments. During the day, some patients cancel their appointments, and some do not show up for their appointments. At the end of the day, the clinic makes an "expected net reward" of $r(x,z)$ if z patients were scheduled on that day and the clinic ended up serving x of these patients during the day. For generality, we do not specify any particular form for $r(\cdot,\cdot)$ for now. The objective of the provider is to schedule arriving appointment requests so that the long-run average expected net reward is maximized.

This problem can be modeled as an Markov decision process (MDP). The decision epochs are the times right after the appointment requests arrive every day, and the system state at decision epoch t is given by $(A^t, \mathbf{X}^t)$. Let Y_j^t represent the number of patients who make their requests on day t and are given appointments for day $t+j$. (For example, Y_0^t is the number of patients who are given same-day appointments on day t.) Thus, $\mathbf{Y}^t = \{Y_j^t : j = 0, 1, \dots, T\}$ is the scheduling "action" taken on day t. Given that there are A^t appointment requests, the set of actions available on day t is $\{\mathbf{Y}^t : \sum_{i=0}^{T} Y_i^t = A^t, Y_i^t \in \mathbb{Z}_+, i = 0, 1, \dots, T\}$ where $\mathbb{Z}_+$ represents the set of all nonnegative integers.[7] We can write up a detailed expression for the transition probabilities from state $(A^t, \mathbf{X}^t) = (a^t, \mathbf{x}^t)$ to state $(A^{t+1}, \mathbf{X}^{t+1}) = (a^{t+1}, \mathbf{x}^{t+1})$ given action $\mathbf{Y}^t = \mathbf{y}^t$, with the system dynamics described above. Now, to evaluate the single-day reward function, we let $U_i^t, i = 0, 1, \dots, T$ be the number of patients who call on day $t - i$ and show up for their appointments on day t. Note that U_0^t depends on Y_0^t; and U_i^t depends on X_{i0}^t, $i = 1, 2 \dots, T$. Then, the net reward obtained on day t given A^t, $\mathbf{X}^t$, and $\mathbf{Y}^t$ is

$$c_0((A^t, \mathbf{X}^t), \mathbf{Y}^t) = r\left(\sum_{i=0}^{T} U_i^t, Y_0^t + \sum_{i=1}^{T} X_{i0}^t\right).$$

Consider a scheduling policy f, and let $\phi_f(a, \mathbf{x})$ be the long-run expected average net reward under policy f given the initial state $A^1 = a$ and $\mathbf{X}^1 = \mathbf{x}$; that is,

$$\phi_f(a, \mathbf{x}) = \lim_{k\to\infty} \frac{\mathbf{E}_f\left[\sum_{t=1}^{k} c_0((A^t, \mathbf{X}^t), \mathbf{Y}^t) | (A^1, \mathbf{X}^1) = (a, \mathbf{x})\right]}{k}.$$

7 It is straightforward to include rejection of the appointment request as another action, but for the convenience of presentation, we do not further explore the rejection option.

A scheduling policy f^* is said to be optimal if

$$\phi_{f^*}(a, \mathbf{x}) = \sup_{f} \phi_f(a, \mathbf{x}), \quad \forall a, \mathbf{x}.$$

In theory, we can solve this MDP problem using one of the standard procedures such as the policy improvement or value iteration algorithms. However, the formulation suffers significantly from the curse of dimensionality. Previous research has considered a range of variants to the model above. We review some recent representative work below.

Liu et al. (2010) developed the first modeling framework as above and proposed heuristic dynamic policies for scheduling patient appointments, taking into account the fact that patients may cancel or not show up for their appointments. Most other prior research does not explicitly model patient cancellation or no-show behaviors, but considers other relevant and complicating factors in practice. Patrick et al. (2008) studied advance scheduling of patients with different priorities to a diagnostic facility. Motivated by the requirement of public healthcare settings, they considered wait-time targets for different patients. They presented analytical results that give the form of the optimal linear value function approximation and the resulting policy. For a similar problem, Gocgun and Ghate (2012) developed an approximate dynamic programming method that uses Lagrangian relaxation and constraint generation to efficiently generate good scheduling policies. Recently, Truong (2015) considered advance scheduling with two classes of patients: regular patients who may wait and urgent patients who need service on the day of arrival. She showed a striking result that the optimal noncommittable advance scheduling policy (which does not have to honor the prior assignment decisions and is easy to compute) is also feasible and optimal for advance scheduling. This is perhaps the first analytical result for the optimal advance scheduling policies.

One common underlying assumption of the work reviewed above is that a single visit completes the whole episode of care. This visit might require services from multiple resources (e.g., physicians, labs, nurse), but all these services are completed within the day of visit. However, some outpatient care programs are multidisciplinary and involve multiple stages of services that span days. In this case, a care itinerary, which describes the appointment days/times for each stage of services, needs to be prescribed for patients when they request care. Diamant et al. (2016) are among the first to study the design of care itineraries; their work has been motivated by a Canadian bariatric surgery program. They developed approximate dynamic programming approaches to solve the resultant MDP, which determines the next service(s) as well as the day to receive it for each patient. We believe that vast research opportunities exist to extend this line of work on the design of patient care itineraries.

Most extant research on the dynamic control of patient flow in ambulatory care considers scheduling patients into *days* upon their appointment requests with the objective to smooth workloads over days. In practice, however, patients are usually informed about their appointment *day and time* when requesting appointments. Some recent research has investigated how to schedule patients successively within a day by deciding whether to accept a new patient (Muthuraman and Lawley, 2008; Chakraborty et al., 2010) or by determining the appointment interval in an "online" fashion for each arrival of a patient (Erdogan and Denton, 2013; Chen and Robinson, 2014). However, there is a lack of research on how to provide patients with an exact appointment time and day upon their requests. This research direction bears significant practical importance and is quite challenging, as it requires taking into account both within-day and across-day dynamics, as described in Sections 10.4.2 and 10.4.3.

10.5 New Trends in Ambulatory Care

In light of the rapidly changing landscape of healthcare, the fast growth of the healthcare market, and the quick development and adoption of medical technologies, several emerging trends in the ambulatory care practice environment provide promising and interesting research opportunities for OM researchers.

10.5.1 Online Market

Online scheduling is being adopted by an increasingly larger percentage of patients and clinics. Some healthcare systems have developed their own online system (e.g., www.questdiagnostics.com), whereas others work with third-party scheduling service vendors, such as www.zocdoc.com and www.docasap.com. These online systems reveal the availabilities of various providers; they also allow patients to provide reviews on providers and their service. These online systems make the access, quality, and cost information much easier for patients to search and compare. Essentially, an Amazon.com-like *online market* for (ambulatory) care is emerging and being used by more and more patients and providers.

Ambulatory care providers are facing many challenges presented by this "new" online market. To effectively manage their operations, providers ought to first understand what (operational) attributes affect patient choice of care options. Some recent studies, for example, Liu et al. (2017), Osadchiy and KC (2017), and Xu et al. (2017), offer insights on how delay to care, in-clinic wait time, perceived quality, and online reviews affect patient choices and, ultimately, demand for physicians. But how patients behave in and use the online healthcare market remains a largely unexplored question.

In addition, providers require effective (scheduling) tools that enable them to be competitive in the online market. To develop these tools, it is critical to take into account patient preferences and choice when making scheduling decisions. A few recent studies develop scheduling protocols for systems that either allow providers to make scheduling decisions based on patients' revealed preferences (e.g., Gupta and Wang (2008) and Wang and Gupta (2011)), or allow patients to choose among various appointment options (e.g., Feldman et al. 2014 and Liu et al. 2016b). These studies are highly relevant to those reviewed in Section 10.4.3, but add one additional layer of complexity to the problem: patient choice behavior. These studies, however, all focus on a single provider's operations (and treat external competition, if any, as exogenous); extensive research opportunities exist in understanding how various providers (should) *compete* in the online market.

10.5.2 Telehealth

One of the biggest changes to health care in the last decade is perhaps telehealth, which encompasses a broad variety of technologies and tactics to deliver *virtual* medical, health, and education services (Center for Connected Health Policy, 2016). For instance, telehealth allows providers to counsel their patients remotely via secure communication systems and enables patients to manage their medications without physically visiting a physician's office. (Telehealth needs to be differentiated from the online market discussed above: the former provides tools to deliver care remotely while the latter offers a platform through which patients compare and choose care.)

We believe that adoption of telehealth could improve quality of care, cut costs, and enhance patient satisfaction. Therefore, both the federal and state governments in the US are leading the way in telehealth expansion, and many forms of care delivered by telehealth are now billable to payers. Consequently, telehealth is experiencing fast growth: It is expected that the global telehealth market will expand at a compound annual growth rate of 14.3 percent through 2020, eventually reaching \$36.2 billion, as compared to \$14.3 billion in 2014 (Lacktman, 2015).

Such fast growth presents opportunities but also challenging questions for providers who adopt telehealth. Specifically, how does the introduction of telehealth affect patient care utilization patterns? How should the providers integrate telehealth visits with their regular in-clinic practices? How should providers manage the health of chronic care patients when telehealth is available? Telehealth enables large healthcare organizations to provide care to overseas patients and expand global markets, but how should this be done without compromising domestic business? Recent research has studied how e-visits affect physician operations, productivity, and patient health (Rajan et al., 2011; Bavafa et al., 2017, 2018) and how teletriage plays a role in healthcare demand management (Cakici and Mills, 2017). But the study of telehealth and its impact on healthcare operations management is still in its infancy and presents significant opportunities for OM researchers.

10.5.3 Retail Approach of Outpatient Care

The US healthcare market has seen a quick rise of retail models for outpatient care, such as retail clinics (e.g., CVS "Minute Clinic") and walk-in urgent care clinics (e.g., CityMD and PM Pediatrics). Since 2000, large retail companies, such as Target, CVS, Kroger, Walgreens, and Walmart have introduced ambulatory clinics located in pharmacies, grocery stores, or other retail settings to offer a fast, convenient walk-in option for low-acuity care. Such clinics are usually staffed with a nurse practitioner (NP). Assisted by this NP, a remote physician may also provide online care to an on-site patient. Retail clinics grow fast in both number and variety of services provided, going beyond urgent care toward more population health and chronic disease management services (Sarasohn-Kahn, 2016). Estimates predict that the US will have more than 2800 retail clinics by 2018 (Nalle et al., 2015).

Compared to retail clinics, walk-in urgent care clinics are often larger and staffed with multiple providers; they can offer more comprehensive urgent-care service to patients, for example, these clinics can provide x-ray services. Urgent-care companies popped up in the 1980s, and have expanded faster after the 2000s as emergency rooms have become more crowded and patients seek alternatives (Li, 2014). There are about 7100 centers in the US and most of them open seven days a week (Urgent Care Association of America, 2016).

Theoretically, these retail and walk-in clinics could help reduce demand for emergency room use for nonurgent conditions and provide some services that would otherwise have to be provided by PCPs. But there are concerns that these clinics, due to their convenience, may also lead to unnecessary care visits due to minor issues, which would otherwise be cared for by patients themselves. These clinics may also break the continuity of care between patients and their own PCPs. We refer readers to Weinick et al. (2010) for a detailed discussion on these clinics.

Beyond the health quality and cost issues, this new retail approach to outpatient care presents a range of operational challenges to various stakeholders. For instance, how should these clinics run to achieve the best operational efficiency, considering that most patients are walk-ins and patient demand has a strong seasonality? Most walk-in urgent care clinics are operated by urgent-care companies, and some retail clinics are owned by a physician group, hospital, or healthcare system. How should the parent health organization plan the locations and resource allocation for these clinics? How might retail clinics owned by retail stores integrate the retail clinics into the management of the whole store? Perhaps the most important question for retail clinics is about how to maintain and improve the current business model, given that most retail clinics have not generated a profit and that even if they do, the profit margins are slim (Costello, 2008).

10.6 Conclusion

Ambulatory care is a critical component in the whole health care service chain, not only because of its large size and patient volume, but also because it is often the entry point for patients to get specialty and inpatient care. With increasing financial pressures under the shift from fee-for-service to pay-for-performance, changing demographics in an aging society, and rising expectations for health services in the movement toward patient-centered care, ambulatory care providers face significant challenges in meeting patient demand that is likely to keep growing in the next several decades. This chapter provides an overview of ambulatory care, introduces representative streams of OM research in this care setting, and discusses new trends and opportunities for future research. Due to the space limit, we are not able to exhaust all relevant topics, but we hope that the contents in this chapter provide a foundation to conduct meaningful OM research in ambulatory care (and its interfaces with other care settings).

References

Ahmadi-Javid, Amir, Zahra Jalali, and Kenneth J. Klassen (2017). Outpatient appointment systems in healthcare: A review of optimization studies. *European Journal of Operational Research* 258, no. 1: 3–34.

Balasubramanian, H., A. Muriel, A. Ozen, L. Wang, X. Gao, and J. Hippchen. (2013). Capacity allocation and flexibility in primary care, in *Handbook of Healthcare Operations Management*, Springer, pp. 205–228.

Batt, R.J. and C. Terwiesch. (2015). Waiting patiently: An empirical study of queue abandonment in an emergency department. *Management Science*, 61 (1), 39–59.

Bavafa, H., L. Hitt, and C. Terwiesch. (2018). The impact of e-visits on visit frequencies and patient health: Evidence from primary care. *Management Science*. Forthcoming.

Bavafa, H., S. Savin, and C. Terwiesch. (2017). Managing office revisit intervals and patient panel sizes in primary care. Working paper. The Wharton School. https://papers.ssrn.com/sol3/papers.cfm?abstract_id=2363685

Begen, M.A., R. Levi, and M. Queyranne. (2012) Technical note—a sampling-based approach to appointment scheduling. *Operations Research*, 60 (3), 675–681.

Begen, M.A. and M. Queyranne. (2011). Appointment scheduling with discrete random durations. *Mathematics of Operations Research*, 36 (2), 240–257.

Berg, B. and B.T. Denton. (2012). Appointment planning and scheduling in outpatient procedure centers, in *Handbook of Healthcare System Scheduling*, Springer, pp. 131–154.

Cakici, O.E. and A.F. Mills. (2017). Calling for care? The risky proposition of teletriage in healthcare demand management. Working Paper, Indiana University Kelley School of Business.

Carroll, A. (2012) The "iron triangle" on health care: Access, cost, and quality. *JAMA*.

Cayirli, T. and E. Veral. (2003). Outpatient scheduling in health care: a review of literature. *Production and Operations Management*, 12 (4), 519–549.

Cayirli, T., E. Veral, and H. Rosen. (2006). Designing appointment scheduling systems for ambulatory care services. *Health Care Management Science*, 9 (1), 47–58.

Center for Connected Health Policy (2016). What is telehealth? http://www.cchpca.org/what-is-telehealth

Chakraborty, S., K. Muthuraman, and M. Lawley. (2010). Sequential clinical scheduling with patient no-shows and general service time distributions. *IIE Transactions*, 42 (5), 354–366.

Chen, R.R. and L.W. Robinson. (2014). Sequencing and scheduling appointments with potential call-in patients. *Production and Operations Management*, 23 (9), 1522–1538.

Cho, S.H., H. Jang, T. Lee, and J. Turner. (2014). Simultaneous location of trauma centers and helicopters for emergency medical service planning. *Operations Research*, 62 (4), 751–771.

Costello, D. (2008). A checkup for retail medicine. *Health Affairs*, 27 (5), 1299–1303.

Denton, B. and D. Gupta. (2003). A sequential bounding approach for optimal appointment scheduling. *IIE Transactions*, 35 (11), 1003–1016.

Deo, S. and I. Gurvich. (2011). Centralized vs. decentralized ambulance diversion: A network perspective. *Management Science*, 57 (7), 1300–1319.

Diamant, A., J. Milner, and F. Quereshy. (2016). Dynamic patient scheduling for multi-appointment health care programs. Working paper. York University.

Erdogan, S.A. and B. Denton. (2013). Dynamic appointment scheduling of a stochastic server with uncertain demand. *INFORMS Journal on Computing*, 25 (1), 116–132.

Evans, M. (2015). Hospitals face closures as a new day in healthcare dawns. *Modern Healthcare*, 45 (8), 8.

Feldman, J., N. Liu, H. Topaloglu, and S. Ziya. (2014). Appointment scheduling under patient preference and no-show behavior. *Operations Research*, 62 (4), 794–811.

Froehle, C.M. and M.J. Magazine. (2013). Improving scheduling and flow in complex outpatient clinics, in *Handbook of Healthcare Operations Management*, Springer, pp. 229–250.

Ge, D., G. Wan, Z. Wang, and J. Zhang. (2013). A note on appointment scheduling with piecewise linear cost functions. *Mathematics Operations Research*, 39 (4), 1244–1251.

Gerchak, Y., D. Gupta, and M. Henig. (1996). Reservation planning for elective surgery under uncertain demand for emergency surgery. *Management Science*, 42 (3), 321–334.

Gocgun, Y. and A. Ghate. (2012). Lagrangian relaxation and constraint generation for allocation and advanced scheduling. *Computers & Operations Research*, 39 (10), 2323–2336.

Green, L.V. and S. Savin. (2008). Reducing delays for medical appointments: A queueing approach. *Operations Research*, 56 (6), 1526–1538.

Green, L.V., S. Savin, and Y. Lu. (2013). Primary care physician shortages could be eliminated through use of teams, nonphysicians, and electronic communication. *Health Affairs*, 32 (1), 11–19.

Gupta, D. and B. Denton. (2008). Appointment scheduling in health care: Challenges and opportunities. *IIE Transactions*, 40 (9), 800–819.

Gupta, D. and L. Wang. (2008). Revenue management for a primary-care clinic in the presence of patient choice. *Operations Research*, 56 (3), 576–592.

Gupta, D. and W.Y. Wang. (2012). Patient appointments in ambulatory care, in *Handbook of Healthcare System Scheduling*, Springer, pp. 65–104.

Hassin, R. and S. Mendel. (2008). Scheduling arrivals to queues: A single-server model with no-shows. *Management Science*, 54 (3), 565–572.

Huh, W.T., N. Liu and V.A. Truong. (2013). Multiresource allocation scheduling in dynamic environments. *Manufacturing & Service Operations Management*, 15 (2), 280–291.

Kaandorp, G.C. and G. Koole. (2007). Optimal outpatient appointment scheduling. *Health Care Management Science*, 10 (3), 217–229.

KC, D.S. (2013). Does multitasking improve performance? Evidence from the emergency department. *Manufacturing & Service Operations Management*, 16 (2), 168–183.

Kong, Q., C.Y. Lee, C.P. Teo, and Z. Zheng. (2013). Scheduling arrivals to a stochastic service delivery system using copositive cones. *Operations Research.*, 61 (3), 711–726.

Lacktman, N. (2015). Five telemedicine trends transforming health care in 2016. https://www.foley.com/five-telemedicine-trends-transforming-health-care-in-2016/

LaGanga, L.R. and S.R. Lawrence. (2012). Appointment overbooking in health care clinics to improve patient service and clinic performance. *Production and Operations Management*, 21 (5), 874–888.

Li, R. (2014). Walk-in urgent-care companies are providing relief to retail landlords. The Wall Street Journal. https://www.wsj.com/articles/walk-in-urgent-care-companies-are-providing-relief-to-retail-landlords-1398048191

Liu, N. (2016). Optimal choice for appointment scheduling window under patient no-show behavior. *Production and Operations Management*, 25 (1), 128–142.

Liu, N., S. Finkelstein, M. Kruk, and D. Rosenthal. (2017). When waiting to see a doctor is less irritating: Understanding patient preferences and choice behavior in appointment scheduling. *Management Science*, 64 (5), 1975–1996.

Liu, N., P. van de Ven, and B. Zhang. (2016b). Managing appointment scheduling under patient choices. Working paper. Columbia University.

Liu, N. and S. Ziya. (2014). Panel size and overbooking decisions for appointment-based services under patient no-shows. *Production and Operations Management*, 23 (12), 2209–2223.

Liu, N., S. Ziya, and V.G. Kulkarni. (2010). Dynamic scheduling of outpatient appointments under patient no-shows and cancellations. *Manufacturing Service Operations Management*, 12 (2), 347–364.

Luo, J., V.G. Kulkarni, and S. Ziya. (2012). Appointment scheduling under patient no-shows and service interruptions. *Manufacturing & Service Operations Management*, 14 (4), 670–684.

Macharia, W.M., G. Leon, B.H. Rowe, B.J. Stephenson, and R.B. Haynes. (1992). An overview of interventions to improve compliance with appointment keeping for medical services. *JAMA*, 267 (13), 1813–1817.

Machlin, S. and S. Chowdhury. (2011). *Expenses and characteristics of physician visits in different ambulatory care settings, 2008*. Agency for Healthcare Research and Quality.

Mak, H.Y., Y. Rong, and J. Zhang. (2014a). Appointment scheduling with limited distributional information. *Management Science*, 61 (2), 316–334.

Mak, H.Y., Y. Rong, and J. Zhang. (2014b). Sequencing appointments for service systems using inventory approximations. *Manufacturing & Service Operations Management*, 16 (2), 251–262.

Mannino, B. (2012). Can ambulatory care fix our costly healthy-care system? FOXBusiness. www.foxbusiness.com/features/can-ambulatory-care-fix-our-costly-healthy-care-system

Medicare Payment Advisory Commission, The. (2016). Ambulatory Care Settings. www.medpac.gov/-research-areas-/ambulatory-care-settings.

Mobin, S.S.N., G.R. Keyes, R. Singer, J. Yates, and D. Thompson. (2013). Infections in outpatient surgery. *Clinics in plastic surgery*, 40 (3), 439–446.

Mundinger, M.O., R.L. Kane, E.R. Lenz, A.M. Totten, W.Y. Tsai, P.D. Cleary, W.T. Friedewald, A.L. Siu, and M.L. Shelanski. (2000). Primary care outcomes in patients treated by nurse practitioners or physicians: a randomized trial. *JAMA*, 283 (1), 59–68.

Murray, M. and C. Tantau. (2000). Same-day appointments: exploding the access paradigm. *Family practice management*, 7 (8), 45–45.

Muthuraman, K. and M. Lawley. (2008). A stochastic overbooking model for outpatient clinical scheduling with no-shows. *IIE Transactions*, 40 (9), 820–837.

Nalle, A., D. Boston, and B. Bhansali. (2015). US Retail Health Clinics Expected to Surge by 2017 According to Accenture Analysis. Accenture Insight Driven

Health. https://www.accenture.com/t20151218T203107__w__/us-en/_acnmedia/PDF-2/Accenture-Retail-Health-Clinics-POV.pdf

Osadchiy, N. and D. KC. (2017). Are patients patient? The role of time to appointment in patient flow. *Production and Operations Management* 26:3: 469–490

Patrick, J., M.L. Puterman, and M. Queyranne. (2008). Dynamic multipriority patient scheduling for a diagnostic resource. *Operations research*, 56 (6), 1507–1525.

Petterson, S.M., W.R. Liaw, R.L. Phillips, D.L. Rabin, D.S. Meyers, and A.W. Bazemore. (2012). Projecting US primary care physician workforce needs: 2010–2025. *The Annals of Family Medicine*, 10 (6), 503–509.

Pugely, A.J., C.T. Martin, Y. Gao, Y., and S.A. Mendoza-Lattes. (2013). Outpatient surgery reduces short-term complications in lumbar discectomy: an analysis of 4310 patients from the ACS-NSQIP database. *Spine*, 38 (3), 264–271.

Rajan, B., A. Seidmann, E.R. Dorsey, K.M. Biglan, and J. Reminick. (2011). Analyzing the clinical and competitive impact of telemedicine-experience with treating Parkinson disease patients via telemedicine, in *2011 44th Hawaii International Conference on System Sciences (HICSS)*, IEEE, pp. 1–10.

Robinson, L.W. and R.R. Chen. (2010). A comparison of traditional and open-access policies for appointment scheduling. *Manufacturing Service Operations Management*, 12 (2), 330–346.

Rubin, G., A. Bate, A. George, P. Shackley, and N. Hall. (2006). Preferences for access to the gp: a discrete choice experiment. *British Journal of General Practice*, 56 (531), 743–748.

Saghafian, S., G. Austin, and S.J. Traub. (2015). Operations research/management contributions to emergency department patient flow optimization: Review and research prospects. *IIE Transactions on Healthcare Systems Engineering*, 5 (2), 101–123.

Samorani, M. and S. Ganguly. (2016). Optimal sequencing of unpunctual patients in high-service-level clinics. *Production and Operations Management*, 25 (2), 330–346.

Sarasohn-Kahn, J. (2016). Retail clinics continue to shape local healthcare markets. HealthcareITNews. http://www.healthcareitnews.com/blog/retail-clinics-continue-shape-local-healthcare-markets

Saultz, J.W. (2003). Defining and measuring interpersonal continuity of care. *The Annals of Family Medicine*, 1 (3), 134–143.

Song, H., A.T. Chien, J. Fisher, J. Martin, A.S. Peters, K. Hacker, M.B. Rosenthal, and S.J. Singer. (2015). Development and validation of the primary care team dynamics survey. *Health services research*, 50 (3), 897–921.

Song, H., M. Ryan, S. Tendulkar, J. Fisher, J. Martin, A.S. Peters, J.P. Frolkis, M.B. Rosenthal, A.T. Chien, and S.J. Singer. (2017). Team dynamics, clinical work satisfaction, and patient care coordination between primary care providers:

A mixed methods study. *Health care management review* 2017 Jan/Mar; 42(1):28–41.

Starfield, B. (1994). Is primary care essential? *The Lancet*, 344 (8930), 1129–1133.

Truong, V.A. (2015). Optimal advance scheduling. *Management Science*, 61 (7), 1584–1597.

Turkcan, A., L. Nuti, P.C. DeLaurentis, Z. Tian, J. Daggy, L. Zhang, M. Lawley, and L. Sands. (2013). No-show modeling for adult ambulatory clinics, in *Handbook of Healthcare Operations Management*, Springer, pp. 251–288.

Urgent Care Association of America (2016). Size of industry. Industry FAQs. http://www.ucaoa.org/?page=industryfaqs

US CDC (2016). National ambulatory medical care survey: 2013 state and national summary tables. https://www.cdc.gov/nchs/data/ahcd/namcs_summary/2013_namcs_web_tables.pdf

US National Center for Health Statistics (2016a). Health, United States, 2015: with special feature on racial and ethnic health disparities. https://www.cdc.gov/nchs/data/hus/hus15.pdf

US National Center for Health Statistics (2016b). National hospital ambulatory medical care survey: 2011 outpatient department summary tables. https://www.cdc.gov/nchs/data/ahcd/nhamcs_emergency/2011_ed_web_tables.pdf

Wang, R., O. Jouini, and S. Benjaafar. (2014). Service systems with finite and heterogeneous customer arrivals. *Manufacturing & Service Operations Management*, 16 (3), 365–380.

Wang, S., N. Liu, and G. Wan. (2016). Managing appointment-based services in the presence of walk-in customers. Working paper. Columbia University.

Wang, W.Y. and D. Gupta. (2011). Adaptive appointment systems with patient preferences. *Manufacturing & Service Operations Management*, 13 (3), 373–389.

Weinick, R.M., C.E. Pollack, M.P. Fisher, E.M. Gillen, and A. Mehrotra. (2010). Policy implications of the use of retail clinics. https://www.rand.org/content/dam/rand/pubs/technical_reports/2010/RAND_TR810.pdf.

Xu, K. and C.W. Chan. (2016). Using future information to reduce waiting times in the emergency department via diversion. Manufacturing & Service Operations Management 18, no. 3 (2016): 314–331.

Xu, Y., M. Armony, and A. Ghose. (2017). The effect of online reviews on physician demand: A structural model of patient choice. Working paper. NYU Stern School of Business.

Zacharias, C. and M. Armony. (2017) Joint Panel Sizing and Appointment Scheduling in Outpatient Care. *Management Science* 63(11):3978–3997.

Zacharias, C. and M. Pinedo. (2014). Appointment scheduling with no-shows and overbooking. *Production and Operations Management*, 23 (5), 788–801.

Zacharias, C. and M. Pinedo. (2016). Managing customer arrivals in service systems with multiple servers. Manufacturing & Service Operations Management 19, no. 4 (2017): 639–656.

11

Inpatient Care

Van-Anh Truong

Columbia University

Inpatients are those who are formally admitted to a hospital for at least one night, taking up a room, a bed, and board. Inpatient areas in a hospital include intensive care units, general nursing wards, delivery wards, and neonatal care units (Hulshof et al. 2012).

Hospitals are most often measured by the size of the inpatient wards, more precisely by the number of beds in these wards. The American Hospital Association's 2017 survey estimates that there are 5,564 registered hospitals in the US and 897,961 staffed beds in these hospitals. Thus, the wards in a hospital contain 161 beds on average (American Hospital Association, 2017).

The management of inpatients is generally accepted to be important for several reasons. As Dong and Perry (2016) first pointed out, and Kc and Terwiesch (2009), Richardson (2002), Trzeciak and Rivers (2003) later showed empirically, delays in admission to inpatient wards lead to an increase in length of stays, higher mortality rates, and increased probabilities for readmission. Second, these delays tend to propagate to units that feed into the inpatient ward, such as the emergency department (ED), intensive care units (ICU), post-anesthesia care units (PACU), and operating rooms (OR) (Jacobson et al., 2006; Argo et al., 2009; McGowan et al., 2007). This problem, called *boarding*, is a major contributor to overcrowding in EDs (Asplin and Magid, 2007; Trzeciak and Rivers, 2003). Third, inefficiencies in inpatient operations leading to longer length of stays (LOS) tend to be costly for hospitals, as they reduce the number of patients that can be served. In 2012, there were 36.5 million hospital stays in the US. The average length of stay was 4.5 days, incurring an average cost of $10,400 per stay (Weiss and Elixhauser, 2012). Overall, hospital inpatient care accounts for a third of all health care expenditures in the US (Pfuntner et al., 2006).

Handbook of Healthcare Analytics: Theoretical Minimum for Conducting 21st Century Research on Healthcare Operations, First Edition. Edited by Tinglong Dai and Sridhar Tayur.

Shi et al. (2015) identify four sources of inpatients for general wards (GW): (1) ED-GW patients are those admitted from the ED, (2) ICU-GW patients are those transferred to general wards from other wards, (3) EL patients are those admitted prior to their day of elective surgeries; and (4) SDA patients are those admitted following their elective surgeries. Note that in their setting, emergency admissions, which are unplanned, make up the largest percentage of total admissions, whereas elective admissions, which can be planned, take up a much smaller percentage.

Inpatients can be further classified (see Shi et al., 2015 and Teow et al., 2012) by their major specialities, for example, Surgery, Cardiology, Orthopedic, Oncology, General Medicine, Neurology, Renal disease, Respiratory, Gastroenterology, Endocrinology, and Obstetrics and Gynecology. Each inpatient ward may be dedicated to a specialty, but patients might be permitted to overflow into another specialty's ward where appropriate.

The management of inpatient wards presents several important challenges. The first is how to model the effects of various policies, such as the timing of discharges, on the availability of beds in general. The second is how to allocate bed capacity among heterogenous patient types, who may differ in priorities, specialities, amount of care required, LOS, and so forth. The third is to how account for LOS in admission decisions.

11.1 Modeling the Inpatient Ward

Queueing theory has been used to model patient flows in various areas of healthcare facilities. Standard queues, such the $M/M/c$ queues, can be used (Banner Health, 2015) to model the inpatient ward (IW). However, various authors have attempted to capture additional characteristics that are unique to the IW. A detailed empirical analysis of IW dynamics is provided by Shi et al. (2015).

At a high level, the IW can be viewed as a queuing network. In this network, beds are considered as servers, and bed requests as customers. Four salient features of this queueing network have been noted:

1) Admission Delays. A patient from an ED who requests a bed in the IW must wait until a bed becomes available (Dai and Shi, 2017).
2) Periodic Discharge Decisions. A patient does not leave upon recovery but must wait until a physician examines and approves the release. These exams take place daily, usually in the morning. Thus, service times are artificially extended in this manner (Dong and Perry, 2016).
3) Discharge Delays. Patients waiting to be discharged are typically further delayed several more hours by paperwork, the necessity of arranging for transportation, coaching by professionals, and so forth. Thus, discharges tend to occur in batches at narrow, highly predictable intervals (Dong and Perry, 2016).

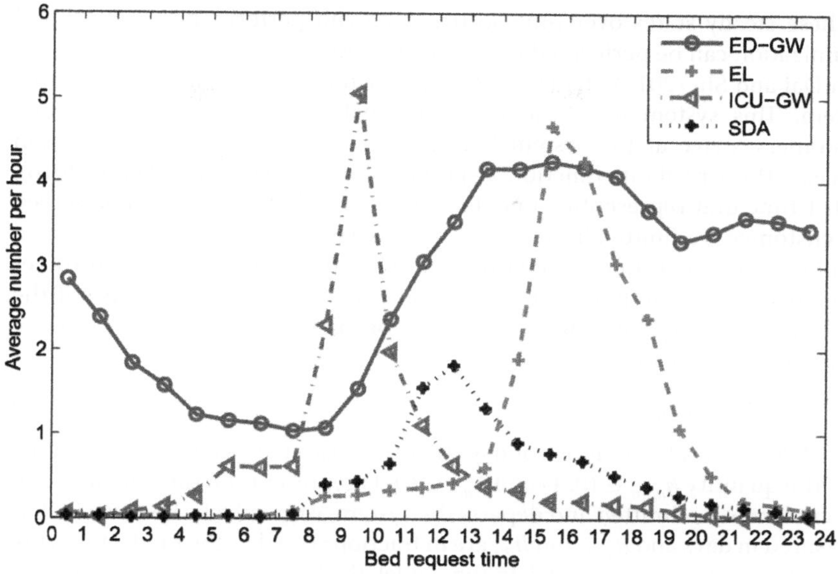

Figure 11.1 From Shi et al. (2015), hourly arrival rate for various admission sources.

4) Non-stationarity. Arrival rates change considerably over the course of a day. Thus, the arrival process must be modeled as time-varying (Dong and Perry, 2016). See Figure 11.1.

Given the above features, two models of the IW have been proposed. The notion of length of stay (LOS) differs subtly between the two models. In addition, only the second model captures admission delays. Both models capture periodic discharge decisions, discharge delays, and non stationary arrivals.

In Dong and Perry (2016), the IW is viewed as a single queue. Patient arrivals follow a nonhomogeneous Poisson process with a strictly positive and periodic arrival-rate function $\lambda(\cdot)$. Arrivals are periodic; that is, $\lambda(t+1) = \lambda(t)$ for all $t \geq 0$, where one unit of time represents one day. Patients are statistically homogeneous, with independent and identically distributed (i.i.d.) service times. Moreover, the service time of each patient is exponentially distributed with mean $1/\mu$. This service time is the actual recovery time, but not the total time that the patient spends in the IW. Inspection is assumed to take place at a specific time point each day. This mode of inspection implies that the total length of stay (LOS) of patients are not i.i.d., even though their service times are i.i.d. For this model, Dong and Perry (2016) develop an analytically tractable, deterministic, fluid approximation to capture patient-flow dynamics. They show that both the stochastic model and the fluid approximation have unique periodic steady states. The corresponding stochastic processes converge to these steady states over time so that long-run performance analysis and optimization can be performed in the steady state.

In Dai and Shi (2017), the IW is a single-customer-class, single server-pool system. This system has N identical, parallel servers in the server pool. Customers arrive at the system following a time-varying periodic Poisson process. The arrival rate function $\lambda(\cdot)$ is periodic as in Dong and Perry (2016), with 1 time unit representing one day. Upon arrival, if there is an idle server, the customer is admitted into service immediately. Otherwise, she waits in an infinite-sized buffer until a server become available. At that point, a customer is removed from the buffer on a first-come, first-served (FCFS) basis if the buffer is not empty. Otherwise, the server becomes idle. A customer service time S follows a model:

$$S = \text{LOS} + h_{dis} - h_{adm}. \tag{11.1}$$

The LOS denotes the number of days that the customer occupies a bed in the IW. The quantity $h_{adm} \in (0, 1)$ and $h_{dis} \in (0, 1)$ represent the time of day when the customer is admitted and departs the system, respectively. Because LOS is measured in days and h_{adm} and h_{dis} are in fractions of a day, the model takes the name *the two-time-scale model.* In the model, the following relationships hold:

$$\text{LOS} = \lfloor T_{dis} \rfloor - \lfloor T_{adm} \rfloor, \quad h_{dis} = T_{dis} - \lfloor T_{dis} \rfloor, \quad h_{adm} = T_{adm} - \lfloor T_{adm} \rfloor$$

where T_{adm} and T_{dis} denote the admission time and departure time, respectively, and $\lfloor x \rfloor$ denotes the largest integer that is less than or equal to x. Dai and Shi (2017) assume that the LOS of each customer follows a geometric distribution with success probability $\mu \in (0, 1)$. Further, LOS and h_{dis} are two i.i.d. sequences, and the two sequences are independent of each other. The sequence h_{dis} follows a general distribution on the interval $(0, 1)$. For this model, Dai and Shi (2017) analyze steady-state time-dependent performance measures, such as the time-dependent mean queue, time-dependent mean virtual waiting time, and time-dependent service level.

11.2 Inpatient Ward Policies

Dai and Shi (2017) analyzed the two-time-scale model to predict the impact of the two terms in the service time model, LOS, and discharge time h_{dis} on system performance. They focused on two processes that track the wait at two time scales. The *midnight customer count* X_k on day k denotes the number of customers in the system at midnight on day k. If we let A_k and D_k denote the total number of arrivals and discharges in day k, respectively, then X_k has the dynamic

$$X_{k+1} = X_k + A_k - D_k, \quad k = 0, 1, \ldots \tag{11.2}$$

The *time-dependent customer count* $X(t)$ tracks the total number of customers in the system at time t. $X(t)$ has the dynamic

$$X(t) = X(0) + A_{(0,t]} - D_{(0,t]}, \tag{11.3}$$

where $A_{(0,t]}$ denotes the cumulative number of arrivals in the period $(0, t]$ and $D_{(0,t]}$ denotes the cumulative number of discharges in the period $(0, t]$.

By studying the above two processes, Dai and Shi (2017) classify the customer wait in the IW into two types. The *overnight wait* results from a mismatch between the daily number of arrivals and discharges. They find that the average fraction of customers experiencing overnight waits does not depend on h_{dis}. On the other hand, the *intra-day wait* results from the mismatches between morning arrivals and afternoon discharges. Reducing LOS can, for example, can increase capacity and thereby reduce the first type of wait, whereas shifting discharges to earlier times (early discharge) can reduce the second type of wait.

11.3 Interface with ED

As previously discussed, delays in admission to the IW are a main contributing factor to ED overcrowding. Therefore, IW policies directly impact this admission delay. From the perspective of the ED, this delay is known as *ED boarding time.*

The model of Shi et al. (2015) focuses primarily on ED boarding time. Their empirical model is more detailed than those of both Dong and Perry (2016) and Dai and Shi (2015).

Shi et al. (2015) grouped IW beds, or servers into $J = 15$ server pools corresponding to J groups of similar wards. There are n_j identical beds in each pool j. Each pool serves patients of various types and classes, where a type is determined by both the source of admission and the medical specialty. There are four admission sources and nine medical specialities, for a combination of $K = 36$ types. A pool may be dedicated to one patient type or can be shared among several types. Patients within a type may be further sorted into classes. Each admission source has an arrival process that is time-dependent and periodic, as in Dai and Shi (2015). Each arriving patient is assigned a type. Then the patient waits in a buffer until she is admitted to a bed. Patients within a type are processed in first-in, first-out (FIFO) order. A patient is *right-sited* if assigned to her designated (primary) server pool and *overflowed* otherwise. A patient can be overflowed only when her waiting time exceeds the *overflow trigger time.* A patient occupies her assigned bed until discharge. The duration of occupancy of the bed is the patient's *service time.* The service time of each patient is modeled similarly to that in Dai and Shi (2015). In addition, patients maybe transferred once or twice between wards.

Compared to Dai and Shi (2015), Shi et al. (2015) broke down ED boarding time into smaller components: a *pre-allocation delay* and a *post-allocation delay*. The pre-allocation delay includes the time needed to "search and negotiate for a bed from a ward." The post-allocation delay includes the time needed for the patient to be discharged from the ED, transportation time from the ED to the bed, and other delays. The authors modeled the pre- and post-allocation delays as log-normal random variables whose parameters depend on the hour when the pre- or post-allocation starts. They also modeled overflow trigger times that are time-dependent.

Shi et al. (2015) fit the above model to data from a large Singaporean hospital. They used this model to predict by simulation the impact of changes in discharge policies and bed capacity on waiting time statistics.

11.4 Interface with Elective Surgeries

Delays in admission to the IW also affect elective operating room (OR) scheduling. For example, Robb et al. (2004) found that in a large university teaching hospital, a lack of IW beds caused up to 62.5 percent of all cancellations of all general OR procedures. Cochran and Bharti (2006) found in an obstetrics hospital that when postpartum beds are full, patients are blocked in the upstream labor and delivery areas. This *blocking* prevents new admissions and delays scheduled inductions. In critical care, where Intensive Care Units (ICUs) are often used at or above nominal capacity (Chan et al. 2011), a shortage of IW beds frequently results in cancellations or rescheduling of elective patients who might need ICU beds after surgery (Kim and Horowitz, 2002).

Queuing models featuring blocking have been studied extensively. See Bretthauer et al. (2011) for a brief review. The authors focusing specifically on healthcare contexts include Hershey et al. (1981), Weiss et al. (1982), Koizumi et al. (2005) and Bretthauer et al. (2011). These models make the assumption that patients are admitted in a greedy manner whenever there is sufficient capacity.

Actively managed scheduling systems, where the decision to admit a patient accounts for resource usage in the IW have been studied by Liu et al. (2016) in a stochastic dynamic setting. They a planning horizon of T days, numbered $t = 1, 2, \dots, T,\ T \leq \infty$. Demand for elective and emergency surgeries that arises over each day t is nonnegative integer-valued random variables denoted by δ_t and ϵ_t, respectively. They assumed that δ_t and ϵ_t are independent and identically distributed (i.i.d.) over time and bounded. Emergency surgeries must be performed on the same day in which they arise, whereas elective surgeries can be waitlisted and performed in the future. Each elective case that is waitlisted incurs a waiting cost of W per day. The waiting cost captures the inconvenience and loss of goodwill in patients due to waiting. It can also capture the loss in productivity for the patient and for society that is caused by delays in treatment. A patient undergoing surgery always proceeds through two main stages. The *upstream stage*, stage 0, takes place on the day when the patient is admitted to the hospital. In this stage, surgery is performed. The patient stays in the upstream stage for no more than a fraction of a day. After receiving surgery in the upstream stage, the patient will move to stage 1, the IW, for recovery and observation. The authors assumed that there is a single bottleneck resource that is consumed by patients in each stage $i \in \{0, 1\}$. They called this resource *stage-i capacity* and denoted it by C_i. For example, capacity might be measured in surgeon time in the entry stage or in number of ICU beds in the IW. Each patient consumes a random amount v^0 of capacity in stage 0, and v^1 of capacity during each day that she remains in stage 1. For each $i \in \{0, 1\}$, v^i is i.i.d. over the patient population and over time. On any given day, if more capacity is required than is available at stage i, then surge capacity will be used, incurring an *overtime cost* of $O_i \geq 0$ per unit. Conversely, if less capacity is required than is available at stage i, an *idling cost* of $L_i \geq 0$ is incurred per unit.

The events of each day occur in the following sequence:

1) At the beginning of day t, there are w_t elective patients on the waitlist. There is no patient upstream because all patients admitted on day $t - 1$ have completed their service at stage 0 on the same day. There are n_t patients in the IW (i.e., at stage 1). Waiting costs are incurred for each of the w_t patients on the waitlist.
2) A random number δ_t of new elective surgery requests arises, bringing the total number of patients in the waitlist to $\overline{w}_t = w_t + \delta_t$ and the total number of patients in the system to $w_t + \delta_t + n_t$, which includes patients waiting for surgery as well as those in the IW.
3) The scheduling manager decides, out of the $w_t + \delta_t$ outstanding elective cases, the number q_t of elective surgeries to fulfill in day t. Immediately after the decision, the number of patients at stage 0 increases to q_t.
4) An additional random number ϵ_t emergency patients arrive and are served at stage 0. Idling and overtime costs are incurred at stage 0 for the service of $q_t + \epsilon_t$ patients.
5) Each patient in stage 0 moves to stage 1. Idling and overtime costs are incurred at stage 1.
6) A random fraction $1 - \xi_t$, $\xi_t \in (0, 1)$, of patients at stage 1 exit the system. They assume that the sequence $\{\xi_t\}_t$ is i.i.d. over time, resulting in geometrically distributed LOS.

The objective is to determine a scheduling policy that minimizes the total discounted cost of the system over the planning horizon, assuming a discount factor of $\gamma \in (0, 1)$.

For the above model, Liu et al. (2016) demonstrated that a formulation that uses the "natural" definition of decision variables does not generate helpful structural results or insights. Instead, they exploited a simple variable transformation to reveal a hidden submodularity structure in the formulation. Building upon this transformation, they proved that the number of patients allowed in the system in each period is monotone in the state variables and in the downstream capacity and thereby generated useful guidelines for adjusting scheduling decisions in practice. In addition, they showed that the total expected cost of the system exhibits decreasing marginal returns as the capacity in each stage increases independently of the other stage, a result that has been confirmed earlier by simulation studies (Bowers, 2013). In an infinite-horizon setting, they examined conditions under which the patient waitlist may grow without bounds. They showed that the number of admissions might be uniformly bounded, even as the number of patients waiting approaches infinity, as long as the waiting costs are low enough. This result may be used to inform the choice of model parameters to ensure that everyone on the waitlist is served.

11.5 Discharge Planning

In the IW, patients cannot simply leave when they are medically ready for discharge. Before each discharge, a physician must examine the patient and review her lab tests, diagnostic results, and so forth. Because physicians have multiple responsibilities, they most often perform these inspection once a day, usually early in the morning (Chan et al., 2016).

To analyze the impact of discharge policies, Chan et al. (2011) proposed a queueing model in which patients, after they complete service, remain in the beds until the time of inspection. See Figure 11.2.

In their model, patients arrive to the system according to a time-varying Poisson process with rate $\lambda(\cdot)$. The rate is cyclic; that is, $\lambda(t+1) = \lambda(t)$, where the unit of time is a day. There are s identical beds. If a patient arrives and a bed is available, the patient will occupy the bed immediately. Otherwise, the patient must wait in an infinite buffer queue until a bed becomes available. Patients are

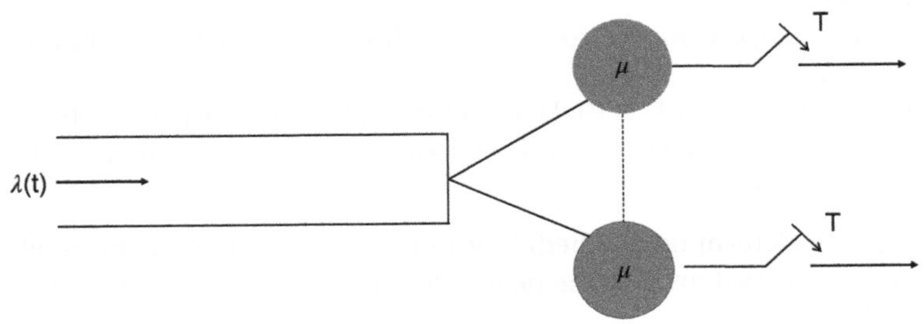

Figure 11.2 $M_tM(T)s$ queueing model with discharge inspection(s) at time(s) T. Adapted from Chan et al. (2016).

assumed to be homogeneous, and each patient's service time is exponentially distributed with rate μ. When service completes, the patient continues to occupy her bed until an inspection occurs. Let $T \in [0, 24]^N$ denote the vector of N inspection rounds on each day, with $T_1 < T_2 < \cdots < T_N$. Then a patient will leave at the first inspection time following completion of service. If a patient finishes service after the last inspection time on a given day, then she must wait until the first inspection time on the following day. No new patient may occupy her bed until she is discharged.

For the above model, Chan et al. (2016) tested the validity of the model assumptions on empirical data. They analyzed the stability of the resulting queue and its equilibrium behavior. They derived explicit characterizations of the queue length and the waiting time processes. They identified inspection times that minimize the expected mean and maximum number of customers in the system, and the probability of waiting. They found that the gains that can be achieved by optimizing the timing of inspections increases with the amplitude of the arrival rate function. Furthermore, system performance improves with more inspection opportunities but with decreasing marginal returns. Finally, when there are multiple equally spaced inspection times, the system performance is robust with respect to the timing of the inspections.

11.6 Incentive, Behavioral, and Organizational Issues

Because the IW lies at the intersection of multiple administrative units, IW management tends to present several difficulties related to behavioral and organizational issues, and incentive incompatibilities.

Conflict between IW admission and discharge. When there is a shortage of beds, IW policies must balance a trade-off between delaying new admissions, by keeping current patients on board for the length of time that they require for optimum recovery, and speeding up admission by discharging current patients earlier. The former action increases wait times, potentially reduces the total number of patients who can be treated, and potentially worsens outcomes for the patients who are made to wait. The latter action potentially reduces the quality of care for admitted patients and increases readmission rates.

Coordination between elective surgery scheduling and IW usage. The surgical suite is the main source of revenue for many hospitals. Often, use of the OR suite is pre-allocated among different departments, then among specific surgeons in those departments. This convention is called block scheduling. With block scheduling, surgeons are free to schedule elective surgeries in their blocks. These elective surgeries are a significant source of demand on

IW beds because many patients spend time in the IW to recover after surgery. Because surgeons might be unaware of or unable to account for the impact of their scheduling decisions on IW usage, the resulting decisions may be suboptimal for the system as a whole.

Resource-use conflicts between departments. As we discussed earlier, IW beds themselves are often pre-allocated among different departments. Patients belonging to a particular department are ordinarily admitted to a bed belonging to that department. Occasionally, there might be cross-admissions, whereby a patient is admitted to an IW bed that does not belong to the patient's department. The number of beds that are allocated to the departments in the long term, as well as the rules that must be set for cross admission, can be a source of conflict among departments. If not properly managed, these decisions can lead to inefficient and unbalanced use of resources.

Discharge timing. The timing of patient discharges is one of the principal ways in which discharges can be optimized to free up IW beds for use by new patients. However, discharge timing is subject to staff availability, which may depend on behavioral and work shift patterns. For example, physicians may be habituated to conducting a morning round of exams on their patients, rather than performing them ad hoc throughout the day. When this is the case, discharges can occur only in the morning, after the exams have concluded for the day. In this way, policies for discharge in general might be limited by behavioral and work shift patterns.

11.7 Future Directions

Extended models are needed for a network of IWs that incorporate routing and overflow of patients among the IWs. Models also need to capture patient transfers between IW wards.

Because patients are heterogeneous in general, analyses need to be extended to capture multiple customer characteristics and multiple priority classes. For example, the LOS differs for different specialties and admission sources (Shi et al., 2013).

The arrival process from EDs can be modeled in greater details. For example, because of nurse batching of bed requests, arrivals can be clustered (Shi et al., 2013) in reality.

Various components, such as the pre- and post-allocation delay, LOS, and discharge can be modeled in greater details to capture second-order effects. For example, the LOS might depend on the arrival time for ED patients (Shi et al., 2013). The duration of discharge exams might depend on the capacity to perform inspections and is not instantaneous in general.

Hithertoo, all models have captured only daily effects. It is important to model day-of-the-week effects.

11.7.1 Essential Quantitative Tools

Queuing analysis has been successfully used to model patient flow through the IW, especially when the IW is viewed as part of a larger network. Queuing analysis is also useful in analyzing stationary policies and simulating the impact of potential changes to policies.

Dynamic programming is an important tool in the analysis of dynamic policies, for example, admission and discharge policies. The difficulty with dynamic programming is the problem of state space explosion in larger, more realistic problem instances, leading to computational intractability.

Although it has not been used so far to study inpatient wards, online optimization is a promising tool to study dynamic policies in richer settings than have been attempted, for example, those involving multiple patient types and stochastic LOS.

11.7.2 Resources for Learners

Queuing models for IWs are studied by Dong and Perry (2016). The interface with EDs is considered in Dai and Shi (2015), Shi et al. (2015), and Shi et al. (2013). The interface with elective surgeries is studied in Liu et al. (2016). Finally, discharge planning has been studied by Chan et al. (2016).

At a strategic level, the capacity planning of inpatient beds has been studied by Best et al. (2015), Utley et al. (2003), Nguyen et al. (2005), Akkerman and Knip (2004), Cohen et al. (1980), and Kao and Tung (1981).

The handbook edited by Hall (2012) contains an informative chapter on bed-assignment and bed-management problems.

References

Akkerman, R., M. Knip. (2004). Reallocation of beds to reduce waiting time for cardiac surgery. *Health Care Management Science* 7(2) 119–126.

American Hospital Association. (2017). Fast facts on us hospitals. www.aha.org/research/rc/stat-studies/fast-facts.shtml.

Argo, J.L., C.C. Vick, L.A. Graham, K.M.F. Itani, M.J. Bishop, M.T. Hawn. (2009). Elective surgical case cancellation in the Veterans Health Administration system: identifying areas for improvement. *The American Journal of Surgery* 198(5) 600–606.

Asplin, B.R., D.J. Magid. (2007). If you want to fix crowding, start by fixing your hospital. *Journal Annals of Emergency Medicine.* 49(2) 273–274.

Banner Health. (2015). Door-to-doc patient safety toolkit. https://www.bannerhealth.com/About+Us/Innovations/DoortoDoc/About+D2D.htm.

Best, T.J., B. Sandıkçı, D.D. Eisenstein, D.O. Meltzer. (2015). Managing hospital inpatient bed capacity through partitioning care into focused wings. *Manufacturing & Service Operations Management* 17(2) 157–176.

Bowers, J. (2013). Balancing operating theatre and bed capacity in a cardiothoracic centre. *Health Care Management Science* 1–9.

Bretthauer, K.M., H.S. Heese, H. Pun, E. Coe. (2011). Blocking in healthcare operations: A new heuristic and an application. *Production and Operations Management* 20(3) 375–391.

Chan, C.W., J. Dong, L.V. Green. (2016). Queues with time-varying arrivals and inspections with applications to hospital discharge policies. *Operations Research* 65(2) 469–495.

Chan, C.W., G. Yom-Tov, G. Escobar. (2011). When to use speedup: an examination of intensive care units with readmissions. Tech. rep., Working paper, Columbia University.

Cochran, J.K., A. Bharti. (2006). Stochastic bed balancing of an obstetrics hospital. *Health Care Management Science* 9(1) 31–45.

Cohen, M.A., J.C. Hershey, E.N. Weiss. (1980). Analysis of capacity decisions for progressive patient care hospital facilities. *Health Services Research* 15(2) 145.

Dai, J.G., P. Shi. (2017). A two-time-scale approach to time-varying queues in hospital inpatient flow management. *Operations Research* 65(2): 514–536.

Dong, J., O. Perry. (2016). A queueing model for internal wards. Working paper.

Hall, R.W. (2012). *Handbook of Healthcare System Scheduling*. Springer.

Hershey, J.C., E.N. Weiss, M.A. Cohen. (1981). A stochastic service network model with application to hospital facilities. *Operations Research* 29(1) 1–22.

Hulshof, P.J.H., N. Kortbeek, R.J. Boucherie, E.W. Hans, P.J.M. Bakker. (2012). Taxonomic classification of planning decisions in health care: a structured review of the state of the art in or/ms. *Health Systems* 1(2) 129–175.

Jacobson, S.H., S.N. Hall, J.R. Swisher. (2006). Patient flow: reducing delay in healthcare delivery. *Discrete Event Simulation of Health Care Systems* 91 211–252.

Kao, E.P.C., G.G. Tung. 1981. Bed allocation in a public health care delivery system. *Management Science* 27(5) 507–520.

KC, D.S., C. Terwiesch. (2009). Impact of workload on service time and patient safety: An econometric analysis of hospital operations. *Management Science* 55(9) 1486–1498.

Kim, S.-C., I. Horowitz. (2002). Scheduling hospital services: the efficacy of elective-surgery quotas. *Omega* 30(5) 335–346.

Koizumi, N., E. Kuno, T.E. Smith. (2005). Modeling patient flows using a queuing network with blocking. *Health Care Management Science* 8(1) 49–60.

Liu, N., V.A. Truong, X. Wang, B. Anderson. (2016). Capacity planning and allocation scheduling with considerations for patients' length-of-stays. Working paper.

McGowan, J.E., J.D. Truwit, P. Cipriano, R.E. Howell, M. VanBree, A. Garson, J.B. Hanks. (2007). Operating room efficiency and hospital capacity: factors affecting operating room use during maximum hospital census. *Journal of the American College of Surgeons* 204(5) 865–871.

Nguyen, J.M., P. Six, D. Antonioli, P. Glemain, G. Potel, P. Lombrail, P. Le Beux. (2005). A simple method to optimize hospital beds capacity. *International Journal of Medical Informatics* 74(1) 39–49.

Pfuntner, A., L.M. Wier, C. Steiner. (2006). Costs for hospital stays in the United States, 2011: Statistical brief #168. Healthcare Cost and Utilization Project (HCUP). https://www.hcup-us.ahrq.gov/reports/statbriefs/sb168-Hospital-Costs-United-States-2011.jsp

Richardson, D.B. (2002). The access-block effect: relationship between delay to reaching an inpatient bed and inpatient length of stay. *Medical Journal of Australia* 177(9) 492–495.

Robb, W.B., M.J. O'sullivan, A.E. Brannigan, D.J. Bouchier-Hayes. (2004). Are elective surgical operations cancelled due to increasing medical admissions? *Irish Journal of Medical Science* 173(3) 129.

Shi, P., M.C. Chou, J.G. Dai, D. Ding, J. Sim. (2015). Models and insights for hospital inpatient operations: Time-dependent ED boarding time. *Management Science* 62(1) 1–28.

Shi, P., JG Dai, D. Ding, J. Ang, M. Chou, X. Jin, J. Sim. (2013). Patient flow from emergency department to inpatient wards: Empirical observations from a Singaporean hospital. Tech. rep., Working paper. 1.3.

Teow, K.L., E. El-Darzi, C. Foo, X. Jin, J. Sim. (2012). Intelligent analysis of acute bed overflow in a tertiary hospital in Singapore. *Journal of Medical Systems* 36(3) 1873–1882.

Trzeciak, S., E.P. Rivers. (2003). Emergency department overcrowding in the United States: an emerging threat to patient safety and public health. *Emergency Medicine Journal* 20(5) 402–405.

Utley, M., St. Gallivan, K. Davis, P. Daniel, P. Reeves, J. Worrall. (2003). Estimating bed requirements for an intermediate care facility. *European Journal of Operational Research* 150(1) 92–100.

Weiss, A.J., A. Elixhauser. (2012). Overview of hospital stays in the United States, Agency for Healthcare Research and Quality. https://www.hcup-us.ahrq.gov/reports/statbriefs/sb180-Hospitalizations-United-States-2012.pdf.

Weiss, E.N., M.A. Cohen, J.C. Hershey. (1982). An iterative estimation and validation procedure for specification of semi-Markov models with application to hospital patient flow. *Operations Research* 30(6) 1082–1104.

12

Residential Care

Nadia Lahrichi[1], Louis-Martin Rousseau[1], and Willem-Jan van Hoeve[2]

[1] *Polytechnique Montréal*
[2] *Carnegie Mellon University*

In this chapter, we provide a perspective on the use of analytics in the context of home care delivery. In particular, we concentrate on operational questions arising from nurse-to-patient assignments and employee scheduling and routing considerations. These questions are highly relevant at the operational level, but tactical and strategic decision-makers can also benefit from quantitative models to provide insight into the trade-offs that exist in healthcare organizations.

One of the most powerful analytical tools for formally representing (modeling) and solving the operational situations listed above is mathematical optimization. As the cornerstone of operations research, optimization-based decision support tools have been widely applied in various industries, including healthcare. One of our goals in this chapter is to provide an overview of the state of the art in optimization technology, and describe what models would be most suitable (and scalable) to home care decision-making.

The chapter will conclude by outlining new perspectives for analytics in home care delivery, made possible by the emergence of mobile technology, based on massive and real-time data collection. The availability of such data, combined with efficient use of machine learning models and algorithms, opens the door to data-driven decision support systems that will assist home care agencies in delivering the best possible care at the most efficient cost, preferably in real time.

12.1 Overview of Home Care Delivery

Home care programs differ from country to country (or even state or province) in the range of services offered and the coverage offered either by insurance companies or the public system. As of 2014, in the United States, there were an

Handbook of Healthcare Analytics: Theoretical Minimum for Conducting 21st Century Research on Healthcare Operations, First Edition. Edited by Tinglong Dai and Sridhar Tayur.

estimated 4,800 adult day services centers, 12,400 home health agencies (80.0% with for-profit ownership and 4.9 million patients who received and ended care any time), and 4,000 hospices (60.2% with for-profit ownership and 1.3 million patients) (CDC, n.d.).

Registered nurses are the most common employees in home health agencies (53.1%) and hospices (48.1%). In the US, home care is a $75 billion dollar a year industry, comprising more than 1.5 million caregivers. Home care workers range from companion caregivers to skilled nurses to occupational therapists. In Canada, the prediction is that by 2020, two-thirds of nurses will be working in the community rather than hospitals, which is a drastic expected increase compared to the current 30 percent (Canadian Nurses Association, 2013). Private and public home care agencies will consequently need to be equipped with efficient tools to deal with the increased demand in home care delivery.

In the following, we distinguish home care and home health care.

12.1.1 Home Care

Home care services (or in-home care) are commonly presented as a service to support activities of daily living (ADL) and instrumental activities of daily living (IADL). ADL refers to activities such as bathing, clothing, transfer, toilet use, feeding, and walking—activities that reflect the patient's ability to heal. IADL refers to everyday tasks such as doing light housework, meal preparation, taking medication, buying groceries or clothing, using the phone, and managing money—tasks that allow the patient to live independently in her community.

These services may be offered to help aging seniors or anyone suffering from an injury, a chronic illness, an accident, or following surgery. It is increasingly an integral part of the post-hospital recovery process, particularly during the first few weeks after discharge.

Home care is usually provided by caregivers who are not certified medically.

12.1.2 Home Healthcare

Home healthcare covers a wide range of activities that differ in the level of required expertise, frequency, and duration. They include wound care for pressure sores or surgical wounds, patient and caregiver education, intravenous or nutrition therapy, injections, and monitoring serious illness and unstable health status. Home care activities determine a patient's care plan, which typically involves doctors, nurses, and other care providers. They may be punctual, limited in duration, or continuous, combining different types of care, sometimes extending several months. In what follows, we use the classification of temporary care (or short term), chronic care (or long term), and specialized programs. Each of these may be accompanied by home care services to support the emotional needs and ADL of the patients.

The structures offering home health care differ by country. Home care programs in Canada, for example, are managed by provincial governments through home and community offices of the patients' health authority (CIHI, n.d.; Govt. of Canada, n.d.). They deliver a wide range of services, including short-term care, long-term care, and other specialized programs. Services may vary from one community center to another.

In most European countries, including France, Italy, Portugal, Spain, and United Kingdom, home healthcare usually falls under the responsibility of a higher government authority, whereas these services are the responsibility of a local government or municipality in Denmark, Finland, and Sweden. For example, in Belgium, the federal public health insurance system finances a set of public and private organizations to provide home care assistance. In some cases, home care and home healthcare may be overseen by different government levels (Tarricone et al., 2008).

In France, a distinction is made between home hospitalization (HAD) (often long-term for patients of all ages with acute or chronic, progressive and/or unstable pathologies who, if not treated by a HAD structure, would be hospitalized in a health facility with accommodation) and nursing home care (SSIAD) (Le site officiel de l'administration française, n.d.). Specialized structures like palliative care, end of life Centre national des soins palliatifs et de la fin de vie, http://www.spfv.fr., or rehabilitation services are also offered. In both France and the US, public structures and private institutions share the home health care market. Private institutions generally have more flexibility than public ones when accepting new patients, which impacts the decision-making process.

The needs assessment is usually based on medical expertise. Some countries may offer a single point of entry to the system: interdisciplinary teams or even agencies will provide guidance through the variety of services and providers (Tarricone et al., 2008).

12.1.2.1 Temporary Care

Temporary care often refers to post-surgery or hospitalization support. The services address specific needs: changing dressings, helping manage medications or ensuring that the recommendations of the care team are being followed. Some structures (such as in France (Le site officiel de l'administration française, n.d.)) offer temporary care also in the case of nonstabilized disease (for example chemotherapy) or rehabilitation care at home.

12.1.2.2 Specialized Programs

Programs including hospice care, palliative care, rehabilitation, and chemotherapy are considered specialized programs. Hospice care is a bundle of comprehensive services for terminally ill patients with a medically determined life expectancy of six months or less. The provided care emphasizes the management of pain and symptoms. Hospice care (NHPCO, n.d.) involves a team approach of expert medical care, pain management, and emotional and spiritual support specifically tailored to the wishes of the patient. Emotional and spiritual support is also extended to the family.

Many hospice care programs nowadays also list palliative care in the range of care and services they provide, as hospice care and palliative care share the same core values and philosophies. Defined by the World Health Organization in 1990, palliative care seeks to address not only physical pain, but also emotional, social, and spiritual pain to achieve the best possible quality of life for patients and their families. Palliative care is acute care delivered in a holistic approach to the person with a severe, progressive, or terminal illness. The goal of palliative care is to relieve physical pain and other symptoms but also to take into account psychological, social, and spiritual suffering. Palliative care extends the principles of hospice care to a broader population that could benefit from receiving this type of care earlier in the illness or disease process. For example, in France more than 25 percent of the interventions offered are palliative care (Ministère des solidaritès et de la santè, 2018).

12.1.3 Operational Challenges

In all the previously described forms, a doctor's order is needed to start the care process (Le site officiel de l'adminitration française, n.d.), (Medicare.gov, n.d.). After the request is received, an appointment is scheduled by the home health agency. Coordination of the care will then be handled by specific staff. In Canada, for example, a case manager will be assigned to the patient, particularly in the context of chronic care. This relationship will ensure successful coordination of care.

Continuity of care is a fundamental principal of the patient-nurse (or team) relationship. Studies show that continuity of care increases patient satisfaction and results in a better standard of care (Sudhakar-Krishnan et al., 2007).

The major operational problems that a manager has to deal with are:

- Who should be assigned as a case manager to each patient?
- How is the provider-to-patient assignment performed?
- How is the coordination between providers satisfied?
- Who should determine the operationalization of the plan care?
- How is staff scheduled?
- How are patients visited; that is, how are providers routed?
- Is the case manager the principal provider?
- How is the continuity of care defined?
- How should the provider deal with uncertainties?
- How should the provider deal with dynamics (patients leave and others arrive)?
- What is the time horizon to consider?

Most providers currently address these problems using their experience. In practice, some managers decide how the assignment is performed, but the provider is responsible for the scheduling and for routing his or her patients.

In most cases presented in the literature, these problems are approached in three phases: First, the assignment of patients is done (sometimes concurrently with a districting of the territory in case of large-scale problems). Second, the scheduling of providers will be performed. Finally, the operational routing will be determined. The second and third phases are often addressed simultaneously, given that routing and scheduling are similar in the home care context.

Mathematical models provide an efficient tool to solve these problems, especially for solving multiple phases at the same time. These mathematical models can be adapted to each home care delivery context. For example, in temporary home care, coordination is usually not a challenge because a case manager is not mandatory. Therefore, the major problem to address is the routing of staff. In the case of coordination of providers, if more than one person needs to visit the patient or to collect medicine/equipment, time windows and length of routes are introduced and may become hard constraints. Each of these problems will be specifically addressed in the following sections. For the sake of generality, we will use the term *provider* for caregivers, nurses, and any other professional/employee who may visit a patient in the course of the home care delivery.

Sahin and Matta (2015) propose a categorization of the operations management decisions in home care structures.

- Long-term: home care service offering specification (not covered in the literature) or global demand forecasting.
- Mid-term: districting and allocation of capacity to districts.
- Short-term: assignment of operators to visits or assignment of operators to patients.
- Very short-term: routing.

Sahin and Matta propose one to three years to characterize long-term decisions and six to twelve months for mid-term decisions; we nuance these durations and relate them to the home care context. In Quebec's context, for example, districting is a long-term decision, as it involves the creation of teams (professionals, team leader, etc). Therefore, the structure is too substantial to be modified regularly. We also point out that the assignment of operators to visits may be a short-term decision, yet in chronic and hospice care, this decision tends to be mid-term for follow-up requirements and continuity of care purposes. For example, in (Wirnitzer et al., 2016), the assignment problem is dealt with at the same time as the scheduling and routing of nurses to ensure continuity of care; they use a monthly horizon to assign, schedule, and route the nurses. We next present a more detailed discussion on the choice of the planning horizon and the continuity of care.

12.1.3.1 Discussion of the Planning Horizon

Determining the length of the planning horizon is crucial for balancing the problem's requirements with the efficiency of determining solutions. Choosing a planning horizon of one day allows for quick adjustments in the dynamic context of home care but makes it very difficult to include continuity of care. Moreover, a daily planning approach might lead to myopic decisions concerning mid-term working time restrictions. For example, in (Trautsamwieser et al., 2014), a one-week horizon is used that takes into account routing and rostering decisions simultaneously but disregards the continuity of care requirement for a longer horizon.

Works that focus only on assignments, usually prioritize continuity of care. Routing is performed as a second step, in which travel times are either ignored or estimated for overtime calculations. As a consequence, the assignment of nurses to patients might be infeasible due to working time restrictions or unavailabilities (e.g., because of holidays or nurse training). While some works impose the continuity of care as a strict requirement (Hertz et al., 2009; Yalçındag et al. 2016), it is also possible to find robust assignments of nurses to patients over a long-term horizon (several months), in which the number of patient-to-nurse reassignments is minimized (Lanzarone et al., 2014).

Another approach to considering continuity of care and routing is to first build weekly routes and then assign each of the routes to the nurses (Wirnitzer et al., 2016; Cappanera et al., 2015). For example, if a patient is visited multiple times in a week, we can build routes such that all visits must be on the same route and are therefore performed by the same nurse (Cappanera et al., 2015).

In (Trautsamwieser et al., 2014), a mathematical programming approach is developed that aims to generate a mid-term nurse roster that seeks the maximal continuity of care considering nurse availabilities, provider-to-patient compatibilities, and daily and monthly working time restrictions. On the basis of a weekly master schedule, the solution provides the assignment of providers to master tours of patient visits throughout a planning horizon of one month.

Other approaches that recommend using a master schedule are presented in (Trautsamwieser et al., 2014, Nickel et al., 2012), which again use a one-month planning horizon. The motivation for using a master schedule is that (in their applications) the home care provider may not want to create the schedule for the next week from scratch. They propose finding a repetitive tour plan that considers all patient requests on a weekly basis.

Lastly, Bennett and Erera (2011) consider a one-year rolling horizon for planning daily visit schedules. They maintain continuity of care by decomposing the problem into single-nurse problems. In their context, each nurse serves one district.

12.1.3.2 Home Care Planning Problem

To summarize, the home (health) care planning problem (H(H)CP) consists of:

- the scheduling of visits to each patient in a time slot (i.e., a day and a time period, morning or afternoon, in the planning horizon),
- the assignment of a caregiver to each of the visits, and,
- the sequence in which the caregivers visit each of their assigned patients in a time slot, considering work regulations.

Although each of these problems can be addressed individually, many applications also address routing and provider-to-patient allocation simultaneously.

12.2 An Overview of Optimization Technology

As the focus of this chapter is the application of mathematical optimization to model and solve home care delivery problems, we first provide an overview of the available optimization technology and the current capabilities.

Optimization methods can be classified in several ways. First, *exact methods* can return provably optimal solutions, and *heuristic methods* may be able to find good solutions but have no guarantee of optimality. Second, *generic optimization methods* need the problem description to be in a specific format, and *dedicated methods* are developed for a specific application. All generic optimization methods require that the problem is represented as a mathematical optimization model, using decision variables, constraints, and one single objective function to be optimized (minimize or maximize). The generic methods differ in the restrictions they impose on the model; for example, linear programming requires that all constraints, and the objective, are linear expressions. This choice impacts the performance of the associated solving methodology; for example, linear programming be solved efficiently for almost any practical problem that fits in the computer's memory.[1]

In Table 12.1 we list and characterize the optimization technologies that will be used in this chapter. We next describe each technology in more detail and provide guidelines for choosing the right technology for the application at hand.

12.2.1 Linear Programming

Linear programming (LP) is among the most efficient and scalable optimization technologies available. It requires that all variables are continuous and that the constraints and objective are linear. This structure allows for development of highly efficient solution methods that provide provably optimal solutions;

1 There exist linear programming models of modest size for which solvers may need more time, although these are rare in practice (Bixby, 2002).

Table 12.1 An overview and characterization of optimization technologies. The third column ("Scalability") represents the typical problem size that is expected to be optimally solved within a reasonable amount of time, for example, several minutes to one hour, as of 2017.

Method	Model Requirements	Scalability
Linear Programming (LP)	linear constraints and objective; continuous variables	millions of variables/ constraints
Mixed Integer Programming (MIP)	linear constraints and objective; continuous or integer variables	thousands of variables/constraints
Constraint Programming (CP)	any algebraic expression allowed; special syntax (e.g., AllDifferent); continuous or discrete variables	thousands of variables/constraints
Heuristics and Dedicated Methods	problem-dependent	problem-dependent; thousands to millions of variables

see (Bixby, 2002) for an overview of the development of linear programming solvers. Nowadays, practical linear programming problems that contain millions of variables and constraints may be solved in seconds or sometimes minutes.

For some problems, a linear program may provide an integer optimal solution, but in general the solution will be fractional. Given that many of the problems discussed in this chapter demand integer decisions, linear programming alone may not be sufficient, and we need a different methodology.

12.2.2 Mixed Integer Programming

In mixed integer programming (MIP), we can extend linear programming models with integer variables (the "mixed" stands for the mix of continuous and integer variables). Although general integer variables are sometimes useful, the most commonly used integer variables are *binary* variables. A binary variable x can represent, for example, whether a specific provider will be allocated to a patient ($x = 1$), or not ($x = 0$). MIP solvers are designed to be exact; as such, they provide a provably optimal solution. They can also be executed to terminate within a given time limit, in which case they provide a heuristic solution (together with a guaranteed maximum distance from the optimum, or optimality gap).

The addition of integer constraints to linear programming makes these problems fundamentally more difficult to solve than LPs. Yet, there has been tremendous progress in solving MIP models over the last decades, and today, MIP models with tens of thousands of variables and constraints can often be solved in a matter of minutes. Because of the nature of this type of problem, more difficult MIP models do exist, but the ongoing improvements in optimization technology continuously push the frontier of scalability and applicability; see Bixby et al. (2004) and Achterberg et al. (2013) for an overview of progress in MIP solving technology.

To date, the most powerful MIP solvers are IBM ILOG CPLEX, Gurobi, and Fico Xpress. Other MIP solvers of good quality include SCIP (which can also handle constraint programming models), MIP-CL, and COIN-CBC.

12.2.3 Constraint Programming

Constraint Programming (CP) has its origins in artificial intelligence and computer science, as it was first developed in the areas of constraint-based reasoning and logic programming (Rossi et al., 2006). Recent CP systems incorporate mathematical optimization techniques as well, and have been increasingly applied to solve optimization problems for operations research and other business applications. In most cases, discrete (finite domain) CP systems are used for this purpose. CP solvers are designed to be exact and provide a provably optimal solution. Like MIP solvers, they can be terminated within a given time limit and return a heuristic solution. Some CP solvers also provide the associated optimality gap, that is, the guaranteed maximum distance from the optimum.

CP models allow variables to take any set of discrete values, and expressions can be of any algebraic form (linear, nonlinear, logical, and even relational). In addition, CP systems offer a library of special expressions, such as the AllDifferent constraint that requires a set of variables to take distinct values. Most systems also offer a dedicated syntax to represent scheduling problems, for example, using the concepts of activities and resources (Baptiste, 2001), or interval variables (Laborie, 2009). Similar to mixed integer programming, CP technology can scale easily to thousands of variables and constraints; CP solvers can be especially effective for applications that contain a scheduling component.

The most powerful CP solvers to date include IBM ILOG CPLEX CP Optimizer, Google OR-tools, Gecode, and Choco. The solver SCIP is a hybrid solver that can handle both MIP and CP models (Achterberg, 2009).

12.2.4 Heuristics and Dedicated Methods

In some cases, the requirements and scale of the problem can be too complex to be solved with a single generic MIP or CP model. In such cases, one typically develops a heuristic approach or a dedicated method that is tailored to the application at hand. Heuristics are usually designed to find good solutions relatively quickly, but they cannot prove optimality or provide a bound on the solution quality.

Heuristics come in different forms. As mentioned above, we can use MIP or CP models with a solving time limit to turn these exact methods into heuristic methods. Another often-used approach is to *decompose* the problem into smaller sub-problems that are easier to handle. For example, a one-year planning problem may be decomposed over time into twelve monthly planning problems. As another example, a large regional staff planning problem may be decomposed into smaller district staffing problems.[2]

It is also possible to develop heuristic methods that do not require an MIP or CP model but instead work directly on problem-specific data structures. Principled approaches such as *local search* can provide a systematic framework for developing heuristics (Martí, 2018). These are often combined with meta-heuristics to further refine the solutions (Gendreau et al., 2010). Popular heuristic methods include Tabu search (Glover, 1997) and simulated annealing (Kirkpatrick et al., 1983).

12.2.5 Technology Comparison

Choosing a specific optimization technology requires a balance between (1) the expectations or requirements of the delivered solution, (2) the solver capabilities in terms of solving time and memory requirements, (3) the time to develop the solution, and (4) the maintenance and flexibility of the solution.

12.2.5.1 Solution Expectations and Solver Capabilities

When the solution is expected to coarsely balance multiple resources—for example, when planning global staffing levels over a long time horizon—linear programming may be suitable, as no detailed integer decisions are required. Because linear programming can be solved efficiently in practice, there are usually no solver limitations in this case.

If instead we need to develop a dispatching tool that generates operational nurse schedules, an MIP or CP-based approach would be needed to handle the discrete decisions. As a rule of thumb, most modelers will first attempt an MIP model, as this technology can provide good results on a wide range of problem classes. For more constrained scheduling and routing applications, however, CP models can perform better than MIP and may be the preferred technology.

In some cases, the requirements and scale of the problem can be too complex to be solved with a monolithic MIP or CP model. In such cases, we typically develop a decomposition approach (in which individual components can still be solved with MIP or CP) or a dedicated method. Popular decomposition methods that have been used in the home healthcare literature include column generation (or branch-and-price) and Benders decomposition (particularly logic-based Benders). Specific examples and references of these decomposition approaches as well as dedicated heuristic methods will be provided in section 12.5.

2 In some cases, it is possible to apply a formal decomposition method that provides provably optimal solutions, for example, using Benders decomposition or column generation.

12.2.5.2 Development Time and Maintenance

Home care solutions often contain a core set of problem characteristics—for which models have been developed in the literature—and additional provider-specific requirements. When the additional requirements are limited or can be handled in a post-processing step, it is often desirable to deploy an off-the-shelf software package that is designed to solve a specific problem class (e.g., employee scheduling or routing). However, many medium- to large-sized organizations have additional needs that are not addressed by commodity solutions, for example, because of their organizational structure or because of physical or legal requirements. In such cases, a tailored solution is often developed by a software consulting firm.

When developing a tailored solution, we typically start with a baseline MIP (or CP) model. This model can usually be based on similar models in the literature and can be quickly adapted to an organization's needs. This allows for a relatively fast delivery of a prototype solution, which is followed by an iterative process of testing and refinement. The overall development process may take several months or more and can result in scalable and detailed solutions. If the solution uses a commercial optimization solver, one should also budget for the solver license.

The alternative would be to develop a new dedicated solution method, perhaps from scratch, or by re-using optimization solvers for sub-parts of the problem. For some problems, for example, certain employee scheduling problems, a dedicated heuristic approach may work well. The development time may be similar to an MIP- or CP-based based solution and does not require the use of a commercial solver. That said, it may be challenging to adapt, extend, or maintain dedicated solutions, especially over a longer time period (e.g., several years). Instead, optimization models can be extended or adapted much more easily by simply changing the model description. Moreover, as optimization models are algebraic, model maintenance and development by multiple people is much easier as well. Finally, the performance of optimization solvers is continuously improving, which means that the same optimization model can provide better solutions or scale to larger instances when updating the solver to a new version.

In the following sections, we present the most common operational challenges in home care, and their respective optimization-based solutions.

12.3 Territory Districting

When applicable, districting is the first problem to solve to tackle the HHCP. In the province of Quebec, for example, where local authorities offer the home care services, a common approach is to divide the territory into districts. Each district will then be staffed (with nurses, social workers, etc.).

A districting problem consists of grouping small geographic areas, called basic territorial units, into larger geographic clusters called districts.

These districts should be balanced (e.g., of equitable size), contiguous, and compact. Typical examples of basic units are census codes, zip code areas, or even aggregated demand points of patients. In home care applications, the districts should have a good accessibility with respect to public transportation and have an equitable workload based on service and travel time (Blais et al., 2003; Benzarti et al., 2013).

Let $J = \{1, \ldots, n\}$ be the set of basic units and d_{ij} the distance between units i and j. In the home care context, it usually represents the road distance (or travel time). Activity measures are defined for each unit: demand (such as the number of patients and frequency of service), service time (total duration of visits), and so forth. The objective is to aggregate these basic units into p districts; p could be either equal to the number of providers (in this case we seek to define one district per nurse), or a smaller number, which we can refer to as teams. These p districts should satisfy the planning criteria of balance, compactness, and contiguity. As highlighted in (Kalcsics, 2015), "the" mathematical model for districting problems does not exist, because of the various design decisions, although there are many commonalities.

Three measures of balance are commonly used. Let w_k be the workload of district k. The first measure of balance B_1 is based on the relative deviation of the district workload w_k from the mean workload $\mu = \frac{\text{Total workload}}{\text{Number of districts}(p)}$:

$$B_1 = |\frac{w_k - \mu}{\mu}|, 1 \leq k \leq p$$

If this balance measure is equal to 0, it ensures that all districts have the exact same workload, which in practice may be difficult to achieve.

The second measure will instead concede a priori a certain relative deviation $\alpha > 0$ from perfect balance and measures only the imbalance exceeding this threshold:

$$B_2 = \frac{1}{\mu} \max \{w_k - (1 + \alpha)\mu, (1 - \alpha)\mu - w_k, 0\}$$

The districts are balanced if the workload is between the lower bound and the upper bound. The value of α should be fixed by management.

A third measure will instead minimize the deviation between the maximum and the minimum workload of districts.

$$B_3 = \max\{w_1, \ldots, w_k\} - \min\{w_1, \ldots, w_k\}$$

The choice of the fairness measure usually depends on the context, and the decision is to be made by the manager.

Districting approaches are commonly based on mixed integer programming or heuristic methods. To reduce the day-to-day traveling distance, one aims to establish contiguity and compactness of the districts. Different measures for contiguity and compactness exist; we refer readers to (Kalcsics, 2015) for more details. A typical districting model is a location-allocation model, which assigns basic units to the "seed" of a district, ideally in order to maximize the compactness of the districts.

To formulate the location-allocation model, we introduce the following decision variables:

- x_{ij} equals 1 if basic unit j is assigned to basic unit i and 0 otherwise; and
- y_i equals 1 if basic unit i is selected as district seed and 0 otherwise.

The model is then formulated as:

$$\min \sum_{i,j \in J} w_i d_{ij}^2 x_{ij} \tag{12.1}$$

$$\text{subject to: } \sum_{j \in J} x_{ij} = 1 \qquad \forall j \in J \tag{12.2}$$

$$\sum_{j \in J} w_j x_{ij} \geq (1 - \alpha)\mu y_i \qquad \forall i \in J \tag{12.3}$$

$$\sum_{j \in J} w_j x_{ij} \leq (1 + \alpha)\mu y_i \qquad \forall i \in J \tag{12.4}$$

$$\sum_{i \in J} y_i = p \tag{12.5}$$

$$y_i, x_{ij} \in \{0, 1\} \qquad \forall i, j \in J \tag{12.6}$$

The constraints ensure that each basic unit is assigned to one district only (12.2), that the workload of each district is within the boundaries (12.3–12.4), and that p district "seeds" are selected (12.5). No explicit measure of compactness is used in this model, however, as the objective is to minimize the total distance.

In (Benzarti et al., 2013), the compactness is integrated as a hard constraint in two ways: by limiting the maximum distance between two basic units that would be assigned to the same district and by minimizing the compactness measure, which is the maximum distance between two basic units assigned to the same district. With this approach, they are able to solve problems in which a maximum of 100 units are to divide into 4 districts.

This type of formulation is useful for a few hundred basic units, but it becomes intractable when the problem size grows. Heuristics approaches then prove to be more efficient, while being flexible enough to include almost any practical criterion and measure for the design of districts.

For example, Blais et al. (2003) use a tabu search algorithm to solve the districting problem for a local community health center in Montreal. The objective is to divide the territory into six districts in order to balance the workload. A tabu search is an iterative method that locally explores the space of solutions.

It starts from an *initial solution* and moves to the others through *one or multiple movements*. In this context, each solution is a feasible districting and is evaluated using a measure (i.e., an objective function).

Blais et al. (2003) also propose a mobility level measure for each solution s:

$$f(s) = \sum_{k=1}^{p} \frac{\sum_{i,j \in D_k | i \leq j} v_i v_j d_{ij}}{n_k(n_k - 1)/2(\sum_{k \in D_k} v_i)^2)}$$

where D_k represents the set of units in district k, v_i is the number of visits in basic unit i, and n_k is the number of basic units included in district k. A low value of $f(s)$ represents a high ease of travel. Their criteria to measure the workload equilibrium is similar to B_2.

12.4 Provider-to-Patient Assignment

We next consider the provider-to-patient assignment problem. First, we introduce workload measures, followed by fairness evaluation, generalized assignment models that allow to model this problem, and we finish with dynamic approaches considering reassignments of new patients.

12.4.1 Workload Measures

Most papers in the literature use only service time (duration of visits) and traveling time to determine a provider's workload (Yalçındağ et al., 2016; Lanzarone et al., 2014; Blais et al., 2003; Carello et al., 2014). In (Hertz et al., 2009), a new workload measure is introduced. The rationale is that all *indirect* duty should be considered, especially for hospice and chronic care. This workload is derived from the notion of case management. Because providers (*case managers, pivot* nurse, or *reference* nurse) have to coordinate care and need to perform work outside the "visit," this work should be accounted for. Four categories of patients are considered:

- Short-term (post-surgery, post-hospitalization, etc.).
- Long-term needing punctual care.
- Long-term needing continuous care.
- Palliative patients.

To scale the workload between these patients, a reference visit to short-term patients (typically 20 minutes) is used, and all other visits are then aligned to this one. For example, a visit to a palliative patient usually requires four times more work. This value was determined with the managers and the care team and may be adapted to adjust to the context.

We note that estimating traveling distances is important in considering assignment models. Yalçındağ et al. (2016) discuss the use of different methods to estimate travel times of caregivers. They compare the Kernel regression technique (based on historical data) to the average (average distance from one patient to all the others) and k-nearest neighborhood search methods. The Kernel regression technique can be successfully used in a two-stage approach that first assigns patients to caregivers and then defines their routes. It needs historical data, though. The average (which is the simplest to use) performs well when the territory to cover is not large.

A limitation to this approach is, however, highlighted in (Lahrichi et al., 2017). Although the approach seems promising when distances are small (e.g., in dense urban territory) it does not seem to perform as well when distances are larger. Accordingly, the authors in this study recommend the use of routing first and then assign.

12.4.2 Workload Balance

To measure workload balance, we introduce w_i the workload of provider i, w^{max} and w^{min}, the maximum and the minimum workloads, respectively. Fairness can be evaluated by minimizing the

- Deviation between max and min: $(w^{max} - w^{min})$
- Maximum workload: w^{max}
- Total workload: $\sum_i w_i$
- Total squared workload: $\sum_i w_i^2$

In other cases, instead of directly optimizing the workload, some authors focus on the deviation between the maximum workload and the average. A target value (if available) could be substituted to the average. For example, for each solution s, the total overload of each provider O_i is equal to the sum of three components:

- Visit load, which corresponds to the deviation between the current load of visits V_i of provider i and the average $\overline{V}$:

$$O_{i1}(s) = \max\{0, V_i(s) - \overline{V}\}$$

- Case load, which corresponds to the deviation between the current load of cases in each category (total number of assignment of patients $\sum_c x_{ic}$ so that patient $c \in C_j$, where C_j is the set of patients of category j) and the average (total number of cases n_j over the number of providers $|I|$). We consider that each additional patient receives the average number of visits $\overline{v}_{ij}$ for its category. Indirect work (through a penalty p_{ji}) is also derived from the category j of the patient. This additional overload is

$$O_{i2}(s) = \sum_{j \in J} \max\left\{0, \sum_{c \in C_j} x_{ic} - \left\lceil \frac{n_j}{|I|} \right\rceil \right\} \cdot \overline{v}_{ij}(s) \cdot p_{ji}$$

- Travel load, which corresponds to the deviation between the current travel T_i of provider i and the average $\overline{T}$

$$O_{i3}(s) = \max\{0, T_i(s) - \overline{T}(s)\}$$

In practice, we use multicriteria optimization, where the objective is to maximize (or minimize) a set of criteria. Our optimization model can optimize only a single objective function, so we introduce weights ω to represent the importance of each criterion. The appropriate values of ω result from discussion with the managers and staff. This type of multicriteria function also provides an efficient tool to test different scenarios: "what-if" one criterion is more important than another, for example.

12.4.3 Assignment Models

We next combine all the above elements in a single optimization model. Here, we provide the assignment model of (Hertz et al., 2009) of operators to patients that includes the most complete workload measure introduced earlier. C is the set of patients to assign, v_c the number of visits required by patient c, and h_{j_c} is the heaviness of a patient of category c (this helps to differentiate between palliative patients and short-term patients, for example). We also define t_{ic} as the travel load of patient c to provider i. The travel load is proportional to the number of visits c requires.

$$\text{Minimize} \sum_{i\in I} \omega_1 \cdot (O_{i1})^2 + \sum_{i\in I} \omega_2 \cdot (O_{i2})^2 + \omega_3 \cdot \left(\sum_{i\in I} (O_{i3})^2 + (\overline{T})^2 \right)$$

subject to

$$\sum_{i\in I} x_{ic} = 1 \qquad \forall c \in C \tag{12.7}$$

$$\sum_{c\in C} v_c \cdot h_{j_c} \cdot x_{ic} - \overline{V} \le O_{i1} \qquad \forall i \in I \tag{12.8}$$

$$\sum_{c\in C_j} v_c \cdot x_{ic} = \overline{v}_{ij} \cdot \sum_{c\in C_j} x_{ic} \qquad \forall i \in I, \forall j \in J \tag{12.9}$$

$$\sum_{c\in C_j} x_{ic} - \left\lceil \frac{n_j}{|I|} \right\rceil \le s_{ij} \qquad \forall i \in I, \forall j \in J \tag{12.10}$$

$$\sum_{j\in J} s_{ij} \cdot \overline{v}_{ij} \cdot h_j \le O_{i2} \qquad \forall i \in I \tag{12.11}$$

$$\sum_{i\in I} \sum_{c\in C} t_{ic} \cdot x_{ic} = |I| \cdot \overline{T} \tag{12.12}$$

$$\sum_{c \in C} t_{ic} \cdot x_{ic} - \overline{T} \leq O_{i3} \qquad \forall i \in I \tag{12.13}$$

$$x_{ic} \in \{0, 1\} \qquad \forall i \in I, \forall c \in C \tag{12.14}$$

$$O_{i1}, O_{i2}, O_{i3} \geq 0 \qquad \forall i \in I \tag{12.15}$$

$$\overline{v}_{ij}, s_{ij} \geq 0 \qquad \forall i \in I, \forall j \in J \tag{12.16}$$

$$\overline{T} \geq 0 \tag{12.17}$$

Constraints (12.7) impose that each patient c is assigned to a provider i. Constraints (12.8), (12.9–12.11), and (12.12–12.13) define, respectively, the visit load, the case load, and the travel load. Variable s_{ij} is used to define the positive deviation between the number of cases obtained by each provider in each category j and the average. Finally, constraints (12.14–12.16) are domain definition.

This model is nonlinear (constraints 12.11) and cannot be handled directly by commercial MIP solvers. Therefore, a heuristic approach is developed in (Hertz et al., 2009). In terms of problem size, they solve problems with more than 1400 patients, 26 staff members, and 36 basic units.

12.4.4 Assignment of New Patients

Carello and Lanzarone (2014) consider a robust assignment of new patients to providers. They use a rolling horizon of 26 periods, and each decision made in a period is fixed for the following ones. Three sets of patients are considered: those not requiring continuity of care, those requiring continuity of care (with a provider already assigned or to be assigned), and those requiring partial continuity of care.

To deal with the dynamics of the arrival of new patients, using a flexible assignment as described in (Hertz et al., 2009) helps the stability of the reassignments. In particular, the authors test one day, three-day, and seven-day assignment periods. Patients from the previous period are fixed, and only new patients are assigned in order to balance the workload. They show that if boundaries are flexible for patient assignment (i.e., providers are already covering for others outside their territory to alleviate for demand variation), then this time interval becomes less critical.

12.5 Task Scheduling and Routing

Task scheduling and nurse routing are most relevant when done in conjunction with the patient-to-nurse allocation. Otherwise, in case the tasks and patients have been allocated to nurses already, determining the associated routes is immediate. From an optimization modeling perspective, the core scheduling/routing of nurses for a single day corresponds to a vehicle routing problem with time windows (VRPTW), in which each of the patient visits is supposed to occur within a given time window. Additionally, we typically need to respect nurse-patient compatibility constraints, workload balancing constraints, and continuity of care constraints for longer time horizons. The VRPTW is known to be a challenging problem class, and the additional constraints typically make it even harder to find provably optimal solutions. Consequently, most of the optimization approaches described in the literature present heuristic methods, although some dedicated exact approaches have been presented as well, as we will see.

One of the first optimization approaches for this problem was presented by Begur et al. (1997), who computed daily nurse schedules/routes based on a master schedule of patient visits. They adapted well-known heuristic methods, including the Clarke-Wright savings heuristics (Clark et al., 1964) as well as route improvement heuristics that were developed for the traveling salesman problem (TSP). However, constraints to ensure continuity of care were not considered explicitly. Another early work, by Cheng and Rich (1998), introduces formal MIP models for the scheduling and routing problem, but uses a problem-specific heuristic for instances of larger scale.

Bertels and Fahle (2006) introduce a heuristic approach that combines linear programming, constraint programming, and metaheuristics. They use CP to generate roster sequences, for which the associated optimal start times are computed by LP. CP is also used to find good initial routes. Route improvements are obtained by simulated annealing and tabu search.

Eveborn et al. (2006) describe an integer programming model for the nurse scheduling/routing problem, based on a set covering formulation. Their model includes patient-nurse compatibility requirements and allows for visits that require multiple staff members. The set covering formulation explicitly lists the possible routes, which are generated to reflect the constraints. Because several other approaches in the literature follow a similar structure, we next present this set-covering model in more detail.

Let I be the set of nurses (caregivers), let V be the set of patient visits, and let J be the set of schedules/routes that can be allocated to a nurse. The set J is pre-computed and contains, in principle, all possible allowed schedules. (Because there are exponentially many schedules, we usually restrict ourselves to a subset of interesting schedules.) Each schedule $j \in J$ has an associated cost vector c_{ij} that reflects the penalty or weight if nurse $i \in I$ follows that schedule, for example, the travel length, possible violation of time windows, patient-to-nurse preference, and so forth. We introduce a binary parameter a_{ijv} to indicate whether nurse $i \in I$ performs visit $v \in V$ in schedule $j \in J$ ($a_{ijv} = 1$) or not ($a_{ijv} = 0$).

We next introduce a binary variable x_{ij} that denotes whether nurse $i \in I$ is assigned to schedule $j \in J$ ($x_{ij} = 1$) or not ($x_{ij} = 0$). The set-covering formulation then ensures that each nurse is allocated to one schedule (12.19) and that each patient visit is performed once (12.20), while minimizing the total cost:

$$\min \sum_{i\in I} \sum_{j\in J} c_{ij}x_{ij} \tag{12.18}$$

$$\text{subject to} \sum_{j\in J} x_{ij} = 1 \qquad \forall i \in I \tag{12.19}$$

$$\sum_{i\in I} \sum_{j\in J} a_{ijv}x_{ij} = 1 \quad \forall v \in V \tag{12.20}$$

$$x_{ij} \in \{0, 1\} \qquad \forall i \in I, j \in J. \tag{12.21}$$

Given the complexity of the resulting model, it is solved heuristically by the repeated matching approach in (Eveborn et al., 2006).

Chahed et al. (2009) present an optimization approach for delivering chemotherapy at home. In this context, the sample lifetime of the product is particularly important, as it varies from two hours to several days. The optimization approach considers both production and distribution; the distribution problem corresponds to the home care scheduling and routing problem, for which Cahed et al. (2009) present an exact branch-and-bound approach, using an MIP model.

In (2012), Rasmussen et al. proposed an exact solution method based on branch-and-price, which is a well-known approach for solving vehicle routing problems. Similar to (Eveborn et al., 2006) they introduced a set-covering model, which is extended with side constraints to represent temporal dependencies. Branch-and-price decomposes the problem into a master problem and a subproblem. The master problem iteratively solves the set-covering problem with a restricted set of variables, after which the subproblem determines whether improving schedules exists. If so, these are added to the master problem and the process repeats. The resulting column generation approach is then embedded in a systematic branch-and-price search to find provably optimal solutions.

Cappanera et al. (2015) presented an MIP model to jointly handle the assignment, scheduling, and routing of home care visits. The model allows multiple patient visits per week and respects patient-nurse compatibilities. Their solution approach relies on weekly patterns of patient visits, which are then allocated to the caregivers.

A different exact approach, based on logic-based Benders decomposition, is proposed by Heching and Hooker (2016). Like branch-and-price, Benders decomposition partitions the problem into a master and a subproblem, but it performs constraint-generation rather than variable-generation. In (Heching et al., 2016), the master problem assigns caregivers to patients (one patient may have multiple visits), which is modeled and solved using MIP. The subproblem then computes the optimal route for each caregiver for each day of the week, which is modeled and solved with CP. If the route/schedule is not feasible, the subproblem returns a Benders cut that forbids that particular assignment.

Both Cappanera et al. (2015) and Heching and Hooker (2016) ensure continuity of care within the one-week planning horizon of their respective models. While longer-term continuity of care can be handled by fixing previous patient-to-nurse assignments in a rolling horizon framework, this may lead to myopic suboptimal solutions. For this reason, Güven-Koçak et al. (2017) presented an optimization approach that aims to better handle long-term continuity of care. Updates to the schedule are processed on a daily basis (usually because of new patients or because existing patients no longer need care), in which case a new schedule is computed that aims to be as consistent with the previous schedule as possible. Thus, the standard objective function to minimize travel time or total cost is now augmented with a penalty for inconsistent nurse-to-patient allocations. They presented an MIP formulation as well as a heuristic solution method to solve the consistent home care delivery problem.

While most optimization methods for home care delivery consider static travel times, Rest et al. (2015) considered time-dependent travel times, which can provide more accurate solutions. They presented a detailed MIP formulation for the problem, as well as a heuristic method based on tabu search.

In the above, we have sketched some of the most common approaches to solving the scheduling/routing problem for home care delivery. We refer to the recent surveys by Fikar and Hirsch (2017) and Cissé et al. (2017) for a more detailed comparison of various approaches and different variants of the rich scheduling/routing literature in this problem domain.

12.6 Perspectives

As we have seen in the previous sections, systematic quantitative models based on optimization technology have proven to be a powerful tool for decision-support in home care delivery. Several avenues remain, however, for improving the efficiency of home health care services. All fields of health care can benefit from continuously improving mobile technologies, and home health care is no exception, as shown by a recent book and survey (Istepanian et al., 2014; Silva et al., 2015). This technological shift will enable new possibilities in the use of advanced predictive and prescriptive analytics tools. In the last part of this chapter, we look at several new, emerging perspectives that rely on data-driven decision-making.

12.6.1 Integrated Decision-Making Under a New Business Model

Over the last few years the home care industry has witnessed the emergence of a new business model. Revenues of private agencies are evolving from a model in which they bill a fee for every service provided to a model in which each patient condition prescribes a fixed amount. Providing high-quality care, while remaining profitable, becomes more challenging as this model is more widely adopted. Most importantly, we can recognize that the individual planning problems, mentioned earlier, are now optimized separately although there are clear interactions between them. For example, admitting certain patients, or certain patient/agency assignment, may require hiring additional staff or lead to highly inefficient routes, which can significantly affect productivity.

These interactions can be made explicit by designing optimization models that span two or more of these decision problems. For example, it is possible to combine the dynamic acceptation of patients with the ongoing employee scheduling and routing problems. The resulting online and stochastic model may be more challenging to solve, but as the algorithmic power of optimization improves and machines get faster, solving these larger models may become routine in the near future.

12.6.2 Home Telemetering Forecasting Adverse Events

Approximately 20 percent of Medicare patients are readmitted shortly after discharge (Jencks et al., 2009). Consequently, insurance companies have established financial penalties for hospital with high readmission rates 30 days after discharge (Huntington et al., 2011). Prediction of adverse events such as hospital readmissions, in the context of home health care patients, can thus have a significant economic impact.

Patients who benefit from home healthcare are initially evaluated by a medical team to assess the level of assistance they will require. Despite the many advantages of home healthcare, one primary medical challenge of home care for patients is the lack of the constant supervision that would be present within an institution. Thus, there is always a risk that the expected medical outcome of a care plan will not be achieved, that the patient will fall and will not be rescued promptly, or that the patient will get confused with medication, leading to deterioration of the health condition and eventually to rehospitalization.

When patients are admitted to a home care agency, they are generally visited by a nurse who will perform an initial needs assessment. Patients may be assigned to a home telemetering (HT) program, if the agency offers such program. While on an HT program, patients answer a periodic questionnaire during which they will be asked to take some vital signs readings. This information is then transmitted to the HHC agency, where a nurse monitors an HT case load. In some experimental cases, patients can wear sensory devices that continuously capture and transmit vital signs.

Based on the patient diagnosed conditions and initial assessment, the care workers create alerts based on acceptable ranges of each measured vital sign, as shown in (Suh et al., 2010).

Sometimes, in more advanced systems, complex rules can be developed to create alerts based on combinations of suspect readings. In all cases, care workers bear the weight of setting up patients with the right set of alerts based on their conditions. The manually engineered rules then need to evolve with each patient's condition in order to remain reliable.

When a vital sign reading is out of the acceptable range, the monitoring nurse can perform one or two of the following actions: (1) call the patient to determine next steps; and/or (2) schedule an in-person visit. The challenge is to prevent costly hospital readmissions and emergency room visits, but there is also a cost to each intervention. To add complexity, most of the alarms are false positives, not leading to adverse events.

Early detection of these events serves the triple aim of improving outcomes: (1) quality of health services; (2) improving health of populations; and (3) reducing costs (Berwick et al., 2008).

Researchers in this field often use linear models such as multivariate logistic regression and the Cox Proportional Hazard (Ross et al., 2008; Hansen et al., 2011; Wallace et al., 2014; Kansagara et al., 2011) because of their understandable nature. Indeed, most of the work so far has been interested in understanding the significant factors that lead to adverse events. Modern machine learning techniques, such as neural networks, have not been adopted yet, although they have demonstrated success in many industries, from computer vision to market finance. One of the challenges of such approaches resides in their interoperability (Zhu et al., 2014). New companies have, however, run case studies, reported in a white paper (Vallée, 2015), that indicate that machine learning approaches could perform significantly better than human-defined alerts, both in terms of sensitivity and specificity.

12.6.3 Forecasting the Wound Healing Process

Today, wound care costs the Canadian health system at least $3.9 billion annually or 3% of total health expenditures (Woundcare Alliance of Canada, n.d.), and approximately $50 billion in the United States (Fife et al., 2012). The portion of these costs dedicated to home care can be significant. For instance, in the case of diabetic foot ulcers, direct-care cost to the Canadian healthcare system of $547 million (2011 dollars) out of which $125M (roughly 23%) was spent in home caring. Public and private agencies must thus be able to assess the necessary effort required to manage each type of wound and each patient, in order to plan the usage of their resources efficiently.

Although there has been some effort to forecast the healing duration of a wound, we have not yet seen any paper reporting the use of modern machine

Table 12.2 Majors factors that influence the wound healing process.

Systemic Factors	Local Factors	Organizational Factors
Deficient eating and hydration	Infection	Absence of specialized nurse
Oxygen deficit	Chronic Wound	Multidisciplinary team
Stress	Wound area	Continuity of care
Bad sensorial perception	Presence of foreign body	Complete evaluation
Age and sex	Hematoma	Following protocol
Obesity	Wound location	
Diabetes, HBP	Necrotic tissues	
Tabagism, alcoholism	Wound pressure	
Auto-immune disease	Wound hydration	
Cultural beliefs	Wound vascularization	
Sexual hormones level	Wound type	

learning techniques to do so. Such methods would require access to a large body of high-quality data in a numerical format. Information on the nature of the wound (type, acuity, area, odor, grade, etc.) would need to be diligently recorded at every visit. Detailed information on the patient would also be quite useful, as many physiological factors, such as obesity, hypertension, and diabetes have a significant influence on wound healing. Table 12.2 lists the major factors that influence the healing of a wound, as stated in several studies (Beitz, 2012; Gould et al., 2015; Guo et al., 2010; Mackavey, 2016; Snyder et al., 2016).

12.6.4 Adjustment of Capacity and Demand

One important challenge faced by home care agencies in many markets is the alignment between their service capacity, that is, the number of productive hours their workforce can provide in a week or a month, and the demand for service that comes from their customers. In particular, it is quite common that peak demand occurs in the morning, because less-mobile patients need help to get the day started while more autonomous customers prefer an early visit so that they can proceed with their daily schedules. Data gathered by the VHA Healthcare[3] shows the spread of thousands of daily visits over each hour of the day, as illustrated in Figure 12.1.

If most of the work is scheduled in the morning, then many caregivers are not needed during the afternoon. This can result in low motivation in the staff and high turnover among the caregivers, who may aim to find full-time

3 www.vha.ca

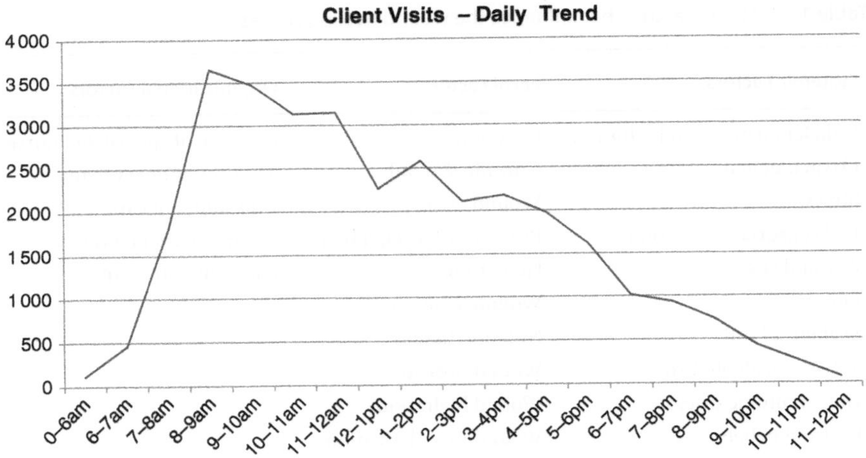

Figure 12.1 Average number of clients visited per daily hour by the VHA Healthcare agency.

positions instead. This problem can be addressed by two possible approaches: (1) hiring part-time caregivers who will willingly work reduced hours; and (2) trying to shift demand to a later period during the day. Both of these approaches come with their own challenges.

It is therefore an arduous task to design and recruit an optimal workforce. Agencies would need to accurately forecast the demand per time period and day of the week, and, using this forecast, they would then need to design a set of work shifts that fit this forecast best as possible. Such approaches are used widely in retail stores and call centers (Van den Bergh et al., 2013); however, in these service industries there is no notion of continuity of care between the employees and the customers. In fact, the assignment of customers to employees is performed each time a new customer requires a service. Dynamic pricing (Zhou et al., 2000), which is widely used in the airline and hospitality industries, may be used as a tool for further development in the delivery of home health care.

References

Achterberg, T. (2009). SCIP: solving constraint integer programs. *Mathematical Programming Computation*, 1, 1–41.

Achterberg, T. and R. Wunderling. (2013). Mixed integer programming: Analyzing 12 years of progress. In *Facets of Combinatorial Optimization: Festschrift for Martin Grötschel* (eds. M. Jünger and G. Reinelt), Springer, pp. 449–481.

Baptiste, P., C. Le Pape, and W. Nuijten. (2001). *Constraint-Based Scheduling—Applying Constraint Programming to Scheduling Problems*, Springer.

Begur, S.V., D.M. Miller, and J.R. Weaver. (1997). An Integrated Spatial DSS for Scheduling and Routing Home-Health-Care Nurses. *Interfaces*, 27 (4), 35–48.

Beitz, J.M. (2012) Predictors of success on wound ostomy and continence nursing certification board examinations: A regression study of academic factors. *Journal of Wound Ostomy & Continence Nursing*, 39 (4), 377–381.

Bennett, A.R. and A.L. Erera. (2011). Dynamic periodic fixed appointment scheduling for home health. *IIE Transactions Healthcare Systems Engineering*, 1 (1), 6–19.

Benzarti, E., E. Sahin, and Y. Dallery. (2013). Operations management applied to home care services: Analysis of the districting problem. *Decision Support Systems*, (55), 587–598.

Bertels, S. and T. Fahle. (2006). A hybrid setup for a hybrid scenario: Combining heuristics for the home health care problem. *Computers and Operations Research*, 33 (10), 2866–2890.

Berwick, D.M., T.W. Nolan, and J. Whittington. (2008). The triple aim: care, health, and cost. *Health Affairs*, 27 (3), 759–769.

Bixby, R.E. (2002) Solving Real-World Linear Programs: A Decade and More of Progress. *Operations Research*, 50 (1), 3–15.

Bixby, R.E., M. Fenelon, Z. Gu, E. Rothberg, and R. Wunderling. (2004). Mixed-integer programming: A progress report, in *The Sharpest Cut: The Impact of Manfred Padberg and His Work* (ed. M. Grötschel), SIAM, MPS-SIAM Series on Optimization, chap. 18, pp. 309–325.

Blais, M., S. Lapierre, and G. Laporte. (2003). Solving a home-care districting problem in an urban setting. *Journal of the Operational Research Society*, (54), 1141–114.

Canadian institute for health information. Home Care. https://www.cihi.ca/en/home-care.

Canadian nurses association. (2013). Optimizing the role of nursing in home care, *Tech. Rep.*, Canadian nurses association.

Cappanera, P. and M.G. Scutellà. (2015). Joint assignment, scheduling, and routing models to home care optimization: A pattern-based approach. *Transportation Science*, 4 (49), 830–852.

Carello, G. and E. Lanzarone. (2014). A cardinality-constrained robust model for the assignment problem in home care services. *European Journal of Operational Research*, 236 (2), 748–762.

Centre national des soins. Palliatifs et de la fin de vie. http://www.spfv.fr.

CDC (Centers for Disease Control and Prevention). US Department of Health and Human Services, National Center for Health Statistics. www.cdc.gov/nchs/fastats/home-health-care.htm. Accessed March 8, 2018.

Chahed, S., E. Marcon, E. Sahin, D. Feillet, and Y. Dallery. (2009). Exploring new operational research opportunities within the home care context: the chemotherapy at home. *Health Care Management Science*, 12 (2), 179–191.

Cheng, E. and J.L. Rich. (1998). A home health care routing and scheduling problem, Tech. Rep. TR98-04, Department of CAAM, Rice University.

Cissé, M., S. Yalçındağ, Y. Kergosien, E. Şahin, C. Lenté, and A. Matta. (2017). OR problems related to Home Health Care: A review of relevant routing and scheduling problems. *Operations Research for Health Care*, pp. 13–14.

Clarke, G. and J.W. Wright. (1964). Scheduling of vehicles from a central depot to a number of delivery points. *Operations Research*, 12 (4), 568–581.

Eveborn, P., P. Flisberg, and M. Rönnqvist. (2006). Laps care—an operational system for staff planning of home care. *European Journal of Operational Research*, 171 (3), 962–976.

Fife, C.E. and M.J. Carter. (2012). Wound care outcomes and associated cost among patients treated in US outpatient wound centers: data from the US wound registry. *Wounds: a compendium of clinical research and practice*, 24 (1), 10–17.

Fikar, C. and P. Hirsch. (2017). Home health care routing and scheduling: A review. *Computers & Operations Research*, 77, 86–95.

Gendreau, M. and J.Y. Potvin. (eds.) (2010). *Handbook of Metaheuristics, Springer.*

Glover, F. (1997). Tabu search and adaptive memory programming—advances, applications and challenges, in *Interfaces in Computer Science and Operations Research, Springer, pp.* 1–75

Gould, L., P. Abadir, H. Brem, M. Carter, T. Conner-Kerr, J. Davidson, L. DiPietro, V. Falanga, C. Fife, and S. Gardner. (2015). Chronic wound repair and healing in older adults: current status and future research. *Wound Repair and Regeneration*, 23 (1), 1–13.

Government of Canada. Home and community health care, https://www.canada .ca/en/ health-canada/services/ home-continuing-care/ home-community-care.html.

Guo, S. and L.A. DiPietro. (2010). Factors affecting wound healing. *Journal of dental research*, 89 (3), 219–229.

Güven-Koçak, Ş., A. Heching, P. Keskinocak, and A. Toriello. (2017). Home Health Care Routing and Scheduling with Consistency. Submitted.

Hansen, L.O., R.S. Young, K. Hinami, A. Leung, and M.V. Williams. (2011). Interventions to reduce 30-day rehospitalization: a systematic review. *Annals of internal medicine*, 155 (8), 520–528.

Heching, A. and J.N. Hooker. (2016). Scheduling Home Hospice Care with Logic-Based Benders Decomposition, in *Proceedings of CPAIOR, Lecture Notes in Computer Science*, vol. 9676, Springer, pp. 187–197.

Hertz, A. and N. Lahrichi. (2009). A patient assignment algorithm for home care services. *Journal of the operational research society*, (60), 481–495.

Huntington, W.V., L.A. Covington, P.P. Center, and L. Manchikanti. (2011). Patient protection and Affordable Care Act of 2010: reforming the health care reform for the new decade. *Pain Physician*, 14 (1), E35–E67.

Istepanian, R., S. Laxminarayan, and C.S. Pattichis. (2014). *M-health*, Springer.

Jencks, S.F., M.V. Williams, and E.A. Coleman, (2009). Rehospitalizations among patients in the Medicare fee-for-service program. *New England Journal of Medicine*, 360 (14), 1418–1428.

Kalcsics, J. (2015). Districting problems. In *Location Science* (eds. G. Laporte, S. Nickel, and F.S. da Gama), chap. 23, pp. 595–622.

Kansagara, D., H. Englander, A. Salanitro, D. Kagen, C. Theobald, M. Freeman, and S. Kripalani. (2011). Risk prediction models for hospital readmission: a systematic review. *JAMA*, 306 (15), 1688–1698.

Kirkpatrick, S., C.D. Gelatt, and M.P. Vecchi. (1983). Optimization by Simulated Annealing. *Science*, 220 (4598), 671–680.

Laborie, P. (2009). IBM ILOG CP Optimizer for Detailed Scheduling Illustrated on Three Problems, in *Proceedings of CPAIOR, Lecture Notes in Computer Science*, vol. 5547, Springer, *Lecture Notes in Computer Science*, vol. 5547, pp. 148–162.

Lahrichi, N., E. Lanzarone, and S. Yalçındağ, (2017). A new decomposition approach for the home health care problem. International Conference in Health Care Systems Engineering, 27–36.

Lanzarone, E. and A. Matta. (2014). Robust nurse-to-patient assignment in home care services to minimize overtimes under continuity of care. *Operations Research for Health Care*, 3 (2), 48–58.

Le site officiel de l'administration française, Hospitalisation et soins à domicile. https://www.service-public.fr/particuliers/vosdroits/N432

Mackavey, C. (2016) Advanced practice nurse transitional care model promotes healing in wound care. *Care Management Journals*, 17 (3), 140–149.

Martí, R., P. Pardalos, and M.G.C. Resende. (eds.) (2018). *Handbook of Heuristics*, Springer.

Medicare.gov. (n.d.), What's home health care? https://www.medicare.gov/what-medicare-covers/home-health-care/home-health-care-what-is-it-what-to-expect.html.

Ministère des solidarités et de la santé, (n.d). L'hospitalisation à domicile. http://solidarites-sante.gouv.fr/soins-et-maladies/prises-en-charge-specialisees/had.

NHPCO (National hospice and palliative care organization, n.d.) https://www.nhpco.org/nhpco-0.

Nickel, S., M. Schröder and J. Steeg. (2012). Mid-term and short-term planning support for home health care services. *European Journal of Operations Research*, (219), 574–587.

Rasmussen, M.S., T. Justesen, A. Dohn, and J. Larsen. (2012). The home care crew scheduling problem: Preference-based visit clustering and temporal dependencies. *European Journal of Operational Research*, 219 (3), 598–610.

Rest, K.D. and P. Hirsch. (2015). Daily scheduling of home health care services using time-dependent public transport. *Flexible Services and Manufacturing* 28(3), 295–525. https://link.springer.com/article/10.1007/s10696-015-9227-1

Ross, J.S., G.K. Mulvey, B. Stauffer, V. Patlolla, S.M. Bernheim, P.S. Keenan, and H.M. Krumholz. (2008). Statistical models and patient predictors of readmission for heart failure: a systematic review. *Archives of internal medicine*, 168 (13), 1371–1386.

Rossi, F., P. van Beek, and T. Walsh. (eds) (2006). *Handbook of Constraint Programming*, Elsevier.

Sahin, E. and A. Matta. (2015). A contribution to operations management-related issues and models for home care structures. *International Journal of Logistics: Research and Applications*, 4 (18), 355–385.

Silva, B.M., J.J. Rodrigues, I. de la Torre Díez, M. López-Coronado, and K. Saleem. (2015). Mobile-health: A review of current state in 2015. *Journal of biomedical informatics*, 56, 265–272.

Snyder, R.J., C. Fife, and Z. Moore. (2016). Components and quality measures of dime (devitalized tissue, infection/inflammation, moisture balance, and edge preparation) in wound care. *Advances in skin & wound care*, 29 (5), 205.

Sudhakar-Krishnan, V. and M.C.J. Rudolf. (2007). How important is continuity of care? *Arch Dis Child*, 92 (5), 381–383.

Suh, M.K.K., L.S. Evangelista, C.A.A. Chen, K. Han, J. Kang, M.K. Tu, V. Chen, A. Nahapetian, and M. Sarrafzadeh. (2010). An automated vital sign monitoring system for congestive heart failure patients, in *Proceedings of the 1st ACM International Health Informatics Symposium*, ACM, pp. 108–117.

Tarricone, R. and A.D. Tsouros. (2008). Home care in Europe, the solid facts, *Tech. Rep.*, World Health Organization Europe.

Trautsamwieser, A. and P. Hirsch. (2014). A branch-price-and-cut approach for solving the medium-term home health care planning problem. *Networks*, 3 (64), 143–159.

Vallée, J. (2015), The effects of machine learning powered remote patient monitoring on home health care, info.alayacare.com/machine-learning-rpm-home-health-care-paper. Alayacare White Paper.

Van den Bergh, J., J. Beliën, P. De Bruecker, E. Demeulemeester, and L. De Boeck. (2013). Personnel scheduling: A literature review. *European Journal of Operational Research*, 226 (3), 367–385.

Wallace, E., E. Stuart, N. Vaughan, K. Bennett, T. Fahey, and S.M. Smit. (2014). Risk prediction models to predict emergency hospital admission in community-dwelling adults: a systematic review. *Medical care*, 52 (8), 751.

Wirnitzer, J., I. Heckmann A. Meyer, and S. Nickel. (2016). Patient-based nurse rostering in home care. *Operations Research for Health Care*, 8, 91–102.

Woundcare alliance of Canada. Confronting the Epidemic of Wounds in Canada. http://wcacanada.ca/.

Yalçındağ, S., A. Matta, E. Sahin, and J. Shanthikumar. (2016). The patient assignment problem in home health care: using a data-driven method to estimate the travel times of care givers. *Flexible Services Manufacturing*, 281, 304–335.

Zhao, W. and Y.S. Zheng. (2000). Optimal dynamic pricing for perishable assets with nonhomogeneous demand. *Management Science*, 46 (3), 375–388.

Zhu, M., L. Cheng, J.J. Armstrong, J.W. Poss, J.P. Hirdes, and P. Stolee. (2014). *Machine Learning in Healthcare Informatics*, Springer.

13

Concierge Medicine

Srinagesh Gavirneni[1] *and Vidyadhar G. Kulkarni*[2]

[1] *Cornell University*
[2] *University of North Carolina at Chapel Hill*

13.1 Introduction

Primary care physician service in the US is in a state of crisis because of the significant shortage of physicians working in this specialty, the aging patient population, the projected increase in the number of office visits following implementation of the Affordable Care Act, and increased patient expectations (Petterson et al., 2012). Under these circumstances, it is not surprising to hear about patients taking six to nine months to find a new primary care physician, or up to two weeks to get an appointment with their current primary care physician. At the same time, these healthcare providers are feeling overworked, unappreciated, and professionally unsatisfied with the incomplete care they provide (Murray et al., 2003). In the third-party payment system prevalent in the US healthcare system, easy access to a primary care physician is an important and necessary first step and must be managed carefully (Forrest, 2003).

Recognizing these inadequacies (Bodenheimer and Pham, 2010) in the current primary healthcare delivery system, some physicians have started offering concierge medicine—a system of fee-based priority access—to better serve the patients who are willing to pay extra for faster appointment scheduling (Alexander et al., 2005). The patients who are unwilling or unable to pay these additional fees (often out-of-pocket) are assigned lower priority in scheduling and may not see any improvement in the care they receive. Since its inception in the early 2000s, concierge medicine has been well received by patients and is being adopted at an increasing speed all across the country. As of 2010, the National Opinion Research Center at the University of Chicago and Georgetown University identifies 756 retainer-based practices, most commonly those of internists (Silva, 2010). A more recent estimate, by the

Handbook of Healthcare Analytics: Theoretical Minimum for Conducting 21st Century Research on Healthcare Operations, First Edition. Edited by Tinglong Dai and Sridhar Tayur.

American Academy of Private Physicians in 2013, estimates the number at over 5,000 (Priddy, 2013).

Concierge medicine is, however, not without its detractors. Critics perceive such fee-based-priority schemes as socially unjust because the schemes determine access to good healthcare based on patients' wealth or income situations (Carnahan, 2006). Although it is true that in concierge medicine the nonconcierge patients are moved behind the "elites" in the queue, supporters argue that nonconcierge patient may benefit in some other manner (e.g. better amenities, higher quality of care, or financial discount). Viewed through this lens, concierge medicine increases social welfare (Lauer and Neil, 2009); thus, this larger pie, if shared appropriately, can result in everyone (service providers, concierge patients, and nonconcierge patients) being better off.

In a typical concierge medicine practice, physicians see both fee-paying patients and those who appear on a conventional fee-for-service basis. Concierge medicine subscribers each pay an annual retainer to the doctor of at least $1,500. For practices associated with MDVIP, a software company that facilitates implementation, about $500 of this fee goes to electronic health records and marketing support. The remainder supplements the doctor's income, and effectively may subsidize at least some of the cost for nonconcierge patients. In the most extreme or purest form of concierge medicine, known as boutique or private physician medicine, physicians cater only to their fee-paying customers, which means that those unwilling to pay the additional concierge fee must choose another doctor (O'Brien, 2013).

Physicians and patients face important and difficult decisions regarding concierge medicine, and we see a need to develop decision support tools that can answer the following questions:

Single-Physician versus Multi-Physician: When a multipractitioner office implements concierge medicine, typically only one or two of its physicians will designate themselves as concierge physicians. Consequently, their patients can choose to sign up for concierge medicine and guarantee themselves timely care with their chosen physician, or not sign up and be assigned, in an ad-hoc manner, to the first available physician when a need for care arises. If a single practitioner office adopts concierge medicine, the patients must either sign up for the concierge approach and pay the retainer or quit this practice and move to a different primary care physician. The decision about whether or not to offer concierge medicine is a difficult one for all practitioners, and it is especially harrowing for sole practitioners, as they will see patients leaving their practice. In a multipractitioner setting, the decision about how many physicians and who, specifically, should switch to concierge mode is an under-explored research question.

Physician Decisions: The physician who chooses to adopt concierge medicine must resolve the following issues: (i) The number of patients she should allow in her concierge practice; (ii) the price she should charge; (iii) the services (e.g., time per visit) she should promise and deliver to the concierge patients; and (iv) the patient mix (age, health condition, etc.) she should target (Gavirneni et al., 2013).

Patient Decisions: When asked to join a concierge-style medical practice, patients should first decide whether to sign up, stay with the practice as a nonconcierge patient, or seek another physician. The key trade-off that must be resolved is between the additional fees they have to pay out-of-pocket and the reduction in the waiting cost experienced because of priority scheduling. The patients are heterogeneous in the cost they attribute to the waiting time, owing to differences in age, health condition, or patience. In fact, it is this heterogeneity in waiting cost that enables the implementation of concierge medicine in the first place.

Society Perspective: Though the physician and patient experience take center stage in our modeling and analysis, we do not forget that impact on society is what matters most in considerations about concierge medicine. There is significant discussion in the media and healthcare circles about the perceived social injustice associated with offering preferred medical care to those who are willing and able to pay. The popular perception is that wealthy patients who join the system will receive better healthcare, whereas the poorer patients will be worse off. This may be the case, but we consider another possibility, namely, that the concierge fees stabilize (or reduce) the cost to conventional patients. We propose and model the possibility that the premium fees collected from the concierge patients are partially transferred, via a discount scheme, to the nonconcierge patients, and show that this eventually results in higher social welfare. Whether such a transfer is practically feasible and actually occurs can be discussed at length, but the fact that concierge medicine is beneficial to society cannot be ignored.

Operations Research offers a wide variety of tools and solution methodologies to address the research issues detailed above. Optimization and simulation can be used to determine optimal resource capacities, quantify and manage uncertainties in the system, and identify recourse actions when a disruption occurs. Inventory theory and scheduling can be instrumental in designing time tables for employees, ensuring adequate supply of materials, and efficiently using diagnostic resources. Statistics and machine learning can be used to monitor quality of service, generate insights into what the organization is excelling at or struggling with, and ensure satisfaction among staff, patients, and physicians. Assortment planning and game theory can be used to understand the competitive landscape, identify what services should or should not be offered, what pricing strategies should be implemented, and how much marketing should be pursued in order to achieve and maintain a leadership position. Service blueprinting can be used to precisely define the service delivery process and identify underlying reasons for service failure when that occurs. Queuing theory can be used to understand the uncertainties in patient arrival rates and physician consulting times and to define appropriate priority schemes. In this chapter, we will illustrate the use of queuing theory in helping us understand the operation, management, and effectiveness of concierge medicine (Gavirneni and Kulkarni, 2014).

We model the service system as a single-server queue with random customer arrivals and service times (Gross and Harris, 1985). The long-run service rate is assumed to be faster than the long-run arrival rate, and the system will eventually reach a steady state. However, short-term imbalances in arrivals and service can result in some customers having to wait before receiving service. The customer willingness to wait varies (Mendelson and Whang, 1990) from one customer to another, and for analytical tractability, we will initially assume that these waiting costs follow uniform and exponential distributions. In Section 6, we apply these models to data from the real world and use Burr distribution (Tadikamalla, 1980) to capture heterogeneity in customer waiting costs. We will analyze the performance of this system under three modes of operation, namely, first-in, first-out (FIFO), minimum cost, and the concierge system.

Our analysis is divided into two different settings, depending on how the customer reacts to the implementation of a concierge option. The first one, which we call the *no abandonment* case, is one in which the customer will not leave the service even though her costs are higher under the concierge setting. In the second setting, which we call the *abandonment* case, a customer is allowed to leave the system (we do not model where she goes) if unhappy with the concierge option. We first show that under *No abandonment*, if the service provider wishes to ensure that *all* the customers are no worse off, then the service provider cannot make any additional revenue from offering the concierge option. On the other hand, if the service provider only wants to ensure that an average customer is no worse off, then she can increase her profits by about 20–100 percent. Under the *abandonment* case, it is imperative that all the remaining customers in the system are no worse off under the concierge option. Even so, the service provider can significantly increase her revenues. In all these cases, we show a wide range of parameter settings in which, the customers and the service provider are no worse off and the total system cost is significantly reduced. By comparing this to the minimum possible system cost, we show that transition to the concierge option eliminates about 73 percent of the inefficiency in the system.

The analytical results concretely establish the conditions under which the concierge option is attractive, yet we acknowledge that they are derived under many assumptions. In order to test whether these results are valid in real-world settings, we collected and analyzed the data associated with adoption of MDVIP service across the country. We show that concierge medicine is adopted in areas (categorized by zip codes) where the median income is larger, the population is older, and income has a larger variance. We applied the queuing models, using the Burr distribution to model heterogeneity in waiting cost, to these zip codes and tabulated participation levels and financial impact. This analysis of the real-world data complements the analytical results in establishing the role that concierge medicine plays in the US healthcare system.

13.2 Model Setup

We model the service offering as a single-server queuing system in which customers arrive according to a PP(λ) (a Poisson process with rate λ). The service times are independently and identically distributed (i.i.d.) random variables with a common mean τ, variance σ^2, and second moment $s^2 = \sigma^2 + \tau^2$. The service provider charges a fee of c dollars to each customer, and these customers are identical in all respects except for the costs they attribute to the waiting time experienced before entering service. We assume that the waiting cost per unit time of the ith customer is H_i and $\{H_i, i \geq 1\}$ is a sequence of i.i.d. continuous non-negative random variables generated from a probability distribution with cdf $G(\cdot)$, pdf $g(\cdot)$, and mean h (Mendelson and Whang, 1990). In particular, we illustrate the main results with the help of two special cases:

Uniform Case: H_i is uniformly distributed over $[0, M]$, i.e., $G(x) = x/M, \quad 0 \leq x \leq M$. In numerical examples, we use $M = 2$.

Exponential Case: H_i is exponentially distributed over $[0, \infty)$ with mean $1/\theta$; that is, $G(x) = 1 - \exp(-\theta x), \quad x \geq 0$. In numerical examples, we use $\theta = 1$.

The service provider is interested in maximizing the revenue it receives while the customers are interested in minimizing their costs. We could also consider modeling customer heterogeneity along the utility the customers receive from the service. This adds another dimension of uncertainty to the model, further complicating analysis, and estimation of the utilities is much more difficult than estimating customer holding cost rates. We thus restrict ourselves to modeling customer heterogeneity using their holding cost rates. We study this system under three different operational settings.

Model FIFO: In this setting, the customers are served in the sequence they arrive. This is the most basic operational strategy. Using the standard results from Gross and Harris (1985), we see that the system is stable if $\rho = \lambda\tau < 1$. The expected queuing time for the FIFO system is given by

$$W = \frac{\lambda s^2}{2(1-\rho)}.$$

The expected total waiting cost of all customers per unit time is given by $C(\text{FIFO}) = \lambda h W$, and the expected revenue per unit time is given by $R(\text{FIFO}) = \lambda c$.

Model MinCost: In this setting, we assume that the system planner knows the waiting cost rates of the individual customers. Suppose the service provider is constrained to implement a nonpreemptive, nonidling policy (i.e., service cannot be interrupted once it starts, and the server cannot be idle if there are customers waiting). Then, to minimize the total waiting costs, it is optimal to serve the customers in decreasing order of their waiting cost rates. That is, when a customer arrives, she will join the queue at a position in which the person ahead has a higher waiting cost rate and the person behind has a lower waiting cost rate. For this system, expected queuing time of a customer with waiting cost rate x can be shown to be (see Kleinrock, 1967)

$$\frac{\lambda s^2}{2(1-\rho)}\frac{1-\rho}{(1-\rho+\rho G(x))^2}.$$

Hence, the total expected cost of all customers per unit time is given by

$$C(\text{MinCost}) = W(1-\rho)\int_0^\infty \frac{xg(x)}{(1-\rho+\rho G(x))^2}dx.$$

The difference in costs between models FIFO and MinCost can be attributed to the fact that the MinCost system tries to remove the highest cost customers first from the system within the constraint of nonpreemption and nonidling. We can show that in the uniform case, we have

$$C(\text{MinCost}) = \lambda M\frac{\lambda s^2}{2(1-\rho)}(\rho+\ln(1-\rho))\frac{\rho-1}{\rho^2},$$

and in the exponential case, we have

$$C(\text{MinCost}) = -\frac{\lambda s^2}{2(1-\rho)}\frac{(1-\rho)\ln(1-\rho)}{\rho\theta}.$$

We computed $C(\text{FIFO})/C(\text{MinCost})$ for the uniform and exponential cases with $M = 2$ and $\theta = 1$, respectively. Thus, in both cases the mean waiting cost rate is one. The improvement of MinCost over FIFO consistently increases with ρ, and the improvement is better under the exponential case than under the uniform case, because the variability of the waiting cost is higher under the exponential case than under the uniform case. The large (150–200%) cost difference between the FIFO system and the MinCost system, especially at higher utilization, demonstrates the need for strategies that can alleviate this inefficiency. We claim that introduction of a concierge option, which essentially segments customers based on their waiting costs, is one possible approach. In the next section, we define the concierge option more precisely, analyze the customer behavior under that option, and compare its performance to these two models.

13.3 Concierge Option—No Abandonment

In this section, we formally introduce the concierge option with no abandonment and perform a detailed analysis of its impact on the customers, the service provider, and the system. A concierge option under which customers receive a differentiated service works as follows: each customer is given a choice of paying an additional fixed charge K and joining an "elite" group of customers. Thus, the total service charge for an elite customer is $c + K$. This is similar to Noar (1969), who study individually and socially optimal policies for controlling arrivals to an M/M/1 system using admission tolls. Yechiali (1972), Stidham (1978), and Mendelson and Yechiali (1981) extend these models to study customer balking behavior for G/M/s systems. These papers do not consider priorities.

In our setting, for this additional fee, the service provider gives the elite customers nonpreemptive priority over the non-elite customers, which reduces the expected queuing time for the elite customers. This is a significantly restricted version of Kleinrock (1967) that allows customers to pay a bribe to secure a position in the queue. One drawback of Kleinrock's model is that it allows unstable policies; that is, left to themselves, greedy customers would not stick to the policy stipulated by the model. Balachandran (1972) accounts for this deficiency and considers Nash equilibrium policies in the case where customers can pay to select a priority in a queuing system based on the congestion information to minimize their own costs. Glazer and Hassin (1986) do a similar analysis in an M/G/1 case. Adiri and Yechiali (1974) study the queue-length-dependent joining behavior of single-class customers in a multipriority M/M/1 queue. They explicitly account for the presence or absence of customer balking (or abandonment). Alperstein (1988) derives further results for the same system. Mendelson and Whang (1990) consider the individually optimal policies for multiclass customers using a multipriority M/M/1 system. They assume that the classes are distinguished by fixed distinct holding cost rates and different utilities for obtaining service. Kim and Mannino (2003) extend their results to the M/G/1 queue. Whereas the aforementioned papers focus on the queue joining (or not) of customers, pricing is the focus of many other research studies. Rao and Peterson (1998) consider the problem of pricing and capacity (service rate) planning in a multipriority queuing system. The recent book by Stidham (2009) deals with the subject of optimal pricing in priority queues. Hassin and Haviv (2003) is an excellent source of general literature on strategic queuing, and chapter 4 therein focuses on information in priority models.

The presence of a fee-based priority option results in the elite customers experiencing shorter waiting times (and cost), but the expected queuing time for the non-elite customers would increase. In order to compensate them for this added inconvenience, the service provider gives a discount of d (which need not necessarily be financial and could be in the form of better amenities or longer time and/or quality of care) in the service charge for the non-elite customers. Thus, a non-elite customer pays $c - d$ for the service. We analyze the effect of the service charge K and the service discount d on customer behavior and the operational performance of the system. We shall see that it is more convenient to use the parameters $u = K + d$ and d, to analyze the concierge option. We can think of u as the cost differential between the elite and the non-elite customers. Therefore, a concierge system can be represented by the pair (u, d) with $u \geq d$.

A (u, d) concierge option has three stakeholders, the elite members, the non-elite members, and the service provider. Define participation level α as the fraction of customers who choose to become elite members for a given (u, d). From here on, we will use α as the decision variable and derive all other quantities as a function of α. In general, for any given α, there are multiple (u, d) values that result in that α, but depending on the stakeholder we focus on, the parameter combination to implement will become clear. We begin by assuming that α is fixed, and then discuss how to choose the optimal α.

13.3.1 A Given Participation Level α

We begin with the following question: How do we choose the concierge system parameters (u, d) to achieve a given participation level α? To answer this question, we model the decision process associated with a customer choosing to become an elite member. She will need to compare the increase in cost of receiving service to the reduction in waiting cost. From her perspective, if she chooses to become an elite member, she will experience a queuing system with arrival process PP($\lambda\alpha$), and the resulting expected waiting time will be (see Gross and Harris, (1985))

$$W_h = W_h(\alpha) = W\frac{1-\rho}{1-\alpha\rho},$$

and the expected waiting time experienced by the non-elite customers is

$$W_l = W_l(\alpha) = W\frac{1}{1-\alpha\rho}.$$

Clearly, $W_h(\alpha) \leq W \leq W_l(\alpha)$. Customer i will choose to become an elite member if (recall that this is the *no abandonment* case)

$$K + c + H_i W_h < c - d + H_i W_l,$$

leading to the condition that

$$H_i > (K + d)/(W_l - W_h) = u/(W_l - W_h).$$

Therefore, if H_i is sufficiently high the ith customer will prefer to pay the premium K and become an elite member. As the waiting costs $\{H_i, i \geq 1\}$ are i.i.d., it stands to reason that in a steady state, every customer in the top 100α percentile of the population will prefer to be an elite member. The precise value of α will depend on u and the distribution of the waiting cost rates. The following theorem shows that any desired level α can be achieved by appropriately setting the value of u. We first define $m(\alpha) = G^{-1}(1-\alpha)$. As the customers in the top 100α percentile of the waiting cost rate distribution choose to become elite customers, we see that $m(\alpha)$ is the minimum waiting cost rate of an elite customer for a given α (or, equivalently, the maximum waiting cost rate of a non-elite customer).

Theorem 13.1 Any level of participation $\alpha \in [0,1]$ can be induced by setting

$$u = u(\alpha) = \frac{\rho W}{1-\alpha\rho} m(\alpha).$$

Proof: Given that customer i becomes an elite member if $H_i > u/(W_l - W_h)$, the proportion of customers choosing to become elite members can be computed as $\alpha = 1 - G(u/(W_l - W_h))$. Substituting for W_h and W_l and solving for u, we get the result. □

13.3.2 How to choose *d*?

The analysis in the previous subsection tells us how to choose $u = K + d$ to achieve the desired participation rate α. Now we focus on the choice of the discount d. Unlike choosing u, the choice of d will depend on what the service provider wants to achieve in terms of her customer's experience. We consider two options: one in which the service provider wants *all* her customers to be better off and the other in which the service provider wants her customers to be better off on *average*.

13.3.2.1 All Customers Are Better Off

If the service provider wishes to ensure that *all* her customers are better off, then the values of K and d can be chosen as follows.

Theorem 13.2 Suppose $u = u(\alpha)$ is chosen to induce a participation rate α. Under this system, *all* customers (elite and non-elite) are no worse-off under the concierge system than under the FIFO system if and only if $d \geq \alpha u(\alpha)$, where $u(\alpha)$ is as defined above.

Proof: Consider a non-elite customer with a fixed cost rate h. This customer is better off under the concierge system than under the FIFO system if $c + hW \geq c - d + hW_l$. Using the definition of w_l given above, this reduces to

$$d \geq \alpha \frac{\rho W}{1-\alpha\rho} h.$$

Because the largest waiting cost rate of a non-elite customer is also $m(\alpha)$, it follows that all non-elite customers are better off if and only if

$$d \geq \alpha \frac{\rho W}{1 - \alpha\rho} m(\alpha) = \alpha u(\alpha),$$

where the last equality follows from the definition of $u(\alpha)$. A similar argument shows that all elite customers are better off under the concierge system than the FIFO system if and only if $K \leq (1 - \alpha)u(\alpha)$. Thus, any $d \in [\alpha u(\alpha), u(\alpha)]$ and the corresponding $K = u(\alpha) - d$ would yield a concierge system that benefits all customers. □

Theorem 13.3 For a given α, the optimal d and K that maximize the service provider's expected revenues per unit time while keeping all customers no worse-off is given by $d = \alpha u(\alpha)$, $K = (1 - \alpha)u(\alpha)$. Under this choice, the service provider obtains the same revenue under the concierge system as under FIFO.

Proof: Because the elite customers arrive according to PP($\lambda\alpha$) and the non-elite customers arrive according to PP($\lambda(1 - \alpha)$), we see that the long run revenue per unit time is given by

$$\lambda\alpha(c + K) + \lambda(1 - \alpha)(c - d) = \lambda c + \lambda(\alpha u(\alpha) - d). \tag{13.1}$$

Here, we have used $K + d = u(\alpha)$. The $d \in [\alpha u(\alpha), u(\alpha)]$ that maximizes this is given by $d = \alpha u(\alpha)$. Under this choice, the revenue rate is λc, which is the same revenue rate under FIFO discipline. Therefore, the service provider is indifferent between the two systems. □

Remark: The theorem above shows that if the service provider is insistent on ensuring that every one of her customers is no worse off after implementing the concierge option, then she cannot make any additional revenues from implementing this option. This lack of profit improvement is probably the reason that most service operations either (i) do not implement a concierge option or (ii) do not attempt to keep all customers happy if they do implement a concierge option.

We investigate whether there exists a (u, d) concierge option under which, compared with the FIFO system, none of the the elite customers is worse off, none of the non-elite customers is worse off, and the service provider is also no worse off. We call such an option a Pareto-improving concierge strategy. For the setting in which all the customers are better off, from Theorems 13.2 and 13.3, we see that the answer is yes if, for a given α, we choose $u = u(\alpha)$, and $d = \alpha u(\alpha)$. Thus, the Pareto-improving region A_{all} is given by $A_{all} = \{(u(\alpha), \alpha u(\alpha)), 0 \leq \alpha \leq 1\}$. Clearly, the service provider never strictly benefits from a concierge option under this model.

13.3.2.2 Customers Are Better Off on Average

Now suppose the service provider wants to ensure that the average (i.e., randomly selected) elite and non-elite customers are happy, but none of them individually need to be happier. Under this setting, the decision process for a customer to choose to become an elite member is the same as in the previous section. The difference is in how the non-elite customers are impacted, especially in the discounts they receive from the service provider. Recall that $m(\alpha) = G^{-1}(1 - \alpha)$ is the maximal waiting cost rate of the non-elite customer for a given α. Let $h_h(\alpha)$ be the average waiting cost rate of an elite (high-priority) customer, and $h_l(\alpha)$ be the average waiting cost rate of a non-elite (low-priority) customer. They can be computed as:

$$h_h(\alpha) = E(H_i|H_i > u/(W_l - W_h)) = \frac{1}{\alpha}\int_{m(\alpha)}^{\infty} hg(h)dh, \tag{13.2}$$

and

$$h_l(\alpha) = E(H_i|H_i \leq u/(W_l - W_h)) = \frac{1}{1-\alpha}\int_{0}^{m(\alpha)} hg(h)dh. \tag{13.3}$$

The next theorem states the condition under which the average (i.e., a randomly chosen) customer of any priority is no worse off under the concierge option.

Theorem 13.4 The expected cost of service for an average low-priority customer in a (u, d) concierge system is no more than that in a FIFO system if

$$d \geq d(\alpha) = Wh_l(\alpha)\frac{\alpha\rho}{1-\alpha\rho}.$$

The expected cost of service for an average high-priority customer in a (u, d) concierge system is no more than that in a FIFO system if

$$K \leq K(\alpha) = Wh_h(\alpha)\frac{(1-\alpha)\rho}{1-\alpha\rho}.$$

Proof: The waiting cost of a randomly chosen low-priority customer is given by $h_l(\alpha)$. Hence, under the (u, d) concierge option, the total expected cost of such a customer in a steady state is given by $c - d + h_l(\alpha)W_l$. Therefore, such a customer fares better under the concierge option if and only if $c + h_l(\alpha)W \geq c - d + h_l(\alpha)W_l$, leading to the condition $d \geq h_l(\alpha)(W_l - W)$. After substituting for W_l and W and simplifying, we get the result. A similar argument regarding a randomly chosen high-priority customer yields the condition $c + h_h(\alpha)W \geq c + K + h_h(\alpha)W_h$, leading to the condition $K \leq h_h(\alpha)(W - W_h)$. This simplifies to the desired condition. □

The next theorem gives the main result about the optimal revenue of the service provider if she plans to keep the average (i.e., randomly chosen) high- and low-priority customers happy.

Theorem 13.5 If $m(\alpha) \leq (1-\alpha)h_h(\alpha) + \alpha h_l(\alpha)$, the optimal K and $d =$ are given by $K^*(\alpha) = (1-\alpha)u(\alpha)h_h(\alpha)/m(\alpha)$, and $d^*(\alpha) = u(\alpha) - K^*(\alpha)$. Otherwise, the optimal K and d are given by $d^*(\alpha) = \alpha u(\alpha)h_l(\alpha)/m(\alpha)$, and $K^*(\alpha) = u(\alpha) - d^*(\alpha)$. In either case, the optimal revenue of the service provider is no less than that in the original system, and it is strictly higher for $\alpha \in (0, 1)$.

Proof: First note that we can use the definitions of $u(\alpha)$, $K(\alpha)$ and $d(\alpha)$ to get $d(\alpha) = \alpha u(\alpha)h_l(\alpha)/m(\alpha)$, and $K(\alpha) = (1-\alpha)u(\alpha)h_h(\alpha)/m(\alpha)$. Because $h_l(\alpha) \leq m(\alpha)h_h(\alpha)$, we see that $d(\alpha) \leq \alpha u(\alpha)$, and $K(\alpha) \geq (1-\alpha)u(\alpha)$. Hence, the region $d \geq d(\alpha)$, $K \leq K(\alpha)$, $K + d = u(\alpha)$ is non-empty for each α. This region can be written more succinctly as

$$u(\alpha) \geq d \geq u(\alpha)\max\{1 - (1-\alpha)h_h(\alpha)/m(\alpha), \alpha h_l(\alpha)/m(\alpha)\}. \tag{13.4}$$

Observe that the max on the right-hand side is achieved by the first term if the theorem condition is satisfied; otherwise, it is achieved by the second term. Regardless, the right-hand side is bounded above by $\alpha u(\alpha)h_l(\alpha)/m(\alpha)$ which is at most $\alpha u(\alpha)$.

The revenue of the service provider is given by Equation 13.1. The service provider maximizes this revenue by choosing as small a d as possible, subject to the condition given by Equation 13.4. Thus, the solution is given by $K^*(\alpha) = (1-\alpha)u(\alpha)h_h(\alpha)/m(\alpha)$, and $d^*(\alpha) = u(\alpha) - K^*(\alpha)$ if the theorem condition is satisfied, and $d^*(\alpha) = \alpha u(\alpha)h_l(\alpha)/m(\alpha)$ and $K^*(\alpha) = u(\alpha) - d^*(\alpha)$ if the theorem condition is not satisfied. In either case, the revenue to the service provider is at least as much as in the original system. In particular, if $\alpha \in (0, 1)$, then $h_h(\alpha) > m(\alpha)$ and $h_l(\alpha) < m(\alpha)$; hence, the new revenue is strictly greater than that in the original system. □

The theorem detailed above illustrates that there exists a (u, d) concierge option under which the average elite customer is no worse off, the average non-elite customer is no worse off, and the service provider sees larger revenue. The next theorem (which we present without proof) formally characterizes the Pareto-improving region. Note that it is independent of c.

Theorem 13.6 The Pareto-improving region A_{avg} is given by

$$A_{avg} = \{(u, d) : d \geq d(\alpha),\ \ K \leq K(\alpha),\ \ d + K = u,\ \ 0 \leq \alpha \leq 1\}.$$ □

Therefore, if $(u, d) \in A_{avg}$, an average stakeholder of any class is no worse off under the concierge (u, d) system than under the FIFO system. Note that $A_{all} \subseteq A_{avg}$. Calculations for the uniform case yield $m(\alpha) = M(1-\alpha)$, $h_h(\alpha) = M(2-\alpha)/2$, $h_l(\alpha) = M(1-\alpha)/2$, and

$$u(\alpha) = MW\frac{(1-\alpha)\rho}{1-\alpha\rho}, \qquad d(\alpha) = MW\frac{\alpha(1-\alpha)\rho}{2(1-\alpha\rho)}.$$

It can be shown that the condition of Theorem 13.5 is satisfied at equality for all $\alpha \in (0,1)$. Thus, the optimal solution is given by $d^*(\alpha) = \alpha u(\alpha)/2$, and $K^*(\alpha) = (2-\alpha)u(\alpha)/2$.

Calculations for the exponential case show that we have

$$u(\alpha) = -\frac{W\rho\ln(\alpha)}{\theta(1-\alpha\rho)}, \quad d(\alpha) = \frac{W\alpha\rho}{\theta(1-\alpha\rho)} \cdot \frac{1-\alpha+\alpha\ln(\alpha)}{1-\alpha},$$
$$m(\alpha) = \frac{-\ln(\alpha)}{\theta}, \quad h_h(\alpha) = \frac{(1-\ln(\alpha))}{\theta}, \quad h_l(\alpha) = \frac{1}{\theta}\left(1 + \frac{\alpha}{1-\alpha}\ln(\alpha)\right).$$

Observe that condition of Theorem 13.5 is not satisfied for any $\alpha \in (0,1)$. Hence, the optimal solution is given by $d^*(\alpha) = \alpha u(\alpha)(\ln(\alpha)-1)/\ln(\alpha)$, and $K^*(\alpha) = u(\alpha) - d^*(\alpha)$.

Note that $d^*(\alpha)$ and $K^*(\alpha)$ are directly proportional to the mean waiting cost rates. The higher the sensitivity of the customers to the waiting costs, therefore, the higher the premium the service provider can charge to elite customers. However, the service provider also has to give a higher discount to keep the average non-elite customers from becoming disgruntled. We further observed that $u(\alpha)$ steadily decreases with α, whereas $d(\alpha)$ first increases and then decreases.

13.3.3 Optimal Participation Level

The above analysis detailed how the customers and the service provider behave for a given participation level α. Here, we will study how the service provider chooses the participation level with the objective of maximizing her expected revenues. For the setting in which *all* customers are better off, the service provider is indifferent among all participation levels because she cannot strictly increase her revenues by adopting a concierge system. However, for the setting in which the customers are better off on average, the service provider decides α by solving the corresponding revenue maximization problem.

Clearly, for a given α, the best revenue for the service provider is obtained by using $K = K(\alpha) = u(\alpha) - d(\alpha)$ and $d = d(\alpha)$. The revenue rate is given by $\lambda c + R(\alpha)$, where $R(\alpha) = \lambda\alpha u(\alpha) - \lambda d(\alpha)$. Thus, the optimization problem for the service provider reduces to the following one dimensional constrained optimization problem: maximize $R(\alpha)$ subject to $0 \le \alpha \le 1$. Let α^* be the optimal solution for the above problem. The concierge option with $(u^* = u(\alpha^*), d^* = d(\alpha^*))$ is optimal for the service provider. Under this system, the service provider charges $K^* = u^* - d^*$ for the expedited service and gives a discount d^* to the non-elite customers to compensate them for the slowdown in their service. For the uniform case, we get

$$R(\alpha) = \lambda M W \frac{\alpha(1-\alpha)\rho}{2(1-\alpha\rho)}.$$

Note that $R(\alpha)/(\lambda c)$ represents the improvement of the revenue for the service provider if she switches from the no-priority system to the concierge system and gets α level participation. It can be shown that the revenue improvement increases with ρ, and is a concave function of α for a given ρ.

The revenue $R(\alpha)$ is maximized at $\alpha^* = (1 - \sqrt{1-\rho})/\rho$. Note that this is independent of M. This yields

$$d^* = d(\alpha^*) = \frac{MW}{2\rho}(1 - \sqrt{1-\rho})^2 \text{ and } u(\alpha^*) = MW(1 - \sqrt{1-\rho}).$$

The optimal revenue is given by $R(\alpha^*) = \lambda d(\alpha^*)$.

For the exponential case, the service provider's revenue is given by

$$R(\alpha) = \frac{\lambda W \alpha \rho}{\theta(1-\alpha\rho)} \cdot \frac{1-\alpha+\ln(\alpha)}{\alpha-1}.$$

This is a unimodal function of α, and its maximum occurs at α^* that has to be computed numerically. The revenue increase $\theta R(\alpha)/(\lambda c)$ as a function of α shows a qualitatively similar behavior as in the uniform case.

It is instructive to study how effective the concierge system is in bringing the waiting cost closer to the waiting cost incurred by MinCost system. To do this we compare the waiting cost gap $C(\text{FIFO}) - C(\text{Concierge})$ with the gap $C(\text{FIFO}) - C(\text{MinCost})$, where $C(\text{Concierge})$ is the total expected waiting cost incurred by all the customers per unit time when the service provider implements the system that maximizes her revenue while keeping the average customers happy (that is, by using the α^* given above). We can think of the ratio

$$\frac{C(\text{FIFO}) - C(\text{Concierge})}{C(\text{FIFO}) - C(\text{MinCost})}$$

as the "efficiency" of the concierge system in bringing the waiting costs closer to the minimum waiting costs. The higher the ratio, the higher the efficiency is. This is not available in closed form, but numerical computation enables us to conclude that the efficiency increases with ρ and ranges from 73–81 percent as the utilization increases from 0 to 1. It is amazing that introduction of a two-priority system brings the waiting costs to within 25 percent of the system with infinite priorities, which is essentially the MinCost system.

The service provider may set a desirable α in several other ways. One possibility is that the service provider simply ignores the impact on the customers and maximizes her revenue (because the customers can't abandon anyway). This reduces to setting $d = 0$ and maximizing $\alpha u(\alpha)$. Surprisingly, in the uniform case it produces the same α^*, but the revenue enhancement is *doubled*. The optimal participation level does change in the exponential case and yields a higher revenue as expected. Another possibility is that the service provider wants to set α such that the average wait for the elite customers is bounded by a given constant, or simply that she wants to keep the elite customer group sufficiently small, say 20 percent, of the total. We have not explored all these possibilities, to save space.

13.4 Concierge Option—Abandonment

So far we have assumed that each customer has only two options: pay K and join the high priority, or join the low priority and receive a discount. In many service environments, though, customers are free to leave the system. The service provider may choose to charge the premium K for the elite customers and give a discount d to the others, but some of the customers may be unhappy with this scheme, as both the options end up increasing their costs. Hence, it is reasonable to assume that some customers may abandon, and we analyze such a scenario in this section. We do not explicitly model where these customers go; they are just no longer part of this service operation.

We now have two probabilities: α is the probability that the customer joins the high-priority (elite) group, and β is the probability that the customer joins the low-priority group. The customers abandon with probability $\delta = 1 - \alpha - \beta$. Thus, the arrival process of the customers is $PP(\lambda(\alpha + \beta))$, and an incoming customer is elite with probability $\alpha/(\alpha + \beta)$ and non-elite with probability $\beta/(\alpha + \beta)$. Recall that W is the expected waiting time in the original system with no priorities. Let W_h^a (W_l^a) be the expected waiting time for the elite (non-elite) customers in the priority system with the abandonment option. We have (using $\rho = \lambda\tau$)

$$W_h^a = W_h^a(\alpha, \beta) = \frac{\lambda(\alpha + \beta)s^2}{2(1 - \alpha\rho)}$$

$$W_l^a = W_l^a(\alpha, \beta) = \frac{\lambda(\alpha + \beta)s^2}{2(1 - (\alpha + \beta)\rho)(1 - \alpha\rho)}.$$

Clearly, if K and d are fixed, that would induce a particular α and β. Here, we ask the question: is there a (K, d) concierge system that can achieve any given probabilities α, β? If there is, we call the pair (α, β) *achievable*. The next theorem answers this question completely.

Theorem 13.7 A pair (α, β) is achievable if $0 \le \alpha + \beta \le 1$ and $\beta \ge \frac{1-\alpha(1+\rho)+\alpha^2\rho^2}{1-\alpha\rho^2}$. It is achieved by setting

$$K(\alpha, \beta) = \frac{m(\alpha)\lambda s^2((1 - \alpha - \beta) + \beta\rho)}{2(1 - \rho)(1 - \alpha\rho)},$$

$$d(\alpha, \beta) = \frac{m(1 - \beta)\lambda s^2(\alpha(\rho(1 - \rho) + (1 - \alpha - \beta)\rho^2) - (1 - \alpha - \beta)))}{2(1 - \rho)(1 - \alpha\rho)(1 - (\alpha + \beta)\rho)}.$$

Proof: Suppose we want to choose a pair (K, d) such that a customer joins the high priority group with probability α, low priority group with probability β, and abandons the system with probability $\delta = 1 - \alpha - \beta$. Then the expected waiting time, $W_h^a(W_l^a)$, in the high (low) priority queue is computed as above. Recall that W is the expected waiting time in the original system with no priorities and no abandonment. Let C be the cost to the ith customer in the original system, C_h be the expected cost in the high-priority queue, and C_l the expected cost in the low-priority queue. Then we have $C = c + H_i W$, $C_h = c + K + H_i W_h^a$, and $C_l = c - d + H_i W_l^a$. First, we consider how to achieve α. We see that the ith customer will join the high-priority queue if $C_h \leq C$; that is, $K \leq H_i(W - W_h^a)$. Substituting for W and W_h^a, we get

$$W - W_h^a = \frac{\lambda s^2(1 - \alpha - \beta(1 - \rho))}{2(1 - \rho)(1 - \alpha\rho)}.$$

Note that $W \geq W_h^a$, always. Thus, inequality $K \leq H_i(W - W_h^a)$ can be achieved if we use the least value of H_i that an elite customer can have, namely, $m(\alpha)$. Hence, we get

$$K = \frac{m(\alpha)\lambda s^2(1 - \alpha - \beta(1 - \rho))}{2(1 - \rho)(1 - \alpha\rho)}.$$

Thus, for a fixed α, β, the above K will induce the correct α.

Next we consider if any β can be achieved. As before, the ith customer will join the low-priority queue if $C_l \leq C$; that is, $d \geq H_i(W_l^a - W)$. Substituting for W and W_l^a we get

$$W_l^a - W = \frac{\lambda s^2(\alpha(\rho(1 - \rho) + \delta\rho^2) - \delta)}{1(1 - \rho)(1 - \alpha\rho)(1 - (\alpha + \beta)\rho)}.$$

Unfortunately, the above difference is not always positive. It is positive if and only if

$$\alpha \geq \frac{1 - \alpha - \beta}{\rho(1 - \rho) + (1 - \alpha - \beta)\rho^2}.$$

This can be rearranged to get the inequality

$$\beta \geq \frac{1 - \alpha(1 + \rho) + \alpha^2\rho^2}{1 - \alpha\rho^2}.$$

Hence, we consider two cases: one in which the inequality above is satisfied and the second in which it is not:

Case 1: In this case, $W_l^a < W$, and the inequality $d \geq H_i(W_l^a - W)$ will be satisfied if we use the smallest value of H_i, namely 0. But this would induce no one to join the low-priority group. Hence, the (α, β) pair cannot be achieved.

Case 2: In this case, $W_l^a \geq W$, and the inequality $d \geq H_i(W_l^a - W)$ will be satisfied if we use the largest H_i the non-elite customer can have, namely, $m(1-\beta)$. As a result, we get

$$d = \frac{m(1-\beta)\lambda s^2(\alpha(\rho(1-\rho)+\delta\rho^2)-\delta)}{2(1-\rho)(1-\alpha\rho)(1-(1-\delta)\rho)}.$$

The constraint $0 \leq \alpha + \beta \leq 1$ is obvious. This proves the theorem. □

Notice that

$$\frac{1-\alpha(1+\rho)+\alpha^2\rho^2}{1-\alpha\rho^2} \geq 0 \;\; \textit{iff} \;\; \alpha \leq \phi(\rho) = \frac{1+\rho-\sqrt{(1+\rho)^2-4\rho^2}}{2\rho^2}.$$

$\phi(\rho)$ is a convex function of ρ that starts at 1 when $\rho = 0$, decreases to 0.75 when ρ increases to 2/3, and then increases to 1 as ρ increases from 2/3 to 1. Consequently, if $\alpha > \phi(\rho)$, any β lower than $1-\alpha$ is achievable. The achievable region is largest when $\rho = 2/3$. We also observed that the proportion of abandoning customers $1-\alpha-\beta$ increases with α and that there exists a threshold value for α above which $\beta = 0$, implying that everyone else abandons.

Note that in the *no abandonment* case, there was only one parameter α, and that fixed the value of $K + d = u(\alpha)$. We therefore had a choice of many K and d combinations. In the *abandonment* case, we have two parameters α and β, and, when they are achievable, they fix the values of $K = K(\alpha, \beta)$ and $d = d(\alpha, \beta)$; that is, we do not have the flexibility of choosing among different K and d values that produce the same α and β. For that reason, we next study how to choose the "optimal" achievable α and β.

13.4.1 Choosing the Optimal α and β

The service provider's revenue per unit time in the original system is λc. The revenue rate in the new system is given by $R(\alpha, \beta) = \lambda c(\alpha+\beta) + \lambda\alpha K(\alpha, \beta) - \lambda\beta d(\alpha, \beta)$. Thus, the service provider maximizes $R(\alpha, \beta)$ subject to

$$\alpha+\beta \leq 1, \;\; \beta \geq \frac{1-\alpha(1+\rho)+\alpha^2\rho^2}{1-\alpha\rho^2}, \text{ and } \alpha, \beta \geq 0.$$

Let α^* and β^* be the solution to the above problem and K^* and d^* the corresponding optimal concierge fees and discounts. We describe some numerical results below. We use $\lambda = 1$, $s^2 = 1$ and $c = 5$ to do the numerical computations. As before, for the uniform case we use $M = 2$, and for the exponential case we use $\theta = 1$. We observed that the optimal premium K charged by the service provider is not that different between the uniform and the exponential cases, implying that the optimal premium is fairly insensitive to the holding cost distribution. We also observed that in all the cases we evaluated, the optimal d is zero. When the service provider charges the optimal premium and offers the optimal discount under the uniform and the exponential cases, no one abandons at extreme values of utilization, and abandonment is highest when the utilization is around 80 percent.

13.5 Correlated Service Times and Waiting Costs

In the development so far we have assumed that the service times $\{S_i, i \geq 1\}$ of the customers are independent of their waiting cost rates, $\{H_i, i \geq 1\}$. In this section, we relax that assumption and instead assume that $\{(S_i, H_i), i \geq 1\}$ is a sequence of i.i.d. bivariate random variables. We assume that $G(\cdot)$ is the marginal distribution of H_i, and τ and s^2 are the marginal first and second moment of S_i. We focus on the abandonment scenario here and, as before, let α be the probability that a customer joins the high-priority queue, and β be the probability that a customer joins the low-priority queue, with $\delta = 1 - \alpha - \beta$ being the probability that the customer abandons the system altogether. Following the notation $h_h(\alpha)$ and $h_l(\alpha)$ of Equations 13.2 and 13.3, we introduce the following notation (using $m(\alpha) = G^{-1}(1 - \alpha)$ as before):

$$\tau_h(\alpha) = \frac{1}{\alpha}\int_{m(\alpha)}^{\infty} E(S_i|H_i = h)g(h)dh, \text{ and}$$
$$\tau_l(\beta) = \frac{1}{\beta}\int_{0}^{m(1-\beta)} E(S_i|H_i = h)g(h)dh.$$

Accordingly, $\tau_h(\alpha)$ is the expected service time of a customer given that he joins the high-priority queue. Similarly, $\tau_l(\beta)$ is the expected service time of a customer given that he joins the low-priority queue. Further, the second moments of the high and low priority customers are given by

$$s_h^2(\alpha) = \frac{1}{\alpha}\int_{m(\alpha)}^{\infty} E(S_i^2|H_i = h)g(h)dh \text{ and}$$
$$s_l^2(\beta) = \frac{1}{\beta}\int_{0}^{m(1-\beta)} E(S_i^2|H_i = h)g(h)dh.$$

We need to compute the appropriate W_l and W_h in a two-priority queuing system where the high-priority customers arrive according to a PP($\lambda\alpha$) and the low-priority customers arrive according to a PP($\lambda\beta$). The first and the second moments of the service time of an arbitrary customer are given by

$$\tau(\alpha, \beta) = \frac{\alpha}{\alpha + \beta}\tau_h(\alpha) + \frac{\beta}{\alpha + \beta}\tau_l(\beta), \text{ and}$$
$$s^2(\alpha, \beta) = \frac{\alpha}{\alpha + \beta}s_h^2(\alpha) + \frac{\beta}{\alpha + \beta}s_l^2(\beta).$$

Hence, the expected waiting times of the high- and low-priority customers in steady state are given by

$$W_h(\alpha, \beta) = \frac{\lambda(\alpha + \beta)s^2(\alpha, \beta)}{2(1 - \lambda\alpha\tau_h(\alpha))}, \text{ and}$$
$$W_l(\alpha, \beta) = \frac{\lambda(\alpha + \beta)s^2(\alpha, \beta)}{2(1 - \lambda(\alpha + \beta)\tau(\alpha, \beta))(1 - \lambda\alpha\tau_h(\alpha))}.$$

The next theorem is the equivalent of Theorem 13.7, and we present it without providing a detailed proof.

Theorem 13.8 The pair (α, β) is achievable if $0 \le \alpha + \beta \le 1$, and $W_l(\alpha, \beta) \ge W$. It is achieved by using $d(\alpha, \beta) = m(1 - \beta)[W_l(\alpha, \beta) - W]$ and $K(\alpha, \beta) = m(\alpha)[W - W_h(\alpha, \beta)]$. The concierge system $(K(\alpha, \beta), d(\alpha, \beta))$ will induce $1 - \alpha - \beta$ fraction of customers to abandon, α fraction of customers to join the elite group, and β fraction to join the non-elite group. □

The revenue to the service provider is $R(\alpha, \beta) = \lambda c(\alpha + \beta) + \lambda\alpha K(\alpha, \beta) - \lambda\beta d(\alpha, \beta)$, and the service provider chooses the α^* and β^* that maximize this revenue. In the system with no priorities, the revenue is λc. Thus, if $R(\alpha^*, \beta^*) > \lambda c$, the service provider will adopt the concierge system; otherwise, she won't.

We illustrate with a concrete example below. For ease of analysis, we focus on the uniform case here. Let $\{X_i, i \ge 1\}$ be a sequence of i.i.d. non-negative random variables, and $\{H_i, i \ge 1\}$ be i.i.d. $U(0, M)$ random variables, independent of the $\{X_i, i \ge 1\}$. We consider two models of dependence: the positive model (so-called because the holding cost and the service times are positively correlated in this model) and the negative model (so-called because the holding cost and the service times are positively correlated in this model). We describe each model separately below.

Positive Correlation. The service time of the ith customer is given by $S_i = H_i X_i$. Thus, we have

$$E(S_i) = \tau = E(H_i)E(X_i) = E(X_i)M/2,$$

$$E(S_i^2) = s^2 = E(H_i^2)E(X_i^2) = E(X_i^2)M^2/3,$$

$$\text{Var}(S_i) = \text{Var}(H_i)\text{Var}(X_i) + \text{Var}(H_i)E(X_i)^2 + \text{Var}(X_i)E(H_i)^2$$
$$= \text{Var}(X_i)M^2/3 + E(X_i^2)M^2/12, \text{ and}$$

$$\text{Cov}(H_i, S_i) = \text{Var}(H_i)E(X_i) = E(X_i)M^2/12.$$

Further, we have

$$W_h(\alpha,\beta) = \frac{\lambda s^2(1+\beta^3-(1-\alpha)^3)}{(1-\rho\alpha(2-\alpha))}, \text{ and}$$

$$W_l(\alpha,\beta) = \frac{W_h(\alpha,\beta)}{1-\rho(\beta^2+\alpha(2-\alpha))}.$$

Negative Correlation. Here, the service time of the ith customer is given by $S_i = (M - H_i)X_i$. The expressions for $E(S_i)$, $E(S_i^2)$ and $\mathrm{Var}(S_i)$ remain the same as in the positive case, however, we get $\mathrm{Cov}(H_i, S_i) = -E(X_i)M^2/12$. The expected waiting times of the high and low priority customers are now given by

$$W_h(\alpha,\beta) = \frac{\lambda s^2(1+\alpha^3-(1-\beta)^3)}{2(1-\rho\alpha^2)}, \text{ and}$$

$$W_l(\alpha,\beta) = \frac{W_h(\alpha,\beta)}{1-\rho(\alpha^2+\beta(2-\beta))}.$$

We tabulated numerical results for these two dependency models using $\lambda = 1$, $M = 2$, and $s^2 = 1$ and varying ρ from .01 to .99 (this sets the values of $E(X)$ and $E(X^2)$). The K^* values in the positive case are slightly higher than those in the negative case, except when ρ is very close to 1. The optimal discount d^* is zero in the positive case, consistent with the independent case. However, it is nonzero (although very small) for the negative case. The positive dependence case seems more likely in practice (patients with higher waiting costs need longer service times); hence, it is more common for the service providers to give no discount. The optimal revenues for the service provider under the two cases are almost the same. However, customer behavior is different between these two models. The abandonment rate is larger in the positive dependence model, whereas the elite participation level is larger for the negative dependence model.

13.6 MDVIP Adoption

Our analytical results clearly demonstrate that introducing concierge medicine has the potential to significantly increase the benefits realized by all parties. The key ingredient to these results is the variance in the costs that consumers attribute to the time waiting before receiving service. In this section, we would like to test whether these results are validated in the real world by analyzing the data associated with adoption of the MDVIP service across the country.

MDVIP was founded in 2000 and is the national leader of personalized, preventive healthcare, what we have been discussing as concierge medicine. Currently adopted by approximately 400 doctors across the country, this service charges patients an annual fee of $1500–$1800 and guarantees them the ability to see their doctors on short notice with same-day or next-day appointments. Further, the patients receive a comprehensive health checkup annually, the ability to communicate with their doctor by email, and a host of other benefits. The fee structure and priority appointments make MDVIP a perfect example of a concierge option in a service offering. Although the fees the MDVIP doctors charge are on a per-year basis, it is not hard to imagine that a patient might convert that cost into a per-visit cost while evaluating whether or not he/she should enroll in this service.

Using data on where MDVIP doctors are located, we can investigate how the adoption is affected by the heterogeneity of customer waiting costs. Needless to say, the costs that customers attribute to waiting are not easily available, but their income and age are good proxies. A customer with a large income is apt to attribute a large hourly cost to the time she spends waiting for service because she sees significant costs associated with lost productive time. An older customer is also apt to attribute a higher cost to waiting time because she is probably more worried about her health and the impact of the delay on the eventual outcome and thus is more likely to attribute a higher cost to the waiting time. Based on the arguments, we formulate the following hypotheses:

Hypothesis 1: Concierge medicine is more likely to be adopted in areas where people have higher incomes.

Hypothesis 2: Concierge medicine is more likely to be adopted in areas where older people live.

Hypothesis 3: Concierge medicine is more likely to be adopted in areas where the variance in incomes is larger.

13.6.1 The Data

At the time we gathered the data, 421 doctors were offering the concierge option located in 260 unique zip codes. For each of these zip codes, we used the website www.zipskinny.com and obtained data on the income distribution, population size, and median age of the population. This data is from the 2000 census, which is the most recent census for which this data is available. We were not able to obtain information for nine of the zip codes and therefore dropped them from our analysis, resulting in 251 remaining zip codes. The median income for these zip codes ranged from $14,095 to $113,788, and the median age ranged from 21.2 years to 63.9 years. The zip code with the largest median income was 20817, covering the area of Bethesda, Maryland; whereas the zip code with the lowest median income was 02903, representing the area of Providence, Rhode Island. The zip code with the highest median age was 33437, representing the area of Boynton Beach, Florida, whereas the zip code with lowest median age was 78705, covering the area of Austin, Texas. The zip code with the smallest population (numbering only 1528) was 02462, covering the area of Newton Lower Falls, Massachusetts. The zip code with the largest population (numbering 77,666) was 94533, covering the area of Fairfield, California. Using the data on income distribution, we were able to compute the variance of income within a zip code. We used the resulting data to test the significance of our hypotheses.

Recall Hypothesis 1 that postulated that concierge medicine is more likely to be adopted in areas where people have higher incomes. To test this hypothesis, we compiled the median incomes of the 251 zip codes in which concierge medicine has been adopted. These values had a mean of 59,347 and a standard deviation of 20,425. To establish the significance of Hypothesis 1, we compared this distribution with the overall US median income of 41,994, resulting in a t-statistic of 13.46 with a p-value close to zero. Thus, we are able to demonstrate, with a high level of confidence, that Hypothesis 1 holds.

Next, we tested Hypothesis 2 that postulated that concierge medicine is more likely to be adopted in areas where older people live. For this purpose, we tabulated the median age in the 251 zip codes where concierge medicine has been adopted. These median values had an average of 37.8 and a standard deviation of 5.48. Comparing this distribution with the overall US median age of 35.3 results in a t-statistic of 7.27 with a resulting p-value of almost zero. Thus, we conclude that Hypothesis 2 also holds with a high degree of confidence.

Hypothesis 3 centers on the role of income variance in the adoption of concierge medicine. The standard deviation in income across the country is \$46,068, whereas the income in the 251 zip codes where concierge medicine is available ranged from \$41,790 to \$147,422 with a mean of \$90,935 and standard deviation of \$23,179. A t-test (resulting in a t-statistic of 30.7) showed that this difference is significant with a p-value of almost zero. Thus, we are able to conclude, with a high degree of confidence, that concierge medicine is more likely to be adopted in areas where the income variance is larger.

13.6.2 Abandonment Model Applied to MDVIP Data

In this section, we apply the queuing model, with the option of customer abandonment as in Section 13.4, to the zip code areas with and without concierge medicine. The computations are based on the assumption that the mean service time is 1/3 of an hour (based on the customary 20-minute appointment slots). We assume that the coefficient of variation of service time is 1 and that the cost per visit to the doctor is \$60. We use income distribution as a proxy for the waiting cost rate distribution. Specifically, if the income of a patient is x dollars per year, we assume that his/her waiting cost rate is $x/2000$ dollars per hour. We do not have a good method of accounting for the influence of age or health condition on the waiting cost rate, so we ignore it in this analysis—although it seems reasonable to assume that the higher the age, the higher the waiting cost rate (because older patients have more serious illnesses).

13.6.2.1 Modeling Heterogeneous Waiting Costs

Although the waiting costs of customers can follow any distribution, it is useful to identify a specific distribution to achieve our research objectives. It is conceivable that the distribution will depend on the service offering and the customers that avail themselves of it. The appropriate waiting cost distribution can be constructed using tools such as customer surveys or other marketing studies, but we will work with the assumption that a patient's income is a good proxy for his waiting cost. The income data is readily available from census surveys, so determining the waiting cost distributions will be relatively easy. Further, existing research on income distribution has demonstrated, rather convincingly, that a Burr (also called Singh-Maddala) distribution accurately captures the variability in income (Gavirneni and Kulkarni, 2016). We present four cases of income distribution (shown in Figure 13.1), which we will use as the basis for our analysis. The first two cases are based on the overall US income and the income distribution averaged across the zip codes where MDVIP service was adopted. The other distributions are (i) a ZIP code in which the income is very high and (ii) a ZIP code in which the income is very low. Figure 13.1 shows the four cumulative functions corresponding to these income distributions. We will use them to illustrate the effectiveness of the proposed concierge strategies. The Burr distribution over $[0, \infty)$ is defined

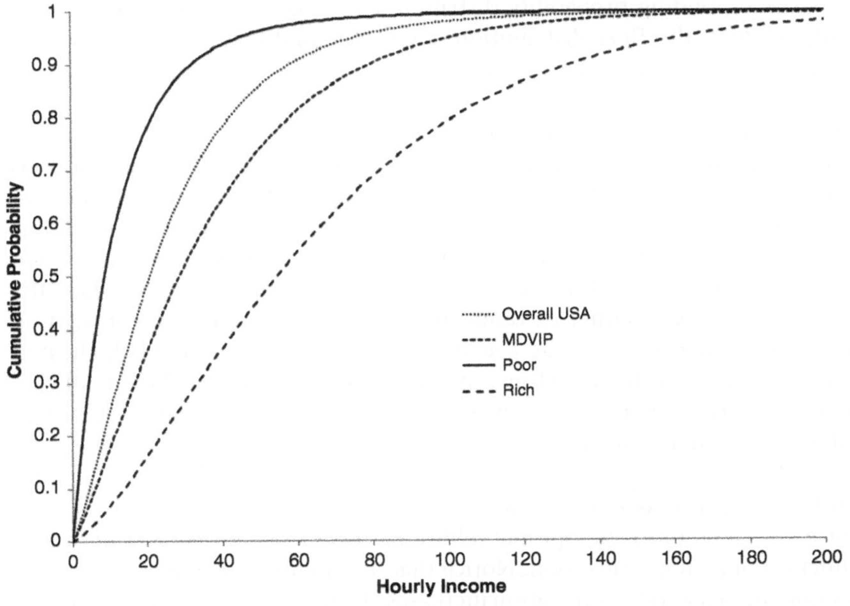

Figure 13.1 Cumulative distribution of incomes in overall U.S., MDVIP, one rich ZIP code and one poor ZIP code areas.

Table 13.1 Burr distribution parameters and the mean and standard deviations of income distributions for various constituencies

Constituency	*a*	*k*	*d*	Mean ($/hr)	Std. Dev. ($/hr)
Overall USA	91.73	5.27	1.33	27.74	24.96
MDVIP ZIP Codes	291.38	12.88	1.25	37.48	32.15
Poor ZIP Code	52.30	4.97	1.07	13.97	16.50
Rich ZIP Code	1205.00	48.36	1.37	66.23	49.58

with parameters $a > 0$, $d > 0$ and $k > 0$ as follows:

$$G(x) = 1 - (1 + (x/a)^d)^{-k}, \quad x \geq 0.$$

See Tadikamalla (1980). Here, a is a scale parameter, in the sense that if X has a Burr distribution with parameters a, d, and K, then cX has a Burr distribution with parameters ca, d, and k. The rth moment of this distribution is finite if $r < kd$ and is given by $a^r kB(k - r/d, 1 + r/d)$, where $B(\cdot, \cdot)$ is the beta function. The mode is $a((d-1)/(kd+1))^{1/d}$ and the median is $2(2^{1/k} - 1)^{1/d}$. The parameters of the best-fitting Burr distributions are given in Table 13.1.

The corresponding probability distributions are given in Figure 13.2. As is clearly evident, the Burr distribution is versatile and able to capture a wide variety of distributions of hourly income.

13.6.2.2 Participation in Concierge Medicine

Figure 13.3 shows the achievable pairs $(\alpha, \alpha + \delta)$ for the four Burr distributions shown in Figure 13.1. For each distribution, the distance between the two curves signifies the proportion of patients who decide to abandon the service provider. Notice that the abandonment fraction is highest when utilization is close to 80 percent. It is worth noting that no one abandons when the utilization is close to either extreme. The percentage of patients who sign up for concierge medicine increases as the utilization increases and is highest at 35 to 45 percent. At the same time, the proportion of patients who do not sign up for concierge medicine and yet stay with the healthcare practice decreases as the utilization increases.

13.6.2.3 Impact of Concierge Medicine

Figure 13.4 illustrates the optimal additional revenues and concierge fees as a function of system utilization. Notice that, for all four income distributions, they both increase as the utilization increases. The concierge fees and additional revenues are larger (by about 10 to 15%) for the MDVIP areas, as compared with the overall US.

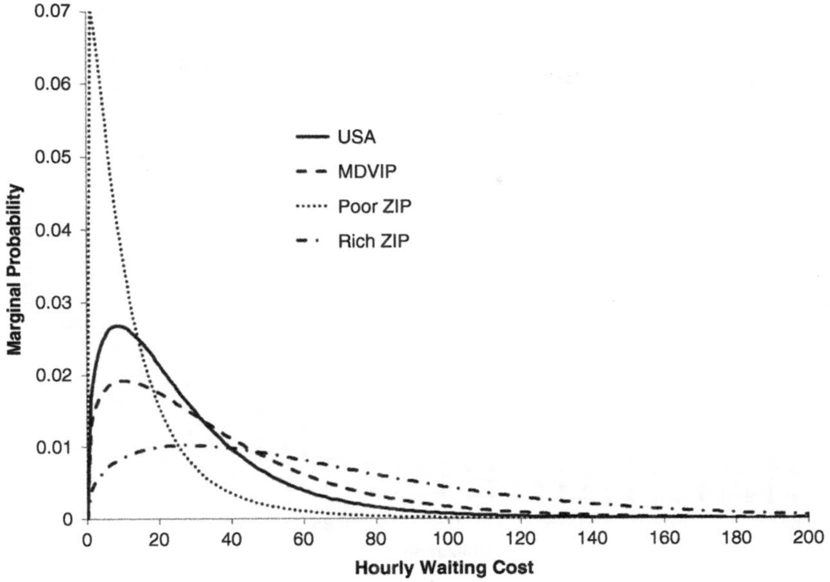

Figure 13.2 The probability distribution functions determined by fitting the Burr distribution to incomes from the various constituencies.

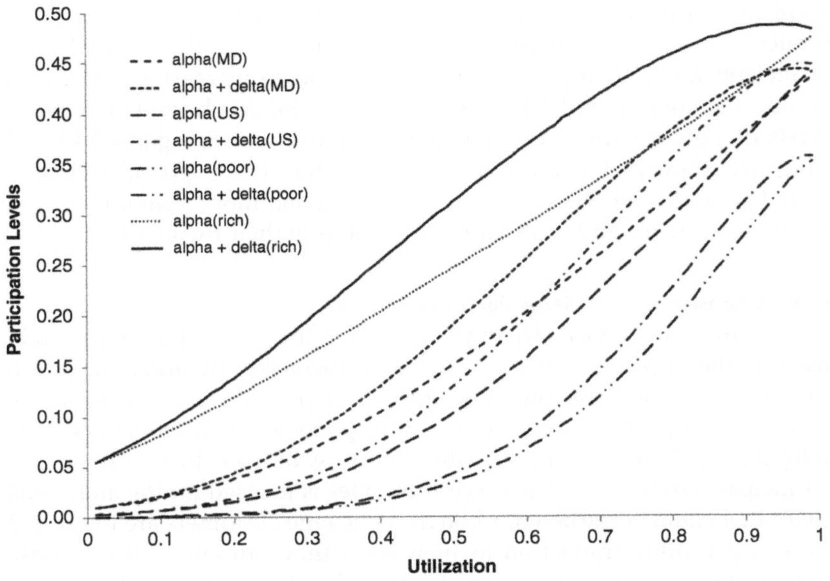

Figure 13.3 The achievable pairs as a function of utilization for the four waiting cost distributions shown in Figure 13.1.

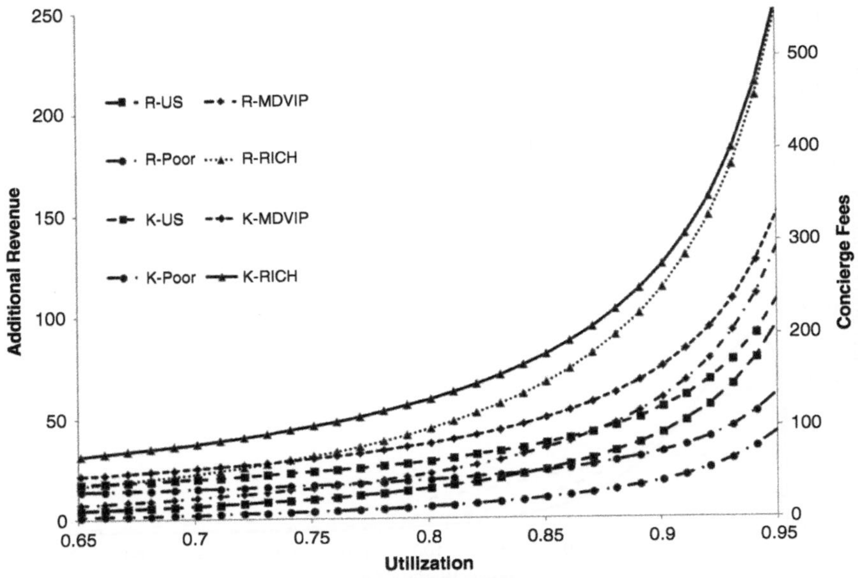

Figure 13.4 Optimal concierge fees and the additional revenues as a function of utilization for the four waiting cost distributions shown in Figure 13.1.

Figure 13.5 shows the reduction in sum of concierge fees and waiting cost that concierge customers experience for the four income distributions. Observe that concierge medicine is more beneficial (in a convex increasing manner) to concierge customers as utilization increases. Further, this benefit is larger in the MDVIP zip code areas, as compared to the overall US. Figures 13.4 and 13.5 together show that as utilization increases, the service provider charges more and garners increasing additional revenues, and more customers enroll in concierge medicine and enjoy larger reductions in their total cost.

13.6.2.4 Choosing the Concierge Participation Level

Ultimately, the service provider must determine the parameters that should be used in the implementation of concierge medicine. In order to inform the decision, we focus on the concierge participation level, which, as we have shown before, has a one-to-one correspondence with concierge fees. In determining these parameters, attention must be paid to the impact on two principal stakeholders. The service provider is focused on the additional revenues that could be garnered, while the concierge customers are interested in the surplus utility (reduction in their cost) they can enjoy. We tabulate these two measures of performance for the *abandonment* cases for system utilizations of 0.85 and 0.95.

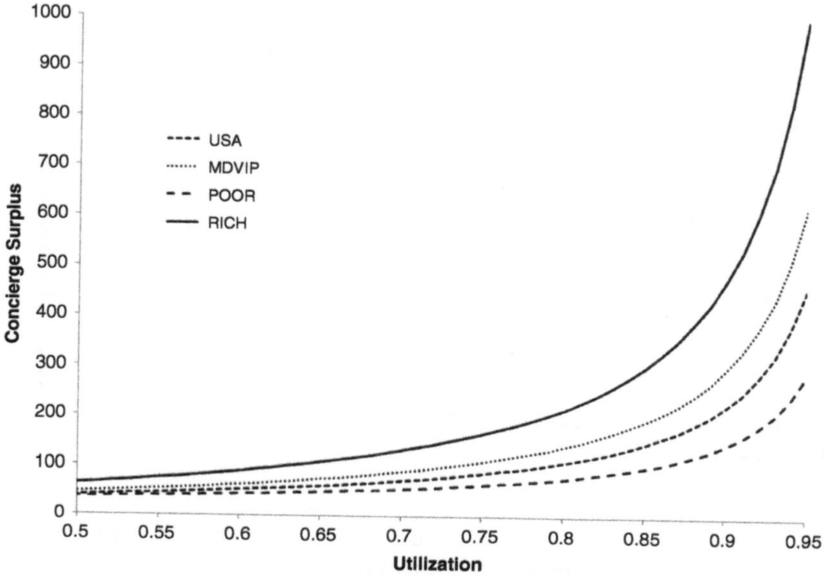

Figure 13.5 Reduction in total cost realized by the concierge customers as a function of utilization for the four waiting cost distributions shown in Figure 13.1.

Figures 13.6 and 13.7 illustrate the additional service provider revenues and concierge customer surplus for the *abandonment* case for the utilizations of 0.85 and 0.95, respectively. Observe that the additional revenues first increase and then decrease with the maximum being achieved around the 30 percent participation level, while the concierge customer surplus is consistently increasing. It seems reasonable to choose the concierge participation level in the range 25–35 percent and select the appropriate concierge fees that achieve this participation level.

13.7 Research Opportunities

We modeled the introduction of a concierge medical practice and evaluated its impact on the patients, the healthcare provider, and society. We observed that the introduction of concierge medicine has the ability to reduce, by as much as 73 percent, inefficiency in the system. Further, we showed that the proposed strategies can be beneficial to everyone if the service provider and the elite customers are willing to share (possibly via a discount) some of their benefits with the non-elite customers. The Pareto-improving region of the parameter space is quite large, and it will not be difficult to find a parameter combination that would be practical to implement. To complement these analytical results

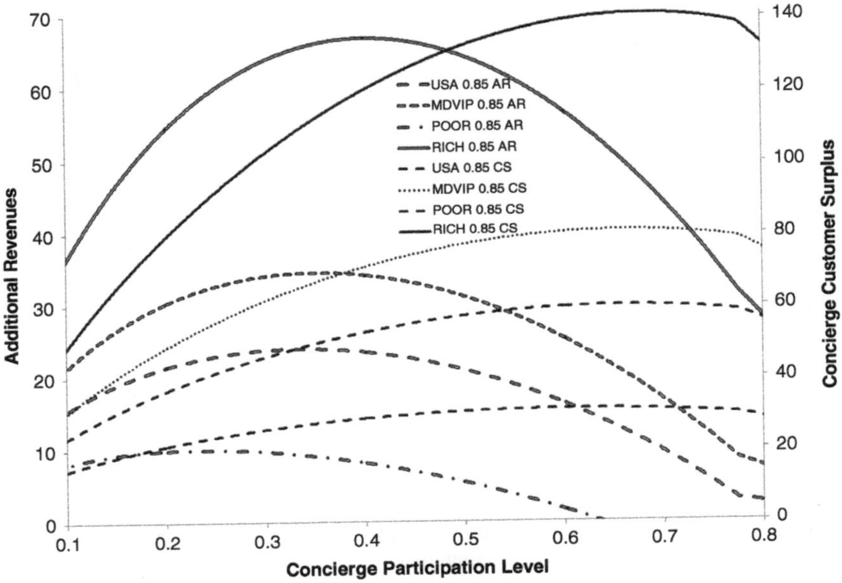

Figure 13.6 Service provider additional revenues and concierge customers' surplus as a function of the concierge participation level for the four waiting cost distributions shown in Figure 13.1. Abandonment is allowed and utilization = 0.85.

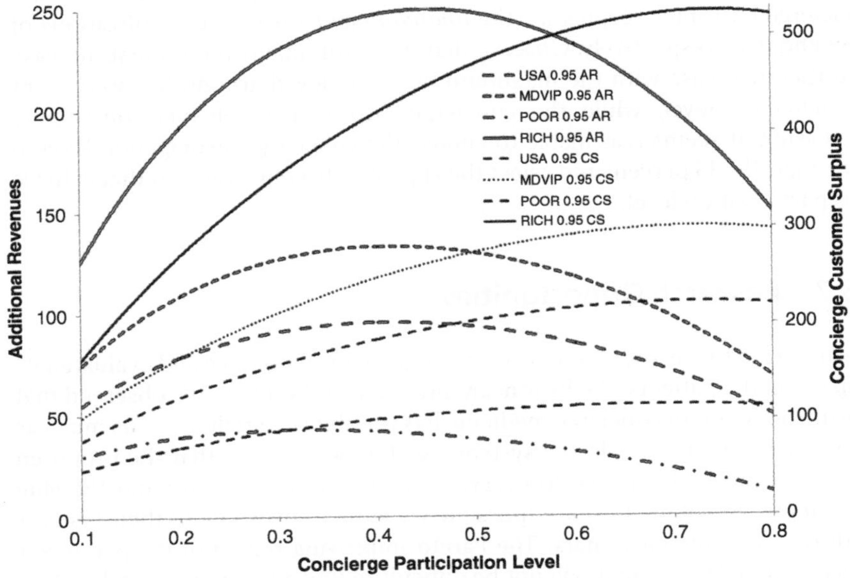

Figure 13.7 Service provider additional revenues and concierge customers' surplus as a function of the concierge participation level for the four waiting cost distributions shown in Figure 13.1. Abandonment is allowed and utilization = 0.95.

with a real-world perspective, we collected data on the adoption of the MDVIP service across the US and observed that it has been adopted in areas where the median incomes are larger, people are older, and the variance in the income is larger. Our computational study showed that by choosing these regions doctors are able to increase their revenues by about 10–14 percent. There are a number of directions for future research.

Three or More Levels of Customer Segmentation: We focused entirely on the setting in which there were only two levels (concierge and non-concierge) of customer segmentation. Although we established that the presence of two segments is able to alleviate 70–75 percent of the inefficiency in the system, we should acknowledge that there is a significant amount of inefficiency still to be alleviated. This can be done by introducing three (e.g., platinum, gold, silver) or more levels of customer segmentation. This will result in more complex queuing models that will need to be carefully analyzed.

Impact of Concierge Medicine on Secondary Care: Technically speaking, concierge medicine is implemented at the primary care level, but it can have an impact on secondary level care as well. In the US healthcare system, in order to receive secondary level care, patients must go through their primary care physicians. If the patient is a concierge patient, the primary care physician carefully monitors the quality and quantity of care the patient is receiving at the secondary care facility. This results in an increase in the load seen by the secondary care provider, and they must be appropriately prepared for it.

Waiting Time Distribution: We focus on the fact that a patient enrolls in concierge medicine with the hope that she will see a significant reduction in average waiting time. Though that may be true for some patients, it is also likely that the enrollment is more motivated by the reduction in worst-case waiting time they would experience. This can be incorporated into the model by associating a cost with a percentile (say 95%) of waiting time distribution. This could be in place of or in addition to the cost associated with average waiting time. The resulting optimization problem would be more complex to analyze, but would be more representative of the real world.

Modeling the Patient Panel: We modeled the queuing system as one in which patients are from an infinite-sized population and each patient seeks service only once. In reality, a primary care physician has a finite-sized panel (ranging from 300 to 2000) from which customers are drawn and often require service more than once. If the patient is enrolled in concierge medicine, they would be treated with high priority at each arrival. That would, of course, result in an increased load on the system. Further, recognizing the higher priority they receive, concierge patients may also seek service more frequently than they would have otherwise. In order to get a more accurate picture of the impact of concierge medicine, these intricacies must be appropriately modeled and analyzed.

References

Adiri, I. and U. Yechiali. (1974). Optimal Priority-Purchasing and Pricing Decisions in Nonmonopoly and Monopoly Queues, *Operations Research*, 22, 1051–1066.

Alexander, G.C., J. Kurlander, and M.K. Wynia. (2005). Physicians in Retainer ("Concierge") Practice—A National Survey of Physician, Patient, and Practice Characteristics, *J. Gen. Intern. Med.*, 20, 1079–1083.

Alperstein, A. (1988). Optimal Pricing Policy for the Service Facility Offering a Set of Priority Prices, *Management Science*, 34, 666–671.

Balachandran, K.R. (1972). Purchasing Priorities in Queues, *Management Science*, 18, 319–326.

Bodenheimer, T. and H.H. Pham. (2010). Primary Care: Current Problems and Proposed Solutions, *Health Affairs*, 29, 799–805.

Carnahan, S.J. (2006). Does Concierge Medicine Promote Health Care Choice, or is it A Barrier to Access? *Stanford Law & Policy Review*, 17, 121–164.

Forrest, C.B. (2003). Primary care gatekeeping and referrals: effective filter or failed experiment? *BMJ*, 326, 692–695.

Gavirneni, S., V.G. Kulkarni, A. Manikas, and A. Karageorge. (2013). Concierge Medicine: Adoption, Design, and Management, *Proceedings of the 2013 Winter Simulation Conference*, 2340-2349.

Gavirneni, S. and V.G. Kulkarni. (2014). Concierge Medicine: Applying Rational Economics to Health Care Queuing, *Cornell Hospitality Quarterly*, 55, 314–325.

Gavirneni, S. and V.G. Kulkarni. (2016). Self-Selecting Priority Queues with Burr Distributed Waiting Costs, *Production and Operations Management*, 25, 979–992.

Glazer, A. and R. Hassin. (1986). Stable Priority Purchasing in Queues, *Operations Research Letters*, 4, 285–288.

Gross, D. and C.M. Harris (1985). *Fundamentals of Queuing Theory*, Second Edition, Wiley, New York.

Hassin, R. and M. Haviv. (2012). To Queue or Not to Queue: Equilibrium Behavior in Queuing Systems. Kluwer Academic Publishers, The Netherlands.

Kima, Y.J. and M.V. Mannino. (2003). Optimal incentive-compatible pricing for M/G/1 queues, *Operations Research Letters*, 31, 459–461.

Kleinrock, L. (1967). Optimum Bribing for Queue Position, *Operations Research*, 15, 304–318.

Lauer, F. and B.A. Neil. (2009). Concierge Medicine: Should Financial Considerations Prevail Over Ethical and Moral Concerns? *Journal of Business & Economics Research*, 7, 9–14.

Marchand, M. G. (1974). Priority Pricing, *Management Science*, 20, 1131–1140.

Mendelson, H. and S. Whang. (1990). Optimal Incentive-Compatible Priority Pricing for the M/M/1 Queue, *Operations Research*, 38, 870–883.

Mendelson, H. and U. Yechiali. (1981). Controlling the GI/M/ 1 Queue by Conditional Acceptance of Customers, *Eur. J. Opnl. Res.*, 7, 77–85.

Murray, M. and D.M. Berwick. (2003) Advanced Access: Reducing Waiting and Delays in Primary Care, *JAMA*, 289, 1035–1040.

Naor, P. (1969). On Regulation of Queue Size by Levying Tolls, *Econometrica*, 37, 15–24.

O'Brien, E. (2013). Why concierge medicine will get bigger. MarketWatch.com, http://www.marketwatch.com, (accessed May 13, 2013).

Petterson, S.M., W.R. Liaw, R.L. Phillips, D.L. Rabin, D.S. Meyers, and A.W. Bazemore. (2012). Projecting US Primary Care Physician Workforce Needs: 2010-2025, *Annals of Family Medicine*, 10, 503–509.

Priddy, M. (2013). AAPP president's update. *American Academy of Private Physicians*, www.aapp.org, (accessed April 2014).

Rao, S. and E.R. Peterson. (1998). Optimal Pricing of Priority Services, *Operations Research*, 46, 46–56.

Silva, C. (2010). Concierge Medicine: a mere blip on Medicare radar, *American Medical News*, amednews.com, (accessed April 23, 2014).

Stidham, S. (1978). Socially and Individually Optimal Control of Arrivals to a G/M/1 Queue, *Management Science*, 24, 1598–1610.

Stidham, S. (2009). *Optimal Design of Queuing Systems*, CRC press, NY.

Tadikamalla, P. R. (1980). A Look at the Burr and Related Distributions, *International Statistical Review/Revue Internationale de Statistique*, 48, 337–344.

Yechiali, U. (1972). Customers' Optimal Joining Rules for the GI/M/s Queue, *Management Science*, 18, 434–448.

14

Markov Decision Processes

Alan Scheller-Wolf

Carnegie Mellon University

14.1 Introduction

If we were to create an idealized analytical tool to assist in healthcare decision-making, we would be hard pressed—at first glance at least—to devise a tool superior to Markov Decision Processes (MDPs). MDPs are *particularly* well-suited for the decisions that need to be made within healthcare when there is (are):

- A high degree of uncertainty, which is at least partially resolved over time, possibly in response to actions the decision-maker takes (i.e., a diagnosis arrived at after a series of tests).
- A well-defined objective or objectives, such as maximizing a patient's longterm health.
- A fundamentally sequential nature; in other words, the decision-maker usually has the ability to select from a series of actions (tests, treatments, medicines, procedures) over time in response to different signals received from the patient, in order to pursue the objective.
- Expectations about *future* signals and actions. Crucially, when choosing an action in the present, the decision-maker must also consider issues such as her future budget, the future possible course of the condition, future potential treatments in response to the future course of the condition, and/or future side effects of current or future treatments.

If we were to get a little greedy, we might design this idealized tool to not only be able to provide the desired course of action (and reaction) to the evolution of the patient or system, but also to have the capability to generate insights into the fundamental rules governing the underlying system (or malady). Once again, this maps quite nicely to the different sorts of results that analysis of an MDP can produce: optimal actions for any given state of the process, structural

Handbook of Healthcare Analytics: Theoretical Minimum for Conducting 21st Century Research on Healthcare Operations, First Edition. Edited by Tinglong Dai and Sridhar Tayur.

results related to the optimal policy, *and* a sensitivity analysis of the importance of different factors to the overall resolution.

It is possibly for these reasons—and the remarkable fit that MDPs have with the needs of healthcare decision makers—that such a flowering of research has been built upon the MDP framework. Over the past decade or so, several surveys or tutorials have written about the application of MDPs to the healthcare field (Schaefer et al., 2004; Alagoz et al., 2010; Steimle and Denton, 2017), along with applications of MDP methodology to problems as diverse as treatment decisions for aortic aneurysms (Mattila et al., 2016), organ transplantation (Alagoz et al., 2004, 2007a,b; Sandikci et al., 2008), cancer treatment (Maillart et al., 2008; Chhatwal et al., 2010; Ayer et al., 2012; Ayvaci et al., 2012; Zhang et al., 2012), chronic disease management(Lee et al., 2008; Shechter et al., 2008; Denton et al., 2009; Kurt et al., 2011; Mason et al., 2014; Zhang and Denton, 2015; Kazemian et al., 2016), guiding steerable needles in surgery (Alterovitz et al., 2008; Sun and Alterovitz, 2014), EMS vehicle dispatching (Maxwell et al., 2010; McLay and Mayorga, 2013a,b; Chong et al., 2016), and hospital operations (Kreke et al., 2008; Helm et al., 2011; Saghafian et al., 2014).

Unfortunately, all is not as well as it might seem *at first glance*: Standard MDPs, despite their wide application and relative success, suffer from several acute shortcomings that can hinder, or even prevent, their employment in certain healthcare domains. It turns out that some of an MDP's greatest strengths can also be significant weaknesses:

- An MDP makes a decision based on observing the condition of the patient or the current state of the system. But sometimes this condition or state can only be ascertained with a significant amount of uncertainty, or, in other words, the true state is only *partially observable*.
- Likewise, in order to be useful, an MDP must be able to map actions to their probable effects:
  - Yet, there may not be enough data to meaningfully evaluate some actions, or again, at least not without significant uncertainty. In such a situation, we may strive to make decisions that will be *robust* to such uncertainty or that can *adapt* as more information is revealed.
  - On the other hand, there may be *too much* information—so much, in fact, that there is little hope of processing it in order to arrive at the best course of action. In this case, we may seek a solution that is *approximately* optimal, and that can be arrived at with a reasonable amount of time and effort.
- Finally, an MDP may produce an optimal policy that is so complex as to be opaque to the practitioner and meaningless to the patient, undermining the trust of both. So we may seek to *constrain* our solutions, to ensure that they are intuitive, yet still near-optimal.

Not surprisingly, researchers have addressed all of these issues, solving some partially and others more fully. Thus, after introducing the basics of MDP modeling through two motivating examples in Section 14.2, we will touch upon the sorts of results that may be obtained using MDPs in Section 14.3. In Section 14.4, we will then discuss how MDPs are being modified and extended, making them even more useful within the field of healthcare operations. In Section 14.5, we look forward to promising future directions and conclude in Section 14.6 with suggestions for further reading.

14.2 Modeling

In this section, we present the fundamental elements of an MDP model—time increments, problem horizon, state space, transition probabilities, actions, and objectives—within the context of two motivating examples from the literature. We will also briefly discuss standard solution techniques.

Motivating Examples: A common healthcare decision modeled with an MDP concerns when to initiate a one-shot treatment or intervention, for instance, when to engage in liver transplantation (Alagoz et al., 2007a) or when to surgically treat an abdominal aortic aneurysm (Mattila et al., 2016). These can be seen as *stopping time* problems: once the decision is made to initiate the treatment (or stop the evolution of the condition), the problem is concluded. We will focus on Alagoz et al. (2007a) below. A good example of a nonstopping time MDP is Chong et al. (2016), in which the authors model emergency medical services (EMS) vehicle dispatching within a larger fleet optimization problem.

Time Increments—Discrete versus Continuous Time: One of the very first modeling decisions that must be made is whether to treat time as a series of discrete periods or as a continuum. Discrete time problems tend to be significantly more tractable, particularly when time must be taken into account when making decisions (for example, patient age is often a factor in cancer treatment decisions, as in Zhang et al. 2012).

With respect to our motivating examples, Alagoz et al. (2007a) is naturally a discrete time model, with organs potentially being offered to the patient each period (i.e., each day). In contrast, Chong et al. (2016) is by nature a continuous time model, as emergency calls occur randomly over time. Nevertheless, since all inter-event times are exponentially distributed, the problem in Chong et al. (2016) can be transformed, via *uniformization* (Lippman, 1975), into an equivalent discrete time formulation. This is a common technique, applicable when all inter-event times are exponential and the maximum transition rate out of any state can be bounded.

In some problems, uniformization cannot be undertaken because the transition rates may be unbounded in certain states, but the authors may still want to transition from continuous to discrete time. In these cases, the transition rates in the unbounded states are often truncated. Saghafian et al. (2014) provides one example; they actually analyzed a *sequence* of bounding systems and proved that the optimal policy for this sequence of systems (each of which *can* be uniformized) converges to that of the original system.

Problem Horizon: MDP problems can be modeled over either a finite or infinite horizon. Sometimes the line between these two models is indistinct: For example, Alagoz et al. (2007a) utilized an infinite horizon model, but all patients eventually transitioned into an absorbing state (either transplantation or death), so although the time until transition can in principle be unbounded, the system will be absorbed in finite time with probability one. Nevertheless, because a patient could be on the wait list for a very large number of periods (e.g., each period could be a day, and the time on the list could be several years), an infinite horizon model is appropriate. In other situations—for example, cancer modeling problems in which there are annual exams (e.g., Ayvaci et al., 2012) and when age might play an explicit role in the decision process—a finite horizon model might explicitly be demanded. In such a case, we will denote the finite horizon length by T.

In still other cases, such as Chong et al. (2016), a nonterminating infinite horizon model may be utilized. This is indicated when it is appropriate (or desirable) to assume *time stationarity*; that is, at all times in the problem horizon, the behavior of the system is independent of any time index. Strictly speaking, this may not be true, as in Chong et al. (2016) time-of-day could reasonably be assumed to influence the rate at which emergency calls arrive or the time it may take to respond to a call, due to traffic. Assuming stationarity may greatly simplify the analysis and may be an acceptable approximation, for example, for service models focusing on times of anticipated peak load.

State: The state must contain all changeable information needed to make decisions within the model. For example, test results, age, patient census, or vehicle location are each elements that might be included. Other *static* factors may also be important for the decision-making process (such as patient gender in diabetes treatment decisions, see Kurt et al. 2011, or blood type for transplant patients, as in Alagoz et al. 2007a); these are usually incorporated by having separate models for patients of these different "types." State may be discrete or continuous. Arguably we live within a discrete world, so everything from test results to locations can be discretized, which is often convenient. But there are problems, such as *partially observable Markov decision processes* (POMDPs, discussed below), for which a continuous state space is essential.

Both Alagoz et al. (2007a) and Chong et al. (2016) have discrete state spaces. The former contains information about the patient and the quality of any organ offered in a period. The latter contains two different types of EMS vehicles; the state tracks the number of vehicles from each class that are currently on a call. In general, we will denote the state at time t by $s_t \in S_t$, where S_t is the state space (which may, in general, vary with time).

Actions: In any state s_t the decision-maker can choose an action $a_t(s_t)$ from a set of feasible actions, $A_t(s_t)$; the feasible actions may depend on the state and the period. In Alagoz et al. (2007a) the possible actions are accept a transplant of an offered cadaveric liver, initiate a living-donor transplant, or wait until the next period. In Chong et al. (2016), the action is to determine whether to send an advanced life support (ALS) vehicle to a low-urgency call if there are no basic life support (BLS) vehicles available or to redirect (drop) the call. (Rules for responding to urgent calls, or non-urgent calls when a BLS vehicle is available, are fixed.)

In a non-uniformized continuous time MDP, owing to the memoryless property, actions need only be taken after state changes. But such changes occur in continuous time, not within discrete periods.

Transitions: For a discrete time MDP, at the end of period t, after action a_t has been chosen in response to state s_t, the system transitions to a new state, s_{t+1}. Typically, this transition is random, governed by a probability matrix that may depend on s_t, a_t and possibly t. We will denote such a transition probability as $\mathbf{P}_t(s_{t+1} = s'|s_t = s, a_t = a) = \mathbf{P}_t(s'|s, a)$ for all $s \in S_t$, $s' \in S_{t+1}$ and $a \in A_t(s)$.

In Alagoz et al. (2007a), these transitions encode the probability that a patient currently in health state s will evolve into health state s' *and* whether or not the patient will be offered a cadaveric organ (and if so, of what quality), in period $t + 1$. In the discrete time process obtained after uniformization in Chong et al. (2016), there is exactly one transition per period—either an arrival of a high-priority or low-priority call, a service completion of one of the vehicles on call, or a dummy transition that corresponds to no event occurring. (Such dummy transitions are an artifact of uniformization.)

Rewards: At any time the decision-maker may receive a reward, usually influenced by the current state and the action chosen and possibly the time; $r_t(s_t, a_t)$. Such a reward may be random, in which case it may be replaced with its expectation. In a discrete time problem, such a reward often is accrued at the end of a period.

In Alagoz et al. (2007a), this reward is the quality of life the patient enjoys in a current state if he or she does nothing or the entire expected future reward if he or she chooses transplantation. In all cases, this reward depends on the patient's current health, and in the case of transplantation, it depends on the quality of the transplanted organ as well. In Chong et al. (2016), rewards are accrued whenever a call for an EMS vehicle arrives and is responded to. This reward depends upon both the type of call (urgent or non-urgent) and the type of vehicle responding (ALS or BLS).

Objective Function: Typically, the objective is to maximize or minimize the reward over the problem horizon. Such a reward may or may not be *discounted*; when a reward is monetary, it is common to discount future rewards because, due to uncertainty and expected inflation, a dollar today may be worth more than an expected dollar sometime in the future. When the objective is related to health, that is, Quality Adjusted Life Years (QALY), it may also be discounted with the rationale that current quality of life may be more valuable than hypothetical future quality, although there is more controversy about this practice (and certainly about estimating such a discount factor). It is also possible to have multicriteria objectives, such as blending cost and QALY, as in Lee et al. (2008); this requires determining a weighting factor to blend the two objectives.

When deciding upon an objective, it is important to understand the perspective of the controller: This could be that of an individual patient concerned with his or her quality of life (Alagoz et al., 2007a), a provider minimizing opportunity costs associated with underutilized resources, penalties arising from congestion costs or canceling scheduled procedures as in Helm et al. (2011), or society at large trying to ensure equitable access to EMS resources, as in McLay and Mayorga (2013a).

In our motivating examples, Alagoz et al. (2007a) sought to maximize the discounted total Quality Adjusted Life Days (QALD), whereas Chong et al. (2016) maximize the long-run average reward accrued by sending different types of vehicles to different emergency calls.

Problem Formulation: Putting everything together yields the MDP recursion. For a finite-horizon discrete time problem, where $V_t(s_t)$ is the optimal expected reward accrued from period t to period T when starting in state s_t, and $0 < \alpha \leq 1$ is a discount factor (without loss of generality, we assume we are maximizing our objective),

$$V_t(s_t) = \max_{a_t \in A_t(s_t)} \left\{ r_t(s_t, a_t) + \alpha \sum_{s' \in S_{t+1}} \mathbf{P_t}(s' | s_t, a_t) V_{t+1}(s') \right\},$$

$$\forall \quad t = 1 \dots T-1, \quad \forall s_t \in S_t. \tag{14.1}$$

$$V_t(s_T) = r_T(s_T). \tag{14.2}$$

It is often easiest to think about MDP recursions backwards. In this light, Eq. (14.2) specifies that the reward received in the final period depends only on that state; there is no action to be taken. Keeping this in mind, Eq. (14.1) expresses that the optimal value starting in time t from any state s_t, $V_t(s_t)$, is the maximum, taken over all feasible actions, of the sum of the expected immediate reward $r_t(s_t, a_t)$ and the total expected discounted reward from period $t + 1$ onward. This expected future reward is calculated by conditioning on which state the process will transition into in period $t + 1$, which depends on the action chosen in period t, and assumes that the *optimal* actions will be chosen from period $t + 1$ onward. Note that we implicitly assume a finite action space in the above; otherwise, the max would be replaced by a sup.

A maximizing action chosen in equation (14.1) is often denoted as $a_t^*(s_t)$. A *policy* is any given rule for choosing actions in any period; this is commonly denoted as π, with an optimal policy denoted as π^*.

When considering *infinite-horizon* problems, we almost invariably assume that the problem is stationary: S_t, A_t, and $\mathbf{P_t}$ all are invariant with respect to t. In this case, under mild assumptions, the existence of an optimal policy with a finite total discounted reward, or average reward, can be established.

Then, for the infinite-horizon discounted reward problem,

$$V(s) = \max_{a \in A(s)} \left\{ r(s,a) + \alpha \sum_{s' \in S} \mathbf{P}(s'|s,a)V(s') \right\}, \qquad \forall s \in S. \tag{14.3}$$

Note here that the same function V appears on each side of the equation.

And, for the infinite-horizon average reward problem,

$$J + V(s) = \max_{a \in A(s)} \left\{ r(s,a) + \sum_{s' \in S} \mathbf{P}(s'|s,a)V(s') \right\}, \qquad \forall s \in S. \tag{14.4}$$

Once again, the same function V appears on both sides of the equation. Here also the scalar J appears, which corresponds to the optimal average reward.

With respect to our motivating papers, Alagoz et al. (2007a) uses a total discounted reward formulation, analogous to Eq. (14.3), while Chong et al. (2016) uses an infinite horizon average reward formulation, analogous to Eq. (14.4).

Although MDPs can certainly be formulated in continuous time, because these are virtually always transformed into a discrete time problem via uniformization (or if this fails, they are often analyzed via a discrete time approximation), we omit discussion of the analogous continuous time recursions. They are available in Puterman (1994).

14.3 Types of Results

After formulation of the problem is complete, different types of results, relying on various analytical techniques, can be obtained from an MDP.

14.3.1 Numerical Results

Numerical solution of an MDP will yield an optimal expected reward and an optimal policy. We will restrict our discussion in this section to discrete time processes with finite state spaces, as these are not only significantly more straightforward to solve, but also comprise the vast majority of healthcare applications. MDPs with continuous state spaces will be discussed below; systems with countably infinite state spaces may be solved by aggregation, truncation, or through derivation of optimal policy structures, which confine the optimal policy to a class that can be evaluated. For a discussion of these latter techniques, please see Puterman (1994).

Finite-horizon problems can be solved simply through the use of backward recursion: First, for every state $s_T \in S_T$, we evaluate Eq. (14.2). Then we evaluate

Eq. (14.1) for all $s_{T-1} \in S_{T-1}$, using the values previously derived for $V_T(s_T)$ for all s_T. We then continue recursively until we have derived $V_1(s_1)$ for all $s_1 \in S_1$, which yields the optimal expected reward for each initial state. During the process, if we likewise record the optimal action in each state, $a_t^*(s_t)$ for all $s_t \in S_t$ and all periods t, we obtain the optimal policy.

For *infinite-horizon problems* our goal for total discounted reward problems is to find a vector $V(s)$ that satisfies Eq. (14.3) and, for average reward problems, to find a scalar J and vector $V(s)$ that satisfies Eq. (14.4). Such problems are typically solved in one of three ways.

Value iteration is an analog to the backward recursion technique described above. We start with any initial value for the reward in each state; for example, $V^0(s) = 0$, where the superscript on V now signifies iteration number, and we are implicitly assuming a stationary problem, obviating the need for subscripts.

Given this initial vector, we solve the analogous equation to (14.1), yielding a sequence of values $V^n(s)$:

$$V^{n+1}(s) = \max_{a \in A(s)} \left\{ r(s,a) + \alpha \sum_{s' \in S} \mathbf{P}(s'|s,a) V^n(s') \right\},$$
$$\forall \quad n = 1 \ldots, \quad \forall s \in S.$$

Under relatively mild conditions such an algorithm will converge in a finite number of iterations in the discounted case when $\alpha < 1$ (or at least converge to a policy within an arbitrary ϵ of the optimal policy). But in the average reward case ($\alpha = 1$), this algorithm could diverge. For this reason, *policy iteration* is used more often, at least for infinite horizon models.

Policy iteration works on the same general principle as value iteration, but instead of updating values at each iteration, it updates policies. It begins with a default policy, π^0, which specifies an action for any given state. Given this set of actions, $a_{\pi^0}(s)$, for the total discounted reward criteria, we then solve for the vector $V^0(s)$ in the series of linear equations:

$$V^0(s) = \left\{ r(s, a_{\pi^0}(s)) + \alpha \sum_{s' \in S} \mathbf{P}(s'|s, a_{\pi^0(s)}) V^0(s') \right\}. \tag{14.5}$$

Using these values for $V^0(s)$, we then find an improved policy π^1 as the set of actions, for each state s, defined by:

$$\pi^1(s) = \arg \max_{a \in A(s)} \left\{ r(s,a) + \alpha \sum_{s' \in S} \mathbf{P}(s'|s,a) V^0(s') \right\}. \tag{14.6}$$

We then substitute $a_{\pi^1}(s)$ into Eq. (14.5), iterating between Eqs. (14.5) and (14.6) until the policies converge. Because there are a finite number of policies over a finite number of states, this algorithm is guaranteed to converge in finite time.

Policy iteration for the average reward criterion is similar; we would start with a policy π^0, solve an equation analogous to (14.4) for J^0 and $V^0(s)$, use an equation analogous to (14.6) to find an improved policy, and then use this policy to solve for updated J^1 and $V^1(s)$, iterating until convergence.

Linear programming can also be used to find optimal rewards and policies; see Puterman (1994) for a discussion and formulations.

14.3.2 Analytical Results

One of the great strengths of MDP modeling is that it affords not only numerical optimization, but also analytical optimization—specifically the possibility of establishing the *structure* of optimal policies. This may be important for at least two reasons. First, numerical optimization of problems with very large or potentially infinite state spaces can be quite challenging, or even intractable, depending on the problem characteristics. In such cases, structural results related to the optimal policy can greatly reduce the search space, potentially rendering the problem tractable. Second, if a conceptually simple optimal policy structure can be established, it can make treatment decisions easier for the practitioner and more intuitive to the patient.

The most common structural result in the healthcare literature is the optimality (under suitable assumptions) of a *control limit* policy. Such a result partitions the state space into disjoint regions, separated by thresholds on values of the state variable. Within each region, one control is the optimal action. For example, under the reasonable assumptions that sicker patients have lower expected QALY and inferior future prognoses (i.e., the transition matrix of patient condition satisfies an *increasing failure rate* condition), control limit policies are shown to be optimal by Alagoz et al. (2007a) for organ transplantation decisions, by Shechter et al. (2008) for the initiation of HIV treatment, by Kurt et al. (2011) for statin initiation, and by Kreke et al. (2008) for hospital discharge decisions. All of these results follow standard induction techniques.

Helm et al. (2011) show the optimality of control limit policies for hospital admissions by verifying that their formulation satisfies conditions, such as convexity and supermodularity. This paper is notable for its utilization of the *event-based* MDP formulation originated by Koole (1998); this formulation has been used in the wider operations literature to prove rather complex structural results (see, for example, Nadar et al. 2014), and could potentially prove valuable within the healthcare domain as well.

While control-limit results are most common, they are not the only type of analytical results obtained. For example, Ayvaci et al. (2012) showed the convexity of QALY in available budget for cancer screening, demonstrating decreasing marginal returns to testing volume. And, using techniques from control theory, Kazemian et al. (2016) showed the separability of the estimation and control operations in their model, rendering it tractable.

14.3.3 Insights

Typically, optimal reward values are used to benchmark the performance of heuristic policies. Such heuristics may be proposed by the authors as simplifications of the optimal policy but are more frequently representations of policies used in practice, for instance, instantiations of treatment guidelines. In these situations, by comparing the optimal policy to current clinical practices, potential shortcomings of the latter may be identified. For example, Ayer et al. (2012) showed the importance of considering other factors in addition to age for initiating breast cancer screenings, and Mattila et al. (2016) showed the importance of considering age when deciding when to operate on abdominal aneurysms. Likewise, Mason et al. (2014) showed the importance of considering age *and* gender when prescribing blood pressure and cholesterol medications. Numerical optimization can also generate other significant insights—for instance, Denton et al. (2009) showed how optimal treatment regimens can dramatically change as different published models of disease evolution are used, and Saghafian et al. (2014) showed how triage procedures can be improved through the joint consideration of urgency *and* complexity.

Finally, numerical results are often also used to illustrate sensitivities to perturbations of problem parameters; this is particularly valuable because such parameters are often difficult (or impossible) to estimate with certainty. Discount factors, for example, are entirely subjective, transition probabilities can be only imperfectly estimated from clinical data, and in some cases even the patient condition is subject to uncertainty. Zhang et al. (2012) provided a nice illustration of sensitivity analysis with regard to different model parameters, within the context of prostate biopsy referrals.

14.4 Modifications and Extensions of MDPs

At this point, we have seen several different ways in which MDPs can be applied to the healthcare domain and some of the results their analysis can produce. Unfortunately, as mentioned above, several aspects of the standard MDP formulation may only imperfectly capture actual healthcare problems. Thus, in their standard form, application of MDPs to some classes of problems may be limited. In this section, we will discuss some of these limitations and how they have, at least partially, been alleviated.

14.4.1 Imperfect State Information

In some healthcare settings, test results can be viewed as largely reliable; thus, the state of the patient (or the system) can be assumed to be known with relative certainty. The size of an aneurysm, for instance, can be accurately determined by a CT scan (Mattila et al., 2016), and knowledge of whether an

EMS vehicle is currently on a call or not is not subject to significant uncertainty (Chong et al., 2016).

But in other domains, the state is not known with certainty—in fact, this may be the entire point of the problem: Cancer screening and biopsy decisions (e.g. Zhang et al. 2012) are made *because* the true state of the patient (i.e., whether he or she has cancer) is unknown. Similarly, but in a different domain, the control of steerable needles may be subject to uncertainty in terms of the actual needle location and orientation because of limitations in medical imaging (Sun and Alterovitz, 2014). In cases such as these, *partially observable Markov decision processes (POMDPs)* may be appropriate models. We will discuss POMDPs only briefly here—readers are referred to Steimle and Denton (2017) for a more detailed discussion of POMDPs in chronic disease treatment and screening.

In a POMDP, the true state of the system at time t (sometimes called the *core state*) can be observed only imperfectly (i.e., it is only *partially observable*). Information about the core state is provided by the *message* or *observation* process. Crucially, core states and observations are linked probabilistically. It is assumed that the probability of a given core state generating a specific observation is known. For example, considering prostate cancer screening in Zhang et al. (2012), it is accepted that a PSA provides only an imperfect indication of whether there is undetected cancer present. But, given a PSA result, the false-positive and false-negative probabilities can be estimated from population models, yielding the relationship between core states (cancer or not) and observations (PSA values).

Therefore, a POMDP can be transformed into an MDP by replacing the core state in the POMDP with a *belief state* in a corresponding MDP. This belief state captures the probability distribution of the true underlying core state, given the sequence of observations received and updated in a Bayesian fashion with each observation. Unfortunately, since the belief state is continuous, exact solution of these models proves to be extremely challenging, save for instances with small state spaces (as in, e.g., Zhang et al., 2012, and Ayer et al., 2012), or situations when optimal policy structure can be established.

Therefore solutions for even moderately-sized POMDPs tend to rely on approximations. The simplest such approximation relies on discretizing the belief space; for a discussion of these techniques, see Lovejoy (1991). But for larger problems, techniques from *Approximate Dynamic Programming* (see Powell, 2007, for a reference), potentially leveraging structural results related to the optimal policy, are usually employed.

14.4.2 Extremely Large or Continuous State Spaces

In addition to POMDPs, standard MDPs can also generate intractably large state spaces, requiring approximation in their solution. Several techniques for this are available; we discuss a few that have appeared in the healthcare literature.

Maxwell et al. (2010) consider the problem of ambulance redeployment, where the controller may choose to redeploy an ambulance while it is en route to a destination. This requires knowledge of how far along in its journey the ambulance is, giving rise to a continuous state space. These authors solved their problem using approximate policy iteration, approximating the value function of their MDP using basis functions (a common ADP technique). Similarly, Lee et al. (2008) used approximate policy iteration combined with simulation to prescribe dialysis treatments, enabling them to incorporate continuous disease trajectories. Sun and Alterovitz (2014) likewise confronted a continuous state space, this time tracking the location of a steerable needle within a patient. They used local optimization for an approximated response function to find locally optimal needle trajectories.

Unlike the previous three papers, Ahuja and Birge (2016) actually assume a discrete state space, but it grows combinatorially. Thus they also developed an approximate solution—at each iteration they found the optimal policy for a finite number of periods and then assume a myopic policy is followed thereafter.

14.4.3 Uncertainty about Transition Probabilities

An MDP is only as good as the underlying model it uses to represent reality. Within the healthcare domain, in particular for disease modeling, a limiting factor for the fidelity of a model is often knowledge of transition probabilities. These limitations can manifest themselves in two different ways.

First, there may be states within the state space for which there is a dearth of data that can be used to estimate the transition probabilities. This is most commonly treated by simply aggregating states within the state space; in Mason et al. (2014), total cholesterol, LDL, and HDL levels are aggregated into macro states corresponding to low, medium, high, and very high. If data were available, and were statistically powerful enough, a finer discretization of the state space would be possible, which could potentially yield a higher resolution model.

Second, different medical studies may yield significantly different models of disease progression. The potential effects of these different models is vividly displayed in Denton et al. (2009), who found strikingly different treatment prescriptions and predicted outcomes across the three published models they used in their MDP. This occurs because each model yields a different relationship between cholesterol levels and the probability of stroke or coronary heart disease.

One potential strategy to combat such uncertainty is to model the system within the framework of a *robust Markov decision process* (RMDP), as in Zhang and Denton (2015). Such a formulation explicitly incorporates possible uncertainty in the transition parameters, using either an uncertainty set or an uncertainty budget. The RMDP is then solved, typically with the objective of maximizing the worst-case reward (i.e., ensuring the best lower-bound outcome is taken over all possible realizations of the uncertain parameters). Zhang et al. (2012) illustrated their model on the problem of glycemic control, where the uncertainty stems from the state transitions between glycated hemoglobin levels. This methodology falls within the general category of *robust optimization*; for a general treatment see Ben-Tal et al. (2009).

A different methodology is utilized to counteract uncertainty in Ahuja and Birge (2016), within the context of medical trials. As opposed to a traditional static experimental design, the authors consider an *adaptive* design, in which patients are assigned to treatment groups based on an updated belief of the underlying efficacy of the treatment. This has the potential benefit of balancing learning about the treatment's effectiveness with improving outcomes among patients in the experimental group.

The authors used a *Bayesian adaptive Markov decision process (BAMDP)*, in which the transition probabilities are assumed to belong to a parametric distribution (Beta) instead of being precisely known. As more trials are completed, more knowledge about the transition probabilities is generated, and the belief about their distribution is updated in a Bayesian fashion. This not only provides a method to optimize the two competing objectives in their problem but also a potential framework to incorporate learning about transition probabilities into a general MDP framework.

Of course, if we simply want to estimate the effect uncertainty about transitions may have on the outcomes of an MDP, a standard sensitivity analysis, as nicely illustrated in Zhang et al. (2012), can be conducted.

14.4.4 Constrained Optimization

Yet another strength of MDPs is that they are amenable to solution via linear programming. As such, if constraints need to be placed on the solution, for example, to ensure equity across patients and EMS responders, they can be incorporated within the linear programming framework, as in McLay and Mayorga (2013a).

Unfortunately, such constraints will, in general, lead to *randomized* policies. Under a randomized policy, there are some states in which multiple actions are prescribed by the optimal policy; the action taken depends on the outcome of a random experiment. While analytically benign, such policies are in many cases practically problematic: No patient wants to think that his or her doctor is flipping coins or rolling dice in order to decide on treatment recommendations. Thus *additional* constraints may be added to an MDP, transforming its formulation from a linear program to a mixed integer program, ensuring nonrandomized solutions. Ayvaci et al. (2012) provided one such example within the context of breast cancer diagnostics subject to budgetary constraints; they enforced integer solutions by adding a set of binary variables to their linear program. Nadar et al. (2016) provided a more detailed example of such a technique outside of the domain of healthcare, which is based on the principles of *disjunctive programming* (Balas, 1998).

14.5 Future Applications

Looking forward, there are several promising themes and venues for future application of MDPs (and their variants) within the healthcare domain.

The Growing Importance of Data: It should surprise no one that one of the most prevalent themes in future application of MDPs in healthcare will center on data. With the increase in availability of more and more granular data on health outcomes, patient behavior, medical system dynamics, traffic modeling, genetic variations, and electronic medical records comes the promise of harnessing this data to make more precise and more customized decisions for both healthcare systems and the individual patients they treat.

A common complaint is that decision-makers have so much data that they don't know what to do with it. If the data is valid and if algorithms can be developed to harvest the data, MDPs (and POMDPs, RMDPs, BAMDPs) can provide the answer to "what to do with it." We could see a future with less and less aggregation of states to provide sufficient statistical power to make predictions of transition probabilities, yielding finer and finer models of disease (or system) evolution.

This will lead to the following:

Increasingly Personalized Medicine: Taken to its extreme, leveraging such data holds the promise of the ability to make informed, valid medical decisions in increasingly specific situations.

1) Does a patient have a set of correlated, interdependent conditions that complicates his or her treatment? Maybe someday we will be able to holistically consider these conditions—and their interplay—within a precise, algorithmic, diagnostic framework.
2) Does a patient have a set of idiosyncratic constraints on his or her treatment, maybe stemming from family or social situations, religious beliefs, or ethical concerns? Maybe one day we will be able to *analytically* incorporate such constraints into a treatment plan, deriving an optimal plan customized to this patient's needs.
3) Ultimately, we could hope to have a truly personalized recommendation for the patient, based on the entirety of data related to the patient's condition, health status, genetic makeup, and medical history: *Personalized medicine.*

If we hope to approach these lofty medical frontiers, it is likely MDPs (and their derivatives) will help get us there. This raises the obvious question of whether we will reach a situation where the MDPs *themselves* are making the medical recommendations, alone or in concert with a practitioner. This is a question researchers are already actively investigating; see Bennett and Hauser (2013), for example.

Improved Decision-Making in Healthcare Systems: At the other extreme, far away from personalized medicine, we have questions of how society as a whole should manage its healthcare assets and expenditures. How can we optimize the functioning of different elements of the healthcare complex—hospitals, EMS vehicles, doctors and nurses, vaccination programs, nutrition, and so forth—both individually and in concert? Several applications of MDP techniques are already starting to answer these questions. As data availability and algorithmic and computational power grow, so too will the reach of MDPs within the control of healthcare assets.

Improved Algorithmic Performance: For the promise implied by the applications described above come to fruition, our ability to leverage data within the MDP framework to make better decisions must keep pace with the availability of this data. Certainly some of the answer may come from increased computing power, but not all. This calls for the continued development of better tools and algorithms within the healthcare domain (POMDPs, ADP, RMDPs, BAMDPs, and combinations thereof).

It *also* calls for more detailed theoretical analysis of models of healthcare systems and patient dynamics. Many of the techniques for solving problems with extremely large state spaces rely on selectively pruning certain actions. Such pruning can be accomplished only if we understand, analytically, which actions are provably suboptimal. Alternately, if we know our optimal policy (or at least a good heuristic) will take a simplified form (such as a control limit policy), we can restrict our search to this smaller class of policies, which can also lead to greatly increased efficiency.

14.6 Recommendations for Additional Reading

Puterman (1994) is a fine general reference on MDPs, supplemented by Koole (1998) for his event-based formulation. For POMDPs in healthcare, the best place to start is the chapter by Steimle and Denton (2017), supplemented with the references therein.

With respect to application papers, Alagoz et al. (2007a) and Chong et al. (2016) provide excellent examples of MDP formulations in healthcare, as well as nice entrées into the organ transplantation and EMS vehicle arenas, respectively. Similarly, Saghafian et al. (2014) offer a nice example of an MDP within the hospital operations domain, while Zhang et al. (2012) provide another clean MDP formulation as well as a fine example of sensitivity analysis.

Kazemian et al. (2016) present a somewhat different perspective on healthcare MDPs, from the optimal control literature; Lee et al. (2008) provide a good example of an ADP application for chronic disease; and Zhang and Denton (2015) are notable for their application of the Robust MDP framework.

These papers can get readers started; specific interest in application and problem domain can provide a further guide.

References

Ahuja, V. and J.R. Birge. (2016). Response-adaptive designs for clinical trials: Simultaneous learning from multiple patients. *European Journal of Operational Research*, 248(2):619–633.

Alagoz, O., H. Hsu, A.J. Schaefer, and M.S. Roberts. (2010). Markov decision processes: A tool for sequential decision making under uncertainty. *Medical Decision Making*, 30(4):474–483.

Alagoz, O., L.M. Maillart, A.J. Schaefer, and M.S. Roberts. (2004). The optimal timing of living-donor liver transplantation. *Management Science*, 50(10):1420–1430.

Alagoz, O., L.M. Maillart, A.J. Schaefer, and M.S. Roberts. (2007a). Choosing among living-donor and cadaveric livers. *Management Science*, 53(11):1702–1715.

Alagoz, O., L.M. Maillart, A.J. Schaefer, and M.S. Roberts. (2007b). Determining the acceptance of cadaveric livers using an implicit model of the waiting list. *Operations Research*, 55(1):24–36.

Alterovitz, R., M. Branicky, and K. Goldberg. (2008). Motion planning under uncertainty for image-guided medical needle steering. *The International Journal of Robotics Research*, 27(11–12):1361–1374.

Ayer, T., O. Alagoz, and N.K. Stout. (2012). OR forum—a POMDP approach to personalize mammography screening decisions. *Operations Research*, 60(5):1019–1034.

Ayvaci, M.U.S., O. Alagoz, and E.S. Burnside. (2012). The effect of budgetary restrictions on breast cancer diagnostic decisions. *Manufacturing & Service Operations Management*, 14(4):600–617.

Balas, E. (1998). Disjunctive programming: Properties of the convex hull of feasible points. *Discrete Applied Mathematics*, 89(1):3—44.

Ben-Tal, A., L. El Ghaoui, and A. Nemirovski. (2009). *Robust Optimization*. Princeton Series in Applied Mathematics. Princeton University Press.

Bennett, C. C. and K. Hauser. (2013). Artificial intelligence framework for simulating clinical decision-making: A Markov decision process approach. *Artificial Intelligence in Medicine* 57(1):9–19.

Chhatwal, J., O. Alagoz, and E.S. Burnside. (2010). Optimal breast biopsy decision-making based on mammographic features and demographic factors. *Operations Research*, 58(6):1577–1591.

Chong, K.C., S.G. Henderson, and M.E. Lewis. (2016). The vehicle mix decision in emergency medical service systems. *Manufacturing & Service Operations Management*, 18(3):347–360.

Denton, B.T., M. Kurt, N.D. Shah, S.C. Bryant, and S.A. Smith. (2009). Optimizing the start time of statin therapy for patients with diabetes. *Medical Decision Making,* 29(3):351–367. PMID: 19429836.

Helm, J., S. Ahmadbeygi, and M. Van Oyen. (2011). Design and analysis of hospital admission control for operational effectiveness. *Production and Operations Management,* 20(3):359–374.

Kazemian, P., J.E. Helm, M.S. Lavieri, J. Stein, and M.P. Van OyenP. (2016). Dynamic monitoring and control of irreversible chronic diseases with application to glaucoma. https://ssrn.com/abstract=2733399 or https://doi.org/10.2139/ssrn.2733399.

Koole, G. (1998). Structural results for the control of queueing systems using event-based dynamic programming. *Queueing Systems,* 30(3):323–339.

Kreke, J.E., M.D. Bailey, A.J. Schaefer, D.C. Angus, and M.S. Roberts. (2008). Modeling hospital discharge policies for patients with pneumonia-related sepsis. *IIE Transactions,* 40(9):853–860.

Kurt, M., B.T. Denton, A.J. Schaefer, N.D. Shah, and S.A. Smith. (2011). The structure of optimal statin initiation policies for patients with type 2 diabetes. *IIE Transactions on Healthcare Systems Engineering,* 1(1):49–65.

Lee, C. P., G.M. Chertow, and S.A. Zenios. (2008). Optimal initiation and management of dialysis therapy. *Operations Research,* 56(6):1428–1449.

Lippman, S.A. (1975). Applying a new device in the optimization of exponential queuing systems. *Operations Research,* 23(4):687–710.

Lovejoy, W.S. (1991). Computationally feasible bounds for partially observed Markov decision processes. *Operations Research,* 39(1):162–175.

Maillart, L.M., J.S. Ivy, S. Ransom, and K. Diehl. (2008). Assessing dynamic breast cancer screening policies. *Operations Research,* 56(6):1411–1427.

Mason, J., B. Denton, N. Shah, and S. Smith. (2014). Optimizing the simultaneous management of blood pressure and cholesterol for type 2 diabetes patients. *European Journal of Operational Research,* 233(3):727–738.

Mattila, R., A. Siika, J. Roy, and B. Wahlberg. (2016). A Markov decision process model to guide treatment of abdominal aortic aneurysms. In *2016 IEEE Conference on Control Applications (CCA),* pages 436–441.

Maxwell, M.S., M. Restrepo, S.G. Henderson, and H. Topaloglu. (2010). Approximate dynamic programming for ambulance redeployment. *INFORMS Journal on Computing,* 22(2):266–281.

McLay, L.A. and M.E. Mayorga. (2013a). A dispatching model for server-to-customer systems that balances efficiency and equity. *Manufacturing & Service Operations Management,* 15(2):205–220.

McLay, L.A. and M.E. Mayorga. (2013b). A model for optimally dispatching ambulances to emergency calls with classification errors in patient priorities. *IIE Transactions,* 45(1):1–24.

Nadar, E., M. Akan, and A. Scheller-Wolf. (2014). Technical note—optimal structural results for assemble-to-order generalized M-Systems. *Operations Research,* 62(3):571–579.

Nadar, E., M. Akan, and A. Scheller-Wolf. (2016). Experimental results indicating lattice-dependent policies may be optimal for general assemble-to-order systems. *Production and Operations Management,* 25(4):647–661.

Powell, W.B. (2007). *Approximate Dynamic Programming: Solving the Curses of Dimensionality* (Wiley Series in Probability and Statistics). Wiley-Interscience.

Puterman, M.L. (1994). *Markov decision processes: discrete stochastic dynamic programming*. John Wiley & Sons, New York; Chichester.

Saghafian, S., W. Hopp, M. Van Oyen, J. Desmond MD, and S. Kronick MD. (2014). Complexity-augmented triage: A tool for improving patient safety and operational efficiency. *Manufacturing and Service Operations Management (MSOM),* 16(3):329–345.

Sandikci, B., L.M. Maillart, A.J. Schaefer, O. Alagoz, and M.S. Roberts. (2008). Estimating the patient's price of privacy in liver transplantation. *Operations Research,* 56(6):1393–1410.

Schaefer, A.J., M.D. Bailey, S.M. Shechter, and M.S. Roberts. (2004). *Modeling Medical Treatment Using Markov Decision Processes,* pages 593–612. Springer US, Boston, MA.

Shechter, S.M., M.D. Bailey, A.J. Schaefer, and M.S. Roberts. (2008). The optimal time to initiate HIV therapy under ordered health states. *Operations Research,* 56(1):20–33.

Steimle, L.N. and B.T. Denton. (2017). *Markov Decision Processes in Practice,* Springer International, Cham, Switzerland.

Sun, W. and R. Alterovitz. (2014). Motion planning under uncertainty for medical needle steering using optimization in belief space. In *2014 IEEE/RSJ International Conference on Intelligent Robots and Systems (IROS 2014),* pages 1775–1781. IEEE.

Zhang, J., B.T. Denton, H. Balasubramanian, N.D. Shah, and B.A. Inman. (2012). Optimization of prostate biopsy referral decisions. *Manufacturing & Service Operations Management,* 14(4):529–547.

Zhang, Y. and B.T. Denton. (2015). Robust Markov decision processes for medical treatment decisions. Working paper.

15

Game Theory and Information Economics

Tinglong Dai

Johns Hopkins University

15.1 Introduction

Game theory provides a powerful analytical basis for modeling and predicting human interactions (e.g., between a patient and a physician). Information economics, on the other hand, is a tool that characterizes how information, or lack thereof, drives decision making. Jointly, these two tools—when obvious conclusions cannot be drawn by mere observation or intuition—help provide a rigorous and scientific understanding of strategic behaviors of producers, consumers, mediators, and regulators of various goods and services instrumental to the functioning of our economy and society. Needless to say, underlying both tools is the assumption that the decision-makers are rational and strategic—possibly to a limited extent—and that they make utility-maximizing calculations by anticipating the other parties are rational and strategic, too.

Perhaps surprising to some, over the brief histories of both tools, starting from high-level descriptive narratives in their early days to a coherent and rigorous set of norms and standards now, much of their theoretic innovation has been and continues to be inspired by the healthcare industry. Below are several examples:

1) **Market for healthcare services**. Among the earliest and most instrumental work in developing what is later known as the "contract theory," a seminal paper, entitled "Uncertainty and the Welfare Economics of Medical Care," by Arrow (1963) studies a unique set of healthcare problems that are due to information asymmetry among healthcare providers, payers, and consumers, often arising out of uncertainties in the "production" of health. Arrow compellingly argues that a sound analysis of healthcare services has to be supported by tools departing from neoclassic economic approaches. For example, it is difficult to imagine that a physician's medical decision-making can be simply modeled as a profit-maximization problem,

Handbook of Healthcare Analytics: Theoretical Minimum for Conducting 21st Century Research on Healthcare Operations, First Edition. Edited by Tinglong Dai and Sridhar Tayur.

as it is in the case of a firm's decision-making problem. A good analytical model must, in one way or another, recognize physicians' inherent altruism in pursing medicine as a profession, a calling. In addition, Arrow argues that the lack of price and quality information makes the healthcare market markedly different from most other markets for goods and services. Since Arrow (1963), the development of contract theory has been inspired by the problems facing the healthcare industry.

2) **Adverse selection–the "lemons."** The concept of "adverse selection" was first formalized by George Akerlof in his 1970 *Quarterly Journal of Economics* paper titled "The Market for 'Lemons': Quality Uncertainty and the Market Mechanism." Of his four examples, the first was the health insurance industry. At that time, Akerlof observed a lack of private insurance options for senior enrollees because of, apparently, the high risk associated with that particular market segment. Theoretically, insurance firms may be able to use actuarial methods to reflect individual customers' varying health risk levels. Why, one may be wondering, couldn't insurance firms simply raise their premiums to match the risk? The answer from Akerlof (1970, p. 492) may be conventional wisdom for insurance professionals but not obvious to the rest of us: "As the price level rises the people who insure themselves will be those who are increasingly certain that they will need the insurance." Information asymmetry arises in this scenario because consumers know their own risk levels better than insurance companies do: "for error in medical check-ups, doctors' sympathy with older patients, and so on make it much easier for the applicant to assess the risks involved than the insurance company." Because of the asymmetric information, no matter how much insurance firms charge for annual premiums, enrollees who willingly accept these premiums will be so risky that a breakeven becomes unlikely. This paper draws much attention to the issue of *adverse selection*—a dark side of consumer choice.
3) **Moral hazard.** Although the notion of "moral hazard"—capturing agents' opportunism after entering into a contractual arrangement—was coined in 1865 in the absence of healthcare (Rowell and Connelly 2012), modern applications of the concept, starting in the 1950s, preeminently include the utilization of health resources (see, e.g., Dickerson, 1959; Arrow, 1963; Pauly, 1968; Zeckhauser, 1970).
4) **Evolution biology.** Game theory became a mathematical discipline because of the publication of *Theory of Games and Economic Behavior* by John von Neumann and Oskar Morgenstern (1944). Since the 1960s, evolutionary biology has become among "the most promising applications of the theory of games at all" (Hyksová 2013, p. 4).
5) **Cancer treatment.** At the Johns Hopkins School of Medicine, among other academic medical centers, game theory is being applied to fight cancer, by

devising the ideal timing to use a targeted therapy disrupting the "cooperation" among metastatic cancer cells (Kianercy et al. 2014).

15.2 Key Concepts

Here we provide a brief introduction to the key concepts in game theory and information economics. Readers are referred to section 15.5 for resources that have proven to be effective for in-depth learning of these concepts.

15.2.1 Game Theory: Key Concepts

Game theory studies strategic interaction (i.e., "a game") between *players* (decision-makers) who choose actions to maximize their own utility values with the anticipation of the other players' strategic responses. As one might expect, how the players will act during the game is closely driven by the rules of the game (e.g., the sequence of the interaction). Game theory formalizes the rules of the game using a *solution concept*. Given a solution concept, one can mathematically predict the way the game will end in what is commonly referred to as an *equilibrium*. The best-known and most widely used solution concept is *Nash equilibrium*, in which each player chooses her actions concurrently and independently, to maximize the player's individual utility without any informational exchanges before or during the one-shot game.

Commonly studied game formats—along with their corresponding solution concepts—may be grouped along several dimensions:

1) **Noncooperative versus cooperative games.** In a *noncooperative game*, all players reason and act independently; by contrast, in a *cooperative game*, some or all players may take joint actions by forming strategic alliances—to the extent permitted by law and other circumstances—that are often referred as *coalitions*. The majority of the game theory literature has been devoted to noncooperative games since the inception of game theory as a mathematical subject, primarily because of the daunting challenge in analyzing cooperative games, especially among multiple asymmetric players—for players to form and commit to coalitions, there must be a binding and stable payoff-allocation scheme. Whereas the operations management (OM) community has been increasingly mastering the art of cooperative games over the past decade (see, e.g., Nagarajan and Sošić, 2009), the field of economics has exhibited an opposite trend: "More recently, cooperative game theory appears to have disappeared from economics" (Samuelson, 2016, p. 122).
2) **Strategic versus extensive games.** A *strategic game* is a one-shot interaction in which all players act concurrently. By allowing multiple opportunities for players to interact, an *extensive game*, also known as a *sequential*

game, captures the scenario in which the players can move according to a given sequence with (possibly limited) knowledge of earlier actions taken by other players.

3) **Complete- versus incomplete-information games.** In a complete-information game, each player is aware of the other players' actions. By contrast, in an incomplete-information game, players act based on partial or no knowledge of the other players' actions. By this definition, a strategic game can never be a complete-information game.
4) **Evolutionary versus nonevolutionary games.** *Evolutionary games* have been among the most exciting game theoretic developments, in its crucial departure—from nonevolutionary games—that players choose their actions not merely based on the structure of game, but based on an *adaptive* process of learning and reasoning, with two central research questions: "Can we expect the dynamic processes shaping behavior in games to lead to Nash equilibria? Can we expect them to lead to refinements of the Nash equilibrium?" (Samuelson, 2016, p. 116).

15.2.2 Information Economics: Key Concepts

According to the *Journal of Economic Literature* classification code JEL: D8 ("Information, Knowledge, and Uncertainty"), information economics covers the following subjects:

JEL: D80 - General
JEL: D81 - Criteria for Decision-Making under Risk and Uncertainty
JEL: D82 - Asymmetric and Private information; Market Design
JEL: D83 - Search; Learning; Information and Knowledge
JEL: D84 - Expectations; Speculation
JEL: D85 - Network Formation and Analysis: Theory
JEL: D86 - Economics of Contract: Theory
JEL: D87 - Neuroeconomics
JEL: D89 - Other,

where D87 ("Neuroeconomics") is an emerging subject driven mostly by the latest medical developments. Our focus in this chapter is the first part of D82 ("Asymmetric and Private information") and D86. For a detailed discussion of market design, readers are referred to chapter 3 ("Market Design" by Itai Ashlagi) of this volume.

The central question in the field of information economics is, how does the lack of information drive decision-makers' behavior? By saying "lack of information," we refer to a scenario that may be one of the following two cases, depending on what the information is about.

15.2.2.1 Nonobservability of Information

The information we speak of cannot be precisely and verifiably obtained, or is prohibitively costly to obtain. As an example, the information may be whether a physician has chosen a correct diagnostic and treatment path for a patient suffering from a given medical condition. The patient's health outcome is not fully determined by a physician's diagnosis and treatment decisions. So it is impossible to perfectly verify whether the physician has made the correct decision, even after the health outcome is revealed—one cannot be certain whether a favorable health outcome is due to the physician's service or the patient's self-healing. In certain cases, even if the physician makes the best medical decision, patient outcome may still be adverse. The lack of information is partially attributed to infeasibility of a "pay only if cured contract" (Dranove and White, 1987).

15.2.2.2 Asymmetric Information

One party has an informational advantage over the other party. This situation can be further divided into several scenarios below:

1) **Credence goods.** One party (often an expert), because of professional training and practical experiences, knows about the condition of the other party (often a client) even better than the other party himself. As a result, there is an opportunity for the informationally advantaged party to choose actions not necessarily aligned with the best interest of the other party. This type of problem is studied by the vibrant *credence goods* (also known as *expert service*) literature (see, e.g., Dulleck and Kerschbamer, 2006, for a thorough review). In the field of health economics, this type of problem has been studied by the "supplier-induced demand" (SID) literature, the inception of which was (again) due to Kenneth Arrow's (1963) seminal paper.
2) **Adverse selection.** Another possibility is that one party has better information about himself than the other party does. As a result, the more informed party may choose actions not mutually beneficial to both parties. This leads to the well-known *adverse selection* problem. For example, Akerlof (1970) outlines the fundamental problem with health insurance, in that individuals with a higher demand for medical services have a higher incentive to sign up for a more expensive health plan, all else being the same. This type of agency problem is there even before two parties form a contractual relationship: a patient can choose not to sign up for a specific insurance plan if the patient decides that the premium is too high given the patient's expected medical expenditure.

   As another example, Jost and Young (2012) document a case in which Boston University Medical Center Hospital (BUMCH) forms a bundled-payment agreement with a health maintenance organization (HMO) in New Hampshire for several pre-defined service bundles (e.g.,

CABG). This contractual arrangement presents an adverse selection issue: because the total hospital and physician charges for each procedure are fixed, the HMO has an incentive to send its riskiest patients to BUMCH, leading to a significant source of financial risk on the provider's side.

3) **Moral hazard.** A third possibility is that after entering into a contractual arrangement, one party might take actions that cannot be perfectly observed by the other party. The observability (or lack thereof) issue might be caused by legal or practical reasons (e.g., the privacy of private citizens) but can also be because monitoring others' actions is prohibitively costly. This brings us back to the famous *moral hazard* problem. In the healthcare setting, moral hazard (along with adverse selection) has been commonly attributed to the over-provision of medical resources (Pauly, 1974). Under the prevailing fee-for-service system in the U.S. healthcare system, a doctor is in general paid more for performing more medical procedures and paid more for performing more difficult (but not necessarily more effective) procedures. As one can imagine, some medical procedures may be abused. For example, percutaneous coronary intervention (PCI) has been systematically overused—a 2014 review of 2.7 million PCI cases identified 13.3 percent of non-acute PCIs as inappropriate (Desai et al., 2015).—partially because of monetary incentives amplified by moral hazard (Dai et al., 2017b).

To understand the above issues presented due to lack of information, we are fortunate to have several theoretic frameworks in place. The most important one, without doubt, is the *principal-agent theory* (aka *contract theory*), developed as a result of the seminal work by Kenneth Arrow in the 1960s and formalized by Sanford Grossman, Oliver Hart, Bengt Holmström, and Paul Milgrom, among other economists. Contract theory presents a unified framework that formalizes the above scenarios. A principal is a player who wishes to complete a service or produce a good but cannot perform the work by him- or herself—possibly because of lack of resources, expertise, or inclination, or a combination of these—whereas an agent is another player who is engaged by the principal to perform the work. Agency issues arise in this scenario because of information asymmetry. If the information asymmetry is about the agent's hidden information (existing even before the agent commits to the relationship), there is an *adverse selection* problem; if the information asymmetry is about the agent's hidden action (chosen after the agent has committed to the relationship), there is a *moral hazard* problem.

To be sure, information asymmetry not only inspires the development of the principal-agent theory, but it also presents interesting game theoretic problems, as previously described in the comparison between complete- versus incomplete-information games. One party's possession of an informational advantage over the other might also affect the way both parties *communicate* with each other (in addition to the way they contract with each other, which is the subject of the principal-agent theory). This type of game can be rigorously analyzed, thanks to the theory of *communication games*. In a communication game between two agents, there must be a *sender* and a *receiver*. The game often cannot be organized in a trivial manner for the sender's *message* to be credible to the receiver. On one hand, if the sender has a better informational position, the problem is commonly referred to as a *signalling game*. Michael Spence (1973), in his pioneering work entitled simply "Job Market Signaling," shows how job market candidates can use their educational experiences to signal their inherent productivity. Certain high-productivity job market candidates, Spencer argues, may choose to be over-educated simply to differentiate themselves from the rest of the pool of candidates, even when their education does not enhance their productivity at all. On the other hand, if the receiver has an information advantage, the sender would be principally concerned about *screening* the receiver's type such that the sender's message would elicit differentiated responses from receivers of different types. The mechanism design framework, in particular, the *revelation principle*, is the principal theoretic foundation in tackling this type of problem.

15.3 Summary of Healthcare Applications

As aforementioned, the birth and refinement of game theory and information economics have been inspired largely by certain distinguishing characteristics of the healthcare industry. Surprisingly, until the past decade, the applications of these tools have been rather limited in the healthcare operations management literature. The relatively thin amount of literature may be partially attributed to the traditional focus of the entire field of operations management; until very recently, most of the healthcare OM literature is devoted to a health provider's optimization problem without accounting for lack of information or other strategic concerns. As the field of OM deepens its understanding of game theory and information economics, we expect to see healthcare applications.

A number of interesting game theoretic applications have emerged over the past few years. By comparison, the applications of information economics in health operations continues to be limited, despite the close relationship between the healthcare context and information economics theory. One possible reason is that the field of health operations has been dominated by more traditional operations research techniques (e.g., mathematical programming, queueing theory, and simulation), which have a whole different set of assumptions regarding the information environment. As more researchers examine issues related to incentives in healthcare operations that are known to be remarkably opaque, information economics is bound to gain more importance in the decades to come.

We now provide a brief summary of healthcare applications. Broadly, game theory and information economics are powerful tools in designing appropriate incentives to align the interests of various stakeholders, including providers, patients, payers, and innovators, among others.

15.3.1 Incentive Design for Healthcare Providers

So and Tang (2000) studied how an outcome-based reimbursement system affects health providers, patients, and pharmaceutical manufacturers. Briefly stated, they examined a health provider who received reimbursement from payers, depending on patient outcome at various stages. For example, consider a case in which the treatment process takes three months to complete. The health provider receives payments from the payer on a monthly basis for each patient, depending on whether each patients' health score meets a prespecified milestone. Moral hazard arises because the patient's healthcare score depends not only on the provider's treatment decision (dosage during each month) but also on random factors that cannot be observed by the payer. Because of moral hazard, the payer has to incorporate the underlying uncertainty in treatment outcome in devising its reimbursement policy.

Relevant to the work by So and Tang (2000), Fuloria and Zenios (2001) studied an outcome-adjusted reimbursement scheme using a principal-agent model. The outcome-adjusted reimbursement for a health provider consists of two parts: (1) a prospective payment at the beginning of each period; and (2) a "carrot-stick" adjustment at the end of each period, based on the number of adverse events (e.g., hospitalizations, infections, and deaths) observed during that period. Patients' health status evolves dynamically over time and can be influenced but not fully determined by the provider's costly interventional efforts. Fuloria and Zenios used Medicare's end-stage renal disease (ESRD) program to illustrate that their proposed scheme leads to significant improvement in patient life expectancy: in one particular case, they show that, maintaining the same budget, the proposed reimbursement scheme leads to a life expectancy increase of 7.8 percent, from 4.1 years to 4.4 years.

In another effort to examine reimbursement design for Medicare's ESRD program, Lee and Zenios (2012) extended Fuloria and Zenios (2001) by incorporating risk adjustment (providers' payments are adjusted by patient risk using age, body mass index, and body surface area) and pay for compliance (providers receive payments for complying with best-practice guidelines). Lee and Zenios considered a single-period, static contracting problem between Medicare and a dialysis provider. Their "empirical principal-agent model" demonstrates that risk adjustment and pay for compliance alone are inadequate for inducing first-best treatment schedules. By contrast, paying for fully adjusted downstream outcome proves to be more effective.

Over the past few years, an increasing number of researchers are examining incentive design. Jiang et al. (2012) considered a healthcare contracting problem in a public healthcare system, for example, between a government agency and an outpatient clinic in United Kingdom. The outpatient clinic is obliged to serve a designated population, but has the freedom of choosing its service capacity, which affects the length of the waiting list. Because the waiting-time data is publicly available, the government has an opportunity to incentivize the clinic to provide an appropriate capacity, using a performance-based contracting scheme. Gupta and Mehrotra (2015) studied the bundled payments for care improvement (BPCI) initiative by the Centers for Medicare and Medicaid Services (CMS). Each bundle corresponds to a well-defined medical condition (e.g., major joint replacement). Healthcare providers are invited to submit proposals, each consisting of a target payment level and a quality threshold. Gupta and Mehrotra modeled each proposer's problem as a constrained mechanism design problem, and provided guidelines for improving CMS's proposal elicitation approach. Under a bundled-payment setting, Adida et al. (2016) characterized health providers' incentive to reject patients deemed as excessively risk, and they provided remedies (e.g., stop-loss protection) for bundled payment schemes. Savva et al. (2018) studied a yardstick-competition scheme in which each healthcare provider (e.g., emergency department) functions as a local monopolist. Each provider receives a payment that depends on its performance metric (e.g., waiting time and cost of care) relative to other providers. Thus, yardstick competition promotes the competition between healthcare providers when demand is elastic and price competition is infeasible.

15.3.2 Quality-Speed Tradeoff

Much of the queueing theory literature is based on the assumption that service providers have fixed capacity levels and do not adjust the service rate based on consumer behavior. The paper by Anand et al. (2011) was not the first one to relax this assumption, but is arguably the most influential one to inspire a large stream of research seeking to answer interesting service design problems. Anand et al. argue that whereas users dislike waiting in line, they may indeed prefer extended interactions with the provider. Therefore, the provider faces a quality-speed tradeoff in choosing an appropriate service rate. Wang et al. (2010) considered a diagnostic service provider's problem in choosing the speed and variability of its service process, and, like Anand et al. (2011), explicitly allow longer service durations to create better service value. Dai et al. (2017a) have extended Anand et al. (2011) by incorporating the effect of health insurance coverage and have jointly model a clinician's financial, operational, and quality incentives. Guo et al. (2017), in another extension, the effect of more extensive healthcare service on reducing unnecessary outpatient visits. For details on this stream of literature, readers are referred to chapter 5 ("Quality of Care" by Hummy Song and Senthil Veeraraghavan) of this volume.

15.3.3 Gatekeepers

The US healthcare system consists of multiple tiers, and interactions among these tiers are of particular interest. Shumsky and Pinker (2003) considered a setting in which a gatekeeper (e.g., a primary care physician) evaluates each customer's condition and decides whether to refer the customer to a specialist. Echoing the results from the health economics literature, they found that the primary care physician may have the incentive to under-refer patients. Deo et al. (2016), for instance, modeled the behavior of "less-than-fully-qualified providers" in India, who may not be able to provide timely diagnosis of tuberculosis. A proper incentive scheme is needed to motivate them to refer their patients to better trained providers.

15.3.4 Healthcare Supply Chain

Chick et al. (2008) studied the supply chain of the influenza vaccine consisting of a government and a vaccine manufacturer and found that traditional supply contracts (e.g., buy-back contracts) do not coordinate the supply chain, because of the random yield associated with the production process. Dai et al. (2016) use commercial contracts between several academic medical centers and major influenza vaccine manufacturers to study the optimal design of pre-booking contracts, by jointly examining three sources of uncertainties in the supply chain: design, delivery, and demand.

Kouvelis et al. (2015) studied the strategic interaction between multiple pharmacy benefit managers (PBMs, e.g., Express Scripts), and a client organization (e.g., an insurance company). Each PBM makes the price and formulary decisions and the client organization chooses one PBM and sets its copayment levels for each tier of drugs. They show the existence and uniqueness of a pure Nash equilibrium.

15.3.5 Vaccination

Motivated by the US influenza vaccine market, Deo and Corbett (2009) studied the Cournot competition among multiple uncapacitated firms with yield uncertainty. They find that yield uncertainty can hinder entry in the market and lead to undersupply of the influenza vaccine. Arifoğlu et al. (2012) studied two sources of demand-sided inefficiencies when the supply of influenza vaccine is limited: (1) Individuals need to incur a "search cost" to be vaccinated. As a result, vaccines are more likely to go to individuals with low search costs instead of those needing the vaccines the most; and (2) as a sufficiently large proportion of the population receives the vaccination, the chance of inflection is low, so unvaccinated individuals receive protection. The first source is a negative externality, and the second source is a positive externality. Jointly modeling both sources, Arifoğlu et al. argued that excessive vaccination is a possible outcome.

15.3.6 Organ Transplantation

A kidney transplant candidate's priority for receiving an organ depends largely on his or her cumulative waiting time. In other words, the queueing discipline for kidney transplantation is, admittedly in an approximate sense, first-come-first-serve (FCFS). Su and Zenios (2004) incorporated patients' individual utility-maximizing problems in organ accept/reject decisions and showed that a last-come-first-serve (LCFS) queueing discipline—albeit practically infeasible—leads to the socially optimal outcome. In another paper also on kidney transplantation, Su and Zenios (2006) considered adverse selection and propose a mechanism-design approach to induce patients' truth-telling report of their types.

Zheng et al. (2018) used a strategic queueing approach to study the welfare impact of an initiative aiming to boost organ supply, employing the donor-priority rule, which grants registered organ donors the priority of receiving organs should they need transplants. They show that the divergence between individual and social optima may lead to reduction in social welfare, despite an increased organ supply under the donor-priority rule. Accordingly, they provide a remedy entailing a "freeze period" after which registered organ donors start enjoying the priority of receiving transplants. Zheng et al. showed that their proposed remedy, when implemented alongside the donor-priority rule, guarantees an increase in social welfare.

15.3.7 Healthcare Network

Addressing the geographic disparities in the US organ transplant system, Ata et al. (2016) modeled the effect of "multi-listing," in which certain patients can be listed in multiple, often very distant, donation service areas (DSAs), as a queueing game among transplant candidates in different DSAs. They characterized the equilibrium outcome under diffusion approximation and show that multi-listing leads to improvement in geographic equity and improves social welfare.

In an emergency care setting, Deo and Gurvich (2011) studied a ambulance diversion problem in which an overcrowded emergency department (ED) may opt to reroute ambulances to another neighboring ED. The classical OM theory views this practice as resource pooling that facilitates sharing of limited medical resources. Deo and Gurvich found that, however, under decentralization, ambulance diversion may not provide the theoretically predicted pooling benefit, due to interhospital strategic interactions. They provide an explanation for the lack of pooling benefit: in equilibrium, hospitals may reject diverted ambulances from other EDs, leading to what they refer to as "defense equilibrium."

15.3.8 Mixed Motives of Healthcare Providers

Dai and Singh (2018) modeled a diagnostic expert (e.g., a physician) as "impurely altruistic," in that the expert cares about both client utility and her own reputation. They show that when the expert's diagnostic skill is not observable, the expert may choose to skip necessary diagnostic tests to signal her type to clients. Paç and Veeraraghavan (2015) modeled a queueing game in which an expert may provide a false diagnosis in an effort to perform unnecessary costly procedures. Analyzing Medicare's pay-for-performance contracts, Bastani et al. (2016) used a principal-agent model to offer insights into two design choices: the use of rewards versus bonuses and the use of single or continuous performance thresholds.

15.4 Potential Applications

Game theory and information economics have become the essential tools in economics. Indeed, nowadays, it is difficult to find an economic theory paper without any modeling of strategic interactions or some sort of information asymmetry. The field of healthcare operations management is different, in that few analytical modeling papers use game theory and information economics. However, we expect our field to follow the trend in economics in decades to come. Next, we identify several areas in which game theory and information economics may lead to fruitful healthcare operations applications.

15.4.1 Micro-Level applications

By micro-level applications, we refer to specific healthcare operational functions, such as ambulatory care, inpatient care, surgical care, and emergency care. Roughly speaking, most of the work along this line assumes either (1) patients will passively follow a predicted behavior pattern, or (2) patients may change their behavior pattern in response to the incentive environment they are in, but their behavior is independent of the operational policy. The dominant analytics tools for these applications, therefore, include scheduling, queueing, and mathematical programming. These tools provide optimal operations rules (e.g., scheduling policies), assuming that a change in the operations rules does not lead to the changes in the users' behavior.

The famous Lucas critique states that one would be naive to expect the users of a system to follow the same pattern after the rules governing the function of the system have changed. As Robert Lucas (1976, p. 41) articulates:

> Given that the structure of an econometric model consists of optimal decision rules of economic agents, and that optimal decision rules vary systematically with changes in the structure of series relevant to the decision maker, it follows that any change in policy will systematically alter the structure of econometric models.

Consider an outpatient care setting for example. In many clinics, when a patient arrives later than her scheduled time, she may still have a higher priority than other patients with later scheduled times. Suppose now that the clinic decides to switch to a more flexible system in which clinicians may choose to see another patient who may have had a later scheduled time slot but who arrived ahead of the patient with an earlier appointment. Following the Lucas critique, one cannot assume that patients' punctuality behavior will remain the same after the introduction of the change.

More broadly, we expect that a comprehensive reflection of this stream of literature, leveraging the powerful Lucas critique, will lead to a new discipline that is not only intellectually exciting, but also has the potential to shape the healthcare practice. By incorporating clinicians' and patients' strategic responses to different operations rules, researchers can go beyond static predictions of policy changes to characterize the system behavior in equilibrium. Thus, the proposed operational remedies can be more sustainable.

Likewise, revisiting this literature by examining the assumptions about the information, or lack thereof, would also lead to more robust managerial insights and recommendations. This does not necessarily mean extending all the existing models to include elements of *information asymmetry*. Rather, in certain cases, the opposite may be true. For example, most of the queueing literature assumes that the length of the queue is invisible to customers joining the queue, which may be a problematic one in the healthcare setting, in which patients are often informed of their actual waiting time in the system and make queue-joining decisions accordingly.

15.4.2 Macro-Level Applications

Traditionally, OM researchers have rejected macro-level problems as too broad and irrelevant to operations. The situation has been evolving over the past few years, as OM researchers start to discover that OR/OM tools, when combined with game theory and information economics, are incredibly powerful not only in modeling the problems facing an individual organization or supply chain, but also in capturing the supply-demand mismatch of society overall. For example, researchers have used game theory and information economics, along with more traditional OR/OM tools, to study macro-level topics ranging from healthcare market structure (Deo and Corbett, 2009) to bundled payment market design (Gupta and Mehrotra, 2015), reimbursement design (Fuloria and Zenios, 2001), and government intervention programs (Arifoğlu et al., 2012). We expect these types of applications to expand in both number and impact as OM researchers deepen their connection with policymakers and help governments make more informed social changes.

15.4.3 Meso-Level Applications

We use *meso-level applications* to refer to healthcare settings that bridge micro-level and macro-level applications. In other words, these applications are beyond the scope of a single-unit or single-supply-chain healthcare setting, but do not implicitly involve the design of a broader marketplace.

Not surprisingly, game theory and information economics have been the primary tool for this type of applications. It is our belief that methodological innovations will become the primary drivers for meso-level applications in the next few decades. Below we list three methodological innovations for potential future applications.

1) **Information design.** This emerging field focuses on the design of information structure that maximizes the utility of an information designer. Typically, the information designer has information but no ability to change the mechanism specific to agents' actions. Information design has attracted much interest from researchers in economics (Kamenica and Gentzkow 2011; Bergemann and Morris 2017) and finance (Glode et al. 2018) but little attention from operations management. We expect information design to become useful in the healthcare domain, particularly because existing empirical research has demonstrated the surprising impact of information availability on the efficiency of healthcare resource allocation: Zhang (2010), for example, showed that when an organ transplant candidate is offered an organ, the candidate's acceptance/rejection probability is significantly influenced by how many times the same organ has been rejected by other candidates beforehand. To increase the probability that limited organ supply can be efficiently utilized, it may make sense for the organ procurement organizations (OPOs) to devise a different information environment, using the principles of information design.
2) **Continuous-time principal-agent theory.** Whereas most of the principal-agent models are discrete-time for tractability reasons—to characterize the equilibrium in such a setting, one that needs to show agents do not deviate from such a continuous-time equilibrium. Recent advances in information economics (e.g., Sannikov 2008), by introducing the notion of *imperfect monitoring*, allow us to define agents' strategies as functions of their imperfect observations. Interestingly, healthcare operations often arise in continuous-time settings, and imperfect monitoring is provided through repeated clinician-patient interactions and increased availability of health data collection tools. There is a hope, then, that more healthcare applications will benefit from the advances in continuous-time principal-agent theory.
3) **Behavioral game theory.** In a recent *Journal of Economic Perspectives* article entitled "Game Theory in Economics and Beyond," Samuelson (2016) contended that a promising direction of game theory lies in providing "new behavioral insights," by leveraging recent advances in behavioral economics. The study of healthcare cannot be truly meaningful unless human behavior is carefully incorporated. Thus, it seems reasonable to expect game theory with behavioral considerations to flourish in modeling healthcare operations problems.

15.5 Resources for Learners

A Primer in Game Theory by Gibbons (1992) is a thorough, exceptionally accessible textbook with many illustrative examples. *A Course in Game Theory* by Osborne and Rubinstein (1994) is another popular textbook with a formal framework of game theory terminologies.

Among numerous textbooks for information economics, we find the following three particularly useful for quickly mastering the basics of the tool: *The Theory of Incentives: The Principal-Agent Model* by Laffont and Martimort (2009), *Contract Theory* by Bolton and Dewatripont (2005), and *The Economics of Contracts: A Primer* by Salanié (2005).

Readers may also find books on industrial organization relevant to their pursuit of game theory and information economics. Although Tirole's (1988) *The Theory of Industrial Organization* is highly regarded as a classical textbook, a more up-to-date and encyclopedic textbook is *Industrial Organization: Markets and Strategies* by Belleflamme and Peitz (2015), which covers many contemporary examples (e.g., social media, online platforms).

References

Akerlof, G.A. (1970). The market for "lemons": Quality uncertainty and the market mechanism. *Quarterly Journal of Economics*, pp.488–500.

Adida, E., H. Mamani, S. Nassiri. (2016). Bundled payment vs. fee-for-service: impact of payment scheme on performance. *Management Science* 63(5):1606–1624.

Anand, K.S., M.F. Paç, S.K. Veeraraghavan. (2011). Quality-speed conundrum: tradeoffs in customer-intensive services. *Management Science* 57(1) 40–56.

Arifoğlu, K., S. Deo, S. Iravani. (2012). Consumption externality and yield uncertainty in the influenza vaccine supply chain: Interventions in demand and supply sides. *Management Science* 58(6) 1072–1091.

Arrow, K.J. (1963). Uncertainty and the Welfare Economics of Medical Care. *American Economic Review*, 53(5), pp. 941–973.

Ata, B., A. Skaro, S. Tayur. (2016). OrganJet: Overcoming geographical disparities in access to deceased donor kidneys in the United States. *Management Science* 63(9):2776-2794.

Bastani, H., J. Goh, M. Bayati. (2016). Evidence of strategic behavior in Medicare claims reporting. Working Paper.

Belleflamme, P., M. Peitz. (2015). *Industrial Organization: Markets and Strategies*. Cambridge, UK: Cambridge University Press.

Bergemann, D., S. Morris. (2017). Information design: a unified perspective. *Cowles Foundation Discussion Paper No. 2075R.*

Bolton, P. and M. Dewatripont. (2005). *Contract Theory*. Cambridge, MA: MIT Press.

Chick, S. E., H. Mamani, D. Simchi-Levi. (2008). Supply chain coordination and influenza vaccination. *Operations Research* 56(6) 1493–1506.

Dai, T., M. Akan, S. Tayur. (2017a). Imaging room and beyond: the underlying economics behind physicians' test-ordering behavior in outpatient services. *Manufacturing Service Operations Management* 19(1) 99–113.

Dai, T., X. Wang, and C. Hwang. (2017b). Clinical ambiguity and conflicts of interest in interventional cardiology decision-making. Johns Hopkins University Working Paper.

Dai, T., S. Singh. (2018). Conspicuous by its absence: diagnostic expert testing under uncertainty. Johns Hopkins University Working Paper.

Deo, S., C.J. Corbett. (2009). Cournot competition under yield uncertainty: The case of the U.S. influenza vaccine market. *Manufacturing Service Operations Management* 11 563–576.

Deo, S. and I. Gurvich. (2011). Centralized vs. decentralized ambulance diversion: A network perspective. *Management Science*, 57(7), pp.1300–1319.

Deo, S., M. Sohoni, N. Jha. (2016). Incentivizing less-than-fully-qualified providers for early diagnosis of Tuberculosis in India. *Indian School of Business* Working Paper.

Desai, N.R., S.M. Bradley, C.S. Parzynski, B.K. Nallamothu, P.S. Chan, J.A. Spertus, M.R. Patel, J. Ader, A. Soufer, H.M. Krumholz, J.P. Curtis. (2015). Appropriate use criteria for coronary revascularization and trends in utilization, patient selection, and appropriateness of percutaneous coronary intervention. *JAMA* 314(19) 2045–2053.

Dickerson, O.D. (1959). The problem of overutilization in health insurance. *Journal of Insurance, pp.* 65–72.

Dranove, D. and W.D. White. (1987). Agency and the organization of health care delivery. *Inquiry*, pp. 405–415.

Dulleck, U. and R. Kerschbamer. (2006). On doctors, mechanics, and computer specialists: The economics of credence goods. *Journal of Economic Literature*, 44(1), pp. 5–42.

Fuloria, P.C., S.A. Zenios. (2001). Outcomes-adjusted reimbursement in a health-care delivery system. *Management Science* 47(6) 735–751.

Gibbons, R. (1992). *A Primer in Game Theory*. Harvester Wheatsheaf. New York.

Glode, V., C. Opp, X. Zhang. (2018). Voluntary disclosure in bilateral transactions. *Journal of Economic Theory*, Volume 175, pp. 652–688.

Guo, P., C.S. Tang, Y. Wang, M. Zhao. (2017). The impact of reimbursement policy on patient welfare, revisit rate and waiting time in a public healthcare system: fee-for-service vs. bundled payment. *Manufacturing & Service Operations Management*. Forthcoming.

Gupta, D., M. Mehrotra. (2015). Bundled payments for healthcare services: proposer selection and information sharing. *Operations Research* 63(4) 772–788.

Hyksová, M. (2013). Several milestones in the history of game theory. http://euler.fd.cvut.cz/~hyksova/ hyksova_milestones.pdf

Jiang, H., P. Zhan, S. Savin. (2012) Performance-based contracts for outpatient medical services. *Manufacturing & Service Operations Management* 14(4) 654–669.

Jost, M.G., D.W. Young. (2012). Boston University Medical Center Hospital. Boston University Teaching Case. Crimson Press.

Kamenica, E., M. Gentzkow. (2011). Bayesian persuasion. *American Economic Review* 101 (10) 2590–2615.

Kianercy, A., R. Veltri, and K.J. Pienta. (2014). Critical transitions in a game theoretic model of tumour metabolism. *Interface Focus*, 4(4), p. 20140014.

Kouvelis, P., Y. Xiao, and N. Yang. (2015). PBM competition in pharmaceutical supply chain: Formulary design and drug pricing. *Manufacturing & Service Operations Management*, 17(4), pp. 511–526.

Laffont, J.J. and D. Martimort. (2009). *The Theory of Incentives: The Principal-Agent Model*.Princeton University Press. Princeton, NJ

Lee, D.K. K., S.A. Zenios. (2012). An evidence-based incentive system for Medicare's End-Stage Renal Disease program. *Management Science*. 58(6) 1092–1105.

Lucas, R. (1976). "Econometric Policy Evaluation: A Critique." In Brunner, K.; Meltzer, A. *The Phillips Curve and Labor Markets. Carnegie-Rochester Conference Series on Public Policy*. 1. New York: American Elsevier. pp. 19–46.

Nagarajan, M. and G. Sošić. (2009). Coalition stability in assembly models. *Operations Research*, 57(1), pp. 131–145.

Neumann, J.V. and O. Morgenstern. (1944). *Theory of Games and Economic Behavior*.Princeton University Press, Princeton, NJ.

Osborne, M.J. and A. Rubinstein. (1994). *A Course in Game Theory*. MIT Press. Cambridge, MA.

Paç, M.F., S. Veeraraghavan. (2015). False diagnosis and overtreatment in services. *University of Pennsylvania* Working Paper.

Pauly, M.V. (1968). The economics of moral hazard: comment. *American Economic Review*, 58(3), pp. 531–537.

Pauly, M.V. (1974). Overinsurance and public provision of insurance: The roles of moral hazard and adverse selection. *Quarterly Journal of Economics*, 88(1), pp. 44–62.

Rowell, D. and L.B. Connelly. (2012). A Historical View of the Term "Moral Hazard." *Insurance Economics*, 65, pp. 3–5.

Salanié, B. (2005). *The Economics of Contracts: A Primer*. MIT Press. Cambridge, MA.

Samuelson, L. (2016). Game Theory in Economics and Beyond. *Journal of Economic Perspectives*, 30(4), pp.107–130.

Sannikov, Y. (2008). A continuous-time version of the principal-agent problem. *Review of Economic Studies* 75(3): 957–984.

Savva, N., T. Tezcan, O. Yildiz. (2018). Can Yardstick Competition Reduce Waiting Times? *London Business School Working Paper*.

Shumsky, R.A., E.J. Pinker. (2003). Gatekeepers and referrals in services. *Management Science.* 49(7) 839–856.

So, K.C., C.S. Tang. (2000). Modeling the impact of an outcome-oriented reimbursement policy on clinic, patients, and pharmaceutical firms. *Management Science* 46(7) 875–892.

Spence, M. (1973). Job market signaling. *Quarterly Journal of Economics*, 87(3), pp. 355–374.

Su, X., S.A. Zenios. (2004). Patient choice in kidney allocation: the role of the queueing discipline. *Manufacturing Service Operations Management* 6(4) 280–301.

Su, X., S.A. Zenios. (2006). Recipient choice can address the efficiency-equity trade-off in kidney transplantation: a mechanism design model. *Management Science* 52(11) 1647–1660.

Tirole, J. (1988). *The Theory of Industrial Organization*. MIT press. Cambridge, MA.

Wang, X., L.G. Debo, A. Scheller-Wolf, S.F. Smith. (2010). Design and analysis of diagnostic service centers. *Management Science* 56(11) 1873–1890.

Zeckhauser, R. (1970). Medical insurance: A case study of the tradeoff between risk spreading and appropriate incentives. *Journal of Economic Theory*, 2(1), pp. 10–26.

Zhang, J. (2010). The sound of silence: Observational learning in the US kidney market. *Marketing Science.* 29(2) 315–335.

Zheng, R., T. Dai, K. Sycara. (2018). Jumping the Line, Charitably: Analysis and Remedy of Donor-Priority Rule. Johns Hopkins University Working Paper.

16

Queueing Games

Mustafa Akan

Carnegie Mellon University

We survey fundamental queueing models and recent healthcare applications. We focus on strategic aspects *of* queueing games. We cover a range of models and their analyses and main results, including observable versus unobservable queues, total system value maximization versus provider revenue maximization, priorities and their implications, incentive-compatibility in queueing systems, time-based competition, and operation of centralized matching markets without transfers.

16.1 Introduction

Queueing theory is the mathematical analysis of customers waiting for service. It answers questions such as: What is the average waiting time? How long is the queue? What is the probability of waiting? How costly is it to reduce waiting? How do these depend on the parameters given?

Queueing analysis is essential for healthcare because delays are ubiquitous. Scientific management of patient flow is essential to improving quality and reducing costs in healthcare. Queueing theory, the intrinsically dynamic and stochastic study of flow systems, is used to model how waiting times depend on capacity utilization and variability.

The following characteristics of healthcare as a service cause waiting (among others):

- Uncertainty: The randomness of arrivals to the system and treatment times.
- Heterogeneity: Wide variety of conditions and symptoms prevent the providers from specifying the work content of the service to be provided for a patient.
- Temporal aspect (inflexible capacity): Improvements in capacity are costly and cannot be brought online quickly.

Handbook of Healthcare Analytics: Theoretical Minimum for Conducting 21st Century Research on Healthcare Operations, First Edition. Edited by Tinglong Dai and Sridhar Tayur.

Delays adversely affect well-being. Waiting is costly in healthcare because patients suffer loss in quality of life until treated; delayed treatment can cause undesirable outcomes because timely information collection could have improved accuracy. Because waiting is costly, it also affects the incentives of all parties involved: patients, physicians, hospitals, insurance companies, and governments.

16.1.1 Scope of the Review

Several review articles cover applications of queueing in healthcare. See Green (2006) and Gupta (2013). The focus of this survey is on optimal design of queueing systems and queueing games in healthcare. The following related topics are omitted in this chapter: simulation/performance analysis, appointment scheduling (see Savin 2006 and Gupta and Denton 2008 for a review), time-varying arrival rates (Armony et al., 2015; Dai and Shi, 2014; Shi et al., 2016; Chan et al., 2017), emergency response, and value of providing delay information (see Whitt, 1999).

The survey is organized into two parts. Section 15.2 performs a review of the most commonly used queueing models in healthcare and points to various directions of extension. Section 15.3 adds strategic behavior to the standard models and offers connections to modeling tools in other fields. We provide some suggestions for further reading throughout.

16.2 Basic Queueing Models

A queueing system consists of the following components:

16.2.1 Components of a Queueing System

- **Arrivals:** This describes how patients arrive at the system. Patients can visit a walk-in clinic, join the transplant queue with end-stage organ failure, make appointments for elective surgery, and so forth. The typical assumption is independent arrivals. This is true in most situations except in the case of natural disasters and the like, where there can be group arrivals.
- **Service:** The service might last different lengths depending on the patient. This could be due to pure randomness in the nature of the service interaction/diagnostic process, or a facility serving a diverse population (e.g., university research hospitals) might need to serve patients with different needs, causing variability in service times.
- **Servers:** The queueing system might have one or more servers. The typical servers in the health system could be primary care physicians, nurses, radiologists, MRI machines, hospital beds, rooms in a nursing home, and so on.

- **Queueing discipline:** This specifies the order in which to serve the customers waiting in line. The most common queueing disciplines used in research are first-in, first-out (FIFO), priority, and processor sharing. Queueing discipline determines how to allocate waiting among different classes of patients in a health system. Ideally, the ordering would strive for efficiency (i.e., minimizing an appropriate aggregate measure of disutility/harm among heterogenous patients) while also maintaining a sense of fairness/equity (if waiting is inevitable). By choosing the scheduling policy carefully, providers can achieve different delay distributions to help implement desired outcomes.

Notation. We could make myriad assumptions regarding the arrival and service processes, number of servers, and so forth. Kendall's queueing notation is a shorthand for classifying queues. In the simplest models it consists of three letters/numbers $\cdot/\cdot/\cdot$, where the first entry denotes the arrival process, the second entry denotes the service process, and the third entry denotes the number of servers, The abbreviations for some commonly used distributions are M for exponential (memoryless), D for deterministic, G for general, and GI for general independent. In addition to the above base notation, more letter/symbols can be appended if other factors are in play, such as when there is a finite waiting room of size K (e.g., $M/M/1/K$) or customer abandonment.

16.2.2 Performance Measures

In analyzing a healthcare queueing system, we are typically interested in one or more of the following performance measures:

- **Waiting time:** This refers to the time spent in the queue until service begins. In an emergency department or in the case of an ambulance, the time until service begins is critical to a patient's health.
- **Sojourn time:** This refers to the time in the queue plus time with the server. In the diagnostic process, patients care about the length of time until an accurate diagnosis is reached, not just about the time until a medical test is administered.
- **Distribution of the waiting time:** The percentage of customers waiting beyond a threshold is a measure of the quality of service that patients and policymakers care about.
- **Expected number of patients in the queue:** The size of the waiting list is of concern to policymakers, especially in countries that have centralized health care systems.
- **Reneging/balking rates:** Balking refers to the situation when an arriving customer chooses not to join the queue. The reason for balking could be exogenous or endogenous (rational). For the latter case, see Section 16.3.4. Reneging means that a customer leaves the system while waiting in the

queue, without completing service. For example, in transplant queues, reneging rates correspond to pretransplant deaths; see Section 16.3.5.

- **Utilization:** Percentage of the time the servers are busy/occupied. A low utilization/occupancy rate for hospital beds might be taken as a sign of excess capacity by the policymakers.
- **Fairness/equity:** Equity refers to the fact that no group of patients enjoys a disproportionate increase in welfare at the expense of all the rest. A major goal throughout is to maximize the efficiency of the healthcare system, subject to an additional set of equity constraints whenever applicable (e.g., organ transplant).

In particular, we provide derivations of the mean performance measures discussed above, such as the mean waiting time and the mean sojourn time.

16.2.3 M/M/1

In the basic model, customers arrive one at a time and are always allowed to enter the system (never turned down), no priority rules exist, and customers are served in the order they arrive. There is a single server. Interarrival and service times are exponential with mean $1/\lambda$ and $1/\mu$, respectively. The utilization of the server is denoted by $\rho := \lambda/\mu$. Stability requires that $\lambda < \mu$; otherwise, the queue length will go to infinity.

Memoryless property: An important feature of an exponential random variable X is that it is memoryless. This property states that for all $x > 0$ and $t > 0$,

$$P(X > x + t | X > t) = P(X > x).$$

That is, the remaining lifetime of X, given that X is still alive at time t, is again exponentially distributed with rate μ.

System state: Since the distribution of the exponential service time is memoryless, the system state is simply the number of customers in the system (queue + server). Let p_n denote the equilibrium probability that there are currently n customers in the system. Equating the flow rate into and out of a single state n, we obtain the balance equations for each system state in the steady state.

$$\lambda p_0 = \mu p_1,$$
$$(\lambda + \mu)p_n = \mu p_{n+1} + \lambda p_{n-1}, \text{ for } n = 1, 2, \dots .$$

Using the fact that $\sum_{n=0}^{\infty} p_n = 1$, we can solve the balance equations to obtain

$$p_n = (1 - \rho)\rho^n, \text{ for } n = 0, 1, 2, \dots . \tag{16.1}$$

Mean waiting time and mean queue length: Let $E[L]$ and $E[Q]$ denote the mean number of customers in the system and in the queue, respectively.

Using the limiting probabilities in Eq. (16.1), we can calculate $E[L]$ as follows:

$$E[L] = \sum_{n=0}^{\infty} np_n = \frac{\rho}{1-\rho}.$$

Little's Law: The second (mean) performance metric of interest is the expected time in system $E[S]$. We can apply Little's Law to compute $E[S]$, which states that

$$E[L] = \lambda E[S].$$

Using this relation between the (expected) time in system and (expected) number in system, we find

$$E[S] = \frac{1}{\mu(1-\rho)} = \frac{1}{\lambda - \mu}.$$

Little's Law makes no assumptions about the interarrival or service time distributions, the queue discipline, or the number of servers (the network topology). Little's Law also applies to a part or parts of the system; for example, we can define the system to just be the queue, not including the server, or a subclass of the arrivals.

Distribution of waiting time: Next, we will derive the distribution of the sojourn time and time in the queue. Consider an arbitrary customer who arrives at the system under stationary conditions. The probability that this customer sees n other people in the system is p_n because of the Poisson arrivals see time averages (PASTA) property. The service time of each of these n customers already in the system is exponential with mean $1/\mu$ because of the memoryless property. Hence, the sojourn time condition on seeing n customers in the system is Erlang-(n + 1) distributed. From this, we can calculate that the sojourn time S is exponentially distributed with parameter $\mu(1-\rho)$. Notice that the sojourn time is magnified by a factor of $1/(1-\rho)$, which goes to infinity as $\rho \to 1$. Therefore, heavily loaded service systems (i.e., $\rho \approx 1$) are quite sensitive to the increases in their load. As for the time in the queue W, it is equal to zero with probability $1-\rho$ (if the system is empty) and exponential with parameter $\mu(1-\rho)$ otherwise. We can also characterize the departure process from an M/M/1 queue to be a Poisson process with rate λ.

16.2.4 M/G/1

In healthcare applications, the Poisson process has been an accurate description of the arrivals. The service times, however, may not always be exponentially distributed. In the M/G/1 queue, the arrival distribution is Poisson, but the distribution of the service time S is general (denoted by G).

System state: Typically, remaining service time depends on the already-attained service, so we do not have a Markov process. To overcome this problem, we can model the system by observing the number of customers just after each departure. Consider the state of the system observed from the perspective of an arriving customer. Let p_n be the limiting probability of there being n tasks in the system or, equivalently, the long-run fraction of time that there are n jobs in the system. Let a_n be the limiting probability of an arrival observing n jobs in the system (or, equivalently, the long-run fraction of arrivals that observe n jobs).

Property 16.1 PASTA (Poisson arrivals see time averages): If the arrival process to the system is a Poisson process, then $a_n = p_n$.

Result 16.1 Pollaczek-Khintchine (PK) formula: For a single-server queue with the PASTA property, mean time in the queue $E[W]$ is given by

$$E[W] = \frac{\rho \frac{E[S^2]}{2E[S]}}{(1-\rho)}.$$

The mean sojourn time $E[T]$ is simply given by $E[T] = \frac{\lambda E[S^2]}{2(1-\rho)} + E[S]$. Notice that the sojourn time is determined by $E[S]$ and $E[S^2]$, the first and second moments of the service time, but does not depend on the the distribution of the service time. Increasing variability lowers the performance of a service system. To convert "times" to "numbers," we can once again use Little's Law. The mean number of customers in the queue is given by $E[Q] = \lambda E[W] = \frac{\lambda^2 E[S^2]}{2(1-\rho)}$. And the mean number of customers in the system is given by $E[L] = \lambda E[T] = \frac{\lambda^2 E[S^2]}{2(1-\rho)} + \lambda E[S]$.

16.2.5 M/M/c

Multiserver queues are used for capacity planning healthcare. A multiserver queuing model is needed to analyze healthcare systems with more than one server, such as hospital units. The M/M/c system contains multiple identical servers. The arrival process is a Poisson with rate λ, and service times are exponential with the same rate μ for each of the c servers. The waiting customers form a single queue; that is, servers face a common pool of arriving tasks. The customer who has waited the longest is served by the next available server. The servers keep working until there are no more waiting customers. Since $c\mu$ is the total service capacity, the utilization (i.e., load) of the system is given by $\rho = \frac{\lambda}{c\mu}$. Stability requires $\rho < 1$; that is, $c\mu < \lambda$.

The limiting probabilities p_n of the number of customers in the system can be found by using a procedure along the lines of that used for the M/M/1 queue. The customers wait only if all servers are busy. The probability that an arriving customer finds that there are more than s customers already in the system is given by

$$\sum_{n\geq s} p_n = \frac{\left(\frac{\lambda}{\mu}\right)^c}{c!}\left(1-\frac{\lambda}{c\mu}\right)^{-1}\left[\sum_{k=0}^{c-1}\frac{\left(\frac{\lambda}{\mu}\right)^k}{k!}+\frac{\left(\frac{\lambda}{\mu}\right)^c}{c!}\left(1-\frac{\lambda}{c\mu}\right)^{-1}\right]^{-1},$$

which is known as the Erlang-C Formula. The probability of delay formula has been used to estimate the number of hospital beds required to achieve a target probability of delay for patients (see Green and Nguyen, 2001, and the review article by Green, 2006).

We do not present the expressions for the mean number in the queue and system as they are well approximated by the following expression for the mean queue length: $E[Q] = \lambda E[W] = \frac{\rho^{\sqrt{2(c+1)}}}{(1-\rho)}$. Other performance measures such as $E[W]$, $E[L]$, and $E[T]$ can be found using Little's law and standard transformation laws.

16.2.6 Priorities

The models discussed so far are serving customers based on FIFO. In healthcare applications where the patients have varying medical urgencies (e.g., in emergency department, organ transplant, and so on), we may want to give priority to some class of patients over others. The scheduling policy determines which customer will be served next when a server becomes available. There are several options:

- **Preemptive priority:** The currently served customer is interrupted when a higher priority customer arrives. The interrupted lower-priority customer resumes service from the point that is left when no more higher-priority customers exist in the system.
- **Non-Preemptive priority:** A higher-priority customer who, upon arrival, finds the server busy with a lower-priority class customer, waits until the lower-priority customer is served.

In preemptive priority policies, the higher-priority class customers are not affected in any way by the existence of the lower-priority class customers. In nonpreemptive priority policies, the higher-priority class customers may need to wait for the residual service time of the lower-priority classes if the server is busy.

The second dimension along which the scheduling policies differ is the amount of information they can use regarding the service times of various customer classes. Scheduling rules that use size/service requirements in determining which customer will be served next influence the distribution of the number of arrivals during one service time.

A **work-conserving (nonidling)** scheduling rule means that the server is not allowed to remain idle while there are still customers to be served in the system.

In what follows, we consider a single server queue to make the analysis simpler. Consider an M/G/1 queueing system with two classes. Let λ_i be the arrival rate of class i customers for $i = 1, 2$. The service times for class i customers have a general distribution with mean $1/\mu_i$ and second moment $E[S_i^2]$. Let $\rho_i = \lambda_i/\mu_i$ be the load due to class i customers. Assume that $\sum\limits_i \rho_i < 1$. Suppose that class 1 customers have higher priority than class 2. Notice that "work in system" is the same for all work-conserving scheduling policies. The server utilization also does not change across all work-conserving polices.

Nonpreemptive priority: We first calculate the expected waiting for the job in service. ρ_i is the probability that the customer in service is of class i. The expected remaining service time of a class i customer is equal to $\frac{E[S_i^2]}{2E[S_i]} = \frac{\mu_i E[S_i^2]}{2}$. The expected waiting for the job in service is then equal to $\sum\limits_i \rho_i \frac{\mu_i E[S_i^2]}{2} = \frac{1}{2}\sum\limits_i \lambda_i E[S_i^2]$.

The time in queue $E[W_1]$ for class 1 customers is then given by

$$E[W_1] = \frac{\frac{1}{2}\sum\limits_{i=1}^{2} \lambda_i E[S_i^2]}{1 - \rho_1}$$

where the denominator $1 - \rho_1$ is due to waiting for only the class 1 jobs already in the queue.

Class 2 customers have to wait for all class 1 customers in the system upon arrival, as well as all class 1 customers who arrive before they start service. Hence,

$$E[W_2] = \frac{\frac{1}{2}\sum\limits_{i}^{2} \lambda_i E[S_i^2]}{(1 - \rho_1)(1 - \rho_1 - \rho_2)},$$

where the $1 - \rho_1 - \rho_2$ in the denominator is due to existing class 1 and 2 customers in the queue and $1 - \rho_1$ is due to class 1 customers arriving afterward (but served earlier because of higher priority). The expected time in system is found by adding the service time $E[T_i] = E[W_i] + 1/\mu_i$.

Preemptive priority: Under preemptive priority, class 1 customers do not need to wait for class 2 customers being served. Therefore, their expected time in the queue is equal to

$$E[W_1] = \frac{\frac{1}{2}\lambda_1 E[S_1^2]}{1 - \rho_1},$$

and their expected time in system is equal to $E[T_1] = E[W_1] + 1/\mu_1$.

Class 2 customers, on the other hand, can be interrupted by class 1 customers during service. Therefore, their time in the queue is given by

$$E[W_2] = \frac{\frac{1}{2}\sum_i^2 \lambda_i E[S_i^2]}{(1-\rho_1)(1-\rho_1-\rho_2)},$$

and time in system is equal to

$$E[T_2] = \frac{1/\mu_2}{1-\rho_1} + \frac{\frac{1}{2}\sum_i^2 \lambda_i E[S_i^2]}{(1-\rho_1)(1-\rho_1-\rho_2)}.$$

Conservation law. The residual service time of all customers in the system is given by $\frac{1}{2}\sum_i \lambda_i E[S_i^2]$. This is a constant that does not change with the scheduling rule.

Hence, the following conservation law holds for mean waiting times in the queue:

$$\sum_i \rho_i E[W_i] = \frac{\rho \sum_i \lambda_i E[S_i^2]}{2(1-\rho)} \tag{16.2}$$

The crucial observation is that the amount of work in the system does not depend on the order in which the customers are served. Also note that if the scheduling policy reduces the response time of some customers, then the response times of other customers would necessarily increase in accordance with conservation laws. The expected steady-state delays of individual service classes are also bounded by the expected delay vectors under absolute (or strict) priority disciplines, which give static preemptive priority to all customers of one class over all others and schedule customers of a given class FIFO (preemptive-resume and -repeat rules perform the same because service times are exponential).

16.2.6.1 Achievable Region Approach

The achievable region approach defines the class of admissible scheduling policies and then characterizes the set of expected delays that are achievable by admissible policies. Using this correspondence between scheduling policies and attainable expected delays, we can transform the stochastic scheduling problem into a simpler problem of choosing expected delays in the achievable set. For instance, we can find the optimal delays (e.g., revenue maximizing, total cost minimizing) within the achievable region, possibly subject to other relevant constraints (e.g., incentive-compatible delays). Finally, we design a scheduling policy that results in the desired optimal delays. The definition of "admissible" depends on the specific setting. The performance measure is typically the mean waiting time in the system or mean number of customers in the queue.

The elements of any achievable (within a certain class of strategies) expected delay vector must satisfy an equality constraint of the type 16.2. Similarly, the expected delays of any single customer class are also bounded by the expected delay vectors under absolute (or strict) priority disciplines that give static priority to customers of one class over all others. For a multiclass M/M/1 queue with preemption, there will be a set of linear constraints, and the achievable region is a polyhedron (cf. Coffman and Mitrani (1980)). Also see Federgruen and Groenevelt (1986) and Shanthikumar and Yao (1992) for further characterizations for multi-class queueing systems.

16.2.7 Networks of Queues

Jackson networks: A Jackson network consists of multiple first-come, first served (FCFS) servers, each with exponential service rate μ_i. Customers arrive at server k from outside with Poisson rate λ_i. Customers who complete service with server k can be routed to server l with probability p_{kl}, or they can leave the system with probability $1 - \sum_l p_{kl}$. The total arrival rate to server k consists of outside arrival plus the inside arrivals.

Jackson networks exhibit the important *product-form* property, which considerably simplifies their solution. It says that

$$P(n_1 \text{customers in server } 1, \ \ldots, n_K \text{ customers in server } K)$$
$$= \prod_{k=1}^{K} P(n_k \text{ customers in server } k).$$

This means that all servers act as if separate $M/M/1$ queues, and the number of customers at the servers is independent.

Types of networks that exhibit product form have been extended beyond Jackson-type networks, including closed Jackson networks, load-dependent servers, and *classed Jackson networks*. However, one requirement for these results is that the service time is associated with the server, not with the customers themselves. In a multiclass queueing network, there are different classes of customers whose service times and routing through the network depend on their class. Such multiclass queueing networks usually render a direct analysis to be intractable. A comprehensive overview of research on queueing networks can be found with Askin (1993) and Hopp and Spearman (2000).

16.2.8 Approximations

In what follows, we review various approximations in the large-capacity asymptotics.

Fluid Models. Fluid models provide useful first-order approximation by replacing random variables with their rates. This gives rise to a deterministic system. The customers in a fluid model are infinitesimal or "fluid." Differential equations describe the evolution of the system state, for example, the number of customers in the queue. Such a model can be constructed through a functional strong law of large numbers argument, or we might posit the fluid model directly and start from there. Solutions are obtained via differential equations (analytical or numerical) or continuous linear programs. The fluid model captures the average behavior of a stochastic queue, which is sufficient in certain applications where capturing the dynamics is the primary goal, such as dynamic health states in organ transplant. It is also used to model situations involving predictable variability, such as early discharge policies.

Diffusion Approximations. Diffusion limits to queueing systems provide a second-order approximation of a stochastic system. These limits help us understand the sensitivity of system performance to temporary overloads that cause customer discontent. The research program with the steps of proving limit theorems; and defining the limiting process is the standard operating procedure in papers on diffusion approximations to queueing systems. For heavy traffic theory, we refer readers to the books by Chen and Yao (2001), Whitt (2002), and Harrison (2013).

In this section, we have illustrated the use of queueing theory, the inherently dynamic and stochastic analysis of flow systems, to model how waiting times depend on demand volume and service capacity. The discussion so far does not account for behavior of strategic agents. Considering rationality in agents is the next step in studying queues in healthcare.

16.3 Strategic Queueing

We use this section to assess standard queueing models introduced in the previous section in an economic environment. We start with forward-looking behavior by consumers. This behavior is basically what defines strategic consumers: They look at their options and their expected future options, and optimize their utility[1]

In healthcare, services are inherently dynamic; interactions take place over time, and populations change as arrivals, departures, abandonments, and other movements occur. At the same time, waiting is costly. This creates an incentive to achieve health status quickly. On the patient side, waiting affects preferences in two ways:

1. Whether to seek healthcare services from a provider or go elsewhere (i.e., join the marketplace or not).
2. Once in the market, how to choose among multiple treatment options (e.g., transplant patients waiting for a better match).

1 A stronger definition is behavior that takes into account the influence on others' behavior. However, we are not covering that direction here.

In response, other actors in the healthcare market (e.g., providers, insurers, government) need to develop strategies that work well with strategic patient behavior. Reference books on rational queueing are Hassin and Haviv (2003) and Hassin (2016).

16.3.1 Waiting as an Equilibrium Device

Health economics literature models the healthcare marketplace as the place where consumers and producers interact (i.e., exchange goods and services). Consumers choose what and how much to consume, maximizing utility, subject to budget constraints, which leads to individual demands and can be later aggregated to obtain market demand. The delay of treatment reduces patients' benefits. If the benefit from being treated is R, delaying treatment by t time periods results in a utility of $e^{-\delta t}R$, where δ is the discount factor. For a fee of p, the consumer can get immediate treatment in the private sector. Consumers' choices are affected by the price p as well as how long they must wait before accessing free care at the public health system. The customer would choose the public sector if $R - p \leq e^{-\delta t}R$, which derives an upper bound on the waiting time that a consumer will tolerate. That is, if waiting is too costly, then the patient will not join the waiting list. For a given distribution of benefits R in the market, the public sector demand D is determined. On the supply side, models are typically based on a production function of waiting time; that is, $t = F(C, D)$, where C represents the resources/capacity and D is the demand for service. The production function is assumed to be increasing in D and decreasing in C. The hospital manager maximizes utility, subject to a general resource budget constraint. The hospital manager's utility depends negatively on waiting times. In equilibrium, the waiting times and prices are such that supply equals demand. In some papers, queue length is equal to demand, as the number of new people added to the waiting list is equal to the number who leave the waiting list by being treated. The demand is rationed so that the patients with the lowest net surplus are not served. (See Lindsay and Feigenbaum (1984), Iversen (1993), Martin and Smith (1999), Barros and Olivella (2005), Siciliani (2005), and the recent survey by Iversen and Siciliani (2011)).

The usual instrument to match supply and demand is the price. Nonprice rationing arises in many diverse situations, including healthcare. For example, prices are illegal for allocating the scarce resource of transplant organs. Indeed, a large literature discusses centralized matching models without transfers. This body of work is based on static models that deal with the matchings among two fixed sets of agents at a specific point in time. We shall not review these here (see the book by Roth and Sotomayor (1990)); we focus instead on the narrower literature on dynamic matching models with queueing in Section 16.3.5. The aforementioned papers do not explicitly model the queue. Instead, they use functional assumptions on the cost function, which are justified as capturing the service capacity constraints and their nonlinear effect on waiting times. Considering a queue structure allows quantification of the costs explicitly and waiting cost reduction via changes in the queueing policy.

16.3.2 Demand Dependent on Service Time

It is possible to measure quality of care by waiting times, as they can be interpreted as a negative form of hospital quality. Another quality attribute that influences patient experiences and clinical outcomes is the time the physician spends with the patient—the longer the service encounter, the higher the patient utility is. Longer service can generate more value because the performance of expert (knowledge-based) services relies on the amount and quality of information collected about the customers.

Longer service means better quality, less risk, or more customization. At the same time, longer service leads to more congestion and increases delays. Service providers face a trade-off between speed and quality. Several authors attempt to optimally resolve the trade-off when customers are strategic (See chapter 5 of this handbook for more general, including nonstrategic, quality–speed trade-off). Anand et al. (2011) study an unobservable M/M/1 queueing model with homogenous customers. The service provider chooses the service rate μ and the price p. The customers' value from the service is a linear decreasing function of service rate: $V(\mu) = V_b + \alpha(\mu_b - \mu)^+$, where V_b and μ_b denote the baseline valuation and baseline service rate (i.e., $V(\mu_b) = V_b$); α is the sensitivity of service quality to its rate (referred to as the customer intensity). The customers arrive according to an exogenous Poisson process with rate arrival rate Λ, which is the potential demand for service. Upon arrival, the customers choose whether to join or balk, based on their forecast of steady-state delays. Since customers are homogenous, their equilibrium joining strategies should yield the same expected payoff. There are three cases: (1) *Full coverage*: If the net benefit is positive when everyone joins, the effective arrival rate λ is equal to potential demand Λ; (2) *Zero coverage*: If a customer who finds the system completely empty prefers not to join (i.e., $V(\mu)$ does not even justify waiting cost during service), then nobody joins; and (3) *Partial coverage*: The equilibrium arrival rate λ makes customers indifferent between joining and not joining, both of which gives them zero utility (in expectation). The authors show that the customer intensity α is a major determinant of the service provider's decision and that the optimal service rate should be neither too fast nor too slow. The authors further analyze the (service rate) competition among multiple service providers and show that higher prices and service quality can result from a more intense competition.

Dai et al. (2017) a physician's service rate and service fee decisions under insurance coverage. A distinguishing feature of healthcare markets is that insured patients often pay less attention to prices because they pay only a fraction of them. The paper investigates the relationship between the physicians' test-ordering behavior and three incentives (financial, operational, and clinical). The service quality $Q(\mu)$ is a decreasing affine function of service rate μ. Demanding more tests means a slower service rate, which increases quality (e.g., probability of a correct diagnosis); however, the marginal improvement is declining with each additional test. Patients are assumed to have the same insurance coverage with zero deductible, a copayment of π, and a coinsurance rate of β. The results continue to hold when patients have different waiting costs or health insurance coverage. Hence, when the nominal service is p, the patient's out-of-pocket payment is just $\pi + \beta(p - \pi)$. The paper focuses on the interesting case where $p \geq \pi$. The potential demand rate Λ is assumed to be large enough to avoid zero or full coverage. Let $W(\mu, \lambda)$ be the patients' mean sojourn time (before a diagnosis is reached), and ω denotes patient's waiting cost per unit of time. In the M/M/1 queue, $W(\mu, \lambda) = 1/(\mu - \lambda)$. The following equation provides the inverse demand relationship and equilibrium (market clearing) condition between W, p and λ: $Q(\mu) = \pi + \beta(p - \pi) + \omega W(\mu, \lambda(\mu, p))$. That is, patients balance three factors while joining the queue: quality, out-of-pocket expense, and waiting time. When the market clears, service quality equals full price of service (fee plus waiting cost). Using the market clearing condition, the induced arrival rate $\lambda(\mu, p)$ can be solved explicitly. The physician's decision variables are service rate μ and the service fee p. In the market equilibrium, the objective is to maximize the revenue rate $p\lambda(\mu, p)$. In social optimization, the objective is to maximize social surplus that is equal to the service quality, less patients' disutility from waiting $\lambda Q(\mu) - \omega\lambda W(\mu, \lambda)$.

Comparing the market equilibrium with the social optimum, Dai et al. (2017) found that (1) the physician always orders more tests than the socially efficient level and that the arrival rate under market equilibrium is lower than socially optimal level. (2) Copayment and coinsurance rates drive the consumption of diagnostic tests in opposite directions: As the copayment π increases, patients are responsible for a large fixed payment. Although p^* is reduced, out-of-pocket expenses still increase, making it necessary to increase the number of tests (μ^* decreases). As the coinsurance rate β increases, patients are responsible for a larger portion of the service fee. This prompts lower p^* and out-of-pocket expenses, making it possible to reduce the number of tests (μ^* increases). (3) The waiting time W^* remains the same under both objectives. The authors also showed that imposing a reimbursement ceiling is insufficient to eliminate overtesting on its own and might lead to undertesting. Misdiagnosis concerns can lead to fewer tests than in the socially efficient level. The authors also show that similar results continue to hold when there is heterogeneity in diagnostic precision over patients. In this case, there are two types of patients, and the rate at which the service quality improves when μ decreases can be either high (α_H) or low (α_H), where $\alpha_H > \alpha_L$. This is an example of a situation where some customers might care more about quality or delays than others, which necessitates different levels of service. The service provider offers a (static) menu of triples of service times, priorities, and prices to heterogeneous customers, based on their valuations.

16.3.3 Physician-Induced Demand

One of the distinguishing features of healthcare market from other service industries is that a patient does not decide treatment. A physician acts on his behalf (the consumer's agent). In the supplier-induced demand (SID) literature,doctors, as service providers, can directly influence patients' usage. Discretionary service times and a positive correlation between service value and service time are common features of expert services. Building on these properties, several papers have studied expert services in the queueing games settings where spending more time on a service adds value but also leads to congestion. Hopp et al. (2007) showed that in services with discretionary tasks, it is sometimes optimal to cut a service prematurely if customers incur a waiting cost that increases with the number of customers in the system. The authors presented situations in which adding capacity can have adverse effects, causing more congestion. In addition, increasing service time variability in some situations may, interestingly, improve system performance.

Debo et al. (2008) modeled a monopolist expert who offers a service with unverifiable duration and hence has the incentive to delay the service. Pac and Veeraraghavan (2015) investigated an expert's pricing and diagnostic decisions where consumers are unsure about the value of the delivered service even after the service is completed. These services are prone to cheating by the expert in the recommended service and service over-provision. They find that congestion induces honesty by acting as a natural fraud cost when consumers are delay sensitive. An expert with less excess capacity is less likely to cheat. Wang et al. (2010) developed a multiserver queueing model of a diagnostic service center where nurses triage patients over the phone and advise the appropriate care. Patients use the nurse line if the perceived value of the diagnostic information outweighs the inconvenience of waiting. The authors use a Brownian motion modeling of the diagnostic accuracy. Starting from an initial value, the belief evolves until it hits the chosen threshold. Because of the inherent uncertainty in the process, the service time varies across patients according to the precision target. The system manager's goal is to choose the appropriate staffing and service depth to balance between the accuracy of advice, callers' wait time, and staffing costs. The authors found that increasing capacity might lead to congestion, which might increase error rates. This counterintuitive outcome comes from the tension between accuracy and congestion. A similar trade-off between judgment accuracy and congestion was also studied by de Vericourt and Sun (2009) and Alizamir et al. (2013).

16.3.4 Joining the Queue

The first level of patient decision that waiting affects is whether to request service or not. Upon arriving at the provider, patients make rational balking decisions (i.e., leaving the system without joining the queue) in order to maximize their expected utility. The system can operate under one of two different information structures, depending on whether or not the customers observe the queue before deciding to join. In the *observable* regime, an arriving customer observes the state of the queue (i.e., number of customers in the system) before deciding on entry. In the *unobservable* regime, customers form expectations about the state of the queue.

16.3.4.1 Observable Queue

Naor (1969) is a seminal paper in the area of pricing service subject to delay. It answers the following questions: Is admission pricing a rational measure? What is the optimal price? How do the outcomes under revenue and social optimization compare?

Customers: Demand arrives according to a Poisson process with fixed rate λ. The process of arrival to the system is exogenous. Customers receive a reward R for completing the service and incur a waiting cost c per unit time. All customers are identical. Customers maximize their expected utility, which is equal to service reward net of a linear delay cost and possible fees for joining the queue. Hence, a type i customer's expected net value of receiving service given an entrance fee of θ and an expected time of wait W in the system is $R - cW - \theta$. Because utilities are additive across customers, social welfare is quantifiable. Customers are risk neutral, and all information is common knowledge.

Service provider charges (static) price θ as a means to control the system under fixed capacity (service rate μ) and FIFO scheduling. This is equivalent to choosing a (static) admission threshold n such that $\theta = R - cn/\mu$ because there is a one-to-one relationship between prices and admission thresholds.

System: The queue is an M/M/1 with infinite waiting room, but customer decision implies an M/M/1/n system with finite waiting room. System size (the balking threshold) n depends on customer preferences, system capacity, and pricing.

- Individual (self) Optimization: Under free admission ($\theta = 0$), the optimal threshold beyond which the customer will not find it in his best interest to enter the queue is given by $\lfloor \mu R/c \rfloor$.
- Social Optimization: The necessary condition for the optimal threshold is that the expected marginal increase in utility due to higher admission probability $\approx$ the expected marginal increase in waiting cost.
- Revenue Maximization: The necessary condition for the optimal threshold is that the marginal revenue increase due to higher admission probability is equal to the marginal revenue decrease due to price reduction.

Comparison of outcomes: Self-optimization overcongests the system because customers do not care about the negative externality they create by joining the queue. Hence, when the marginal customer joins the queue at the socially optimal solution, the marginal system profit is negative owing to the externality. The revenue-maximizing system is smaller than the socially optimal because a monopolist cares about the marginal customer's net utility but not about the average utility of all customers served, which is higher. Edelson and Hildebrand (1975) shows that revenue maximization coincides with social optimization in a no-balking (unobservable) queue. Hiding the queue and charging a static price that corresponds to the socially optimal threshold would simply extract all surplus.

16.3.4.2 Unobservable Queue

If the system state is unobservable, then customers forecast steady-state waiting and, hence, their join/balk decision is *state-independent*. Edelson and Hildebrand (1975) consider a no-balking M/M/1 queue. Therefore, customers must make a decision to join before observing the state of the system. The authors show that revenue maximization coincides with social optimization. The system manager's objective in the *unobservable* regime corresponds to social welfare maximization because all surplus can be extracted from the customers via fees. Hassin (1986) compared performance with balking (Naor (1969)) versus no balking (Edelson and Hildebrand (1975)) under the objective of maximizing revenue versus social welfare. Chen and Frank (2001) considered uniform dynamic pricing. With homogenous customers, the revenue maximizing threshold is equal to the socially optimal threshold because price extracts surplus from every admitted customer. See Borgs et al. for the closed-form solution (via the lambert W function) of the optimal threshold.

Mendelson (1985) considered an unobservable queue in which customers have heterogenous valuations. He compared the optimal price p (equivalently, the arrival rate λ) and capacity μ under three objectives functions: self optimization, net value maximization (i.e., social optimization), and profit maximization. Because there is no balking, stability requires $\lambda < \mu$. The users' valuations are summarized by a value function $V(\lambda)$, which represents the *total* value corresponding to the arrival rate λ. Value function $V(\lambda)$ aggregates across users who choose to join the queue. $V(\lambda)$ is increasing and strictly concave. From $V(\lambda)$, users' demand curve can be derived. We can think of the individual valuations as drawn from a distribution with cumulative distribution function (cdf) $F(\cdot)$. Let the market potential arrival rate be Λ. Among the potential customers who arrive, only those with valuations above a cut-off $\underline{v}$ will choose to join. The effective arrival rate is $\lambda = \Lambda(1 - F(\underline{v}))$. What is the cut-off $\underline{v}$? The marginal value function $V'(\lambda)$ is downward sloping and corresponds to the valuation of the marginal (i.e., cut-off) user. Hence, we have the mapping between the aggregate value function value function $V(\lambda)$ and value distribution $F(\cdot)$ as follows: $\lambda = \Lambda(1 - F(V'(\lambda)))$, or equivalently, $V'(\lambda) = \overline{F}^{-1}(\lambda/\Lambda)$.

As in Naor (1969), customers have linear (identical) waiting cost v per unit time. Let $W(\lambda, \mu)$ denote the expected waiting time. Individual (self) optimization: Customers join if and only if their expected utility from doing so is positive. For the marginal customer, who is indifferent between joining or not, the following equilibrium condition holds: $p = V'(\lambda) - vW(\lambda, \mu)$.

- Under Free Admission ($p = 0$), the marginal customer has value equal to the expected waiting cost: $V'(\lambda) = vW(\lambda, \mu)$.
- Social Optimization: The necessary condition for the optimal arrival rate λ is that the marginal value because of the higher $\lambda \approx$ the marginal waiting cost increase; that is, $V'(\lambda) = vW(\lambda, \mu) + v\lambda\frac{\partial W(\lambda,\mu)}{\partial \lambda}$. The socially optimal price $v\lambda\frac{\partial W(\lambda,\mu)}{\partial \lambda}$ is equal to the externality, in other words, the marginal waiting cost they impose on other customers.
- Profit Maximization: For fixed capacity μ, or, the short-run view, the necessary condition for optimal λ is that $V'(\lambda) = vW(\lambda, \mu) + v\lambda\frac{\partial W(\lambda,\mu)}{\partial \lambda} - \lambda V''(\lambda)$. The optimal price $v\lambda\frac{\partial W(\lambda,\mu)}{\partial \lambda} - \lambda V''(\lambda)$ accounts for the drop in marginal value due to higher λ as well as the marginal delay cost.

When capacity μ is jointly optimized with price (equivalently λ), or, the long-run view, then the optimal price is equal to the marginal capacity cost when $W(\lambda, \mu)$ is a function only of $\mu - \lambda$, for instance, M/M/1.

The customers have identical waiting costs in both Naor (1969) and Mendelson (1985). Mendelson and Whang (1990) consider multiple customer classes and construct an incentive-compatible static priority pricing to maximize total system value. Each customer class i is characterized by its delay cost v_i, value function $V_i(\lambda)$, and processing time distribution $H_i(\cdot)$. The service requirements are stochastic and heterogeneous.[2] Class i comprises a continuum of atomistic customers with heterogeneous values. Customers' waiting costs and service requirements are privately known. The service provider offers a static menu of prices and (nonpreemptive) priority policies. Customers choose whether to join or balk as well as the priority level independently (as opposed to colluding, for example, a class-based decision structure where a single representative makes a decision on behalf of the entire class). In particular, they choose the price-delay menu pair that maximizes their net utility (value minus disutility of waiting and price). Therefore, the system manager must take into account incentive-compatibility constraints while designing the optimal menu. Under full information, where the system manager can tell customer types apart, the $c\mu$ rule (which is known to minimize the total expected delay

2 Mendelson (1985) considers a special case where all customers are ex-ante homogeneous with respect to service requirements and waiting costs.

cost rate under linear costs—cf. Cox and Smith, 1961) is optimal. Under incomplete information, the system manager cannot observe the characteristics of customers. Nevertheless, externality pricing allows implementation of the first best solution, even with heterogenous customers who differ on valuations. The literature on social welfare-maximizing scheduling rules under incomplete information has been extended to convex customer delay costs by van Mieghem (2000) and convex-concave delay costs by Akan et al. (2012b).

Afeche (2012) is similar to Mendelson and Whang (1990) in that it takes the usual approach of endowing classes with atomistic customers who differ, in each class, on their valuation (downward sloping demand curves). However, unlike his predecessors, he focuses on profit maximization. Afeche (2012) considered a system with two customer classes with different (linear) delay costs. The system manager does not know individual customers' types. The solution methodology involves work conservation laws and mechanism design. Operationally feasible waiting times must be within the achievable region (cf. Section 16.2.6.1). Incentive compatibility requires that the class i customer has no incentive to buy class j service, from which we can obtain bounds on the waiting times that do not depend on price. The optimal solution partitions the demand rate space and identifies the optimal scheduling policy in each region. Afeche (2012) showed that profit maximization may lead to some alternative scheduling rules, such as injecting strategic delay (intentionally delaying some classes) and pooling different classes.

16.3.5 Waiting for a Better Match

The second way in which disutility of waiting affects preferences is by trading-off delay and quality of the match. There is an extensive matching literature in economics—and missing from static models is the waiting cost. Currently, only a few dynamic matching models have been studied in the matching literature with a queueing structure.

From the operations point of view, several researchers have studied the problem of accepting/declining organs for transplant (Alagoz et al., 2004; Alagoz et al., 2007a; David and Yechiali, 1985; Hornberger and Ahn, 2007). These papers optimize a particular patient's welfare and hence do not have an equilibrium characterization (where each patient would solve his own option value problem). The impact of patient choice has been studied by Su and Zenios (2004, 2005, 2006) and Ata et al. (2016) in the context of kidney allocation. Transplant center-level queues are studied by Delasay and Tayur (2017). Previous research that seeks to provide an optimal match between organs and patients by considering factors, such as organ failure and dynamic health status, captures the evolution of the population of transplant patients as a multiclass fluid model of overloaded queues. A continuous time deterministic model of the organ allocation system consists of K classes of patients and J classes of organs. Patient class can represent the patient's age, gender, and medical urgency. The state of the transplant waiting list at time t is the vector of patients in each class. Patients of class k arrive at rate λ_k. Organs of type j arrive at rate μ_j, and a fraction is allocated to patient classes. Patients who receive organs exit the queue. Patients can also flow out of class k because of death (too sick to transplant) or a change in dynamic health characteristics (e.g., laboratory values in the blood), in which case they become another class. The state evolution is governed by differential equations, giving rise to optimal control problems with state constraints. Zenios et al. (2000) considered kidneys where the driving trade-off is efficiency-equity and develop a dynamic index policy for kidney allocation. Akan et al. (2012a) studied livers transplantation incorporating the dynamic evolution of patient health and analyze the trade-off between medical urgency and efficiency. For further research on optimization of the organ allocation problem, see chapter 9 of the handbook.

The organ allocation system is a one-sided economy because body parts do not have preferences and only the patient can reject an organ offer. Leshno (2017) studies a similar scenario: a one-sided overloaded queue for public housing applications. Social welfare maximization requires agents to be matched to the houses in their preferred location. However, agents may find it optimal to get a house in an unpreferred location as opposed to waiting for a long time.

In a two-sided economy, agents on both sides of the market would have preferences about whom to match (e.g., child adoption; cf. Slaugh et al., 2016). Baccara et al. (2017) characterized the optimal mechanism in a setting with binary types (i.e., two classes of agents on both sides of the market). The two sides of the market are symmetrical. Every period, a pair of agents arrives at the market, one on each side. Because preferences are assortative and satisfy a super-modularity condition, matching compatible pairs is always optimal. Hence, there will always be a finite stock (i.e., admission threshold) of a single class of remaining agents on each side at all times. The stationary distribution (which is uniform as $\rho = 1$) of the two-sided queue with threshold n on each side corresponds to that of a single-sided M/M/1/2n system. The authors derive the socially optimal thresholds and finds that the individually optimal (i.e., decentralized) solution is excessively congested, (à la Naor (1969). Afeche and Akan (2017) advance a two-sided queueing model with two-sided incentives (i.e., selfish agents on both sides).[3] Two types of customers arrive at both ends of the queue from independent Poisson processes at rates λ_1, λ_2, respectively. The paper answers the following questions: Who should wait? What is the right system size? What are the corresponding prices? How do these differ under revenue maximization and social optimization? Doval (2016) instead focused on how to define a dynamic stability notion and showed

3 There is also a literature on two-sided queues without incentives, which we do not review here.

that dynamically stable allocations may fail to exist in two-sided economies, whereas they always exist in one-sided economies.

Competition

Service operations management literature has long considered time-based competition (see, e.g., Cachon and Harker, 2002; Bernstein and Federgruen, 2004; Allon and Federgruen, 2007, 2008). The arrival rates to each firm are a function of the service levels of all the firms, which compete on price and service levels simultaneously. The setting is not intrinsic to the healthcare application but applies to any service industry with time-sensitive customers. In health economics, Siciliani (2005) and Brekke et al. (2008) studied the impact of hospital competition on waiting times. Siciliani (2005) modeled a duopolistic market where a general practitioner refers the patients to the hospital with the lowest waiting time. The objective of the altruistic general practitioner is to choose how many patients λ_i to send to hospital i to maximize the total social welfare from treatment, less the waiting costs: $U(\lambda_1, \lambda_2) - \lambda_1 W_1 - \lambda_2 W_2$, where W_i is the waiting time at hospital i, and U is assumed to be a quadratic function and contains the measure of substitutability between the two hospitals. Solving for the general practitioner's problem yields the demand for each hospital as a function of W_1 and W_2. The hospitals choose the supply of care and waiting time to compete for patients. The hospital utility function contains a production cost for supply of care and disutility for waiting times. The paper shows that substitutability among hospitals reduces supply of care in equilibrium and results in longer waits.

Brekke et al. (2008) modeled hospitals competing in a spatially differentiated market. They considered two types of patients who differ in their benefit from treatment: high segment and low segment. The waiting time competition is based on the Salop model,[4] where the hospitals have different locations and waiting times. Patient choice is extended with respect to the standard models of rationing by waiting time (cf. section 16.3.1) for the high segment to include from which provider to demand care. The low patient segment can either seek treatment from the closest hospital or seek no treatment at all. The utility of type i patient located at x to seek treatment from the hospital located at z_i is $U_i(x, z_i) = V_i - cW_i - t|x = z_i|$, where V_i is the benefit of segment i, c is the waiting cost parameter and t measures travel disutility. The hospitals simultaneously announce waiting times, but they cannot differentiate the two patient segments in terms of waiting times. The authors characterized the optimal price and waiting time for society and determine when competition

4 See Salop (1979) for the n-firm variant of Hotelling's duopoly model: Firms are evenly distributed around a circle of circumference one. Consumers are distributed uniformly around the same circle. Each firm competes directly with the two neighbors. The solution allows comparative statics on n.

is desirable. They showed that introducing competition to this market leads to higher waiting times only if the high patient segment is large enough in the population.

In countries with single payer health markets, policymakers are concerned with waiting lists. One way for the government to regulate the healthcare sector is through reimbursement systems to providers. Andritsos and Aflaki (2015) presented a model of competition with nonprofit as well as for-profit hospitals. Following the general approach in the time-based competition literature, Jiang et al. (2017) studied the effects of introducing performance-based incentives for patient access to care in the presence of provider competition.

16.4 Discussion and Future Research Directions

The field of queueing has a rich theory for modeling dynamic stochastic interactions, which can help patients, doctors, and policymakers to make informed decisions. And thanks to collaborative efforts of researchers in operations management, computer science, statistics, economics, and medicine, queueing theory has been successfully applied to real-world healthcare problems. Queueing theory also provides a particular framework and established machinery for studying dynamic matching mechanisms, which have not received much attention in the existing literature because of their complexity.

References

Afeche, P. (2013). Incentive-Compatible Revenue Management in Queueing Systems: Optimal Strategic Delay. *Manufacturing & Service Operations Management.* 15(3) 423–443.

Afeche, P. and M. Akan (2017). Pricing in a Two-sided Market with Time-sensitive Customers and Suppliers. Working paper.

Akan, M., O. Alagoz, B. Ata., F.S. Erenay, and A. Said. (2012). A Broader View of Designing the Liver Allocation System. *Operations Research.* Vol. 60, No. 4. pp. 757–770.

Akan, M., B. Ata and T. Olsen. (2012). Congestion-Based Leadtime Quotation for Heterogenous Customers with Convex-Concave Delay Costs: Optimality of a Cost-Balancing Policy Based on Convex Hull Functions. *Operations Research.* Vol. 60 No. 6. pp. 1505–1519.

Alagoz, O., L.M. Maillart, A.J. Schaefer, and M.S. Roberts. (2004). The optimal timing of living-donor liver transplantation. *Management Science* 50(10), 1420–1430.

Alagoz, O., L.M. Maillart, A.J. Schaefer, and M.S. Roberts. (2007a). Choosing among cadaveric and living-donor livers. *Management Science* 53(11), 1702–1715.

Alizamir, S, F. de Vericourt, and P. Sun. (2013). Diagnostic accuracy under congestion. *Management Science* 59(1) 157–171.

Allon, G., A. Federgruen. (2007). Competition in service industries. *Operations Research* 55(1) 37–55.

Allon, G., A. Federgruen. (2008). Service competition with general queueing facilities. *Operations Research.* 56(4) 827–849.

Anand, K. S, M F. Pac, S. Veeraraghavan. (2011). Quality-speed conundrum: trade-offs in customer- intensive services. *Management Science* 57(1) 40–56.

Andritsos, D. A. and S. Afiaki. (2015). Competition and the Operational Performance of Hospitals: The Role of Hospital Objectives. *Production and Operations Management.* Vol. 24, No. 11, pp. 1812–1832.

Armony M., S. Israelit, A. Mandelbaum, Y.N. Marmor, Y. Tseytlin, G.B. Yom-Tov. (2015). Patient flow in hospitals: A data-based queueing science perspective. *Stochastic Systems* 5(1): 146–194.

Askin R.G. (1993). *Modeling and analysis of manufacturing systems.* Wiley, New York.

Ata, B., Y. Ding, and S.A. Zenios. (2017). KDPI-Dependent Ranking Policies: Shaping the Allocation of Deceased-Donor Kidneys in the New Era. Stanford University. Working paper.

Baccara, M., S. Lee, and L. Yariv (2016) Optimal Dynamic Matching. Working paper.

Barros, P. and P. Olivella. (2005). Waiting lists and patient selection. *Journal of Economics and Management Strategy*, 15: 623–46.

Bernstein, F., A. Federgruen. (2004). A general equilibrium model for industries with price and service competition. *Operations Research* 52(6) 868–886.

Brekke, K., L. Siciliani, O.R. Straume. (2008). Competition and waiting times in hospital markets. *Journal of Public Economics* 92(7) 1607–1628.

Borgs, C., J.T. Chayes, S. Doroudi, M. Harchol-Balter, and K. Xu. (2014). The optimal admission threshold in observable queues with state dependent pricing. *Probability in the Engineering and Informational Sciences*, 28, 101–119.

Cachon, P.C. and P.T. Harker. (2002) Competition and outsourcing with scale economies. *Management Science*, Vol. 48, No. 10, 1314–1333.

Chan, C.W., J. Dong, L.V. Green (2017). Queues with Time-Varying Arrivals and Inspections with Applications to Hospital Discharge Policies. *Operations Research* 65(2): 469–495.

Chen, H. and D. Yao. (2001). *Fundamentals of Queueing Networks: Performance, Asymptotics, and Optimization,* Springer.

Coffman, E.G. Jr.,, I. Mitrani. (1980). A characterization of waiting time performance realizable by single-server queues. *Operations Research.* 28(3) 810–821.

Chen, H., M. Frank. (2001). State dependent pricing with a queue. *IIE Transactions* 33, 847–860

Dai, T., M. Akan, and S. Tayur. (2017). Imaging Room and Beyond: The Underlying Economics Behind Physicians' Test Ordering Behavior in Outpatient Services. *Manufacturing & Service Operations Management* 19 (1). 99–113.

Dai, J.G., P. Shi. (2014). A two-time-scale approach to time-varying queues for hospital inpatient flow management. Cornell University, Ithaca, NY. *Operations Research* 65(2), pp.514–536.

David, I. and U. Yechiali. (1985). A time-dependent stopping problem with application to live organ transplants. *Operations Research* 33(3), 491–504.

de Vericourt, F and P. Sun. (2009). Judgement accuracy under congestion in service systems. Working Paper.

Debo, L.G., L.B. Toktay, L.N. Van Wassenhove. (2008). Queuing for expert services. *Management Science* 54(8) 1497–1512.

Delasay, M. and S. Tayur (2017) Conditions of participation: Inducing organ discards and patient deaths on transplant waiting lists. Carnegie Mellon University. Working paper.

Doval, Laura. 2015. A Theory of Stability in Dynamic Matching Markets, Working paper.

Edelson, N. M., and Hildebrand, D. K., 1975, Congestion Tolls for Queuing Processes, *Econometrica* 43, 81–92.

Federgruen A., H. Groenevelt. 1988. Characterization and optimization of achievable performance in general queueing systems. *Operations Research* 36(5) 733–741.

Green, L. (2006). Queueing analysis in healthcare. In *Patient Flow: Reducing Delay in Healthcare Delivery*. Edited by Randolph W. Hall. Springer, pp. 281–308.

Green LV, Nguyen V (2001). Strategies for cutting hospital beds: the impact on patient service. *Health Services Research* 36(2):421–42.

Gupta, D. (2013). Queueing models for healthcare operations. In *Handbook of Healthcare Operations Management*, B.T. Denton (ed.), Springer, New York.

Gupta D., B. Denton. (2008). Appointment scheduling in health care: Challenges and opportunities. *IIE Transactions* 40:800–819.

Harrison, J.M. (2013). Brownian Motion and Stochastic Flow Systems. Wiley Series in Probability and Mathematical Statistics. John Wiley and Sons, Inc., New York.

Hassin, R. (1986). Consumer information in markets with random product quality: the case of queues with balking. *Econometrica* 54, 1185–1196.

Hassin, R. (2016). *Rational Queueing*. CRC Press.

Hassin, R. and M. Haviv. (2003). *To Queue or Not to Queue: Equilibrium Behavior in Queueing Systems.* International Series in Operations Research & Management Science. Kluwer Academic Publishers, MA.

Hopp, W.J., S.M.R. Iravani, G.Y. Yuen. (2007). Operations systems with discretionary task completion. *Management Science* 53(1) 61–77.

Hopp W.J., L. Spearman. (2000). *Factory Physics.* McGraw-Hill Higher Education, New York.

Hornberger, J.C. and J.H. Ahn. (1997). Deciding eligibility for transplantation when a donor kidney becomes available. *Medical Decision Making* 17(2), 160–170.

Iversen, T. (1993). A Theory of Hospital Waiting List, *Journal of Health Economics,* 12, pp. 55–71.

Iversen, T. and L. Siciliani. (2011). Non-Price Rationing and Waiting Times, in *Oxford Handbook of Health Economics,* 649–670, Oxford University Press.

Jiang, H., Z. Pang, and S. Savin. (2017) Improving Patient Access to Care: Performance Incentives and Competition in Healthcare Markets, Working Paper.

Lindsay, C.M. and B. Feigenbaum. (1984): Rationing by Waiting Lists, *American Economic Review* 74(3), pp. 404–417.

Leshno, J.D. (2017). Dynamic Matching in Overloaded Waiting Lists Working paper. Columbia University.

Martin, S. and P. C. Smith (1999). Rationing by Waiting Lists: An Empirical Investigation, *Journal of Public Economics,* 71, pp. 141–164.

Mendelson, H. 1985. Pricing Computer Services: Queueing Effects. *Commun. ACM.* 28 (3), 312–321.

Mendelson, H., and S. Whang. 1990. Optimal Incentive-Compatible Priority Pricing for the M/M/1 Queue. *Operations Research.* 38 (5), 870–883.

Naor, P. 1969. The Regulation of Queue Size by Levying Tolls. *Econometrica.* 37 (1), 15–24.

Pac, M.F., S. Veeraraghavan (2015). False diagnosis and overtreatment in services Working Paper, The Wharton School.

Roth, A. and M. Sotomayor (1990). Two-Sided Matching: A Study in Game-Theoretic Modeling and Analysis. Cambridge University Press.

Salop, S.. 1979. Monopolistic Competition with Outside Goods. *The Bell Journal of Economics,* Vol. 10, No. 1, 141–156.

Savin, S. (2006). Managing Patient Appointments in Primary Care in Patient Flow: Reducing Delay in *Healthcare Delivery.* Edited by Randolph W. Hall. Springer, pp. 123–150.

Slaugh, V.W., M. Akan, O Kesten, U. Unver. (2016). The Pennsylvania Adoption Exchange Improves Its Matching Process. *Interfaces.* Vol. 46 Issue 2, March-April 2016, pp. 133–153.

Siciliani, L. (2005). Does more choice reduce waiting times. *Health Economics* 14/1: 17–23.

Shi P., M. Chou, J.G. Dai, D. Ding, J. Sim. (2016). Models and insights for hospital inpatient operations: Time-dependent ED boarding time. *Management Science* 62(1):1–28.

Van Mieghem, J.A. (2000). Price and Service Discrimination in Queueing Systems: Incentive Compatibility of Geμ Scheduling. *Management Science* 46 (9), 1249–1267.

Wang, X., L.G. Debo, A. Scheller-Wolf, S.F. Smith. (2010). Design and analysis of diagnostic service centers. *Management Science* 56(11) 1873–1890.

Whitt, W. Improving service by informing customers about anticipated delays. *Management Science* 45(2):192–207, 1999.

Whitt, W. (2002). *Stochastic-Process Limits: An Introduction to Stochastic-Process Limits and Their Application to Queues*. Springer.

Su, X. and S. Zenios. (2004). Patient choice in kidney allocation: The role of queueing discipline. *Manufacturing Service Operations Management* 6(4), 280–301.

Su, X. and S. Zenios. (2005). Patient choice in kidney allocation: A sequential stochastic assignment model. *Operations Research* 53(3), 443–455.

Su, X. and S. Zenios. (2006). Recipient choice can address the efficiency-equity trade-off in kidney transplantation: A mechanism design model, *Management Science* 52(11), 1647–1660.

Zenios, S.A., G.A. Chertow, and L.M. Wein. (2000). Dynamic allocation of kidneys to candidates on the transplant waiting list. *Operations Research* 48(4), 549–569.

17

Econometric Methods

Diwas KC

Emory University

17.1 Introduction

The healthcare industry faces important challenges, including rising costs, increasing complexity, and quality issues, while confronting increased demand for limited resources. For most of the advanced economies that foresee demographic changes associated with a shrinking workforce, aging population, and the attendant complexity of disease management, the resulting socioeconomic and public health challenges are particularly pressing.

Meeting these challenges calls for more efficient models of care delivery, well-informed governmental policies, and innovative new products and services. In this regard, data can play a crucial role in uncovering new insights and in allowing the various stakeholders including patients, providers, payers, and policymakers to make more informed decisions.

To that end, the healthcare industry generates significant amounts of data, such as transactional data that is often the natural byproduct of care provision. Data sources range from RFID-enabled tracking devices used to monitor patient flows and resource usage within a hospital to connected devices, such as pacemakers that relay biometric data to a cardiologist's office. More commonly used sources of data include hospital-level claims data submitted to payers for reimbursement, as well as the online reviews of providers by individual patients.

The growing availability of novel data sets can help to uncover important actionable insights. But used incorrectly, data can also misinform and mislead. In examining a statistical relationship between a set of variables, one has to be aware of possible confounding in general. In healthcare, sources of confounding tend to be quite extensive, not least because it is difficult to fully account for all the factors that impact the complex human body. Moreover, there are many nuances to the underlying incentive structures, un-observability of the actions

Handbook of Healthcare Analytics: Theoretical Minimum for Conducting 21st Century Research on Healthcare Operations, First Edition. Edited by Tinglong Dai and Sridhar Tayur.

of different parties, and organization and delivery of healthcare, all of which tend to confound an accurate estimation of the underlying relationships.

The first half of this chapter provides an overview of some challenges, especially due to unobserved factors, in establishing causality. We will explore the importance of accounting for unobserved variables, and the utility of exogenous variation, using instrumental variables and difference estimators as examples. The second half of the chapter presents structural estimation methods that can be used to generate prescriptive recommendations based on the empirical analysis.

17.2 Statistical Modeling

Suppose we are interested in estimating the causal effect of a treatment T on an outcome of interest Y. For example, T could be the use of an experimental diabetes drug, and Y could be a measure of physiological performance (e.g., the HbA1c measure, which provides the average level of blood glucose over a two- to three- month period). Alternatively, if we are interested in comparing the quality of care (Y) across two different hospitals, T could be the assignment of patients to one of the hospitals (the treatment group), with the patients assigned to the other hospital serving as the comparison (control) group. In general, the estimation of a statistical relationship such as that between the treatment and outcome is preceded by theory or a reasoned argument that leads the researcher to expect the relationship to go in a certain direction. For instance, the treatment hospital in question might have recently invested in new processes that reduce medical error, which we hypothesize improves quality of care.

From a set of N total patients treated at either hospital, for any given patient i, let Y_i denote a measure of quality of care. This could be the thirty-day survival rate, early recovery, or improved physiological functioning. For the purposes of discussion, we will assume that a higher value for Y_i indicates a higher quality of care. Suppose we believe that the relationship between T and Y is given by:

$$Y_i = X_i'\beta + u_i, \tag{17.1}$$

where $X_i = \begin{bmatrix} 1 & T_i \end{bmatrix}'$ and u_i represents the residual stochastic error term.

Then β is given by minimizing the sum of squared residuals, $u_i = Y_i - X_i'\beta$, which would yield the ordinary least squares (OLS) estimate:

$$\beta = arg \min_b E[(Y_i - X_i'b)^2].$$

From the first order conditions:

$$E[X_i(Y_i - X_i'b)] = 0.$$

Therefore, our OLS estimate is given by:

$$\hat{\beta} = E[X_i X_i']^{-1} E[X_i Y_i]. \quad (17.2)$$

In our example, X_i includes only the single regressor T_i. Therefore, the coefficient associated with T, $\hat{\beta}_1$ is given by

$$\hat{\beta}_1 = Cov(Y_i, T_i)/Var(T_i)$$

where $Cov(Y_i, T_i)$ represents the covariance between the outcome measure and the treatment, and $Var(T_i)$ represents the variance in treatment. We can think of the coefficient as an estimate of variation in the outcome attributed to the variation in the treatment variable, normalized by the variance of the treatment variable. As we hypothesize that the treatment hospital offers a higher quality of care, we expect that $\beta_1 > 0$.

17.2.1 Statistical Inference

If $E[u_i|X_i] = 0$, then the conditional independence ensures that our estimate is unbiased. This also implies that $E[u_i X_i] = 0$, which makes the estimator consistent. That is, in large samples, the estimator converges to the true value (i.e., $plim\hat{\beta} = \beta$). In order to draw statistical inferences on the estimated value of $\hat{\beta}$ using OLS on Eq. (17.1) (e.g., is it statistically different from 0?), we need the individual observations (i) to be independent and identically distributed. Then, the asymptotic variance of the error term u_i is given by the variance matrix:

$$Var(u_i) = \sigma^2 I_N,$$

where I_N is a rank N identity matrix. The independence of the observations means that there is no autocorrelation; therefore, the nondiagnoal elements of the variance matrix are zero. If the observations are identically distributed, then there is no heteroscadisticity (i.e., the variance in outcome does not depend on the specific values of X_i), so the diagonal terms in the matrix are the same. There is a direct relationship between the variance of the error term and the variance of the estimator given by

$$Var(\beta) = \sigma^2 (X'X)^{-1}.$$

Finally, although normality of the error terms is not strictly required for OLS, it can make inferencing more convenient.[1] In particular, if $u_i \sim N(0, \sigma^2 I_N)$, then the estimator is also normally distributed as follows:

$$\hat{\beta} \sim N(\beta, \sigma^2 (X'X)^{-1}) \quad (17.3)$$

1 In addition, when the error terms are normally distributed, the maximum likelihood estimator is also the OLS estimator.

17.2.2 Biased Estimates

Suppose instead that the true causal relationship between Y and T is given by the following:

$$Y_i = X_i'\beta_{true} + \delta_i + \epsilon_i \tag{17.4}$$

where $u_i = \delta_i + \epsilon_i$, and δ_i represents an important variable that impacts the outcome measure, but has been excluded from the regression analysis. If it were to be included in the regression model, then we would obtain a regression coefficient associated with δ_i. However, as this variable has been omitted, estimating the model by OLS and replacing Y_i by (17.4) would yield the following:

$$\hat{\beta} = E[X_iX_i']^{-1}E[X_iY_i]$$
$$\hat{\beta} = E[X_iX_i']^{-1}E[X_i(X_i'\beta_{true} + \delta_i + \epsilon_i)]$$
$$\hat{\beta} = E[X_iX_i']^{-1}E[X_i(X_i')]\beta_{true} + E[X_iX_i']^{-1}E[X_i\delta_i] + E[X_iX_i']^{-1}E[X_i\epsilon_i].$$

Since ϵ_i is a residual of a regression on X_i, it is uncorrelated with it, so the last term in the expression is zero. This yields:

$$\hat{\beta} = \beta_{true} + E[X_iX_i']^{-1}E[X_i\delta_i].$$

In the case of a bivariate regression model, with just the treatment variable T_i as a regressor in X_i, we have

$$\hat{\beta} = \beta_{true} + Cov(T_i, \delta_i)/Var(T_i). \tag{17.5}$$

We can make a few noteworthy observations from Eq. (17.5) above. First, β_{true}, which represents the true underlying relationship between T and Y, is the estimate that we hope to recover. However, the estimated value $\hat{\beta}$ is equal to the true value only as long as the expression $Cov(T_i, \delta_i)/Var(T_i)$ is equal to zero. If $Cov(T_i, \delta_i)/Var(T_i) \neq 0$, our estimated parameter $\hat{\beta}$ is *biased*.

Second, examining the second term on the right hand side of Eq. (17.5), we see that $Cov(T_i, \delta_i)/Var(T_i)$ is equal to zero as long as δ_i is uncorrelated with T_i (i.e., $Cov([T, \delta_i] = 0)$. This means that even if a number of unobserved factors influence the outcome, as long as the treatment T_i is independent of these factors, our estimate for the treatment effect will be unbiased. For example, the patient's age might strongly determine the patient's clinical outcome. However, if age is not a factor in the patient's assignment to the treatment or control group, our estimate will continue to be unbiased, even if we exclude age from the regression model.

Third, the sign of the correlation between treatment assignment and unobserved factors informs us about the direction of bias. For example, suppose the patient is assigned to the treatment group whenever the patient's physiological condition (captured by δ_i) is high. In other words, healthier patients are systematically directed to the treatment hospital. Without loss of generality, suppose that a higher numerical value of δ_i signals higher health. Therefore,

$Cov(\delta_i, Y_i) > 0$, because a high-health patient is predisposed to a higher quality outcome.

If healthier patients are systematically directed to the treatment hospital, then $Cov(T_i, \delta_i) > 0$. Given this, the second term on the right side of Eq. (17.5) will be positive, which would bias the coefficient upward. We would overestimate the actual impact of being treated at hospital T. The intuition for this is straightforward: if healthier patients are more likely to be treated at hospital T, this would have the effect of improving the average outcome at hospital T relative to the population average, independent of the actual quality of care at hospital T.

Conversely, consider the opposite scenario where the treatment group is systematically treating sicker patients (i.e., δ_i small). For example, many teaching hospitals tend to draw high-risk patients who cannot be treated at other hospitals. Such a set of conditions would have the effect of biasing the coefficient downward (as $Cov(T_i, \delta_i) < 0$). In other words, the hospital appears worse than it actually is. Further, if the goal of the empirical analysis is to test the hypothesis that treatment assignment improves quality, the hypothesis may still be validated if the estimated coefficient is positive (even if it is biased). This is because removing the bias would increase the estimated effect, further strengthening the hypothesis.

In addition to the treatment assignment (T_i), the researcher may have other variables associated with observation i at her disposal. Some of these factors could be patient-level, such as age, gender, race, and the results of physiological tests. Other factors might be temporal (e.g., day of week and month of year of treatment), or specific to the care provision (e.g., who was the attending physician and whether the hospital was busy at the time of treatment). Including these variables as controls in our regression model would allow us to estimate the relative effects of these factors on the treatment outcome, which, in addition to examining the treatment effect, may also be of interest. For example, we might be interested in comparing the magnitudes of the effects of age versus treatment assignment on outcome quality. Importantly, some of these control variables might be correlated with the treatment assignment. Consequently, including these controls would help to minimize the bias in the estimate of the treatment effect. Let the vector W_i denote the set of controls associated with patient i. Let us also augment the vector $X_i = \begin{bmatrix} 1 & T_i & W_i \end{bmatrix}'$.

The effect of the k-th element in X_i is given by the k-th element of estimated coefficient vector $\hat{\beta} = E[X_i X_i']^{-1} E[X_i Y_i]$. Specifically, β_k provides an estimate for the effect of element x_{ik} on the outcome, controlling for everything else. Thus, β_k is given by

$$\beta_k = Cov(y_i, \tilde{x}_{ki}) / Var(\tilde{x}_{ki}),$$

where, $\tilde{x}_{ki}$ is the residual obtained from regressing x_{ki} against the remaining elements in X_i. In other words, the coefficients β_k can be thought of as the effect of coefficient k on the outcome, attributed to the variation in k after the variation in outcome because of all the other covariates has been extracted.

In practice, even after including a large set of controls (W_i), there might still be factors that influence the outcome measure Y_i but are not observed by the econometrician. For example, there might be important measures of patient severity that impact outcome. If these unobserved variables are correlated with the treatment assignment, then the OLS approach will not be adequate to make claims of causality.

17.3 The Experimental Ideal and the Search for Exogenous Variation

Given the issue of bias at hand, consider the following thought experiment. Suppose we randomly assign any given patient i to either the treatment or the control group (say, based on the toss of a fair coin). Given the random assignment, by definition, the assignment of the patient to treatment or control should not be correlated with unobserved (or observed) factors at the patient level. That is, $Cov[T_i, \delta_i] = 0$. This means that our estimate for $\hat{\beta}$ is unbiased in Eq. (17.5). Our goal is to recover β_{true} rather than account for all of the factors, including δ_i, that affect outcome. Hence, even though various measures of severity affect outcome, under random treatment assignment, their lack of observability in our analysis has no impact on our ability to recover β_{true}. In practice, no one would flip a coin to determine the treatment plan for a sick patient (due to various clinical, ethical, or legal issues). Thus, this approach of deliberately and randomly assigning patients to treatment represents more of an experimental ideal. In the absence of such an experiment, we would like to consider practical approaches that appear to emulate the experimental ideal.

17.3.1 Instrumental Variables

One approach is natural experiments, in which comparable units of subjects are randomly assigned into treatment and control groups. The econometrician may then be able to exploit the naturally occurring exogenous variation in the treatment assignment to identify the treatment effect.

For example, in an emergency, a patient is likely to go to the nearest available hospital for treatment. This means that emergency patients who live closer to the treatment hospital are more likely to be assigned to the treatment group compared to patients who live closer to the control hospital. The travel distance to the hospital therefore serves to effectively randomize patients into the treatment and control groups. By then comparing the quality outcomes at the two hospitals, we may be able to estimate the effect of T. In this case, travel distance is called an *instrumental variable*.

An instrumental variable (denoted z_i) must satisfy the two conditions of relevance and exogeneity. The relevance condition requires that the instrument and the treatment condition be correlated. That is, $Cov(z_i, T_i) \neq 0$. In other words, the instrument must drive the assignment to the treatment group. The exogeneity condition requires that the instrument not be correlated with the error term (u_i in Eq. 17.1, such that $Cov(z_i, u_i) = 0$). This means that we have to be able to rule out any direct effect of the instrumental variable on the outcome. Specifically, z_i should not directly influence outcome (Y_i) in the sense that we would consider including them on the right side of Eq. (17.1).

The relevance condition can be easily examined through a statistical relationship between the treatment assignment and z_i. However, in general, we cannot statistically test the exogeneity condition, which has to be argued theoretically.[2]

Let z_1 denote a single valid instrument that satisfies the conditions of exogeneity and relevance. Let $Z_i = \begin{bmatrix} 1 & z_{1i} & W_i \end{bmatrix}'$ be a column vector that includes the constant term, the single instrument (z_{1i}), and the set of controls (W_i). Then, given that the number of endogenous regressors ($dim[T] = 1$) is equal to the number of instruments ($dim[z_1] = 1$), the IV estimator is considered to be ***just identified***, and is given by:

$$\hat{\beta}_{IV} = (Z'X)^{-1}Z'y \tag{17.6}$$

Given N independent observations, the dependent variable Y is an $N \times 1$ vector, and X is a $N \times K$ vector of K endogenous and control variables. In the just identified case, Z is also an $N \times K$ vector of K instruments and control variables. In order to estimate the treatment effect, the number of instruments has to be greater than or equal to the number of endogenous regressors. (If there are more instruments than endogenous regressors, then the IV estimator is said to be *over-identified.*) In the case of multiple instruments and endogenous regressors, both the Z vector and X vector would be augmented by the set of instruments and endogenous regressors respectively, and the IV estimator is

$$\hat{\beta}_{IV} = (X'P_ZX)^{-1}Z'y,$$

where

$$P_Z = Z(Z'Z)^{-1}Z'.$$

A typical implementation of an instrumental variable estimator is through a two-stage least squares (2SLS) approach, where the first stage equation employs the instruments and the other covariates to predict the treatment. In the second stage, the predicted treatment ($\hat{T}_i$) is used as an explanatory variable alongside

2 If there are multiple instrumental variables, then we could run a J-test for over-identifying restrictions. This is a test that examines whether all the instruments are exogenous, given that at least one of the instruments is exogenous. As such, it cannot be used to examine whether all instruments are exogenous.

the other X_i to predict Y_i. The coefficient in the predicted treatment assignment ($\hat{T}_i$) is the IV estimate.[3]

It is noteworthy that the estimation of β_{IV} is attributed to the portion of the variation in the treatment that is truly exogenous. That is, variation in the instrument(s) drives the variation in the treatment, which in turn drives the outcome. Consequently, if the correlation between the instrument and the treatment is weak, then we cannot extract enough meaningful exogenous variation in the treatment assignment to identify the underlying effect. Instruments that have a low correlation with the treatment assignment after accounting for the other controls are called *weak instruments*. Weak instruments incur the risk of inaccurate estimates for the treatment effect. See Stock, Wright, and Yogo (2002) for a more in-depth exposition on this issue of weak instruments. The F-statistic in the first-stage regression, based on including and excluding the instruments, can be used to determine if the instrument(s) is weak. A rule of thumb is that the instrument(s) should significantly predict the treatment assignment, based on an F-statistic value of 10 or better.

Finally, given that the instrument already pseudo-randimizes the treatment assignment, why is it still necessary to include the other controls in the regression model if the the goal is to estimate the treatment effect? There are three reasons for this. First, the pseudo-randomization may be applied after groups of comparable subjects have been identified. In other words, assignment is random conditional on observable subject characteristics. Second, even when the randomization is independent of observable group characteristics, the use of controls in the model can allow the researcher to compare the treatment estimates with and without the controls. If the treatment assignment is truly random, the estimates with and without the additional controls should be similar. Finally, even if the observed controls are uncorrelated with the treatment assignment, they may help generate more precise estimates of the causal effect because the controls may improve the explanatory power for the outcome (Y_i), leading to lower residual error variance. Given the correspondence between the residual standard error (σ) and the standard error of the estimator (e.g., see Eq. (17.3)), this will have the effect of improving the efficiency of the estimator (i.e., a smaller number of observations N are required to improve the consistency). For a more in-depth treatment of instrumental variables, Agrist, Imbens, and Rubin (1996) provide an excellent reference.

17.3.1.1 Example 1 (IV): Patient Flow through an Intensive Care Unit

Patients who undergo a major surgical procedure, such as a coronary artery bypass grafting (CABG), require increased care and monitoring immediately

3 Manually estimating the IV estimator as described here will not provide the correct standard error for the treatment effect in the second stage OLS regression. However, 2SLS procedures in standard software packages like Stata and SAS will provide the correct standard errors.

following surgery. To care for these and other high-acuity patients, the intensive care unit (ICU) offers an increased level of care, with expensive medical equipment, high nurse-to-bed ratios, full-time attending anesthesiologists, and the availability of on-call clinical specialists. For this reason, the ICU is one of the more expensive resources within a hospital. Consequently, the ICU tends to operate at high levels of average occupancy, leading to scarce beds for new arrivals. The lack of available beds may lead the ICU to discharge existing patients to a step-down unit sooner, in order to free up capacity for new arrivals into the ICU. However, there is a risk that the patients who are discharged earlier than usual may not have had sufficient recovery in the ICU. Consequently, these patients may be at a higher risk of an adverse outcomes upon discharge, resulting in a revisit (or bounce-back) into the ICU. The figure below illustrates this important dynamic:

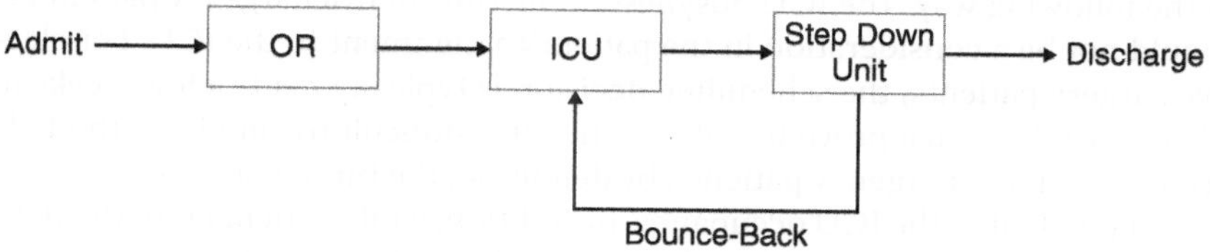

An important question for hospitals is, does this faster discharge lead to a significant increase in the bounce-back rate into the ICU? To empirically examine this effect, a researcher would collect data on all patients discharged from the ICU, and note whether any given patient bounced back or not. Let Y_i be a binary outcome variable with a value of 1 if patient i bounced back and 0 otherwise. Data would be collected on the length of stay (LOS_i) for patient i. This is our explanatory variable (or the continuous analog of the treatment condition described above). Finally, additional data would be collected on the patient's clinical conditions, like her level of clinical recovery, renal sufficiency, physiological function, and so forth. Let's denote these variables as well as other observed temporal factors associated with patient i's care, by X_i. The empirical specification would then be:

$$Y_i = X_i'\beta + \gamma LOS_i + \delta_i + \epsilon_i \tag{17.7}$$

Equation (17.7) has a dichotomous outcome variable, and the equation is often estimated by a logistic or probit regression. A linear probability model is sometimes used. Regardless of the underlying statistical transformation, the selection bias issue remains the same. γ provides the estimation for the effect of LOS on the likelihood of a bounce-back, and a value of $\gamma < 0$ suggests that a shorter LOS leads to an increased risk of bounce-back.

This estimation of γ is subject to the confounding described earlier. Specifically, factors not included in X_i, such as unobserved measures of severity (δ_i) or a faster recovery, will lead the patient to be discharged sooner, independent of the other observed factors. So, if $E[\delta_i|LOS_i] \neq 0$, our estimation for γ will be biased.

In this case, the experimental ideal would entail selecting patients from the ICU, randomly increasing or decreasing their *LOS*, and then observing incidences of bounce-back. As this is not clinically advisable, ethical, or legal, the econometrician can turn to an instrumental variable (IV) instead.

A reasonable choice of IV is the occupancy level of the ICU, or its measure of busyness associated with patient *i*'s stay, denoted by $BUSY_i$ (see KC and Terwiesch 2011 for a detailed analysis of this topic, including a detailed description of the *BUSY* variable). The relevance condition of the IV is justified as follows: when the ICU is busy, it tends to discharge patients faster. This can be easily verified with the data. The exogeneity condition requires that $BUSY_i$ not directly drive the outcome (other than indirectly through LOS_i). This can be reasoned in the following way. The ICU busyness at the time of discharge for patient *i* is should not be a consideration in the patient's assignment to the ICU. For elective surgery patients, the scheduling decision is typically made a few weeks in advance of the actual procedure date, when it is difficult to anticipate the ICU occupancy. For emergency patients, by definition, the timing of surgery should be independent of the ICU occupancy. In addition, while patient *i* is in the ICU, the arrival of new patients (thus driving *BUSY*) is also a random occurrence, independent of patient *i*'s clinical readiness for discharge. Thus, in general, we do not expect the unobserved factors (δ_i) that could affect both LOS_i and Y_i to be correlated with ICU occupancy.[4]

With the measure $BUSY_i$ established as an instrumental variable, we can exploit the naturally varying levels of occupancy in the ICU to exogenously drive changes in the *LOS*. This variation in *LOS* is then used to inform the estimate of γ. In this case, given that $BUSY_i$ is a binary instrumental variable, we can obtain the IV estimator as the ratio between the difference in outcomes across the patients discharged during busy and nonbusy periods, and the difference in length of stay for the patients discharged during busy and nonbusy periods as follows

$$\gamma_{IV} = \frac{E[Y_i|BUSY_i = 1] - E[Y_i|BUSY_i = 0]}{E[LOS_i|BUSY_i = 1] - E[LOS_i|BUSY_i = 0]}.$$

The above estimator is called the Wald estimator and provides a clear illustration of the utility of a binary instrumental variable to pseudo-randomize patient assignments. KC and Terwiesch (2011) found the effect of LOS reduction by a day to increase bounceback likelihood by 16 percent. Chan et al. (2012)

---

4 It may be possible that a higher workload for the staff can impact the quality of care delivered. However, the ICU workload is already typically high because of its 90 percent average utilization, so we do not expect the variation in workload to be significant. Moreover, given the strict nurse-to-bed ratios (2:1) in some states, care delivery should not be impacted, as nurse staffing will be increased to meet new demand.

similarly found that a faster discharge increases the likelihood of an adverse outcome. Other studies that involve occupancy-based measures that drive outcomes include Kuntz et al. (2014), who found a nonlinear effect of occupancy on clinical outcomes, and Chan et al. (2016), who the day of hospital admission as an instrumental variable to show that early discharges from the hospital have adverse patient outcomes, increasing mortality rates by 9 percent for select patient types.

17.3.1.2 Example 2 (IV): Focused Factories

The focused factory is a longstanding principle in operations management. By reducing a firm's product portfolio and focusing operations on a smaller number of products, the firm can gain through repetition and specialization, resulting in improved performance in the form of increased productivity, reduced production cost, or higher quality of product.

The late 1990s and early 2000s saw a three-fold increase in the number of specialty hospitals (GAO, 2003), which cater only to patients with a specific set of clinical conditions, for example, cardiac, orthopedic, or women's health. These specialty hospitals were found to be more profitable, and patients also appeared to have superior outcomes, when compared to patients in general hospitals. The proponents of specialty hospitals claimed that these hospitals were essentially focused factories and had developed a superior delivery system through specialization. Opponents of these specialty hospitals countered that they gained from cherry-picking the lower-risk and profitable patients who were predisposed to improved outcomes. This debate came to a head in 2005 when the US Congress issued a temporary moratorium on the construction of new specialty hospitals, citing the GAO study that more research was needed to fully understand the underlying drivers of performance.

To examine these effects, consider a simple case of two hospitals, one of which is focused. Let's denote this hospital the treatment hospital, and $FOCUS_i = 1$ if patient i is assigned to the focused hospital and 0 if the patient is assigned to the general, nonfocused hospital.

To isolate the effect of cherry-picking and to estimate the benefit of focus, consider the following specification that examines the effect of focus on the length of stay (LOS_i) for patient i:[5]

$$LOS_i = \alpha + X_i'\beta + \gamma FOCUS_i + \delta_i + \epsilon_i.$$

X_i is a set of patient controls that possibly drive LOS_i. Our interest is in estimating γ, the effect of focus on length of stay. δ_i denotes unobserved (to the researcher) patient level factors, such as severity.

5 Revenue per patient in the US follows a prospective payment system and is fixed based on the diagnosis-related group (DRG) for the patient. A shorter LOS means fewer resources, hence lowered cost and higher profit per patient for the hospital.

If there is cherry-picking by the focused hospital then $Cov(FOCUS_i, \delta_i) \neq 0$, and our estimate will be biased.

To generate an unbiased estimate for γ, we could use the differential distance as an instrumental variable. This differential distance is defined as $diffDist_i = distance_{i,FOCUS_i=0} - distance_{i,FOCUS_i=1}$, where $distance_{i,FOCUS_i}$ is the travel distance for the patient i to get to either a focused or nonfocused general hospital.

If the differential distance increases, then the patient will need to travel a longer distance to the general hospital, compared to the travel distance to the focused hospital. Thus, we expect the differential distance to be positively correlated with the likelihood of selecting a focused hospital. We can argue for the exogeneity condition on the grounds that individuals (when they bought their homes many years ago), likely did not decide where to live based on the proximity to a specialty hospital's current or future site. Therefore, we expect that on average, the differential distance is uncorrelated with any factors that could lead to cherry-picking. That is,

$$Cov[\delta_i, diffDist_i] = 0.$$

These two conditions mean that the differential distance can serve as a valid instrument to estimate the operational gains achieved through focus at specialty hospitals, independent of the effects of cherry-picking. For example, KC and Terwiesch (2012) developed a set of continuous measures for focus and found that focus at the hospital level (defined as the ratio of cardiac patients to all inpatients) and at the department level (defined as the ratio of CABG patients to all cardiac patients) is associated with a reduction in length of stay for cardiac and CABG patients, respectively. However, once selection effects are accounted for, the effect of department-level focus decreases, and the effect of hospital-level focus disappears. Huckman and Clark (2012) also examined the effects of focus, finding positive spillover effects across related clinical specialties. This IV approach based on distance had been previously used by McClellan et al. (1994) to determine whether intensive treatment of patients with Acute Myocardial Infarction (AMI) leads to better four-year survival outcomes. They found that after accounting for selection effects, survival benefits from intensive treatment are minimal.

17.3.2 Difference Estimators

Empirical researchers are often interested in evaluating the efficacy of various programs, estimating the results of policy interventions or simply comparing two time periods separated by an important event, such as the introduction of a new product or service. These situations typically involve a treatment group, which is evaluated at a specific point in the pre-policy period and again in the post-policy period. A control group to whom the policy does not apply, forms the basis of comparison, and is also evaluated at the same two points in time.[6]

Ideally, subjects are randomly assigned to the treatment and control groups, and if the sample is large, the estimate based on a comparison of the two groups at the two points in time is unbiased. However, subjects are not usually randomly assigned, and even when randomly assigned, the treatment and control groups tend to draw from a small sample (leading to randomly generated significant differences between groups because of the small number of subjects). Accordingly, there will be observable differences in outcomes between the two groups prior to the policy implementation. In this type of situation, the difference-in-differences (or D-in-D) estimator can help to provide an unbiased effect of treatment. The D-in-D estimator adjusts for the prepolicy differences by subtracting from each subject's prepolicy outcome value. Specifically,

$$\Delta Y_i = Y_i^{pre} - Y_i^{post}$$

is the first difference in outcome for each subject in either treatment or control group across the two time periods of evaluation. The D-in-D estimator is then

$$\hat{\beta}_{D-in-D} = [\overline{Y_{i \in T}^{post}} - \overline{Y_{i \in T}^{pre}}] - [\overline{Y_{i \in C}^{post}} - \overline{Y_{i \in C}^{pre}}],$$

where $\overline{Y_{i \in T}^{post}}$ is the average outcome in the treatment group post-policy. Essentially, the D-in-D estimator corrects the change in outcome for the treatment group (denoted T) by subtracting from it the change in outcome for the control group denoted C (hence the name "difference in differences"). The estimator effectively states that had the policy not been implemented, the observed change across the two groups would have been the same. From regression, the D-in-D estimator is given by

$$\Delta Y_i = \alpha + \beta T_i + u_i,$$

where $\Delta Y_i = Y_i^{post} - Y_i^{pre}$, and $T_i = 1$ if subject i is assigned to the treatment group and 0 otherwise. β is the D-in-D estimator.

Alternatively, let Y_{it} be the outcome for subject i in period t ($t = pre$ denotes the prepolicy period and $t = post$ denotes the postpolicy period). Then,

$$Y_{it} = \alpha + \beta_1 1_{t=post} + \beta_2 1_{i \in T} + \beta_3 [1_{t=post} \times 1_{i \in T}] + \epsilon_{it},$$

where 1 is an indicator function denoting either the treatment assignment or the postpolicy period. Estimating β_3 in the above equation by OLS would yield the D-in-D estimator.

6 Temporal variations are sometimes more intuitive, so our exposition is based on temporal changes. However, the treatment and control groups do not necessarily have to be evaluated across time. For instance, we can also make comparisons across two different geographical regions, instead of two time periods. In either case, the estimation methodology remains the same.

The D-in-D estimator is predicated on the assumption that in the absence of the policy, the observed changes in the treatment and control groups will be identical. In other words, any baseline trends in Y_i across the two groups should be parallel; otherwise, our estimate of β_3 might just be picking up the effects of the difference in trends. Thus, it is a good idea to check for any trend differences between the two groups prior to the policy implementation, especially in the immediate prepolicy period. Tests of robustness may also involve examining additional comparison groups, or examining any changes in observable factors that are not expected to result from the policy intervention.

Finally, even though the D-in-D estimator allows for observable differences between the treatment and control groups prior to the policy, it is important that the policy implementation is not driven by these observed preexisting differences in outcome. Such targeting of policy application based on observed differences could mean that the treatment group is disproportionately worse-off (better-off) immediately prior to the policy. If the outcome has a tendency to revert to the mean, then the D-in-D estimator would overestimate (underestimate) the effect of the policy, resulting in an Ashenfelter dip (Ashenfelter and Card 1985).

17.3.3 Fixed Effects Estimators

Fixed effects models involving panel data can be considered to be a generalization of the D-in-D model, with the modification that there are more than two periods of observation, and more than two comparison groups. The benefit in employing fixed effects comes from the larger number of periods being examined, along with the larger number of subjects, which can lead to more precise and possibly more generalizable results. The fixed effects for the time periods and for the individual subjects can be implemented using dummy variables (akin to the policy and treatment assignment binary variables in the D-in-D estimation). A typical fixed effect panel regression would be estimated by

$$Y_{it} = \alpha + \rho_i + \tau_t + T_{it}\beta + \epsilon_{it}.$$

Y_{it} is the outcome for subject i measured at time t. ρ_i and τ_t denote the subject and time fixed effects, respectively. The estimator β turns on the intrasubject variation over time, specifically the differences between the prepolicy and the postpolicy time periods. The key benefit of this approach is that any unobserved heterogeneity at the subject level is subsumed by the fixed effect and therefore will not confound the estimates. However, if treatment is not random, there is still the issue that the results may be confounded by selection bias. That is, if a selective sample were assigned to the treatment groups, observing the subjects over time would not allow us to correct for factors that led to the subjects being selected in the first place.

17.3.3.1 Examples 3-4 (D-in-D): Process Compliance and Peer Effects of Productivity

Staats et al. (2017) employed a D-in-D estimator to evaluate the impact of a hand-hygiene monitoring system on improving hand-hygiene practices among healthcare professionals. The treatment assignment was whether the hospital where the healthcare worker was employed had implemented a hand-hygiene monitoring system that used RFID technology to monitor worker movement and compliance with hand hygiene processes. Workers in hospitals where the system was not implemented formed the control group. The outcome was whether the individual healthcare worker was compliant in practicing hand hygiene. By comparing hand-hygiene behavior in the pre- and post-implementation periods across the two groups, the paper found that compliance increased following implementation but was not sustained in the longer term.[7]

Song et al. (2017) similarly employed a D-in-D estimator to examine whether providing public relative performance feedback (RPF), in which physician rankings on predetermined productivity criteria are openly shared, has the effect of improving worker productivity. They compared two different emergency departments, one of which implemented RPF (the treatment group), and the other of which did not (the control group). By comparing differences in service processing times (the outcome variable) in the emergency departments before and after the implementation of RPF, Song et al (2017) found that RPF led to an 8.6 percent improvement in physician productivity.

17.4 Structural Estimation

Structural estimation begins with the understanding that observed empirical data are the result of a data-generating process that is dictated by an underlying economic theoretical model. The goal of the econometrician is then to uncover the parameters of the economic model. A key distinguishing feature of structural estimation, as described by the Cowles Foundation for Research in Economics, is that the model parameters are invariant. In other words, the economic model, in conjunction with the estimated model parameters, can be used to generate counterfactuals in examining various possible operational or policy interventions. This prescriptive component of structural estimation is what makes it particularly appealing. In healthcare, structural estimation methods can be used to explore the decision-making behavior of agents (patients, providers, payers, and policymakers) under uncertainty. They can also help the

---

7 The paper also uses an alternative data source, in addition to that generated from the monitoring system, to fully account for compliance changes in the pre- and post-implementation periods.

understanding of healthcare marketplace dynamics and allow researchers to examine the impact of governmental policies.

Standard economic or operations management theory guides the relationship between the outcome variable(Y), the explanatory variables (X), and the unobserved variables (δ). The theoretical arguments lead to a relationship:

$$Y = f(X, \delta, \beta),$$

where $f()$ is a known function, and β represents model parameters that need to be estimated. Often, theory dictates a relationship that is deterministic. Given randomness in observed outcomes Y, X, and δ, the researcher further imposes restrictions on the joint probability distributions of X and δ. The combination of the economic model and the statistical assumptions guide the generation of a maximum likelihood specification:

$$L(\beta) = L(\beta|Y, X), \tag{17.8}$$

and the model parameters are given by

$$\beta = arg\ max\ log\ L(y, x).$$

Conceptually, the likelihood function tells us for any given value of β how likely it is that the observed data is consistent with the data predicted by the economic model and the statistical assumptions. The goal then is to find the specific value of β that maximizes the likelihood.

17.4.1 Example 5: Managing Operating Room Capacity

Hospital operating room (OR) capacity is a scarce resource, and effective utilization of OR capacity is important to managing costs and maintaining effective patient flow through the hospital. For a patient needing surgery, the scheduling staff needs to determine the amount of time to reserve the OR (or OR capacity). An important challenge in this task is that the actual procedure time is not known with certainty in advance. At best, the decision-maker may draw on historical procedure times to inform the probability distribution of OR time.

Allocating excess capacity would mean that the OR becomes idle. Allocating insufficient capacity would mean that when the surgery runs over, it would have a knock-on effect, disrupting the schedules of subsequent procedures. In other words, there are attendant costs of both overage and underage. Knowing these costs would be helpful in understanding the trade-offs in the decision-making process. It could also facilitate out-of-sample predictions for future capacity allocation decisions.

The newsvendor model, in which the decision-maker allocates capacity in the face of demand uncertainty and the attendant costs of overage and underage provide a fitting and parsimonious economic modeling framework for this problem (see Olivares et al., 2008, for more details). A crucial maintained assumption is that the decision-maker orders the newsvendor optimal amount.

Let $\hat{Q}$ represent the observed OR time, and let Q^* be the theoretical optimal. We know from the newsvendor model that:

$$F(Q^*) = C_u/(C_u + C_o) = 1/(1 + \gamma), \tag{17.9}$$

where F is the CDF of demand, which is the (realized) OR time, and C_u and C_o are the costs of underage and overage, respectively. The critical ratio γ may depend on the type of procedure, physician, and patient conditions, and can be further parameterized as:

$$\gamma = \gamma(Z; \alpha), \tag{17.10}$$

where Z represents observed factors, and α is the set of parameters to estimate.

Likewise, the probability distribution function F could depend on a number of factors like case complexity, day of the week, and the physician assigned. Thus, $F = F(X; \eta)$ represents the fact that the CDF comes from a family of distributions, depending on observed covariates X and the parameters to be estimated η. Therefore, the optimal capacity is given by maximizing the likelihood function:

$$Q^*(X_i, Z_i, \alpha, \eta) = F^{-1}\left[\frac{1}{1 + \gamma(Z_i, \alpha)}; (X_i, \eta)\right].$$

The two sets of model parameters (η and α) can be estimated in two separate stages. In the first stage, the demand distribution parameters (η) can be obtained using maximum likelihood of the observed demand realizations, or the duration of observation i (D_i) of OR capacity used. This allows us to fix the demand distribution based on the estimated parameters $\hat{\eta}$. Once that is done, in the next stage, we can use nonlinear least squares or maximum likelihood to estimate the equation:

$$Q_i = Q^*(X_i, Z_i, \alpha, \hat{\eta}) + e_i.$$

Specifically, for observed capacity decision X_i, the error is then $e_i = Q_i - Q*$. This assumes that the decision made is equal to the optimal newsvendor amount, after adjusting for an idiosyncratic perturbation. The recovered parameters α can then be plugged into Eq. (17.10) to obtain the critical ratio.

17.4.2 Example 6: Patient Choice Modeling

A topic of interest to various stakeholders in the healthcare industry is understanding the drivers of patient choice. That is, when presented with a number of different healthcare providers, what are the factors that lead the patient to select a specific provider? When aggregated at the market level, individual patient choices inform us about market share and overall demand for specific providers. This information is useful in facilitating more effective matching of supply and demand in healthcare.

In this example, we examine the availability of government-offered universal care on the hospital choice behavior of previously uninsured patients. Data include observed hospital choices by patients, both in periods when they were uninsured and in periods when they were insured.

In the most general form, the utility U_{iht} that patient i gets from visiting hospital h at time t is

$$U_{iht} = X'_{iht}\beta + D_{ht} + e_{iht},$$

where X_{iht} is a vector of patient-level controls, including demographic and clinical factors, as well as hospital–patient specific variables such as the travel distance incurred by patient i in getting to hospital h. Apart from these drivers, other unobservable factors (unobserved by the econometrician but observable to patients) can also impact patient utility. These could include factors such as the hospital's unobserved reputation, level of engagement in the community in terms of marketing activities, availability of free ambulatory service, emergency room patient flow process, perceived quality of care, friendliness of staff, and so forth. In order to account for these factors, we can include time-varying hospital fixed effects, D_{ht}. These hospital fixed effects, which are a set of dummy variables that represent the average patient preference for hospital h in time period t, are allowed to vary in each time period to fully absorb unobserved hospital characteristics that might affect patient choice. e_{iht} is the extreme value distributed i.i.d. error term. Given the i.i.d. extreme value error terms, we can obtain convenient closed form expressions for the patient choice probabilities. Specifically, the probability of patient i selecting hospital h at time t is

$$Pr_{iht}(\beta;D) = \frac{exp(X'_{iht}\beta + D_{ht})}{\sum_{h' \in H} exp(X'_{ih't}\beta + D_{h't})}.$$

The maximum likelihood yields both individual patient-level and time-varying drivers as well as population-level preferences for specific hospitals (D_{hm}). The recovered dummy variables D_{hm} can then be regressed using generalized least squares (see Nevo 2000 for a discussion on this) against hospital characteristics (e.g., whether the hospital is privately owned or public), indicator variables denoting time period (pre- or postpolicy), and interaction between the hospital characteristics and time dummies as follows:

$$D_{ht} = \alpha_1 Public_h + \alpha_2 Post_t + \alpha_3 Public_h * Post_t + e_{ht}.$$

From the model above, we can examine the population-level preference for public hospitals ($\alpha_1 > 0$), and whether universal insurance (post-policy) has the effect of changing population-level preferences for public hospitals.

In particular, $\alpha_3 < 0$ would indicate that public hospitals fall out of favor following universal healthcare.

17.5 Conclusion

In this chapter, we have briefly described two approaches to conducting econometric research in healthcare operations. In the first half, we discussed confounding, especially due to omitted variables and sample selection.

Estimating causality in healthcare operations is often confounded by various forms of endogeneity. Randomized treatment assignments can help to mitigate the confounding but are often impractical, expensive, and time-consuming and may raise questions of equity (e.g., is it fair to deny treatment to a patient who could possibly benefit from it?). However, the researcher may be able to employ natural variation in observed empirical data. Such variation can arise from natural experiments or from past policy interventions. By employing the appropriate econometric methodology, we may use such historical data to draw causal inferences.

Instrumental variables exploit naturally occurring exogenous variation to identify the effect in question. The key to using instrumental variables, of course, is identifying a clever instrument. A deep understanding of the healthcare operations context, understanding of the theoretical motivation, and the source of confounding is the first step in coming up with a list of possible IVs. Policy reforms, observed circumstantial variation in the subjects being studied, or even truly random geopolitical or weather-related events may motivate a useful instrumental variable. Similarly, D-in-D estimators exploit temporal (and sometimes spatial) changes in subjects. Basically, two comparable groups (treatment and control) are evaluated at a period prior to an intervention and again in the period following the intervention. Assuming that the treatment assignment is independent of any underlying baseline or trend in group outcomes, we can estimate the impact of the treatment as the difference of two differences: the first difference is between the treatment and control groups in the pre-intervention periods, and the second difference is between the treatment and control groups in the post-intervention period.[8] D-in-D estimators are often used in program evaluations or in estimating the effect of a policy intervention. Similarly, panel estimators exploit temporal (and sometimes spatial) changes in subjects to estimate within-subject changes in outcome. These estimators turn on the intrasubject variation over time, and thereby allow us to effectively control for subject-specific sources of unobserved heterogeneity. However, care should be taken in ensuring that the treatment assignment is not confounded by subject-specific factors. Field

8 We may also view the first difference as the pre-post difference in the treatment group.

experiments, in which an intervention is made across randomly selected units of analysis (e.g., hospitals, doctors, or patients) and in which outcomes are tabulated post-intervention are well-suited for a difference-in-difference analysis. However, if the sample sizes are small, there may still be significant differences across treatment and control groups. For an in-depth treatment of program evaluation and natural experiments, readers are referred to Angrist and Krueger (1999).

In the second half of this chapter, we briefly discussed structural estimation methods. Structural methods specify a data generating process defined by an underlying economic theory, and statistical relationships between observed and unobserved variables. In a structural estimation, the primitives of the underlying economic model are derived, with the goal of evaluating out-of-sample policy interventions. Reiss and Wolak (2005) provide an excellent source of the underlying principles of structural estimation, complete with illustrative examples, primarily from industrial organization. Train (2003) also provides an in-depth study of structural models, especially those involving models of discrete choice.

The growing availability of novel sources of data in healthcare suggests new opportunities for developing and using econometric models to help inform decision-making. For example, patient tracking technologies now enable us to develop detailed time and motion studies in worker productivity. RFID tracking of resources can allow us to manage the fulfillment and location of critical resources more effectively.

Healthcare Internet of Things (IOT) devices, for example, implanted medical devices, can provide biomarkers to assess patient risk, helping to inform clinical decision making. As new models of care delivery are implemented and new products are developed, data can help compare alternative models of care delivery and provide insights into improving the delivery process. Government policies play a critical role in regulating healthcare markets and in providing appropriate incentives to providers and patients. In this regard, data can help evaluate the efficacy of policies. Finally, the advent of personalized medicine could allow us to account for the sources of patient-level heterogeneity in making recommendations tailored to individual patients.

References

Angrist, D., W. Imbens, and B. Rubin. (1996). Identification of causal effects using instrumental variables. *Journal of the American Statistical Association* 91 (434), 444–455.

Angrist, D., and A.B. Krueger. (1999). Empirical strategies in labor economics. *Handbook of Labor Economics* 3: 1277–1366.

Ashenfelter, O. and D. Card. (1985). Using the longitudinal structure of earnings to estimate the effect of training programs. *Review of Economics and Statistics* 67 (4), 648–60.

Bartel, A.P. and Chan, C., and S.-H. Kim. (2014). Should Hospitals Keep Their Patients Longer? The Role of Inpatient Care in Reducing Post-Discharge Mortality. NBER Working Paper No. w20499. Available at SSRN: https://ssrn.com/abstract=2499341

Chan, C.W., V.F. Farias, N. Bambos, and G.J. Escobar. (2012). Optimizing intensive care unit discharge decisions with patient readmissions. *Operations Research* 60 (6), 1323–1341.

Clark, J.R. and R.S. Huckman. (2012). Broadening focus: Spillovers, complementarities, and specialization in the hospital industry. *Management Science* 58 (4), 708–722.

U.S. General Accounting Office (GAO). (2003). Specialty hospitals: Geographic location, services provided, and financial performance. Report to congressional requesters, GAO, Washington, DC.

KC, D.S., and C. Terwiesch. (2011) The effects of focus on performance: Evidence from California hospitals. *Management Science* 57 (11), 1897–1912.

KC, D.S. and C. Terwiesch. (2012). An econometric analysis of patient flows in the cardiac intensive care unit. *Manufacturing & Service Operations Management* 14 (1), 50–65.

KC, D.S. S. Venkataraman, and T.T.I. Kim. (2016). Are Patients Patient? Choosing Emergency Care under Universal Healthcare. Available at SSRN: https://ssrn.com/abstract=2847705.

Kuntz, L., R. Mennicken, and S. Scholtes. (2014). Stress on the ward: Evidence of safety tipping points in hospitals. *Management Science* 61 (4), 754–771.

McClellan, M., B.J. McNeil, and J.P. Newhouse. (1994). Does more intensive treatment of acute myocardial infarction in the elderly reduce mortality? Analysis using instrumental variables. *JAMA* 272 (11), 859–866.

Nevo, A. A Practitioner's Guide to Estimation of Random-Coefficients Logit Models of Demand. (2000). *Journal of Economics & Management Strategy* 9.4 (2000): 513–548.

Olivares, M., C. Terwiesch, and L. Cassorla. (2008). Structural estimation of the newsvendor model: an application to reserving operating room time. *Management Science* 54 (1), 41–55.

Reiss, P. and F. Wolak, (2007). Structural Econometric Modeling: Rationales and Examples from Industrial Organization, in J. Heckman and E. Leamer (eds.), *Handbook of Econometrics*, vol. 6A Elsevier. New York:

Song, H., A.L. Tucker, K.L. Murrell, D.R. Vinson. (2017). Closing the Productivity Gap: Improving Worker Productivity through Public Relative Performance Feedback and Validation of Best Practices, *Management Science*, forthcoming.

Staats, B.R., H. Dai, D. Hofmann, K.L. Milkman. (2017). Motivating process compliance through individual electronic monitoring: An empirical examination of hand hygiene in healthcare. *Management Science* 63(5), 1563–1585.

Stock, J.H., J.H. Wright, and M. Yogo. (2002). A survey of weak instruments and weak identification in generalized method of moments. *Journal of Business & Economic Statistics* 20 (4), 518–529.

Train, K. (2003). *Discrete Choice Methods with Simulation*. Cambridge University Press.

18

Data Science

Rema Padman

Carnegie Mellon University

18.1 Introduction

Data science is conceptualized currently as a mashup of many disciplines to extract value from data (Saltz and Stanton, 2018; Cao, 2017; Fawcett, 2015; Kayyali et al., 2013; Kruse et al., 2016; Russell et al., 2010). Enabled by the explosive advances in information, communication, and decision technologies in recent decades, digitization is dramatically transforming every industry sector in economies worldwide, from manufacturing and retail to transportation and hospitality services, resulting in the creation of large volumes of data (L'Heureux et al., 2017). In no industry is this more disruptive or potentially transformative than the healthcare sector for many reasons, including the diversity of users and usage, technologies, data sources and types, heterogeneity of content, lack of interoperability among the software systems that collect and manage data, and insufficient standards across the data generation, collection, analysis, and usage spectrum (Raghupathi et al., 2014).

Healthcare today is so complex that it has surpassed the human mind's capacity to operate without aid (Figure 18.1). The greatest challenge is to take the appropriate information and apply it to individual patients or a population at the time when the information is needed. Drawing on multiple disciplines, such as statistics, machine learning, operations research, information technologies, computer science, and economics, data science offers a rich lens to investigate new opportunities to enhance data-driven healthcare decision-making from the perspectives of multiple stakeholders. This chapter provides some background on the rapid digitization of healthcare in the clinical and consumer healthcare settings and the resultant availability of vast amounts of digital data for analysis, inference, and decision-making. This background is followed by a brief overview of some data science approaches and methodologies that are powering the transformation of healthcare decision-making. Three examples

Handbook of Healthcare Analytics: Theoretical Minimum for Conducting 21st Century Research on Healthcare Operations, First Edition. Edited by Tinglong Dai and Sridhar Tayur.

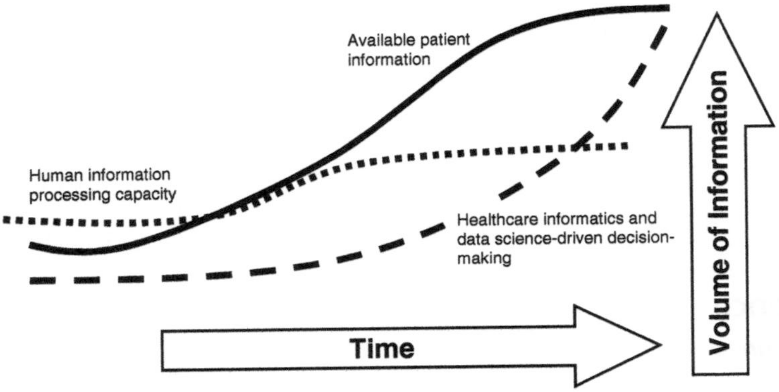

Figure 18.1 Data and information are the key drivers of healthcare decision-making.

illustrate the opportunities and challenges in this domain. Finally, the chapter concludes with some future directions for research and practice.

18.1.1 Background

The healthcare industry lagged behind most sectors of the economy during much of the digitization explosion. Although financial healthcare information systems have been in use for many decades in the United States, the Health Information Technology for Economic and Clinical Health (HITECH) Act of 2009 accelerated the deployment of information systems for clinical decision-making at the point of care delivery, such as electronic health records (EHR) and computerized provider order entry (CPOE) applications. In less than a decade, the move from a primarily paper-based healthcare delivery system to one where nearly every individual has a digital record of her care has been a historic, disruptive, health information technology (IT) transformation. From fewer than one in ten hospitals and one in six physicians using EHRs in 2009, today more than 95 percent of all hospitals and 80 percent of all physicians use certified EHRs, leading to slowly improving impacts on quality, safety, and efficiency of care in slightly more than 80 percent of studies reported in the clinical setting (DeSalvo and Washington, 2016). Alongside this, advances in personal computing technologies and mobile connectivity have resulted in clinically-oriented mobile apps with significant uptake by clinicians (Kayyali et al., 2013).

However, much of chronic, preventive, and wellness care happens outside formal clinical care delivery settings, in settings such as the home and workplace (Swan, 2013). Recent, unprecedented growth in consumer devices, including smartphone applications, wearable sensors, and Internet of Things (IoT) devices, and in social media platforms, including discussion forums on

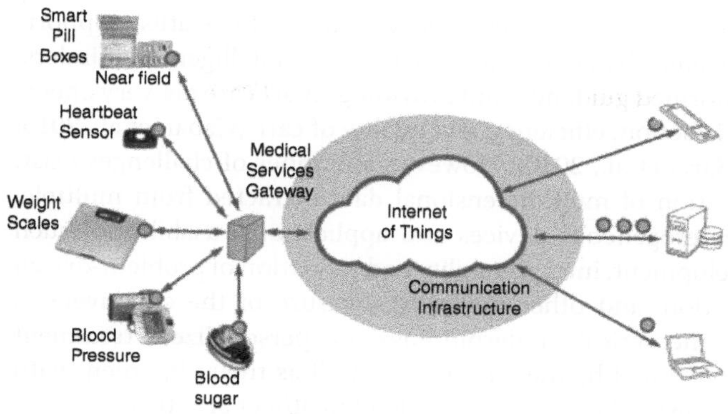

Figure 18.2 Smart and connected health.

specific health conditions, are generating large volumes of user-generated health data from new settings (Figure 18.2). These include personal stories, streaming vitals, symptoms, medication compliance, exercise routines, time and location stamps, and food habits recorded by individuals to help monitor their general health and lifestyle habits at a granular level (Fawcett, 2015; Swan, 2013). With more than 250,000 M-health apps available in 2016, estimates suggest that five to ten gigabytes of health information per individual will be recorded in electronic data repositories, not including genomic information (Starren et al., 2013). Finally, the *All of Us* Research Program announced recently by the National Institutes of Health (Collins et al., 2015) "*is a historic effort to gather data from one million or more people living in the United States to accelerate research and improve health. By taking into account individual differences in lifestyle, environment, and biology, researchers will uncover paths toward delivering precision medicine*" (NIH, n.d.). Studies indicate that 25 percent of cancer patients, 33 percent of people with Alzheimer's disease, 50 percent of arthritis sufferers, and 66 percent of people with asthma do not respond to their drugs (Spear et al., 2001), and need new approaches to improve adherence. The proposed novel and ambitious initiatives, digital platforms, resulting data, and their analysis via data science have the potential to change the paradigm of healthcare delivery.

Whereas medical care has been based mostly on measurements taken during clinical visits, new methods that monitor patients remotely will allow health-care providers to gain a more holistic understanding of a patient's longitudinal health status across the continuum of care, which is currently not possible from the snapshot taken during an office encounter. Innovative methods and tools are needed for a range of decisions, such as responding to different treatment regimens; assessing individual and population level risk; detecting anomalies and preventing deterioration in patient behavior or health status; supporting communication and shared decision-making via intelligent reminders, notifications, and informed guidance; and providing smart care delivery operations to improve satisfaction, efficiency, and quality of care (Caban et al., 2015; Knorr et al., 2009; Saria et al., 2010). However, a number of challenges exist, including harmonization of multidimensional data extracted from multiple, nonstandardized, heterogeneous devices and applications; usability of such streaming data; development, interpretability and validation of problem-driven prediction, visualization, and other methods; measure of the effectiveness, sustainability, and theoretical underpinnings of personalized treatment interventions recommended by the analytics, as well as their alignment with organizational workflows (Zhang et al., 2015; Raghupathi et al., 2014).

Extensive literature on the data science process includes studies on the harmonization, cleaning, and preprocessing of raw data from diverse sources, followed by its modeling and analysis, evaluation for performance and accuracy, and visualization and presentation for easy interpretation and use (Figure 18.3). The modeling and analysis approaches comprise machine learning and data mining, operations research and statistics, natural language processing and text analysis, video and image processing, and personalization and recommendation methods, among others. As the granularity and volume of available information on each individual increase, attribute-ranking and selection techniques are critical for selecting a concise set of relevant attributes to reduce the dimensionality of the analytics space before the models are built (Figure 18.4). In the healthcare context, embedding them in decision support tools and software platforms to leverage the "big data" from medical and self-care encounters to support decision-making, both at the population and individual levels, is an important endeavor (Swan et al., 2018). For example, predictive analytics explore data in a variety of ways, from predicting patient mortality and hospital readmissions (Saria et al., 2010) to applying algorithms to uncover new statistical patterns in disease progression or postoperative complications for minimizing them through appropriate interventions (Lin et al., 2001; Lin et al., 2017). Prediction, classification, clustering, and association are some of the widely used data science methods that have significant value for this domain (Saltz et al., 2018).

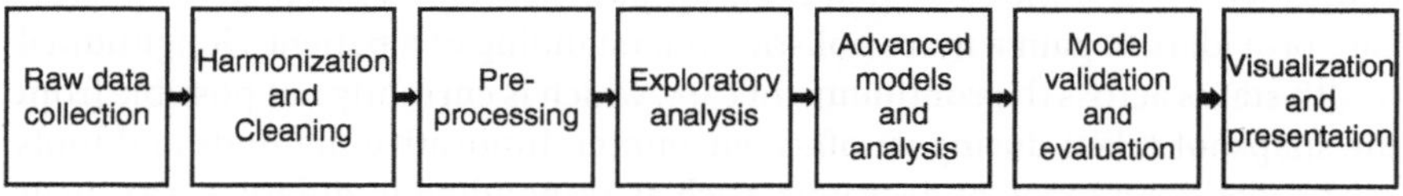

Figure 18.3 Data science process.

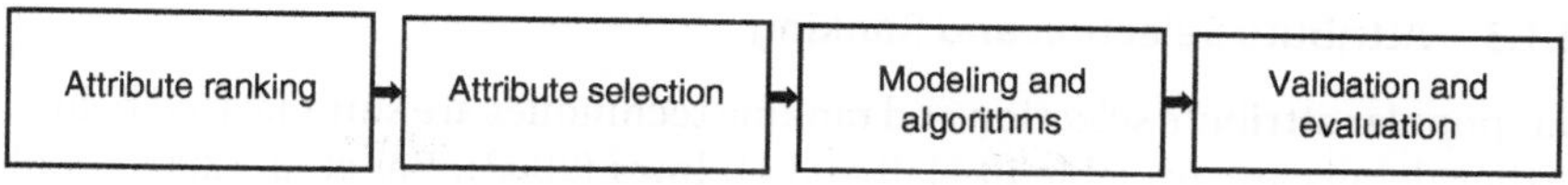

Figure 18.4 Key steps in the analysis process.

18.1.2 Methods

This section briefly summarizes some widely used methods for the steps in Figure 18.4. Saeys et al. (2007) provided a literature review of several attribute selection methods employed in Bioinformatics, particularly attribute-ranking techniques such as information gain (IG) and relief algorithms. These methods provide quick estimates of relevant attributes and are techniques that are commonly used in attribute ranking. More recent developments on selection and classification, particularly those relevant to healthcare informatics, are reported in Hall et al. (2003). Techniques such as the Markov blanket attribute selection method and correlation-based feature selection (CFS), for instance, that can be employed to model attribute dependencies have also been studied (Aliferis et al., 2010; Bai et al., 2008). In the modeling setting, Roumani et al. (2013) discuss unbalanced data sets and their challenges, where the outcome variable is a rare event.

Traditional methods in machine learning include classification and unsupervised learning (Bishop, 2006; Hall et al., 2003; Witten and Frank, 2011). Classification refers to the method of labeling unknown data to target variables through training a classification model using labeled data. Logistic regression and naïve Bayes are examples of classification algorithms (Saltz et al., 2018). Unsupervised learning refers to identification of latent groups in the data (Kaufmann et al., 2008). Unlike classification, which is also called *supervised* learning, unsupervised learning does not have true labels, and users need to predefine the number of latent groups. K-means and hierarchical clustering are two of the most common unsupervised learning algorithms (Saltz et al., 2018). Zhang et al. (2014) used a variant of the K-means clustering algorithm to design more efficient *order sets* from historical order data in a pediatric inpatient setting (see also Gartner et al., 2017). Order sets are groups of relevant orders traditionally clustered together by clinical experts and used within CPOE, requiring significant labor- and knowledge-intensive effort in maintenance and update. Zhang et al. (2014, 2017) demonstrated that creation of order sets can be automated using optimization and machine learning algorithms, such that the resulting data-driven order sets require less physical and cognitive workload in development and match the workflow-generated order data. In addition to these classical approaches, many advanced machine learning algorithms have been developed and applied over the years to facilitate a more efficient and safer healthcare system.

18.1.3 Attribute Selection and Ranking

Four popular attribute selection and ranking techniques are summarized below. Further details are available in Hall and Holmes (2003), Bai et al. (2009), and Gartner et al. (2015), among others.

18.1.4 Information Gain (IG) Attribute Ranking

Given the prior probability $p(n)$ for each outcome $n \in N$, we can compute the information entropy $H(N)$ and the conditional information entropy $H(N|a)$ of N of the attribute $a \in A$ with values $v \in V_a$; that is, $H(N) = -\sum_{n\in N} p(n)\ ln\, p(n)$, and $H(N|a) = -\sum_{v\in Va} p(v) \sum_{n\in N} p(n|v)\ ln\, p(n|v)$, which measures the uncertainty associated with the attribute (Sharma and Yu 2009). This information is sufficient to compute the information gain $IG(a)$ of each attribute $a \in A$ as $IG(a) = H(N) - H(N|a)$. The higher the information gain $IG(a)$ of an attribute $a \in A$, the more valuable the attribute is assumed to be for classifying N. $IG(a)$ can be sorted in decreasing order to obtain an attribute ranking and, commonly, the attributes with the highest $IG(a)$ are selected for classification.

18.1.5 Relief-F Attribute Ranking

This is a class of fast feature selection algorithms that is efficient for binary classification problems (Robnik-Šikonja et al., 2003). The result is a quality measure of each attribute Q_a which can, similar to $IG(a)$, provide an attribute ranking. This attribute ranking can be split into a ranking of (1) clinical attributes and (2) a ranking of socio-demographic/-economic attributes but is not capable of detecting redundant attributes.

18.1.6 Markov Blanket Feature Selection

The Markov blanket feature selection method uses conditional independence relations between the class variable and all other attributes, thus detecting redundant attributes. A Markov blanket is a specific type of Bayesian network that encodes this conditional independence in a graph (Bai et al., 2008; Tsamardinos et al., 2003). Specifically, the Markov blanket of a vertex $v \in V$ is a minimal subset of vertices containing vertex v, its direct parents and direct children, as well as all direct parents of the children of v. The Markov blanket of vertex v contains all the variables needed to predict the value of that variable because v is conditionally independent of all other variables given its Markov blanket. Methods to develop the Markov blanket include the grow-shrink approach (Margaritas 2003) and the incremental association search (Tsamardinos et al., 2003).

18.1.7 Correlation-Based Feature Selection

This method selects attributes that individually correlate well with the outcome and have low intercorrelation with other individual attributes. The intercorrelation of two nominal attributes a and b is computed from the symmetrical uncertainty, $SU(a,b)$, between two attributes using conditional entropies; that is, $SU(a,b) = 2.(H(a) + H(b) - H(a|b))/(H(a) + H(b))$. Then, the attribute subset A_i^* is selected, which maximizes the normalized sum of conditional symmetrical uncertainties between each attribute and the outcome variable; that is, $A_i^* = argmax_{A' \subset A} SU(a,b)/sqrt(\sum_{a \in A'} \sum_{b \in A' \backslash a} SU(a,b))$ (Hall et al., 2003).

18.1.8 Classification

Three commonly used classification methods are outlined below. For each method, the model is trained from a data set of labeled training samples, where the true value of the outcome variable is known to the method. The prediction of the outcome by the trained classifier on a holdout set of test data samples is compared against the known value to identify performance measures such as prediction accuracy (proportion of correctly classified samples), true positive rate, and false positive rate. All performance indicators are measured using k-fold cross-validation (Witten et al., 2011). The learning curve of a classifier that displays prediction accuracy as a function of the training set is an additional useful quality measure (Mackay, 2003; Perlich et al., 2003).

Naive Bayes, Bayesian networks, and decision trees (also called classification trees) represent different approaches to learning and are relatively fast, state-of-the-art algorithms often used in data mining applications (Margaritis, 2003). For each method, the classifier is learned from a dataset of labeled training instances. This means that the true class of each instance is known to the classification method. The classifier is later applied to a separate dataset of unlabeled test instances. Here, the true outcome of each instance is unknown to the classification method and must be predicted.

The Naïve Bayes and Bayesian Network methods learn a probabilistic model from the training data, compute the posterior probability that the instance belongs to each outcome $n \in N$ given the attributes A, and assign the instance to the class with highest posterior probability. The decision tree method, instead, learns a tree-structured set of decision rules from the training data and uses these rules to predict the outcome. Each method is summarized below.

Naïve Bayes: The Naïve Bayes classifier assumes that all of an instance's attributes $a \in A$ are conditionally independent given the class value n. Under this assumption, the prior probability $p(n)$ of each class value $n \in N$ is learned from the training data by maximum likelihood estimation; that is, $p(n)$ is set equal to the proportion of training examples that belong to class $n \in N$.

Similarly, the conditional likelihood of each attribute value $v_{i;a}$ given each class value $n \in N$ is learned from the training data by maximum likelihood estimation; that is, $p(v_{i;a}|n)$ is set equal to the proportion of training examples of class $n \in N$ that have value $v_{i|a}$ for attribute $a \in A$. The classifier then assigns the class value n^*_i to the test instance i, which maximizes the likelihood function; that is, $n^*_i = argmax_{\ n} \in (p(n) \prod p(vi, a|n))$.

Bayesian Networks: The Naïve Bayes classifier can be extended to a Bayesian network classifier where the set of conditional independence assumptions is encoded in a graph. As in the Naïve Bayes approach, the conditional probabilities are learned from the training data, but are conditioned not only on the class, but also on any other parents of the given attribute a in the graph. Similar to the Naïve Bayes classification, a new instance i is assigned to the class n^*_i that maximizes the likelihood function; that is, $n^*_i = argmax_n \in {}_N$ $\{p(n) \prod p(vi, a|n), \prod a\}$.

Decision Trees: Decision tree learners automatically learn a decision tree from labeled training data. Various methods can determine the structure of a decision tree from data (Hall and Holmes, 2003; Quinlan, 1986). In the first step, the attribute a^* with the maximum information gain is selected out of the set of attributes A. Based on a^*, which becomes the root node, the set of instances is divided into subsets; each one contains different values $v \in V_{a^*}$ of attribute a^*. Each value is represented by an edge. If in any subset I_v only one outcome value exists, the attribute value v is assigned to that outcome. Otherwise, the attribute with the next higher information gain is selected from the attribute set and linked to the outcome by an edge. Recursively, it is split further on each subset of attribute values.

18.2 Three Illustrative Examples of Data Science in Healthcare

The following section summarizes three examples of data science in healthcare drawn from prior research that highlight the interplay between information technology, data, statistical and machine learning methods and their evaluation in complex decision-making contexts. They include medication reconciliation for improving patient safety (Hasan et al., 2008, 2011), dynamic prediction of medical risks for clinical care (Ganssauge et al., 2016, 2017), and practice-based clinical pathway learning for evidence generation and practice improvement (Zhang et al., 2015; Zhang and Padman, 2015, 2016).

18.2.1 Medication Reconciliation

Medication reconciliation is defined as "A process for obtaining and documenting a complete and accurate list of a patient's current medications upon admission, and comparing this list to the physician's admission, transfer, and/or discharge orders to identify and resolve discrepancies" (IHI, 2008). This is an important patient safety goal for avoiding adverse drug events resulting from omissions, duplications, dosing errors, or drug interactions. As a third of US adults take five or more medications at any time, studies report that adverse drug events result in more than 1.5 million injured patients in hospitals, more than 700,000 emergency department visits and more than 100,000 hospitalizations every year, at a financial cost as high as $3 billion a year (da Silva et al., 2016). Studies also suggest that 50 percent of medication errors in hospitals result from a failure to reconcile medications at various transition points including admission, transfer between units, and discharge (Barnsteiner, 2005). Consequently, the Joint Commission recommends a process-oriented medication reconciliation approach for creating the most accurate list of all medications a patient is taking, using reconciliation forms to be completed and verified at every encounter with the healthcare entity (Geller et al., 2005). This is a laborious and inconsistent approach and dependent on fallible memories and behaviors of all stakeholders (Aspden, 2006).

However, information technology and data analytics can play a major role in supporting medication reconciliation unobtrusively. Electronic health records (EHRs), prescribing systems, and computerized physician order entry (CPOE) applications provide a mechanism to store large volumes of medication data in a structured and easily accessible format, and alert prescribers about potentially harmful interactions using decision-support tools with preprogrammed rules. However, the usefulness of these alerts depends on the accuracy of the stored patient information, which depends on the robustness of the reconciliation process to many factors, including a patient's accurate recall, complex medication regimens, unconnected prescribing systems, and others (Aspden, 2006).

Hence, detecting potential omissions of medications from a patient's list from the extensive data repositories is an opportunity for data science to improve medication reconciliation and patient safety. For example, in prior research (Hasan et al., 2008, 2011), collaborative filtering (CF) has been proposed as a methodology for answering the following question: *if a patient's medication list is incomplete, what drugs are most likely to be missing?* In most other applications, the goal of collaborative filtering is to make predictions and provide recommendations about products to an individual based on the observed choices of similar individuals. Successful applications of collaborative filtering include movie recommendations used by Netflix and product recommendations on amazon.com (Linden et al., 2003). The collaborative filtering methods for medication reconciliation produce an ordered list of drugs considered to have the highest likelihood of being omitted from a patient's record. From a translational perspective, the ordered list of potentially omitted drugs can be used to develop individualized memory aids, embedded in decision-support tools, that can improve recall and strengthen reconciliation efforts (Hasan et al., 2011). Patients can be queried about whether they are taking drugs that are likely to have been omitted and/or that may cause serious adverse drug events.

As developed in Hasan et al. (2008, 2011), a patient's medication list can be considered as a set of entities, where each entity represents a drug. The most granular view of a drug entity is a brand name drug with a specific dose and route (e.g., Advil Oral Tablet 200 mg). It can also be viewed in more general terms, such as a brand name drug (e.g., Advil), as a generic chemical name (e.g., Ibuprofen), or more generally as a member of a therapeutic class (e.g., non-narcotic analgesics). In all cases, the complete and accurate medication list of all patients in a population can be represented as a matrix $M = \{m_{ij}\}$, for patients $i = 1, \cdots, I$ and drugs $j = 1, \cdots, J$, and where

$$m_{ij} = \begin{cases} 1 & \textit{drug} - \textit{entity } j \textit{ occurred in medication list of patient } i \\ 0 & \textit{otherwise} \end{cases}$$

A simpler representation of the medication list is a set of lists l_i, where l_i constitutes the set of drug entities e_j for a given patient i and $e_j \in l_i$ if and only if $m_{ij} = 1$. However, a patient's true medication list l_i is often incomplete, hence prescribers observe a partial list, denoted by $\tilde{l}_i$. A collaborative filtering approach can be used to predict whether specific drugs have been omitted from an individual's medication list based on the known medications of similar individuals and the observed list of medications for that patient. Many computational and statistical methods for collaborative filtering have been reported in the literature, each with its own advantages and challenges (Ekstrand et al., 2010). In each case, the algorithm assigns a score p_j for each drug not observed in the partial list. Drug entities are sorted in decreasing order based on this score, assuming that the entity with the highest score is the one with the highest chance of being missing from the partial list.

For example, K-nearest neighbors (KNN) is a widely-used, memory-based machine learning approach for collaborative filtering (Ekstrand et al., 2010). Given an observed partial list, we find the K training lists $\boldsymbol{l}_1 \cdots \boldsymbol{l}_K$ that are closest to it according to some distance metric. The Ochiai similarity measure (Bolton, 1991) is a binary form of cosine similarity that compares the observed partial list $\tilde{\boldsymbol{l}}_i$ with each of the lists $\boldsymbol{l}_{-i}$ in the data set used for training the collaborative filtering model. If a is the number of drug entities that are present is both lists, b is the number of drug entities present in $\tilde{\boldsymbol{l}}_i$ but not in $\boldsymbol{l}_{-i}$ and c is the number of drug-entities present in $\boldsymbol{l}_{-i}$ but not in $\tilde{\boldsymbol{l}}_i$, the Ochiai similarity measure is computed as: $Dist(\tilde{l}_i, l_{-i}) = \sqrt{\left(\frac{a}{a+b}\right)\left(\frac{a}{a+c}\right)}$. Scores for the missing entities can be now assigned using majority vote of the K nearest neighbors (Hasan et al., 2008, 2011).

Evaluation of the collaborative filtering method using a k-fold cross-validation approach (Witten et al., 2011; Wasserman, 2004) can determine how successfully it predicts the missing medications. The model is trained using k-1 folds of the medication data and tested on the holdout sample using a leave-one-out strategy. In the test set, one drug is randomly removed from each patient's medication list to create the observed list, and the model's prediction of the missing drug and its position in the ranked candidate list of potential missing drugs is aggregated across all patients in the test set. Performance measures, such as the median and mean rank of the omitted drugs in the ordered list, can be compared across many algorithms. This solution can be further improved by contextualizing the ordered list of missing candidate drugs that considers, for example, the expected consequence such as the potential for future harm if the missing drug is not identified and included in the record, particularly in the context of the immediate prescribing decision. Finally, the best algorithms can be implemented in decision-support tools to present the list of potentially missing drugs in a patient's record to the clinician at the time of prescribing and as a memory aid to the patient to improve medication reconciliation.

18.2.2 Dynamic Prediction of Medical Risks

In many clinical settings, a patient is followed over a long period of time with multiple visits and repeated measurements (Barrett, 2017; Ganssauge et al., 2016). Measurements are often recorded in EHR systems and reflect the patient's state that is dynamically changing over time due to disease progression, treatments, medications, and further factors (Ganssauge et al., 2016). Dynamic models that account for the continually changing states of the patient's health and exploit the longitudinal nature of patient data are critical to capture the nuances of care delivery and health outcomes, particularly mortality, hospitalizations, and so on. In contrast to static models, dynamic models provide the opportunity to update an individual prediction when a patient's condition progresses over time and covariates, such as laboratory measurements, are observed longitudinally. In mortality prediction, for example, the objective is to calculate at the landmark s the probability of surviving longer than a fixed horizon w given that the individual has survived until s and some time-dependent covariates $X_i(s)$ have been observed; that is,

$$P(T_{surv,i} > s + w | T_{surv,i} > s, X_i(s))$$

Many statistical methods are available in the literature that deal with such a dynamic setting (Barrett et al., 2017; Fisher et al., 1999; van Houwelingen, 2007; van Houwelingen et al., 2012). The Cox proportional hazards model with time-dependent covariates offers one option to integrate longitudinal observations into the analysis of survival data (Lin et al., 1989). However, this method is used mainly for exploring the relationship between time-dependent covariates and the event of interest, so the ability to predict is usually lost unless the future distribution of the time-dependent covariates is known. Therefore, predictions might be feasible using covariates, such as age, but hard to justify if covariates such as time-varying blood pressure are included. Several methods for this task are summarized in Ganssauge (2016), and an extension of the Cox model for dynamic predictions uses a landmarking approach by fitting Cox models at different landmarks and combining the models to one single "super model" (van Houwelingen et al., 2012) is applied in the specific context of predicting dialysis outcomes.

To apply a data science approach, Dynamic Bayesian Networks (DBNs), drawn from the machine learning literature, constitute another class of models that can be used for prediction when longitudinal variables are present (Ganssauge et al., 2016). A DBN is a temporal extension of a Bayesian Network (BN) and generalizes hidden Markov models and Kalman filters (Murphy, 2002). The joint probability distribution of a set of random variables is modeled over time by introducing discrete time slices. Dependencies between random variables within each time slice are captured similarly to a BN, but in addition, dependencies between consecutive time slices are modeled and enable the representation of stochastic processes. Advantages of DBNs are the capability of representing complex interactions between variables, the simple integration of expert knowledge, native handling of missing values, and utilization of all previous observations to infer the current belief about a set of random variables (Murphy, 2002; Russell et al., 2010). Several clinical applications of DBNs can be found in literature, such as diagnosis of pneumonia for patients in the intensive care unit (Charitos et al., 2009), and a comprehensive review of further applications of DBNs in clinical research is reported in Orphanou et al. (2014).

The identification and early mitigation of individual risk is a challenging task for physicians who often make treatment decisions under severe time and cost constraints. Robust models that support risk assessment of adverse events, such as mortality, can help to identify early warning signals of increased risk, enable clinicians to target such patients, and allow more informed discussions about future treatment options (Cohen et al., 2010; Doi et al., 2015). DBNs provide a simple approach to integrate expert knowledge, handle missing values, and allow complex interactions of covariates by specifying joint probability distributions.

A Bayesian Network (BN) is defined by a pair (G, P) where G is a directed acyclic graph and P specifies the joint probability distribution of a set of random variables $X = \{X_1, , \dots , X_n\}$ (Pearl, 1988; Koski, 2009). The nodes N of G correspond to the random variables, and the directed edges $E \subseteq N \times N$ express dependencies between the variables. A BN provides a compact representation of the joint distribution by factorization into conditional probability distributions (CPDs) $P(X) = \prod_{j \in N} P(X_j | \pi(X_j))$ where $\pi(X_j)$ denotes the parents of X_j in

G. Random variables are allowed to be hidden, and the associated CPDs can be of arbitrary form. If realizations of some random variables are observed, probabilistic inference can be used to update the beliefs about the state of any other X_j (Koski, 2009).

A DBN is a temporal extension of a BN and allows the modeling of probability distributions over semi-infinite collections of random variables $(Z_0, Z_1, \ldots)$ (Murphy, 2002). Thus, a set of random variables can be represented conveniently at different time points, and a stochastic process can be modeled. Time is discretized into distinct time slices t, and for each time slice, a set of random variables is given by Z_t. Dependencies can be modeled within each time slice (intraslice arcs) and between time slices (interslice arcs). Usually, the Markov property is assumed, and the parents of a node j in t (i.e., $\pi(Z_{j,t})$) have to be located in the same or previous time slice. If $Z_{i,t-1}$ is a parent of $Z_{i,t}$, this node is called persistent. Furthermore, the structure of the network is assumed to be invariant for all time slices. A DBN is then defined by a pair $(B_0, B_\rightarrow)$, where B_0 is a BN and $B_\rightarrow$ is a two-slice temporal Bayes net. B_0 defines the initial distribution of Z_0 at $t = 0$ and $B_\rightarrow$ specifies the distribution of the random variables for subsequent time points by $P(Z_t Z_{t-1}) = \prod_{i \in N} P(Z_{i,t} | \pi(Z_{i,t}))$, where $Z_{i,t}$ is the i-th node in time slice t. It is possible to "unroll" a DBN to a BN for a fixed number of time slices and apply the common inference algorithms. Algorithms that exploit the repetitive structure of a DBN can decrease computational complexity. Both structure and parameters of the CPDs are either learned from data or specified, using expert knowledge (Friedman et al., 1998; Murphy, 2002; Ganssauge et al., 2016).

Ganssauge et al. (2016) report on the results of developing a DBN model to predict mortality of patients on dialysis. Despite substantial advances in the treatment of end-stage renal disease, mortality of hemodialysis patients remains unacceptably high. Several models exist that predict mortality for this population and identify patients at risk. However, the models focus mainly on patients at a particular stage of dialysis treatment, such as the start of dialysis, and use only the most recent patient data. Generalization of such models for predictions in later periods can be challenging because disease characteristics change over time and the evolution of biomarkers is not adequately incorporated. Dynamic methods allow updates of initial predictions when patients progress in time and new data is observed. Comparison of DBN to regularized logistic regression models and a Cox model with landmarking indicates that the DBN achieves satisfactory performance for short-term prediction horizons but needs further refinement and parameter tuning for longer horizons and that the Cox model with landmarking provides the best predictions. Additionally, there are many risk factors showing strong effect on one-year mortality that are common across all three modeling methods.

The implications of these findings for dynamic predictions and their extensions to similar problems for other health conditions are manifold.

First is the observed decrease of prediction performance for later landmarks (van Houwelingen et al., 2012). Studies have shown that model performance declines as the prediction horizon increases, and the data is also more uncertain, hence short- and medium-term predictions are applicable to chronic disease progression (Soyiri et al., 2013). Second, risk factors may change over time, and the modeling approach needs to accommodate this requirement. Finally, use of observational data may introduce several biases that need to be mitigated using appropriate statistical techniques (Myers et al., 2016).

18.2.3 Practice-Based Clinical Pathway Learning

Evidence-based medicine is "the conscientious, explicit, and judicious use of current best evidence in making medical decisions about the care of individual patients" (Sackett, 2000). It is a critical prerequisite for achieving coordinated, patient-centered, and effective healthcare. However, validated models, methods, and tools required to apply evidence-based medicine at the point of care, particularly those that accommodate insights from current practice, are lacking (Zhang et al., 2015). An important source for medical evidence is clinical pathways, indicating the most widely applicable order of treatment interventions for specific health conditions or particular patient groups (Rotter et al., 2010; Huang et al., 2012, 2014). Clinical pathways translate best available evidence into practice, have been shown to reduce in-hospital complications, and reduce length of stay and medical expenses (Rotter et al., 2010), and are widely used in US hospitals.

Clinical pathways are developed from clinical practice guidelines (CPGs), which list recommendations for various treatments based on evidence from randomized clinical trials (RCTs) or the consensus opinions of clinical experts. However, the strength of such evidence differs by clinical area and mostly target the "average patient." While innovations in chronic care delivery are beginning to leverage advanced analytic models and methods to obtain new insights on care quality, outcomes, and cost, predictions generated by the algorithms appear like a "black box" to time-constrained clinicians, with limited relevance to actual medical decision-making (Poelmans et al., 2010). To provide decision-support recommendations on clinical interventions that are personalized and predictive, healthcare service delivery can benefit greatly from learning potentially useful insights from large amounts of highly granular data collected daily in electronic health records as part of routine care delivered in multiple, diverse settings and presented such that they are credible and interpretable at the point of decision-making (de Clercq et al., 2001; Egho et al., 2013; Peleg, 2013).

In the United States, the National Guideline Clearinghouse (NGC), maintained by the Agency for Healthcare Research and Quality (AHRQ) of the Department of Health and Human Services, is a publicly available repository of evidence-based clinical practice guidelines created by professional healthcare organizations (AHRQ Guideline Index, 2015). In the United Kingdom, the National Institute for Health and Care Excellence (NICE) publishes clinical, public health, social care, safe staffing, and medications practice guidelines (NICE, n.d.). NICE guidelines cover 23 broad clinical conditions, each of which further extends to subconditions. As of 2015, the number of CPGs in the US National Guideline Clearinghouse is 2,382. On the other hand, the number of diagnostic codes in ICD-10 is 69,823. Hence, there is a clear shortage of CPGs for the number of clinical conditions that exist in the medical domain. As information technology (IT) gains widespread adoption in healthcare, it offers an opportunity to develop practice-based clinical pathways that learn from actual patient care data, and can be validated and deployed much faster than traditional CPGs (de Clercq et al., 2001).

An important problem in this context is to learn the *most common* data-driven clinical pathways from EHR data (Zhang et al., 2015). Given the retrospective data on patients with chronic conditions and their multiple visits to providers, learning the high-volume pathways and predicting the most probable interventions at any stage in the pathway have the potential to identify best practices, modify consensus guidelines, and impact research and practice on health and organizational outcomes, quality of care, and patient satisfaction (Zhang et al., 2015; Rotter, 2010). Figure 18.5 summarizes the process of developing clinical pathways from large volumes of data that can subsequently be evaluated by clinical experts before deployment for frontline practice (Zhang et al., 2015).

Zhang et al. (2015) also present a methodology to learn data-driven clinical pathways that include data transformation, followed by identification of latent patient subgroups and clinical pathway extraction. They evaluated the resulting pathways by comparing their methodology with an existing solution called HeuristicMiner (Weijters et al., 2006), using patient data on chronic kidney disease in the outpatient setting. For instance, each patient *p*'s medical visit $Visit^p$ comprises many types of events, *i*, such as the type of visit, diagnoses, procedures, and medications that allow the construction of a visit sequence. $Visit_n^p\{V_i\}$, $i=1, 2, \ldots I$ events, $n = 1, 2, \ldots N_p$, is the nth visit of patient *p*, where

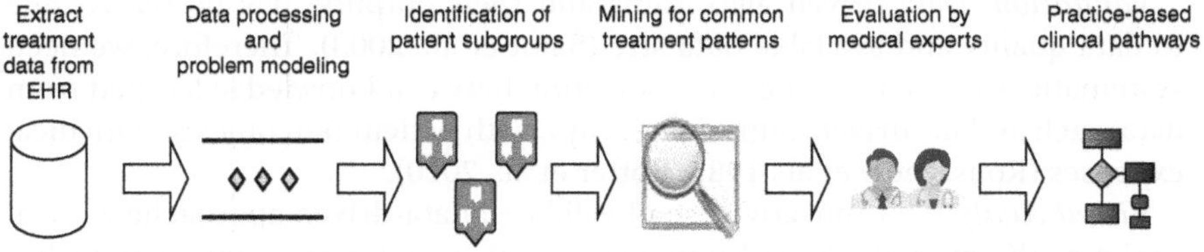

Figure 18.5 Practice-based clinical pathway development process (Zhang and Padman, 2015).

I is the number of event types and N_p is the number of visits of the patient. Once a unique visit sequence is generated for each patient, the longest common subsequence (LCS) measure is applied to measure similarity among sequences (Elzinga, 2008). It is computed as $LCS(x, y) = max\{|u|: u \in S(x, y)\}$, where $|u|$ is the length of the longest common subsequence for the pair of sequences (x, y), and S (x,y) is the nonempty set of subsequences of sequences x and y. A distance measure based on LCS is defined as $dLCS(x, y) = |x| + |y| - 2LCS(x, y)$, where $|x|$ is the length of sequence x and $|y|$ is the length of sequence y. Hierarchical clustering on the $dLCS$ distance matrix produces multiple latent patient subgroups. A second-order, discrete, time homogeneous Markov chain model identifies the transition sequences to which frequency and transition probability thresholds are applied to extract the most common pathways (Karlin, 2014; Norris, 1999; Rabiner et al., 1986).

Analysis of an EHR extract of 1,576 patients with chronic kidney disease patients generated 31 distinct subgroups differing in patterns of visit events (Zhang et al., 2015). Subsequent prediction of acute events such as hospitalization, future clinical pathways, and best-practice treatment decisions using hidden Markov models for the subgroups show that it is possible to leverage current sources of clinical big data to deliver standardized but personalized predictions (Zhang and Padman, 2015, 2016). Visualization of the pathways and subsequent predictions of the most probable interventions at any stage have the potential to better aid healthcare providers and researchers to identify discrepancies between actual practices and CPG, assess outcomes for treatments that are compliant or otherwise with best practices, and facilitate shared decision-making with patients (Yang et al., 2006; Zhang et al., 2017). Some extensions of this problem in care delivery settings are detailed below.

Workflow Mining: An understanding of healthcare providers' workflows and the demands of their patients is essential, although not sufficient, for successful application of CPG in practice. EHR data contains valuable information on care delivery patterns of clinicians, allowing healthcare organizations to compare them against clinical practice guidelines (Zhang et al., 2015, 2016), identify treatment variations, and build IT components such as CDS and health portals (Jung et al., 2014). Future work needs to explore innovative use of EHR data for workflow mining (Aalst et al., 2003; Lin et al., 2001; Vankipuram et al., 2011).

Validation: Data-driven algorithms and their outputs may be biased due to data quality and available data size (Saint et al., 2003). Therefore, we need systematic ways of assessing the association between knowledge learned from data, such as data-driven clinical pathways, with patient outcomes and medical expenses (Rousseeuw et al., 1987; Rotter et al., 2010).

Visual Analytics: Innovative use of validated data-driven approaches, visual analytics (Keim et al., 2008; Klimov et al., 2015), and mobile applications has the potential to facilitate more efficient employment of CPGs by healthcare providers (Chomutare et al., 2011; Mosa et al., 2010), leading to high-quality care for patients (West et al., 2015; Zhang et al., 2015). Future studies that advance further development and appropriate use of these data-driven CPGs in the context of decision support-enabled care delivery are needed to help healthcare organizations achieve continuous quality improvement, better patient outcomes, and reduced costs (Rotter et al., 2010).

18.3 Discussion

18.3.1 Challenges and Opportunities

While exciting developments are ongoing in the areas of new models, methods, and applications of data science in research and practice, solutions to several challenges have to be addressed as well. In the specific context of using data science methods for healthcare decisions, these include enhancing the interpretability and usability of solutions so that end users can access the insights provided by data science and convert them to impactful actions (Lisboa 2013). Key to the successful deployment of these insights are the following: visual analytics that allow explorations of solutions for accuracy, sensitivity, and robustness; user-friendly human–computer interfaces that display the results of algorithms; and trust and transparency with the methods and their implementations in software tools and platforms for credibility. In addition, several critical trade-offs have to be considered, such as complexity of the methods versus usability, bias versus variance in data processing and variable selection, efficiency of classification versus usefulness of the solution via explanation capability that may require added variables and features, and explanations versus the ambiguity that may be introduced by lack of parsimony in modeling the problem. Specifically, multidimensional visualizations that display health risk predictions must present several components: risk assessment from population, individual, and intervention perspectives; ability to measure confidence in risk predictions; relative importance of individual risk factors; and additional clinical context that may improve translational value (Harle et al., 2012). Finally, every data science project in the healthcare setting has to deal with data quality, privacy, confidentiality, and security issues. Although there is a large and growing literature and many solutions proposed for these issues, new types of structured and unstructured clinical and financial data—including from individuals and healthcare devices and services, social determinants of health and wellness, games for health, and use of artificial intelligence assistants—will generate unique and unanticipated risks and quality issues. New and validated models of trade-offs between risks and utility and their translation to practice will facilitate the data science process for improving healthcare.

Research on precision medicine, population health, integrative care delivery, and self-health management, among others, are gathering increasing momentum, powered by new data collection, storage, management, and analysis methods and technologies. Methods for risk measurement and prediction, identifying the causes of individual differences, evaluating new biological markers for diseases, detecting diseases and new health threats early, and correlating new data and measurements with health outcomes offer significant opportunities for new research at the interface of data science methods and information and computing technologies (Raghupati et al., 2014). Facilitating translational delivery by creating platforms—for instance, to test and evaluate new therapies and population health strategies for common and rare diseases—that leverage new communication and decision technologies such as cognitive computing, quantum machine learning (Wittek, 2014), artificial intelligence gamification, and deep learning and simulation-optimization with machine learning will support progression from predictions to decision-making and executing actions. Embedding new insights into actual workflows, learning from the resulting data streams, and providing a feedback loop to continuously improve healthcare decisions is the ultimate objective of a data-driven, learning healthcare system.

18.3.2 Data Science in Action

Successful transformations of practice in some pioneering healthcare organizations using data science approaches are slowly beginning to be reported in the literature. These span the range of predictive analytics from clinical improvements and quality and patient safety monitoring to fraud and waste monitoring, as undertaken by United Healthcare, the largest insurer in the US. Similarly, the FIRE analytics program at MD Anderson Cancer Center in Texas integrates clinical, financial, genomic, operational, and other types of structured and unstructured data to support precision medicine and improve cancer care (Davies 2015). Express Scripts (n.d.), the largest pharmacy benefit management organization in the US, delivers several million prescriptions to the home and retail pharmacies and uses advanced methods to analyze this data, both for individual patients and for populations and healthcare organizations, so they can provide alerts for adverse drug events, monitor prescription-filling behaviors, and evaluate adherence to medication regimens.

As Steinhubl et al. (2015) reported, advances in mobile health technologies and applications are another exciting frontier for new ventures in research and practice. From wearable sensors that collect medical-grade personalized information to monitor health and wellness (Poh et al., 2010) to medical technology developments, such as the "lab on a chip" smartphone application that supports medical testing at home (Sackmann et al., 2014) to photometric diagnostics for dermatology (Janda et al., 2013), a new range of novel tools are generating large volumes of data for analysis. Furthermore, new startups powered by data science are creating innovations in diagnosis, treatment, self-health management, and point-of-care testing. These innovations include providing personalized nutritional recommendations by applying machine learning to analyze gut microorganisms, next-generation infusion pumps enhanced with real-time monitoring, and clinical oncology pathways that consider patients' stress levels, which are being evaluated in pilot studies. The insights from these data streams combined with their incorporation into the workflow of routine care as actionable tasks for consumers, patients, providers, and health systems have the potential to transform healthcare worldwide.

18.3.3 Health Data Science Worldwide

The medical landscape in Africa is experiencing a revolution with the advent of ehealth and mobile health for public health and medical consultations, enabling the use of data science embedded in decision support tools for clinical care (Mosa et al., 2012). In India, the HealthHiway initiative is anticipated to provide a comprehensive national health data network to exchange and share patient data in a secure and efficient manner, and allow decision support services to be deployed efficiently. Furthermore, applications, such as Internet of Things (IoT) devices used in a portable imaging platform for screening and diagnosing common eye problems, wearable cardiac monitor with advanced analytics to provide diagnosis and monitoring in remote areas, and low-cost pathology tools, can use the network to exchange data and decisions between patients and providers who are located far from each other. The National Health Service in the UK has a goal to enroll 10 percent of the patient population to use apps and online services for routine care, generating vast amounts of data for analytics and decision-making. Similar efforts are ongoing in many other parts of the world, including sharing of information across boundaries, such as between Australia and Germany.

18.4 Conclusions

The rapid digital revolution in healthcare combined with significant advances in medical and consumer technologies, and developments in advanced analysis of high dimensional, high volume, and complex data is anticipated to power a transformation of healthcare delivery. Though data science is still in the early stages of definition, development, and use, early implementation and results by healthcare-related organizations indicate both major challenges and opportunities in the US and worldwide. This chapter highlights a few, illustrates the potential with three specific examples, summarizes some successes in the industry, and reviews similar efforts around the world.

References

van der Aalst, W.M.P., B.F. van Dongen, J. Herbst, L. Maruster, G. Schimm, A.J.M.M. Weijters. (2003). Workflow mining: A survey of issues and approaches. *Data & Knowledge Engineering* 47(2):237–267.

AHRQ Guideline Index 2015. (n.d.). Available from: http://www.guideline.gov/browse/index.aspx?alpha=A.

Aliferis, C.F., A. Statnikov, I. Tsamardinos, S. Mani, X.D. Koutsoukos. (2010). Local causal and Markov blanket induction for causal discovery and feature selection for classification part I: Algorithms and empirical evaluation. *Journal of Machine Learning Research* 11(1):171–234.

Aspden, P., J. Wolcott, L. Bootman, and L.R. Cronenwett. (2006). *Preventing Medication Errors* National Academies Press, Washington, DC.

Bai, X., R. Padman, J. Ramsey, P. Spirtes. (2008). Tabu search-enhanced graphical models for classification in high dimensions. *INFORMS Journal on Computing* 20(3):423–437.

Barrett, J.K., M.J. Sweeting, A.M. (2017). Dynamic Risk Prediction for Cardiovascular Disease: An Illustration Using the ARIC Study (n.d.). In *Disease Modelling and Public Health, Handbook of Statistics* 36, Eds. Rao et al. Elsevier.

Bishop, CM (2006) Pattern Recognition and Machine Learning (Springer, New York).

Bolton, H. C. (1991). On the Mathematical Significance of the Similarity Index of Ochiai as a Measure for Biogeographical Habitats. *Australian Journal of Zoology*, 39, 143–156.

Caban, J.J., D. Gotz. (2015). Visual analytics in healthcare—opportunities and research challenges. *Journal of the American Medical Informatics Association (JAMIA)*. 22(2):260–262. PubMed PMID: 25814539.

Cao, L. (2017). Data Science: A Comprehensive Overview. *ACM Computing Surveys*, Vol. 50, No. 3, Article 43.

Charitos, T., L.C. van der Gaag, S. Visscher, K.A. Schurink, P.J. Lucas. (2009). A dynamic Bayesian network for diagnosing ventilator-associated pneumonia in ICU patients. *Expert Systems with Applications* 36(2):1249–1258.

Chomutare, T., L. Fernandez-Luque, E. Arsand, G. Hartvigsen. (2011). Features of mobile diabetes applications: review of the literature and analysis of current applications compared against evidence-based guidelines. *Journal of Medical Internet Research*. 13(3): e65. PubMed PMID: 21979293. Pubmed Central PMCID: 3222161.

Cohen, L.M., R. Ruthazer, A.H. Moss, M.J. Germain. (2010). Predicting six-month mortality for patients who are on maintenance hemodialysis. Clinical Journal of the American Society of Nephrology 5(1):72–79.

Collins, F.S., H. Varmus (2015). A new initiative on precision medicine. *New England Journal of Medicine*. 372(9):793–795.

da Silva, B.A., M. Krishnamurthy. (2016). The alarming reality of medication error: a patient case and review of Pennsylvania and National data. *Journal of Community Hospital Internal Medicine Perspectives* 6: 31758.

Davies, C. (2015). Impactful analytics: MD Anderson Cancer Center's drive for better insights. Ovum Consulting, Product code: IT0011-000364

de Clercq, P.A., A. Hasman, J.A. Blom, H.H. Korsten. (2001). Design and implementation of a framework to support the development of clinical guidelines. *International Journal of Medical Informatics* 64(2-3):285–318. PubMed PMID: 11734393.

DeSalvo, K., V. Washington. (2016). By The Numbers: Our Progress In Digitizing Health Care, *Health Affairs* Blog September 29, 2016, http://healthaffairs.org/blog/2016/09/29/by-the-numbers-our-progress-in-digitizing-health-care/, Copyright ©2016 *Health Affairs* by Project HOPE - The People-to-People Health Foundation, Inc.

Doi, T., S. Yamamoto, T. Morinaga, K. Sada, N. Kurita, Y. Onishi. Risk Score to Predict 1-Year Mortality after Haemodialysis Initiation in Patients with Stage 5 Chronic Kidney Disease under Predialysis Nephrology Care. PloS one 2015; 10(6):e0129180.

Egho, E, Jay N, Raïssi C, Nuemi G, Quantin C, Napoli A. An Approach for Mining Care Trajectories for Chronic Diseases. *Artificial intelligence in medicine.* 2013;7885:258–267.

Ekstrand, MD, J. T. Riedl and J. A. Konstan Collaborative Filtering Recommender Systems Foundations and Trends in Human–Computer Interaction Vol. 4, No. 2 (2010) 81–173.

Elzinga, Cees H. (2008). Sequence analysis: Metric representations of categorical time series. Technical Report, Department of Social Science Research Methods, Vrije Universiteit, Amsterdam.

Express Scripts. (n.d.). www.express-scripts.com

Fawcett, T. Mining the Quantified Self: Personal Knowledge Discovery as a Challenge for Data Science. (2015). *Big Data.* DOI: 10.1089/big.2015.0049

Fisher, L.D., D.Y. Lin. Time-dependent covariates in the Cox proportional-hazards regression model. *Annual Review of Public Health* 1999; 20:145–157.

Friedman, N., K. Murphy, S. Russell. (1998). Learning the structure of dynamic probabilistic networks. *Proceedings of the 14th Conference on Uncertainty in Artificial Intelligence.* Morgan Kaufmann, Madison, WI. San Francisco.

Ganßauge, M., R. Padman, A. Karambelkar, P. Teredesai. (2016). Exploring dynamic risk prediction for dialysis patients. *Proceedings of AMIA 2016.*

Gartner, D., R. Kolisch, D.B. Neill, and R. Padman. (2015). Machine Learning Approaches for Early DRG Classification and Resource Allocation. *INFORMS Journal on Computing*, 27(4).

Gartner, G., Y. Zhang, R. Padman. (2017), Cognitive Workload Reduction in Hospital Information Systems—Decision Support for Order Set Optimization. Forthcoming in *Health Care Management Science.*

Geller, K.H., J.L. Guzman. JCAHO 2005 national patient safety goals: medication reconciliation. http://www.fojp.com/Focus_2005_1.pdf.

Hall, M.A., G. Holmes. (2003). Benchmarking attribute selection techniques for discrete class data mining. *IEEE Transactions on Knowledge and Data Engineering* 15(6):1437–1447.

L'heureux, A., K. Grolinger, H.F. Elyamany, and M.A.M. Capretz (2017). Machine learning with big data: Challenges and approaches. *IEEE Access* 5: 7776–7797.

Harle, C., D. Neill, R. Padman (2012). Development and Evaluation of An Information Visualization System for Chronic Disease Risk Assessment. *IEEE Intelligent Systems* 2012:27(6):81–85.

Huang, Z., W. Dong, L. Ji, C. Gan, X. Lu, H. Duan. (2014). Discovery of clinical pathway patterns from event logs using probabilistic topic models. *Journal of Biomedical Informatics* 47:39–57.

Huang, Z, X. Lu, H. Duan. (2012). On mining clinical pathway patterns from medical behaviors. *Artificial Intelligence in Medicine* 56(1):35–50.

Jung, C., R. Padman. (2014). Disruptive Digital Innovations in Health Care Delivery: The Case for Patient Portals and Online Clinical Consultations. In: Agarwal R., W. Selen, G. Roos, R. Green, eds. *The Handbook of Service Innovation*: Springer.

Karlin, S. (2014). *A First Course in Stochastic Processes.* Academic Press, Cambridge, MA.

Kayyali, B, S. Knott, S.V. Kuiken. (2013). *The big-data revolution in US health care: Accelerating value and innovation.* McKinsey & Company, New York. https://www.mckinsey.com/industries/healthcare-systems-and-services/our-insights/the-big-data-revolution-in-us-health-care

Keim, D.A., F. Mansmann, D. Oelke, H. Ziegler. (2008). Visual Analytics: Combining Automated Discovery with Interactive Visualizations. *Lecture Notes in Computer Science* 5255:2–14.

Klimov, D., A. Shknevsky, Y. Shahar. (2015). Exploration of patterns predicting renal damage in patients with diabetes type II using a visual temporal analysis laboratory. *Journal of the American Medical Informatics Association (JAMIA).* 22(2):275–89. PubMed PMID: 25352568.

Knorr, T., L. Schmidt-Thieme, C. Johner. (2009). Identifying patients at risk. In: Gaul, W., H. Bock, T. Imaizumi, A. Okada, eds. *Cooperation in classification and data analysis.* Berlin: Springer; 2009. pp. 131–140.

Koski, T, J. M. Noble. *Bayesian networks: An introduction.* Wiley, Chichester.

Kruse, C.S., R. Goswamy, Y. Raval, S. Marawi. (2016). Challenges and Opportunities of Big Data in Health Care: A Systematic Review. In Eysenbach, G., ed. *JMIR Medical Informatics* 4(4):e38. doi:10.2196/medinform.5359.

Kaufman, L., P.J. Rousseeuw. (2008). Finding Groups in Data: An Introduction to Cluster Analysis. John Wiley & Sons, Inc., Hoboken, NJ.

Lakshmanan, G.T., S. Rozsnyai, F. Wang. (2013). Investigating Clinical Care Pathways Correlated with Outcomes. *Lecture Notes in Computer Science* 8094:323–338.

Lin, D.Y., L.J. Wei. (1989). The robust inference for the Cox proportional hazards model. Journal of the American Statistical Association 84(408):1074–8.

Lin, F., S. Chou, S. Pan, Y. Chen (2001). Mining time dependency patterns in clinical pathways. *International journal of medical informatics* 62(1):11–25.

Lin, Y.-K., H. Chen, R. A. Brown, S.-H. Li, and H.-J. Yang (2017). Healthcare Predictive Analytics for Risk Profiling in Chronic Care: A Bayesian Multitask Learning Approach. *MIS Quarterly* (41:2), pp. 473–495.

Linden, G., B. Smith, J. York (2003). Amazon.com recommendations: Item-to-item collaborative filtering. *Internet Computing, IEEE* 7(1):76–80.

Lisboa, P.J.G. (2013). Interpretability in Machine Learning - Principles and Practice. In: Masulli F., Pasi G., Yager R. (eds) Fuzzy Logic and Applications. WILF 2013. Lecture Notes in Computer Science, vol 8256. Springer, Cham.

Mackay, D.J.C. (2003). *Information Theory, Inference, and Learning Algorithms*. Cambridge University Press, Cambridge, UK.

Margaritis, D. (2003). Learning Bayesian network model structure from data. PhD thesis, School of Computer Science, Carnegie Mellon University, Pittsburgh, PA.

Mosa, A.S., I. Yoo, L. Sheets. (2012). A systematic review of healthcare applications for smartphones. *BMC medical informatics and decision-making* 12:67. PubMed PMID: 22781312. Pubmed Central PMCID: 3534499.

Murphy, K.P. (2002). Dynamic Bayesian Networks: representation, inference and learning. Dissertation. Berkeley: University of California.

Myers, L., J. Stevens. (2016). Using EHR to Conduct Outcome and Health Services Research. In: *Secondary Analysis of Electronic Health Records*. Springer, Cham.

NICE (National Institute for Health and Care Excellence; n.d.). www.nice.org.uk/guidance

NIH (National Institutes of Health; n.d.) The future of health begins of All of Us. https://allofus.nih.gov/

Norris, J.R. (1999). *Markov Chains*. Cambridge University Press, Cambridge, UK.

Orphanou, K., A. Stassopoulou, E. Keravnou. (2014). Temporal abstraction and temporal Bayesian networks in clinical domains: a survey. *Artificial Intelligence in Medicine* 60(3):133–49.

Peleg, M. (2013). Computer-interpretable clinical guidelines: a methodological review. *Journal of biomedical informatics* 46(4):744–63. PubMed PMID: 23806274.

Pearl, J. (1988). *Probabilistic reasoning in intelligent systems: networks of plausible inference*. Morgan Kaufmann, San Francisco.

Perlich, C.C., F. Provost, J.S. Simonoff. (2003) Tree induction vs. logistic regression: A learning-curve analysis. *Journal of Machine Learning Research* 4(1):211–255.

Poelmans, J., G. Dedene, G. Verheyden, H.V.D. Mussele, S. Viaene, E. Peters. (2010). Combining business process and data discovery techniques for analyzing and improving integrated care pathways, *Lecture Notes Computer Science.* 6171. 505–517.

Poh, M.Z., N.C. Swenson, R.W. Picard. (2010. A wearable sensor for unobtrusive, long-term assessment of electrodermal activity. *IEEE Transactions on Biomedical Engineering* 57:1243–1252. (PubMed: 20172811).

Quinlan, J.R. (1986). Induction of decision trees. *Machine Learning,* 1(1), pp.81–106.

Rabiner, L., B.H. Juang (1986). An introduction to hidden Markov models. *IEEE ASSP Magazine.* Vol 3: 4–16.

Raghupathi, W., V. Raghupathi. (2014). Big data analytics in healthcare: promise and potential. *Health Information Science and Systems* 2:3. doi: 10.1186/2047-2501-2-3.

Robnik-Šikonja, M., I. Kononenko. (2003). Theoretical and empirical analysis of ReliefF and RReliefF. *Machine Learning* 53(1):23–69.

Rotter, T., L. Kinsman, E. James E, et al. (2010). Clinical pathways: effects on professional practice, patient outcomes, length of stay and hospital costs. *The Cochrane database of systematic reviews.* (3):CD006632.

Roumani, Y., J. May, D. Strum, and L. Vargas. (2013). Classifying highly imbalanced ICU data. *Health Care Management Science* 16(2):119–128.

Rousseeuw, P. J. (1987). Silhouettes: A graphical aid to the interpretation and validation of cluster analysis. *Journal of Computational and Applied Mathematics* 20:53–65.

Russell, S.J., P. Norvig, E. Davis. (2010). *Artificial intelligence: a modern approach. 3rd ed.* Prentice Hall, Upper Saddle River, NJ.

Sackett, D.L. (2000). *Evidence-based Medicine: How to Practice and Teach EBM, vol. xiv, second ed.*, Churchill Livingstone, Edinburgh; New York.

Sackmann, E.K., A.L. Fulton, D.J. Beebe. (2014). The present and future role of microfluidics in biomedical research. *Nature* 507:181–189.

Saint, S., T.P. Hofer, J.S. Rose, S.R. Kaufman, L.F. McMahon Jr. (2003). Use of critical pathways to improve efficiency: a cautionary tale. *The American Journal of Managed Care.* 9(11):758–65. PubMed PMID: 14626473.

Saltz, J.F., J.M. Stanton. (2018). *An Introduction to Data Science*, SAGE Publications.

Saria, S., A.K. Rajani, J. Gould, D. Koller, A.A. Penn. (2010). Integration of early physiological responses predicts later illness severity in preterm infants. *Science translational medicine* 2(48):48ra65–48ra65.

Saeys, Y., I. Inza, P. Larrañaga. (2007). A review of feature selection techniques in bioinformatics. *Bioinformatics* 23(19):2507–2517.

Soyiri, I.N., D.D. Reidpath. (2013). An overview of health forecasting. *Environmental Health and Preventative Medicine* 18:1–9.

Spear, B.B., M Heath-Chiozzi, J. Huff. (2001). Clinical application of pharmacogenetics. *Trends in Molecular Medicine* 7(5): 201–204.

Starren, J., M.S. Williams, E.P. Bottinger. Crossing the Omic ChasmA Time for Omic Ancillary Systems. (2013). *JAMA Viewpoint, March* 27, 2013.

Steinhubl, S.R., E.D. Muse, E.J. Topol. (2015). The emerging field of mobile health *Science Translational Medicine* 7.

Sharma, M.J., S.J. Yu. (2009). Benchmark optimization and attribute identification for improvement of container terminals. *European Journal of Operational Research* 201(2):568–580.

Swan, M. (2013). The quantified self: Fundamental disruption in big data science and biological discovery. *Big Data* 1, 2, 85–99.

Tsamardinos, I., C.F. Aliferis, A. Statnikov. (2003). Algorithms for large scale Markov blanket discovery. Russell, I., Haller, S., eds. *Proceedings of the Sixteenth International Florida Artificial Intelligence Research Society Conference* AAAI Press, Menlo Park, CA, 376–381.

van Houwelingen, H.C., H. Putter. (2012). *Dynamic Prediction in Clinical Survival Analysis.* Boca Raton: CRC Press.

van Houwelingen, H.C. (2007). Dynamic prediction by landmarking in event history analysis. *Scandinavian Journal of Statistics* 34(1):70–85.

Vankipuram, M., K. Kahol, T. Cohen, V.L. Patel. (2011). Toward automated workflow analysis and visualization in clinical environments, *Journal of Biomedical Informatics* 44 (3) 432–440. PubMed PMID: 20685315.

Wasserman, L. *All of Statistics: A Concise Course in Statistical Inference.* Springer.

West, V.L., D. Borland, and W.E. Hammond. Innovative information visualization of electronic health record data: a systematic review. *Journal of the American Medical Informatics Association* 22, no. 2 (2014): 330–339.

Wittek, P. (2014). *Quantum Machine Learning: What Quantum Computing Means to Data Mining*. Academic Press. ISBN 978-0-12-800953-6.

Witten, I.H., E. Frank. (2011). *Data Mining 2 Practical Machine Learning Tools and Techniques, 3rd ed.* Morgan Kaufmann, San Francisco.

Yang, W.W., I.J. Chiang. (2006). EBCPG: A visualized evidence-based clinical practice guideline system. *Studies in health technology and informatics* 122:465–70. PubMed PMID: 17102301.

Zhang, Y., R. Padman. (2017). An Interactive Platform to Visualize Data-Driven Clinical Pathways for the Management of Multiple Chronic Conditions. *Studies in health technology and informatics.*

Zhang, Y., R. Padman, J.E. Levin. (2014). Paving the COWpath: data-driven design of pediatric order sets. *Journal of the American Medical Informatics Association (JAMIA).* 21(e2):e304–311.

Zhan, G.Y., R. Padman, N. Patel. (2015). Paving the COWPath: Learning and Visualizing Clinical Pathways from Electronic Health Record Data. *Journal of Biomedical Informatics.* 58: 186–197.

Zhang, Y., R. Padman. (2015). Innovations in Chronic Care Delivery Using Data-Driven Clinical Pathways. *American Journal of Managed Care*, special issue on Health Information Technology 21(12):e661–e668.
Zhang, Y., R. Padman. (2016). Data-Driven Clinical and Cost Pathways for Chronic Care Delivery. *American Journal of Managed Care*, special issue on Health Information Technology 22(12):294–298.

Index

Handbook of Healthcare Analytics: Theoretical Minimum for Conducting 21st Century Research on Healthcare Operations, First Edition. Edited by Tinglong Dai and Sridhar Tayur.